Using UNIX, Special Edition

Ernest Ackermann
Steve Glines
Ralph Roberts
Peter Kuo
Eddie Kee
Frank de Monbrun
George Mayleben
Marvin Tanner
Kamran Husain
Ben Hunsberger

With Contributing Authors:

Keith Blanton
Mary Ann Pike
William A. Tolhurst

Technical Edit By:

Larry Schumer
Chris Negus

que

D1317200

Using UNIX, Special Edition

Copyright© 1994 by Que® Corporation

Library of Congress Catalog No.: 94-65890

ISBN: 1-56529-619-2

97 96 95 94   5 4 3 2 1

Interpretation of the printing code: the rightmost double-digit number is the year of the book's printing; the rightmost single-digit number, the number of the book's printing. For example, a printing code of 94-1 shows that the first printing of the book occurred in 1994.

Publisher: David P. Ewing

Associate Publisher: Michael Miller

Publishing Director: Joseph B. Wikert

Managing Editor: Michael Cunningham

Product Marketing Manager: Ray Robinson

Dedications

To Diane: Without your support and patience, these chapters would not have been possible. And to Patty Brooks of Que for putting up with all the hassle needed to obtain software to develop the TCP/IP chapter of this book.

—Eddie Kee

This work wouldn't have been possible without the support, understanding, and help of my family: Lynn, Karl, and Oliver.

—Ernie Ackermann

To my daughters, who still want me to write a UNIX for Kids book.

—Steve Glines

Credits

Publishing Manager
Brad R. Koch

Acquisitions Editors
Angela J. Lee
Sarah Browning

Acquisitions Coordinator
Patty Brooks

Product Director
Robin Drake

Developmental Editor
Ella Davis

Technical Editors
Larry Schumer
Chris Negus

Production Editors
Alice Martina Smith
Jodi Jensen

Editors
Lori Cates
Midge Stocker

Editorial Assistants
Michelle Williams
Theresa Mathias

Command Reference Author
Ben Hunsburger

Command Reference Tech Editor
Steve Pryor

Command Reference Editors
Linda Seifert
Danielle Bird

Book Designer
Paula Carroll

Cover Designer
Dan Armstrong

Production Team
Stephen Adams
Jeff Baker
Laurie Casey
Brook Farling
Teresa Forrester
Joelynn Gifford
Dennis Clay Hager
Carla Hall
Bob LaRoche
Tim Montgomery
Aren Munk
Nanci Sears Perry
Caroline Roop
Dennis Sheehan
Amy L. Steed
Michael Thomas
Johnna VanHoose
Sue VandeWalle
Mary Beth Wakefield
Lillian Yates

Indexer
Michael Hughes

Composed in *Stone Serif* and *MCPdigital* by Que Corporation

About the Authors

Ernest Ackermann enjoys writing about, using, administering, and teaching others about UNIX systems. He currently administers a network of about 1,500 registered users. Over the past few years, he has become involved in providing Internet access to his campus, Mary Washington College, Fredericksburg, VA. He is currently professor of Computer Science, Associate Director of Academic Computing, and serves as the primary campus contact for Internet services. In these capacities, he is active in support and planning activities. Ernie can be reached on the Internet at `ernie@oregano.mwc.edu` or on CompuServe at 71157,3672.

Steve Glines is a world-renowned UNIX consultant and author. This is his third book on UNIX.

Ralph Roberts contributed the chapters on hardware and software considerations, single-user installations, loading UNIX applications, and running DOS and Windows applications. Ralph lives in the mountains near Asheville, North Carolina, and has been writing about computers since 1978. He is the author of over 40 books and thousands of articles, including *The UNIX Desktop Guide to Emacs* (published by Que's sister company, Hayden Books).

Peter Kuo, Ph.D., is the first Canadian Enterprise Certified NetWare Engineer and a Certified NetWare Instructor. His areas of expertise include advanced NetWare topics such as network management, IBM, and UNIX connectivity issues. Peter is a SysOp on NetWire (CompuServe), supporting many advanced sections for Novell, such as Connectivity, Network Management, NetWare 4.x, Client Software, and OS/2 Requester. He is also a member of Novell's Professional Developer's Program.

Eddie Kee has been working with computers and networks for 15 years. He is a principal of a networking and computer consulting firm in northeastern Ohio and is a member of IEEE, ACM, DECUS, and local computer groups. He specializes in integrating multiple computer architectures and platforms, network management, systems management, and graphical user interface programming. Other interests are woodworking and house-building. He is married to a very understanding and supportive wife, Diane. He can be reached through CompuServe at 73165,526.

Frank de Monbrun wrote the introductory chapters for *Using UNIX*, Special Edition. Recently retired from the U.S. Navy, Frank manages day-to-day computer operations for a Fortune 1000 company. His experience ranges from operating and maintaining various electronics and computer systems to teaching physics and digital theory. He has worked with a wide variety of computer hardware and operating systems and has taught classes in DOS, UNIX, and assorted military and commercial applications. The author of a variety of technical references used as military standards throughout the world, Frank resides in Indiana with his wife Rose and sons Joshua and Aaron. This is Frank's first book for Que Corporation.

George Mayleben is a native of Pittsburgh, Pennsylvania and a graduate of the University of Minnesota with a Bachelor of Science degree in Business. He became involved with computers while employed with the Bell System and acquired his knowledge of UNIX from AT&T sources. He was the UNIX Product Manager for Insight Technology Systems in Wausau, Wisconsin before he formed George W. Mayleben and Associates. George and his associates service UNIX computers, install larger computer systems, provide administrative support, support industry computer applications, and conduct seminars. George has written numerous articles about UNIX, mechanization, ergonomics, and other facets of the computer market.

Marvin Tanner is trained by Microsoft University and Novell Education. He has a master's degree in Public Administration (Management) and has 15 years of computer industry experience. Currently, he is a professor of Computer Information Systems at Merritt College in Oakland, California and a consultant with Network Services Group in San Francisco, California.

Kamran Husain is an independent consultant with experience in UNIX systems programming, X-Windows and Motif, and Microsoft Windows; he specializes in real-time systems applications. He is an alumnus of the University of Texas at Austin. Kamran offers training and consulting services through his company, MPS Inc., in the Houston area. He can be reached at mpsi@aol.com.

Ben Hunsberger has worked for the only SCO APC (Advanced Product Center) in Indiana for the past nine years. He is the Service Manager and senior technical advisor. Ben is an SCO ACE (Advanced Certified Engineer) and a coauthor of Que's *Introduction to UNIX*, Second Edition, and *Inside SCO UNIX* (published by New Riders Publishing).

Keith Blanton is cofounder and vice president of research and development for Atlanta Innovation, Inc., a firm that provides engineering services for new product development. His professional specialties include digital signal processing, computer graphics, advanced algorithm and software development, and evaluation of new technologies. He holds six patents for his work in computer speech synthesis, optical character recognition, and flight-simulator image generation. He received his S.M. and S.B. degrees in electrical engineering from the Massachusetts Institute of Technology.

Mary Ann Pike is a technical writing consultant in southwestern Pennsylvania. She has a B.S. in electrical engineering and an M.A. in professional writing from Carnegie Mellon University. She has been on the Internet for at least 10 of the past 16 years and hopes that everyone will have an Internet connection at home eventually.

William A. Tolhurst is cofounder and vice president of engineering for Atlanta Innovation, Inc., a firm that provides engineering services for new product development. His professional specialties include environment simulation, hardware design, signal processing, computer graphics, software development, and project management. Tolhurst received his B.S. in electrical engineering from the University of San Antonio.

Acknowledgments

I want to acknowledge the fine people at Que who helped me through the process of working on this project. They are **Angie Lee**, who served as my principal contact and put up with my questions and notes; **Brad Koch**, who got me involved in the project; and **Sarah Browning**, who set the original terms of the project and deadlines. ——Ernie Ackermann

I'd like to thank **Brad Koch** for always thinking of me when the topic of UNIX comes up. I'd also like to thank all my clients for letting me make lots of mistakes on their systems; without those mistakes, I wouldn't know half as much as I do now. ——Steve Glines

Que would like to thank **Chris Negus** and **Larry Schumer** for their efficiency and hard work in providing the tech edit—and so much more—for this book. Their contributions and assistance are greatly appreciated.

Chris Negus, in 12 years of consulting for AT&T Bell Laboratories, UNIX System Laboratories, and Novell, has authored a variety of books and manuals on the UNIX operating system. As a member of the development teams for UNIX System V Releases 2.1 through 4.2, he produced networking and administration documentation.

Larry Schumer cowrote the UNIX Desktop product documentation for UNIX System Laboratories. For over a decade, Larry has provided technical support and documentation for the UNIX operating system. As Vice President of Technology for C & L Associates, Larry is working as a consultant with Novell on its UnixWare product manuals and support materials.

Chris and Larry own a consulting firm, C & L Associates, in Salt Lake City, that specializes in UNIX services.

Trademarks

All terms mentioned in this book known to be trademarks or service marks have been appropriately capitalized. Que cannot attest to the accuracy of this information. Use of a term in this book should not be regarded as affecting the validity of any trademark or service mark.

Contents at a Glance

Introduction to UNIX

Installing UNIX

Controlling UNIX

UNIX Tools

Using the Internet

Working with Applications

UNIX Networking

UNIX Multiuser Systems

Appendix

Command Reference

Contents

6 Using the UNIX Command Environment   115

7 Understanding UNIX File and Directory Systems   137

11 Managing Multiple Processes   217

12 Using the *vi* Editor   245

13 Working with E-Mail 279

14 Using UNIX Remote Communications   311

V Using the Internet   339

15 Understanding the Structure of the Internet   341

16 Finding and Using Internet Resources 379

18 Using *ftp* and *telnet* with the Internet   443

19 Using USENET

23 Running DOS Applications 567

24 Running Windows Applications 581

VII UNIX Networking 591

25 UNIX Networking Concepts 593

VIII UNIX Multiuser Systems   689

29 Understanding Multiuser Concepts   691

30 UNIX Administration in a Multiuser Environment 701

Introduction

This decade has been the fastest growth period for the most complex of technologies: computer science. In glaring contrast to the explosion of computer applications and capabilities has been the lack of advance in operating systems. One must reason that either there has been no need for improvements in existing operating systems or that there is a lack of motivation for the development of new and better operating systems.

The first argument is quickly refuted by examining the operating systems available today. To state that these have no limitations and need no improvement is to ignore the obvious. All but one have their own idiosyncrasies that plague novice and expert alike.

The second argument can be discredited with just one word: UNIX.

When existing operating systems are compared, UNIX stands unmistakably above the rest. All operating systems have express limitations in one area or another—many operating systems are constrained by limitations in many areas—but UNIX has risen above the rest to provide the novice and the computer scientist alike with an operating platform second to none. The worst anyone could ever claim about UNIX was that it was an unforgiving, unfriendly operating system, difficult to use and hard to master. Until now.

UNIX has evolved over the years to become the premier operating system used by hundreds of thousands of people throughout the world. This is not an accident. The earlier versions of UNIX were indeed harder to manipulate than other operating systems, but in spite of this, UNIX managed to amass a distinguished following in academic and scientific circles. These professionals realized not only what a powerful, flexible, and manageable operating system UNIX was, they also realized its potential to be the best operating system ever. Their efforts have culminated in the UNIX of today, with its marvelous utilities, bundled with the newest communications capabilities and graphical user interfaces (not one, but two).

The UNIX of today promises to revolutionize again the personal computer industry and perhaps redirect its growth. UNIX has evolved from a minicomputer operating system to one that crosses all hardware configuration lines. There is no reason to think that this evolution will stop. UNIX may well become the standard for what most users dream of—eventual, complete standardization and compatibility of all computer systems, regardless of size or power.

Who Should Use This Book?

If the preceding claims sound incredible to you, it's likely you are not a UNIX user. But the fact that you're reading this now indicates that you are at least interested in knowing more about the operating system your friends told you was too difficult to learn. You have come to the right source. Que's *Using UNIX*, Special Edition, will prove an invaluable asset to your library of computer references. Although this publication is not intended to provide merely a cursory examination of UNIX capabilities, the beginning UNIX user should not shy away from delving into its chapters. The information presented is complete, concise, and accurate without being overwhelming. Novices and experts alike will enjoy both material and presentation because it's detailed enough to keep you from getting into trouble. Better yet, it's complete enough to get you out of trouble if you somehow manage to get stuck.

From the basics and introduction to the UNIX operating system, to its treatment of advanced manipulation techniques, this book is for everyone interested in knowing UNIX better. You learn about the developmental history of the operating system and find new and exciting applications of control provided through the addition of the GUIs in USL's SVR4.2. Utilities, network environments, system administration, and communications concepts are taught simply and effectively. In short, this book has it all, and this book does it all.

> **Note**
>
> If you want to start exploring UNIX on an even more basic level, look at *Introduction to UNIX*, Second Edition (published by Que Corporation).

How To Use This Book

You may prefer to read this book from cover to cover. The information progresses from simple to complex as you move through the chapters. However, because the information is separated into nine parts, plus an appendix, each with its own particular emphasis, you can choose to read only those areas that appeal to your immediate needs. But don't let your immediate needs deter you from eventually giving attention to each chapter as you have time. You'll find a wealth of information in them all!

Following is a brief look at the contents of each chapter in *Using UNIX*, Special Edition:

Part I, "Introduction to UNIX," does just that: introduces you to UNIX.

■ Chapter 1, "What Is UNIX?," provides insight into the history of UNIX development and a brief discussion of its capabilities and characteristics and introduces some of the different versions of UNIX.

Part II, "Installing UNIX," gives you basic information about hardware and software.

■ Chapter 2, "Hardware Issues," addresses concerns you are likely to have: what hardware is needed to run UNIX and what is not, and the differences you are likely to encounter when making decisions about your platform.

■ Chapter 3, "Software Issues," gives you a feel for what to look for in software that can run on UNIX and how that compatibility issue can be best dealt with by configuring UNIX in advance.

■ Chapter 4, "Single-User Installations," describes the general process for installing, configuring, and troubleshooting UNIX on a single-user system (no networks, dumb terminals, and so on).

Part III, "Controlling UNIX," presents the basics you need to know to accomplish work with UNIX.

■ Chapter 5, "Manipulating the GUI," describes basic window, mouse, and keyboard functions of the UnixWare Desktop GUI. It also explains how to manipulate files and folders.

■ Chapter 6, "Using the UNIX Command Environment," speaks to the subtle nuances of UNIX command syntax, execution from the command prompt, parsing, command interpretation, and command feedback.

- Chapter 7, "Understanding UNIX File and Directory Systems," details the UNIX file-system structure and organization, file-naming conventions, and directory hierarchy.

- Chapter 8, "Managing Files and Directories," teaches you how to navigate the UNIX file system successfully. Management of files and directories is covered here in detail.

- Chapter 9, "Printing," covers all the bases from issuing print commands, checking printer status, canceling print jobs, and dealing with common printing problems.

Part IV, "Working with UNIX Command Line Tools," advances your skill levels with UNIX. You learn to make your time with UNIX productive.

- Chapter 10, "Understanding UNIX Shells," introduces you to the magical world of UNIX shells, the powerful capabilities that exist through the use of shell scripting, and the different shells you may encounter with different versions of UNIX.

- Chapter 11, "Managing Multiple Processes," explores the capabilities of UNIX when you run more than one process at a time. You learn how to initiate and manage those multiple processes as well as how to control and stop them.

- Chapter 12, "Using the *vi* Editor," instructs you how to use UNIX's visual editor to edit text files.

- Chapter 13, "Working with E-Mail," presents everything you need to learn before you can communicate successfully with other UNIX users using the e-mail utility.

- Chapter 14, "Using UNIX Remote Communications," shows you how UNIX can access another UNIX system across the hall or around the world using its remote communications capabilities. You learn about the remote login feature that allows you to log in to another UNIX system.

Part V, "Using the Internet," introduces you to that vast and sometimes intimidating group of computer users collectively known as the Internet. As you learn in these chapters, the Internet is nothing more than a larger version of what you already are familiar with.

- Chapter 15, "Understanding the Structure of the Internet," provides information on how to access systems on the Internet. Topics include system name and address structures as well as system administration.

- Chapter 16, "Finding and Using Internet Resources," describes the organizations responsible for maintaining the Internet. It includes tips on locating Internet services.

- Chapter 17, "Using Internet E-Mail," teaches you how to communicate over the Internet using e-mail.

- Chapter 18, "Using *ftp* and *telnet* with the Internet," describes the file transfer and remote login utilities: `ftp` and `telnet`.

- Chapter 19, "Using USENET," shows you how to access USENET to read and post news items on the Internet.

- Chapter 20, "Determining the Level of Internet Service You Need," describes basic Internet services, such as network navigation aids and teleconferencing, and explains how to choose connection attributes based on how you use the Internet.

- Chapter 21, "Making Connections Beyond the Internet," describes how to navigate various commercial computer services, such as CompuServe, AppleLink, and America Online.

Part VI, "Working with the Applications," explains some things you should consider when you load UNIX applications, DOS applications, and Windows applications on your UNIX system.

- Chapter 22, "Loading UNIX Applications," contains information on installing single-user and multiuser UNIX applications.

- Chapter 23, "Running DOS Applications," shows you how to run DOS applications under UNIX using various DOS emulators.

- Chapter 24, "Running Windows Applications," describes programs that emulate Windows under UNIX and explains how to use these emulators to load and run Windows applications.

Part VII, "UNIX Networking," contains information about specific UNIX commands and configuration files needed to communicate between UNIX systems.

- Chapter 25, "UNIX Networking Concepts," is invaluable to those who are installing or maintaining a UNIX network. The chapter discusses networking concepts, protocols, OSI models, and internetworking devices and techniques.

- Chapter 26, "UNIX in a NetWare World," provides tips and techniques for integrating UNIX clients and UNIX servers into a NetWare environment. Installation, instruction, tuning, troubleshooting, and configuration are discussed.

- Chapter 27, "TCP/IP," talks about properly integrating TCP/IP (the backbone of your networking strategy) into multivendor, multiplatform environments.

- Chapter 28, "UNIX Administration in a Networked Environment," fosters the skills you need for basic administration of the UNIX system in a networked environment. You learn how to work with local and remote hosts, optimize UNIX performance, and institute security measures.

Part VIII, "UNIX Multiuser Systems," provides information on using and administering multiuser UNIX systems.

- Chapter 29, "Multiuser Concepts," explains how UNIX provides access to the system for simultaneous users.

- Chapter 30, "UNIX Administration in a Multiuser Environment," helps you develop your administrative skills by showing you how to optimize performance, provide help for users, perform routine tasks, manage system security, and effectively back up a multiuser system.

Part IX, "Command Reference," provides you with hundreds of UNIX commands and explains how to use the commands.

The single appendix, "Resources for UNIX Users and Administrators," lists news groups, interest groups, and ftp sites on the Internet as well as other resources.

Conventions Used in This Book

This book uses several special conventions of which you should be aware. These conventions are listed here for your reference.

UNIX is a case-sensitive operating system; that means that when this book instructs you to type something at a command or shell prompt, you must type exactly what appears in the book *exactly as it is capitalized*. This book uses a special typeface for UNIX commands and filenames to set them off from standard text. If you are instructed to type something, what you are to type appears in **bold in the special typeface**. For example, if the book instructs you to type **cat** and press <Return>, you must press the letters <c>, <a>, and <t> and then press <Return>.

At times, you are instructed to press a key such as <Return>, <Tab>, or <space>. Angle brackets surround the name of the key to distinguish the name of the key from a command you may have to type. Keys sometimes are pressed in combination; when this is the case, the keys are represented in this way: <Ctrl-h>. This example implies that you must press and hold the <Ctrl> key, press the letter <h>, and then release both keys.

> ### Note
>
> When you press the key whose name appears in angle brackets, you do *not* type the angle brackets.
>
> This book uses a convention for key names that may differ from what you are accustomed to. To avoid confusion in the case-sensitive UNIX environment, this book uses lowercase letters to refer to keys when uppercase letters may be the norm. For example, this book uses the form <Ctrl-c> instead of the form Ctrl-C (the latter form may make literal readers wonder whether they should press <Ctrl> *and* <Shift> *and* <c>).

Some examples show a listing with a portion of the screen after you type a specific command. Such listings show the command or shell prompt (usually a dollar sign, $) followed by what you type in bold. Do *not* type the dollar sign when you follow the example on your own system. Consider this example:

```
$ lp report.txt & <Return>
  3146
$
```

You should type only what appears in bold on the first line (that is, type **lp report.txt &** and then press <Return>). The remainder of the listing shows UNIX's response to the command.

When discussing the syntax of a UNIX command, this book uses some special formatting to distinguish between the required portions and the variable portions. Consider the following example:

```
lp filename
```

In this syntax, the *filename* portion of the command is variable; that is, it changes depending on what file you want the lp command to work with. The lp is required; it is the actual command name. Variable information is presented in *italics*; information that must be typed exactly as it appears is presented in nonitalic type.

In some cases, command information may be optional; that is, it is not required for the command to work. Square brackets ([ ]) surround those parts of the command syntax that are optional. In the following example, notice that the *filename* parameter is variable *and* optional (it is in italics as well as surrounded by square brackets); however, to use the optional -l parameter, you must type it exactly as it appears (it is not in italics; it is a *literal* option):

```
is [-l] filename
```

Tips, notes, and cautions appear in specially formatted boxes to make the information they contain easy to locate. Longer discussions not integral to the flow of the chapter are set aside as sidebars (shaded blocks of text with a bold heading).

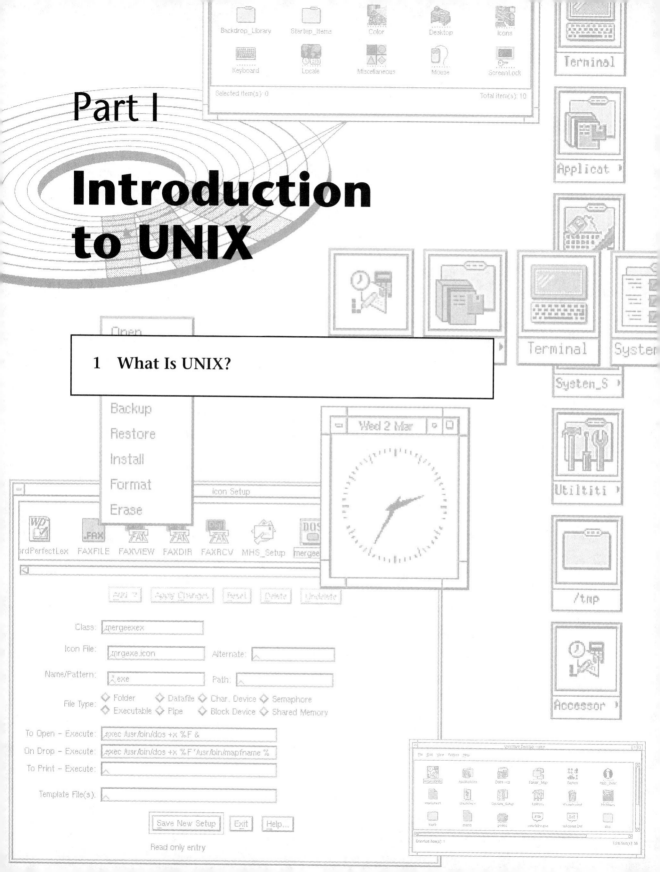

Part I

Introduction to UNIX

1 What Is UNIX?

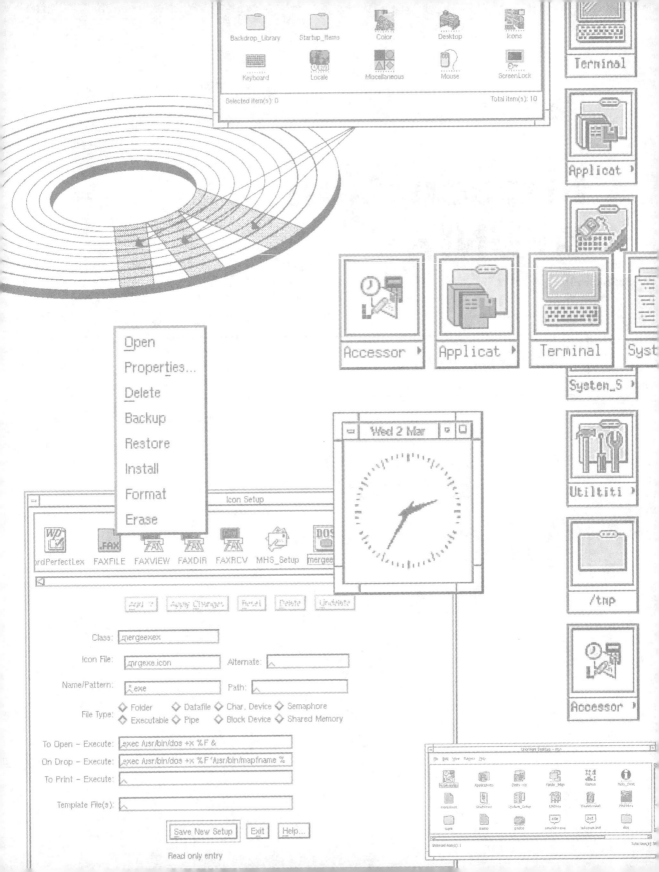

Backdrop_Library   Startup_Items   Color   Desktop   Icons

Keyboard   Locale   Miscellaneous   Mouse   ScreenLock

Selected item(s): 0   Total item(s): 10

Terminal

Applicat ▸

Accessor ▸   Applicat ▸   Terminal   Syst

System_S ▸

Utiltiti ▸

/tmp

Accessor ▸

Open
Properties...
Delete
Backup
Restore
Install
Format
Erase

Icon Setup

rdPerfectLex   FAXFILE   FAXVIEW   FAXDIR   FAXRCV   MHS_Setup   mergee

Wed 2 Mar

Add ▾   Apply Changes   Reset   Delete   Undelete

Class: _mergeexex

Icon File: _mrgexe.icon   Alternate: ▵

Name/Pattern: *.exe   Path: ▵

File Type: ◇ Folder ◇ Datafile ◇ Char. Device ◇ Semaphore
◇ Executable ◇ Pipe ◇ Block Device ◇ Shared Memory

To Open – Execute: _exec /usr/bin/dos +x %F &

On Drop – Execute: _exec /usr/bin/dos +x %F '/usr/bin/mapfname %

To Print – Execute: ▵

Template File(s): ▵

Save New Setup   Exit   Help...

Read only entry

## Chapter 1

What Is UNIX?

UNIX is arguably the most versatile and popular operating system today. This chapter explains why you may want to select UNIX instead of one of the other operating systems available. It also provides details about the different versions of UNIX covered by this book. Additionally, you'll find information covering UNIX System Laboratories' revolutionary System V, Release 4.2 (SVR4.2) and how flexible GUIs enhance the UNIX operating system.

Why Use UNIX?

If you have a computer, you must have an operating system (OS). An *operating system* is a complex set of computer codes that provides the operating process protocols, or laws of behavior. Without an operating system, your computer would sit idle, unable to interpret and act on your input commands or run a simple program.

Because your computer cannot function without an OS, you will want the best one available that can run the applications you need. Factors you want to consider include the OS's capability, versatility, compatibility, and expandability. This chapter looks at each of these factors in more detail.

Most computer systems today can function with more than one OS. The selection of an operating system is important for a number of reasons. First, application programs are coded to run under a particular operating system, so the choice of an OS determines the selection of programs available. Second, features vary among operating systems, limiting the types and uses of peripheral hardware. Finally, each operating system uses a specific format when transferring data so that one operating system may not be able to read disks created by another operating system.

Although there are many operating systems available, many operate only on one or two specific hardware configurations and are not easily customized to

This chapter covers the following topics:

- Why use UNIX?

- Versions of UNIX in this book

- An overview of the features of UNIX

- A brief history of UNIX

Introduction to UNIX

meet the changing needs of the user. UNIX, however, is the one operating system that crosses these boundaries to provide a powerful, versatile, and flexible platform that can grow and change as users' needs do.

You will want to use UNIX because it is the only operating system today that can provide multitasking, multiprocessing capabilities for multiusers on virtually any hardware platform. No other operating system gives you these same features with the power and ease of manipulation that UNIX enjoys.

UNIX Versions Covered in This Book

The name *UNIX* can mean many things. It is one of the most context-specific terms used in the computer industry today. To better understand what is meant when someone uses the word *UNIX*, you must know which version of the operating system they are referring to.

Although versions of UNIX are offered by many different vendors, these versions fall into one of two major categories: UNIX System V and Berkeley Software Distribution (BSD). UNIX System V is the version developed by the creators of UNIX: AT&T Bell Laboratories. Berkeley UNIX was associated with the version of UNIX developed and proliferated by the University of California at Berkeley. The most popular version of BSD UNIX was sold by Sun Microsystems on its powerful workstations.

With UNIX System V Release 4, AT&T and Sun Microsystems merged their two version of UNIX into UNIX System V. Because of this merger and the rallying of the industry around the UNIX System V standard, UNIX System V is now considered the standard UNIX system.

This book focuses on UNIX System V (although there are some examples of utilities that originally came from the BSD world). In particular, because Novell Inc. now owns UNIX System V (after recently purchasing AT&T's spin-off company UNIX System Laboratories), this book focuses on Novell's shrink-wrapped UNIX product: UnixWare. UnixWare, based on UNIX System V Release 4.2 and including NetWare connectivity, contains the latest UNIX system technology and is expected to carry UNIX into the future.

For more information on the history and development of the UNIX variants listed here, turn to "A Brief History of UNIX," at the end of this chapter.

USL UNIX SVR4.2

Undoubtedly the best thing to happen to the UNIX OS was the development of System V, Release 4.2 (SVR4.2). Created and introduced by UNIX System Laboratories (USL), SVR4.2 combines the power and capabilities of UNIX with a "user-affectionate" graphical user interface (GUI). The result is an operating system that can be easily navigated by computer novices or radically customized by system administrators and other experts.

Before the release of SVR4.2, UNIX users saw only a command-line prompt (a simple dollar sign) after logging into the system. With no guidance evident on the screen, inexperienced users frequently were intimidated into forsaking UNIX in favor of other, better-known operating systems. No doubt this contributed to UNIX's reputation as an unfriendly operating system throughout its early years. Although experience and word of mouth dispelled some user reluctance, it was a reputation dying a slow death until now.

SVR4.2 provides the user with a GUI called *the UNIX Desktop*, based on the X-Windowing system developed at the Massachusetts Institute of Technology (MIT). The Desktop is comprised of windows and icons that can be manipulated by the mouse or keyboard. By selecting icons, you can run applications or services and otherwise configure your system or operating environment. The GUI actually "sits" on top of the OS, providing a layer of protocols that allow the user to interact with the computer using fewer keystrokes and UNIX-specific commands. One look at a typical GUI, like the one shown in figure 1.1, and you will agree that it's a marked improvement over the earlier UNIX command-line prompt.

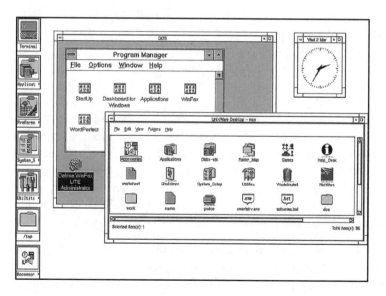

Fig. 1.1
The UNIX Desktop GUI (Motif).

Flexible GUI

The UNIX GUI offers the flexibility of customizing the look and feel of your computer's operating environment. You make the selection between *OPEN*

LOOK and *Motif* GUIs when setting up your UNIX desktop. The OPEN LOOK GUI is supported by UNIX System Laboratories and Sun Microsystems. The Motif GUI is a standard environment promoted by the Open Software Foundation. Personal experience alone determines which of these environments is best for you; each provides a slightly different way of managing the Desktop's windows and your mouse.

User preferences about color scheme, hardware functions, size of windows or folders, and the appearance of icons (to name a few options) can be changed and recorded at will. More advanced functions can be altered, too, such as sound, icon spacing, text-editing options, and so on. You make these changes to the look and feel of your Desktop with a simple point-and-click of your mouse.

You can quickly and easily change almost every aspect of the UNIX Desktop to suit your own desires. Navigating through the operating system is almost mundane without having to recall specific UNIX commands and their unforgiving syntax rules. Never has the UNIX operating system been simpler to modify and manipulate than now, thanks to the GUIs bundled in SVR4.2.

An Overview of UNIX Features

The benefits derived from using the UNIX operating system stem from its power and flexibility. These are the result of the many features built into the system, ready for you to use as soon as you turn the system on. The following sections examine these features more closely.

Multitasking

The word *multitasking* describes exactly what UNIX does that no other operating system could do before it: run a number of applications at the same time. Recently, other operating systems and *operating environments* (which add an additional layer of protocols on top of the underlying operating system) claim to have developed multitasking capabilities, but those claims are open to debate. Arguably, what they have instead is a *task-switching* capability, quite unlike UNIX's multitasking feature that processes tasks simultaneously.

To better understand the multitasking capability of UNIX, examine it from another view. The microprocessor in your computer can do only one thing at a time, but it is capable of completing those individual tasks in periods of time so short they are difficult to comprehend. For example, typical microprocessors today operate at clock speeds of 20 to 60 MHz (megahertz) and faster. What this means is that they are capable of *transferring* from 20 to 60 *million bits per second*! When *processing* a complete set of instructions, the speeds are much faster, typically 30 nanoseconds (*billionths* of a second). The human mind cannot detect the difference between so short a delay and something occurring simultaneously. In short, it *appears* that tasks are performed at the same time.

UNIX monitors processes waiting to run, as well as those currently running, and schedules each process to have equal access to the microprocessor. The result is that open applications *appear* to be running concurrently (in reality, there are delays of only billionths of a second between when the processor executes a set of instructions from one application and when it is scheduled by UNIX to devote time to that process again).

It is the ability to allocate time to open applications that sets UNIX apart from all other operating systems. The others merely switch the processor's time to one *single* task or another instead of allocating equal processing time for each application the user has open. Usually, this switch can be accomplished only after closing or otherwise temporarily suspending (*minimizing*) the active application to run a second one. This is why these operating systems and operating environments are said to have a task-switching capability as opposed to a true multitasking feature.

Using a real-world example may further explain this feature. Suppose that, while working in a spreadsheet application, you discover that the current month's information has not yet been merged from the database to the spreadsheet application. Typically, this takes some minutes to accomplish, so you start the process. Then you switch to another window in UNIX to work on a report you are preparing.

Before you finish the report, you switch back to the original UNIX window to check on the progress of your spreadsheet-merge process. Seeing that it is not yet complete, you switch back to the report window, only to realize that some of the information you want to include is located in a letter you wrote some time ago. So you open yet another window, select the file containing your letter, extract the information you need by using a copy utility, and return to the report, where you paste the copied information in place—all the while using the same word processing package. UNIX informs you that your merge process is now complete, so you close your word processing windows and return to the original spreadsheet window to finish your work there.

You can readily see the benefits of having true multitasking capabilities. Besides reducing dead time (time in which you can't continue working on an application because a process has not yet finished), the flexibility of not having to close application windows before opening and working in others is infinitely more convenient.

Multiprocessing

Although some people in the computer industry today draw a distinction between the terms *multitasking* and *multiprocessing*, there is not really a substantive difference. All applications require *processing* of instructions by the microprocessor and it must be argued that each *task* is broken down by the microprocessor into a number of executable sets of instructions, or *processes*. Hence, with no discernible distinction between the two terms, *multitasking* and *multiprocessing* can be used interchangeably.

Multiuser

The concept of many users accessing applications or processing power from a single PC was only a dream a few short years ago. UNIX helped develop that dream into reality. UNIX's capability of allocating microprocessor time to many applications at once naturally lent itself to serving many people at once, each running one or more applications. The truly remarkable feature of UNIX and its multiuser, multitasking features is that more than one person can work in the same version of the same application at the same time, from the same or separate terminals. Don't confuse this with multiple users updating the same *file* simultaneously, a feature that is potentially confusing, potentially hazardous, and positively undesirable.

Again, a real-world scenario will help further your understanding of this feature. Imagine a company whose personnel are networked to a UNIX system. While one employee places the finishing touches on outgoing correspondence, another produces a company roster. Still another uses the same word processing package to ready a view-graph presentation by importing pictures from a graphics package while the boss extracts information from a database for a report he's preparing—using (you guessed it) the *same* word processing application.

Down the hall in accounting, three data-entry clerks are updating files in the same accounting database; in the mailroom, the supervisor updates the shipping file that simultaneously updates the accounting database. At the same time, the system administrator sets up an account for a new employee and inactivates a second system account for an employee who is away on an extended leave of absence.

Although it may be difficult to imagine this scenario, it is being repeated thousands of times each day in offices throughout the world that utilize the UNIX operating system. Many systems are configured for scores of people to access; others are set up with only a few user accounts. You'll find both ends of the spectrum when you talk about UNIX system configurations: from the single user with the UNIX operating system on a PC to thousands of students and faculty at a school making use of UNIX services and applications night and day. There are no limits to this UNIX multiuser capability—except in the mind of the skeptic.

Programmable Shells

The *programmable shell* is another feature that makes UNIX what it is: the most flexible operating system available. Within the framework of the shell is a whole new world available to those adventurous enough to master the nuances of UNIX command syntax.

Although you shouldn't be discouraged from attempting exciting forays into the Bourne, C, or Korn shell, you should understand that, without proper guidance and preparation, shell programming can be a difficult lesson in frustration. Make sure that you have a reliable reference manual at hand (like the one you're reading now) and that you have the phone number of a good system administrator or other UNIX expert in case you get bogged down.

For those who anticipate the rewarding experience of directing a powerful operating system like UNIX, the importance of command syntax in UNIX cannot be overstated. (*Syntax* is nothing more than the order and form of a command line.) The UNIX shell scans each command line to determine whether the formation and spelling are consistent with its protocols.

The shell's scan process is termed *parsing*: the commands are broken down into more easily processed components. Each component is interpreted and executed—including those special characters that convey additional meaning to the shell. These special characters are further expanded into their proper command processes and executed.

Although many UNIX system versions include more than one type of shell, they all function essentially the same. A shell works as the interpreter between the user and the *kernel* (the heart, or brain, of the UNIX operating system). The primary difference between the three available shells (GUIs are not considered to be shells here for simplification) lies in command-line syntax. Although it's not a severe limitation, you will encounter difficulties if you try to use C shell commands or syntax in the Bourne or Korn shell.

Perhaps the simplest of scenarios to help further your understanding of UNIX shell programming is that of *background processing*. You should back up all or parts of your system files at one time or another; if those files and their associated directories are of substantial size, the backup process can take a considerable amount of time.

With a simple shell program consisting of a line or two of command arguments, a backup process can run concurrently with other operations you may want to do (or *need* to do, since the backup process can take quite some time). After programming the shell and starting the backup process, you can simply open a different window to access the desired application and begin your work there. When the background processing is completed, UNIX signals that the job is finished.

UNIX shell programming serves as many different functions as there are people willing to attempt it. Many use this feature to personalize their system and make it more user friendly. Others find it helpful in streamlining many of the applications they run by allowing them to perform a number of processes in the background so that they are free to work in others.

Some users go even further by devising programs that link processes or applications, so that they can reduce their work load to perhaps a single session of data entry and have the system update numerous software packages at once. The only limit to what can be done in UNIX shell programming exists in the user's mind.

Device Independence

The ability of your computer system's peripherals to operate on a stand-alone or independent basis may not, at first glance, seem important. When you view it from a multiuser UNIX environment, however, it becomes fundamental to a productive work place. To understand the importance of device independence, you must first understand how other systems view attached peripherals and how UNIX views them.

Until recently, computer systems could generally support peripherals such as printers, terminals, disk drives, and modems. The technology explosion has added to this list other devices too numerous to list. Difficulties are encountered when the user cannot utilize a peripheral because of an operating systems inability to access the device. This inability can be the result of incompatible system architecture, operating system addressing limitations, and so on.

UNIX sidesteps the problem of adding new devices by viewing each peripheral as a separate file. As new devices are required, the system administrator adds the required link to the kernel. This link, also known as the *device driver*, ensures that the kernel and the device merge in the same fashion each time the device is called on for service.

As new and better peripherals are developed and delivered to the user, the UNIX operating system will allow immediate, unrestricted access to their services after the devices are linked to the kernel. The key to device independence lies in the adaptability of the kernel. Other operating systems allow only a certain number or a certain kind of device. UNIX can accommodate any number of any kind of device because each device is viewed independently through its dedicated link with the kernel.

Communications and Networking

UNIX's superiority over other operating systems is equally evident in its communications and networking utilities. No other operating system includes these capabilities, and no other operating system has the built-in flexibility of these same features. Whether you need to talk with another user through a mail utility or download megafiles from another system across the nation, UNIX provides the means to do so.

Internal messaging or file transfer can be accomplished through a number of UNIX commands, including `write`, `calendar`, `mail`, and `mailx`, as well as `cu` and `uucp`. These commands are examined more closely in later chapters. As an aid to understanding these capabilities, it is helpful to understand that information exchange *by users on the same system* (also called *internal* communications) is accomplished by terminal-to-terminal communication, e-mail, and an automatic calendar that serves as a scheduler/information manager.

An extension of UNIX communications is found in the `cu` and `uucp` commands (used for *external* communications). Not only does UNIX allow for file and program transfer, it gives system administrators and technicians a window of access to another system. Through this remote-access capability, one technician can effectively service many systems, even when those systems are located across great distances.

The latest and most popular means of communicating involves electronic bulletin boards. Not all systems are set up for users to access a bulletin board service, but those that are connected to a network (like `uucp`, ARPANET, Berknet, and so on) will find a forum for their questions as well as their personal articles. Exchanges that take place in these electronic auditoriums are often the most helpful and informative because of the wide range of professional abilities represented.

Networking in UNIX needs little explanation. The communications capabilities inherent in the operating system were designed to support many tasks and many users over many miles. UNIX quite naturally evolved in the professional marketplace as the operating system of choice thanks to the same characteristics that gave it premier status in the scientific community and academia.

Open Systems Portability

In the never-ending quest for standardization, many organizations have taken a renewed interest in the direction in which operating systems are developing. UNIX has not gone unnoticed. The drive to standardize UNIX stems from the many UNIX variants currently available. You learn more about how those variants were developed in the following section.

Efforts have been made to combine, collate, and otherwise absorb all versions of UNIX into a single, all-encompassing version of the operating system. Initially, the effort met with guarded enthusiasm and some effort was expended on coming to terms with blending the different versions. As with many noble efforts, this one was doomed to failure because no single developer was willing to sacrifice part of what they had already invested into their particular version. (Sad to say, many developers still feel that way.)

However, the continued existence of varieties of UNIX is not necessarily cause for alarm. In spite of the different varieties, all are still inherently superior to all other operating systems available today because each contains the same elements described in the preceding pages.

Portability is merely the ability to transport an operating system from one platform to another so that it still performs the way it should. UNIX is indeed a portable operating system in that sense. Initially, UNIX could operate on only one specific platform, the DEC PDP-7 minicomputer. Today, the many variants of UNIX can operate in any environment and on any platform, from laptops to mainframes.

Portability provides the means for different computer platforms running UNIX to accurately and effectively communicate with any of the others without the addition of special, pricey, after-market communications interfaces. No other operating system in existence can make this claim.

A Brief History of UNIX

When Novell Inc. purchased UNIX System Laboratories from American Telephone and Telegraph Corporation (AT&T) in 1993, they gained the ownership of the registered trademark recognized as UNIX and, therefore, controlled the rights to who can use it for advertising or other commercial purposes. Although AT&T was the creator of the UNIX operating system, many other companies and individuals have attempted to improve the basic idea over the years. The following sections examine a few of the leading variants in use today.

AT&T

Ken Thompson was a computer programmer who worked for Bell Labs at AT&T. In 1969, a group of people working under Ken's direction developed an operating system that was flexible and completely compatible with programmers' varied needs. Legend tells how Ken, who had been using the MULTICS operating system, dubbed this new product *UNIX* as he joked with others on his development team. He was lampooning the MULTICS multiuser operating system—UNIX was derived from *uni*, meaning *one* or *single*, followed by the homophone *X*. Perhaps the greater joke in this bit of folklore lies in the fact that MULTICS is remembered by few users today as a viable multiuser operating system, while UNIX has become the *de facto* industry standard.

BSD

Berkeley Software Distribution, University of California at Berkeley, released their first version of UNIX, based on AT&T's Version 7, in 1978. BSD UNIX, as it is known throughout the industry, contained enhancements developed by the academic community at Berkeley designed to make UNIX more user friendly.

The user-friendly "improvements" in BSD UNIX were an attempt to make UNIX appeal to common, ordinary folk as well as to advanced programmers who liked its flexibility in conforming to their changing demands. In spite of being less than 100-percent compatible with AT&T's original UNIX, BSD did accomplish its goals: the added features enticed common users to use UNIX. BSD has become the academic standard.

USL

USL, or UNIX System Laboratories, was a company spun off by AT&T from the organization that had been developing the UNIX Operating System since the early 1980s. Before it was purchased by Novell in 1993, USL produced the source code for all UNIX System V derivatives in the industry. However, USL itself did not sell a shrink-wrapped product.

USL's last release of UNIX was UNIX System V Release 4.2 (SVR4.2). The significance of SVR4.2's contribution to the UNIX community is its use of a graphical user interface, or GUI. Until recently, when a user started the system and logged in, he or she was presented with only a command prompt. Novices were intimidated enough to move on to other operating systems that appeared more user friendly.

USL's GUI (called the UNIX Desktop) provides the familiar windowed environment seen on a majority of computers today. Navigating within the operating system is simply a matter of point-and-shoot: you use your mouse cursor to open and close applications, configure the system, and access other system services. USL's contribution of SVR4.2 could prove to be an historical milestone for the UNIX operating system, helping it overcome the stigma of an unfriendly and difficult-to-use operating system.

SVR4.2 also marked USL's first entry into the off-the-shelf UNIX marketplace. In a joint venture with Novell, USL produced a shrink-wrapped version of SVR4.2 called UnixWare. With Novell's purchase of USL, Novell has shifted the focus of USL (now part of Novell's UNIX Systems Group) from source-code producer to UnixWare producer.

UnixWare represents the most significant chance to date for standardizing a low-cost, mass-market UNIX operating system. Leveraging its ownership of the UNIX System V source-code product and USL's development team with its proven marketing strength, Novell has the opportunity to solidify the UNIX industry plagued by too many UNIX variants.

Standard Versions of UNIX

Although the AT&T, BSD, and USL versions are given more attention in this book, a few other versions of UNIX must not go unmentioned. All versions of UNIX have given parts of themselves to the newer versions, but they all have one thing in common: the UNIX core. The UNIX *core*, or basic set of operating system instructions, is what gives UNIX its characteristics. Users become accustomed to the way UNIX can be handled and develop an appreciation for it. This breeds a loyalty in UNIX users that results in the careful preservation of the original UNIX flexibility, centered around the core. In spite of the many versions, differences, and improvements, UNIX is UNIX is UNIX.

Microsoft developed their UNIX version, called XENIX, in the late 1970s and early 1980s, during the peak of the personal computer revolution. Processing power available in PCs began to rival that of existing minicomputers. With the advent of Intel's 80386 microprocessor, it soon became evident that XENIX, which had been developed specifically for PCs, was no longer necessary. Microsoft Corporation and AT&T merged XENIX and UNIX into a single OS called System V/386 Release 3.2, which can operate on practically any common hardware configuration. XENIX is still available today from Santa Cruz Operation (SCO), a codeveloper with Microsoft, whose efforts to promote XENIX in the PC market have made this version of UNIX one of the most successful commercially.

Sun Microsystems has contributed greatly to UNIX marketability by promoting the Sun OS and its associated workstations. Sun's work with UNIX produced a version based on BSD. Interestingly enough, AT&T's SVR4 is compatible with BSD, too—no doubt an offshoot of AT&T and Sun Microsystems' collaboration in UNIX System V Release 4.0.

Finally, IBM's venture into the world of UNIX yielded a product called AIX (Advanced Interactive Executive). Although AIX is not as well-known as some other UNIX versions, AIX performs well and has no problem holding its share of the operating system market. It is perhaps the old mindset that any UNIX version is an unfriendly, unforgiving OS that has kept AIX from a better market reception.

Summary

UNIX has a long tradition of serving the scientific and engineering community. Although in recent years it has made significant inroads into business applications, it has not made significant moves into the mass market.

With UNIX SVR4.2, represented in the marketplace by Novell Inc. as UnixWare, UNIX is making its first big play at mass-market distribution. With a new graphical user interface designed to make UNIX more accessible to new users, UnixWare takes UNIX's multiprocessing, multiuser, and networking strengths and makes them easier to use.

The major UNIX versions, UNIX System V and BSD, are merging more and more. As vendors, software developers, and users continue to rally around the UNIX System V standard from Novell, the confusion of choosing which UNIX to use will diminish.

Now that you're sold on UNIX, Chapter 2, "Hardware Issues," will help you understand how to choose the hardware you need for your UNIX system.

Part II

Installing UNIX

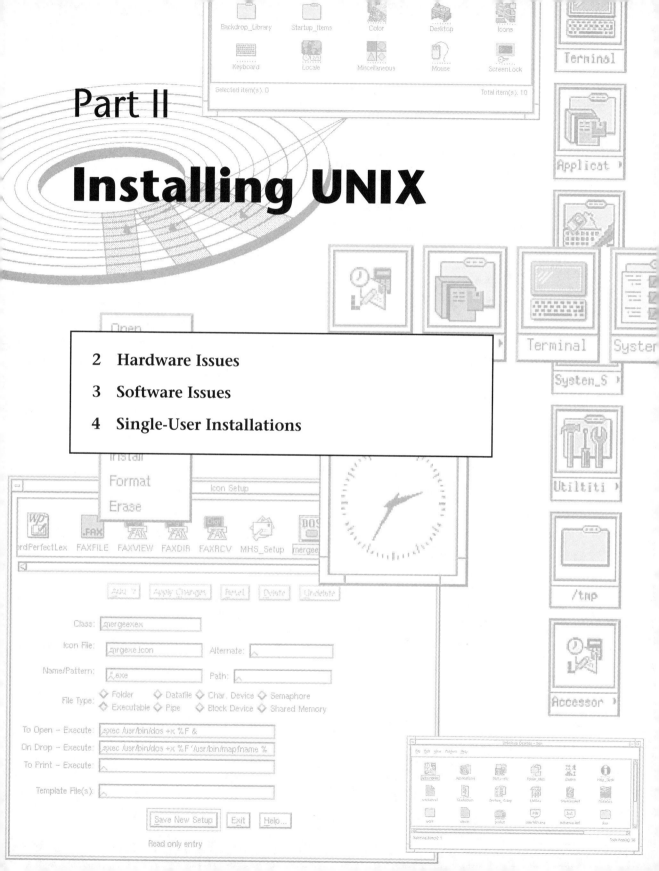

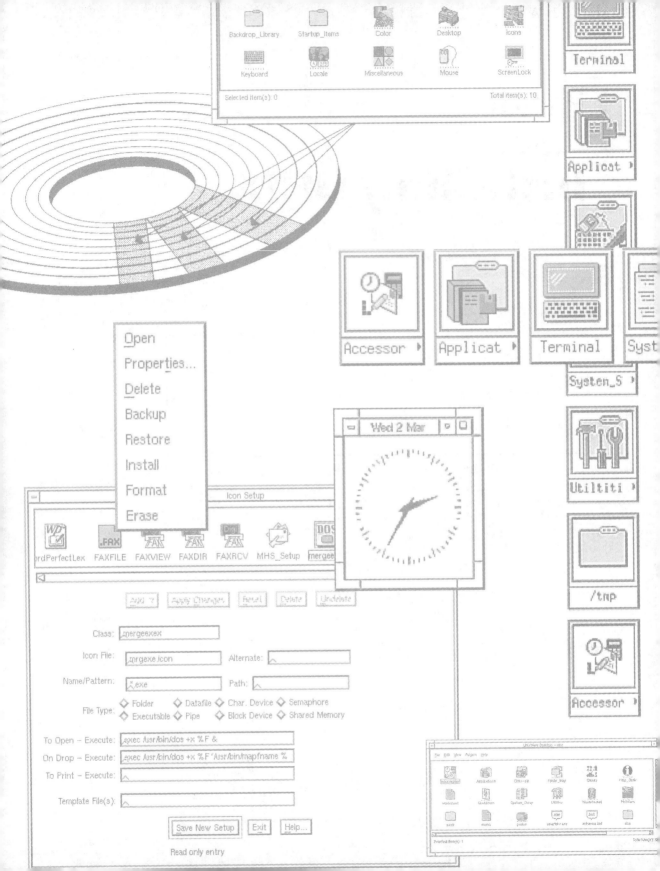

Chapter 2

Hardware Issues

A computer—any computer—is part of a *system*. The operating system software, your application program, the keyboard you type on, the terminal or monitor in front of you, the computer itself—all these form the complete system. The parts of the computer system you actually can touch—real physical devices like keyboards and disk drives and monitor screens—are called *hardware*.

A *system administrator* is the person in charge of a UNIX system. He or she adds new users, enables various pieces of hardware for system access, installs new software packages, maintains the security and integrity of the system, and keeps the system fine-tuned. UnixWare systems have a system owner instead of a system administrator because UnixWare is designed to be maintained by the user/owner of the system. If your UnixWare system is networked to other systems, you can think of the person maintaining the network as the system administration.

Even if you are only setting up UNIX for your personal use on a desktop computer, the job of system administrator is an all-important one. If yours is a stand-alone system, by default, the system administrator job and its attached responsibilities fall on your shoulders. Whether you are involved in the administration of a large UNIX system with many other users or just enjoying the benefits of UNIX on your own workstation or personal computer, this chapter helps you with the hardware-related considerations.

The good news is that you don't have to be a UNIX guru, adept in the arcane arts of alchemy and the magical language of C, spoken only by programmers and gold-hoarding dragons in deep, dark caves. This chapter gives you the general basics of hardware you need to understand a UNIX system. The chapter also clarifies the difference between *workstations* and *PCs* and CISC and RISC (and shows you what these mysterious letters really mean). By doing so, it helps you choose the level of hardware necessary for the intended use of your system.

This chapter covers the following topics:

- Hardware terms

- Description of system hardware

- Description of peripheral hardware

- How to choose hardware

II

Installing UNIX

Key Terms Used in This Chapter

This chapter starts by reviewing some key terms. Just knowing the jargon immediately dissipates a lot of the mystery about computer systems. Table 2.1 lists some terms you should be familiar with before you continue reading.

Table 2.1: Hardware-Related Terms

Term	Definition
hardware	The physical parts of a computer system such as screens, keyboards, disk drives, the central processing unit (CPU), and all other electrical and mechanical devices.
system hardware	Any component of a computer used in the actual action of computing, like the integrated circuit chips of the CPU and working memory.
peripheral hardware	The parts of a computer that provide input and output, including the keyboard, printer, modems, your mouse, and your display screen.
binary	The numbers in base 2 used internally by computers to represent values. Binary numbers are 0 and 1 and correspond to *off* and *on*.
instruction	A binary pattern the central processing unit decodes and executes to compute a task. A set of instructions forms a *program*, also called *software*.
CISC	Complex Instruction-Set Computing (CISC) microprocessors are the most common type today. They include the Intel 80386, 80486, and Pentium family, and the CPU chips used in the Apple Macintosh series. CISCs have multiple addressing modes and many variable-length instructions (which require more effort by the chip to decode and execute).
RISC	Reduced Instruction-Set Computing (RISC) is now the most common type of CPU in new workstations. The RISC microprocessor design features simple methods of decoding instructions, memory addressing, and other ways of boosting hardware performance; software such as program compilers require more sophistication when intended for use with RISC chips than software intended for CISC chips.
bit	An acronym for Binary digIT. A bit is a binary 0 or 1.
byte	A pattern of bits stored and manipulated as a unit. In an 8-bit computer, there are 8 bits per byte, 16 in a 16-bit machine, 32 in a 32-bit computer, and so forth.

Term	Definition
Random-Access Memory	Also called *RAM*. Two other terms for RAM are *virtual memory* and *working memory*. RAM is an electronic storage area—usually contained within integrated circuit chips—that the CPU addresses when storing and retrieving data and program instructions. All contents of working memory are lost when the computer is turned off, hence the need to *boot* computers each time power is turned on by reloading the operating system and application programs back into memory from some permanent storage area such as a hard disk or tape.
Read-Only Memory	Also called *ROM*. This is memory the computer can only read, or retrieve values from; it cannot use it to store new values. The contents of ROM chips are not lost when power is turned off. ROM chips are used in some computers to retain boot-up information or small, often-used programs. Sometimes, ROM integrated circuits are referred to as Application Specific Integrated Circuits (ASICs).
CPU	The Central Processing Unit (CPU) is the heart of any computer. The CPU has the circuitry that does the actual computing actions; most of this circuitry is contained in a microprocessor integrated circuit chip. The IBM-compatible or Intel-based personal computer (after the name of the company that makes the chip) uses such chips as the 80386, 80486, and the new Pentium chip. Other computers running UNIX (such as Sun and the new DEC Alpha workstations) employ more powerful RISC chips.
MPU	Multiple Processing Units (MPUs) consist of several CPUs in parallel, adding speed and power to a UNIX computer.
workstation	A computer used as a terminal on a UNIX system that can supply local computing power as well as tap into the system's computing capacity. A workstation can also be used as a stand-alone system.
terminal	A device used to send and receive data and commands to and from a computer system. A terminal cannot be used as a stand-alone system.
X terminal (or *X-Windows terminal*)	A more advanced display device that allows the use of a graphical user interface such as X-Windows itself or one based on the X-Windowing system, such as OPEN LOOK or Motif.
printer	A piece of peripheral hardware that takes output from a computer system and puts it on paper.
modem	A device that connects two computers or a computer and an input/output device. Modems are most often used in making connections from remote locations through telephone lines.

II

Installing UNIX

(continues)

Table 2.1 Continued	
Term	**Definition**
hard disks	Mechanical devices that allow the permanent storage of large amounts of data and programs, which are then fed into working memory as needed.
floppy disks	"Floppies" are small removable disks. The most common are the 5.25-inch and 3.5-inch sizes.
tape	A device that uses magnetic tape cassettes of various sizes for storage and retrieval of very large amounts of data and programs. Often used to back up the entire system.
optical drives	Drives that use small platters, similar to those in your stereo CD-ROM player. Some optical drives also play music using the same laser technology. There are three kinds of optical drives: the standard ROM (Read-Only Memory), WORM (Write Once, Read Many), and the full-fledged drive that permits reading and writing just as you do to a standard hard disk, albeit slower.
CRT	A Cathode Ray Tube (CRT) is the television-like screen that most terminals have. CRTs can be black and white, monochrome (a single color), or show hundreds and even thousands of colors.
keyboard	The most common interface with computers; the typewriter-like bank of keys attached to your terminal or workstation.
mouse	A pointing device used by numerous application programs and in graphical user interfaces such as X-Windows and Microsoft Windows to speed and make easier your input to and output from a computer.
network adapter	A device allowing a computer to communicate with other computers over a network.

The parts of a computer system you can actually touch are called *hardware*. The terms *hardware* (also called *equipment*) and *software* (also called *programs*) are the two terms you hear most often from people who work with computers.

The definition really is that simple; hardware is any computer or its associated equipment. The equipment can be sitting in some remote computer room or on your desktop. IBM-compatible personal computers, Apple Macintoshes, Sun workstations, DEC terminals, printers, modems—all are hardware. So are the components that make up these machines: all the nuts, bolts, circuit boards, lights, and wiring. The term *hardware* is an all-inclusive term that refers to any physical device in any computer system.

Hardware can (and should) be divided into two general categories: *system hardware* and *peripheral hardware*. Anything used for actual computing is system hardware; attachments that allow input and output are peripheral hardware. The next sections explain this in more detail so that you can understand why knowing the difference can help you.

Understanding System Hardware

The most important part of system hardware is the CPU, or Central Processing Unit. In desktop systems like the IBM-compatible personal computer, the CPU is often a single microprocessor integrated circuit chip, such as the Intel 80486 or Pentium. Larger computers can have several microprocessor chips operating in parallel for greater computing power (these machines have MPUs, or Multiple Processing Units). Along with the chips, circuit boards, and other electronic components that make up a computer's CPU are various other items of system hardware. These include system memory, power supplies, and various peripheral-controller circuit boards.

Computers vary widely in the types and configurations of system hardware but the standard components just described are almost always there. However, just because a device is contained within the computer's case doesn't mean it's automatically defined as system hardware. Disk and tape drives are major exceptions: these are really items of peripheral hardware because the computer inputs to and receives data from these devices.

The personal computer or UNIX-based workstation on your desk also has a microprocessor chip, but its CPU *is not* system hardware if that PC is connected to a larger system. Rather, the entire machine is considered peripheral hardware because it serves as a terminal to a larger system. In other words, the main controlling computer in a UNIX system is system hardware; your desktop unit, even though it may have stand-alone computing capability, is just an auxiliary.

The CPU

The Central Processing Unit has been called the "heart" of a computer. You can also refer to it as the computer's "brain." The CPU handles all the arithmetic and logic operations that lets a computer think and feel.

The "intelligence" shown by a computer is, of course, not the cognitive type humans possess. In fact, a CPU is not smart at all, being in reality only a switch (albeit an extremely fast, exceptionally sophisticated switch). The CPU recognizes and properly routes the many strings of binary electrical signals flying around inside the computer—and does so millions of times every second. An appropriate analogy of a CPU's actions is to liken it to a switcher in a busy rail yard. The CPU reads the values of "trains" of signals and puts them on the right track. Once a string has been properly manipulated, the CPU switches the "trainload" of newly computed data back to wherever it must next travel.

CPUs understand only switching; they don't have any internal information about how to make your system do word processing, solve spreadsheets, play games, or perform any other useful task. Programs instruct CPUs, step by step, how to do useful work. Programs are explained in the next chapter but for now, you must know only that programs and the CPU work together.

Computers keep getting smaller and more powerful. A small desktop computer today easily outperforms the room-sized monster computers of the 1960s and 1970s. The secret is the integrated circuit called a *microprocessor*, a unit not much larger than your thumb containing millions of transistors and other electronic parts, that serves as a computer's CPU. Because the circuit itself is on a small chip of silicon inside the microprocessor's case, integrated circuits (ICs) are most often referred to as *chips*. Essentially, the terms *microprocessor* and *CPU* are interchangeable.

The faster a CPU can recognize program instructions and respond with a switching action, the more work a computer accomplishes in a given time. Faster and faster microprocessor chips continue to be developed and introduced. Yet there are physical limits on these circuits that determine how many switching actions per second they can complete without burning to a crisp. One way around these limitations is the MPU concept. By adding more CPUs to a computer and dividing the work into parallel streams, an MPU can accomplish a greater number of tasks in a shorter time than a single CPU can do. MPUs are becoming more common in higher-end UNIX computers today.

> **Note**
>
> The next release of UnixWare will be a multiprocessor version. With this version, you can enjoy the benefits of a multiprocessor operating system on common, Intel-based computers at relatively low prices.

A program sends series of *instructions* to the CPU, causing the CPU to exert its arithmetic, logical, and control capabilities to do useful work. A single instruction is a *binary code*, a string of 1s and 0s that the CPU recognizes as various types of switching commands.

The major difference between, for example, an Apple Macintosh and an IBM-compatible personal computer is the design of their CPUs. Although both may accept the same-length byte as a program instruction, they react to that byte differently. The same holds true for a microprocessor in a Sun workstation as opposed to one in a DEC Alpha. This is the underlying reason why a program written for a PC does not run on a Macintosh and vice versa.

Memory

A program is nothing more than a series of steps that the CPU retrieves in a predetermined order. Each step is a binary string, and these strings must be stored where the computer can find and read their values into the CPU. And after a result has been computed, this value (data) must also be stored. This storage place is the computer's *working memory*, or *RAM* (Random-Access Memory).

RAM is a collection of electrical binary storage units in integrated circuit chips. There are, at a minimum, usually thousands and quite often now *millions* of these units in every memory chip. Each unit stores one byte of data. A million bytes is referred to as a *megabyte*. The size of the byte or string of binary numbers used by the computer depends on its design, and these vary from 8 to 16 to 32 to 64 bits and higher—but they are always in some multiple of 8.

As long as power is applied to the chip, each unit "remembers" the last binary string placed into it. If the power goes away (as when the computer is turned off), the memory contents are emptied. This is one reason why permanent memory storage devices, such as hard and floppy disks, are necessary.

About Memory Capacity

UNIX system computers today contain millions of bytes of working memory. Programs often have thousands or even millions of steps. To make byte capacity, or quantity, less awkward to write or speak, prefixes are used to help you handle large numbers. A *kilobyte*, which is abbreviated as K or KB, is 1024 bytes. A megabyte, abbreviated M or MB, is 1024 kilobytes. The multiples are not in even thousands (1024 is a power of 2 and is converted from the binary system). The conventional memory in IBM-compatible computers, for example, is 640KB. However, if you multiply this number by 1,024 (the actual size of a kilobyte) you find that the value is 655,360 bytes.

RAM, or working memory, sounds wonderful—and it is—but there are several limitations. The worst is its *volatility*. This means that RAM requires electrical power at all times to retain the values stored in it. Any interruption to power—even such a minor blip that you barely notice the lights in your office dim—can destroy programs and data. RAM is also expensive compared to other methods of storage.

So a computer needs other types of memory. All UNIX computers require that some initial information be available as soon as power is available. That information can't be left in RAM because those memory locations are purged by the loss of power. The answer is ROM (Read-Only Memory).

ROM memory chips are similar to RAM chips except that, when they are written to by a special programming device at the factory, they permanently retain the values put into their memory locations. A computer can only read values in ROM memory; it cannot write to them. The values in ROM are *always there*, even after the power is turned off.

ROM is often used to retain a computer's *booting*, or startup, information. This information is in the form of a small initialization program that executes the procedures required to bring the computer to operational readiness.

ROMs, because they come preprogrammed for a specific application, are expensive and good only for that one purpose. RAM is less expensive, but only relatively so when compared to ROM. Mass permanent storage of data is not practical on ROM, and you can't cram enough RAM into a system to hold the hundreds of megabytes of programs and data that even a small UNIX system needs to access. Mass storage in the system is handled by magnetic devices, such as hard and floppy disks. These devices are peripheral hardware instead of system hardware, and are explained later in this chapter.

Controller Cards

Think of *controller cards* as gateways. Controller cards (see fig. 2.1) are printed circuit cards that plug into the system's bus (the bus is a circuit that connects controller cards to the computer's CPU). Each card controls a piece of peripheral hardware, allowing the CPU to address that hardware and route binary strings to and from the device.

Disk drives have controller cards, as do tape drives and video displays hooked directly to the main computer. If you use a remote terminal, it is likely hooked up through a serial I/O card. (I/O means *input/output*; *serial* is the way the data is sent in a sequential binary string with one bit following another.)

Printers are often connected through another type of controller card called a parallel interface. The word *parallel* describes how the data is sent. (*Parallel* means that each bit of the byte is sent at the same time down parallel lines, like the front line of a football team advancing on kickoff. This method allows faster transfer of data but is limited by the length of cables that can be used.) Devices using parallel interfaces are usually restricted to being in the same room as the main computer; serial lines can run all over the building.

Network adapter cards allow for even faster and more distant transfer of information in and out of the main computer. They let the CPU send data over coaxial lines or twisted pairs of wires at very fast rates. The speed depends on the *bandwidth* of the network system. Bandwidth is measured in Mbps (mega-bytes per second). A bandwidth of 2.5 Mbps can (theoretically) pass data at 2.5 million bytes per second. The actual speed depends on how many users are on the system at any one time and on all the other tasks the main computer's CPU is attending to at the time.

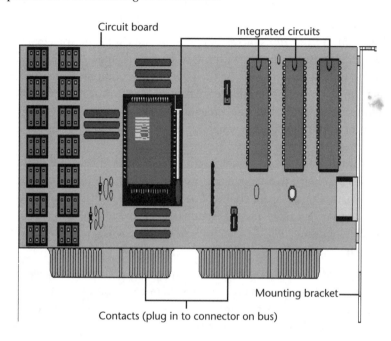

Circuit board   Integrated circuits

Mounting bracket

Contacts (plug in to connector on bus)

Fig. 2.1
A controller card
has several
integrated circuits
and other
components.

True, 2.5 million bytes per second sounds fast but it is not especially so in the world of networking. One of the more common network controller cards used in UNIX systems is the *Ethernet* card. Such a card offers a top speed of 10 Mbps. And even faster systems are now becoming available.

Some controller cards let the CPU handle more than one device. The SCSI (Small Computer System Interface, pronounced *scuzzy*) is a type of controller card often found in UNIX computers. It allows peripheral devices to be "daisy chained," that is, hooked up one after the other like elephants holding each other's tails in a circus parade. In this way, the CPU can address several devices through one controller card. You can have, for example, two hard disks, a tape drive, and an optical scanner in the daisy chain, all of which are accessible to the CPU.

Understanding Peripheral Hardware

CPUs, RAM, controller cards, and other items are interesting, but you are more concerned (and rightly so) with getting your work done. When it comes right down to it, you don't care whether the CPU receives program instructions in binary strings or in little hearts and flowers symbols—just so long as the report you have to turn in to the boss this afternoon is printed.

Unless data is passed to and from the outside world in a meaningful manner, a computer is nothing more than useless circuitry. The devices making this transfer of data possible are what you employ to get useful work from the system. These devices are referred to as *peripheral hardware*.

The first and most obvious pieces of peripheral hardware are the keyboard and screen you use to interact with the system. You type work on the keyboard and monitor its progress on the screen. The computer takes your input and acts on it, returning completed work as output. If you want a more permanent record than data on the screen, the computer can route that output to a printer to put the data on paper (a process often referred to as making a *hard copy*). Alternatively, you can have the computer write the data to a file on the hard disk for later retrieval. Later, the contents of the hard disk can be automatically copied to a tape in the system's *backup tape drive* as a safety precaution. (Making backup copies of data helps prevent the possibility that you will lose work you've already completed because of a system malfunction or accidental erasure.) All these actions, of course, are accomplished with the aid of peripheral hardware.

Peripheral hardware is used for computer input/output (often referred to as I/O). You and all other users on a UNIX system communicate with the system hardware through peripheral hardware. In fact, peripherals are the only components of a computer system you directly operate: they are the go-betweens for you and the CPU.

Disk Drives

A *disk drive* is a peripheral hardware device that enables the storage of extremely large amounts of instructions and data. Although they are often contained within the same case as system hardware, disk drives are really input/output devices and thus are peripheral hardware.

Disk drives are of two basic types: *floppy disks* (also referred to as *removable disks*) and *hard disks* (see fig. 2.2). Hard disks in typical UNIX systems can store hundreds of megabytes of data and programs. Loading a new application program from disk into working memory usually takes only a few seconds, as does opening a data file for the application program to manipulate.

Disk drives are so named because they store binary information on spinning disks called *platters*. The disks are inside the case of the disk drive and cannot be removed. A special circuit converts the binary strings of 1s and 0s that come in over the data bus to magnetic patterns written onto the disk. The recording and playback process is somewhat similar to that used in a cassette tape recorder or your home entertainment VCR. Both types of devices selectively magnetize areas of an oxide coating in order to store information. Oxides, of course, are a type of rust (the action of oxygen combining with a substance). In the case of cassette tape recorders, the oxide coating is on flexible film pulled past the record and playback heads. A hard disk has the coating on a spinning metal platter. A floppy disk also has oxide on a piece of plastic film but the film is a round, flexible (floppy) platter.

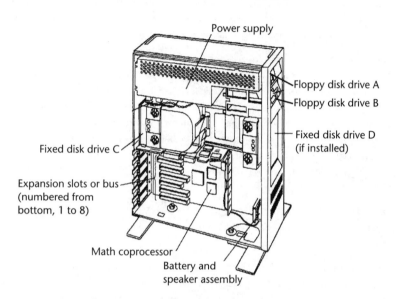

Fig. 2.2
An interior view of a computer, showing floppy and hard disk drives.

The important difference between tapes and disk drives (the difference that makes disks especially practical for use in computers) is that disks can do *random seeking*. Tapes are sequential devices. To get to data stored on a specific area of tape, you must go past all the tape preceding the desired area. If the data is near the end of the tape, you waste a lot of time searching for the right place on the tape.

Hard and floppy disks have data stored in concentric circles (called *tracks*) on the disk. It is easy for the CPU to cause the disk's read/write heads to jump, in a random-access fashion, to the proper circle and then read the right data as it spins by. Most hard disks now have seek times measured in mere milliseconds. (*Seek time* is the time it takes the disk drive to find the requested data.) Because disk drives are random-access devices, the computer's CPU can read or write to a specific location in the same way as it does to locations in working memory.

More About Disks

The oxide coating on disks is a special material that is easily magnetized. Such a coating contains literally billions of particles, each of which is capable of acting like a tiny magnet. As you may recall from your high school science class, every magnet has two poles: a north pole and a south pole. Because of this configuration, magnets are perfect binary storage devices. Polarized north, the bit they contain is a 1; polarized south, the bit is read as a 0. Because there are billions of particles to magnetize, all of which are tiny magnets, disks can store massive amounts of binary information.

The conversion of electrical signals to and from magnetism on the disk's surface is done by the drive's *head*. This device is rapidly and precisely positioned over the spinning disk. It exerts a precise magnetic force on the particles beneath it, polarizing them properly to match the binary string of 1s and 0s being stored. These binary strings, of course, correspond to the letters, numbers, and various control characters used by you and your application programs. When the head magnetizes the clumps of oxide coating into north-pole or south-pole orientations (in other words, it is recording), the head is *writing* the disk. If the head is simply reporting what is already recorded, it is *reading* the disk.

Large disks can, and often do, have more than one platter, greatly increasing storage space. Each platter has its own head that reads and writes to that particular spinning disk only.

After data has been written to a hard or floppy disk, it is very stable. Because the binary values are stored by magnetism, the disk retains its information even when the electrical power is off. After the computer is powered on again and booted up, the head moves over the spinning disks and the drive electronics can then convert the stored magnetic data back into binary strings ready for use by the CPU or RAM.

Preciseness counts for a lot in hard disk design. Because platters spin at speeds close to 3,600 revolutions per minute, there has to be a system of recording data onto the disk so that the head can reposition itself exactly over that specific location and accurately retrieve the binary data. The system that was devised divides each disk into concentric *tracks*. Each track is further divided into many *sectors* (see fig. 2.3). The electronic head controller positions the head by the track/sector "address" to accurately read and write data or program instructions to and from the disk. Any of millions of positions are quickly and accurately found—in mere thousandths of seconds.

A special UNIX program sets up track and sector information on a hard disk before the disk is used the first time. You do not have to learn this procedure because disk formatting is automatically done by the UNIX installation program.

Many UNIX systems and desktop personal computers use small removable disks, called *floppy disks*. Floppy disks are available in 5.25-inch and 3.5-inch sizes and range in capacity from about 128KB to several megabytes. The 3.5-inch size is rapidly becoming the most popular, usually in a 1.44MB capacity.

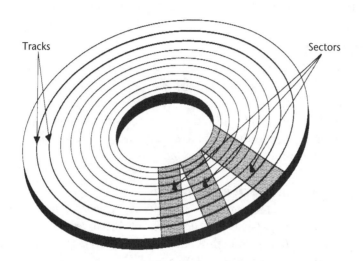

Tracks

Sectors

Fig. 2.3
Concentric tracks and sectors provide an "address" so that the head can find specific locations.

Tape Drives

Tape drives are devices that use special tape cassettes for the storage and retrieval of data and programs. There are various sizes and capacities of tapes, ranging from 40MB up to several *gigabytes* (hundreds of megabytes). The most popular type of cassette uses quarter-inch tape.

Like your home cassette recorder, tape drives are sequential devices, meaning that all the data preceding the desired data must pass by the read/write head before the desired data is found and can be retrieved. If new data is to be written to the tape, the tape must be forwarded past all previously recorded data. Because of this limitation, the most common use for tape drives is for full system backups. Should a hard disk crash, as sometimes they do, then the mirror image of that disk can be reloaded from tape onto the repaired or new drive, with very little data lost.

Another use for tape drives is becoming more and more important: near-line storage. *Near-line* is a take-off of the term *online*. To have something online means that it is available to the computer at all times. Near-line means that the data is close to the computer and, if needed, can be read from tape reasonably quickly.

The perfect use for near-line storage is in pulling vast amounts of old data from the hard disk and storing it away on tape (just as you store last year's paperwork for financial and sales records in banker's boxes after tax season). Should you ever need something from the old data, load the correct tape and retrieve it back to hard disk. If you are a system administrator, the near-line technique is a godsend to you in keeping plenty of storage room on your system for all its users.

Yet another use of tape drives involves graphics programs. Of all the types of data you use on computers, graphics take up the most room. Graphics data includes artwork, photographs, typesetting program files, and so forth. A color photograph scanned into the computer can easily take up several megabytes of disk space. After the job requiring that photograph is done, moving it from disk to tape frees a lot of room.

CD-ROMs and Optical Drives

A relatively new category of storage device is the *optical drive*. This category includes CD-ROM, Magneto-optical, and WORM drives. CD-ROM drives are similar to your home entertainment CD audio player. The discs even look the same. CD means *compact disc*; ROM means exactly what you know it means: *Read-Only Memory*. A CD-ROM drive, whether playing music or connected to your computer, can only read the disc. Magneto-optical drives are new types of drives that combine magnetic media with optical technology to produce an optical drive that both reads and writes. A laser (the optical part) heats the magnetic particles before a magnetic field is applied. Another type of drive, the WORM drive (Write Once, Read Many), lets a computer write data on the disc only once but the data can be read back any number of times.

A big advantage optical drives have over other mass-storage devices is that they are removable. You can have any number of discs you want, making them as handy as tape drives for both backup and near-line storage functions. Unlike tapes and like hard disks, optical drives allow random access. They are also much faster than tape drives, although not quite as fast as hard disk drives. Access times for optical drives are measured in the high milliseconds as compared to access times for hard disks.

More About Magneto-Optical Drives

The way optical drives read and write are two distinct and unrelated processes. Writing uses the laser as a heat source; reading uses it just as a light source. Recording is done on a thin layer of a magnetic alloy embedded within the clear disk. This alloy (usually terbium-iron-cobalt) is resistant to magnetic change at normal temperatures. But when the laser heats it to 200 degrees Centigrade, the alloy takes on a magnetic polarity. Just as with a conventional hard drive, binary data is stored as 1s and 0s by polarizing the alloy.

In reading data, the magneto-optical drive uses the laser as a source of polarized light. The beam bounces off the reflective recorded layer and intensity changes are measured. Because polarized light reflected from areas of opposite magnetic polarity rotates in opposite directions, the proper binary bit is passed back to the computer.

Another reason to have an optical drive in your system is the thousands of pieces of software and databases available on CD-ROM, making access of hundreds of megabytes of new data or programs quick and easy. Prices for the various types of optical drives continue to drop, making them viable additions to both UNIX and personal computer systems.

Terminals

The *terminal* is the most often used piece of peripheral hardware in a UNIX system. The terminal, as its name suggests, is an end point of the computer system. Beyond the terminal, the computer expects to find human eyes and fingers.

Terminals consist of a Video Display Unit (a VDU) and a keyboard. The VDU includes a cathode ray tube, much like that in a television, and the associated circuitry that allows it to display the letters, numbers, and symbols sent by the computer (output). On earlier UNIX systems, the terminal's display unit was sometimes a paper-printing mechanism, like a teletype (tty) printer. Today, however, you find mostly color CRT screens.

Although most VDUs today employ cathode ray tubes as their display device, newer technologies are allowing flat screens that use liquid-crystal or gas-plasma techniques to display computer output. Whatever technology is used, the video display screen shows text or graphics under the CPU's control. The VDU is actually only an output device. Some people refer to VDUs as terminals, but they are not. Only after a keyboard is added can the combination be called a terminal.

The other half of a terminal is a *keyboard*. The keyboard by itself is only an input device. You type letters and numbers by pressing keys in various sequences, but nothing comes back to you unless a VDU is also present. Then the computer echoes back the words and numbers you typed, as well as the result of the computations your input may have asked for. Keyboards can be in the same physical case, or enclosure, as the VDU or attached to the VDU by a curled cord.

A UNIX system may have from one to hundreds of terminals connected to it. From your point of view, the terminal is the standard peripheral used to provide keystroke input and receive visual output. The concepts of *standard input* and *standard output* are important in UNIX, as you discover in using the operating system. For now, all you have to understand is that typing at the keyboard is considered standard input; the letters, numbers, and symbols displayed on the screen is standard output.

Many UNIX systems have a *system console terminal*, the primary terminal for starting a UNIX system's operation. Usually, the person responsible for system administration uses the system console. On single-user UNIX systems, the user terminal and the system console is the same terminal. In fact, as you see in Chapter 4, "Single-User Installations," that terminal can actually be *many* terminals at once.

Note

If you're running UnixWare on a PC, your "terminal" is actually your keyboard and monitor. You can connect other terminals to your PC through its serial (COM) ports.

Printers

Printers are the way you obtain a permanent copy (often called *hard copy* because it's a physical item—paper) of output. Output can be anything from an instruction manual to a letter to your company's monthly sales report. Printers are output-only devices. A UNIX system can have several printers and you can print even to those in remote locations.

▶ For more information about printers and how to access them, refer to Chapter 9, "Printing."

One reason for having several printers on a system is that today's printers are specialized. A UNIX system commonly has a laser printer for high-quality output such as correspondence and graphics, and a dot-matrix printer for high-volume reports such as accounting audit-trails.

Laser printers are becoming commonplace (see fig. 2.4). Their output rivals that of commercial typesetters. Large dot-matrix printers, on the other hand, are perfect for high-volume output where quality is not a necessity (see fig. 2.5). Some dot-matrix printers run at hundreds of lines a minute. Your system administrator can tell you what printers are on the system and how you can route output to them.

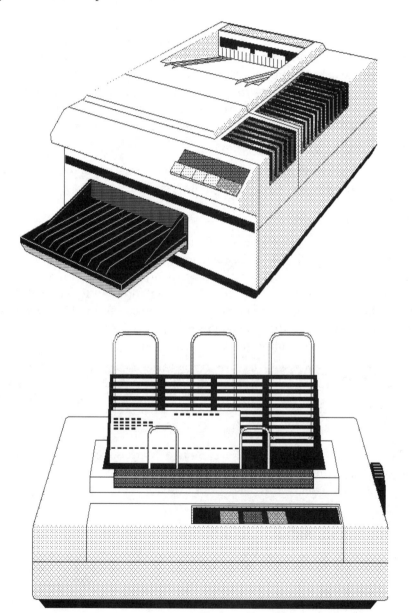

Fig. 2.4
A laser printer.

Fig. 2.5
A dot-matrix printer.

II

Installing UNIX

Modems

UNIX systems do not have to be restricted to a single room or even to a single building. Both the system and your terminal can be hooked to the regular telephone lines by a device called a *modem*. Your terminal can then control the UNIX system across the state, country, or even the world! With a modem, you can access many UNIX systems, including the thousands on the Internet, the world's data highway.

The word *modem* is derived from the terms *mo*dulate and *dem*odulate. Modulation is a method of sending information through a signal imposed on top of a carrier wave. Radio and television systems work by transmitting modulated signals. Your radio or TV demodulates those signals. The technique is the same with a modem but the carrier wave is different. Radio and television stations modulate radio frequency waves; modems use the telephone lines to modulate sound waves.

Modems add an exciting dimension to any system, even a local-only personal computer. With a modem, you can literally access the world.

The Mouse

Another trend in computer systems is the growing popularity of the Graphical User Interface (GUI). A GUI is a software system such as X-Windows or Microsoft Windows that makes computer operation easier by using small symbols (called *icons*) and other pictorial representations. Instead of typing a long and hard-to-remember command to start a program, you simply move a pointer on the screen to that program's symbol. When the pointer and symbol coincide, clicking a button activates the program.

> **Note**
>
> UnixWare is a GUI-based version of UNIX.

The device you use to manipulate the pointer on-screen is called a *mouse*. If you have a good imagination, you can visualize the curved, tapered body of the mammalian rodent when you look at this input device. The trailing connection wire, of course, is the mouse's tail.

A small rubber ball on the bottom of the mouse rolls as you move it on your desktop; this movement is translated into movements of the arrow pointer on the screen. When the arrow touches a symbol you want to activate, press the left mouse button (the standard way to indicate your choice to the computer). The other button or buttons (depending on whether you have a two-button or three-button mouse) do various things, depending on the application you are running and how the buttons themselves are programmed.

After you get used to using the mouse, you'll love it. You simply point and click to do many computer operations without ever touching the keyboard.

Choosing the Right Level of Hardware

Choosing the right level of hardware for your UNIX system depends on such factors as the number of users to be supported and the types of applications to be run. All this translates into requirements for working memory, hard disk storage space, the types of terminals needed, and so forth.

▶ For more information about software drivers, see Chapter 3, "Software Issues."

One persistent misconception about UNIX is that the systems are large, complex ones costing hundreds of thousands of dollars. This is not necessarily so. In fact, the majority of UNIX systems today consist of personal computers and workstations (both of which are discussed in detail in the following two sections). These UNIX installations are often for only a single user, although they may also be tied into a larger UNIX system or systems.

If you're using a version of UNIX such as UnixWare on a personal computer or on a UNIX-based workstation in a single-user configuration, you are the system administrator. It's your responsibility to understand the system well enough to do the administrative duties required to keep it operating at an optimum level. These duties include keeping enough space on the hard drive, backing up regularly, making sure that all devices attached to the system have the proper software drivers, installing and configuring software, and so forth.

Choosing the level of hardware you need depends on your budget and the number of users to be supported. Table 2.2 gives you a basic overview of some system options; table 2.3 presents the hardware requirements for each of these same configurations.

II

Installing UNIX

Table 2.2: Basic Guidelines in Choosing the Level of Hardware

Type	Advantages	Disadvantages
PC	Intel 80386 and 80486 personal computers are readily available and prices keep dropping. Many versions of UNIX run on PCs and tie into Novell and other DOS networks. A PC and an Intel-platform UNIX like UnixWare is a good combination for a workstation that stands alone or is connected to a network or a larger UNIX system. Such a system can more easily emulate DOS and Windows because of the Intel chip. *Good choice* for the private individual who wants to move up to a more powerful operating system, or as a "cheap" work-station for a power user (either stand-alone or networked to a larger system).	Lacks the speed and power of a RISC-based system. It is harder to expand for other users to provide adequate system resources.
RISC workstation	Fast and powerful. Uses a reduced instruc-tion set CPU optimized for UNIX operation. Can handle CPU-intensive tasks like CAD/CAM (Computer-Assisted Drafting/Computer Assisted Modeling), desktop publishing, and similar jobs better than personal computers. *Good choice* for engineers or any power user who does a lot of CPU-intensive tasks.	More expensive than PCs. Requires more UNIX skills in setting up and administering. Does not run DOS applications easily.
Larger systems	Larger UNIX systems are designed for dozens, even hundreds of users. They are faster, have a lot more resources in working memory and disk storage, and are easier to expand than PCs and RISC workstations. *Good choice* for a system that must support several users at the same time.	Greatly expensive and require a lot of administration.

Table 2.3: Hardware Considerations

Item	What You Need To Know
PC	Any IBM-compatible personal computer with an Intel 80386 or higher chip probably will work fine with most Intel-platform versions of UNIX today, including Novell's UnixWare or SCO UNIX. A reasonable configuration for running the operating system plus several applications requires 16MB of RAM and a 340MB hard drive. More of both is better. If you already have the PC, additional hardware is not needed unless you want to add terminals for additional users. (Remember: UNIX turns your PC into a powerful multiuser, multitasking computer.)

Item	What You Need To Know
RISC workstation	Typically, you buy RISC workstations from the workstation manufacturer (DEC, Hewlett-Packard, IBM, and Sun, to name the most common). The manufacturer supplies a version of UNIX optimized for their workstation (like Sun's Solaris). You choose the quality of the graphics display, size of hard disk, amount of working memory, and so forth that your suite of proposed applications requires. Usually, the workstation comes as a complete unit and the purchase of additional hardware is not necessary unless you want to add terminals for additional users. And, of course, you might need a printer.
Larger systems	Larger systems require many more hardware decisions. In addition to the server, you must decide what kind of terminals individual users need for their jobs (character-based or graphics-based such as X terminals). System memory requirements go up based on the average number of users on the system at any one time, and so forth.

Setting up a larger system requires considerable knowledge of UNIX to track all the details and make sure that the proper system and peripheral hardware is chosen. As the system administrator, you may oversee the entire selection process; you should seek the help of outside consultants for specific choices and initial installation. After the system is up and running, the regular routines of system administration are much less of a burden. After procedures are established, almost anyone can handle such duties as enabling new users, doing backups, monitoring the security of the system, and installing new software packages with the aid of helpful scripts supplied by the vendor.

▶ Chapter 22, "Loading UNIX Applications," gives more information about using scripts to install software packages.

As to the smaller types of UNIX systems (UNIX on personal computers and RISC workstations), the PC is the hardest to implement because the PC platform has so many minor variations (as described in the following section). Workstations, on the other hand, are relatively easy to implement because the vendor provides you with a complete package, including a version of UNIX tailor-designed for your particular workstation.

PCs (CISC)

The IBM PC-compatible personal computer is truly ubiquitous. Today, machines sporting Intel's powerful 80486 chip are routinely advertised in your local paper for less than $1,000. Computers are, indeed, cheap. Your total investment in software (programs) can easily exceed what the PC hardware costs.

The Intel family of microprocessors used in these computers (which are initially mostly DOS-based) are CISC (Complex Instruction Set Computing)

II

Installing UNIX

devices. CISCs have multiple addressing modes and many variable-length instructions. The variable-length instructions require the chip to exert more effort in decoding and executing the instructions, but so many tens of millions are being sold that the PCs using them continue to drop in price and rise in computing power.

The almost unimaginable proliferation of PCs that has put them into your local department stores at incredibly low prices has also pushed computers more into the realm of consumer electronics and away from what little standardization that ever existed. Just because you can purchase a 486SX25 system including monitor and printer for less than $1,000 does not mean you want it for a UNIX system.

UNIX is a powerful operating system that demands much of the hardware it runs on. It pushes a PC to heights of efficiency and productivity undreamed of by DOS or any other single-tasking operating system. Because of their wide variance in internal configuration, not all PCs are suitable for UNIX.

The best method of determining which PC to buy is simply to consult the UNIX vendor whose product you want to install. SCO, the makers of SCO UNIX, and Novell, makers of UnixWare, provide lists of certified computers by brand that have been tested with SCO UNIX and UnixWare, respectively. Non-name-brand PCs are usually less expensive than name brands; their vendors are usually helpful in supplying you with basic specifications of memory, hard disk size, and CPU recommended.

In this age of cheap PCs and with many versions of UNIX designed to take them to their fullest potential, adding PC-based workstations to a UNIX system (or creating a powerful stand-alone system) is a joy in creation. For very little money, you'll find that the personal computer can be turned into a powerful and useful UNIX system.

One thing that has accelerated the trend to use PCs with UNIX is the extreme cheapness and wide use of IBM-compatible personal computers and networks. Some companies and institutions run a dual network system by tying their PCs together over a Novell-type network and then into the UNIX system. It was no accident that Novell purchased the rights to UNIX recently from AT&T; UNIX and PCs are a powerful combination. Individual users can now run their DOS and Windows programs on their desktop PC and use that same PC as a terminal to access a UNIX system for electronic mail, run application programs too big to run on a PC, and all the other advantages of UNIX. It's the best of both worlds. In fact, UnixWare allows you to run DOS and Windows at the same time as you run UNIX. Both your UNIX and DOS/Windows applications appear on the screen simultaneously.

Workstations (RISC)

RISC workstations, like those made by DEC, Hewlett-Packard, IBM, Sun, and many others, use RISC (Reduced Instruction Set Computing) chips. A RISC workstation has *real* power because the chip is optimized for UNIX operation. The RISC workstation provides all the advantages of UNIX locally and can also tie into the main system. As you learn later in this book, you can run DOS and Windows applications as well. With a RISC workstation, you can have literally dozens of tasks going at the same time on both your local system and on the main UNIX system. It takes a little getting used to, but you become almost frighteningly productive.

The trend today for power users on UNIX systems is away from terminals and towards workstations. A *workstation* is a stand-alone computer, often with its own disk drives and other peripherals, that also can serve as a terminal on the system. The advantages of a workstation are many. If you have a workstation, you have both local computing power and access to the power of the entire system.

RISC workstations are *optimized* for running UNIX and the leading UNIX applications. You'll often find a design engineer doing the CPU-intensive tasks of CAD/CAM using a workstation. The publishing of newspapers, magazines, and books is another area in which workstations appropriately lend their power towards faster and more efficient operation.

Times have and are changing, though. Back in the late 1980s, the average workstation was about ten times faster than a personal computer. It was also about ten times more expensive. Today, that gap has narrowed dramatically. An average workstation may be only two or three times faster than the average PC and cost only two or three times as much. Some top-end PCs that use the new Pentium chip are beginning to rival RISC workstation performance.

The bottom line is that workstations are still better overall than a PC-based UNIX system, but the lower costs and increasing performance of PCs make them attractive alternatives for the majority of jobs in which time is not quite so critical.

▶ Chapter 23, "Running DOS Applications," and Chapter 24, "Running Windows Applications," explain how Merge makes UNIX work with DOS.

▶ For more about productivity, see Chapter 4, "Single-User Installations."

II

Installing UNIX

Summary

This chapter presented some basic information about hardware. No one expects you to be a computer expert, but a little knowledge about hardware goes a long way in easing the task of learning UNIX—and in choosing the proper level of software for your system.

The next chapter discusses the other major part of a computer system: the software.

Chapter 3

Software Issues

A UNIX computer system—like all other computer operating systems—consists of software that interacts with computer hardware. Hardware, as you saw in the preceding chapter, is a collection of electrical, electronic, and electro-mechanical devices doing work under control of the CPU. The CPU, in turn, receives its instructions from binary strings of 1s and 0s that it recognizes and reacts to according to the microprocessor chip's instruction set. These binary-string instructions are program steps or, as programs are often called, *software*.

This chapter introduces you to the software concepts on a UNIX system and helps you understand what you need to know to use the UNIX system. It includes the general rules and procedures for choosing, understanding, and using software and for configuring UNIX in advance so that software applications run properly.

An Introduction to Software

Programs usually reside in *files* stored on a hard disk when not in use. If you call for a program by typing its name on the command line or by pointing and clicking with a mouse on an icon in a Graphical User Interface (GUI, pronounced *gooey*), the software is *loaded* into RAM. This means that the CPU was instructed to copy the program file into working memory and begin executing its program steps. The program then takes over, sending instructions to the CPU. An active program is referred to as a *running* program.

In this chapter, you learn answers to the following questions:

■ What is software?

■ What is system software?

■ What is development software?

■ What is application software?

II

Installing UNIX

UNIX is a multiuser, multitasking operating system. Several people (users) can be logged in and running programs at any one time. These users, singly or collectively, may very well run more than one task at the same time. Hence the terms *multiuser* and *multitasking*.

Your running program doesn't control the CPU totally. Programs in a UNIX system share CPU time. The CPU jumps from program to program, executing a few steps of each in sequence. Because the CPU does millions of steps per second, this *time slicing* is not noticeable under normal operating conditions. Only when a lot of users are on the system, or someone is doing a very CPU-intensive task, do you notice the system slowing down.

A quick overview of how software and hardware work together is in order. An overview will help you more easily understand the detailed views later in this chapter and in other chapters.

Software used with a UNIX-based system is divided into three basic types:

- System and utility software

- Development software

- Application software

System and utility software are those programs that run the UNIX operating system and provide various utility services such as copying files, printing, and so forth. You are working with the operating system when you log into the system, load a program, or just list the files in your home directory. To liken UNIX to a hotel, the operating system is equivalent to the desk clerk, manager, hotel detective, and housekeeping staff. More on all this later.

Carrying on the hotel analogy, the second major area of UNIX software—development software—is similar to the architects, carpenters, plumbers, and electricians planning and building new additions to the hotel or modifying the existing structure. In other words, development software are the programs and libraries of routines that allow programmers to devise and add new software to the system.

Application programs are those you use to do useful work. These are like the entertainers in the hotel lounge and the various conventions that use the ballroom from time to time. Application programs come and go, but while they are there, they do your job, whether that job is word processing, accounting, or database management.

Key Terms Used in This Chapter

The rest of this chapter looks at the three broad areas of UNIX software in more detail, but first you should become familiar with some terms. Table 3.1 lists some common software terms with brief definitions.

Table 3.1: Software-Related Terms	
Term	**Definition**
software	A collection of program steps that instruct a computer how to accomplish various tasks.
system software	Programs comprising the operating system and associated housekeeping programs (those that keep the system running correctly and efficiently) and utility programs.
operating system	System software that handles routine repetitive tasks and resource allocation. UNIX is an operating system.
utilities	Small system programs for doing things like listing file directories or viewing the contents of files. There are hundreds of utilities in UNIX.
development software	A set of programs and routine libraries used by programmers to design and write new programs for the system.
application software	Programs you use to accomplish actual work. These include software for word processing, accounting, database management and so on.
compiler	A development program that takes a text file of program steps written by a human programmer and turns (*compiles*) those steps into binary code the CPU can recognize and accept as program instructions or *machine executable code*.
source code	A text file of program instructions typed by a programmer. Source code is acted on by a compiler, which turns it into machine executable code.
SCCS	Source Code Control System (SCCS) is add-on software you can purchase for UNIX that tracks source-code files from programmers on the system, making sure that only the most current files for a project are incorporated in the new program.
accounting software	Programs used to track the financial side of a company or institution's operation.
order-entry software	Software that tracks and manages customer orders.

(continues)

II

Installing UNIX

Table 3.1 Continued	
Term	**Definition**
inventory-control software	Programs that keep track of a company's physical inventory.
database-management software	An application designed for the management of information. The files from this application are called *databases*.
spreadsheets	A valuable software tool in accounting that organizes information into rows and columns like an accountant's columnar pad or tablet.
CAD/CAM	Computer Aided Design/Computer Assisted Modeling (CAD/CAM) programs are used for mechanical and architectural drawing, circuit design, stress modeling, and other engineering activities.
word processing	One of the most widespread uses of computers is for the creation and editing of text. Word processing software is used for this activity.

Understanding System Software

A lot of computer tasks that occur constantly are repetitive. Take, for example, what happens whenever you type the first letter of a command to be executed. Your terminal converts the key you pressed into a binary string. The string of 1s and 0s travels through the data bus to the CPU.

The CPU stores the information in a temporary memory location and, at the same time, echoes it back to the terminal. The CPU then waits for your next character or for the end-of-line control character that signals you've pressed the <Return> key and that no more data is coming (in other words, "execute this command, thank you"). The terminal causes the letter you typed to appear on the screen. You type the next letter and it, too, echoes to the screen. Finally you press <Return> and the CPU accesses the program steps it needs to execute your command.

This procedure may sound simple enough, but there are many repetitive steps involved. This is true for most fundamental computing tasks. Copying files, printing, video display, receiving keyboard input, reading and writing data to the hard disk, and thousands more little things are handled by the operating system and system utilities.

If a design scheme were not implemented, every application program would also have to contain the routines for these simple tasks, making those programs longer and more expensive. Instead, application programmers rely on being able to "farm out" all these small repetitive tasks to the operating system.

Operating System Software

UNIX is an operating system—a very good and powerful operating system. A computer controlled by UNIX can accommodate several users at the same time and run a multitude of tasks simultaneously. It is the operating system software that allows a computer's hardware and software to work together. Figure 3.1 shows a screen where a user has just logged on to a system with several other users already using it.

```
fiction  tty06    1:46am    4    4    2  -bash
info     tty07    1:46am    4    2       menu menu1
market   tty05    1:46am    5    3    2  -sh
menu     tty08    1:48am    3    2       menu menu1
print    tty01    1:49am    1    4    2  -ksh
ralph    tty6b    1:51am         3       sort
root     tty11    1:48am    3    4    2  -ksh
yam      tty10    1:47am    1    3    1  yam call inittb
yam2     tty09    1:47am    4    3    1  yam port tty6B call inithv96
------------------------------------------------------------------
Today is Monday, the twenty-fourth day of January, nineteen ninety-four.
In twenty-six seconds, the time will be eight minutes before two AM,
Eastern Standard Time. Sunrise is at sixteen minutes before eight AM;
sunset is at thirty minutes after five PM. The Moon is Waxing Gibbous
(88% of Full).

The more we disagree, the more chance there is that at least one of us
is right.
------------------------------------------------------------------
Filesystem                         MB Used  MB free  MB total  % full
/                                      153       51       204     74%
up 0 days 0:39:03    booted Mon Jan 24 01:12:33 1994
------------------------------------------------------------------
/usr/ralph>
```

Fig. 3.1
A UNIX user has just logged on to the system, showing a customized initial screen.

The UNIX operating system—whatever brand your system uses—consists of the programs and routines that translate data from input devices and send it to output devices. The operating system also handles data and program storage in working memory and the hard disks, coordinates the many processes running on the computer at any one time, and allocates system resources to the users and processes currently on the system. In general, the operating system oversees everything going on within the bounds of the system and makes sure that "the trains run on time," so to speak.

Basically, the UNIX operating system provides two very important functions: a standard programming environment for software developers and a standard working environment within which end users such as yourself can run application programs.

The fact that the operating system, with its hundreds of services, is already in place is a true boon to programmers. The programmer writes a new application program without worrying about the thousands of low-level steps needed to display characters and read an exact sector of the hard disk. The programmer simply calls on the operating system for these low-level routines and the finished application program includes these calls.

In essence, the operating system is a foundation on which you can build. It's similar to a convention center attached to that hotel used as an example earlier in this chapter. You may want to rent a room in the center and put on, say, a comic-book show. To accomplish this, you need support. Tables must be brought in on which the dealers can display their boxes of comics for sale. The room must have lights—and heat in the winter or air conditioning in the summer. A public address system is necessary for announcements. In a typical convention center, you pay the rent and all those services are provided.

UNIX provides the room, tables, lights, heat, public address system, and so forth for application programs. It serves as the bridge between the hardware and your program.

Utilities

To continue with the hotel convention center example: if you needed a banner put up, you could call maintenance and they'd send over a carpenter. The carpenter has a toolbox full of all sorts of tools for building, maintaining, and repairing things. UNIX and other operating systems also have toolboxes full of tools. These tools are called *utility programs*, or *utilities*. Most versions of UNIX today come with over 200 of these useful little programs.

Utilities are not operating system software, even though they come bundled with the operating system in many cases. Utilities don't do the low-level, housekeeping chores the operating system does; utilities call on those services just like application programs do. In fact, utilities can be considered mini-application programs. Instead of large, complicated jobs like word processing or accounting, utilities perform simple tasks like listing a file directory (see fig. 3.2), letting you quickly view a file, or generating calendars (see fig. 3.3).

By using utilities, you and other users on the system can manage files, directories, user environments, security, and many other computer considerations. Specific utilities and how they operate are discussed throughout this book.

```
eliz            emacs           emacs.rv        fax.zip         fifth
format.doc      garbo.p         german          gettys.pun      gif
gnu.bk          guide.txt       hart            hart.csc        horse
ideas           in.zip          inet            internet.bk     internet.bkr
joinus          kermit.zip      label           label.pr        larry2
lavonda.cov     lavonda.spr     leowhite        letter.akb      letter.rwr
letters         levy            linda.3         linda.bk1       linda.bk2
linda.ns        linda.ol        linda.per       linda.r         linda.tor
mailer.rz       manguide.doc    markoff         markoff.asc     markoff.spr
mcp.sty         mouse.com       msg             neb             nebula
newnum          news.exe        news.fil        news.lab        nims
nuts            oberonm.zip     opt             pack.mcw        pack.msw
pack.sq         pack.wpf        pi2000          pix1.gif        pix2.gif
ponder          portlan         pow.pro         psx.cfg         ralph.eps
resakb          review          rodger.inv      sb.bat          sb5
script          scriptbook.get  sen.fax         seth            sign
simson.adr      spew.c          sprint          survey.zip      swift
system          tallunix        talmage         tax             taxes
temp            temp.prn        terms.spr       tmp             top25
trash           turbobasic.zip  tv.cfg          uniteach.cov    uniteach.ol
unix.cov        util            vet             vi.ref          vimous.arc
vpix            wayne.st        whois           whois.asc       whois.prn
whois.spr       wines           world.ltr       xdtinitial.xde
/usr/ralph>
```

Fig. 3.2

Listing the files in a directory is done with the ls utility program.

```
/usr/ralph> cal
Mon Jan 24 01:53:31 1994
        Dec                     Jan                     Feb
 S  M Tu  W Th  F  S     S  M Tu  W Th  F  S     S  M Tu  W Th  F  S
          1  2  3  4                       1              1  2  3  4  5
 5  6  7  8  9 10 11     2  3  4  5  6  7  8     6  7  8  9 10 11 12
12 13 14 15 16 17 18     9 10 11 12 13 14 15    13 14 15 16 17 18 19
19 20 21 22 23 24 25    16 17 18 19 20 21 22    20 21 22 23 24 25 26
26 27 28 29 30 31       23 24 25 26 27 28 29    27 28
                        30 31
```

Fig. 3.3

The useful cal utility can give you a calendar for any month from January of the year 1 to December of the year 9999.

II

Installing UNIX

Configuring UNIX in Advance

A good system administrator anticipates new software packages and increased user loads. He or she keeps the system tuned for optimal operation by keeping adequate hard disk storage space, setting configuration parameters such as the numbers of processes the system can accommodate at any one time, and generally handling all problems related to the use of always-limited computer resources. (It is, as you may have already discovered, an immutable law of the universe that disk usage expands to fill available space.)

Advance configuration may also include creating and mounting a new file system, setting up file permissions for various users, and installing appropriate device drivers. The requirements depend on the type of software package or general enhancement to the system that you plan.

More details are available elsewhere in this book, but a lot of the planning information you need is contained within the new application's documentation or can be obtained from the software vendor. Planning for new additions is always a good idea for something as complex as a UNIX system, where each new set of processes must coexist with those already running.

Understanding Development Software

Development software is the second of the three basic types of software on a UNIX system. Programmers use development software to create new programs and to manage the process of creation. As a typical user of a UNIX system, you may not use development software at all. You should, however, be aware of it and understand its basic use. A lot of the mystery of a UNIX system rapidly disappears if you have even a surface understanding of all the components, both software and hardware, that comprise the total system. The following sections briefly introduce development software.

Compilers

In the previous chapter, you were introduced to program steps. *Program steps* are instructions in the form of binary strings of 1s and 0s that the CPU recognizes as part of its instruction set and to which it responds with an appropriate action. You most likely are not a programmer (nor probably ever want to be one), but without even thinking about it, you no doubt conclude that writing a program consisting of many thousands of 8, 16, 32, or 64-digit strings of 1s and 0s (the number of digits depends on the CPU) is an incredible pain in the neck.

As programmers know, there is an easier way: *high-level languages*. A high-level language is a way to describe processing steps in language and symbols much simpler to type than massive rows and columns of 1s and 0s. This symbolic description is also known as *program code*. Such programming languages as Fortran, COBOL, BASIC, Pascal, C, and C++ are examples of high-level languages.

A programmer writes program source code in a high-level language using a text editor. In the UNIX world, the two most popular text editors for programming are vi and some version of emacs (such as GNU emacs). The coded "words" contained in the source program are specialized notations for the steps the programmer wants the computer to carry out. If you look at a file containing source code (and you easily can because they are standard text files), it may very well look like Greek to you, but programmers read it like a romance novel.

After a programmer has completed editing the source-code file for a program written in a high-level language, the file cannot be immediately executed. As you saw in the last chapter, computers understand binary values rather than words and symbols. So the source-code file must be turned into an executable program of binary strings the CPU can recognize and act on. This is done by a special development program called a *compiler*.

The compiler translates the written source code into a set of binary instructions and data the CPU can use. In their binary form, programs are in the CPU's native tongue. This native tongue depends on who manufactured the microprocessor chip (Intel, Motorola, and so forth). A compiler translates (*compiles*) operating-system software source programs, utilities source programs, application source programs, or any program into executable form.

Compiled programs are often referred to as *binaries* because they are no longer in text form. There is a file directory in most UNIX systems named /bin (for *binary*). Many of the system's executable programs are stored in /bin.

This directory of executable binaries is always on the path available to UNIX users. If you know the name of the program you want to use, you simply type its name and press <Return>. The computer then knows to find the program, load it into RAM, and begin execution. Should the program be in a directory not on the path, unless it's in your current directory, you must type the complete path information in front of the program's name so that the system knows where to find the program. You may already be familiar with directory paths from using MS-DOS. (In fact, there are a number of similarities between DOS and UNIX because UNIX influenced the development of DOS. DOS, alas, only has a small subset of the power of UNIX.)

There are many computer languages (compilers): BASIC, ADA, Fortran, COBOL, and Lisp are just a few. The most common compiler available in UNIX systems is the C compiler. C is a programming language that has been adapted to many different hardware platforms. UNIX is written in the C language.

Computer languages such as C and the newer C++ (pronounced *see plus plus*) may not excite you at all. But all you need to understand is that UNIX can be functionally implemented, or *ported*, to any computer that supports a C compiler. Thus, UNIX runs on everything from tiny laptops to massive supercomputers. And the application programs written for UNIX are just as portable.

II

Installing UNIX

> ### Note
>
> A portable program, by the way, does not mean that you can simply copy one binary to another system and expect it to run. But you *can* take its source-code files and compile them on a specific computer and the program usually runs fine (minor modifications to the source code are usually necessary).

Recently, various companies in the UNIX field have formed organizations to standardize UNIX more. They hope that standardization will eventually allow different brands of UNIX running on the same type of CPU to exchange binary programs without the necessity of recompiling. The goal is to fulfill the age-old dream of being able to distribute shrink-wrapped UNIX programs on store shelves just like DOS and Macintosh applications are sold.

Because there are competing organizations at the moment, there remains more than one "standard" version of UNIX, but progress is being made. The recent purchase by Novell of the basic rights to UNIX from AT&T and Novell's subsequent relaxing of license requirements have opened UNIX up far more than it has ever been before.

Source Code Control System (SCCS)

The most popular development software system in UNIX—SCCS— is, like UNIX itself, well-suited for several people to work on simultaneously. Programmers plan out large application programs and parcel out the tasks among several programmers. Each person edits his or her source-code files. The completed series of source-code files are compiled and the application's binary or binaries are created. If everything goes as planned, all the right source files are run through the compiler and the project is completed. Of course, when has anything *ever* gone according to plan?

What's needed is a method for tracking the source code for projects and making sure that the right files in their most current versions are available for compiling. A utility is available for many UNIX systems: Source Code Control System (SCCS). A single project can have hundreds of source-code files, each representing a small portion of the final program. Each programmer tests and modifies his or her portion of the source files several times before the program is completed. SCCS identifies the most current version of each source-code file to enable the newest version to be incorporated into the program. Figure 3.4 shows a directory listing of some source-code files; figure 3.5 lets you peer inside one of these files.

Fig. 3.4

A directory listing of a collection of source-code files. Together, these files compile into the GNU text utilities.

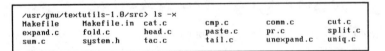

```
/usr/gnu/textutils-1.8/src> ls -x
Makefile     Makefile.in  cat.c        cmp.c        comm.c       cut.c
expand.c     fold.c       head.c       paste.c      pr.c         split.c
sum.c        system.h     tac.c        tail.c       unexpand.c   uniq.c
```

```
      writeline (thisline[0], stdout, 1);

   /* Step the file the line came from.
     If the files match, step both files.  */
   if (order >= 0)
     thisline[1] = readline (thisline[1], streams[1]);
   if (order <= 0)
     thisline[0] = readline (thisline[0], streams[0]);
  }

/* Free all storage and close all input streams. */
for (i = 0; i < 2; i++)
  {
    free (lbl[i].buffer);
    if (ferror (streams[i]) || fclose (streams[i]) == EOF)
      {
        error (0, errno, "%s", infiles[i]);
        ret = 1;
      }
  }
if (ferror (stdout) || fclose (stdout) == EOF)
  {
    error (0, errno, "write error");
```

Fig. 3.5
Part of a source-code file written in the high-level language C.

Program documentation and definitions are usually also incorporated into SCCS. SCCS also can track the dependencies of the source programs (when one source file refers to another in order to complete its function). SCCS is a kind of combination source-code librarian and project-management system for programs.

The *make* Program

The job isn't over when all the source files have been compiled and an executable binary created. Application programs—especially complex ones that do a lot of things—are in an almost constant state of change. One user finds a *bug* (bugs are mistakes in the program that cause glitches in operation). Another user needs the program to do something it can't now do, thus requiring a minor modification. Yet another would like the program to do a certain step slightly differently. So one or more programmers have to change the appropriate source-code text files.

UNIX has a powerful program called make. This program is useful in situations like the one just described (in which several source files are being acted on by different people from time to time). The make program automatically keeps track of source-code files that have changed and causes them to be recompiled if required.

Each program's library of source-code files has a text file named Makefile (by convention). The Makefile file contains the names of all the source-code files that make up the program, their interdependencies, and instructions to the compiler on how to regenerate the program. Figure 3.6 shows part of a typical Makefile file.

Fig. 3.6

Part of a Makefile
file.

```
expand.c fold.c head.c \
paste.c pr.c split.c sum.c tac.c \
tail.c unexpand.c uniq.c version.c

DISTFILES = Makefile.in system.h $(SOURCES)

PROGS = cat cmp comm cut expand fold head \
paste pr split sum tac tail unexpand uniq

all: $(PROGS) $(LIBPROGS)
.PHONY: all

install: all
        $(INSTALL) $(PROGS) $(bindir)
.PHONY: install

tags: $(SOURCES)
        ctags $(SOURCES)

TAGS: $(SOURCES)
        etags $(SOURCES)
```

This automated method of program generation saves programmers from the necessity of remembering to recompile every time they make a change in the source code. And because several source-code files may depend on another source file, changes made to the latter file without proper recompilation of all the others can make for unexpected results. The programmer making the change may not even be aware of these dependencies. In other words, make diminishes the chances of human error.

All these development software features make a UNIX system an excellent choice for developing application software for a wide range of computers and operating systems. Programs for DOS and the Apple Macintosh are often developed on UNIX systems. Once the source code is complete, it can be copied over to the appropriate operating system and compiled there, thus providing a program that runs on DOS or the Mac.

Understanding Application Software

System software and development software are all very nice but, unless you're a programmer, they get none of *your* everyday work out.

Application software is the software you use to do your daily computer work. Application software includes word processors, spreadsheets, database managers, various accounting programs, and many other specialized programs. From your point of view, application software does the useful work; the system software supports that work.

The range of application software is growing. You may use programs used by hundreds or thousands of other UNIX users. Other programs you use may be unique to your location or even unique to you. The next sections look at some of the popular categories of UNIX application software.

Word Processing

The most widely used application on a UNIX system (indeed, on most computer systems) is word processing. From the editing programmers do to create source-code files to letters to reports to the various forms of desktop publishing and electronic typesetting, the manipulation of words in many forms is what is done most frequently on UNIX systems.

Although no word processors are included with the UNIX operating system, third-party vendors such as WordPerfect and FrameMaker have versions of their word processing and desktop publishing applications available for UNIX systems. The closest thing to word processing that comes with UNIX is the troff text-formatting command that contains special text-formatting macros you can use with text files created with the vi text editor.

► Refer to Chapter 12, "Using the vi Editor," for details about vi and emacs.

UNIX usually comes with several built-in editors, including the programmer-oriented text editors vi and emacs. Actually, calling emacs just a text editor does not do it justice. The emacs editor is essentially a way of life for those who love it. You can do *anything* with emacs, including reading and sending electronic mail, running other programs, playing games, writing *and* compiling programs, and even editing text (see fig. 3.7). Should you become fascinated with emacs, check out *UNIX Desktop Guide to emacs* (published by Que's sister company, Hayden Books).

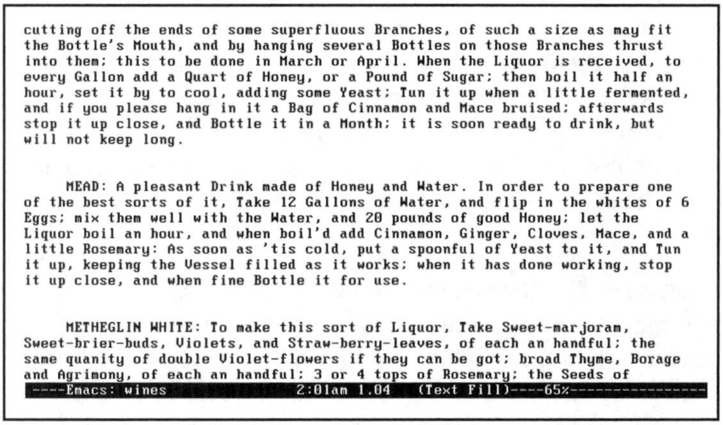

II

Installing UNIX

```
cutting off the ends of some superfluous Branches, of such a size as may fit
the Bottle's Mouth, and by hanging several Bottles on those Branches thrust
into them; this to be done in March or April. When the Liquor is received, to
every Gallon add a Quart of Honey, or a Pound of Sugar; then boil it half an
hour, set it by to cool, adding some Yeast; Tun it up when a little fermented,
and if you please hang in it a Bag of Cinnamon and Mace bruised; afterwards
stop it up close, and Bottle it in a Month; it is soon ready to drink, but
will not keep long.

     MEAD: A pleasant Drink made of Honey and Water. In order to prepare one
of the best sorts of it, Take 12 Gallons of Water, and flip in the whites of 6
Eggs; mix them well with the Water, and 20 pounds of good Honey; let the
Liquor boil an hour, and when boil'd add Cinnamon, Ginger, Cloves, Mace, and a
little Rosemary: As soon as 'tis cold, put a spoonful of Yeast to it, and Tun
it up, keeping the Vessel filled as it works; when it has done working, stop
it up close, and when fine Bottle it for use.

     METHEGLIN WHITE: To make this sort of Liquor, Take Sweet-marjoram,
Sweet-brier-buds, Violets, and Straw-berry-leaves, of each an handful; the
same quanity of double Violet-flowers if they can be got; broad Thyme, Borage
and Agrimony, of each an handful; 3 or 4 tops of Rosemary; the Seeds of
----Emacs: wines            2:01am 1.04   (Text Fill)----65%----------------
```

Fig. 3.7
A text file being edited with emacs.

For correspondence and document-oriented word processing, there are several good word processing applications available for UNIX systems—including the ubiquitous WordPerfect, beloved by every secretary between here and Utah.

The formatting and editing of longer documents is ably covered by such page-composition programs as FrameMaker and Interleaf. FrameMaker's text-editing capabilities, by the way, were originally developed from emacs.

The UNIX operating system itself provides a plethora of text-manipulation utilities. These let you do everything from count the words in a file (wc) to allowing you to globally search and change words or phrases in a whole series of documents without ever loading those documents into a word processing program (sed). Other useful utilities include troff, which prepares a file for typesetting, and style, which checks your writing style.

Accounting

Accounting software is used to track the financial side of company operations. Most accounting packages consist of several distinct parts. Although the exact makeup varies, standard accounting applications usually include accounts payable, accounts receivable, general ledger, fixed assets, and payroll modules. By the time a company has a dozen employees and a dozen accounts, the company can benefit from a computerized accounting system. If the company gets any larger than that, it *has* to have computerized accounting.

Order Entry

Order-entry software is a specialized form of an accounting program that handles the tracking and management of customer orders. Any company that sells a product, whether the sales are wholesale or retail, can implement an order-entry system. Most order-entry systems can track an order until the order is filled and shipped. It is not uncommon for order-entry software to tie into accounting and inventory software. Applications that plan materials requirements are often linked to order-entry applications to track the goods ordered.

UNIX is an especially good choice for order entry because of its multiuser nature. Terminals for the people taking orders over the phone, in the shipping department, in the warehouse, on the account-receivables person's desk, and so on, make sure that every bit of data concerning an order gets into the system and is acted on properly. If Joe Smith calls from Topeka wanting to know where his order is, a simple query to the order-entry system details his order's status. In the meantime, data is being fed into other accounting program modules such as inventory control and accounts receivable. New stock can be ordered when needed and no one is allowed to get too far behind in paying for goods received.

Good order-entry software also facilitates the shipping of orders by printing picking lists (a list telling the warehouse people what items to pull and send to shipping), packing lists (a list that goes in the box to tell the customer what has been sent), and mailing labels.

Inventory Control

Inventory-control applications provide a crucial role in accounting for materials. Inventory control provides information about items, quantities, bills of materials, stocking levels, inventory turns, inventory values, and more. It is hard to picture a modern business of any size remaining competitive without inventory-control software.

Machine Control

In today's modern manufacturing and testing environments, machine-control applications provide a means to coordinate a complex operation with a minimum of human intervention. Machine-control applications automate factory floors, give directions to robots, monitor alarm-system switches, and perform many other specialized control tasks. Machine-control applications make extensive use of I/O that is not *user* input and output. Much of a machine-control application's I/O is associated with sensors, machine interfaces, and other computers.

Database Management

Database-management applications provide a means for users to design data forms and enter information into the forms. The forms provide a uniform method for entering and viewing a particular category of information. The actual storage file or files for each form is called the *database.* One of database management's strong suits is its capability to assume responsibility for the complex nature of storing information while presenting an easy-to-use interface.

Database management is another of the many tasks that UNIX is uniquely suited for. The multiuser, multitasking nature of UNIX makes it easy to have a lot of terminals and a lot of other I/O sources feeding information into a database. Although database management can be done on a large scale using a Novell network and DOS machines, UNIX is far more flexible for such a task. Even the newer operating systems OS/2 and Microsoft NT (which are oriented more toward one user doing several tasks than several people doing one related task) fall short of UNIX for this type of application.

When information (data) is in the database, the user of a database-management application can query, modify, relate, and report the stored information. The user may work directly with the database-management software in an *ad hoc* mode, or the user may work with programmer-developed, stand-alone applications that use the active core, or engine, of the database-management software.

Many database managers support Structured Query Language (SQL). SQL is a standard method for managing databases without regard to the exact database engine that supports the particular database. Through SQL, two different database-management programs can exchange data. If SQL interests you, pick up a copy of *Using SQL* (published by Que Corporation).

Spreadsheets

The spreadsheet is one of the biggest success stories in software. Millions of users find their spreadsheet software a valuable tool for business. Spreadsheets get their name from the concept of the accountant's columnar pad or tablet. The tablet is ruled with rows and columns to provide boxes for entries. The use of boxes, or *cells*, keeps entries neat, aligned, and segregated.

Spreadsheet software takes the idea of the accountant's columnar pad and adds provisions that take advantage of the computer. Not only can each cell contain a literal value, like the accountant's entry, but the cells can also contain formulas that use the contents of other cells. When a value is changed in a formula-referenced cell, the value of the cell containing the formula changes accordingly.

CAD/CAM

UNIX has been popular in the scientific and engineering professions for many years. A popular family of application programs that has roots in these professions is CAD/CAM. CAD (Computer Assisted—or Aided—Design) and CAM (Computer Assisted Modeling) harness the computer for tasks that previously required many hours of tedious work by humans who drafted large blueprint-type drawings on paper. CAD/CAM is used for mechanical and architectural drawing, circuit design, stress modeling, printed circuit-board layout, prototyping, and other engineering activities.

▶ Chapter 4, "Single-User Installations," describes the productive concept of stand-alone workstations.

CAD/CAM is an area in which powerful workstations, such as those manufactured by DEC, Hewlett-Packard, IBM, Sun, and others, are exceptionally beneficial. These desktop units are stand-alone UNIX systems in their own right, even though they are oriented more toward a single user doing several tasks.

Putting It All Together

Installing a new application on a UNIX system is not always the simple process it is in, for example, DOS. UNIX applications often run several copies of themselves at the same time and have to allocate resources such as data files properly. They also must avoid such conflicts as allowing two users to write data to the same file simultaneously, a definite and potentially disastrous no-no.

Application documentation is usually good about spelling out specifications. Unlike DOS applications, all the drivers you need to implement the software may not be included with the application. UNIX systems vary widely. It is one of the jobs of the system administrator to find sources for all the parts and pieces (drivers and so forth) needed to implement a new package.

> **Tip**
>
> The best time to accomplish all the necessary planning is at the instant you purchase the new package. The vendor should be an expert on making the software run on all types of systems. Make the vendor spell out what is needed for your system and where to get it.

New hardware devices also require drivers, so make sure that the manufacturer supplies one for your system. There is nothing as frustrating as having users screaming to use the new laser printer, which the system can't print to because the right driver is not installed. Tying your UNIX system into a network also requires the installation of software drivers.

If a user wants to install a DOS or Windows application, you must implement some sort of *DOS emulation*, a program that runs Microsoft Windows applications within the UNIX system.

▶ Chapter 23, "Running DOS Applications," and Chapter 24, "Running Windows Applications," describe the implementation of emulation software.

Merge is a software feature included with UnixWare and other System V Release 4.2 systems. With Merge, you can run entire Windows or DOS operating environments within a single window on the UnixWare GUI. For more information on Merge, see *Introduction to UNIX* (published by Que Corporation).

Summary

This chapter gave you an overview of the types of software found on a UNIX system. There are three major types of software on a UNIX system: system and utility software, development software, and application software.

II

Installing UNIX

The operating system handles routine, repetitive tasks and makes application development easier by providing basic low-level services. In addition, UNIX boasts literally hundreds of handy utility programs that help you in tasks such as listing directories, printing, viewing the contents of files, and counting words in files.

Application software are the programs that do the real work on a computer—*your* work. Application programs include word processing, accounting, order entry, inventory control, machine control, database management, financial spreadsheets, and CAD/CAM—all of which are ideally suited for UNIX.

In the next chapter, you learn about the beauty of single-user UNIX installations and how they can dramatically increase your productivity.

Chapter 4

Single-User Installations

This chapter introduces you to the concept of the single-user UNIX installation and how it can dramatically increase your personal productivity. Although single-user installations are most often UNIX operating systems installed on personal computers or RISC (Reduced Instruction Set CPU) workstations, several of the techniques in this chapter are also useful for productivity enhancement on standard terminals attached to a larger UNIX system.

Too many people have the mistaken perception that UNIX systems are only for lots of users each running one application program per user. A roomful of data-entry persons busily punching numbers into their terminals from stacks of invoices fits this vision. Although UNIX can handle such multiuser, clerk-type jobs wonderfully well, that is *not* where its real power and potential lie for the individual *power user*. A power user is someone who gets as much work as he or she can out of a computer in the shortest amount of time possible. A UNIX single-user installation is a power user's dream come true.

The term *single-user installation* refers to a UNIX system configured in both hardware and software for use by a single individual. The system described in the preceding paragraph, used by many people, is a *multiuser* system. Single-user installations are *multitasking* systems. One person running several jobs at one time is the definition of multitasking, which also applies to this chapter's main topic.

No matter what kind of UNIX system you log in to, from a solitary laptop to systems spanning the world, the single-user installation concept gives you power and techniques to manipulate the system to your best advantage.

This chapter covers the following topics:

- Terms relating to single-user systems

- Understanding single-user systems

- Using single-user systems

II

Installing UNIX

Key Terms Used in This Chapter

The first thing you should do before you continue reading is become familiar with some terms. Table 4.1 lists some common terms with brief definitions.

Table 4.1: Installation-Related Terms	
Term	**Definition**
single-user installation	A UNIX system meant to be used by a single person, either as a workstation tied into a larger UNIX system or as a stand-alone computer.
multiuser installation	A UNIX system that allows several simultaneous users, usually a computer with several terminals attached.
multitasking	An operating system with the capability to run several programs simultaneously (in the case of a single-user installation, for the same user).
pseudo terminal	A terminal emulated by software only, that is, one that does not exist as actual hardware.
multiscreen	A terminal having the capacity of displaying several pseudo terminals, either on-screen at once or by switching back and forth between them.
Graphical User Interface (GUI)	A visually oriented operating system (or program) that allows the use of a mouse or other point-and-click device to choose programs by icons or visual symbolism rather than typing commands.
X-Windows	A popular GUI on UNIX systems and the base technology for other GUIs on UNIX (such as Motif and OPEN LOOK).
Microsoft Windows	The most widely used GUI on computers based on Intel 80386, 80486, and Pentium CPU chips.
workstation	A computer used as a terminal on a UNIX system but which supplies local computing power as well as the ability to tap into the system's computing capacity. A UNIX-based workstation is also a single-user installation and may or may not be connected to a larger UNIX system.

Understanding the Single-User Concept

Computers were invented to get more work done in a shorter length of time than unassisted humans can do on their own—and computers do that well. Accounting applications crunch numbers far faster than is possible using pencil and paper—or even adding machines and calculators. Word processors have turned the typewriter into an endangered species. CAD/CAM software has retired drafting tables and rubber erasers by scores of thousands.

Consider this: If the computer does one task well, shouldn't it be able to do several tasks well *at the same time* and allow *several people* to use it at once? The answer, as far as UNIX is concerned, is *yes*. Combining these multitasking and multiuser talents of UNIX into a single-user installation is the basis for the productivity-enhancing techniques covered in this chapter.

Multiuser versus Multitasking

The UNIX operating system, by design, does many tasks simultaneously. It can run multiple programs at once by *slicing*, or dividing, CPU time. Each task, depending on its priority, gets a few microseconds of the CPU's attention, which acts on a few steps in that task's program's instructions before the CPU turns to the next program to run a few steps, then the next, and so on all the way back around the circle of programs running. The CPU, essentially nothing more than a dumb but complex switching device, never realizes that the millions of steps it executes every second are for many different programs instead of just one.

It is through the magic of CPU time-sharing that computers utilizing the UNIX operating system can run many programs simultaneously and support more than one user. Other types of operating systems are much more limited; the CPU may be devoted to only one main task. For example, if you run the WordPerfect word processing program on DOS, that is the only application the entire system can handle (with the possible exception of some printing occurring in the background if a spooler program is installed).

The "single-mindedness" of DOS is not the fault of the computer it runs on, but rather the internal design of that operating system. The same computer, an IBM PC-compatible (sometimes called a *clone*), using one of the Intel family of microprocessor chips (80386, 80486, or Pentium) can run UNIX and perform multitasking in a multiuser environment. Even a "cheap" PC—say an old 386 20 MHz computer, ancient and slow by today's standards—supports six to eight users comfortably if it runs one of the several versions of UNIX available for the Intel platform. That same machine can support more than 20 users, although it does tend to bog down with such heavy usage. The newer 486s and Pentiums do even better.

II

Installing UNIX

> **Note**
>
> To use a PC with multiple users, you must either take turns with the keyboard and monitor or connect terminals to the PC through the PC's serial ports. By using a serial-ports board (a device that adds multiple serial ports to your PC), you can connect 8, 16, or even 32 or more users to a single PC. Remember that the more users using the computer at the same time, the worse the performance.

To use an approximate figure, an IBM-PC running UNIX can perform 10 to 20 times the work of the same machine running under a single-user operating system like DOS. Even Microsoft Windows, the GUI that runs under DOS and is touted as a productivity enhancement, is limited when compared to UNIX. Windows lets you load a number of programs at the same time; by pressing the <Alt-Tab> key combination, you cycle through all these programs. With some minor exceptions, you are limited to running one main application at a time with Windows. The others merely crouch patiently in working memory, waiting like lazy sheep dogs until you need them again. Good sheep dogs would be out there keeping the flock together, even when you were not watching. UNIX has good sheep dogs.

Even though UNIX lets a PC do 10 times the work of the same machine running DOS, or a Macintosh running Apple's System 7 operating system, or any other single-user operating system, your immediate reaction may be "So what? There aren't 10 people using my PC. At most, there is only me, myself, and I—and we do only one thing at a time."

As indicated at the start of this chapter, people tend to confuse the concepts of multiuser and multitasking. Several people all doing one thing each but using the same computer seems an easy enough idea to grasp, but what about you doing 6 or 12 or 18 things at once?

This concept is a little harder to grasp and, admittedly, requires a change in the mindset with which you look at ways of accomplishing your daily work. Most people tend to focus on one task at a time, a narrowness that fits both single-user operating systems like DOS and the older manual methods of paper and pencil.

It is human nature to look at any job as a sequence of tasks to be accomplished. You pick up the potato, you wash the potato, you peel the potato, you slice the potato. You pick up the next potato, you wash that potato—and so forth, all in sequence. But if your cousins Fred and Sally help, with Fred washing, Sally peeling, and you slicing, the job goes faster because it is now being done in *parallel* instead of in sequence. That's a form of multiuser operation.

What if your job involves virtual potatoes on a computer, so to speak? On a UNIX system, Fred could do part, Sally could do part, and you could put the finishing touches in place. This is called *workgroup* computing. Once more, the job goes faster because a good portion of the tasks are being performed concurrently with other tasks.

On your stand-alone PC or workstation, Fred and Sally don't exist; there is only you. To get the same parallel approach, you can set up the job as several concurrent processes and rotate through them, feeding them whatever information is required to keep the jobs going. Although you don't achieve 100 percent parallel operation, you *will* save a lot of time and get your work out sooner. You become a one-person workgroup.

Now you should look at the two major types of computer systems that make the UNIX single-user installation concept possible: UNIX on personal computers and UNIX on RISC workstations.

UNIX on Personal Computers

The IBM PC-compatible (often referred to as an *Intel-platform computer* because Intel manufactures the CPU) is a computer you may already own or have access to at your workplace. These computers are almost ubiquitous these days. By changing the computer's operating system from DOS to UNIX, you can gain many benefits.

Times have changed dramatically in the computer world. UNIX and most "serious" computing was once the province of large mainframes and mini-computers. Those manufacturers looked down their noses at the lowly PC.

True, there were some successful implementations of UNIX on early PCs. XENIX, a brand of UNIX from the Santa Cruz Operation (SCO), has been available for the IBM PC from the early 1980s. Many thousands of those installations still exsist, and SCO today is still a dominant force in the UNIX desktop market. But most big UNIX manufacturers didn't want to touch the desktop market. What happened? The IBM-compatible PC gained in popularity and sales at an explosive rate. Networking allows these relatively cheap little boxes to be tied together, replacing large expensive mainframe computers. Now, the PC *is* the market and all the UNIX vendors are scrambling to "capture the desktop."

You can currently buy a Pentium-based computer (Intel's latest and fastest CPU) with a huge hard disk for less than the original IBM PC cost in 1982 dollars. The Pentium and the 486 and 386 chips, as well as the chips in Apple's Macintosh, have the power and speed to run full-fledged implementations of UNIX.

UNIX vendors have noticed this massive shift in the computer world and are competing for their share of the market. PC users looking for a 32-bit multitasking operating system now have a number of good choices. OS/2 2.1 and Windows NT are not UNIX but they are vying with versions of UNIX for market share.

New Intel-based high-end versions of UNIX are being introduced and pushed from such vendors as Novell Inc. (the Novell Network people) who recently purchased UNIX System Laboratories (USL) from the inventor of UNIX, AT&T. Because of the link between the original UNIX and AT&T, Novell's version of UNIX, UnixWare, is considered the original UNIX.

Other UNIX manufacturers also have versions of UNIX for Intel-based PCs. SunSoft Inc. (the software subsidiary of the workstation manufacturer, Sun Microsystems Inc.) released Solaris for the IBM PC-compatible recently. And SCO shipped updated versions of its SCO UNIX and Open Desktop versions of UNIX. And the legendary Steve Jobs (cofounder of Apple), who now owns NeXT Inc., has just released NexTStep for Intel processors, a PC version of the company's object-oriented UNIX operating system.

Why the rush to the desktop to replace DOS and Windows? Pure numbers. Some industry analysts predict market sales of Intel-based personal computers will exceed over $30 million a year, as opposed to perhaps $300,000 in sales of RISC-based workstations.

To make UNIX more attractive, and to make it easier for DOS and Windows users moving up to UNIX, most UNIX vendors have adapted their operating systems so that they run the more than 20,000 DOS and Microsoft Windows applications currently on the market. If you move to a single-user UNIX installation, you can have all the advantages of a multiuser, multitasking operating system and still use all the applications you already know. And you can use several of them at the same time! Or even run several copies of the same program at once. For example, if you were working on an instruction manual, you could have all the chapters or sections of the manual open at the same time.

RISC Workstations

The RISC-based (Reduced Instruction-Set Computing) UNIX workstation continues to drop in price, although it is still higher than the average Intel-based personal computer. The RISC chip optimizes a workstation to run UNIX. RISC workstations are usually markedly faster than personal computers. Sun's SPARCstations, DEC's Alpha series, and the IBM RS/6000 workstations currently lead the field.

> **Tip**
>
> Although a workstation does more for you, its price may still be prohibitive. But like the prices of PCs, workstation prices continue to drop and their manufacturers continue to offer more "bang for the buck" with ever-faster machines and more and more features.

Using the Single-User Installation Concept

The single-user installation concept boils down to working in parallel instead of wasting time with sequential steps. In short, you can do several jobs at the same time.

A UNIX-based computer gives the single user the ability to perform more than one task simultaneously. You can start one task and move on to the next. You can have massive numbers of data files open all at once. You can have all this and plenty of time for a long lunch.

One simple secret about how to accomplish this—once you have a UNIX system on your desktop or tie into one through a terminal—is to turn yourself into several users. The following sections explain.

Multiscreens and Additional Terminals

A *multiscreen* is a terminal that can display several pseudo terminals, either by putting them all on the screen at the same time or by switching back and forth between them. A *pseudo terminal* is one that does not exist physically even though the computer *thinks* it does. It's not nice to fool the motherboard, but the technique is much to your benefit.

To more quickly help you understand the advantages of multiscreen operation, look at your personal computer and imagine UNIX running on it as a single-user installation. You log in to the system and are up and running in UNIX as a single user. Just about the same as in DOS, isn't it? "Where," you ask, "is all this power I was promised?"

What you have is called a *console* screen. Larger UNIX systems have a console screen from which the system administrator controls the system and a varying number of separate terminals for all other users. UNIX running on a personal computer or other stand-alone workstation combines the console and user terminal into just one screen (although you can easily add several external terminals, even to a PC).

▶ Chapter 11, "Managing Multiple Processes," explains how to start programs in the background.

Actually, a single-screen login in UNIX gives you a lot more power than DOS by itself. You can start tasks running and relegate them to the background by adding the ampersand symbol (&) to the end of the command. UNIX lets you have *foreground* and *background* tasks and switch between them. A foreground task is displayed on the screen; a background task runs without outputting anything to the screen until it finishes. You can instruct background tasks to route their results through any of the standard output devices attached to the UNIX system as peripheral hardware (for example, to the printer, to your display screen, or to a file on your hard disk).

Many of the major application programs you use for accounting, word processing, and other work do not lend themselves easily to being run as background tasks. They often demand the foreground. How can you run several major applications at once when you have only one foreground? Simple: add more foregrounds.

The multiscreen function adds pseudo screens for you. Because the manufacturers know PCs will be used, most versions of UNIX designed for the Intel platform come with the multiscreen feature in place. In SCO UNIX and UnixWare, for example, you can have up to 12 multiscreens; you access them by pressing the <Alt> key in combination with one of the function keys (<F1> through <F12>).

When you initially log in to SCO UNIX or UnixWare, you are on the first screen, corresponding to the key combination <Alt-F1>. Pressing <Alt-F2> replaces the current screen with another screen that displays a log-in prompt. You can now log in to the system *again*. Any UNIX system allows you to have multiple sessions of "yourself"—that is, you can log in under one user name and password on as many terminals as you can find.

The major advantage to multiscreens is that, when you switch to a new multiscreen, the one that is replaced does not stop its processing. If, for example, you have a database program running in a multiscreen, and you're building a new index, which takes, perhaps, hours if the database is large, it continues to build its index even when you switch to another multiscreen.

Although logging in as multiple copies of yourself is nice, on a single-user installation, it may be more convenient and efficient to establish a number of "users," each with his or her own home directory. Each pseudo user (they're all you, remember) has a specific purpose for specific types of jobs. One might be where all word processing takes place, another might handle accounting functions, and so forth. The following example shows the results of the who command, which lists all the users currently logged in to the system. Remember that all these "users" can be logged in to a single stand-alone computer.

```
$ who <Return>
print       tty01           Jan 23 09:47
desk        tty02           Jan 25 08:13
author      tty03           Jan 17 12:36
auto        tty04           Jan 10 08:55
market      tty05           Jan 23 08:41
yam         tty06           Jan 24 10:32
dosterm     tty07           Jan 15 13:46
fiction     tty08           Jan 22 10:31
info        tty09           Jan 22 10:29
menu        tty10           Jan 18 11:22
emacs       tty11           Jan 23 10:19
root        tty12           Jan 23 08:49
ralph       tty6b           Jan 11 13:33
```

In this example, there are 12 multiscreens, or 12 "users" logged on at once. You rotate through them by pressing the appropriate <Alt> and function key combination.

You are not limited to using UNIX on a PC. Older terminals are cheap and plentiful at electronic flea markets, computer conventions, and hamfests. This author has picked them up for as little as $25. They work fine on the serial port of your personal computer. Although most PCs have only one or two serial ports, serial-port extenders that can give you 8, 16, or more ports are readily available. Even on a PC, you can add terminals relatively easily and inexpensively.

If you add two terminals, you can log on as 14 users at any one time: the 12 multiscreens plus the two terminals. Currently, there are terminals and soft- ware that permit multiscreens on the terminal as well. The possibilities are tremendous.

Even on a conventional terminal, like a cheap used or surplus one, you have access to the power of the single-user installation concept. You can have several background processes running at the same time one is running in the foreground. Although they are less featured than multiscreens or a GUI, old- style terminals can still add to your productivity with UNIX.

Some terminals are designed to run X-Windows. Adding one of these to your single-user system adds all the benefits described in the following section on GUIs.

GUIs

Another way to do a lot of jobs at once is by using a graphical user interface designed for UNIX, such as X-Windows. X-Windows comes with UnixWare and is similar to Microsoft Windows and the Macintosh operating system, either of which you may be familiar with. X-Windows allows you to have several applications on the screen at once in separate windows, although only one is running full bore.

There is a major difference between X-Windows and the GUIs on the more limited DOS and Mac operating systems. X-Windows lets you run almost any number of applications independently. It's like having a lot of mini-terminals on your UNIX system, all right where you can see them.

In a single-user UNIX installation, you can have several "users" on different multiscreens, all running X-Windows and all having multiple applications active in their X-Windows session.

> **Caution**
>
> X-Windows is a memory hog. Too many sessions with too many applications can slow your system down to a crawl. With a little moderation, you will find yourself doing a lot of things all at once with this wonderful single-user installation concept.

Summary

Thinking of UNIX systems as being for many people, each doing a single task, is incomplete logic. UNIX systems also work very well in the single-user installation concept. As a single-user installation site, you can accomplish dramatically more work on the computer in a shorter time.

UNIX can do several things at once because the CPU slices its attention among the running tasks (also called *time sharing*). The multitasking and multiuser power of UNIX greatly benefit the single user. Multiscreens make use of that power by letting there be several copies of *you* on the system. And Graphical User Interfaces are another way to accomplish several tasks at once.

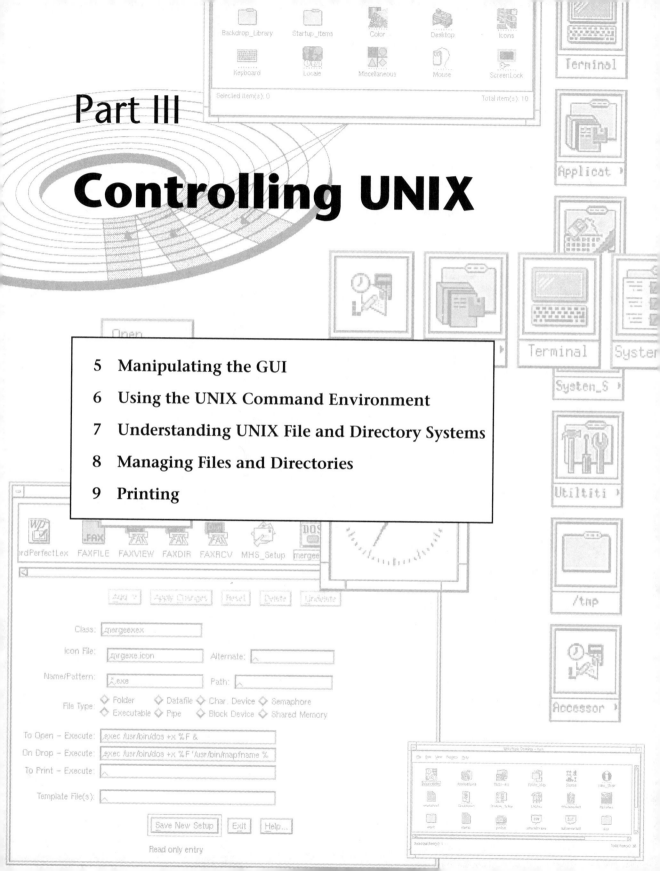

Part III

Controlling UNIX

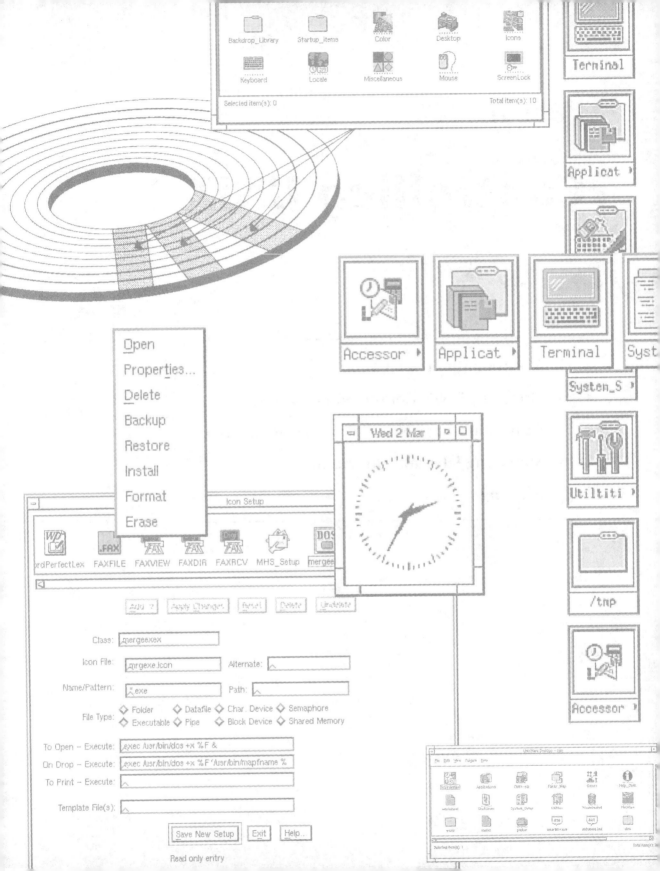

Chapter 5

Manipulating the GUI

Today the latest versions of the UNIX system all have graphical user interfaces (also referred to as GUIs). GUIs let you use the UNIX system in a way that is more intuitive than the standard shell command-line interface that was the hallmark of the first UNIX systems.

Instead of trying to remember commands and options, you can work with the mouse and keyboard to manipulate the elements of the GUI. If you want to start an application, you simply move the mouse pointer so that it's pointing to an icon representing the application, and double-click the mouse button. The GUI provides ways for you to adjust its look-and-feel; you can change the colors of the backdrop, windows, and borders, adjust the way the mouse buttons work, change key assignments, and so on.

Until UNIX System V Release 4.2 (SVR4.2) and UnixWare, vendors received the UNIX system with no GUI built in. Therefore, several different GUIs emerged from vendors when they put UNIX on their computer hardware. Recently, however, the UNIX industry has rallied around several graphical standards: the X-Windows system with Motif or, to a lesser extent, OPEN LOOK. X-Windows is the windowing system and Motif and OPEN LOOK are the look-and-feels. Motif and OPEN LOOK add the colors, mouse controls, and window-managing functions to the basic windowing technology.

The GUIs described in this chapter are Motif and OPEN LOOK (with the X-Windows system underneath). These two GUIs are delivered with UnixWare. If you are using a UNIX system with a non-standard GUI, the descriptions in this book may not match your system.

This chapter contains the following information:

- Working with the mouse to manipulate the GUI

- Changing the mouse buttons and functions

- Using the keyboard to navigate the GUI

- Adapting attributes of the GUI, such as colors and icon alignment

- Using standard GUI tools to do simple tasks and to become more comfortable with the GUI

III

Controlling UNIX

Starting the GUI

When you add a user to a UnixWare system, you can select whether that user is a desktop or a non-desktop user. If you are a desktop user, you are set up to use the GUI and have it start up automatically when you log in. If you are a non-desktop user, you are simply presented with a shell command-line prompt on login.

A desktop user also has the choice of having Motif or OPEN LOOK assigned as the look-and-feel. If you were already assigned a login account as a desktop user, simply log in. By default, the GUI starts up with the Motif look-and-feel, as shown in figure 5.1.

Fig. 5.1
Starting the GUI
(Motif).

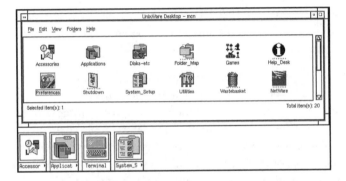

The examples in this chapter use the Motif GUI environment. If, when you log in, you see either a command-line prompt or the OPEN LOOK interface, you may want to change to a desktop-and-Motif user to make it easier to follow the examples.

If you are a non-desktop user, have the system owner change your user account to that of a desktop user by way of the User Setup icon. If you are a desktop user, but you want to change either the GUI environment or whether the GUI starts up at login, see "Controlling Your Desktop," later in this chapter, for instructions.

Understanding the X-Windows System

The X-Windows system, usually simply called X, is a windowing system that can operate on a variety of computer hardware and software platforms. X lets you open windows and work with information between the application and your keyboard and mouse. Also, you can open several windows at a time with X, so that you can work with several applications simultaneously.

If you had only X running, your screen would look empty. You would see a grey background with a letter *X* representing your mouse pointer, which you could move around. If you started an application, there would be no border around it and no way of managing the elements on the screen. Figure 5.2 is an example of an X application without a window manager running.

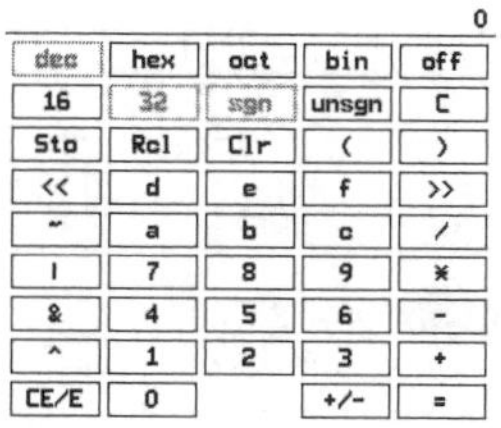

Fig. 5.2
An example of an X application (without borders).

It is the *window manager* that adds the full graphical interface you are used to seeing. The window manager provides the look-and-feel, such as Motif or OPEN LOOK for the GUI. After the window manager starts up, the borders appear, the menus work, and the mouse pointer is fully activated. See "Selecting OPEN LOOK or Motif" (the following section) for further information on UNIX window managers.

What sets X apart from other windowing systems is that X is designed to operate over networks. X communicates to networking protocols instead of directly to the computer's operating system. As a result, after you are connected to a network, any applications run on the network can be displayed on your screen.

What X's networking capabilities mean to you is that you can run applications from the company's super-computer or your coworker's PC and work with them using the window manager, colors, and mouse buttons you have set to your preferences.

Selecting OPEN LOOK or Motif

When you log in to UNIX, as noted earlier, the GUI starts up with the Motif look-and-feel by default. To change the GUI used with your login or select whether the GUI starts up at login time, use the Desktop Preferences icon.

> **Note**
>
> The procedure for changing your GUI and making sure that it starts up automatically is included here so that you can turn on the GUI and set it to Motif. Most of the examples in this chapter are based on the Motif GUI. If you don't know how the mouse, windows, or icons operate yet, you may want to skip ahead in this chapter and come back to this procedure.

III

Controlling UNIX

To change the default GUI or to select the GUI to start automatically when you log in, follow these steps:

1. Move the mouse pointer so that it is on the Preferences icon in the UnixWare desktop window and double-click the mouse button. The Preferences window appears as shown in figure 5.3.

Fig. 5.3
The Preferences window.

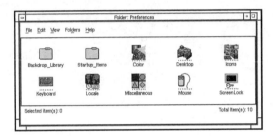

2. Move the mouse pointer to the Desktop icon and double-click the mouse button. The Desktop Preferences window appears as shown in figure 5.4.

Fig. 5.4
The Desktop Preferences window.

3. Choose the login options you want by clicking on the buttons next to GUI Environment and Start Desktop at Login options. The following options are available:

   ■ *GUI Environment.* Click on OPEN LOOK or Motif. The GUI environment you select takes effect the next time you start the GUI (usually this is when you log in).

   ■ *Start Desktop at Login.* Click on Yes or No. By default, Yes is selected, so the GUI starts automatically when you log in. If you select No, you see a standard UNIX command-line prompt (after which you can start the GUI as described in "Starting the GUI Manually," later in this chapter.)

4. Click on Apply. The changes are applied the next time you start the GUI. Usually, this means you have to quit the Desktop and log in again.

Comparing Motif and OPEN LOOK

Both the Motif and OPEN LOOK look-and-feels are built into UnixWare. The windows and icons that appear on your screen are the same, regardless of the GUI environment you choose. The controls and appearance of the two GUI environments, however, are different.

Figure 5.5 shows the UnixWare Desktop window in Motif mode.

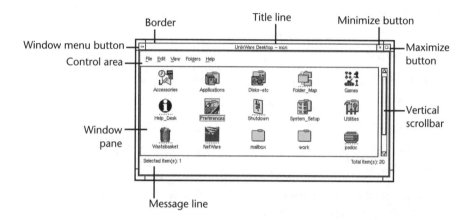

Fig. 5.5
The UnixWare Desktop window (Motif).

The features of a Motif window used in UnixWare are described in the following list:

■ *Border.* Use the border to resize the window with the mouse.

■ *Title line.* Lists the name of the window, including special information such as the folder name on a folder window. A folder is synonomous with a directory from the command line.

■ *Window menu button.* Click on this button to display the window menu.

■ *Window menu.* After you have clicked on the window menu button, the window menu displays the following window functions:

> *Close.* Stops the application associated with the window and removes the window from the screen.

> *Lower.* Places the window behind any other windows it covers.

> *Maximize.* Expands the window to fill the entire screen.

III

Controlling UNIX

Minimize. Sets the window aside as an active icon along the bottom of the screen.

Size. Changes the size of a window.

Move. Prepares the window to move to another location. Use the arrow keys to move the window and the Enter key to set it in place.

Restore. Restores an iconized window to its original form. (Not available on an open window.)

- *Control area.* Contains buttons that let you select the functions available with the window.

- *Minimize button.* Sets the window aside as an active icon along the bottom of the screen.

- *Maximize button.* Expands the window to fill the entire screen.

- *Window pane.* The area of a window in which you display and input information.

- *Vertical scrollbar.* Used to scroll to information above or below the current window pane.

- *Horizontal scrollbar* (not shown). Used to scroll to information to the left or right of the current window pane.

- *Message line.* The area in which messages from the application are displayed.

With UnixWare, both Motif and OPEN LOOK are implemented within the same window manager. That window manager is based on an interface called *Moolit* (a combination of Motif and OPEN LOOK). Although the two interfaces look different, the Motif purist will find that the Motif look-and-feel acts a lot like OPEN LOOK. To use the Motif window manager instead, see "Using *mwm* (Motif Window Manager)," later in this chapter.

There are advantages and disadvantages to both interfaces. To see the difference between the Motif and OPEN LOOK look-and-feels, compare figure 5.5 to figure 5.6.

If you use OPEN LOOK, you'll find it annoying that every time you want to maximize (full) or minimize (close) an application you have to pull down the window menu. Motif lets you click buttons in the upper-right corner of the window to do those functions.

After a window is iconized, OPEN LOOK lets you only reopen it. Motif lets you quit (close) or reopen (restore) an iconized window. If you want to resize a window in OPEN LOOK, you must click the mouse pointer on one of the corners and drag it. In Motif, you can grab any part of the border to resize it.

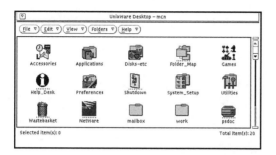

Fig. 5.6
The UnixWare
Desktop window
(OPEN LOOK).

If you compare the window menus of the two interfaces, you see that the same functions are sometimes called different things. Each also has a function not available with the other. Table 5.1 compares the window menus of Motif and OPEN LOOK.

Table 5.1: Motif versus OPEN LOOK Window Functions	
Motif	**OPEN LOOK**
Restore	(Not available)
Move	Move
Size	Resize
Minimize	Close
Maximize	Full
Lower	Back
Close	Quit
(Not available)	Refresh

The only window manager function not available with Motif is the Refresh function. Use Refresh to redraw your screen if it becomes garbled.

Using Pop-Up Windows

As you use UNIX GUI applications, you will notice that a different kind of window sometimes appears. For example, if you add a user, rename a file, or change GUI properties, a *pop-up window* appears.

III

Controlling UNIX

Pop-up windows are usually used for entering information related to a specific function. Figure 5.7 shows a Motif pop-up window used to add a user to UnixWare. Figure 5.8 shows the same window with the OPEN LOOK look-and-feel.

Fig. 5.7
A pop-up window (Motif).

Fig. 5.8
A pop-up window (OPEN LOOK).

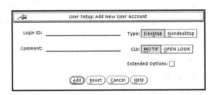

Instead of having buttons in the control area at the top of the window, pop-up windows have buttons at the bottom of the window. Typically, a button on a pop-up window represents a single action. For example, a button lets you apply a change, create a file, or cancel the operation.

The "pushpin" is an excellent feature of the OPEN LOOK look-and-feel not offered with Motif. Every pop-up window in OPEN LOOK has a pushpin in the upper-left corner (see fig. 5.8). By clicking on the pushpin, you pin the window so that it doesn't disappear when a function is completed. Click on the pushpin again when you're ready to cancel the window. In Motif, the window simply disappears when the function is done.

Tip

The pushpin is convenient if you are repeating several actions on a pop-up window. For example, if you are adding several users at a time to UnixWare, you can pin the window so that you don't have to reopen the window after you add each new user.

Using *mwm* (Motif Window Manager)

In UnixWare 1.1, a Motif window manager (the mwm command) is included so that you can use it to replace the Moolit window manager (olwm command) used by default. Users coming from a pure Motif environment may prefer the Motif window manager because it lets them use Motif configuration files for setting preferences and differs slightly in how mouse actions are done.

Follow these steps to replace the `olwm` with the `mwm` window manager:

1. Set the GUI Environment to Motif, as described in "Selecting OPEN LOOK or Motif," earlier in this chapter.

2. Open the `.olinitrc` file in your home directory using any text editor. (To use the graphical Text Editor, double-click on the Accessories icon, double-click on the Text Editor icon, click on the File button, click on Open, click on `.olinitrc`, and click on Open. The Text Editor window opens with the `.olinitrc` file ready to edit.)

3. Find the line that contains the single line `olwm`, and change it by adding several lines to read as follows:

   ```
   if[$XGUI="MOTIF"]then
       mwm&
   else
         olwmfi
   ```

   As a result, when you start the desktop and the GUI is set to Motif, the Motif window manager starts (`mwm`). Otherwise, the OPEN LOOK window manager (`olwm`) runs.

4. Save the changes. (In the Text Editor, click on File and click on Save. Then click on File and click on Exit to quit.)

5. Type the following command from a terminal window:

   ```
   cp /usr/X/lib/system.mwmrc $HOME/.mwmrc
   ```

This action places a copy of the Motif resource file (`.mwmrc`) in your home directory. Use `/usr/X/lib/example.mwmrc` to copy an expanded version of the file.

The next time you log in to UnixWare, the GUI starts up with the Motif (`mwm`) window manager.

Starting the GUI Manually

Some UNIX users like to work primarily from the shell (the UNIX command line) and only start the GUI when they need it. To do this, you must have been added as a desktop user and have the GUI set to *not* start at login.

To start the GUI manually from a UNIX command line after you are logged in, type the following:

```
$ /usr/X/bin/desktop
```

III

Controlling UNIX

The GUI starts in a few moments. Then run the desktop command again. The GUI should start this time.

Operating the Mouse

The mouse is a device you operate with your hand to move a pointer around on your screen. By moving this mouse pointer to different places on the screen and clicking the mouse buttons, you can work with the windows, menus, and icons that appear on your screen.

Although there are many different types of mice and other pointing devices, the most popular are the ones that roll around on a pad on your desk and fit in your hand. For PCs, the mouse typically has two (or sometimes three) buttons. A cable runs from your mouse to the computer and plugs into a serial port or some special mouse port.

Mouse Types

The types of mice supported by UnixWare are defined by how they are connected to the computer. Often the mouse comes with your PC and plugs into a serial port (COM1 or COM2). UnixWare, however, also supports the PS/2 and bus mouse types. When you install UnixWare, you define the type of mouse connected to your system.

Tip

Most people rarely change the type of mouse they use. If you defined the wrong mouse type or want to change it, you can do so using the mouseadmin command from a Terminal window. The mouseadmin command lets you change the display terminal associated with the mouse (usually the console), the mouse device (such as tty00 for COM1) and the mouse type (serial, PS/2, or bus). You must have superuser permission to use the mouseadmin command (type **su** and the root password). The mouseadmin command does not work without superuser permission.

Mouse Buttons

The left mouse button is the one you use the most. That's the button that a right-handed person's index finger falls on. If you are left-handed, have a different number of mouse buttons, or don't like the functions assigned to the buttons, you can change those assignments. See the section "Mouse Attributes" later in this chapter for information on changing the various attributes of your mouse.

Mouse Functions

There are three major functions assigned to your mouse buttons: Select, Paste, and Menu. You may notice that there are more functions than there are buttons if you have a two-button mouse. That's because to get the Menu function on a two-button mouse, you must use the mouse in conjunction with the <Shift> and <Ctrl> keys on your keyboard. To use other mouse functions, you must use the <Alt>, <Shift>, and <Ctrl> keys in conjunction with the mouse buttons. The mouse functions are outlined in the next section.

Select Function

Most work is done with the Select function, assigned to the left button on your mouse. As you use your mouse to complete procedures described in this book, procedures usually assume that you know how to use the Select function. For example, a procedure may say "click on the icon" as opposed to saying "move the pointer to the icon, press the Select mouse button, and release."

The actions you take with the Select mouse button are outlined in the following list:

- *Click.* Move the pointer to an object and quickly press and release the Select button. Use the click action to select an icon or activate a window.

- *Double-click.* Move the pointer to an object and quickly press and release the Select button twice. Use the double-click action to open a file, start an application, or select a word of text.

- *Triple-click.* Move the pointer to an object and quickly press and release the Select button three times. Use the triple-click action to select a line of text in a text area.

- *Drag.* Hold down the Select button and drag the pointer to a new location. Use the drag action to highlight an area of text or select a group of icons in a folder window.

- *Drag-and-drop.* Hold down the Select button on an icon, drag the pointer to another area of the screen, and release the Select button. Use the drag-and-drop action to drop a file icon on a folder (to move it to a new folder), on a printer (to print the file), or on a Wastebasket icon (to delete the file).

The Select button can be used in conjunction with certain keyboard keys. You can perform special functions along with click and drag-and-drop functions. For example, if you are working with file icons inside folders, the following list of special functions describes what you can do with files and folders.

III

Controlling UNIX

- *Drag-and-drop with no keys pressed.* Moves that item to the new folder.

- *Drag-and-drop while holding down the <Alt> key.* A copy of that item is placed in the new folder.

- *Drag-and-drop while holding down the <Ctrl> and <Alt> keys.* A link to that item is placed in the new folder.

- *Click while holding down the <Ctrl> key.* The item is selected or unselected (toggled). Use this action to select and unselect multiple icons in a folder window.

Menu Function

Use the Menu function to pull down a menu from the menu bar or from an icon. On a three-button mouse, Menu is assigned to the right button. On a two-button mouse, you must hold down the <Ctrl> and <Shift> keys as you click the right (Select) mouse button. This is inconvenient, considering that most users have a two-button mouse and that Menu is the second most important function.

There are several cases in which the only way you can access a feature is using the Menu function. For example, if you are working with floppy disks in your Disks-etc folder, the only way you can request to format a floppy disk is to click on Menu from the Disk icon and then select Format from the menu.

Click on Menu on an icon (the right button on a three-button mouse or <Ctrl-Shift>-right button on a two-button mouse) to see an icon menu. Figure 5.9 shows the icons menu for the Disk_A icon.

Fig 5.9
The Menu button is used to display an icon menu.

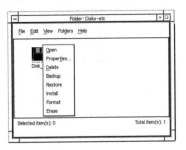

If you are using a two-button mouse, change the assignments so that Menu is on the right button. This is described in the "Mouse Attributes" section, later in this chapter.

Paste Function

The Paste function lets you cut and paste text between windows that support Motif cut-and-paste functions. Many applications however, do not support this function.

To use Paste, highlight an area of text by pressing the left mouse button and moving it across the text. Next, click the right mouse button in the spot where you want the text to be pasted. The text is copied to the new location. This works in Terminal windows and Text Editor windows.

Other Mouse Functions

Using the mouse buttons in conjunction with the <Ctrl>, <Shift>, and <Alt> keys, you can use other mouse functions. Many of these functions don't do anything in the UnixWare GUI, but may be implemented in specific applications.

The following list contains the alternative mouse functions you can get using mouse/keyboard combinations.

Function	Key	Mouse Button
Adjust	<Ctrl>	Select
Toggle	<Ctrl>	Select
Extend	<Shift>	Select
Duplicate	<Alt>	Select
Link	<Ctrl-Alt>	Select
Constrain	<Shift-Alt>	Select
Cut	<Alt>	Paste
Copy	<Ctrl>	Paste
Scroll by panning	<Shift>	Paste
Set menu default	<Alt>	Menu

Mouse Attributes

You can change any of the *attributes* (button and keyboard assignments) related to your mouse. To change either the number of mouse buttons (from two to three) or how the functions are assigned to each button, follow these steps:

1. Double-click on the Preferences icon in the UnixWare Desktop window. The Preferences folder appears.

III

Controlling UNIX

2. Double-click on the Mouse icon. The Mouse Modifiers Preferences window appears, as shown in figure 5.10.

Fig. 5.10
The Mouse
Modifiers Prefer-
ences window.

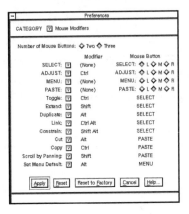

3. Click on either Two or Three to use the two-button or three-button mouse assignments for your mouse. (Consider using the three-button mouse assignment, even if you have a two-button mouse. This puts the Menu feature on the right mouse button.)

4. Click on the arrow button next to any of the function names to change the keyboard modifier used to get the function. Then click on <Shift>, <Ctrl>, and/or <Alt>.

   You may want to do this to simplify the keystrokes needed for a function you do often.

5. Click on Apply to have the new Mouse Modifiers take effect.

Changing the Window with the Mouse

Now that you are familiar with the UnixWare mouse functions, you can try a few to become comfortable working with the GUI.

- *Reshape the window.* You can reshape any window using your mouse. Place the mouse pointer on a corner or a border of a window, hold down the mouse button, and move the pointer to reshape the window. When you release the mouse button, the window is the new size.

- *Lower the window.* When you have several windows open, they usually cover each other. You can move a window behind any other windows it may be covering. To lower a window, click on the Window menu button of a window and then click on Lower. The window moves behind any windows it is covering.

- *Move the window.* To move a window to another area of the screen, use your mouse on the window header area (also called the *title line*). Hold down the mouse button with the pointer on the window header area, move the mouse until the window is where you want it, and then release the mouse button.

- *Reduce the window to an icon (iconize it).* If there is a window you want to set aside for the moment, but don't want to quit completely, you can reduce the window to an icon on your screen. Click on the small box (the one that contains a small dot) in the upper-right corner of the window. This is referred to as the minimize button. The window disappears and an icon representing the window appears on the bottom of the screen.

  You also can iconize a window using the window menu button. Click on the Window menu button and then click on Minimize to reduce the window to an icon.

- *Restore the window.* After you have iconized a window, restore the window by double-clicking on the icon.

- *Quit the window.* If you are finished with a window, you can quit the window using the window menu. Click on the Window menu button and then click on Close. (If you are using the OPEN LOOK look-and-feel, click Quit rather than Close. Close iconizes the window in OPEN LOOK.)

Using the Keyboard

Sometimes it's quicker to use the keyboard instead of the mouse to do some functions. Also, if you prefer, you can use the keyboard exclusively to work with your GUI and never even touch your mouse.

Use the procedures in the following sections to work with the graphical elements on your GUI using your keyboard.

Handling Windows

You work with the windows on the GUI using different function-key combinations. Here are a few examples:

- *Go to the next window.* With several windows open on-screen, hold down the <Alt> key and press the <Esc> key. The next window, or iconized window, is highlighted. Repeat the sequence to step forward through all the windows on-screen.

III

Controlling UNIX

■ *Go to the previous window.* With several windows open on-screen, hold down the <Shift> and <Alt> keys and press the <Esc> key. The previous window, or iconized window, is highlighted. Repeat the sequence to step backward through all the windows on-screen.

■ *Use the Window menu.* Hold down the <Shift> key and press the <Esc> key. The window menu appears for the current window. From that point, you can choose any of the basic window functions (Restore, Move, Size, Minimize, Maximize, Lower, or Close) by pressing the arrow keys until you highlight the function and then pressing the space bar.

■ *Use window functions.* You can request window functions directly without opening the window menu. With a window selected, use the following function keys to do basic window functions:

Restore. Hold down <Alt> and press the <F5> function key.

Move. Hold down <Alt> and press the <F7> function key.

Size. Hold down <Alt> and press the <F8> function key.

Minimize. Hold down <Alt> and press the <F9> function key.

Maximize. Hold down <Alt> and press the <F10> function key.

Lower. Hold down <Alt> and press the <F3> function key.

Close. Hold down <Alt> and press the <F4> function key.

■ *Go to the next window (same application).* Sometimes a single application has several windows open. For example, within the Mail application you may have the Mail Reader and Mail Manager windows open. To move among windows in the same application, hold down the <Alt> key and press the <F6> key.

■ *Go to the previous window (same application).* To go to the previous window in the same application, hold down the <Shift> and <Alt> keys and press the <Esc> key.

Working within a Window

After you have selected the window you want, you can use the functions within that window from the keyboard instead of using the mouse:

■ *Moving the focus between pane and buttons.* When you open a window, the *focus* (highlighted area) is either on the first button in the control area or in the window pane. To toggle between the buttons and the window pane, press the <F10> function key. In a folder window, you can toggle between the File button being lit and an icon in the pane being lit (selected).

- *Moving the focus (within an area).* After an item is highlighted in the pane or the control area, you can move among items in that area using the arrow keys. To select a different item (icon or button), use the up-, down-, left-, or right-arrow keys. As you use the arrow keys, you see different items highlighted.

- *Selecting buttons.* Notice that each of the buttons on a window has a single letter of the button name underlined. By holding down the <Alt> key and pressing that letter (when the window is selected), you request that function. For example, with a folder window active, you see the buttons shown in figure 5.11.

    To use any of these functions, hold down the <Alt> key and press f (for File), e (for Edit), v (for View), d (for Folders) or h (for Help). In each of these cases, a menu appears for the function from which you can select the action you want. In other cases, such as on pop-up windows, an action might just occur (such as an Apply or a Cancel).

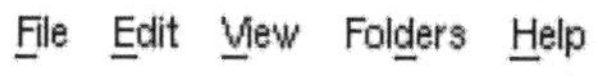

File   Edit   View   Folders   Help

Fig. 5.11
Menu buttons with a folder window active.

- *Acting on icons.* After you have selected an icon in a folder window, you can request actions on that icon (usually a file or folder) by selecting a function from the icon's menu. With the icon highlighted, hold down the <Ctrl> button and press <m>. A menu appears for the icon. Use the arrow keys to move to the function you want and press the space bar to select it.

    You use this action to choose the Open menu item. This starts the application (if it is an application) or opens the file in a text editor (if it is a text file).

Requesting Mouse Functions from the Keyboard

Keyboard keys can be used instead of the mouse to do standard mouse functions, such as Select, Adjust, Menu, or Drag-and-Drop:

- *Select function.* Use the space bar instead of the Select mouse function. The space bar doesn't implement all Select mouse functions. For example, you can't press the space bar twice quickly to "double-click" on an icon. You can, however, use the space bar to select a menu item or a button that is currently highlighted.

III

Controlling UNIX

■ *Adjust function.* Hold down the <Ctrl> key and press the ampersand (&) to select multiple items. For example, if an icon is highlighted in a folder window, move to another icon using the arrow keys, and then press <Ctrl-&> to highlight that icon, too. Use Adjust to unhighlight an icon as well.

■ *Menu function.* Hold down the <Ctrl> key and press <m> to open a menu for a selected item. The item must already be selected before you can use <Ctrl-m> to open its menu.

■ *Drag operation.* To use the keyboard to drag an item from one place to another, first select the item (usually a file or folder icon). Next press the <F5> function key. The icon changes color. Press the arrow keys until the item reaches the new location.

■ *Drop operation.* After you have dragged an item where you want it to go, press the <F2> function key to drop the item.

■ *Copy operation.* To copy an item from one location to another (usually a file or folder), hold down the <Alt> key and press the space bar with the item selected. Next, move the item to the new position and press <F2> to drop it. A copy of the item appears in the new location.

Changing Screen Resolution

The first time you log in to UnixWare, the screen appears at a resolution that works with all standard VGA video boards: 640×480 pixels. The resolution determines how many dots fit on the screen. The higher the resolution, the more dots.

Most video boards today support higher resolutions. Higher resolutions allow you to fit more on your screen and makes the screen elements appear less jagged. Unfortunately, UnixWare doesn't include a graphical way to change your screen resolution. It does, however, include a command for telling the system what kind of video board you have and the resolution you want to run.

To change video resolution to suit your video board, perform the following steps. Before you run the procedure, however, you should know the size of your screen, the type of video board (in particular what chip set it uses), the amount of RAM on the board, the number of colors it supports (16 or 256), and the video resolution it supports.

1. Double-click on the Accessories icon in the UnixWare Desktop window. The Accessories window appears.

2. Double-click on the Terminal icon in the Accessories window. A Terminal window appears.

3. Type **su** and then the root password to obtain superuser permission.

4. Type **/usr/X/adm/setvgamode**. You are asked for the following information:

   - *The type of video board.* There are hundreds of entries to choose from. Use the highest resolution available with the greatest number of colors (usually 256). If your video board is not mentioned specifically, read the manual that comes with the board to find out what type of graphics chips it uses and match a similar entry.

   - *The size of the monitor.* Some standard monitor sizes are 14", 15", 17", 20", and 21", as measured diagonally.

   - *The video RAM.* To take full advantage of the RAM (random-access memory) on the video board, you must specify it here.

5. After you have selected your video settings, setvgamode asks you whether you want to test the settings. Try this test. If you don't, the next time you log in, your screen appears garbled if you have made the wrong selections.

6. Exit the GUI.

7. Log in again to see the new screen resolution.

> **Note**
>
> Increasing the screen resolution causes the icons in your folder windows to squish together. Increase the number in the first box of the File Icon Grid Size in the Desktop Preferences window to increase the distance between the icons. You may have to realign the icons the next time you open the folder window by clicking on View and then clicking on Align.

Controlling Your Desktop

Almost all features of your screen, mouse, and keyboard have attributes associated with them that you can change. The way that icons align, the colors on each part of a window, and the functions assigned to your mouse can all be adapted to suit the way you use your GUI.

The Preferences folder provides access to most of the things you can change on your screen. Open the Preferences folder by double-clicking on the Preferences icon in the UnixWare Desktop window. After you open individual Preference windows for specific functions, the word Preferences appears in the title bar, but the window is distinguished from others by the name next to the Category button. The Preferences window appears as shown in figure 5.12.

Fig. 5.12
Opening the
Preferences
window.

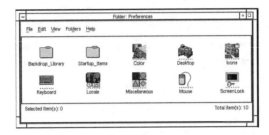

The Backdrop_Library contains icons representing graphics you can use for the backdrop of your screen. Startup_Items is where you drop applications you want to start automatically when you log in. Color enables you to change the colors on your screen. Icons lets you change how iconized windows appear on your screen.

Keyboard preferences enable you to change how window controls are mapped into the keyboard. Locale lets you change country-specific and language-specific attributes. Miscellaneous enables you to change a few odd attributes, such as whether keyboard shortcuts are displayed on menus or whether the system beeps when errors occur.

Changing the Backdrop and Colors

You can change the backdrop on-screen to a solid color or you can use a graphic to fill the screen. You can also change the colors of other window elements.

Changing Colors

To change the color of your screen's backdrop to a solid color, use the Color Preferences window. This is used for other elements on your screen as well. First open the Preferences window as described previously. Then double-click on the Color icon. One of the two windows shown in figures 5.13 and 5.14 appears. If your video is configured to display 16 colors (the default), the Color Preferences window in figure 5.13 appears. For 256 colors, the Color Preferences window in figure 5.14 appears.

Fig. 5.13
The Color
Preferences
window (16
colors).

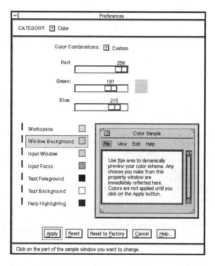

Fig. 5.14
The Color
Preferences
window (256
colors).

In the Color Preferences window, click on the area of the sample screen you want to change, such as the background. Then select the color either by clicking the box of the color you want (16 colors) or by moving the three slide bars with your mouse to create the color you want (256 colors).

Click on Apply. The new colors immediately take effect.

If you want to change to a preset combinations of colors, click on the down-arrow button next to the words Color Combinations. Then click on one of the color combinations listed.

Changing Pictures

Using the Backdrop_ Library, you can insert a picture as the background of your screen. Several graphics, in GIF format, are included with UnixWare. You can use graphics in any of the following formats for your backdrop:

- Sun Rasterfile

- Portable Bit Map (PBM)

- Faces Project

- GIF Image

- X Pixmap

- X Bitmap

To change the picture on your backdrop, do the following:

1. Open the Preferences window.

2. Double-click on the Backdrop_ Library icon. The Backdrop_Library Folder appears as shown in figure 5.15.

3. Drag-and-drop any of the GIF files in the folder on the Backdrop_Items icon. The backdrop immediately changes to the new picture.

Fig. 5.15
The Backdrop
Library folder.

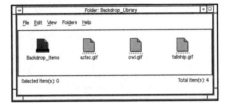

If you want to use a different picture, drop it on the Backdrop_Items icon and it will display After you have dropped several items into the Backdrop_Items icon, you should be aware of a bit of strange behavior. The next time you log in, the GUI selects one of the items you dropped on the Backdrop_Items icon as the backdrop. At each future log in, the GUI rotates to another picture.

To see which pictures are active with the Backdrop_Item icon, click the Menu mouse button on the icon. When the menu appears, click on List Items. The list of active backdrop pictures is displayed.

To clear all active pictures from the Backdrop_Item icon, click the Menu mouse button on the icon. When the menu appears, click on Delete All Items. The active backdrops are cleared. This, however, doesn't clear the current picture from the backdrop.

To clear the current picture from the backdrop, double-click on the Backdrop_Items icon. The screen returns to the solid color you set on your Color Preferences window.

Changing the GUI Appearance

There are dozens of attributes of the GUI you can change from Preferences windows. The procedure for changing these attributes is the same in each case:

1. Double-click on the Preferences icon. The Preferences window opens.

2. Double-click on the specific preference icon that contains the attribute you want to change.

3. Select the specific change you want to make.

4. Click on Apply to activate the change.

Table 5.2 lists the attributes you can change, the specific Preferences window you must open to make the change, and a description of your options.

Table 5.2: Changing GUI Preferences

Attribute	Preference Window	Description
GUI Environment	Desktop	Select either OPEN LOOK or Motif. This changes the entire look-and-feel of the GUI.
Desktop at Login	Desktop	Select either Yes or No to indicate whether the Desktop starts up when you log in.
Desktop Appearance	Desktop	Select either 2D or 3D. 3D gives the appearance of greater depth on the windows, icons, buttons, and menus.
Show Full Path Names	Desktop	Select Yes or No. If you select Yes, instead of showing the single folder name when you open a folder window, the header displays the full path name of the folder.
File Icon Grid Size	Desktop	Click on the up and down arrows to increase or decrease the space between icons in your folder windows. It is important to do this if you have increased your screen resolution. The default is 84 pixels wide and 62 pixels high for each icon.
Default Folder Window Size	Desktop	Click on the up and down arrows to change the number of icons displayed the first time you open a folder window. By default, a folder window displays two rows and five columns of icons.

III

Controlling UNIX

(continues)

Table 5.2   Continued

Attribute	Preference Window	Description
Location	Icons	Click on Top, Bottom, Left, or Right to have iconized windows align on one of those four parts of the screen. By default, iconized windows appear on the bottom of the screen.
Border	Icons	Click on Show or Don't Show to determine whether icon borders are displayed or not. (This preference only applies to the OPEN LOOK look-and-feel.)
Basic Settings	Locale	Click on the location (country, continent, or city) that indicates the way the language, numbers, and dates are represented. American English is the default.
Specific Settings	Locale	Click on the down-arrow button for any specific locale setting you want to change. Settings that can change include the display language, input language, numeric format, and date and time format. Most basic settings don't give you a choice of specific settings to change.
Beep	Miscellaneous	Click on Always, Notices Only, or Never. The Always option tells the system to beep at every illegal action; the Notices Only option says to beep only when a message window appears; and the Never option says to never beep.
Window Layering	Miscellaneous	Click on Individually or As a Group. The As a Group option says that when you have a main window and a pop-up window(s) on the screen, and you move the main window, the pop-up window(s) move with it. The Individually option lets you move the windows separately.
Select Mouse Press	Miscellaneous	Click on Displays Default or Displays Menu. In OPEN LOOK mode, this defines whether clicking on a Menu button displays the default action or displays the menu. (This option isn't used in Motif mode.)

Attribute	Preference Window	Description
Help Model	Miscellaneous	Click on Input Focus or Pointer. This defines whether help is displayed based on the current input focus or on where the pointer is pointing when you press the <F1> function key. The help text you get isn't part of the basic help text, but rather some left-over OPEN LOOK text that the programmers forgot to get rid of.
Input Area	Miscellaneous	Click on Click SELECT or Move Pointer. This sets whether you must click on a window or simply move the pointer to it for the window to become active.
Mnemonics	Miscellaneous	Click on one of four settings to define whether mnemonics (the <Alt>-letter functions associated with each menu item and button) are on or off. Selections also define whether the mnemonic, when on, is underlined, highlighted, or not shown.
Accelerators	Miscellaneous	Click on Off, On-Show, or On-Don't Show to define whether keyboard accelerators are on or off and, if on, whether they are shown. This applies to the <Alt>-function keys, such as those on the window menu.

There are dozens of keyboard preferences you can change using the Keyboard Preferences window. Change these preferences if you don't like the keys you have to press to get the keyboard functions described earlier in this chapter. Many of these functions don't appear to do anything in UnixWare, but were simply implemented to meet the Motif specifications.

Changing GUI Resources

Most of the preferences you change in the GUI are stored in the .Xdefaults file (for the olwm window manager) or the .mwmrc file (for the mwm window manager). Specific applications (word processing programs, spreadsheets, and others) also store their preferences in these files.

In the X-Windows system, these preferences are called *resources*. Figure 5.16 shows examples of some resources that may appear in the .Xdefaults file in your home directory.

III

Controlling UNIX

Fig. 5.16

X resources in the
.Xdefaults file.

A resource consists of the name of the resource, a colon (:), and the value. The three values shown in figure 5.16 represent values you can change from the GUI:

- Text Background defines the color of the text background in a window pane.

- beep indicates that the system should beep at every illegal action on the GUI.

- iconGravity indicates that iconized windows should be aligned on the bottom of the screen (south).

You should know about these specific files because there are times when an application will tell you to put resources into one of these files. Also, if you are brave, you can do some more fine-tuning of your resources by changing values in this file.

Caution

If you change any resources in your .Xdefaults file, exit the desktop and log in again for them to take effect. If you change any preferences from the Preferences window after you change the .Xdefaults and before you restart the GUI, your changes are lost.

Automatic Application Startup

Another way you can control the way your GUI appears when you log in is to define some applications to start up automatically. The Startup_Items icon (in the Preferences folder) simply represents a folder that you drop applications into. When the GUI starts, the applications you dropped on Startup_Items are started up.

A handy application to have started automatically is the Terminal window. To see how the Startup_Items icon works, try setting up a Terminal window to start automatically as shown in the following procedure:

1. Double-click on the Preferences icon in the UnixWare Desktop window to open the Preferences folder.

2. Double-click on the Accessories icon in the UnixWare Desktop window to open the Accessories folder.

3. Drag-and-drop the Terminal icon from the Accessories folder onto the Startup Items icon in the Preferences folder.

> ### Note
>
> A link is made to the Terminal icon in the Accessories folder. There is not an extra copy of the Terminal icon on the system, but simply a pointer to the original one.

4. Exit the GUI.

5. Log in to the GUI again. The Terminal window opens a few moments after the GUI starts.

> ### Note
>
> By default, the system waits 30 seconds before starting up items in the Startup Items folder. This waiting period was created to avoid a condition on some slower computers. The application would try to start before the GUI was completely started and the application would fail. With a faster system, you can shorten this waiting period without a problem.

Using the GUI Tools

After you have mastered the basic features of the GUI, try a few of the simple accessories that come with UnixWare. This will help you become comfortable with the GUI before you have to deal with more difficult applications.

Using the Clock

The Clock application displays the current time in digital or analog format. There are a few things you can do with the clock, such as set an alarm or change properties of the clock.

To start the clock, open the Accessories folder (double-click on the Accessories icon in the UnixWare Desktop window) and then double-click on the Clock icon. The clock appears, as shown in figure 5.17.

III

Controlling UNIX

Fig. 5.17
The analog clock.

The clock displays the time, the current day, date, and month.

To set an alarm, click the Menu mouse button somewhere on the clock face. Select Set Alarm from the menu. The Set Alarm window appears, as shown in figure 5.18.

Fig. 5.18
The Set Alarm
window.

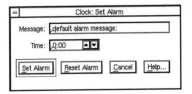

Triple-click in the box next to Message to select the entire message. Type a new message over the old one. Next, use the arrow keys or type over the information in the box next to Time to indicate the time you want the alarm to go off. Click on Set Alarm to set the alarm to go off at the specified time. You can also move to different fields with the Tab key.

Figure 5.19 is an example of a message notice that appears as a result of the clock alarm.

Fig. 5.19
A clock message.

There are also attributes of the clock you can change. To change clock attributes, click the Menu mouse button somewhere on the clock face. Then select Properties from the menu. The Clock Properties window appears as shown in figure 5.20.

Fig. 5.20
The Clock
Properties
window.

Click on the type of chimes you want to accompany the clock: Traditional or Ship's Bells. By default, there is no chime with the clock. Click on Analog or Digital. Click on Second or Minute ticks to show a second hand, or simply an hour and minute hand, respectively. Click on Apply to apply the changes immediately.

Using the Calculator

The Calculator is a simple, graphical version of a handheld calculator. To start the Calculator, open the Accessories folder (double-click on the Accessories icon in the UnixWare Desktop window) and then double-click on the Calculator icon. The calculator appears as shown in figure 5.21.

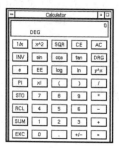

Fig. 5.21
The calculator.

Try a few simple calculations. Click on numbers. Click on an operation (/ for division, * for multiplication, – for subtraction, or + for addition), then click the equal sign (_). As you do the calculations, the numbers change in the pane at the top of the calculator.

Using the Terminal Window

The Terminal window lets you get to the traditional UNIX system shell command-line interpreter (often simply called *the shell*). Because the GUI was added to UNIX System V in Release 4.2 and the shell has been around for decades, there are many things you must still go to the shell to do. For example, some advanced administration must be done from the shell.

For a complete description of shell commands, see the Command Reference at the end of this book.

To start the Terminal window, open the Accessories folder (double-click on the Accessories icon in the UnixWare Desktop window) and then double-click on the Terminal icon. The Terminal window appears as shown in figure 5.22.

III

Controlling UNIX

Fig. 5.22
The Terminal
window.

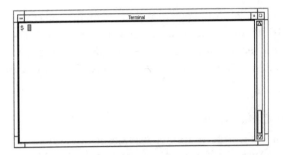

In the Terminal window is a prompt (a dollar sign, $, by default) with a cursor next to it, ready to accept input. To become familiar with the shell, type a few UNIX commands. Figure 5.23 shows the results of typing each of the following commands, followed by <Enter>: pwd, ls, date, and who -u.

Fig 5.23
A few UNIX
commands in the
Terminal window.

The pwd command shows that the present working directory is /home/mcn; ls shows a listing of files within that directory; date displays the current date; and who -u shows a listing of all users logged into your system (only the user named zorb).

Changing Terminal Properties
You can change certain properties relating to your Terminal window. To display the Terminal Properties box and change some Terminal window properties, do the following:

1. Click the Menu mouse button on any part of the Terminal window pane. The menu shown in figure 5.24 appears.

2. Click on Properties. The Terminal (xterm) Properties window appears as shown in figure 5.25.

   ■ *Visual Bell.* Click here to use a visual bell (the window pane flashes) rather than an audible bell (a beep) when you do an illegal action.

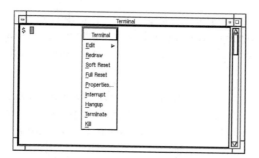

Fig. 5.24
The Terminal
menu.

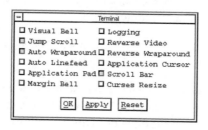

Fig. 5.25
The Terminal
(xterm) Properties
window.

- *Jump Scroll.* Click here to have the window scroll a full screen at a time rather than a line at a time when big blocks of text are being sent to the screen.

- *Auto Wraparound.* Click here to have text wrap around automatically when you type at the shell command line. Otherwise, text appears to overwrite itself when you reach the end of a shell command line.

- *Auto Linefeed.* Click here to have a carriage return added each time you type a newline, vertical tab, or new page. Newline, vertical tab, and new pages are all codes that may appear in your text.

- *Application Pad.* Click here to use the keypad as input.

- *Margin Bell.* Click here to have a bell ring each time you type near the right margin.

- *Logging.* Click here to have your entire Terminal session logged in a file called XtermLog.*xxxxx* (where *xxxxx* is replaced by a unique set of characters). Everything the screen displays and everything you type are captured in the log file. Each time you open a new Terminal window, a new, unique log file is created.

III

Controlling UNIX

■ *Reverse Video.* Click here to reverse the foreground and background colors. If you have black text on a white background, clicking here changes changes to white text on a black background.

■ *Reverse Wraparound.* Click here to reverse wraparound. Reverse wraparound lets you backspace to the line above (as opposed to only being able to backspace to the beginning of the current line).

■ *Application Cursor.* Click here to allow arrow keys to be used in the Terminal window.

■ *Scrollbar.* Click here to have a scroll bar appear on the right side of the Terminal window.

■ *Curses Resize.* Click here to be allowed to resize the Terminal window while applications based on the cursor interface are running. An example of a cursor application is the vi editor.

4. Click on OK to apply the changes.

Using Edit Properties

There are some convenient cut-and-paste features built into the Terminal window. To use these editing properties, follow this procedure:

1. Click the Menu mouse button. The Terminal window menu appears.

2. Click on Edit and then click on Stay Up. This makes it so the little Edit menu does not go away the next time you click your mouse. The Edit menu appears as shown in figure 5.26.

3. Placing your cursor at the start of a section of text you want to copy, hold down the Select mouse button, move the cursor to the end of the text you want to copy, and release the mouse button. The text is highlighted.

Fig. 5.26
The Terminal Edit menu.

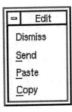

4. Click on Copy in the Edit menu.

5. Move the cursor to the location where you want to insert text. (You have to use keyboard keys if you are in the shell or using the vi text editor.)

6. Click on Paste in the Edit menu. The text is inserted at the point of the cursor.

Instead of copying and pasting, you can simply *send* the data. First highlight the text you want to send and then click on Send in the Edit menu. The text is sent to wherever your cursor was located. Make sure that you are in input mode in your editor when you send the text .

Summary

In this Chapter, you learned how to use the Graphical User Interfaces that come with UnixWare. You learned how to use the mouse as an efficient way to make selections and active icons. You explored the differences between the Motif and OPEN LOOK look-and-feels for UnixWare and learned how to make one or the other of these modes the default when you log in.

You also learned how to make UNIX aware of your preferences. You can now change the backdrop that appears on your screen to either a solid color or a graphics image. You learned which Preferences windows contain specific options that control other aspects of the appearance and operation of your Desktop. Finally, you explored a few of the built-in tools, such as the Clock and Calculator, and discovered how to use the Terminal window to access the shell command-line prompt.

III

Controlling UNIX

Chapter 6

Using the UNIX Command Environment

As a new user or novice system administrator (or system owner in UnixWare), you have been given a login ID and a password. Because UNIX is a multiuser operating system, it must be able to distinguish between users and classes of users. UNIX uses your login ID to establish a session in your name and to determine the privileges you have. UNIX uses your password (which you should never tell anyone—not even the system administrator) to verify who you are.

Because any user can log in to any terminal in theory (there *is* an exception), UNIX begins by displaying a login prompt on every terminal. When you log in to a terminal, you own the session on that terminal until you log out. When you log out, UNIX displays the login prompt for the next user. Between logging in and logging out, UNIX makes sure that all the programs you run and any files you might create are owned by you. Conversely, UNIX does not allow you to read or alter a file owned by another user unless that user or the system administrator has given you permission to do so. Your login ID and password allow UNIX to maintain the security of your files and those of others.

> **Note**
>
> When UnixWare starts, the Graphical Login screen appears. You enter the same information at the Graphical Login screen as you do at the UNIX login prompt.

The system administrator assigns every user a user ID and a temporary password as well as a group ID, a home directory, and a shell. This information is kept in a file named /etc/passwd, which is owned and controlled by the

This chapter covers the following topics:

- UNIX command processing

- UNIX command parsing

- UNIX command feedback

III

Controlling UNIX

system administrator (the system owner in UnixWare). Once you have successfully logged in, you can change your password, which is then encrypted in a form that even the system administrator can't unravel. If you forget your password, the system administrator can issue you another temporary password but will never know what you change it to. You can change your password with the `passwd` command. In UnixWare, use the Password Setup window, shown in figure 6.1. To open the Password Setup window, click on the Password Setup icon (located in the System Setup window).

Fig. 6.1
The UnixWare
Password Setup
window.

Understanding UNIX Command Processing

▶ You learn a lot more about the standard shells in Chapter 10, "Understanding UNIX Shells."

After you log in, UNIX places you in your home directory and runs a program called a *shell*. A shell is really nothing more than a program designed to accept commands from you and execute them. Many kinds of programs can be used as shells but there are several standard shells available with almost all versions of UNIX. The following section introduces shells; for now, assume that the system administrator assigned one of the standard shells to your account.

If you use UnixWare, the UnixWare Desktop starts after you log in. To get to a command line and run a shell, you open a Terminal window by clicking on the Terminal icon (located in the Accessories folder). Figure 6.2 shows the Terminal window, which you can use just like a standard shell prompt.

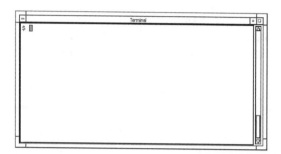

Fig. 6.2
The UnixWare
Terminal window.

Shells

The most common shell programs are the Bourne shell, the C shell, and the Korn shell. To the novice user, the Bourne and Korn shells look identical (indeed, the Korn shell grew out of the Bourne shell). The C shell was developed at the University of California at Berkeley as a shell more suitable for programmers than the Bourne shell. The Korn shell has all the features of the C shell but uses the syntax of the Bourne shell. If all this sounds confusing at the moment, don't worry. You can do a lot without knowing or worrying about the shell you are using.

In their simplest forms, the Bourne and Korn shells use the dollar sign ($) as the standard prompt; the C shell uses the percent sign (%) as the prompt. Fortunately (or not, depending on your disposition), these prompts can be changed so that you may or may not see either the dollar or the percent sign when you first log in.

The Environment

Before you see the shell prompt, UNIX sets up your default environment. The UNIX *environment* contains settings and data that control your session while you are logged in. Of course, as with all things in UNIX, you are completely free to change any of these settings to suit your needs. Your session environment is divided into two components: The first component controls your terminal, or more properly, the behavior of the computer's port, to which you connect the cable from your terminal. The second component is called the *shell environment*. It controls various aspects of the shell and any programs you run. You should first know about your terminal environment.

> **Note**
>
> UnixWare runs on a PC—the "terminal" is actually your monitor and keyboard. You may or may not have other terminals connected to your UnixWare system.

Setting the Terminal Environment

Your login session actually consists of two separate programs that run side by side to give you the appearance of having the machine to yourself. Although the shell is the program that receives your instructions and executes them, before the shell ever sees your commands, everything you type must first pass through the relatively transparent program called the *device driver*.

The device driver controls your terminal. It receives the characters you type and determines what to do with them—if anything—before passing them on to the shell for interpretation. Likewise, every character generated by the shell must pass through the device driver before being delivered to the terminal. This section is first concerned with how to control the behavior of your device driver.

UNIX is unique in that every device connected to the system looks, to a program, just like every other device, and all devices look like files. It is the task of the different device drivers in your system to accomplish this transformation. A hard disk in the system behaves very differently from your terminal yet it is the job of their respective device drivers to make them look identical to a program.

For example, a disk has blocks, sectors, and cylinders, all of which must be properly addressed when reading and writing data. Your terminal, on the other hand, accepts a continuous stream of characters, but those characters must be delivered to the terminal in an ordered and relatively slow manner. The device driver orders this data and sends it to you at 1200, 2400, 9600 or higher *baud* (a unit of measure that stands for bits per second) and inserts stop, start, and parity bits in the data stream.

Because your terminal is always connected to the system, the device driver allows you to define special characters, called *control characters*, that serve as end-of-file and end-of-line markers for your shell. The device driver also allows you to define control characters that send signals to a running process (such as the interrupt signal which can, in most cases, stop a running process and return you to the shell). Figure 6.3 shows one way that the UNIX kernel, your shell, and your device driver behave.

Fig. 6.3
The interaction of the UNIX kernel, the shell, and the device driver.

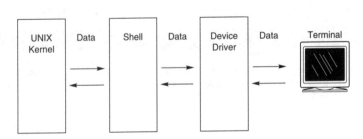

Dozens of parameters can be set for your terminal but most of them are handled automatically. However, there are a few parameters and modes you should know about.

The device driver has two modes of operation called "cooked" and "raw." In *raw mode*, all the characters you type pass directly to either the shell or a program run by the shell. Programs like editors and spreadsheets require raw mode and set it up automatically. When such programs end, they normally reset your terminal to cooked mode—but not always. When your terminal is in raw mode, it will not respond to control keys like the interrupt key.

When your terminal is in *cooked mode*, every key you type is interpreted by the device driver. Normal keys are stored in a buffer until the end-of-line key is pressed. In most cases, the end-of-line key is the <Enter> or <Return> key (however, this key can be changed). When the device driver receives the end-of-line character, it interprets the entire line before passing the interpreted or "parsed" line on to the shell or application program. Table 6.1 lists the most important control keys.

Table 6.1: Control Keys

Key Name	Description
Interrupt	Use the interrupt key to interrupt the execution of a running program. When you give UNIX a command and press the end-of-line key, a program normally runs until normal completion. If you press the interrupt key, you send a signal to the running program, telling it to stop. Some programs ignore this signal; if your terminal is in raw mode, the control key passes directly to the program and may not have the desired effect. The UNIX convention is to use the <Del> key as the interrupt key. Many UNIX sites change this key to <Ctrl-c> for the convenience of people familiar with MS-DOS and other systems that use this key combination.
Erase	The erase control key is usually defined as the <Backspace> key. When you press the erase key, it deletes the last character in the buffer. The erase key works just like the backspace key on a typewriter. On some terminals and systems, there is confusion between the <Del> and <Backspace> keys. If the erase key has been defined as <Del>, the interrupt key has probably been defined as <Ctrl-c>.
Kill	The kill key (normally defined as the @ character) is used to delete everything in the buffer before it passes to the shell or application program. Unlike what happens when you press the interrupt key, you don't see a new shell prompt when you press the kill key. The device driver simply waits for you to type more text.

(continues)

III

Controlling UNIX

Table 6.1 Continued	
Key Name	Description
End-of-line	The end-of-line control key tells the device driver that you have finished entering text and want the text interpreted and passed on to the shell or application program. Normally, this control key is the <Enter> or <Return> key. Note that this key is usually defined as the new-line character. Your terminal may return the new-line character, the carriage-return character, or both.
End-of-file	UNIX treats all devices as though they were files; because your terminal is a source of virtually unlimited characters, UNIX provides a way for you to signal you are done with your login session. When the shell sees an end-of-file character, it exits; you see the login prompt again. Traditionally the end-of-file character is the <Ctrl-d> character.

The command used to both set these parameters and display them is stty. The stty command stands for *set teletype*. In the "old days," a teletype terminal was the only terminal available; a lot of UNIX terminology is left over from this era. For example, your terminal is defined as a *tty device* with a name like tty14. To display all your present settings, type **stty -a** from the command line and press <Return>. If you use this command in a UnixWare Terminal window, you see something like the following:

```
speed 9600
rows = 47; columns = 88; ypixels = 664; xpixels = 710;
intr = DEL; quit = ^¦; erase = ^h; kill = @;
eof = ^d; eol = <undef>; eol2 = <undef>; swtch = <undef>;
start = ^q; stop = ^s; susp = ^z; dsusp = ^y;
rprnt = <undef>; flush = <undef>; werase = <undef>; lnext =
<undef>;
-parenb -parodd cs8 -cstopb hupcl cread -clocal -loblk -parext
-ignbrk -brkint -ignpar -parmrk -inpck -istrip -inlcr -igncr icrnl
-iuclc
ixon -ixany -ixoff -imaxbel
isig icannon -xcase echo echoe echok -echonl -noflsh
-tostop -echoctl -echoprt -echoke -defecho -flusho -pendin -iexten
opost -olcuc onlcr -ocrnl -onocr -onlret -ofill tab3
```

Notice that on this system, the interrupt key (intr) is defined as DEL and the kill key is @. Although you can set all the settings listed here, as a matter of practicality, users usually only reset the interrupt and kill keys. For example, if you want to change the kill key from @ back to ^C (<Ctrl-c>), use the following command:

```
stty kill '^C'
```

Tip

If you want a certain setting to take effect every time you log in, place the command in your `.profile` file (located in your home directory) if you're running the Korn or Bourne shell. For the C shell, place the command in your `.login` file.

Note

If your terminal is behaving strangely, reset it to a "most reasonable" setting by giving the command **stty sane**.

Setting the Shell Environment

Part of the process of *logging in*, that is, of creating a UNIX session, is the creation of your environment. All UNIX *processes* (as running programs are called) have their own environment separate and distinct from the program itself. It could be said that a program runs from within an environment. The UNIX environment, called the *shell environment*, consists of a number of variables and their values. These variables and values allow a running program, like a shell, to determine what the environment looks like.

Environment refers to things like the name of your shell, your home directory, and what type of terminal you are using. Many of these variables are defined during the login process and either cannot or should not be changed. You can add or change as many variables as you like as long as a variable has not been marked "read only."

Variables are set in the environment in the form *VARIABLE=value*. The meaning of *VARIABLE* can be set to anything you like. However, many variables have predefined meanings to many standard UNIX programs. For example, the TERM variable is defined as being the name of your terminal type as specified in one of the standard UNIX terminal databases. Digital Equipment Corporation for years made a popular terminal named the VT-100. The characteristics of this terminal have been copied by many other manufacturers and often emulated in software for personal computers. The name of such a terminal type is vt100; it is represented in the environment as TERM=vt100.

Many other predefined variables exist in your environment. If you use the C shell, you can list these variables with the printenv command; with the Bourne or Korn shell, use the set command. Table 6.2 lists the most common environment variables and their uses. Note that some of these variables can be changed and some cannot be changed. The first column in the table shows what you type at the command line. The second column describes the variable and how it's used.

III

Controlling UNIX

Note

If you want an environment variable defined every time you log in, place the definition in your `.profile` file (located in your home directory) if you're running the Korn or Bourne shell. For the C shell, place the definition in your `.login` file.

Table 6.2: Common Environment Variables

Variable	Description
HOME=/home/*login*	Sets your home directory, the location from which you start out. Replace *login* with your login ID. For example, if your login ID is zorb, HOME is defined as /home/zorb.
LOGNAME=*login*	LOGNAME is automatically set the same as your login ID.
MAILCHECK=*seconds*	Replace *seconds* with the number of seconds representing the interval of time when the shell is to check for mail. For example, if you enter **MAILCHECK=600**, the shell checks for mail every 600 seconds.
PATH=*path*	The *path* variable represents the list of directories through which the shell looks for commands. For example, you can set the path like this: PATH=/usr:/bin:/usr/local/bin.
PS1=*prompt*	PS1 is the primary shell prompt. It defines what your prompt will look like. If you don't set it to anything specific, your prompt is the dollar sign (**$**). If you prefer, you can set it to something more creative, for example, PS1="Enter Command >" displays Enter Command > as your command-line prompt.
PWD=*directory*	PWD is automatically set for you. It defines where you are in the file system. For example, if you checked PWD (by entering **echo $PWD** at the command line) and UNIX displays /usr/bin, you are in the /usr/bin directory.
SHELL=*shell*	SHELL identifies the location of the program that serves as your shell. For example, you can set SHELL in your `.profile` or `.login` file as SHELL=/bin/ksh to make the Korn shell your login shell.
TERM=*termtype*	Sets the name of your terminal type, as specified by the terminal database. For example, you can set TERM in your `.profile` or `.login` file as TERM=vt100.

Earlier in this section, you were introduced to the TERM variable. If your terminal does not respond properly, ask your system administrator for help in defining the proper terminal. You learn how to modify variables in the environment later in this chapter.

Note

In UnixWare, TERM is automatically set correctly for your monitor and keyboard. You have to set the TERM variable only if you attach a terminal to your UnixWare system through a serial port.

Perhaps the single most important variable in your environment is the PATH variable. The PATH variable contains a colon-delimited string that points to all the directories that contain the programs you use. The order in which these directories are listed determines which directories are searched first. The list order is important on systems that support several different forms of the same command. For example, your system may contain commands from the Berkeley version of UNIX as well as those conforming to standard UNIX System V. Your system may also have locally created commands you may want to access. For example, your PATH variable may contain the following values:

```
/usr/ucb:/bin:/usr/bin:/usr/local/bin
```

This statement instructs your shell to explore the /usr/ucb directory first. The /usr/ucb directory contains, by convention, all the Berkeley versions of standard UNIX commands. If the shell finds the command in the first directory it searches, it stops searching and executes that command. The /bin and /usr/bin directories contain all the standard UNIX System V and UnixWare commands. The /usr/local/bin directory often contains the local commands added by the system administrator (or the system owner in UnixWare).

If you intend to create your own commands, you can modify the PATH variable to include directories that contain your own commands. How you do this depends on which shell you use. For example, if you use the Bourne or Korn shell, you can add a directory to your PATH variable by giving the following command:

```
PATH=$PATH:newpath
```

When you place a $ in front of the name of a variable, its current value is substituted. In this command, the $PATH variable represents whatever the current path is; the colon and the newpath parameters add to the current path.

Several other ways of manipulating variables in your environment are described in the next section. For now, it is sufficient to say that the shell environment contains variables and functions and that these objects can be manipulated by both shells and application programs. Application programs can access and modify the environment, but they generally manipulate variables within the program. Shells, on the other hand, can only manipulate variables in the environment.

III

Controlling UNIX

Understanding the UNIX Process

A running program in UNIX is called a *process*. Because UNIX is a multi-tasking system, many processes can run at the same time. To distinguish between processes, UNIX assigns each new process a unique ID called a *process ID*. The process ID is simply a number that uniquely identifies each running process.

When UNIX is instructed to run a program (that is, to create a process), it does so by making an exact copy of the program making the request. In the simplest case, you request that a program be run by instructing your shell; the shell makes a fork request to the UNIX kernel.

Fork and *exec*

A *fork* is the process of cloning an existing process. UNIX creates all new processes through the mechanism of forking. When a process is forked, an almost exact duplicate of an existing process (including its environment and any open files) is created; what keeps the duplicate from being exactly the same as its parent application is a flag that tells the forked process which is the parent and which is the child. Because all processes are created in this fashion, all processes have a parent process and a parent-process ID. Every process running on a UNIX system can trace its lineage back to init, the mother of all processes. init itself, process ID 1, is the only process run directly by the UNIX kernel that you as a user have any contact with. Every process you create during a session has your login shell as an ancestor, and your login shell has init as its parent.

After a process has successfully forked, the child process calls the exec routine to transform itself into the process you requested. The only thing that changes after an exec function is the identity of the running process; the environment of the new process is an exact copy of the environment of its parent. This process is shown in figure 6.4.

Fig. 6.4
Forking, or cloning, an existing process.

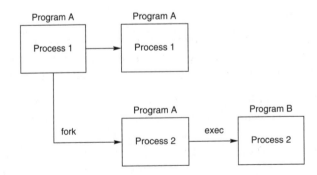

Standard Input and Output

Every new process is created with three open "files." Because UNIX treats files and devices exactly the same, an open "file" can be either a real file on a disk or a device such as your terminal. The three open files are defined as standard input, standard output, and standard error output. All UNIX commands, as well as application programs, accept input from the standard input and place any output on the standard output. Any diagnostic messages are automatically placed on the standard error output (see fig. 6.5).

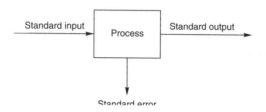

Fig. 6.5
How a process accepts input and places output.

When you first log in, the standard input, output, and error files are attached to your terminal; any programs you run (processes you create) inherit your terminal as the three open files.

Understanding UNIX Command Parsing

Parsing is the act of splitting the command line, or what you type, into its component parts for processing. In UNIX, parsing constitutes a lot more than simply splitting the command line. The command string is first split into its component parts, the filenames expanded if you used any wild cards, shell variables expanded, I/O redirection set up, and any command groupings or subshells set up and command substitution performed. Only then can the command line as you typed it be executed. If these terms are new to you, you'll find explanations of them, in the order they are performed, later in this chapter. You must first start, however, with the basic command syntax.

▶ See Chapter 10, "Understanding UNIX Shells," for more information about I/O redirection.

Commands, Flags, and Parameters

To execute a UNIX command, you merely type the name of the file. The command to list files is `ls`; you can find a file by that name in the `/bin` directory. If `/bin` is listed in your PATH variable (and it should be), your shell will find it and execute it. Some UNIX commands are not independent files. These commands are built into the shells themselves. For example, the `cd` (change directory) command is built into most shells and is executed directly by the shell without looking up a file. Read the documentation for the shell

III

Controlling UNIX

you are using to determine what commands are executed internally or exter-
nally. Some shells have a command file that contains commands executed
directly by the shell.

Flags

If a command is to execute properly, you must present it to your shell in the
proper fashion. The command name itself must be the first item on the line;
it is followed by any flags and parameters. *Flags* (sometimes called *options*) are
single letters preceded by a dash (-) that modify the behavior of a command.
For example, the list command, ls, simply lists the names of the files in the
current directory in alphabetical order. By adding various flags, you can list
the contents of a directory in many different ways. You can list files and all
their attributes with the "long" flag, -l. This command takes the following
form:

    ls -l

The -l is the flag. When you want to use more than one flag, simply string
the flags together as in ls -lF (the -F flag shows an asterisk, *, if the file is
executable, an @ sign if the file is a symbolic line, and a slash, /, if the file is a
subdirectory). The manual page for every command usually lists all the modifying flags and their meanings before describing any parameters. Flags can
also be listed separately; the shell parses them before passing them on to the
program. For example, you can write the ls -lF command as ls -l -f.

One type of flag signals that the next parameter has some special meaning.
For example, the -t flag in the sort command is used to indicate that
the next character is a field separator. If you want to sort the /etc/passwd
file, whose fields are separated by colons (:), you can give the following
command:

    sort -t: /etc/passwd

In the case of the sort command, the -t flag is needed only if the file uses a
field separator other than the default. The default field separator is defined in
the IFS (Inter Field Separator) environment variable. The shell uses the IFS
variable to parse the command line so that the shell knows to use the standard field separator unless the -t flag indicates otherwise.

Parameters

Flags must be presented to the command before any other parameters.
Parameters are strings separated by any of the characters defined in the IFS
environment variable. The default string in IFS is a space, a tab, and a
newline character. You can place any number of field-separator characters
between parameters; when the shell parses the command line, it reduces

these characters to one character before proceeding. For example, if a command is followed by three spaces and a tab character and then the first parameter, the shell automatically reduces the three spaces and a tab to one tab character:

```
command<sp><sp><sp><Tab>parameter
```

becomes

```
command<Tab>parameter
```

Parameters are usually either filenames or a string that instructs the command to perform some function. If a parameter contains an embedded space, the string must be placed in quotation marks to prevent the shell from expanding it. The following command line contains two parameters; the shell will attempt to find the word *New* in a file named York:

```
grep New York
```

If the intent is to find the string *New York* in the standard input, the command must be written as follows:

```
grep "New York"
```

In this case, the string *New York* is passed to the grep command as one parameter.

Filename Generation

Most modern operating systems (including all versions of UNIX and DOS) support the use of wild cards for file and string searches.

The * Wild Card

The asterisk (*) is the most universal wild card used. It simply means *any and all characters*. For example, the string a* means all files beginning with *a*. You can use as many asterisks in a single expression as you need to define a set of files. For example, the expression *xx*.gif defines any filename with the extension gif that has xx anywhere in the rest of the name. Matches include the filenames abxx.gif, xxyyzz.gif, and the simple name xx.gif.

The ? Wild Card

The question mark (?) represents a single occurrence of any character. Thus the string ??? represents all files consisting of just three letters. You can generate a list of files with three-letter extensions with the string *.???. For example, if you are searching a directory containing graphic images as well as other data, the following command lists all files with extensions like tif, jpg, and gif as well as any other files with three-letter extensions:

```
ls *.???
```

The [ ] Expression

Sometimes you must be more selective than either of the more general-purpose wild cards allow. Suppose that you want to select the files job1, job2, and job3 but not jobx. You cannot select the right files with the ? wild card because it represents one occurrence of any character. You can, however use job[123] as the file descriptor. Like the question mark, items inside square brackets ([]) represent exactly one character. You can describe a discrete series of permissible values such as [123] which permits only the characters 1, 2, or 3; you can also describe a range of characters such as [A-Z] which represent any character between uppercase A and uppercase Z, inclusive.

> **Note**
>
> When expressing ranges, remember that what is included in the range depends on the character set used. Most UNIX systems use the ASCII character set but some systems use the IBM EBCDIC character set. The range you specify is between the characters specified by the character set's sort sequence.

You can also specify a set of ranges. For example, if you want to specify only alphabetic characters, you can use [A-Z,a-z]. In the ASCII character set, there are special characters between ASCII *Z* and ASCII *a*; if you specified [A-z], you include those special characters in your request.

> **Note**
>
> If you place a filename wild card or expression inside quotation marks, filename expansion is suppressed during command-line parsing. For example, if you type ls *, you get all files in the current directory. On the other hand, if you type ls "*", you probably get the error message file not found because you are instructing ls to search for a file named *.

Shell Variable Substitution

You learned about shell variable expansion in the first part of this chapter when you set your PATH variable to PATH=$PATH:*newpath*. The shell replaced $PATH with the current values of the PATH variable. Shells are really interpreted languages almost like BASIC; the shell variable is the primary object manipulated. Because shell variables are frequently manipulated, each shell provides methods of testing and defining the shell variables.

Shell variables are stored as strings. When two variables are placed together, their respective strings are *concatenated*. For example, if you have two variables, X=hello and Y=world, the expression XY results in the string `helloworld`. If you gave the following command, the shell would parse the two parameters and the values of X and Y (the two strings `hello` and `world`) would be substituted before being passed to the `echo` command:

```
echo $X $Y
```

The `echo` command would then print out `hello world`. Note that if you place a dozen <Tab> characters between $X and $Y, the output results are still the same.

If the substitution could be ambiguous, the shell picks the most obvious substitution—often with unpredictable results. For example, if you type **echo $XY** the shell substitutes `helloY`. If you also had a variable XY, its value would be substituted instead. To get around these ambiguities, the shell has a simple mechanism to allow you to define exactly what you mean. If you type **${X}Y** the shell substitutes the value of X before appending the character *Y* to the string.

The Bourne and Korn shells have a rich collection of shell-variable expansion techniques that perform various tests on the variable before making the substitution. See the manual pages for `sh` and `ksh` for more details.

Command Substitution

After the shell performs its substitution of variables, it scans the line once more for commands to be run before the command line is finally ready. *Command substitution* means that UNIX substitutes the results of a command for a positional parameter. This is specified in the following way:

```
command-1 parameter 'command-2'
```

Be careful in the use of quotation marks (") and apostrophes ('). Table 6.3 lists which marks perform what results.

▶ For more details on shell programming, refer to Chapter 10, "Understanding UNIX Shells."

III

Controlling UNIX

Table 6.3: Quotation Marks and Apostrophes	
Symbol	**Meaning**
"	The double quotation marks disable filename generation and suppress parameter expansion. However, shell-variable and command substitution still take place.
'	The apostrophe disables all parsing; whatever is enclosed within the apostrophes is passed on as a single parameter.
`	The accent grave, or back quote, implies command substitution. Whatever is enclosed within accent graves is executed as though the command was performed on a line by itself. Any output placed on the standard output replaces the command. The command line is then parsed again for parameters.

Consider the following command line:

```
echo "Today\'s date and time are `date`"
```

It produces this output:

```
Today's date and time are Sun May 09 14:35:09 EST 1994
```

To make the `echo` command behave properly, the `'`s (in *Today's*) in the preceding command was preceded by a backslash (\), also called the *escape character*. Virtually every non-alphanumeric character on your keyboard has some special meaning to the shell. To use any of the special characters in a string and to prevent the shell from interpreting the character, you must "escape" the character, that is, you must precede it with the escape character \. If you want to pass the backslash character itself, for example, type \\. To pass a dollar sign to a command, type \$, and so on.

> **Note**
>
> In a UnixWare Terminal window, the escape character is not necessary in front of the apostrophe. If you enter **echo "Today's"** in UnixWare, you get what you expect: Today's.

Command Groups, Subshells, and Other Commands

You terminate a simple command with a carriage return. If you want to place more than one command on the command line before pressing <Return>, you can delimit individual commands with a semicolon (;). When the shell parses the command line, it treats the semicolon as it would an end-of-line character. If you type the following string, the shell executes each command sequentially as though you had typed each on a line by itself:

```
command-1;command-2;command-3
```

For example, in a UnixWare Terminal window, you can enter **clear;ls** to clear your screen *and* display a directory listing.

Command Groups

If you want to redirect input or output to all the commands as a group, you can do so by making the command line a command group. A *command group* is defined as any number of commands enclosed in curly braces ({ }). For example, the following command string directs the output of both commands to the file `output-file`:

```
{ command-1;command-2 } > output-file
```

Any form of redirection can also be used. The output of a command group can be placed on a pipe as in the following example:

```
{ command-1; command-2 } ¦ command-3
```

In this case, the output of *command-1* is fed into the pipe; then the output of *command-2* is fed into the same pipe; *command-3* sees just one stream of data.

> **Note**
>
> Commands run in a command group run in the current shell. That means that they may modify the environment or change directories.

Subshells

When you run a series of commands as a command group, those commands run in the current shell. If one of the commands modifies the environment or changes the directory, the changes are in effect when the command group finishes running. To avoid this problem, run a command group in a subshell. A *subshell* is a clone of the present shell; because child processes cannot modify the environment of their parent process, all commands run in a subshell have no effect on the environment when the command group finishes. To run a command group in a subshell, replace the curly braces {} with parentheses (). The command-group example used in the preceding section would become the following:

```
( command-1; command-2 ) ¦ command-3
```

Only *command-3* runs in the current shell but the output of the subshell is piped into the standard input of *command-3*.

Background Processing

Because UNIX is a multitasking operating system, there are several ways of running commands in the background. The simplest form of background processing allows you to run a command concurrently with a command in the foreground. Other methods place commands deeper and deeper in the background.

The & Operator

Normally when you run a command, the shell suspends operation until the command is complete. If you append the & sign to the end of a command string, the command string runs concurrently with the shell. By placing the ampersand after a command string, the shell resumes operation as soon as the background command is launched. Unless you use I/O redirection with the background command, both the background command and the present

III

Controlling UNIX

shell expect input from, and produce output to, your terminal. Unless your background command takes care of I/O itself, the proper syntax for background processing is as follows:

```
command-string < input-file > output-file &
```

Because the background process is a child of your shell, it is automatically killed when you log out. All child processes are killed when their parent dies.

The *nohup* Command

To place a command deeper in the background than the & operator allows, use the nohup command (which stands for *no hang up*). The nohup command takes as its arguments a command string. However, the nohup command must be used in conjunction with the & operator if you want the command to be actually placed in the background. If a command is run with nohup in the foreground, the command is immune to being killed when you disconnect your terminal or hang up a modem (its original purpose).

The syntax for the nohup command is as follows:

```
nohup command-string < input-file > output-file &
```

The *batch* and *at* Commands and the *cron* Daemon

If you run a command with the nohup command, the command executes immediately. If you want to run the command at a later time or on a "time available" basis, you must invoke the services of the cron daemon.

The cron daemon is a command run in the background by UNIX—or, more specifically, by init, the master program. The function of cron is to provide scheduling services. You can ask cron to run a program at a specific time, periodically, at a particular time every day, or whenever the load on cron permits. The use of the at and batch commands and the cron daemon must be explicitly permitted or denied by the system administrator; if they don't work, ask your system administrator for help.

To schedule tasks with UnixWare, you use the Task Scheduler, shown in figure 6.6. With the Task Scheduler, you can schedule any task to run on specific days, at specific times, or to repeat constantly over an interval of time.

The *at* Command

The at command expects a time or date as a parameter and takes any number of command strings from its standard input. When the at command detects an end-of-file marker, it creates a Bourne shell script for execution at the time you specified. The at command is flexible about the types of dates and times it accepts. For example, if you enter the command **at now + 1 day**, the next commands, taken from the standard input, are executed tomorrow at this time. One way to use the at command is from within a shell script.

Fig. 6.6
The UnixWare
Task Scheduler
window.

A *shell script* is nothing more than a file containing all the commands necessary to perform a series of commands. The name of the file then becomes your own addition to the UNIX command language. See Chapter 10, "Understanding UNIX Shells," for more information. One way of using the at command is as follows:

```
at now + 1 day <<XX
command-1
command-2
XX
```

When placed in a shell script, these lines let you conveniently run one or more commands the next day. To run different commands, simply change the lines between the first and last line. You can run any number of commands from this script.

The *batch* Command

The batch command is the logical equivalent of at now. If you attempt to use the at now command, you see an error message that says something like now has passed. The batch command works exactly as at now would work if it were logically possible, with one minor exception: the cron daemon maintains a separate queue for commands generated by at, batch, and cron. This means that the system administrator has control over how many commands can run at any one time using the services of the cron daemon.

The *crontab* Command

One of the best uses of the cron daemon is in automating the maintenance of a system. With cron, the system administrator can set up automatic backups of your system every night at 4 AM, Monday through Saturday. You install, delete, and list commands you want run in this fashion with the crontab command.

III

Controlling UNIX

> **Note**
>
> UnixWare's Backup window lets you schedule backups by automatically running the Task Scheduler. Backups can be scheduled to run for any cycle, such as every day, every week, and so on.

To run commands periodically, you must create a file in the `crontab` format. The `crontab` file consists of six fields separated by spaces or tabs. The first five fields are integers specifying minutes (0 through 59), hour (0 through 23), day of the month (1 through 31), month of the year (1 through 12), and day of the week (0 through 6, with 0 referring to Sunday). The sixth field is a command string. Each numeric field can contain an inclusive range of numbers such as `1-5` to indicate Monday through Friday, or discrete sets of numbers such as `0,20,40` to indicate that an instruction should be run every 20 minutes. A field can also contain an asterisk to indicate all legal values. The following example runs the `calendar` command every 20 minutes starting at midnight Monday and ending at 11:40 PM Friday.

```
0,20,40 * * * 1-5 calendar -
```

> **Note**
>
> The hyphen at the end of this command makes the calendar do its work for *all* users on a system. Although you can invoke the calendar without the hyphen, it's recommended that you use it.

If you name this file `cronfile`, you can install it in the `cron` system by issuing the command **crontab cronfile**.

The `cron` daemon has a time granularity of one minute; the system administrator may place limits on the number of commands allowed to be run at any one time. Just because you ask `cron` to run an `at`, `batch`, or `crontab` file does not mean that it will run at precisely the time you have indicated.

Understanding Command Feedback

UNIX provides instant feedback for commands that abort for one reason or another. In most cases, errors are limited to misspellings of the command name or badly formed filenames. If you attempt to run a nonexistent command, UNIX replies with this message:

```
command: command not found
```

If you try to use a nonexistent filename, UNIX responds with this message:

```
command: file: No such file or directory
```

If the error is caused by something other than a command-line error, the command itself usually reports what happened—although not always in an easily decipherable form.

If you attempt to run a command with nohup and you have not redirected the standard error, UNIX automatically places any error messages in a file named nohup.out in the directory from which the command was run.

Because commands run by cron have less urgency, any errors—indeed, any output placed on the standard output and not redirected—is sent to you through electronic mail.

Summary

The shell is the primary interface between you and the UNIX operating system. Although a shell can be almost any executable program, several standard shells are either supplied with UNIX or are freely available in both source code (written in C) or already compiled for your machine. All UNIX shells can be viewed as highly sophisticated, special-purpose programming languages containing all the usual constructs found in a programming language. The special purpose of UNIX shell languages is to tie together the many small commands and utilities found in the UNIX environment. By making use of I/O redirection and background processing, the shell languages allow you to write complex programs with a minimum of effort.

III

Controlling UNIX

Chapter 7

Understanding UNIX File and Directory Systems

The words *UNIX file system* have two different and often conflicting meanings: the file system of disks and mechanisms by which the disks are strung together, and the logical file system the user sees and manipulates. This chapter is about the logical UNIX file system you see and manipulate.

Every physical and logical entity in UNIX is represented as a file in the UNIX file system. The physical entities include disks, printers, and terminals; logical entities include directories and, of course, ordinary files—the kind that store documents and programs.

This chapter covers the following topics:

- UNIX filenames
- Types of UNIX files
- File permissions
- UNIX directory structure

Understanding Filenames

Note

The commands demonstrated in this chapter are entered at the command line. To get to a command line in UnixWare, open a Terminal window by clicking on the Terminal icon, located in the Accessories folder.

In UNIX, you must distinguish between a filename and a path name. A *filename* consists of a simple series of contiguous letters, numbers, and certain punctuation marks. Filenames cannot contain spaces or any character that represents a field separator. For example, the filename johns.letter is valid; johns letter is not.

III

Controlling UNIX

A filename cannot contain any characters that have special meaning to the shell. These special characters are listed here:

```
! @ # $ % ^ & * ( ) [ ] { } ' " \ / | ; < > `
```

Actually, you *can* use any of these characters but you would have a hard time accessing the files they represent. It should also be obvious that you shouldn't use backspace characters in a filename—although you could if you tried very hard.

Most early versions of UNIX limited filenames to 14 characters. UNIX System V Release 4 and UnixWare allow an almost unlimited number of characters in a filename but only the first 14 are significant; the Berkeley version of UNIX allows 64 characters in a filename. Because one of the goals of UNIX is portability, in the interests of writing portable programs and shell scripts, you should limit yourself to 14-character filenames.

Although a filename is only 14 characters (in most cases), a *path name* can be any number of characters. In UNIX, files don't exist in a vacuum: they exist in a directory. The highest directory is called the *root directory* in UNIX and is symbolized by the slash character (/). If a file named fred exists in the root directory, its absolute path name is /fred. Users are assigned a "home" directory by the system administrator when their accounts are set up. If a user named Fred is assigned a directory named /home/fred, all files Fred creates are attached to the directory /home/fred. An absolute path name for one of Fred's files might be /home/fred/freds.file.

There is another kind of path name: a relative path name. A *relative path name* unambiguously points to a file relative to the current directory. If Fred is in his home directory, the filename freds.file is also a relative path name, relative to his current directory. To find out which directory is your current directory, use the command pwd (which stands for *print working directory*).

You can define a file anywhere in the UNIX file system with relative path names by using the two pseudonyms found in all directories. The single dot (.) refers to the current directory; the double dot (..) refers to the parent directory.

If Fred is in /home/fred, he can point to /fred by using ../../fred. The first double dot points to /home (the parent directory of /home/fred); the second double dot points to the parent directory of /home—namely, the root. The pseudonym for the current directory, the single dot, comes in handy if you want to move files. If Fred wants to move `/fred` to his current directory, he can do so with absolute path names by using this command:

```
mv /fred fred
```

Alternatively, Fred can use the pseudonym for the current directory by using this command:

```
mv /fred .
```

All UNIX commands operate on path names. In most cases, the path name you use is the name of a file in the current directory. The default path name points to your current directory. If Fred is in his home directory, `/home/fred`, all three of the following are equivalent:

```
command freds.letter
command /home/fred/freds.letter
command ./freds.letter
```

> **Note**
>
> Although there is a difference between filenames and path names, directories are files too. When naming directories, remember that they have the same name limitations as ordinary files.

Looking at Types of Files

There are just four basic types of files: ordinary files, directories, links, and special files. There are several kinds of ordinary files, links, and special files and a large number of standard directories. Each is described in the following sections.

Ordinary Files

Ordinary files are what you spend most of your time manipulating. Ordinary files can contain text, C language source code, shell scripts (programs interpreted by one of the UNIX shells), binary executable programs, and data of various types. As far as UNIX is concerned, a file is a file. The only difference that UNIX knows about are files marked as executable. *Executable files* can be executed directly, provided, of course, that the file contains something to execute and that it is in your search path.

Executable files are *binary files*, that is, files that execute machine code and shell scripts. The UNIX `file` command looks at the data in a file and makes a

reasonable guess as to what's inside. If you type **file *** , you might see
something like this:

```
cdfront:     C program text
reid1:       ascii text
rlong.a:     data
screen:      commands text
srg:         ELF 32-bit LSB executable 80386 Version 1
vuimg.exe:   DOS executable (EXE)
```

All the files named in the first column are ordinary files that contain different
kinds of data. All the files are located within a directory.

Directory Files

Directories are files that contain the names of files and subdirectories as well
as pointers to those files and subdirectories. Directory files are the only place
that UNIX stores names of files. When you list the contents of a directory
with the ls command, all you are doing is listing the contents of the directory file. You never touch the files themselves.

When you rename a file with the mv command and that file is in the current
directory, all you are doing is changing the entry in the directory file. If you
move a file from one directory to another, all you are doing is moving the
description of the file from one directory file to another, provided, of course,
that the new directory is on the same physical disk or partition. The sidebar
on the next page explains this.

Links

Ordinary *links* aren't really files at all. They are simply directory entries that
point to the same i-node. The i-node table keeps track of how many links to
a file there are; only when the last directory reference is deleted is the i-node
finally released back to the free pool. Obviously, ordinary links cannot cross
device boundaries because all the directory references point to the same
i-node.

UNIX System V Release 4, UnixWare, and the Berkeley versions of UNIX
have another kind of link called a *symbolic link*. For such a link, the directory
entry contains the i-node of a file that is itself a reference to another file
somewhere else in the logical UNIX file system. A symbolic link can point
to another file or directory on the same disk, another disk, or to a file or
directory on another computer. One major difference between an ordinary
link and a symbolic link is this: With ordinary links, every link has equal
standing (that is, the system treats every link as though it were the original
file) and the actual data is not deleted until the last link to that file is deleted.

With symbolic links, when the original file is deleted, all symbolic links to that file are also deleted. Symbolically linked files do not have the same standing as the original.

Other than these subtle differences between links and files, links are treated and accessed exactly as though you were accessing the file directly.

Directories and Physical Disks

Every file in a UNIX system is assigned a unique number called an *i-node*. The i-node is stored in a table called the *i-node table*, which is allocated when the disk is formatted. Every physical disk or partition has its own i-node table. An i-node contains all the information about a file, including the address of the data on the disk and the file type. File types include such things as ordinary files, directories, and special files such as the device drivers for other disks.

The UNIX file system assigns i-node number 1 to the root directory. This gives UNIX the address on disk of the root-directory file. The root-directory file contains a list of file and directory names and their respective i-node numbers. UNIX can find any file in the system by looking up a chain of directories, beginning with the root directory. The contents of the root-directory file might looks like this:

```
1       .
1       ..
45      etc
230     dev
420     home
123     .profile
```

Notice that the files . (dot) and .. (double dot) are represented in the directory. Because this is the root directory, . and its parent directory .. are identical. The contents of the /home directory file look different:

```
420     .
1       ..
643     fred
```

Notice that the i-node of the current directory, ., matches the i-node for /home found in the root-directory file and that the i-node for the parent directory, .., is the same as that of the root directory.

UNIX navigates its file system by chaining up and down the directory file system. If you want to move a file to a directory on another physical disk, UNIX detects this by reading the i-node table. In such a case, the file is physically moved to the new disk and assigned a new i-node on that disk before being deleted from its original location.

As with the mv command, when you delete a file with the rm command, you never touch the file itself. Instead, UNIX marks that i-node as free and returns it to the pool of available i-nodes. The file's entry in the directory is erased.

III

Controlling UNIX

Special Files

Every physical device associated with a UNIX system, including disks, terminals, and printers, is represented in the file system. Most, if not all, devices are located in the /dev directory. For example, if you are working on the system console, your associated device is named /dev/console. If you are working on a standard terminal, your device name may be /dev/tty01. Terminals, or serial lines, are called *tty devices* (which stands for *teletype*, the original UNIX terminal). To determine what the name of your tty device is, type the command **tty**. The system responds with the name of the device you are connected to.

Printers and terminals are called *character-special devices*. They can accept and produce a stream of characters. Disks, on the other hand, store data in blocks addressed by cylinder and sector. You can't access just one character on a disk; you must read and write entire blocks. The same is usually true of magnetic tapes. This kind of device is called a *block-special device*. To make life even more complex, disks and other block-special devices must be able to act like character-oriented devices, and so every block device has a matching character device. UNIX makes the translation by reading data being sent to a character device and translating it for the block device. This happens without you doing anything.

There is at least one other type of special device you may run into: a FIFO (first-in-first-out buffer), also known as a *named pipe*. FIFOs look like ordinary files; if you write to them, they grow. But if you read a FIFO, it shrinks in size. FIFOs are used mainly in system processes to allow many programs to send information to a single controlling process. For example, when you print a file with the lp command, the lp command sets up the printing process and signals the lpsched daemon by sending a message to a FIFO.

You will find one device-special file very useful: the *bit bucket*, /dev/null. Anything you send to /dev/null is ignored—useful when you don't want to see the output of a command. For example, if you don't want to see any diagnostic reports printed on the standard error device, you can pour them into the bit bucket with the following command:

```
command-2> /dev/null
```

File Permissions

File permissions mean more in UNIX than just what permissions you have on a file or directory. Although permissions determine who can read, write, or execute a file, they also determine the file type and how the file is executed.

You can display the permission on a file with the long form of the list command, `ls -l`. The `-l` flag tells the `ls` command to use the long listing. If you type **`ls -l`**, you might see a directory listing that looks like this:

```
drwx------  2 sglines   doc      512 Jan  1 13:44 Mail
drwx------  5 sglines   doc     1024 Jan 17 08:22 News
-rw-------  1 sglines   doc     1268 Dec  7 15:01 biblio
drwx------  2 sglines   doc      512 Dec 15 21:28 bin
-rw-------  1 sglines   doc    44787 Oct 20 06:59 books
-rw-------  1 sglines   doc    23801 Dec 14 22:50 bots.msg
-rw-r-----  1 sglines   doc   105990 Dec 27 21:24 duckie.gif
```

> **Note**
>
> To see file permissions with UnixWare's Graphical User Interface (GUI), open the
> *folder* (UnixWare's name for *directory*) containing the file and click on the file's icon.
> Then click on the File button to display the File menu. Click on Properties to open the
> Desktop: File Properties window, shown in figure 7.1. This window shows the same
> information as the `ls -l` command, but in easy-to-read, labeled sections.

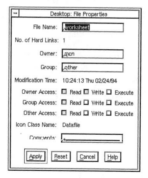

Fig. 7.1
Viewing permissions with the UnixWare Desktop: File Properties window.

This listing shows virtually everything that can be known about a file from the directory entry and the i-node of the file. The first column shows the file permissions, the second column shows the number of links to a file (or extra blocks in a directory), the third column shows who owns the file. (In UNIX, ownership has three possibilities: the owner, the owner's group, and everyone else. Ownership is detailed later in this section.) The fourth column shows the group to which the file belongs. The fifth column shows the number of bytes in the file, the sixth column shows the date and time of creation, and the seventh column shows the name of the file itself.

The permission field (the first column) is broken into four subfields:

```
- rwx rwx rwx
```

III

Controlling UNIX

The first subfield defines the file type. A normal file has a dash (-) as a place holder; directories are marked with a d. Table 7.1 shows the permissible values for the file-type subfield.

Table 7.1: Valid Entries for the File-Type Subfield

Character	Meaning
-	Ordinary file
b	Block-special file
c	Character-special file
d	Directory
l	Symbolic link

The next three subfields show the read, write, and execute permissions of the file. For example, an rwx in the first of these subfields means that the file has read, write, and execute permission for the *owner*. The next subfield shows the same information for the *group ownership* of the file; the third subfield shows the permissions allowed for *everyone else*.

These permission fields can show more information; in fact, there are several attributes packed into these three fields. Unfortunately, what these attributes mean is determined by the version of UNIX you use and whether or not the file is executable.

If the file is not executable and you use UNIX System V Release 4 or UnixWare, you can specify that the system use *mandatory file locking* (where the file is automatically set to read-only when it is opened). If the file is executable, you can also specify that the file set the user or group ID on execution.

Note

Normally, a running program is owned by whoever ran it. If the user-ID bit is on, the running program is owned by the owner of the file. This means that the running program has all the permissions of the owner of the file. If you are an ordinary user and the running program is owned by the root user, that running program has automatic permission to read and write any file in the system regardless of your permissions. The same is true of the set-group-ID bit.

The *sticky bit* can also be set in these subfields. The sticky bit tells the system to save a copy of a running program in memory after the program completes. If the program is used often, the sticky bit can save the system a little time because the program does not have to be reloaded into memory from disk each time someone runs it.

You can change permissions on any file you have write permission for by using the chmod command. This command has two different syntaxes: absolute and relative. With *absolute permissions*, you define exactly what the permissions on a file will be in octal, or base 8. The permissions you want are added together to arrive at a number that defines the permissions. Table 7.2 lists the valid octal permissions.

Table 7.2: Absolute Octal Permissions Used with the *chmod* Command

Octal Value	Permissions Granted
0001	Execute permission for the owner
0002	Write permission for the owner
0004	Read permission for the owner
0010	Execute permission for the group
0020	Write permission for the group
0040	Read permission for the group
0100	Execute permission for all others
0200	Write permission for all others
0400	Read permission for all others
1000	Sticky bit on
2000	Group-ID bit on if the file is executable; otherwise mandatory file locking is on
4000	User-ID bit on if the file is executable

III

Controlling UNIX

To give a file read and write permissions for everyone, you must add the required permissions together, as in the following example:

0002	Write permission for the owner
0004	Read permission for the owner
0020	Write permission for the group
0040	Read permission for the group
0200	Write permission for all others
0400	Read permission for all others
0666	Read and write permission for everyone

To give a file these permissions, use the following command:

```
chmod 666 file
```

Relative permissions use a slightly different format. With relative permissions, you must state the following:

1. Who you are giving permissions to

2. What operation you intend (add, subtract, or set permissions)

3. What the permissions are

For example, if you give the command **chmod a=rwx file**, you give read, write, and execute permission to all users. The commands are summarized in table 7.3.

Table 7.3: Relative Permissions Used with the *chmod* Command

Value	Description
Who	
a	All users (the user, his or her group, and all others)
g	Owner's group
o	All others
u	Just the user

Value	Description
Operator	
+	Adds the mode
-	Removes the mode
=	Sets the mode absolutely
Permission	
x	Sets execute
r	Sets read
w	Sets write
s	Sets set-user-ID bit
t	Sets the sticky bit
l	Sets mandatory locking

If a file has been marked as having the set-user-ID bit on, the permissions displayed by the ls -l command look like this:

```
-rws------  1 sglines     3136 Jan 17 15:42 x
```

If the set-group-ID bit is added, the permissions look like this:

```
-rws--S---  1 sglines     3136 Jan 17 15:42 x
```

If you then turn on the sticky bit for the file, the permissions look like this:

```
-rws--S--rws--S--T  1 sglines     3136 Jan 17 15:42 x
```

Note

Mandatory file locking is available only on some versions of UNIX, such as UNIX System V Release 4 and UnixWare.

Looking at UNIX Standard Directories

You are already familiar with the concept of directories. When you log in, the system places you in your home directory. The PATH environment variable is

III

Controlling UNIX

set to point to other directories that contain executable programs. These other directories are part of the standard UNIX directory structure.

Unfortunately, what constitutes the standard directories depends on which version of UNIX you use. There is the "classic set of directories" and what can be called the "emerging standard set of directories." Both are described in the following sections.

Classic UNIX Directories

Before UNIX System V Release 4 (for example, UNIX System V Release 3.2 and earlier), most versions of UNIX settled on a regular system of organizing the UNIX directories that looked like this:

```
/
      /etc
      /lib
      /tmp
      /bin
      /usr
            /spool
            /bin
            /include
            /tmp
            /adm
            /lib
```

The /etc directory contains most of the system-specific data required to *boot*, or bring the system to life. The /etc directory contains such files as passwd and inittab, necessary for the proper operation of the system.

The /lib directory contains a library of functions needed by the C compiler. Even if you don't have a C compiler on your system, this directory is important because it contains all the shared libraries that application programs may call. A *shared library* is loaded into memory only when the command calling it is run. This arrangement keeps executable programs small. Otherwise, every running program would contain duplicate code and would require a lot more disk space to store and a lot more memory to run.

The /tmp directory is used for temporary storage. Programs that use /tmp generally clean up after themselves and delete any temporary files. If you use /tmp, be sure to delete any files before logging out. Because the system automatically deletes the contents of this directory periodically, do not keep anything you might need later in this directory.

The /bin directory keeps as a minimum all the executable programs needed to boot the system. It is usually home for the most commonly used UNIX commands. Note, however, that an executable program does not have to be a binary as the name *bin* implies. Several smaller programs in /bin are, in fact, shell scripts.

The /usr directory contains everything else. Your PATH variable contains the string /bin:/usr/bin because the /usr/bin directory contains all the UNIX commands that aren't in the /bin directory. This arrangement has an historical precedence. In the early days of UNIX, hard disks weren't very big. UNIX needs at least the /etc/tmp/ and /bin directories to bootstrap itself. Because the disks of the early UNIX era could hold only those three directories, everything else was on a disk that could be mounted after UNIX was up and running. When UNIX was still a relatively small operating system, placing additional subdirectories in the /usr directory was not much of a burden. It allowed a moderately sized UNIX system to exist with just two disks: a root disk and a /usr disk.

The /usr/adm directory contains all the accounting and diagnostic information needed by the system administrator. If both system accounting and diagnostic programs have been turned off, this directory is effectively empty. As an ordinary user, you should not have access to /usr/adm.

The /include directory contains all the source code used by #include statements in C programs. You will have at least read permission for this directory because it contains all the code fragments and structures that define your system. You should not modify any of the files in this directory because they were crafted (carefully, you can assume) by your system vendor.

The /spool directory contains all the transient data used by the lp print system, the cron daemon, and the UUCP communications system. Files "spooled" to the printer are kept in the /spool directory until they are printed. Any programs waiting to be run by cron, including all the crontab files and pending at and batch jobs, are also stored here.

The /usr/lib directory contains everything else that is part of the standard UNIX system. In general, the /usr/lib directory represents the organized chaos hidden beneath the relatively well-disciplined UNIX system. This directory contains programs called by other programs found in /bin and /usr/bin as well as configuration files for terminals and printers, the mail system, cron, and the UUCP communications system.

The /usr directory contains all the subdirectories assigned to users. The general convention is this: If your login ID is mary, your home directory is /usr/mary. This arrangement made a lot of sense when disks were small and expensive but with the advent of very large disks at (relatively) inexpensive prices, there are better ways of organizing UNIX, as evidenced by the new directory structure discussed in the next section.

III

Controlling UNIX

UNIX System V Release 4 and UnixWare Directories

One of the problems with the classical structure of UNIX is that backing up your data files is difficult with a fragmented /usr directory. There are three different levels of backup generally required in a system: the basic system itself, any changes to the tables that define the basic system for a specific site, and, of course, user data.

The basic system can be backed up only once; changes to the controlling tables must be backed up only when there are changes. User data changes all the time and should be backed up frequently. UNIX System V Release 4 attempts to resolve backup problems through a radically new directory system, shown here:

```
/
      /etc
      /sbin
      /bin
      /spool
      /tmp
      /var
      /lib
      /home
      /usr
```

The /bin, /etc, /tmp, and /spool directories have the same function as they do in the classic structure. User directories are moved out of /usr and placed in /home so that you can back up just the /home directory to save all user data. System definition tables are moved into the /var directory so that whenever the operation of the system changes, you can back up only that directory.

What is new is that all system programs are moved into the /sbin directory. All the standard UNIX programs are in /usr/bin, which is linked to /bin. For compatibility, all the classic directories are maintained with symbolic links. The /usr directory, which no longer contains user data, has been reorganized to make sense from the chaos that once was the /usr/lib directory.

From a user's point of view, little about the directory structure has changed with System V Release 4. Most changes are for the benefit of system administrators.

Summary

In this chapter, you examined how UNIX uses files and directories and how the file-permission system protects your data. You learned how to change the permissions on files and directories and what the meaning of a special file is. Finally, you looked at the purpose and names of the most common directories found in UNIX.

Chapter 8

Managing Files and Directories

The vast majority of UNIX commands manipulate files and directories. Indeed, UNIX shell scripts are particularly adept at manipulating files and directories. File manipulations that would be difficult in a conventional language (even in C) are easy from within a shell. This is largely because of the rich selection of file-manipulation commands available in UNIX.

File-manipulation commands can be roughly grouped into two categories:

- Commands that manipulate files as objects

- Commands that manipulate the contents of files

This chapter concentrates on commands that manipulate files as objects: commands that move, rename, copy, delete, locate, and change the attributes of files and directories. The chapter also takes a quick look at commands that manipulate the contents of files.

Listing Files

The basic command to list files is ls. The way ls displays files depends on what version of UNIX you are using and how you are using the command.

If you use the ls command in a pipe, every file is displayed on a line by itself. This is also the default for some versions of UNIX like SCO UNIX. Other versions of UNIX list files in several columns. For most uses, the columnar format is more convenient; systems that list files one per row often have an alternative command, usually named lc, for *list in column format*.

This chapter
includes the
following topics:

- Listing files

- Organizing files

- Copying files

- Moving and
renaming files

- Removing files
or directories

- Viewing the
contents of a
file

- Compressing
files

- Manipulating
files with the
GUI

III

Controlling UNIX

The behavior of the `ls` command is modified with the use of flags that take the form `-abcd`. Again—and unfortunately—what the flags do depends on which version of UNIX you use. In general, versions of the `ls` command fall into two categories: versions of `ls` derived from UNIX System V and those derived from Berkeley. Because the Berkeley UNIX systems are slowly giving way to UNIX System V, this chapter concentrates on the flags used by System V. If you are in doubt about which version of `ls` you have, consult the manuals for your system or try the command `man ls`. If you are using a GUI, view the `ls` manual page in the Fingertip Librarian.

Flags used with the `ls` command can be concatenated or listed separately. This means that the following commands are effectively identical:

```
ls -l -F
ls -lF
```

The flags used with `ls` are listed here in alphabetical order:

Flag	Description
-a	List all entries. In the absence of this option, or the -A option, entries whose names begin with a period (.) are not listed. UNIX has a way of "hiding" files: all files that begin with a period are, by default, not listed. Files that begin with a period are generally files used to customize applications. For example, .profile is used to customize the Bourne and Korn shells; .mailrc is used to customize your electronic mail. Because almost every major command you use has a startup file, your home directory would look cluttered if the ls command listed them all by default. If you want to see them, use the -a flag.
-A	Same as -a, except that . and .. are not listed. Recall from Chapter 7, "Understanding UNIX File and Directory Systems," that . is a pseudonym for the current directory and .. is a pseudonym for the parent directory. Because these filenames begin with a period, the -a flag lists them. If you don't want to see these pseudonyms, use the -A flag instead. This option is not supported in UnixWare or UNIX System V Release 4.2.
-c	Use time of last edit (or last mode change) for sorting or printing. UNIX maintains three time and date stamps on every file: the file creation date, the date of last access, and the date of last modification. Normally, files are listed in ASCII order. (ASCII order is alphabetical order, except that capitals are sorted before lowercase letters.)
-C	Force multicolumn output with entries sorted down the columns. For some versions of UNIX, such as UnixWare, this is the default format of ls when output is to a terminal. In some other versions of UNIX, the lc command is supplied to list files in multiple columns.
-d	If the argument is a directory, list only its name (not its contents); often used with the -l flag to get the status of a directory. Normally, the contents of a directory are listed if a directory name is explicitly listed or implied with the use of a wild card. Thus, the simple command ls lists just the directory names themselves but ls * lists files, directories, and the contents of any directories encountered in the current directory.

Flag	Description
-F	Mark directories with a trailing slash (/), executable files with a trailing asterisk (*), and symbolic links with a trailing at sign (@). A directory listed with the ls -F command may look like this: `bin/` `list.names*` `other.names@` `plain.file` From this listing, you can see that `bin` is a directory, `list.names` is a program (that is, it is executable), `other.names` is a file symbolically linked to some other file in another directory, and `plain.file` is an ordinary file.
-i	Print each file's i-node number (i-nodes are described in Chapter 7, "Understanding UNIX File and Directory Systems") in the first column of the report. If you list files that are linked, notice that both files have the same i-node number.
-l	List in long format, giving mode, number of links, owner, size in bytes, and time of last modification for each file. If the file is a special file, the size field instead contains the major and minor device numbers. If the time of last modification is greater than six months ago, the month, date, and year are shown; otherwise, only the date and time are shown. If the file is a symbolic link, the path name of the linked-to file is printed preceded by the characters ->. The UNIX System V version of ls -l prints the group in addition to the owner. You can combine -l with other options, such as -n to show user and group ID numbers instead of names.
-n	List the user and group ID numbers, instead of names, associated with each file and directory. Usually, only the names are listed. If you are setting up networking products, such as TCP/IP, it is useful to know ID numbers when you are setting up permissions across several systems.
-q	Display nongraphic characters in filenames as the character ?. For ls, this is the default when output is to a terminal. If a file has accidentally been created with nonprintable characters, the -q flag displays it.
-r	Reverse the order of sort to see files in reverse alphabetic order or oldest-file-first order, as appropriate.
-s	Give the size of each file, including any indirect blocks used to map the file, in kilobytes (Berkeley) or 512-byte blocks (System V).
-t	Sort by time modified (latest first) instead of by name. If you want to see the oldest file first, use the combination of flags -rt.
-u	Use time of last access instead of last modification for sorting (with the -t option) or printing (with the -l option).
-b	Force printing of nongraphic characters to be in the octal \ddd notation. This is more useful than the -q flag because it allows you to figure out what the characters are.
-x	Force multicolumn output with entries sorted across rather than down the page.

There are more options than those shown here but they are not available on all versions of UNIX or they behave differently on various systems. When in doubt, consult the ls manual pages for your system.

Organizing Files

There are no fixed rules for organizing files in UNIX. Files do not have extensions (such as EXE for executables) as they do in MS-DOS. You can (and perhaps should) make up your own system of naming files but the classic system of organizing files in UNIX is with subdirectories.

More and more, however, UNIX applications that have come from the DOS world are bringing their conventions to UNIX. Although they may not require it, applications encourage you to name files that you use with their applications with certain extensions. For example, WordPerfect for UNIX uses the .wp extension. The UnixWare GUI recognizes many of these DOS extensions and displays files with appropriate icons when it encounters them in a folder window.

If you are going to write your own private commands, a useful way to organize your directories is to mimic UNIX's use of the /bin, /lib, and /etc directories. Create your own private directories with these names and follow the UNIX tradition of placing executable commands in your bin directory, subsidiary commands in your lib directory, and initialization files in your etc directory. Of course, there is no requirement that you do this but it is one way of organizing your files.

You create directories with the mkdir command. Its syntax is simple:

```
mkdir directory-name
```

In this syntax, directory-name is replaced by the name you want to assign to the new directory. Of course, you need write permission in the directory before you can create a subdirectory with mkdir, but if you are making a subdirectory within your home directory, you should have no problem.

Suppose that you have written three programs called prog1, prog2, and prog3, all of which are found in $HOME/bin. Remember that $HOME is your home directory; if you want your private programs to run as though they were a standard part of the UNIX command set, you must add $HOME/bin to your PATH environment variable. Do this with the following command in the Bourne or Korn shell:

```
PATH=$PATH:$HOME/bin;export PATH
```

In the C shell, you use this command:

```
setenv PATH "$PATH $HOME/bin"
```

> **Note**
>
> Remember that $HOME is the placeholder for the complete path that refers to your home directory. If your home directory is /home/ams, $HOME/bin is interpreted as /home/ams/bin.

If your programs call subsidiary programs, you may want to create sub-directories within your $HOME/lib directory. You can create a subdirectory for each program. The private command pgm1 could then explicitly call, for example, $HOME/lib/pgm1/pgm1a.

Similarly, if your command pgm1 requires a startup table, you could name that table $HOME/etc/pgm1.rc; your data can be in your $HOME/data/pgm1 directory.

Copying Files

The command for copying files is cp *from to*. You must have read permission for the file you are copying from and write permission for the directory (and the file, if you are overwriting an existing file) you are copying to. Other than that, there are no restrictions on your ability to copy files.

Here are a few things to watch out for as you copy files:

- If you copy a file and give it the name of a file that already exists and for which you have write permission, you overwrite the original file.

- If you give the name of a directory as the destination of the cp com-mand, the file is copied into that directory with its original name. For example, if you give the command **cp *file directory***, the file is copied into *directory* as *directory/file*.

- You can copy a list of files into a directory with the command cp *file1 file2 file3 ... directory*. If the last item in the list is not a directory, you see an error message. Likewise, if any element in the list other than the last item is a directory, you see an error message.

- Be careful when you use wild cards with the cp command because you can copy more than you intend.

III

Controlling UNIX

Moving and Renaming Files

In UNIX, moving and renaming files are accomplished with the same command: mv. The syntax and rules are the same for mv as they are for the copy command, cp. That is, you can move as many files as you want to a directory but the directory name must be last in the list and you must have write permission to that directory.

One thing you can do with mv that you can't do with cp is move or rename directories. When you move or rename a file, the only thing that happens is that the entry in the directory file is changed (unless the new location is on another physical disk or partition, in which case the file and the contents of the directory are physically moved).

If you try to use rm (for *remove*) or cp without options on a directory, the command fails and displays a message telling you that the item you are dealing with is a directory. To remove or copy directories, you must use the -r flag (for *recursive*) with rm and cp. The mv command, however, moves directories quite happily.

Removing Files or Directories

The command to remove a file is rm. To delete a file you don't own, you need both read and write permission. If you own the file, you are allowed to delete it, provided that you haven't closed off your own permission to the file. For example, if you turn off write permission to a file by typing **chmod 000 *file***, you must open permission again with the chmod command (by typing **chmod 644 *file***, for example) before you can delete it.

If you accidentally type **rm ***, you delete all the files you have permission to delete in the current directory; you do not delete the subdirectories. To delete subdirectories, you must use the recursive option (-r).

Some versions of rm stop and ask whether you really want to delete files that you own but don't have at least write permission for. Other versions of rm prompt you for any files marked for removal with wild cards. Indeed, you can write a macro or shell script that gives you a second chance before actually deleting a file.

If your version of rm balks at removing files you own but don't have write permission for, you can partially protect yourself from accidentally deleting everything in your directory by following these steps:

1. Create a file named 0. In the ASCII string sequence, the number 0 is listed before any files that begin with letters; if you give the command `rm *`, the file named 0 is the first file `rm` attempts to remove.

2. Remove all permissions from the file named 0 by giving the command `chmod 000 0`. This command removes read, write, and execute permissions for everyone, including yourself.

If your version of `rm` balks at removing the 0 file when you type `rm *`, you have the chance to think about what you just did. If you didn't intend to delete everything in your directory, press <Del> or <Ctrl-c> to kill the `rm` process. To test this out, try removing just the file named 0. Don't use `rm *` because, if your version of `rm` doesn't stop at the file 0, you will erase all the files in your directory!

A better way to protect yourself from accidentally deleting files is to use the `-i` flag with `rm`. The `-i` flag stands for *interactive*. If you give the command `rm -i filename`, you are asked whether you really want to delete the file. You must answer yes before the file is actually deleted. If you give the command `rm -i *`, you must answer yes for every file in your directory. This should give you enough time to think about what you really wanted to do.

Caution

Think before you delete files. When you delete a file (in most versions of UNIX), it's gone and the only way to recover a lost file is from a backup. You did make a backup—didn't you?

If you use the `rm -i` command frequently, there are two ways to implement it: write a shell script or create a shell function. If you write a shell script, remember that the shell searches for commands in the directories listed in your PATH variable in the order in which they are listed there. If your $HOME/bin directory is listed last, a shell script named `rm` will never be found. You can place your $HOME/bin directory first in the PATH variable's list or create a new command like `del`. If you create a shell script called `del`, you must mark it as executable with the `chmod` command before the shell can recognize it. When you create your `del` command, you need to give it only one command: `rm -i $*`. If you then give the command `del *`, the shell translates it into `rm -i *`.

Another way to accomplish the same task is with an alias. An *alias* takes precedence over commands that must be looked up; you can think of it as an internal shell command.

▶ Shell functions are discussed in detail in Chapter 10, "Understanding UNIX Shells."

III

Controlling UNIX

▶ The vi editor
is discussed in
Chapter 12,
"Using the
vi Editor."

To add an alias if you are using the C shell, you must edit the file named
.cshrc. You can use any text editor, such as the vi editor, to edit this file.
For the C shell, add these lines to the top of your .cshrc file:

```
rm ()
{
/bin/rm -i $*
}
```

To add an alias to the Korn shell, add the following line to your $HOME/.kshrc
file:

```
alias rm 'rm -i $*'
```

If you tried to delete a directory with the rm command, you were told that it
was a directory and that it could not be deleted. If you want to delete empty
directories, use the rmdir command (just as with MS-DOS). UNIX offers
another way to delete directories and their contents but it is far more dangerous. The rm -r command recursively deletes any directories and files it encounters. If you have a directory named ./foo that contains both files and
subdirectories, the command rm -r foo deletes the foo directory and its contents, including all subdirectories.

If you give the command rm -i -r, each directory that the rm command
encounters triggers a confirmation prompt. You must answer yes before the
directory and its contents are deleted. If you left any files in the directory you
were attempting to delete, rm balks just as it does if you attempt to remove
the nonempty directory with the rm command with no options.

Viewing the Contents of a File

Almost every UNIX command prints to the standard output. If the command
takes its input from a file, after manipulating the file in some way, the command prints the file to your screen. The trick in choosing a UNIX command
is in how you want the file displayed. There are three standard commands
you can use: cat, more, and pg

Using *cat* To View a File

For displaying short ASCII files, the simplest command is cat (which stands
for *concatenate*). The cat command takes a list of files (or a single file) and
prints the contents unaltered on the standard output, one file after another.
Its primary purpose is to concatenate files (as in cat file1 file2>file3) but it
works just as well to send the contents of a short file to your screen.

If you try to display large files using `cat`, the file scrolls past your screen as fast as the screen can handle the character stream. One way to stop the flow of data is to alternatively press <Ctrl-s> and <Ctrl-q> to send start and stop messages to your screen. Or you can use one of the page-at-a-time commands: `more` or `pg`.

Using *more* To View a File

Both `more` and `pg` display one screenful of data at a time. Although they both do roughly the same thing, they do it differently. Both `more` and `pg` determine how many lines your terminal can display from the terminal database and from your `TERM` environment variable.

The `more` command is the older of the two and is derived from the Berkeley version of UNIX. It proved so useful that, like the `vi` editor, it has become a standard. Although `more` has remained functionally the same, it has been rewritten a number of times and behaves slightly different on different versions of UNIX. This section covers just the basics of the command.

The simplest form of the `more` command is `more` `filename`. You see a screenful of the file. If you want to go on to the next screenful, press the <spacebar>. If you press <Return>, only the next line is displayed. If you are looking through a series of files (with the command `more` `file1 file2 ...`) and want to stop to edit one, you can with the `e` or `v` command. The `e` command within `more` uses whatever editor you have defined in your `EDIT` environment variable; the `v` command uses whatever editor has been defined in the `VISUAL` variable. If you have not defined these variables in your environment, `more` defaults to the `ed` editor for the `e` command and the `vi` editor for the `v` command. The `more` command has only one real drawback: you can't go backwards in a file and redisplay a previous screen. You can do this with `pg` however.

Using *pg* To View a File

The `pg` command is relatively new to UNIX System V and may not be available on versions based on the Berkeley distribution. One disadvantage to the `pg` command is that you cannot use an editor on a file being displayed. However, `pg` makes up for this deficiency by allowing you to move both forward and backward through a file.

The `pg` command works almost the same way that `more` does. To page through a file, give the command `pg` `filename`. One screenful of data is displayed. To advance to the next screen, press <Enter> rather than the <spacebar> as you did with the `more` command.

III

Controlling UNIX

The pg command has other options too. To move forward one line in the text, press the letter <l> (el); to scroll forward a half-screen, press the letter <d>. If you want to reverse direction, precede the command with a hyphen (–): Press – and <Return> to display the previous screen, and so on. The pg command also has a handy online help page; to display it in the middle of displaying a file, press the letter <h>.

Both the pg and more commands allow you to search for strings in the file being displayed. The pg command, however, allows you to search backwards through the file as well. The search syntax is /string. The pg /string command searches backwards through the file. With both the pg and more commands, if a string is found, a new page is displayed with the line containing the matching string at the top of the screen.

Both the more and pg commands allow you to escape to the shell with the ! command. When you escape to the shell with the ! command, you are actually in a subshell; you must exit the subshell just as you would if you were logging out from a session. Press <Ctrl-d> or enter the exit command to return to the same screen in more or pg from which you escaped.

Viewing Files in Other Forms

Other commands display the contents of files in different forms. For example, if you want to look at the contents of a binary file, display it with the od command (which stands for *octal dump*). The od command displays a file in octal notation, or base 8. By using various flags, the od command can display a file in decimal, ASCII, or hexadecimal (base 16).

Octal, Decimal, and Hexadecimal Notation

Representing binary data is an intriguing problem. If the binary data represents ASCII, you have no problem displaying it (ASCII is, after all, what you expect when you look at most files). If the file is a program, however, the data most likely cannot be represented as ASCII characters. In that case, you have to display it in some numerical form.

The early minicomputers used 12-bit words. Today, of course, the computer world has settled on the 8-bit byte as the standard unit of memory. Although you can represent data in the familiar decimal (base 10) system, the question becomes what to display: a byte, a word, 32 bits? Displaying a given number of bits compactly requires that base 2 be raised to the required number of bits. With the old 12-bit systems, you could represent all 12 bits with four numbers (represented by 2^3, which was the octal, or base 8, format). Because early UNIX systems ran on these kinds of minicomputers, much of the UNIX notation is in octal. Any byte can be represented by a three-digit octal code that looks like this (this example represents the decimal value of 8):

```
\010
```

Because the world has settled on an 8-bit byte, octal is no longer an efficient way to represent data. Hexadecimal (base 16 or 2^4) is a better way. An 8-bit byte can be represented by two hexadecimal digits; a byte whose decimal value is 10 is represented as 0A in hexadecimal.

The od command gives you a choice of how you want binary data to be displayed. It all depends on the flags you use. The following chart summarizes the flags you can use with the od command:

Flag	Description
-b	Displays each byte as a three-digit octal number. This is the default.
-c	Displays the ASCII character if the byte can be interpreted as ASCII. Otherwise, it displays bytes according to the codes used in the C language: null (or zero) as \0, backspace as \b, form feed as \f, newline as \n, return as \r, and tab as \t. Any byte that cannot be interpreted by these rules is displayed as a three-digit octal number in the form \nnn.
-d	Displays each word (two bytes) as an unsigned decimal integer from 0 to 65535.
-o	Interprets each word (2 bytes) as octal.
-s	Interprets each word (2 bytes) as signed decimal from –32768 to +32767.
-x	Displays each byte as a two-character hexadecimal digit.

Some versions of UNIX also provide an hd command that prints data in hexadecimal by default. You can combine flags in the od command with useful and occasionally interesting results.

Searching for Files

If you can't find a file by looking with the ls command, you can use the find command. The find command is an extremely powerful tool. As a result, it is one of the more difficult commands to use. The find command has three parts, each of which may consist of multiple subparts. The parts are as follows:

1. Where to look

2. What to look for

3. What to do when you find it

III

Controlling UNIX

If you know the name of a file but don't know where in the UNIX file structure it is located, the simplest case of the find command works:

```
find / file -name -print
```

Be careful searching from the root directory: on large systems, it can take a long time to search every directory beginning with the root directory and continuing through every directory and disk (and remotely mounted disk) before finding what you are looking for.

> **Note**
>
> A -xdev option is available in UnixWare and other SVR4.2 systems. This option disregards devices, including remote file systems. It's a much more efficient way to search your whole local file system.

It may be more prudent to limit the search to at most one or two directories. For example, if you know that a file is probably in either the /usr or /usr2 directory, use this command instead:

```
find /usr /usr2 -name file -print
```

There are many different options you can use with find; the following chart lists just a few:

Command	Description
-name *file*	The *file* variable can be either the name of a file or a wild-carded filename. If it is a wild-carded filename, every file that matches the wild cards is selected for processing.
-links *n*	Any file that has *n* or more links to it is selected for processing. Replace *n* with the number you want to check.
-size *n*[c]	Any file that occupies *n* or more 512-byte blocks is selected for processing. A c appended to *n* means to select any file that occupies *n* or more *characters*.
-atime *n*	Select any file that has been accessed in the past *n* days. Note that the act of looking for a file with find modifies the access date stamp.
-exec *cmd*	After you select a list of files, you can run a UNIX command that uses the selected files as an argument. You use two simple rules with -exec: the name of a selected file is represented by {}, and the command must be terminated by an escaped semicolon. An escaped semicolon is represented by \;. For example, if you are looking for all files larger than one megabyte, give the following command: `find /home -size 1000000c -exec ls -l {} \;`

Command	Description
	This command prints out (using the long form) every file larger than one megabyte in the /home directory.
-print	This is the most often-used instruction. It simply prints the name and location of any selected files.

The `find` command allows you to perform many logical tests on files as well. For example, if you want to find a selection of filenames that cannot be collectively represented with wild cards, you can use the *or* option (`-o`) to obtain a list:

```
find /home ( -name file1 -o -name file2 ) -print
```

You can combine as many selection criteria as you like with the `find` command. Unless you specify the `-o` option, `find` assumes that you mean *and*. For example, the command `find -size 100 -atime 2` means find a file that is at least 100 blocks in size *and* that has been accessed in the past two days.

Changing File Time and Date Stamps

Each UNIX file maintains three time and date stamps: the date of the file's creation, the date of the file's last modification, and the date of the last access. Only the file creation date cannot be changed artificially except by deliberately copying and renaming a file. Whenever a file is read or opened by a program, the file's access date stamp is modified. As mentioned in the preceding section, using the `find` command also causes the access date to be modified.

If a file is modified in any way (that is, if it is written to—even if the file is actually not modified), both the file modification and file access date stamps are updated. The date stamps on a file are useful if you need to selectively back up only files that have been modified since a given date. The `find` command can be used for this purpose.

If you want to modify the date stamps on a file without actually modifying the file, you can do so with the `touch` command. By default, the `touch` command updates with the current system date both the access and modification date stamps on a file. By default, if you attempt to touch a file that does not exist, the `touch` command creates the file.

You can use the `touch` command to fool a command that checks for dates. For example, if your system runs a backup command that only backs up files modified after a particular date, you can touch a file that hasn't been changed recently to make sure it is backed up.

The `touch` command has three flags you can use to modify its default behavior:

Flag	Description
-a	Updates only the file's access date and time stamp.
-m	Updates only the file's modification date and time stamp.
-c	Prevents touch from creating a file if it does not already exist.

The default syntax for `touch` is `touch -am` *filelist*.

Compressing Files

If space is tight on a system or if you have large ASCII files that are stable, you can reduce the size of the files by compressing them. The standard UNIX utility for compressing files is `pack`. The `pack` command can compress an ASCII file by as much as 80 percent. Compression is also a good thing to do before you mail a file or back it up.

The standard UNIX compression utilities consist of `pack`, `unpack`, and `pcat`. If a file is successfully compressed with the command `pack` *filename*, the compressed file is named *filename*`.z` and the original file is deleted. To restore the compressed file to its original components, use the `unpack` *filename* command. Note that you do not have to append the `.z` to the filename when you uncompress a file. The `.z` extension is assumed by the `unpack` command.

If you want to keep the file in its compressed form but want to use the data in a pipeline, use the `pcat` command. The `pcat` command works just like the `cat` command but expects a compressed file as input, decompresses it, and then prints it on the standard output.

For example, if you have compressed a list of names and addresses stored in a file named `namelist`, the compressed file is named `namelist.z`. If you want to use the contents of the compressed file as input to a program, use the `pcat` command to begin a pipeline:

```
pcat namelist ¦ program1 ¦ program2 ....
```

You may run into several other compression utilities. None of them have the status of a standard UNIX utility but are common enough to deserve mention. The `compress`, `uncompress`, and `zcat` commands are based on software thought to be in the public domain and readily accessible. Many UNIX vendors ship the `compress` utilities along with the `pack` utilities. The `compress` command has a better compression algorithm than `pack` but because its legal status is in limbo (someone has claimed patent infringement), it may not be available on your system. Another freely distributed compression utility is `gzip`. The `gzip` command has none of the potential legal problems of `compress` but is not (as yet) as widely distributed.

Manipulating Files with the GUI

If you are using UnixWare or another System V Release 4.2 system, chances are you are working with its Graphical User Interface (GUI). All the file manipulations you do with commands from the shell can be done with mouse actions from the GUI.

The UnixWare GUI, also referred to as *the Desktop*, displays the contents of your directories in what are called *folder windows* (the term *folder* is used instead of the word *directory*). Within these folder windows, the files, subfolders, and applications are represented by icons.

Every icon has certain attributes associated with it. One attribute that every icon has is an open action (that is, an action that takes place when you double-click the mouse pointer on it). When you open a text file, that text file is opened in a Text Editor window. When you open an executable file, that file is run as a program.

This chapter, however, is concerned with how you manage the file, directory, and application icons that appear in your folder windows. These actions include how to list, copy, delete, and move these items in your folder windows.

Figure 8.1 shows an example of a UnixWare folder window named `myfiles` that exists in your home folder. Note that you can get to this same folder (although you would call it a *directory*) from a command line by typing **cd $HOME/myfiles**.

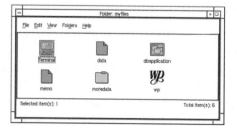

Fig. 8.1

Displaying a UnixWare folder window.

III

Controlling UNIX

There are six items in the myfiles folder window example. The files memo and data are generic data files—simple text or data files that do not have execute permissions turned on. The dbapplication file, on the other hand, is a file with execute permissions turned on. If you double-click on the first two items, they open in a Text Editor window. If you double-click on the third item, it runs as an application.

The icon named moredata represents a folder icon. By double-clicking on that icon, you open it. A new folder window appears, displaying the contents of the moredata folder.

The other two icons represent special applications the GUI knows about. The GUI knows that any file named wp with execute permissions turned on is a WordPerfect application. Likewise, any file named Terminal with execute permissions turned on is assumed by the GUI to be the Terminal window application.

> **Note**
>
> To create the Terminal icon, the /usr/X/bin/xterm file was linked to the name Terminal in this folder. You can tell that it is a linked file because a line of dots appears under the icon.

Listing Files with the GUI

You can change the way files appear in a folder window using the View menu. After selecting View, you can select the Sort and Format menu items to select how the icons are sorted and how they appear.

To list files in the GUI, follow these steps:

1. Click on the View menu, located at the top of the folder window. The View menu appears.

2. Click on either Sort or Format. Following is a list of the choices presented after you select either Sort or Format:

   ■ **Sort:** After you select this option, you can click on one of the following options to further define the sort: Click on By Type to sort the icons by type (folders, then applications, then data files). Click on By Name to sort in ASCII order (alphabetical order, with capital letters preceding lowercase letters). Click on By Size to sort by the size of the contents of the file. Click on By Time to sort by when the file was last modified.

■ **Format:** After you select this option, you can click on one of the following options: Click on Icons to display icons and names (the default, as shown in fig. 8.1). Click on Short to show tiny icons and names. Click on Long to show a long listing that includes a small icon, permissions, ownership, and date last modified. (Long output is similar to output from the ls -l command.)

Organizing Files with the GUI

Unlike using UNIX from the command line, the UNIX GUI *does* recognize some naming conventions for identifying what a file contains. A data file with the extension .wp is interpreted as a WordPerfect data file; an executable file named 123 is the Lotus 1-2-3 application, and so on.

You can see what icons and actions are assigned to different files in the GUI by looking at the Icon Setup window. Starting from the UnixWare Desktop window, open the Icon Setup window by double-clicking on System Setup and then double-clicking on Icon Setup. The Icon Setup window appears as shown in figure 8.2.

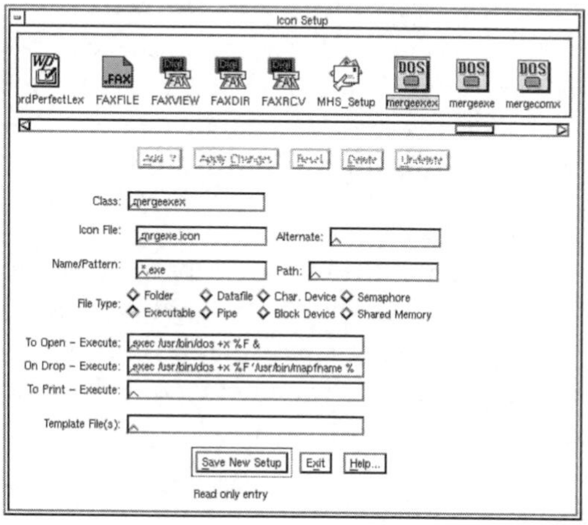

Fig. 8.2
Displaying the Icon Setup window.

Click on the icon in the top pane that you are interested in. Then look in the Name/Pattern text box in the lower part of the window for the names that are matched in the GUI to assign to the icon.

To organize your personal files, you can create your own folders within existing folder windows. To create a new file, click on the File menu at the top of any folder window and then click on New. A File:New window appears. Click on the Folder icon, type the name of the new folder, and click on Create.

The new folder appears in your current folder window. (Actually, you have created a subdirectory in the current directory; you can see this setup from the command line as well as in the GUI.)

The UnixWare GUI does not use a concept like the PATH variable you learned about earlier in this chapter. In the GUI, you can't run an application from any directory or folder as you can from the command line. To run an application, open the folder that contains that application (typically the Applications folder) and double-click on the application's icon.

Copying Files in the GUI

To copy files from one folder to another, use your mouse. First, open both folders: the folder that contains the file you want to copy and the folder in which you want the copy to appear. Press and hold the <Alt> key on your keyboard, move the mouse so that the pointer appears on top of the file icon you want to copy, press the left mouse button, move the mouse to the new folder, and release the mouse button and the <Alt> key. A copy of the file appears in the new folder.

Moving and Renaming Files in the GUI

To rename a file within a folder window, click on the icon you want to rename to select it, click on the File menu at the top of the folder window, click on the Rename option, type the new name for the file, and click on the Rename button. The new name appears with the icon in the folder.

To move a file from one folder to another, use the mouse. First, open both folders: the folder that contains the file you want to move and the folder to which you want to move the file. Simply drag-and-drop the file from the old folder to the new one: position the mouse pointer over the file icon you want to move, press the left mouse button and hold it down, move the mouse to the new folder, and release the mouse button.

Removing Files and Folders

To remove, or delete, a file or folder from a folder window, click on the item you want to delete, click on the File menu, and click on Delete. The file or folder disappears from the folder window.

Tip

If you deleted a file by mistake, you can recover it with the GUI by using the Wastebasket. From the UnixWare Desktop window, double-click on the Wastebasket icon. The Wastebasket window opens with the deleted file in it. Simply drag-and-drop the file back to its original location to retrieve it.

Viewing the Contents of Files in the GUI

Unlike in the UNIX shell, in the GUI, data files are associated with applications. As noted earlier, when you double-click on a data-file icon, the GUI assumes you want to open it in a Text Editor window. Special data files can be associated with specific applications using the Icon Setup window described earlier in this chapter.

Summary

Managing files and utilities in UNIX is a relatively simple chore. Organizing files into directories is easy. Finding, moving, copying, renaming, and deleting files and directories are simple with the commands find, mv, cp, and rm. Looking at the contents of a file is a different matter. You can look at the contents of a simple ASCII file with cat, more, or pg. You can look at the structure of binary files with the od command. Looking at the contents of files in any other manner requires one or more of the specialized UNIX filters. How you want to look at a file determines your choice of filters. And if all your file creation and manipulation has left you short of space, you can compress your files with the pack command. You can still use the packed data with the pcat command or unpack it with the unpack command.

If you are lucky enough to be using a UNIX system with a GUI, such as UnixWare, many basic file-management actions are simplified. You can list files by clicking the mouse on menu buttons. You can copy and move files by dragging-and-dropping them on a new location. The GUI also supports concepts not in the UNIX shell, such as associating data files with applications. As more graphical applications are added to UnixWare, more applications and data files will be bundled together to simplify actions that used to be done using pipes and arrows from the command line.

Chapter 9

Printing

Although everyone thought that the computer revolution would result in the paperless office, it hasn't. More paper is used today than was used 20 years ago. When UNIX was in its infancy, Bell Labs used it to produce technical documentation. As a result, UNIX has a great many utilities designed around printing (or at least formatting data to be printed). This chapter concentrates on the mechanics of actually printing a file.

Because printers are relatively slow, they are called *spooled devices*. When you print a file in UNIX, the file doesn't go directly to a printer; instead, it goes to a *queue* to wait its turn to be printed. If your file is the first in the queue, it prints almost immediately.

Because UNIX has been around for so long, it supports many different print devices, including everything from old daisywheel and dot-matrix printers to laser PostScript printers.

There are two different printing systems common to UNIX systems. The older is called the *lpr system* and the newer is called simply the *LP system*. The older lpr system is quickly giving way to the newer LP system, but for the sake of completeness, this chapter describes both.

Sending a File to a Printer

Sending a file to a printer is easy. In the old lpr system, each printer had its own command. The command for sending a file to the default printer is `lpr` *filename*. Of course, you can put the `lpr` command in a pipeline so that the output of a series of commands is sent directly to the printer.

If the system has more than one printer, the commands to send files to the various printers are `lpr1`, `lpr2`, and so on. Ask your system administrator which command goes with which printer. In the old lpr system, once you

In this chapter, you learn about the following topics:

- Sending a file to a printer

- Checking printer status

- Canceling a print job

- Dealing with problems

- Printing from the GUI

III

Controlling UNIX

sent a file to a printer, that was the end of it. The file was eventually printed, but if you wanted to stop printing for some reason (if you sent the wrong file to the printer, for example), you had to ask the system administrator for help because there weren't any controls in the old system.

The older lpr system is mentioned first because many newer systems mimic the lpr system for backward compatibility. Even though you may be on a system that supports the LP printer system, you may still be able to use the lpr command. UnixWare and other System V Release 4.2 systems support the lpr command, although the lp command is much more commonly used.

Printing Files in the LP System

Simple printing of files in the LP system is easy. To send a file to the default printer, use the following command:

```
lp filename
```

From within a pipeline, you can pipe a file to the default printer. The following is an example of sorting the contents of a file and then piping it to lp:

```
sort file1 ¦ lp
```

If you are not sure what your default printer destination is, type **lpstat -d**. This command tells you the name of the default printer destination. If no default printer is set, have the system administrator set it with the lpadmin -d printer command, where printer is replaced by the default printer name.

When you use the lp command, you get a job-ID number. The job-ID is the handle you can use to manage the job once it has been spooled. For example, if you want to print a file called printfile, you type this command:

```
lp printfile
```

The system responds with a message like this:

```
request id is laser-1431
```

This message tells you that the job will be printed on a printer named internally laser and that its job number is 1431. This message also tells you that the default printer (or class of printers) is called laser.

In the LP print system, each printer is given a descriptive name. The system administrator can also give a name to a class of printers and name the class as the default printer. This arrangement is useful in large installations in which one printer cannot handle the print load. Suppose that a system has five printers: three dot-matrix printers used as the default and two laser printers. The system looks as though it has seven printers attached if the system administrator defines the line printers as a class and the laser printers as a class. Table 9.1 shows a logical view of this system.

Table 9.1: Logical View of Printer Groups

Physical Printers	Logical Printer Groups
printer1	
printer2	printer (default class)
printer3	
laser1	
laser2	laser (class)

The system administrator can define an individual printer or a class of printers as the default. If the system administrator has defined a class of printers as the default, your print job is printed on the first available printer in the class. The print spooler maintains a balance between all the printers in a class.

If you want to print a file on a specific printer (other than the default), you must use the destination flag, `-d`, followed by the name of the destination printer. Using an example from table 9.1, if you gave the command `print -d laser file`, the `file` is printed on either `laser1` or `laser2`—whichever is free when your job is ready to be printed. If you want to print the file specifically on `laser2`, specify this with the following command:

```
lp -d laser2 file
```

You can use a number of other options (flags) to control how your job is printed. For example, the system administrator may allow or disallow a banner page to be printed on a printer. The default banner page is printed with users' login names so that the owners of print jobs can be identified. You can change what is printed on the banner page with the `-t` flag followed by a string of characters in quotation marks. The flags most commonly used with the `lp` command are summarized in table 9.2.

Table 9.2: Flags Used with the _lp_ Command

Flag	Description
-c	Forces `lp` to make a copy of the file you want to print. Without the `-c` option, if you modify a file before it is actually printed, the modified file is printed. The `-c` flag forces `lp` to make a copy of the file at the time you request the file to be printed. If you print from the end of a pipeline, this flag is ignored because the output of the pipeline is automatically copied into the spool area.

III

Controlling UNIX

(continues)

Table 9.2 Continued	
Flag	**Description**
-H *command*	Spools a print request to a printer and places the request on hold. The option also is used to print a request immediately or resume a held print request. If you want to hold a print job, use this command: lp -H hold *file*. Although you still get a job ID, the actual printing of the job is suspended until a new command to resume printing is received. To actually print the suspended job, use the lp -i *job-id* -H resume command. Note that the -i flag is used to change the status of a pending job. If you have a job in the queue and it has not yet been printed, you can put it on hold with the lp -i *jobid* -H hold command. For example, if you have a pending job named laser-1320, you can put it on hold with lp -i laser-1320 -H hold and resume it with lp -i laser -1320 -H resume. *Note:* A system administrator can use the -H option to bypass the queue and print a job immediately: lp -H immediate *file*. With this command, as soon as the current print job is done, *file* is printed.
-m	Causes mail to be sent to your account when the job finishes being printed. This option is most useful when you are running long jobs in the background or over-night. See also the -w flag.
-n*number*	Tells lp to print more than one copy of the file. For example, to print four copies of a file, enter lp -n4 *file*.
-o*option*	Signals that an option string follows (there are many printer-specific options you can enable). Note that not all options apply to every printer; even those printers that have the capability to perform some of the options may not be able to use the options because the system administrator has not implemented them. (As you might have guessed, the LP system requires a lot from the system administrator.) The most common lp request with the -o option is -onobanner. This option tells lp not to print a banner page with the print job. If many people are using a printer, banner pages help identify who sent each print job and when. Using -onobanner saves paper if you are the only one using a printer. Other requests you can use with the -o option are specific to the type of printer you are using and are not supported by all printers. Consult your system administrator for other options available with your printer. Some of the options you may be able to use are listed here:

cpi=*n*	Sets the characters per inch to a specific number (*n*). This number could be 10 (for pica type), 12 (for elite type), or a larger number to compress more characters into the space.

Flag	Description	
	length=*n*	Sets the length of page, based on number of lines, inches, or centimeters. Replace *n* with a number plus i (for inches), c (for centimeters), or nothing (for lines). The values 66, 10i, and 20c indicate 66 lines, 10 inches, and 20 centimeters, respectively.
	lpi=*n*	Sets the number (*n*) of lines per inch on the page.
	nofilebreak	If multiple files are sent, this request says not to insert a form feed between the files as they are printed.
	width=*n*	Sets the page width, based on number of inches or centimeters. These values are described with the length request.
-s		The silent option. Normally, the lp command reports your print job-ID on the standard output (usually at your terminal). If you don't want to see this, use the -s option.
-t*title*		Prints *title*, where *title* is a string of characters surrounded by quotation marks, on the banner page along with your login name. If the printer has been instructed not to print a banner page, this flag overrides the no-banner default.
-w		Sends a message to your screen when your job finishes printing. If you are not logged in when the job is finished, the lp spooler sends you mail instead. See also the -m flag.

The LP print spooler system continues to evolve. On the newest versions of LP, you can specify the type of form to be used to print a job with the -f flag. The system administrator defines which form is on which printer and is notified if a request for a different form is received. If no printer is available with the type of form you have requested, the job is automatically put on hold. When the system administrator changes the forms on a printer, he or she can then release all the print jobs requesting that form.

With the newest version of LP, you can also request that a particular type font be installed on a printer. A *type font* can be a different daisy wheel or laser-printer cartridge. If the system administrator has not defined the printers to have specific fonts, this option is ignored. You specify the font you want mounted with the -s flag. The following command requests that the roman font be mounted on the default printer before your file is printed:

```
lp -S roman file
```

III

Controlling UNIX

Because of the diversity of different printer, word processing, and graphic design programs, there is always a potential conflict between the output of a program and the input expected by a printer. For example, a word processor may expect to print on an old daisywheel printer but you may have replaced all the daisywheels with laser printers. The type of file to be printed is called the *content-type*. You can specify the content-type of your file with the -T *content-type* flag.

The system administrator has defined the content-type that each printer can print, and the LP spooler automatically directs your file to a printer with the right content-type. There are also a large number of filters that the system administrator can use to convert one content-type to another. If the content-type of a word-processing file is Diablo, for example, and the desired printer has the PostScript content-type, the system administrator can define a filter that makes the translation. If you don't want the LP system to use a filter, you can make the demand with the following command:

```
lp -T diablo -r file
```

The -r flag instructs the LP system not to use a filter even if one is available but to wait for a printer with the desired content-type to become available.

A common option for printing a particular content-type, however, is the PostScript content-type. If you have a PostScript file and want to print it on a PostScript printer, type the following command:

```
lp -T postscript file
```

> **Caution**
>
> Although many UNIX systems support the latest version of the LP system, only large installations or installations with sophisticated system administrators have taken the time and trouble to implement forms, character sets, or content-type applications.

Checking Printer Status

As you may have guessed, the LP system is complex—it has to be, given the demands placed on it. To determine the status of the LP system, use the lpstat command. The lpstat command by itself lists all the pending jobs you own.

The output of the simple lpstat command looks like this:

```
printer-407    user 2103    Feb 1 10:23    on printer
printer-512    user 42200   Feb 1 10:27
laser-517      user 35974   Feb 1 10:35
```

This listing tells you that your job `printer-407` is currently being printed on a printer named `printer`. Your other job destined for that printer, `printer-512`, is in the queue and may or may not be the next job to run on `printer`. The next job listed, `laser-517`, is in the queue for the printer named `laser`.

By using `lpstat -a` *printer* you can see whether the printer is currently accepting print jobs. For each printer, the print jobs are, by default, printed in the order in which they were sent. The order is reflected by the number following the printer name (for example, job `printer-407` will print before job `printer-512` on the printer named `printer`; there is only one job for the printer named `laser`).

The third column in the output from `lpstat` tells you how many characters are in the print file. You can use this information to determine roughly how long it will take to print the job. The fourth column tells you when the LP system received the job.

The `lpstat` command can, with the right combination of flags, tell you everything you want to know about the LP print system. For example, if you are far from the printer, you can't see whether the printer is currently running. The command `lpstat -r` reports the status of the print daemon `lpsched`. The `lpsched` daemon is a process that runs all the time on your system to manage the distribution and scheduling of print jobs on your system. If it's not running, you're not printing.

Several useful flags and their meanings are summarized in table 9.3.

> **Tip**
>
> To get the status of a list of printers, present the list as a single parameter. That means the list may be comma delimited (`pr1,pr2,pr3`) with no spaces or that the list may be space delimited and enclosed in quotation marks (`"pr1 pr2 pr3"`).

III

Controlling UNIX

Table 9.3: Flags Used with the *lpstat* Command

Flag	Description
`-a[list]`	Prints the acceptance status of all or a list of print queues. The print spooler has a double-gate system: print jobs are accepted or rejected from a queue and printers are marked as enabled or disabled. If a queue is accepting jobs but the printer is disabled, jobs accumulate in the queue without being printed. If, on the other hand, a print queue is rejecting print jobs but the printer is enabled, the remaining jobs already in the queue are printed but no further jobs are accepted. Only the system administrator can change the status of the print queues.

(continues)

Table 9.3 Continued	
Flag	**Description**
-c[*list*]	Shows a list of printer classes and their members.
-d	Displays the name of the default printer.
-o[*list*]	Displays the output status of all pending print jobs. The *list* parameter can be a mixture of printer names, class names, and print request IDs.
-p[*list*]	Displays the enable/disable status of all or a list of printers.
-r	Displays the status of the LP print daemon.
-s	Displays a status summary of the LP system, including the following: ■ Status of the scheduler ■ System default printer ■ Printer class names and their members ■ A list of printers and their associated device names
-t	Lists on-screen all available information about the printers and print jobs on your system. On large systems with many printers, this report may run several screen lengths.
-u[*list*]	Prints the status of all user print requests. The *list* parameter is a list of login IDs.
-v[list]	Displays a list of printers and the names of their associated devices as specified in the /dev directory if the printer is connected to the local system. For a remote printer, the system name the remote printer is connected to is listed.

Canceling a Print Job

One of the problems with the older lpr print system was that it was impossible for a user to cancel a print job once it was requested. The system administrator had to be notified and the problem handled with care. In the LP system, the task of canceling print requests is a lot easier.

When you make a print request, the lp command returns a print-job ID. This ID is used to manipulate the print job and cancel it. If you have forgotten the job's ID, use the lpstat command to list your current print jobs and then locate the job ID. If your job is not currently being printed, you can cancel it with the cancel *job-id* command. If your job is currently being printed, you can cancel it with the cancel *printer* command. For example, to print the file printfile, type this command:

```
lp printfile
```

The system responds with this message:

```
request id is laser-1431
```

Cancel the print request with this command:

```
cancel laser-1431
```

If the `lpstat` command shows that the job you want to cancel is currently being printed, you can stop printing and cancel the job with this command:

```
cancel laser
```

Note, however, that many printers have buffers that can hold several pages of text. When you cancel a print job, all you have done is stop the transmission of data to the printer. The printer continues to print until all the data in its buffer is printed. This can be a problem with laser printers because they do not begin printing a new page until they receive an end-of-page signal or detect a form-feed signal. Check your printer's manual or ask your system administrator for help.

Troubleshooting

Cannot access the file.

If `lp` gives you this message when you request to print a file, there are several things that may be wrong. You may have typed the filename incorrectly or you may not have read permissions to the file.

Requests for printer are not being accepted.

The administrator probably disabled the printer to do maintenance. Turn it on again (with superuser permission) with the `accept` *printer* command.

Print job is queued, but nothing prints.

This is by far the most common problem. Check that the printer is not disabled. If it is, enable it (with superuser permission) with the `enable` *printer* command. If it's a local printer, make sure that the cable is plugged in and the printer is turned on and online. If it's a remote UNIX printer, make sure that your network connection to the remote system is active. (Typically, typing **/usr/sbin/ping -s** system, where *system* is the name of the remote system to which the printer is connected, tells you whether you can reach the remote system at all over TCP/IP networking.) Finally, the print scheduler may be corrupted for some reason. You may have to reboot the system to fix the problem.

The print job prints, but it's garbage.

You're probably using the wrong filter. If you are printing a PostScript file, for example, and you don't use the `-T postscript` option on the `lp` command line, you will probably get reams of PostScript code as output. Once you figure out the appropriate filters, create a shell script that contains those filters so that you don't have to remember them again.

III

Controlling UNIX

Printing from the GUI

The Desktop graphical user interface that comes with UnixWare and other UNIX SVR4.2 systems has dramatically simplified the setup and use of printing in UNIX. Most standard printing can be done using your mouse and icons.

As someone printing from the GUI, you can probably assume that your system administrator has already added several printers to your system. To see the printers available on your system, open the Printer Setup window by following these steps:

1. Double-click on the System Setup icon in the UnixWare Desktop window. The System Setup window appears.

2. Double-click on the Printer Setup icon. The Printer Setup window appears (see fig. 9.1).

Fig. 9.1
Displaying the Printer Setup window.

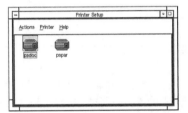

In this example, you can see that two printers are currently configured. One is called psdoc (a PostScript printer connected to a remote system) and one is pspar (a PostScript printer connected to your parallel port).

To make these printers available for printing from the GUI, you can place icons for these printers in convenient folders. For example, if you keep your documents in a folder called docs, you can place a printer icon in that folder. To do this, drag-and-drop the printer icon from the Printer Setup window to the desired folder. The printer icon appears in the new folder. Figure 9.2 shows the docs folder after both printer icons have been dropped there.

Fig. 9.2
Moving printer icons to convenient locations in document folders.

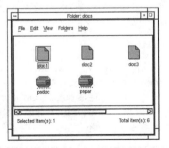

To actually print to a printer icon, drag-and-drop a document file on top of the printer icon. A Printer: Request Properties window appears (see fig. 9.3).

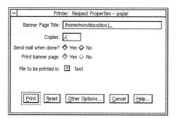

Fig. 9.3
Using the Printer:
Request Properties
window to
customize the
print request.

You can change the title on the banner page (the default is the name of the file) or the number of copies to be printed (the default is 1). You also can elect to send mail when the job is printed or elect to print or not print a banner page.

If you are printing a text file, simply click on the Print button at the bottom of the window to send the print job to the printer. If the file is not just text, you can use the Printer: Request Properties window to select various filters. Click on the arrow next to the File to be printed is: line and select one of the following options:

- **Text.** This filter prints plain text and wraps around text that goes beyond the current page width.

- **Text (no word wrap).** This filter prints text, but lets it run off the page if it goes beyond the current page width.

- **PostScript.** This filter is used to print PostScript files.

- **HP PCL.** This filter is used to print files in Hewlett-Packard PCL format.

- **Troff Output.** This filter is for printing files in troff output format. Unfortunately, you can't just print a troff file with this option. You must have already used the troff command (for example, /usr/ucb/troff -man *file* > *outfile*) to send the troff output to an output file before you can print the output file this way.

Once you click on the Print button at the bottom of the Printer: Request Properties window, you get a confirmation message that the file has been sent.

III

Controlling UNIX

Another way to print from the GUI is to use the Print menu option. In a folder that contains the file you want to print, click on the file's icon to select the file. Then click on the File menu option at the top of the folder window and then click on the Print option. The Printer: Request Properties window appears again. Complete the print request just as you would if you were printing from a drag-and-drop operation.

Summary

The lp command is the standard UNIX interface for printing files. From the command line, you can use lp to print to many different types of printers and to request many different options. Later, you can check the status of your print jobs with the lpstat command. If you change your mind and want to cancel a print job, you may do so with the cancel command.

UnixWare and UNIX System V Release 4.2 use a graphical means for printing files. Using simple drag-and-drop actions, you can print regular text files as well as those in PostScript, HP PCL, and troff output formats.

Part IV

Working with UNIX Command-Line Tools

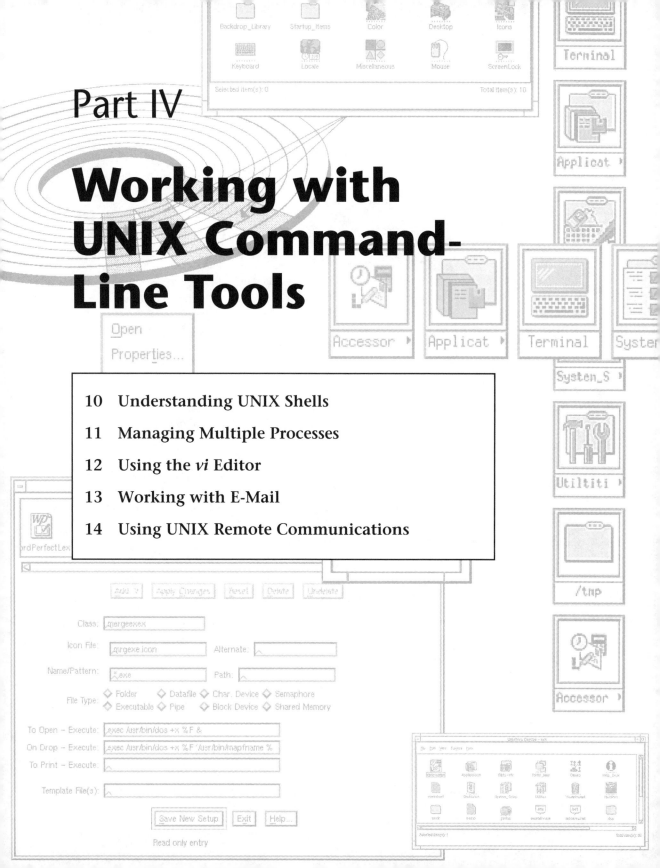

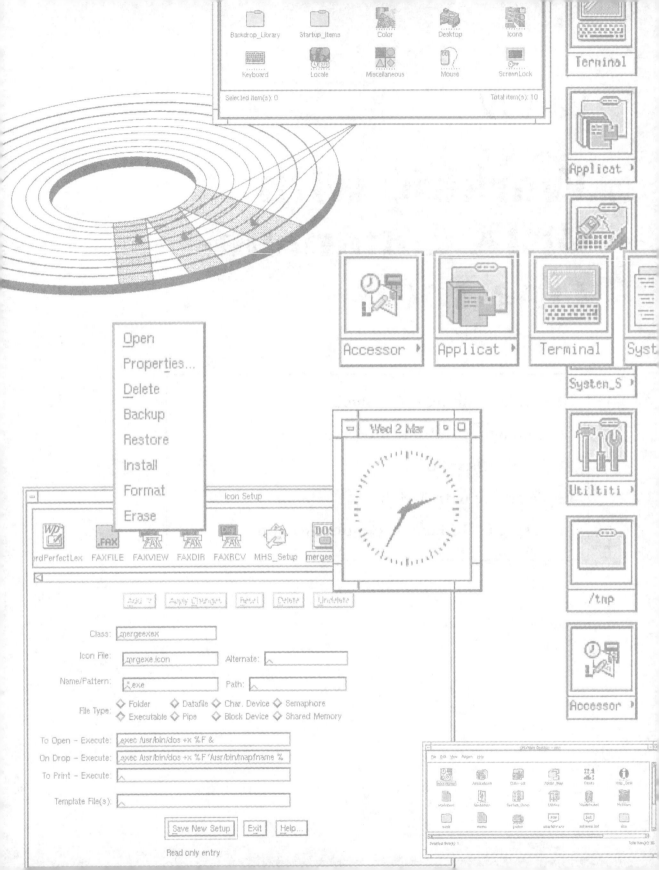

Chapter 10

Understanding UNIX Shells

A *shell* is a program that interprets commands and acts as an interface to the UNIX operating system. When you log in, a shell is started to deal with your commands. This shell is called the *login shell*. From then on, whenever you type a command and press <Return>, the shell examines the command and takes appropriate action. You can use some of the features and concepts associated with the shell to write programs called *shell scripts* or *shell procedures*. These scripts are easy to construct and test. They are also useful in creating commands tailored to your own needs.

If you're running UnixWare, the UnixWare Desktop starts after you log in. To get to a command line and run a shell, you open a Terminal window by clicking on the Terminal icon (located in the Accessories folder).

This chapter concentrates on how to use the shell so that you can gain more flexibility and power in working with UNIX.

This chapter covers the following topics:

■ What a shell is and what it does

■ Basic shell features

■ The three most common shells

■ How to create and execute shell scripts

■ How to program with shell scripts

■ How to customize your shell and environment

Examining UNIX Shells

Every command you type is interpreted by the shell and passed on to the operating system. When you log in to a UNIX system, a program, called your *login shell*, is started automatically. It runs constantly, monitoring and interpreting your commands. For example, if you wanted to print the files in the current directory whose names end with the characters *txt*, you would type this command and press <Return>:

```
lp *txt
```

The shell interprets the command by first constructing a list of the names of files in the current directory whose names end with txt and then sends that list to the program lp, which prints the files. It's the shell's job to get commands, interpret them, and make sure that the correct programs are started.

The shell is a program. It is not part of the kernel or internal workings of the operating system. It does, however, interact very closely with the operating system. You can write a program to use as a shell; it isn't impossible but it is best left to professional systems programmers. Although shells may differ in some of their properties, UNIX users have come to expect a standard set of features available in any shell. The following list identifies these features; the next few sections give examples of how you can use them to enhance your work:

- Redirecting input and output

- Completing filenames with wild cards

- Connecting processes

- Arranging for processes to run in the background

Redirecting Input and Output

Many programs expect input from the terminal or keyboard; many programs send their output to the terminal screen. UNIX associates keyboard input with a file named stdin; it associates terminal output with a file named stdout. You can *redirect* input and output so that instead of it coming from or going to the terminal, it comes from a file or is sent to a file.

You use the < (less than) symbol to redirect input into a command or program so that it comes from a file instead of the terminal. Suppose that you want to send a file named info by electronic mail to someone whose address is sarah. Instead of retyping the contents of the file to the `mail` command, give this command to use file `info` as the input (stdin) to the `mail` command:

```
mail sarah < info
```

You use the > (greater than) symbol to redirect the output of a program to a file. Instead of the output going to the terminal screen, it is put into a file. The command `date` displays the current time and date on the terminal screen. If you want to store the current time and date in a file named `now`, give the following command:

```
date > now
```

Caution

If the file named on the right side of the > already exists, it is overwritten. Be careful not to destroy useful information this way.

If you want to append information to an existing file, use the two-character >> symbol. To append the current date to a file named `report`, enter the following command:

```
date >> report
```

Following is a slightly more lengthy example. Suppose that the file named `sales` consists of sales data; the first field of each line contains a customer ID code. The first command line puts the output of the `date` command into a file named `sales_report`. The second command line uses the `sales` file as input to the `sort` command and appends the output to the `sales_report` file. The last line sends the `sales_report` file to users `sarah` and `brad` by electronic mail.

```
date > sales_report
sort < sales >> sales_report
mail sarah brad < sales_report
```

Caution

Be careful not to redirect the same file as both input and output to a command. Most likely, you'll destroy the contents of the file.

Table 10.1 summarizes the redirection symbols used in UNIX.

Table 10.1: Summary of Redirection Symbols		
Symbol	**Meaning**	**Example**
<	Take input from a file	`mail sarah < report`
>	Send output to a file	`date > now`
>>	Append to a file	`date >> report`

Completing Filenames with Wild Cards

As the shell interprets your commands, it recognizes some characters as wild cards. When you use wild cards, you don't have to type out the complete name of a file. You can also use wild cards to represent a collection of files. Wild cards can be used to represent any sequence of characters, a single character, or a range of characters. Wild cards are used for filename completion.

The Asterisk Wild Card

Use the asterisk character (*) to represent any sequence of characters. For example, to print all files in your current directory whose names end with .txt, enter the following command:

```
lp *.txt
```

Pay attention when using the asterisk wild card. If you enter the following command, you print all files whose names end with txt:

```
lp *txt
```

The file named reportxt is included with the files printed with the second command but not the first. If you enter the following command, the shell passes the name of every file in your directory, as well as the single file named txt, to the command lp (the file named txt in your directory is passed twice to lp):

```
lp * txt
```

In the last example, the lp command first prints the files represented by the *; that is, it prints all files. The lp command then moves to the second item in the list of files it is to print (UNIX interprets the space character between the * and txt as a delimiter—in effect, as a comma in an English command). The lp command processes txt as the name of the next file it is to print.

The * symbol can be used anywhere in a string of characters. For example, if you want to use the ls command to list the names of all files in your current directory whose names contain the characters rep, enter the following command:

```
ls *rep*
```

UNIX lists files with such names as frep.data, report, and janrep. There is one exception: files whose names start with a period or dot (.) aren't listed. To list files whose names start with a period (often called *hidden* files), you must specify the leading period. For example, if you have a file named .reportrc and want to see it listed, enter the following variation of the preceding command:

```
ls .*rep*
```

The Asterisk Wild Card Can Be Dangerous

Be careful using the asterisk wild card when you are deleting or removing files. The command rm * removes all the files in your directory! An all-too-common mistake is to accidentally delete all files when you mean to delete a collection of files with a common suffix or prefix. If instead of entering rm *txt (which would remove all files whose names end with txt), you enter rm * txt, UNIX first deletes all files and then attempts to delete a file named txt. But at that point there aren't any files left. For safety, use the -i option with rm if you use the asterisk for filename completion. The rm -i *txt command prompts you for confirmation before each file is deleted.

The Question Mark Wild Card

Use the question mark (?) wild card to represent a single character. Suppose that you have the files report1, reportb, report10, reportb3, report.dft, and report.fin in your current directory. You know that the lp rep* command will print all the files, but to print just the first two (report1 and reportb), enter the following command:

```
lp report?
```

To list the names of all files whose names are three characters long and end with the character x, enter this command:

```
ls ??x
```

This command lists a file whose name is tax but not one whose name is trax.

You can also represent a single character by enclosing a range of characters within a pair of square brackets: []. To list the names of all files that begin with an uppercase letter, use this command:

```
ls [A-Z]*
```

Suppose that you have files named sales.90, sales.91, sales.92, and sales.93 and you want to copy the first three to a subdirectory named oldstuff. Assuming that the subdirectory oldstuff exists, enter the following command to accomplish this task:

```
cp sales.9[0-2] oldstuff
```

Table 10.2 summarizes the filename completion characters, otherwise known as wild cards.

Table 10.2: Summary of Filename Completion Characters		
Character	**Example**	**Meaning**
?	lp sales.9?	Represents a single character. The example prints a collection of files whose names are in the form sales.*yy*, where *yy* represents a year in the nineties (sales.90, sales.91, and so on).
[ ]	rm sales.9[0-3]	Represents a single character in a range. The example removes the collection of files whose names are sales.90, sales.91, sales.92, and sales.93.
*	cat sales* > allsales	Represents any collection of characters except a period when it is the first character in a filename. The example combines into a file named allsales all files whose names begin with sales.

Connecting Processes with Pipes

Frequently, you need to use the output of one program or command as the input of another. Instead of entering each command separately and saving results in intermediate files, you can connect a sequence of commands by using a *pipe*. The UNIX pipe character is a vertical bar (¦).

To sort a file named allsales and then print it, enter the following single command:

```
sort allsales ¦ lp
```

The name *pipe* is appropriate. The output of the program on the left of the pipe (the vertical bar) is sent through the pipe and used as the input of the program on the right. You can connect several processes with pipes.

To print a sorted list of the data in all files whose names begin with `sales`, enter the following command:

```
cat sales* | sort | lp
```

Arranging for Processes To Run in the Background

The shell allows you to start one process and, before the first one completes, start another. When you do this, you put the first process "in the background." You put a process in the background by using the ampersand (&) character as the last character on the line containing the command you want to run in the background. Consider the following command:

```
sort sales > sales.sorted &
```

If you enter this command, you see a number on the screen. This number is the *process ID number* (also called a *PID*) for the process you put in the background. The PID is the operating system's way of identifying that process.

To copy a collection of files whose names end with the characters `.txt` to a subdirectory named `oldstuff` and, without waiting for that process to finish, print a sorted list of the data in all files whose names begin with `sales`, enter the following two commands:

```
cp *.txt oldstuff &
cat sales* | sort | lp
```

Note

Put jobs in the background when you don't want to wait for one program to finish before starting another. You can also put jobs in the background when you have a collection of tasks in which at least one can run on its own. Start that one and put it in the background.

Looking at Different Shells

The shell is a program that starts when you log in and interprets your commands. Because it serves as the primary interface between the operating system and the user, many users identify the shell with UNIX. They expect the shell to have the properties mentioned in the first part of this chapter and they expect the shell to be programmable. Remember that the shell is not part of the kernel of the operating system; with enough background in systems programming and knowledge of the UNIX operating system, you can write a program that can become a shell.

Although many different shells have been created, there are three prevalent shells: the Bourne shell, the C shell, and the Korn shell. They all have the features discussed so far. The Bourne shell is the oldest and the others have some features not in the Bourne shell.

The Bourne shell, known as sh, is the original UNIX shell. It was written by Steve Bourne with some help and ideas from John Mashey, both of AT&T Bell Laboratories. It is available on all UNIX systems and is considered the "standard" shell. The executable program for this shell is in the file /bin/sh. When you use this shell, you usually see a $ prompt. The fact that the Bourne shell is available on all UNIX systems and that it has all the properties described in the preceding sections—as well as the fact that it has powerful programming capabilities—make this a widely used shell. The examples in the next section are written so that they can be used with the Bourne shell.

▶ For more infor-
mation about
the *vi* editor,
refer to Chap-
ter 12, "Using
the *vi* Editor."

The C shell, known as csh, was developed by Bill Joy at the University of California at Berkeley. The students and faculty at Berkeley have had a great deal of influence on UNIX. Two results of that influence are the C shell and the vi text editor. The Bourne shell has superior programming capabilities, but the C shell was developed to reflect the fact that computing was becoming more interactive. The executable program for this shell is in the file /bin/csh. When you use this shell, you usually see a % prompt. The syntax of the C shell closely resembles the C programming language. This is one reason that shell scripts written for the C shell often cannot run under the Bourne or Korn shell. But the C shell has some desirable features not available in the Bourne shell: command editing, command history, and command aliasing. These features are also available in the Korn shell and are described later in this section.

The Korn shell, known as ksh, was developed by David Korn at AT&T Bell Laboratories. It was developed to include some of the interactive features of the C shell while maintaining the programming capabilities of the Bourne shell. The Korn shell is compatible with the Bourne shell (*compatible* in the sense that shell scripts written to run in the Bourne shell can be run in the Korn shell). The executable program for this shell is in the file /bin/ksh. When you use this shell, you usually see a $ prompt. This shell, like the C shell, includes the features command editing, command history, and command aliasing.

> **Note**
>
> UnixWare's Personal Edition does not come with the Korn shell. However, it *does* come with the Windowing Korn shell (the file /bin/wksh). The Windowing Korn shell contains all the features of the Korn shell as well as the ability to create graphical shell scripts.

Command editing means that after you type a command—and before you press <Return>—you can edit or change parts of the command without having to retype most of it. To edit a command, press <Esc> to get into editing mode and then use any of the line-movement commands from the vi editor to modify the command. You can use <Backspace> to go back to the portion of the command you want to change and other vi commands such as x to delete a character, r to replace a character, and so on.

The *command history* feature allows you to look back at previously entered commands and recall them. This feature saves you the time and trouble of retyping commands. When you combine this feature with command editing, you can easily correct mistakes in complicated commands and deal effectively with some repetitive tasks. In both shells, the history command displays the list of past commands the shell has saved. The commands are numbered. To execute command 10, for example, type **r 10** if you use the Korn shell or **! 10** if you use the C shell.

Command aliasing allows you to define a name for a command. Consider this example: The command man displays UNIX documentation or manual pages. To make the word help an alias, or alternative, for man, enter this command:

```
alias help=man
```

Now you can enter **help cp** or **man cp** to display UNIX manual pages about the cp command. Aliases can also be used with commands that have options or arguments. For example, if you want to list the names of all the files in the current directory sorted in descending order by the time they were last modified (so that the most recent files are at the bottom of the list), you can use this command:

```
ls -art
```

The ls command is the command to list files; the -a option specifies all files, the -t option sorts by time last modified, and the -r option arranges the files in reverse, descending order. That's a lot to remember. You can assign the alias timedir to this complex command with the following command:

```
alias timedir="ls -art"
```

The quotation marks (" ") are necessary because the shell expects the alias for `timedir` to be terminated by a space or <Return>. If you enter **timedir**, you get the directory listing you want.

> **Note**
>
> Setting an alias from the command line keeps that alias in effect only for the current session. To have the alias active whenever you log in, include the alias definition in the file `.profile` if you use the Bourne or Korn shell; keep it in the file `.login` if you use the C shell.

Which Shells Are Available?

All UNIX systems have the Bourne shell. You may also have the C shell or the Korn shell available to you. If your prompt is `$`, you're most likely using either the Bourne or Korn shell. If your prompt is `%`, you're most likely using the C shell. To determine which shell you are using, enter the following command:

```
echo $SHELL
```

The `echo` command prints whatever follows the word *echo* to the terminal screen. `SHELL` is a variable, maintained by the shell, which holds the name of your current shell; `$SHELL` is the value of that variable.

To see whether the C shell is available, enter the following command:

```
csh
```

If you see the percent sign (`%`) as the prompt, the C shell is available and running (enter **exit** to return to your previous shell). If you get an error message, the C shell isn't available to you. To determine whether the Korn shell is available, follow the same steps but use **ksh** instead of `csh`. If you see the `$` prompt, you have either the Korn or C shell available.

The shell you use as a login shell is specified in the password file. Each login ID is represented by a record or line in the password file; the last field in the record specifies your login shell. To change your login shell, you must change that field. The act of changing to another shell is relatively easy. Before you change shells, however, decide whether learning a new syntax and operating method—as well as some incompatibility problems—are worth the change. See your system documentation for detailed information on your shell's syntax.

> **Caution**
>
> Never directly edit the password file (/etc/passwd) in UNIX System V Release 4 or later (including UnixWare). Because of the security features added to these releases, the password file should be manipulated only with the appropriate commands. For UnixWare, use the User Setup window (the User Setup icon is located in the System Setup folder) to change the login shell. For System V Release 4, use the usermod command (you must be the root user). For example, to change to the Korn shell using usermod, enter **usermod -s /bin/ksh *user*** where *user* is replaced by the user ID of the user for which you're changing the shell.

A variety of other shells are available; some are proprietary and others are available on the Internet or through other sources. One worth noting is Bash; it is freely available and is similar to the Korn shell. Before adopting a shell from another source, consider such issues as whether the shell has bugs or errors you can live with and who will support that shell in terms of system resources, documentation, installation, and so on.

Working with UNIX Shells

The shell accepts commands, interprets them, and arranges for the operating system to execute the commands in the manner you specify. In the previous sections, you saw how the shell interprets special characters to complete filenames, redirects input and output, connects processes through pipes, and puts jobs or processes in the background.

You can type commands at the terminal or they can come from a file. A *shell script* is a collection of one or more shell commands in a file. To execute the commands, you type the name of the file. The advantages to this approach are as follows:

- You don't have to retype a sequence of commands

- You determine the steps to accomplish a goal once

- You simplify operations for yourself and others

By using variables and keywords, you can write programs that the shell can interpret. This is useful because it allows you to create general shell scripts you or others can use in a variety of situations. In the next section, you look at creating shell scripts and shell programming.

Creating a Shell Script

Suppose that after you log in, you regularly like to see who is logged in to your system, run a program named `calendar` that displays your appointments for today and tomorrow, and print the current date and time. To do all that, you enter the following commands:

```
who
calendar
date
```

If you put these three commands into a file named `whatsup` and make that file executable, you have a shell script you can execute just like any other command. The file `whatsup` must be a text file. You can use the UNIX text editor `vi` or a word processor (provided that you can create an ASCII or text file with it) to put the commands in the `whatsup` file. To make the file executable, enter this command:

```
chmod +x whatsup
```

With UnixWare, you can create shell scripts from the Desktop by using the Text Editor (see fig. 10.1). The Text Editor icon is located in the Accessories folder.

Fig. 10.1
The UnixWare
Text Editor
window.

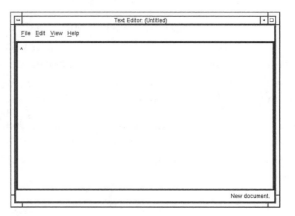

The command `chmod` modifies or sets the permissions for a file. The `+x` option makes the file executable, that is, it makes the file work just like a standard UNIX command. Putting commands into the file and making the file executable are both one-time operations. From that point on, you can type **whatsup** and press <Return> to execute your shell script. You can use the shell script just like any other command. For example, to print the results of the `whatsup` command, enter this:

```
whatsup ¦ lp
```

To put the results of the `whatsup` command into a file named `info` for future reference, enter this command:

```
whatsup > info
```

To review, follow these steps to create a shell script you can use whenever you want:

1. Use a text editor such as `vi`, UnixWare's Text Editor, or a word processor to put the shell commands into a text or ASCII file. In the preceding example, the commands were put in the file named `whatsup`.

2. Make it so that you have execute permission on the file. Use `chmod +x` *filename* (for example, `chmod +x whatsup`).

3. Test the command by typing the name of the file and pressing <Return>.

After using this process a few times, you'll see how easy it is to create useful scripts. Of course, the hardest part is figuring out which shell commands to use and how to use the shell's programming capabilities to express the steps you need to carry out.

You can test a shell script and see all the steps it goes through by entering the following command:

```
sh -x scriptname
```

In this syntax, `scriptname` is the name of the file that holds the script you're considering. The `sh -x` command displays all the steps the script goes through and is useful when you are trying to debug a script.

Using *echo*

You can use the `echo` command to display informative messages about what is happening in a shell script. The `echo` command displays its *arguments*, that is, whatever follows the word *echo*, on the terminal screen. Putting a string of characters in quotation marks ensures that all the characters are displayed. You also can redirect the results of `echo` to a file.

```
echo "Please stand by ..."
```

The preceding command displays the following line on the terminal screen:

```
Please stand by ...
```

The following command puts `Please stand by ...` in the file `messg`:

```
echo "Please stand by ..." > messg
```

The echo command can make users feel like something is happening when they enter a command (a particularly good idea if the command doesn't give any output for several seconds or longer). The echo command is also useful when you want to trace a shell script. Using the echo command at key points tells you what is happening in a script. Here is the file whatsup with an echo command or two added:

```
echo " Let's see who is on the system."
who
echo " Any appointments? "
calendar
date
echo " All done"
```

When you run the whatsup file, you see the following:

```
$ whatsup <Return>
 Let's see who is on the system.
sarah      tty01     Dec 20 08:51
brad       tty03     Dec 20 08:12
ernie      tty07     Dec 20 08:45
 Any appointments?
12/20      Sales meeting at 1:45
12/21      party after work!
Mon Dec 20 09:02 EST 1993
 All done
$
```

Using Comments

It is always possible that after you write a shell script and don't use it for a while, you'll forget what the shell script does or how it accomplishes its task. Put comments in your shell scripts to explain the purpose of the task and how the task is achieved. A *comment* is a note to yourself or whoever is reading the script. The shell ignores comments; they are important to and for human beings.

The pound-sign character (#) signals the beginning of a comment to the shell. Every character from the pound sign to the end of the line is part of that comment. Here is how you might comment the shell script whatsup:

```
# Name:     whatsup
# Written:  12/19/93, Patty Stygian
# Purpose:  Display who's logged in, appointments, date
    echo "Let's see who is on the system."
    who            # See who is logged in
    echo " Any appointments? "
    calendar       # Check appointments
    date           # Display date
    echo " All done"
```

Run the shell script again and you see the same results as before. The comments don't change the behavior of the shell script in any way.

Writing Programs with the Shell

To write programs using the shells, you must know about variables and control structures. Don't let either of these terms scare you off. A *variable* is an object that at any one time has one of possibly many different values assigned to it. *Control structures* specify the way you can control the flow of execution of a script. There are two basic types of control structures: decision structures (such as if..then..else structures or case structures) and iterative structures or loops (such as a for loop or a while loop). With a *decision structure*, you choose a course of action from one or more alternatives, usually depending on the value of a variable or the outcome of a command. With an *iterative structure*, you repeat a sequence of commands.

Variables in Shell Programs

To use variables, you must know how to give a variable a value and how to access the value stored in a variable.

Using the value of a variable is straightforward, but there are four ways of giving a variable a value:

- Direct assignment

- Using the read command

- Using command-line parameters

- Substituting the output of a command

Using Direct Assignments. The most direct way to give a variable a value is to write an expression such as this one:

```
myemail=edsgar@crty.com
```

This expression gives the variable myemail the value edsgar@crty.com. Do not include spaces to the left of the equal sign (=) *or* immediately to the right of the equal sign. The direct-assignment method of assigning a value to a variable is of the following form:

```
variable-name=variable-value
```

If *variable-value* contains blanks, surround the value with quotation marks. To assign an office address of Room 21, Suite C to the variable myoffice, for example, use the following command:

```
myoffice="Room 21, Suite C"
```

The shell retrieves the value of the variable whenever it sees a dollar sign ($) followed by the name of a variable. You can see that when the following two statements are executed:

```
echo " My email address is $myemail"
echo " My office is $myoffice"
```

Suppose that you frequently copy files to a directory named /corporate/info/public/sales. To copy a file named current to that directory, you have to enter this command:

```
cp current /corporate/info/public/sales
```

To make this easier, you can assign the long directory name to the variable corpsales with the following expression:

```
corpsales=/corporate/info/public/sales
```

Now to copy the current file to that directory, you issue this much shorter command:

```
cp current $corpsales
```

The shell replaces $corpsales with the value of the variable corpsales and then issues the copy command.

Using the *read* Command. The read command takes the next line of input and assigns it to a variable. The following shell script extends the preceding example to ask the user to specify the name of the file to be copied. The read command pauses the script and waits for input from the keyboard. When <Return> is pressed, the script continues. If <Ctrl-d> (sometimes represented as <^d>) is entered while the read command is waiting for input, the script is terminated.

```
# Name: copycorp
# Purpose: copy specified file to
#          /corporate/info/public/sales
     corpsales=/corporate/infor/public/sales
     echo "Enter name of file to copy"      # prompt user
     read filename                          # get filename
     cp $filename $corpsales                # do the copy
```

Using Command-Line Parameters. When the shell interprets a command, it attaches variable names to each item on the command line. The *items* on the command line are the sequences of characters separated by blanks or tab characters. (Use quotation marks to signal that a collection of characters separated by spaces represents one item.) The variables attached to the items in the command line are $0, $1, $2, and so on up through $9. These ten variables correspond to the positions of the items on the line. The command name is

$0, the first argument or parameter for the command is $1, and so on. To demonstrate this concept, consider the following sample shell script named shovars:

```
# Name:      shovars
# Purpose:   demonstrate command-line variables
      echo $0
      echo $2 $4!
      echo $3
```

Now suppose that you enter this command:

```
shovars -s hello "look at me" bart
```

The output of the shell script is as follows:

```
shovars
hello bart!
look at me
```

In this output, the first line is the command's name (variable $0), the second line is the second and forth arguments (variables $2 and $4). The last line is the third argument (variable $3).

Following is a more serious example. This shell script deletes a file but first copies it to the directory /tmp so that you can retrieve it if necessary.

```
# Name:    safrm
# Purpose: copy file to directory /tmp and then remove it
#          from the current directory
# first copy $1 to /tmp
    cp $1 /tmp
# now remove the file
    rm $1
```

If you type **safrm abc def** and press <Return>, only the file abc is removed from the current directory because the safrm shell script deletes only variable number 1. You can, however, represent all the parameters on the command line with $*. Make safrm more general by replacing each occurrence of $1 with $*. If you then enter **safrm abc def xx guio**, all four files (abc, def, xx, and guio) are removed from the current directory.

Substituting the Output of a Command. You can assign to a variable the result of an executed command. To store the name of the current working directory in a variable named cwd, for example, enter this command:

```
cwd='pwd'
```

Notice that pwd, the print working directory command, is surrounded by accent graves, or backquotes (`), and *not* by apostrophes (').

The following shell script changes the name of a file by appending the current month, day, and year to the filename:

```
# Name:        stamp
# Purpose:   rename file: append today's date to its name
# set td to current date in form of mmddyy
      td='+%m%d%y'
# rename file
      mv $1 $1.$td
```

In this example, the variable td is set to the current date. In the final line, this information is appended to variable $1. If today is February 24, 1995, and you use this script on a file called myfile, the file is renamed (moved) to myfile.022495.

Special Shell Variables

The shell keeps track of a number of special variables. You can see what they are with the env command, which lists the variables available to you within your *working environment*. Following is an abbreviated list of what you might see when you enter **env**:

```
HOME=/usr/wrev
SHELL=/bin/sh
MAIL=/usr/mail/wrev
LOGNAME=wrev
PATH=/bin:/usr/bin:.
TZ=PST8PDT
PS1=$
TERM=vt100
```

Any of these special variables can be used in the same way you use any other shell variable. Table 10.3 defines the special variables.

Table 10.3: Environment Variables	
Variable Name	**Meaning**
HOME	Full path name of your home directory
PATH	Directories the shell searches for commands
SHELL	Name of your current shell
MAIL	Full path name of your mailbox
LOGNAME	Your login name
TZ	Time zone for the date command
PS1	System prompt
TERM	The type of terminal you are using

The variable HOME always specifies your home directory. When you log in, you are in your home directory. Occasionally, you use the cd command to move to other directories. To change to the directory /usr/local/games, for example, enter **cd /usr/local/games**. To get back to your home directory, all you have to do is enter **cd**. You can use the HOME variable when you are writing shell scripts that specify files in your home directory. Instead of writing a command such as grep $number /usr/wrev/sales/data.01, it is better to write the command as grep $number $HOME/sales/data.01. Here are three reasons why it's better to do this:

■ The command line is easier to read.

■ If your home directory is moved, the command still works.

■ $HOME always represents the home directory of whoever is using the command. If you write the command using $HOME, others can use it as well.

The variable PATH lists the directories in which the shell searches for commands. The shell searches those directories in the order they are listed. If PATH=/bin:/usr/bin/:., whenever the shell interprets a command, it first looks in the directory /bin. If it can't find the command there, the shell looks in the directory /usr/bin. Finally, the shell searches the directory . (remember that the period represents your current directory). When you enter **cal** to print this month's calendar, the shell first looks in /bin. Because the command isn't there, the shell then looks in /usr/bin and finds it.

Note that if you had a personalized command named cal, the shell would never find it; the shell would execute the cal command in /usr/bin first whenever you gave the command. Give your commands names that aren't the same as system commands.

You may want to put all your shell scripts in one directory and change the PATH variable to include that directory. This arrangement enables you to execute your shell scripts from whatever directory you happen to be in. To do this, follow these steps:

1. Create a directory to hold the scripts. Use the mkdir $HOME/bin command to create the bin subdirectory in your home directory.

2. Move each shell script to that subdirectory. For example, to move a shell script named stamp to your bin subdirectory, use the mv stamp $HOME/bin command.

3. Add the script subdirectory to your PATH variable with the PATH=$PATH:$HOME/bin command. Do this in your .profile file so that the change takes effect every time you log in to your system.

You need to create that directory and modify the PATH variable only once. On some systems, a directory called /usr/local/bin is created by the system administrator (or system owner in UnixWare) to hold "local" commands and scripts that aren't part of the standard UNIX package but that have been added locally and are available to all users. In this case, you should expect that /usr/local/bin is also part of PATH.

The variable MAIL contains the name of the file that holds your electronic mail. Whenever mail comes into the system for you, it is put into the file specified by the MAIL variable. If you have a program that notifies you when new mail has arrived, it checks the file associated with the MAIL variable.

The variable PS1 holds the string of characters you see as your primary prompt. The *prompt* is the string of characters the shell displays whenever it is ready to receive a command. You see how you can change this variable—and any of the others—in the section "Customizing UNIX Shells" at the end of this chapter.

The variable TERM is used to identify your terminal type. Programs that operate in full-screen mode, such as the text editor vi, need this information.

The variable TZ holds a string that identifies your time zone. The date program and some other programs require this information. The computer system keeps track of time according to Greenwich Mean Time (GMT). If the TZ variable is set to PST8PDT, the time and date is determined as Pacific Standard Time (PST), 8 hours west of GMT, with support for Pacific Daylight Savings Time (PDT). Your computer system automatically changes between daylight savings time and standard time.

The variable LOGNAME holds your login name, the name or string of characters that the system associates with you. Among the things the LOGNAME variable is used for is to identify you as the owner of your files, to identify you as the originator of any processes or programs you may be running, and to identify you as the author of mail or messages sent by the write command.

The following example is an extension of the shell script safrm introduced earlier in this chapter. In this new version, the LOGNAME variable is used to remove all the files you own from the directory /tmp. To do that, the shell script uses the command find. The find command has a number of options; the shell script uses this find command line:

```
find /tmp -user $LOGNAME -exec rm {} \;
```

The first parameter, /tmp, is the directory to search. The option -user indicates that you want to search for all files that belong to a specified user. Before the command is executed, the shell replaces $LOGNAME with the current user's login name. The option -exec indicates that the following command is to be applied to every file found by the find program. In this case, the rm program is used to remove the found files. The pair of curly braces {} represent the position of each filename passed to the rm command. The last two characters, \;, are required by the find command (an example of using the backslash to pass a character on to a program without being interpreted by the shell). Add this command line to the shell script to obtain a program that removes files safely and also cleans up anything a user has in the /tmp directory over 10 days old.

```
# Name:      safrm
# Purpose:   copy files to directory /tmp, remove them
#            from the current directory, clean up /tmp,
#            and finally send mail to user
# first copy all parameters to /tmp
    cp $* /tmp
# remove the files
    rm $*
# create a file to hold the mail message
#   The file's name is set to msg
#   followed by process ID number of this process
#   For example, msg1208
    msgfile=/tmp/msg$$
# construct mail message
    date > $msgfile
    echo "These files were deleted from /tmp" >>$msgfile
# get list of files to be deleted from tmp
# -mtime +10 gets all files that haven't been
# modified in 10 or more days, -print displays the names.
    find /tmp -user $LOGNAME -mtime +10 -print >> $msgfile
# remove the appropriate files from /tmp
    find /tmp -user $LOGNAME -mtime +10 -exec rm {} \;
# mail off the message
    mail $LOGNAME < $msgfile
# clean up
    rm $msgfile
```

Using Special Characters in Shell Programs

You have seen how the shell gives special treatment to certain characters such as >, *. ?, $, and several others. What do you do if you don't want those characters to get special treatment? This section provides a few answers.

You can use the apostrophe, or single quote ('), to make the shell ignore special characters. Surround the string of characters with a pair of apostrophes, as in this example:

```
grep '^Mary Tuttle' customers
```

The result of this grep command is that the lines in the file customers that begin with Mary Tuttle are displayed. The caret (^) tells grep to search from the beginning of the line. If *Mary Tuttle* was not placed within apostrophes, it might be interpreted literally (or as a pipe symbol on some systems). In addition, the space between Mary and Tuttle isn't interpreted by the shell when it occurs within the apostrophes.

You can also use quotation marks (") to make the shell ignore *most* special characters, with the exception of the dollar sign ($) and the accent grave, or backquote (`). In the following example, the asterisks, spaces, and the greater-than sign are treated as regular characters because the string is surrounded by quotation marks:

```
echo " ** Please enter your response —>"
```

In this next example, however, $LOGNAME evaluates correctly but there is no value for $5:

```
echo " >>>Thanks for the $5, $LOGNAME"
```

Use the backslash (\) to make the shell ignore a single character. For example, to make the shell ignore the dollar sign in front of the 5, issue this command:

```
echo " >>>Thanks for the \$5, $LOGNAME"
```

The result is what you expect:

```
>>>Thanks for the $5, wrev
```

Programming with Control

There are two primary control structures in shell programming: *decision structures* and *iterative structures*. In decision structures, such as if...then...else and case, you can have the shell script decide which commands to execute based on the value of an expression (such as a variable, the properties associated with a file, the number of parameters in a script, or the result of executing a command). In iterative structures, such as for and while loops, you can execute a sequence of commands over a collection of files or while some condition holds. The following sections use examples that are not too complicated yet demonstrate the essentials of programming with some control.

Using *case*

The case structure is a decision structure that allows you to select one of several courses of action, based on the value of a variable. Here is a short menu program.

```
# Name:      ShrtMenu
# Purpose:  Allow user to print a file, delete a file,
#            or quit the program
# Display menu
     echo "Please choose either P, D, or Q to "
     echo " [P]rint a file"
     echo " [D]elete a file"
     echo " [Q]uit"
# Get response from user
     read response
# Use case to match response to action
     case $response
     in
        P¦p) echo "Name of file to print?"
             read filename
             lp $filename;;
        D¦d) echo "Name of file to delete?"
             read filename
             rm $filename;;
          *) echo "leaving now";;
     esac
```

The syntax of the case statement is as follows:

```
case word     in
   pattern) statement(s);;
   pattern) statement(s);;
   ......
   esac
```

The *word* parameter is matched against each of the *pattern* parameters, starting with the pattern at the top of the list. The statements that execute if *word*
matches a pattern are terminated by *two* semicolons (;;). The end of the case
statement is marked by the word esac (yes, that's *case* spelled backwards).

In the sample menu, the vertical bar was used to give a choice for a match.
For example, P¦p means that either an uppercase or lowercase letter *P* is considered a match.

The *pattern* * is used to represent all other patterns not explicitly stated. If
the user presses any key besides <P>, <p>, <D>, or <d>, he or she exits from
the menu.

The following example uses a case statement that makes a selection based on
the number of parameters that the shell represents as $#.

```
# Name:      recent
# Purpose:  list the most recent files in a directory
# If user types recent <return> then the names of
#    the 10 most recently modified files are displayed
# If the user types recent n <return> then the names of
#    the n most recently modified files are displayed
# Otherwise user is notified of incorrect usage
#
```

```
# Case based on number of parameters
    case $# in
        0) ls -lt ¦ head ;;
                # ls -lt lists names of file in order of
                # most recently modified
                # head displays the first 10 lines of a file
        1) case $1 in
            [0-9]*) ls -lt ¦ head -$1 ;;
            *)echo "Usage: recent number-of-files";;
            esac;;
        *) echo "Usage: recent number-of-files";;
    esac
```

Understanding Exit Status

When a shell command executes, it is either successful or not. If you use the command grep "American Terms" customers to see whether the string American Terms is in the file customers, and the file exits, you have read permission to the file, and American Terms is in the file, the shell command has executed *successfully*. If any of those conditions isn't true, the shell command executes *unsuccessfully*. The shell always reports back about the status of the termination of a command, program, or shell script. The value reported back is called the *exit status* of a command and is represented by the variable #?. If you enter the following commands, you will see the value of $?.

```
grep "American Terms" customers
echo $?
```

> **Note**
>
> If $? has a value of 0, the previous command was successful; otherwise the command was not successful.

Following is an example in which the exit status of the command who¦grep $1 is used in the case statement:

```
# Name:     just.checking
# Purpose:  Determine if person is logged in
# Usage:    just.checking login_name
#
case 'who ¦ grep $1 > /dev/null' in
    0) echo "$1 is logged in.";;
    *) echo "$1 is not here. Try again later.";;
esac
echo "Have a great day!"
```

If you enter **just.checking rflame** and rflame is logged in, you see the following:

```
rflame is logged in.
Have a great day!
```

If `rflame` is not logged in, you see these lines:

```
rflame is not here. Try again later.
Have a great day!
```

Using the *if* Structure

The `if...then...else...fi` structure is a decision structure that allows you to select one of two courses of action based on the result of a command. The `else` portion of the structure is optional. One or more commands go in place of the ellipsis (...). Provided that the exit status of the last command following the `if` is zero (that is, the command executed successfully), the commands following the `then` and preceding the `else` (if there is one) are executed. Otherwise, the commands following the `else` are executed.

In other words, one or more commands are executed. If the last command was successful, the commands in the `then` portion of the statement are performed and then the commands following the `fi` (the end of the structure) are executed. If the last command wasn't successful, the commands after the `else` are performed.

Here is a familiar example that behaves exactly the same as when it was written using the `case` statement:

```
# Name:     just.checking
# Purpose:  Determine if person is logged in
# Usage:    just.checking login_name
#
if
    who ¦ grep $1 > /dev/null
then
    echo "$1 is logged in."
else
    echo "$1 is not here. Try again later."
fi
echo " Have a great day!"
```

Using the *test* Command

Many of the shell scripts used in this chapter expect the user to behave nicely. The scripts have no check to see whether the user has permission to copy or move files or whether what the user was dealing with was an ordinary file rather than a directory. A command named `test` can deal with these issues as well as some others. For example, `test -f abc` is successful if `abc` exists and is a regular file. You can reverse the meaning of a test by using an exclamation point (!) in front of the option. For example, to test that you do *not* have read permission for file `abc`, use `test ! -r abc`. Table 10.4 lists several options for the `test` command.

Table 10.4: Options for Using the *test* Command with Files

Option	Meaning
-f	Successful if file exists and is a regular file
-d	Successful if file is a directory
-r	Successful if file exists and is readable
-s	Successful if file exists and is not empty
-w	Successful if file exists and can be written to
-x	Successful if file exists and is executable

Here is an example of the use of the test command:

```
# Name:     safcopy
# Purpose: Copy file1 to file2
#          Check to see we have read permission on file1
#          If file2 exists then
#                if file2 is a file we can write to
#                then warn user, and get permission to proceed
#                else exit
#          else
#                copy file
#
# Check for proper number of arguments
  case $# in
     2) if test ! -r $1       # cannot read first file;;
        then;;
              exit (1)       # exit with non-zero exit status;;
        fi;;
        if test -f $2         # does second file exist?;;
        then;;
          if test -w $2       # can we write to it?;;
          then;;
              echo " $2 exists, copy over it ? (Y/N)";;
              read    resp  # get permission from user;;
              case $resp in;;
                   Y¦y)    cp $1 $2;;  # go ahead;;
                     *) exit(1);;       # good bye!;;
              esac;;
          else;;
              exit (1)       # Second file exists but can't write;;
          fi
        else                 # Second file doesn't exist so go
                             # ahead and copy!;;
          cp $1 $2;;
        fi;;
     *) echo "Usage: safcopy source destination";;
        exit (1);;
  esac
```

You can also use the `test` command to test numbers. To determine whether a value in the variable `hour` is greater than 12, use `test $hour -gt 12`. Table 10.5 lists some options you can use with `test` when you are comparing numbers.

Table 10.5: Options for Using the *test* Command when Comparing Numbers

Option	Meaning
-eq	equal
-ne	not equal
-ge	greater than or equal
-gt	greater than
-le	less than or equal
-lt	less than

The following example shows these options used to display a timely greeting:

```
# Name:      greeting
# Purpose:   Display Good Morning if hour is less than 12
#                    Good Afternoon if hour less than 5PM
#                    Good Evening if hour is greater than 4PM
# Get hour
    hour='date +%H'
# Check for time of day
    if test $hour -lt 12
    then
        echo "Good Morning, $LOGNAME"
    else
        if test $hour -lt 17
        then
            echo "Good Afternoon, $LOGNAME"
        else
            echo "Good Evening, $LOGNAME"
        fi
    fi
```

Using Iterative Structures

Iterative control structures allow you to write shell scripts that contain loops. The two basic types of loops are `for` loops and `while` loops. With `for` loops, you specify a collection of files or values to use with some commands. To copy all the files whose names end with the characters `.txt` to the directory `textdir`, for example, use the following `for` loop:

```
for i in *.txt
do
      cp $i textdir/$i
done
```

The shell interprets the statement `for i in *.txt` and allows the variable `i` to take on the name of any file in the current directory whose name ends with `.txt`. You can then use the variable `$i` with any statements between the `do` and the `done` keywords.

The next example prints a collection of files, each with its own banner page. It also sends mail to the user concerning the status of the print requests. The characters `$*` represent all the parameters given to the shell command.

```
# Name:        Prntel
# Purpose:     Print one or more files
#              each with own title page
#              Notify user which were sent to the printer
#              and which were not.
#              Do this for all parameters to the command
for i in $*
do
      if lp -t $i -dlasers $i > /dev/null
      then
            echo $i >> printed
      else
            echo $i >> notprinted
      fi
done
# end of loop
if test -s printed
then
      echo "These files were sent to the printer " > mes
      cat printed >> mes
      mail $LOGNAME < mes
      rm mes printed
fi
if test -s notprinted
then
      echo "These files were not sent to the printer " >mes
      cat notprinted >> mes
      mail $LOGNAME < mes
      rm mes notprinted
fi
```

A while loop looks at the exit status of a command in the same way the `if` statement looks at it. The following script notifies a user when he or she has received new mail. The script makes the assumption that if the mailbox changes, the user has new mail. The script uses the command `diff` to compare two files and then reports on the differences. If the files are the same, the exit status is zero (the command is successful).

```
# Name:        checkmail
# Purpose:     Notify user if their mail box has changed
# Suggestion:  Run this in the background
# get a size of mail box for comparison
    cp $MAIL omail          # Get set for first time through
# MAIL is a "special" variable indicating the user's mailbox
# while omail and $MAIL are the same, keep looping
    while diff omail $MAIL > /dev/null
    do
        cp $MAIL omail
        sleep 30            # sleep, pause for 30 seconds
    done
# There must be a change in the files
    echo "New mail!!" ¦ write $LOGNAME
```

You can see that some of the commands and concepts used with if statements can be transferred to while loops. The difference is, of course, that
with while loops you are dealing with an iterative, repetitive process.

Customizing UNIX Shells

The shell starts when you log in. Other sections in this chapter have shown
you that certain special variables are given values by the shell to help define
your shell environment. Some of these variables are set by the shell. You
can change those settings and give other variables values by editing the file
.profile if you are using the Bourne or Korn shell. If you are using the C
shell, set the variables by editing the file .login. If you are using the Korn or
C shell, you can also use command aliasing to define aliases for commands.
Whenever you issue a command, a new shell starts; it inherits many of the
characteristics—or much of the environment—of the existing shell. Two
things to note about the new shell are as follows:

- The new shell runs in your current directory. The pwd command returns
  the same value within a shell as it gives before the shell was started.

- The new shell receives many of its variables from the existing shell.
  There are ways to make sure that variables set in the existing shell are
  exported to the new shell.

Exporting Variables to the New Shell

When you create shell variables or give existing variables values, they exist
in the running shell. A variable set in the login shell is available to all
command-line arguments. A variable set within a shell has that value only
within that shell. The value disappears or is reset when you exit that shell.
Consider the following example.

From the command line, enter these two commands, pressing <Return> after each:

```
today=Thursday
echo $today
```

Suppose that the echo command displays Thursday. Now suppose that you write and execute the following shell script named whatday:

```
# Name: whatday
# display the current value of the variable today
    echo "Today is $today."
# set the value of today
    today=Friday
# display the current value of the variable today
    echo "Today is $today."
```

Now enter the following four commands from the command line:

```
chmod +x whatday
today=Thursday
whatday
echo $today
```

The following lines appear on the screen:

```
Today is .
Today is Friday.
Thursday
```

The value of the variable today in the login shell is Thursday. When you execute the shell script whatday, you see that initially the variable today is not defined (as shown by the display Today is .). Then the today variable has the value Friday in the shell. When the whatday script terminates, you return to the login shell and today has its original value Thursday.

In order to give the variable today the same value it has in the login shell when the shell script whatday starts, use the command export. This command "exports," or passes on, the variables from one shell to subsequent shells:

```
export today
```

Now any shell started from the login shell inherits the value of the variable today. Add the export command to the preceding sequence of commands as shown here:

```
today=Thursday
export today
whatday
echo $today
```

You see the following output:

```
Today is Thursday.
Today is Friday.
Thursday
```

Notice that the value the variable receives in the shell started by the `whatday` script isn't carried back to the login shell. Exportation or inheritance of variable values goes only in one direction: from a running shell *down* to the new shell—never back up. That's why when you change your current directory inside one shell, you're back to where you started when that shell terminates.

You can export any variable for one shell down to another shell by using the following syntax:

```
export variable-name
```

In this syntax, `variable-name` is the name of the variable you want to export. To change your terminal type from its current setting to a vt100, for example, enter the following commands to make the new value of `TERM` available to all subsequent shells or programs:

```
TERM=vt100
export TERM
```

When you make changes to or set shell variables in the `.profile` file, be sure to export them. For example, if you want the `PATH` variable to be `PATH=/bin:/usr/bin:/usr/local/bin:.`, set it in the `.profile` file and follow it with this `export` command:

```
export PATH
```

To change the shell prompt, you must set a value for `PS1` in the file `.profile`. To change it from `$` to `Ready $`, for example, use a text editor to put these lines in the file `.profile`:

```
PS1="Ready $"
export PS1
```

Note

Changes you make to `.profile` or `.login` don't take effect until you log out and log in again.

Defining Command Aliases

If your login shell is the Korn or C shell, you can define command aliases. Command aliases are useful for defining commands you use regularly but for which you don't want to bother remembering the details. Command aliases are also useful for enhancing your working environment with a set of useful tools. This command assigns the alias `recent` to a command that lists the 10 most recently modified files in the current directory:

```
alias recent="ls -at¦head"
```

To avoid typing your command aliases each time you log in, put them in the `.login` file if you are using the C shell. If you are using the Korn shell, put the command aliases in a file called `.kshrc`; then edit your `.profile` file and add the line `ENV=.kshrc;export ENV`. The command aliases will now be available to you when you're in your login shell.

Summary

This chapter explained how to use the shell. The *shell* is the interface between the user and the UNIX operating system. It has many features and can be used to enhance your environment and productivity. Using these features takes some practice but is worth the effort.

In the next chapter, you learn how to control multiple processes.

Chapter 11

Managing Multiple Processes

UNIX is a multiuser and multitasking operating system. *Multiuser* means that several people can use the computer system simultaneously (unlike a single-user operating system such as MS-DOS). *Multitasking* means that UNIX can work on several tasks concurrently; it can begin work on one task and take up another before the first is finished.

Taking care of several users and multitasking are the jobs of the operating system. In most systems, there is only one CPU and one collection of chips that make up main memory or RAM. The system may have more than one disk or tape drive for secondary memory and several input/output devices. All of these must be managed and shared between several users. The operating system creates the illusion that each user has the computer system dedicated to himself or herself.

In this chapter, you see how to do the following:

- Start multiple processes
- Schedule multiple processes
- Monitor the state of the system
- Manage processes

Understanding Multitasking

As previously mentioned, it is the job of UNIX to create the illusion that when you make a request, you have the system's undivided attention. In reality, hundreds of requests may have been handled between the time you pressed <Return> and the system responds to your command.

Imagine having to keep track of dozens of tasks that you are trying to deal with simultaneously. You have to share the processing power, storage capabilities, and input and output devices among several users or several processes belonging to a single user. UNIX monitors a list—also known as a *queue*—of tasks waiting to be done. These tasks can include user jobs, operating-system tasks, mail, and background jobs. UNIX schedules "slices" of system time for each task. By human standards, each *time slice* is extremely short—a fraction of a second. In computer time, a time slice is adequate for a program to process hundreds or thousands of instructions. The length of the time slice for each task may depend on the relative priority of each task.

UNIX works on one task from the queue for a while, puts the task aside to begin work on another task, and so on. It then returns to the first task and works on it again. UNIX continues these cycles until it finishes a task and takes the task out of the queue or until the task is terminated. In this arrangement, sometimes called *time-sharing*, the resources of the system are shared among all the tasks. Naturally, time-sharing must be done in a reliable and efficient manner.

Chapter 10, "Understanding UNIX Shells," showed that you can put or run a program *in the background*. While the program runs in the background, you can continue entering commands and working with other material. This is a feature of multitasking: UNIX employs the time-sharing method to balance your immediate commands *and* the ones running in the background. This chapter shows that there are other ways to schedule jobs or tasks so that they can run without your attention.

The UNIX operating system has the primary responsibility of handling the details of working with several users and several tasks. As a user, you have the power to specify which programs you want to run. Some UNIX commands let you specify when you want a job or a process to start. You also have the option to monitor your processes as well as see what other processes are currently running. In some cases, you can change the relative priority of jobs. And you can always terminate your processes if the need arises. If you are a system administrator, you have all these capabilities plus the responsibility and power to initiate, monitor, and manage processes belonging to the operating system or any user.

Table 11.1 lists the commands that make possible the controlling of the multiuser and multitasking capabilities of UNIX.

Table 11.1: Multiuser and Multitasking Commands	
Command	**Action**
at	Executes commands at a given time
batch	Executes commands when system load allows
cron	Executes scheduled commands
kill	Stops processes
nice	Adjusts the priority of a process before it starts
nohup	Allows a process to continue after you log out
ps	Displays process information
renice	Adjusts the priority of a running process
who	Displays the system's logged users

Initiating Multiple Processes

You can start a program running by typing its name and then pressing <Enter> or <Return>. You can also start programs from files that contain shell commands. Running programs can interact with many different parts of the system. A program may read from or write to files, manage its information in RAM, or send information to printers, modems, or other devices. The operating system also attaches information to a process so that the system can keep track of and manage it.

A *process* is a running program. A process is different from a program. In one sense, a process is more than a program because a program is only a set of instructions; a process is dynamic because it uses the resources of a running system. On the other hand, a single UNIX program can start several processes.

UNIX identifies processes by assigning a *process ID number* (PID) to each process. UNIX keeps track of a process with its PID.

Starting Multiple Processes

Chapter 10, "Understanding UNIX Shells," explained that your login shell is always running. Whenever you type a command and press <Return>, you start at least one new process while the login shell continues to run. For example, if you enter the following command, the file named report.txt is sent to the lp program:

```
lp report.txt
```

When the lp program completes its task, you see the shell prompt reappear. In that time, both the login shell and the lp command were running; you initiated multiple processes in that case. The shell waited until the lp command was finished before putting the shell prompt back on the screen.

Starting a Background Process

You can run a process as a background job by giving the command to start a process and placing an ampersand (&) after the command. For example, if you type the command **lp report.txt &** and press <Return>, the shell responds immediately with a number: the PID for that process. The shell prompt reappears without waiting for the process to complete. Here is a sample of what you would see:

```
$lp report.txt & <Return>
3146
$
```

In this example, 3146 is the PID of the process started by the lp command.

Note

If you are using the Korn shell (ksh), a job ID number appears in brackets along with the PID when you place a command in the background. Although the PID is a system-wide process ID, the job ID is related only to processes executed in the current shell. The output from a background command may look like this:

```
[1]    3146
```

You refer to the job ID by using a percent sign. To kill a running process in the preceding example, type one of the following commands:

```
kill -9 %1
```

or

```
kill -9 3146
```

Regardless of whether or not you run the lp command in the background, the process associated with the lp command is started from the current shell.

The `lp` process is a *child process* of the current shell. This example points to a common relationship between processes: that of parent and child. Your current shell is the *parent process* and the running `lp` process is a child process. Usually, a parent process waits for one or more of its child processes to complete before it continues. If you want the parent to continue without waiting for the child to finish, attach the ampersand (&) to the command that *spawns* the child process. You can continue with other work or commands while the child runs.

> ### Note
>
> If you are working from a character terminal or a remote login, your current shell is usually your login shell. However, if you are using a virtual terminal or a Terminal window from a GUI, a separate shell is associated with each of those sessions.

Using Pipes To Start Multiple Processes

Another way to start multiple processes is to use one or more *pipes* on a command line. To print a long listing of the 10 most recently modified files in your current directory, enter this command:

```
ls -lt ¦ head ¦ lp
```

This command starts three processes simultaneously—and they are all children of the current shell. A pipe works this way: commands on either side of the vertical bar (¦) begin at the same time. Neither is the parent of the other; they are both children of the process that was running when they were created. In this sense, you can think of commands on either side of the pipe symbol as *sibling processes*.

Some programs are written so that they themselves spawn several processes. One example of this is the `spell` command that lists the words in a document that UNIX can't find in a system dictionary. The `spell` command spawns some child processes. Suppose that you enter the following command:

```
spell final.rept > final.errs &
```

You will see the following results displayed:

```
1286
$
```

Here, 1286 is the PID of the `spell` process; the $ prompt indicates that the shell is ready to handle another command from you. Even though `spell` may spawn some children and wait for them to complete, you don't have to wait.

In this example, the current shell is the parent of spell, and spell's children can be thought of as grandchildren of the login shell. Although a parent can wait for its children, grandparents don't.

All these examples show how it's possible for a user to start multiple processes. You can wait until child processes are finished before continuing or not. If you continue without waiting for the child process to complete, you have made the children background processes. The following section looks at some UNIX commands you can use to schedule processes to run at specified times or at a lower relative priority.

Using the Scheduling Commands

The UNIX environment provides many ways to handle command execution. UNIX lets you create lists of commands and specify when they are to be run. The at command, for example, takes a list of commands typed at the keyboard or from a file and runs them at the time specified by the command. The batch command is similar to the at command, but batch runs commands when the system finds time for them rather than allowing the user to specify a particular time. The cron command allows for commands to be run periodically.

All scheduling commands are useful for running tasks at times when the system is not too busy. They're also good for executing scripts to external services—such as database queries—at times when it is least expensive to do so.

Running Commands at Specified Times with *at*

To schedule one or more commands for a specified time, use the command at. With this command, you can specify a time, a date, or both. The command expects two or more arguments. At a minimum, you specify the time you want the command or commands executed and the command or commands you want to execute.

The following example performs its job at 1:23 AM. If you are working in the wee hours of the morning before 1:23 AM, the command is done today. Otherwise, it is done at 1:23 tomorrow morning. The job prints all files in the directory /usr/sales/reports and sends a user named boss some mail announcing that the print job was done at 1:23 AM.

```
at 1:23 <Return>
lp /usr/sales/reports/* <Return>
echo "Files printed, Boss!" ¦ mailx -s"Job done" boss <Return>
<^D>
```

> **Note**
>
> The ^D symbol means that <Ctrl-d> was pressed to end the process. Press and hold the <Ctrl> key and then press the <d> key; then release both keys. (UNIX uses the ^D symbol to represent the end of a file.)

Commands to be scheduled by at are entered as a list of commands on the line following the at command; the list of commands are terminated with <Ctrl-d>.

After you terminate the at command, you see a display similar to the following:

```
job 756603300.a at Wed Dec 21 01:23:00 1994
```

This response indicates that the job will execute at 1:23 as specified. The job number, 756603300.a, identifies the job. If you decide you want to cancel the job, do so by using the job number associated with it.

If you have several commands you want to schedule using at, it is best to put them in a file. If the name of the file is getdone, for example, and you want to schedule the commands for 10:00 AM, enter the following command:

```
at 10:00 < getdone
```

Remember that the less-than symbol (<) means to use the contents of the getdone file as input to the at command.

You can also specify a date for an at job. For example, to schedule a job at 5:00 PM on January 24, enter these commands:

```
at 17:00 Jan 24 <Return>
lp /usr/sales/reports/* <Return>
echo "Files printed, Boss!" ¦ mailx -s"Job done" boss <Return>
<^D>
```

The jobs you schedule with at are put into a queue that the operating system checks periodically. You don't have to be logged in for the job to be executed. The at command always runs in the background, freeing resources but still accomplishing the job. Any output produced by the commands in your at job is mailed to you.

To see which jobs you scheduled with at, enter **at -l.** Working with the preceding examples, you would see the following results:

```
job 756603300.a at Wed Dec 21 01:23:00 1994
job 756604200.a at Tue Jan 24 17:00:00 1995
```

Only *your* at jobs are listed.

To remove a scheduled at job, enter **at -r** followed by the job number. For example, to remove the second job just listed, enter this command:

```
at -r 756604200.a
```

Table 11.2 summarizes the different ways of using the at command.

Table 11.2: Summary of *at* Commands	
Format	**Action**
at *hh:mm*	Schedule job at the hour (*hh*) and minute (*mm*) specified
at *hh:mm month day year*	Schedule job at the hour (*hh*), minute (*mm*), *month*, *day*, and *year* specified
at -l	List scheduled jobs
at -r *job_id*	Cancel job with job number matching *job_id*

Running Long Tasks with *batch*

UNIX has more than one command for scheduling tasks. The preceding section describes the at command, which gives you the power to decide when a task will run. However, it is always possible that the system can be loaded down with more jobs scheduled at one time than it can comfortably handle. The batch command lets the operating system decide an appropriate time to run a process. When you schedule a job with batch, UNIX starts and works on the process whenever the system load is not too great. Jobs run under batch execute in the background, just as those run with at.

The format for the batch command is to enter the list of commands on the lines following the batch command; you terminate the list of commands with <Ctrl-d>. You can put the list of commands in a file and then redirect the input to batch to come from the file. To sort a collection of files, print the results, and notify user Boss that the job is done, enter the following commands:

```
batch <Return>
sort /usr/sales/reports/* ¦ lp <Return>
echo "Files printed, Boss!" ¦ mailx -s"Job done" boss <Return>
<^D>
```

The system returns the following response:

```
job 7789001234.b at Wed Dec 21 11:43:09 1994
```

The date and time listed are the date and time you pressed <Ctrl-d> to complete the batch command. When the job is complete, check your mail: anything that is normally displayed on the screen by the commands is mailed to you.

Tip

It is useful to put commands you want to run with at or batch in a file so that you don't have to retype them. To use batch to schedule the commands in the file getdone, enter this command:

```
batch < getdone
```

Scheduling Commands with *cron* and *crontab*

Both at and batch schedule commands on a one-time basis. To schedule commands or processes on a regular basis, you indirectly use the program cron. You specify the times and dates you want to run a command in crontab files. Times can be specified in terms of minutes, hours, days of the month, month of the year, or day of the week.

The cron program is started only once, when the system is booted. Individual users should not have permission to run cron directly. Also, the system administrator shouldn't start cron by typing the name of the command; cron should be listed in a shell script as one of the commands to run during a system boot-up sequence.

Note

In UnixWare, the cron program is started by the /etc/dinit.d/S75cron shell script. That script is started by the command /etc/dinit from the /etc/inittab file.

Once started, cron (short for *chronograph*) checks queues for at jobs to run and also checks to see whether regular users or the root have scheduled jobs using crontab files. If there is nothing to do, cron "goes to sleep" and becomes inactive; it "wakes up" every minute to check whether there are commands to run. You can see how important and useful this facility is; in addition, cron uses very few system resources.

In UnixWare or other System V Release 4.2 systems, crontab files are stored in the /usr/spool/cron/crontabs directory.

Setting Up a Schedule of Commands with *crontab*

Use the crontab command to install a list of commands that will be executed on a regular schedule. The commands are scheduled to run at a specified time (such as once a month, once an hour, once a day, and so on). The list of commands to be performed on the specified schedule must be included in the crontab file, which is installed with the crontab command. Once you install the crontab file, cron reads and executes the listed commands at the specified times. The crontab command also enables you to view the list of commands included in the file and cancel the list if you want.

Before you install your crontab file with the crontab command, create the file containing the list of commands you want to schedule by using a text editor such as vi or the graphical Text Editor that comes with UnixWare. The crontab command handles the placement of the file. Each user has only one crontab file, created when the crontab command is issued. This file is placed in a directory that is read by the cron command.

Each user has one crontab file, stored in the /usr/spool/cron/crontabs directory. That file is given the user's name. If your user name is mcn and you use a text editor to create a file called mycron and install it by typing **crontab mycron**, the file /usr/spool/cron/crontabs/mcn is created. (In this example, the mcn file is created, or overwritten, with the contents of mycron, which may contain entries that launch one or more commands.)

> **Note**
>
> For a user to be able to use the crontab command, that user must be listed in the /etc/cron.d/cron.allow file. When you add a user to UnixWare with the User Setup icon, the user is automatically added to this file. If you add a user from the command line (by using the useradd command), the user is not automatically added to that file. As the root user, you must add the new user to the cron.allow file with a text editor.

> **Note**
>
> Once you have created your crontab file, modify it using only the crontab command. Don't try to replace or modify the file that cron examines (that is, the /usr/spool/cron/crontabs/*user* file) by any other means than by using the crontab command.

Each line in the crontab file contains a time pattern and a command. The command is executed at the specified time pattern. The time pattern is divided into five fields separated by spaces or tabs. Any output that usually appears on the screen (that is, information that isn't redirected to `stdout` or `stderr`) is mailed to the user.

Following is the syntax for the commands you enter in a file to be used by `crontab`. The first five fields are time-option fields (you must specify all five of these fields; use an asterisk `*` in a field if you want to ignore that field). Table 11.3 lists the time-field options available with `crontab`.

```
minute hour day-of-month month-of-year day-of-week command
```

> **Note**
>
> Technically, an asterisk in a `crontab` field means "any valid value" rather than "ignore the value." For example, consider this `crontab` entry: `2 0 1 * * date`. This entry says to run the `date` command at two minutes after midnight (zero hour) on the first day of the month. Because the month and day-of-the-week fields are both asterisks, this entry runs on the first day of every month and any day of the week that the first of the month happens to land on.

You can have as many entries as you want in a `crontab` file and designate them to run at any time you want. This means that you can run as many commands as you want in a single `crontab` file.

Table 11.3: Time-Field Options for the *crontab* Command

Field	Range
minute	0 through 59
hour	0 through 23 (midnight is 0)
day-of-month	1 through 31
month-of-year	1 through 12
day-of-week	0 through 6 (Sunday is 0)

To sort a file named `/usr/wwr/sales/weekly` and mail the output to a user named `twool` at 7:30 each Monday, use the following entry in a file:

```
30 07 * * 01 sort /usr/wwr/sales/weekly ¦mailx -s"Weekly Sales" twool
```

This commands specifies the *minute* as 30, the *hour* as 07, any day of month with the *, any month of year with another *, and the *day-of-week* as 01 (which represents Monday).

Notice that there is a pipe between the `mailx` and `sort` commands in the previous example. The command field can contain pipes, semicolons, arrows, or anything else you can enter on a shell command line. At the specified date and time, `cron` runs the entire command field with a standard Bourne shell (`sh`).

To specify a sequence of values for one of the first four fields, use commas to separate the values. Suppose that you have a program, `chkquotes`, which accesses a service that provides stock quotes and puts the quotes in a file. To get those quotes at 9:00 AM, 11:00 AM, 2:00 PM, and 4:00 PM on Monday, Tuesday, and Thursday of every week—and definitely on the 10th of March and September—use the following entry:

```
* 09,11,14,16 10 03,09 01,02,04 chkquotes
```

Put the command lines into a file using `vi` or some other editor that allows you to save files as text files. Assume that you put your commands in a file named `cronjobs`. To use `crontab` to put the file where `cron` can find it, enter this command:

```
crontab cronjobs
```

Each time you use `crontab` this way, it overwrites any `crontab` file you may have already launched.

The `crontab` command has three options: The `-e` option *edits* the contents of the current crontab file. (The `-e` option opens your file using the `ed` editor or whatever is assigned to the `EDITOR` variable in your shell.) The `-r` option *removes* the current `crontab` file from the `crontabs` directory. The `-l` option *lists* the contents of the current `crontab` file.

In all of these cases, `crontab` works with the `crontab` file that has your login name. If your login name is `mcn`, your `crontab` file is `/usr/spool/cron/crontabs/mcn`. The `crontab` command does this automatically; you don't need to know this fact to use the `crontab` command.

The system administrator and the users share responsibility for making sure that the system is used appropriately. When you schedule a process, be aware of the impact it may have on the total system. UNIX allows the system administrator tó grant access to the `at`, `batch`, and `cron` commands to all users, specific users, or no users (or to deny access to individual users). If you find that you don't have access to `at`, `batch`, or `crontab`, talk with your system administrator.

Troubleshooting

The commands you put in your crontab file don't work.

The cron command runs your crontab entries using the Bourne shell (sh). Your entry fails if you use shell features not supported by sh. For example, the Korn shell (ksh) allows you to use a tilde (~) to represent a home directory or the alias command to designate aliases for certain commands. These aren't recognized by the sh shell and cause your crontab entry to fail if you rely on them.

When you try to use the at command, you are told you don't have permission to use it.

Have your system administrator add your login ID to the /etc/cron.d/at.allow file.

You tried to use the at now command to run a command immediately.

No matter how fast you type, at now always responds with the message ERROR: Too late. The best alternative is to use the batch command to run the command for you. You can, however, use at now +1 min to run the command in a minute. After you press <Return>, type fast to enter your command before the minute expires.

Reporting on and Monitoring the Multitasking Environment

You know that UNIX is a multiuser, multitasking operating system. Because so many people can do so many things with the system at the same time, the system administrator and users find it useful to determine who is using the system and what processes are running.

It's important to know that others can keep track of the commands you enter. Most users can't access your files without your permission, but they can see the names of commands you enter. The system administrator or someone with the root password can peruse all your files. Although you don't have to be paranoid about privacy on a UNIX system, you should know that the system can be monitored by anyone who wants to take the time to do it. The information you can gain about what is going on in the system is more useful than just satisfying curiosity: by seeing what jobs are running, you can appropriately schedule your tasks. You can also see whether a process of yours is still active and whether it is behaving properly.

Finding Out Who Is On the System with *who*

The purpose of the who command is to find out who is logged on the system. The who command lists the login names, terminal lines, and login times of users currently logged in. The who command is useful in many situations. For example, if you want to communicate with someone on the computer using the write command, find out whether that person is on the system by using who. You can also use the command to see when certain users are logged in to the computer to keep track of their time spent on the system.

Using *who* To List Users Logged in to the System

To see everyone who is currently logged in to the system, enter who; you see a display similar to the following:

```
$ who <Return>
root          console      Dec 13 08:00
ernie         tty02        Dec 13 10:37
bkraft        tty03        Dec 13 11:02
jdurum        tty05        Dec 13 09:21
ernie         ttys7        Dec 11 18:49
$
```

This listing shows you that root, ernie, bkraft, and jdurum are currently logged in. It shows that root logged in 8:00 AM, bkraft at 11:02, and jdurum at 9:21. You can also see that ernie is logged in to two terminals and that one login occurred at 6:49 PM (18:49) two days earlier (which may be some reason for concern or it may just be ernie's usual work habits).

Using Headers in User Listings

There are several options available with who, but this chapter describes how to use only two to monitor processes on the system:

-u   Lists only *users* who are currently logged in

-H   Displays *headers* above each column

These options enable you to get more information about the users currently logged in. The headers displayed with the -H option are NAME, LINE, TIME, IDLE, PID, and COMMENTS. Table 11.4 explains the terms appearing in the heading.

Table 11.4: Output Format for the *who* Command	
Field	**Description**
NAME	Lists the user's login name.
LINE	Lists the line or terminal being used.

Field	Description
TIME	Lists the time the user logged in.
IDLE	Lists the hours and minutes since the last activity on that line. A period (.) is displayed if activity occurred within the last minute of system time. If more than 24 hours elapsed since the line was used, the word old is displayed.
PID	Lists the process ID number of the user's login shell.
COMMENT	Lists the contents of the comment field if comments have been included in /etc/inittab or if there are network connections. (See the following note.)

Note

You probably won't see the COMMENT field filled in very often in any recent UNIX systems. In the old days, processes that let you log in to UNIX (getty or uugetty) were started directly from entries in the /etc/inittab file and usually listened for login requests from a particular terminal. The COMMENT field might identify the location of the terminal and tell you who was logged in and what terminal they were sitting at. Today, processes that listen for login requests are typically handled by the Service Access Facility and are no longer listed in /etc/inittab.

The following example uses both the -u and -H options and shows the response UNIX returns:

```
$ who -uH <Return>
NAME      LINE       TIME         IDLE   PID    COMMENTS
root      console  Dec 13 08:00    .     10340
ernie     tty02    Dec 13 10:37    .     11929  Tech-89.2
bkraft    tty03    Dec 13 11:02   0:04    4761  Sales-23.4
jdurum    tty05    Dec 13 09:21   1:07   10426
ernie     ttys7    Dec 11 18:49   old    10770  oreo.coolt.com
$
```

You can infer from this listing that the last session associated with ernie is from a network site named oreo.coolt.com and that there hasn't been any activity in that session in over 24 hours (which could signal a problem). The session for root and the first one for ernie have both been accessed within the last minute. The last activity on the session for bkraft was four minutes ago; it has been one hour and seven minutes since any activity was reported on the session for jdurum. Also note that this listing includes the PID (process ID number) for the login shell of each user's session. The next section shows how you can use the PID to further monitor the system.

Reporting on the Status of Processes with *ps*

The command ps reports on the status of processes. You can use it to determine which processes are running, see whether a process has completed, see whether a process is "hung" or having some difficulty, see how long a process has run, see the resources a process is using, determine the relative priority of a process, and find the PID (process ID number) needed before you can kill a process. All this information is useful to a user and very useful to a system administrator. Without any options, ps lists the PID of each process associated with your current shell. It is also possible to see a detailed listing of all the processes running on a system.

Monitoring Processes with *ps*

A common use of the ps command is to monitor background jobs and other processes on the system. Because background processes don't communicate with your screen and keyboard in most cases, you use the ps command to track their progress.

The ps listing displays four default headings as indicators of the information in the fields below each heading: PID, TTY, TIME, and COMMAND. Table 11.5 explains these headings.

Table 11.5: Headings in the Output of *ps*	
Field	**Explanation**
PID	The process identification number.
TTY	The terminal on which the process originated.
TIME	The cumulative execution time for the process in minutes and seconds.
COMMAND	The name of the command being executed.

Suppose that you want to sort a file named sales.dat, save a copy of the sorted file in a file named sales.srt, and mail the sorted file to a user named sarah. If you also want to put this job in the background, you enter the following command:

```
sort sales.dat ¦ tee sales.srt ¦ mailx -s"Sorted Sales Data" sarah &
```

To monitor this process, enter **ps** and see a display such as this one:

```
    PID TTY     TIME COMMAND
  16490 tty02   0:15 sort
```

```
16489 tty02    0:00 mailx
16492 tty02    0:00 ps
16478 tty02    0:00 sh
16491 tty02    0:06 tee
16480 tty02   96:45 cruncher
```

You see the accumulated time and PID for each of the processes started with
the command. You also see information for your login shell, sh, and for ps
itself. Notice that all the commands in the pipe are running at once—as you
would expect (this is the way the pipe mechanism works). The last entry is for
a command that has been running for over one hour and a half. If that is a
problem, you may want to terminate the process by using the kill command, described later in this chapter. If you enter **ps** and see only the
following listing, you know the previous job you put into the background is
complete:

```
PID    TTY     TIME COMMAND
16492 tty02    0:00 ps
16478 tty02    0:00 sh
16480 tty02   99:45 cruncher
```

> **Note**
>
> Use ps occasionally to check on the status of a command. However, if you use ps
> every second, waiting to see whether the background job is complete, there isn't
> much sense putting the job in the background in the first place.

Obtaining More Information about Processes with *ps*

Sometimes, you need to know more about your processes than what the default ps listing provides. To generate additional information, you can invoke
some of the options listed in table 11.6.

Table 11.6: Commonly Used Options for the *ps* Command	
Option	**Action**
-e	Shows information about all processes, not just the ones started from your terminal.
-f	Displays a *full* listing.
-l	Displays a *long* listing.
-t *tlist*	Restricts the listing to data about the time processes associated with the terminals specified in *tlist*.

The ps command gives only an approximate picture of process status because things can and do change while the ps command is running. The ps command gives a snapshot of the process status at the instant the ps command executed. The snapshot includes the ps command itself.

In the following examples, three commands are shown. The first command is the login shell (sh). The second command is sort (used to sort the file named inventory). The third command is the ps command you are currently running.

To find out what processes you are currently running, use the following command:

```
$ ps <Return>
PID   TTY     TIME      COMMAND
65    tty01   0:07      -sh
71    tty01   0:14      sort inventory
231   tty01   0:09      ps
```

To obtain a full listing, use the following command:

```
$ ps -f <Return>
UID      PID   PPID  C   STIME      TTY     TIME   COMD
amanda   65    1     0   11:40:11   tty01   0:06   -sh
amanda   71    65    61  11:42:01   tty01   0:14   sort inventory
amanda   231   65    80  11:46:02   tty01   0:00   ps -f
```

There are a few things to note about this full listing. In addition to the PID, the PPID is listed. The PPID is the process ID number of that process's *parent* process. In this example, the first process listed (PID 65) is the parent of the following two. The entry in the fourth column (the column headed C) gives the amount of CPU resources a process has used recently. In selecting the next process to work with, the operating system chooses a process with a low C value over one with a higher value. The entry in the STIME column is the time at which the process started.

To monitor every process on the system and get a full listing, enter **ps -ef**. (By piping the command through the grep $LOGNAME command, the processes belonging to your login name are displayed while all others are filtered out.) To see a full listing of all your processes, enter this command:

```
ps -ef ¦ grep $LOGNAME
```

To list processes for two terminals (for example, tty01 and tty02), use the following command:

```
$ ps -t "01 02" <Return>
PID   TTY     TIME    COMMAND
32    tty01   0:05    sh
36    tty02   0:09    sh
235   tty02   0:16    vi calendar
```

In this example, the -t option is used to restrict the listing to the processes associated with terminals tty01 and tty02. Terminal tty02 is running the shell command (PID 32) and using vi to edit the calendar (PID 235). The cumulative time for each process is also listed. If you are using shells from a graphical interface (the xterm command or a Terminal window), use device names pts001, pts002, and so on with the -t option to see the processes from those sessions.

Sometimes a process is marked as <defunct>. This means that the process has terminated and its parent process has been notified, but the parent hasn't acknowledged the fact that the process is "dead." A process like that is called a *zombie process*. It is possible that the parent is busy with something else and the zombie will soon disappear. If you see a number of defunct processes or defunct processes that linger for some time, this is a sign of some difficulty with the operating system.

Controlling Multiple Processes

UNIX gives you the power to run several processes concurrently. It also allows a user or an administrator to have control over running processes. This control is advantageous when you need to do the following:

- Initiate a process that continues after its parent has quit running (use the nohup command)

- Schedule a process with a priority different than other processes (use the nice command)

- Terminate or stop a process (use the kill command)

Using *nohup* with Background Processes

Normally, the children of a process terminate when the parent dies or terminates. This means that when you start a background process, it terminates when you log out. To have a process continue after you log out, use the nohup command. Put nohup at the beginning of a command line:

```
nohup sort sales.dat &
```

This sample command tells the sort command to ignore the fact that you log off the system; it should run until the process completes. In this way, you can initiate a process that can run for days or even weeks. Furthermore, you don't have to be logged in as it runs. Naturally, you want to be sure that the job you initiate behaves nicely (that is, that it eventually terminates and doesn't create an inordinate amount of output).

When you use nohup, the command sends all the output and error messages of a command that normally appear on the screen to a file named nohup.out. Consider the following example:

```
$ nohup sort sales.dat & <Return>
1252
Sending output to nohup.out
$
```

The sorted file *and* any error messages are placed in the file nohup.out. Now consider this example:

```
$ nohup sort sales.dat > sales.srt & <Return>
1257
Sending output to nohup.out
$
```

Any error messages are placed in the file nohup.out but the sorted sales.dat file is placed in sales.srt.

When you use nohup with a pipeline, you must use nohup with each command in the pipeline:

```
nohup sort sales.dat ¦ nohup mailx -s"Sorted Sales Data" boss &
```

Scheduling the Priority of Commands with *nice*

Use the nice command to run a command at a specific scheduling priority. The nice command gives you some control over the priority of one job over another. If you don't use nice, processes run at a set priority. You can lower the priority of a process with the nice command so that other processes can be scheduled to use the CPU more frequently than the nice job. The superuser (the person who can log in as the root user) can also raise the priority of a process.

The general form of the nice command is as follows:

```
nice -number command
```

The priority level is determined by the *number* argument (a higher number means a lower priority). The default is set to 10. If the *number* argument is present, the priority is incremented by that amount up to a limit of 20. If you enter this command, the sort process starts with a priority of 10:

```
sort sales.dat > sales.srt &
```

If you want to start another process, say with the lp command, but give preference to the sort command, you can enter the following:

```
nice -5 lp mail_list &
```

To give the `lp` command the lowest possible priority, use this command:

```
nice -10 lp mail_list &
```

Only the system administrator can increase the priority of a process. To do that, the system administrator (or someone logged in as the root user) uses a negative number as the argument to `nice`. Remember: the lower the `nice` value, the higher the priority (up to a maximum priority of 20). To give a job "top priority," the superuser initiates the job as follows:

```
nice --19 job &
```

The ampersand (&) is optional; if *job* is interactive, the system administrator wouldn't use the ampersand.

Scheduling the Priority of Running Processes with *renice*

The `renice` command is available on some systems; it allows you to modify the priority of a running process. Berkeley UNIX systems have the `renice` command; it is also available in the /usr/ucb directory in UNIX System V systems for compatibility with Berkeley systems. With `renice`, you can adjust priorities on commands as they execute. The format of `renice` is similar to that of `nice`:

```
renice -number PID
```

To change the priority on a running process, you must know its PID. To find the PID of all your processes, enter this command:

```
ps -ef ¦ grep name
```

In this command, *name* is replaced by the name of the running process. The `grep` command filters out all processes that don't contain the name of the process you are looking for. (If there are several processes of that name running, you have to determine the one you want by looking at the time it started.)

The entry in the second column of the `ps` listing is the PID of the process. In the following example, there are three processes running for the current user (in addition to the shell). The current user's name is `pcoco`.

```
$ ps -ef ¦ grep $LOGNAME <Return>
  pcoco 11805 11804   0 Dec 22    ttysb    0:01 sort sales.dat >sales.srt
  pcoco 19955 19938   4 16:13:02 ttyp0    0:00 grep pcoco
  pcoco 19938     1   0 16:11:04 ttyp0    0:00 sh
  pcoco 19940 19938 142 16:11:04 ttyp0    0:33 find . -name core -exec rm {} ;
$
```

To lower the priority on the process with PID 19940 (the find process), enter this command:

```
renice -5 19940
```

As you would expect, the following are true about renice:

- You can use renice only with processes you own

- The system administrator can use renice on any process

- Only the system administrator can increase the priority of a process

---

Caution

This caution is for the system administrator: Change priorities only on jobs you have created. Don't modify priorities on system programs unless you know what you are doing.

Terminating Processes with *kill*

Sometimes, you want or need to terminate a process. Here are some reasons for stopping a process:

- It is using too much CPU time

- It is running too long without producing expected output

- It is producing too much output, either to the screen or to a disk file

- It appears to have locked a terminal or some other session

- It is using the wrong files for input or output because of an operator or programming error

- It is no longer useful

Most likely, you will come across a number of other reasons as well. If the process to be stopped is a background process, you use the kill command to get out of these situations.

To stop a command that is not in the background, press an interrupt key such as <Del>, <Break>, <Ctrl-c>, or <Ctrl-d>, depending on the type of shell you are using. When a command is in the background, pressing an interrupt key does not stop it. Because a background process is not under terminal control, keyboard input of any interrupt key is ignored. The only way you can stop background commands is to use the kill command.

Normal Termination of Background Processes

The `kill` command sends signals to the program to demand that a process be terminated or killed. To use `kill`, use either of these two forms:

```
kill PID(s)

kill -signal PID(s)
```

To kill a process whose PID is 123, enter **kill 123**. To kill several processes whose PIDs are 123, 342, and 73, enter **kill 123 342 73**. Using a *signal* option, you can do more than simply kill a process. Other signals can cause a running process to reread configuration files or stop a process without killing it. Valid signals are listed in the `/usr/include/sys/signal.h` file. As an average user, however, you will probably use `kill` with no signal or, at most, with the -9 signal (the I-mean-it-so-don't-ignore-me signal, described in the next section).

> ### Caution
>
> Use the correct PID with the `kill` command. Using the wrong PID can stop a process you want to keep running. If you are the system administrator, you can kill *any* process; remember that killing the wrong process or a system process can have disastrous effects.

If you successfully kill the process, you get no notice from the shell: the shell prompt simply reappears. You see an error message if you try to kill a process you don't have permission to kill or if you try to kill a process that doesn't exist.

Suppose that your login name is `chris` and that you are currently logged in to `tty01`. To see the processes you have running, enter **ps -f** and see the following response:

```
UID     PID   PPID  C    STIME      TTY     TIME   COMMAND
chris    65    1     0    11:40:11   tty01   0:06   -sh
chris    71    65    61   11:42:01   tty01   0:14   total_updt inventory
chris    231   65    80   11:46:02   tty01   0:00   ps -f
chris    187   53    60   15:32:01   tty02  123:45  crunch stats
chris    53    1     0    15:31:34   tty02   1:06   -sh
```

Notice that the program `total_updt` is running at your current terminal. Another program, `crunch`, is running on another terminal and you think that it has used an unusually large amount of CPU time. To kill that process, it may be sufficient to enter this simple command:

```
kill 187
```

To kill the parent of that process, enter this command:

```
kill 53
```

You may want to kill a parent and its child if you are the system administrator and see that someone left their terminal unattended. You can kill a clock process that the user has running (the child process) and the login shell (the parent process) so that the unattended terminal is no longer logged in.

Stopping the parent of a process sometimes terminates the child process as well. To be sure, stop the parent *and* its children to halt all activity associated with a parent process. In the preceding example, enter **kill 187 53** to terminate both processes.

> **Tip**
>
> If, for some reason, your terminal "locks up," log in to another terminal, enter **ps -ef ¦ grep $LOGNAME**, and kill the login shell for the locked terminal.

Unconditional Termination of Background Processes

Issuing the `kill` command sends a *signal* to a process. UNIX programs can send or receive over 20 signals, each of which is represented by a number. For example, when you log out, UNIX sends the hangup signal, signal number 1, to all the background processes started from your login shell. This signal kills or stops those processes *unless* they were started with nohup (as described earlier in this chapter). Using nohup to start a background process lets the process ignore the signal that tries to stop it. You may be using programs or shell scripts written to ignore some signals. If you don't specify a signal when you use `kill`, signal 15 is sent to the process. The command `kill 1234` sends signal 15 to the process whose PID is 1234. If that process is set to ignore signal 15, however, the process doesn't terminate when you use this command. However, you can use `kill` in a way a process "can't refuse."

The signal 9 is an unconditional kill signal; it *always* kills a process. To unconditionally kill a process, use the following format:

```
kill -9 PID
```

For example, suppose that you enter **ps -f** and see the following response listing:

```
UID     PID   PPID  C   STIME      TTY     TIME    COMMAND
chris   65    1     0   11:40:11   tty01   0:06    -sh
chris   71    65    61  11:42:01   tty01   0:14    total_updt inventory
chris   231   65    80  11:46:02   tty01   0:00    ps -f
chris   187   53    60  15:32:01   tty02   123:45  crunch stats
chris   53    1     0   15:31:34   tty02   1:06    -sh
```

To kill process 187, you normally enter **kill 187**. If you then enter **ps -f** again and see that the process is still there, you know the process is set up to ignore the kill command. Kill it unconditionally with **kill -9 187**. When you enter **ps -f** again, you see that the process is no longer around.

A disadvantage to using this version of the kill command is that kill -9 does not allow a process to finish what it is doing before it terminates. If you use kill -9 with a program that is updating a file, you loose the updated material. Use the powerful kill -9 command responsibly. In most cases, you do not need the -9 option; the kill command issued without arguments stops most processes.

Terminating All Background Processes

To kill all background jobs, use the following command:

```
kill 0
```

Commands that run in the background sometimes initiate more than one process; tracking down all the PID numbers associated with the process you want to kill can be tedious. Because the kill 0 command terminates *all* processes started by the current shell, it is a faster and less tedious means of terminating processes. Type the jobs command to see what commands are running in the background for the current shell.

Managing Processes in the GUI

There are graphical equivalents to many of the command-line tools for managing processes if you are using the UnixWare Graphical User Interface (GUI). The Task Scheduler window, described in Chapter 6, "Using the UNIX Command Environment," lets you set up processes that the cron program runs at designated times. If you use a GUI, you can always open a Terminal window and run any of the commands described in this chapter from there.

One convenient feature of the GUI for starting processes is the Startup Items folder. This feature lets you designate certain commands to start automatically when you log in to the system and start the GUI. Here's how it works:

1. Double-click on the Preferences icon in the UnixWare Desktop folder. The Preferences window appears, including the Startup Items folder icon.

2. Open the folder containing the command you want to run each time you log in. For example, to open a Terminal window each time you log in (a handy thing to do), open the Accessories folder.

3. Drag-and-drop the icon representing the command on the Startup Items folder.

4. To see that the command is set up to start when you log in, double-click on the Startup Items folder. The Startup Items folder opens. Figure 11.1 shows a Startup Items folder that contains two commands that will start automatically when you log in: the screen lock and a Terminal window (a shell).

Fig. 11.1
Opening the Startup Items window.

After you complete these steps, the next time you log in, a Terminal window opens and the screen-lock program starts up and locks the screen as appropriate.

Summary

This chapter presented the commands you need to manage multiple processes. You saw that you run multiple processes whenever you put jobs in the background with the ampersand (&) or when you use pipes. You can schedule jobs at a specific time with the command at, at a time the system feels is appropriate with the command batch, and at regularly scheduled times with cron and crontab.

You looked at how to monitor your own and other user's processes with the who command; you learned how to get useful information about your processes with the ps and ps -f commands and how to get the same information about all processes on the system with the ps -ef command. You also learned how to modify the priority of a process by using nice before the command starts or renice after it is running.

Background processes are usually terminated when you log out, but you can set them up to continue after you log out if you put nohup on the line before the name of the command. Finally, you looked at the kill command, which allows you to terminate running processes.

There are graphical means of managing processes, as well as command-line methods. In addition to the Task Scheduler (the GUI version of the cron program), the Startup Items folder lets you start up specific processes each time you log in.

The next chapter describes effective use of the text editor vi to create and modify text files. It also includes a summary of other popular text editors.

IV

UNIX Tools

Chapter 12

Using the *vi* Editor

In previous chapters, you have seen how convenient and advantageous it is to have sequences of commands or shell programs stored in a file. You probably have the need to create data, e-mail, lists, memos, notes, reports, and so on; you use some type of text editor to do these tasks. You may have several editors or word processors available on your UNIX system to help you with those tasks. In order to put commands or shell programs in a file, however, you need an editor that can save your work in a *text file*—a file in ASCII format. UNIX comes with a standard text editor called vi that you can use for all but the most complex writing and editing projects.

Your UNIX system may have other text editors; UnixWare offers the graphical Text Editor. Two standard, non-graphical text editors are ed and ex, both line-oriented editors. When you use them, you work with only one line at a time. On the other hand, vi and Text Editor are full-screen editors; when you use them, you see a screen's worth of information so that you can make changes or additions in context. This chapter doesn't discuss ed or ex very much because you'll find vi easier to use.

You may have other text editors available on your system. Two popular ones are emacs and pico. The chapter closes with a survey of some popular text editors.

In this chapter, you learn the following:

- Basic vi commands

- How to create new files and modify existing files

- How to set the vi environment

- What other editors are available

Introducing *vi*

UNIX was developed in an environment in which the user's terminal was a teletype or some other slow, hard-copy terminal; video display monitors generally were not used. A natural editor for that environment was a *line-oriented editor*—one with which the user sees and works on one line of text at a time. Two line-oriented editors are on UNIX systems today: ed and ex.

In its early days, UNIX was made available to universities essentially free. Students and faculty at several universities made many contributions to the UNIX working environment. Several notable improvements came out of the University of California at Berkeley. One of these was a *full-screen editor*—one that lets you work with a screenful of information at once rather than a single line. That full-screen editor is called vi (pronounced *vee eye*), which stands for *visual*. The time was right for the transition to screen-oriented work. Users were working with video terminals rather than hard-copy devices.

Unless you're running UnixWare on a PC, you are most likely working on a terminal or X-terminal (a terminal capable of displaying graphics). With a PC running UnixWare or an X-terminal, you may be working in one of several *windows*; you've probably also had some experience using a word processor. Naturally, you expect some sort of full-screen editor. Although vi may not be the perfect editor, you will find it may be the most expedient tool to use in many situations.

> **Note**
>
> This chapter doesn't cover all the features of vi—that would take more space than is available! In fact, there are entire books written just on vi. Instead, you learn the commands to do most necessary editing tasks. If you want to know about the more advanced features of vi and advanced text-editing operations, consult the Reference Manual supplied with your system. You don't have to become a vi expert to use it.

What is *vi*?

The vi editor is probably the most popular, full-screen UNIX text editor (there are even versions available for DOS). Because it is part of the standard UNIX environment, it has been learned and used (to one degree or another) by millions of UNIX users. You find that it starts quickly and can be used for both simple and complex tasks. As you would expect, you use it to enter, modify, or delete text; search or replace text; and copy, cut, and paste blocks of text. You also see that it can be customized to match your needs. You can move the cursor to any position on the screen and move through the file you're editing. You use the same methods with any text file, regardless of its contents. All the files vi produces and all the files UNIX commands work with are ASCII or text files.

The vi editor is not a word processor or desktop publishing system. There aren't any menus and virtually no help facilities. Word processing systems usually offer screen and hard-copy formatting and printing such as representing text as **bold**, *italic*, or underlined—vi doesn't. Other UNIX commands can perform some of these functions (for example, lp can print and nroff can format text). In addition, you may have access to a word processor on your system.

The vi editor operates in two modes. In *command mode*, your keystrokes are interpreted as commands to vi. Some of the commands you use allow you to save a file, exit vi, move the cursor to different positions in a file, and modify, rearrange, delete, substitute, and search for text. In *input* or *text-entry mode*, your keystrokes are accepted as the text of the file you are editing. When vi is in input or text-entry mode, the editor acts as a typewriter. In an editing session, you can freely switch between modes. You have to remember the mode you're using and know to change modes. Some people find this uncomfortable at first; there is a learning curve you must deal with. With a little practice, however, you'll find vi extremely convenient for editing UNIX ASCII files.

Understanding the Editing Process

You *edit* text by either creating new text or modifying existing text. When you create new text, you place the text in a file with an ordinary UNIX filename. When you modify existing text, you use the existing filename to call a copy of the file into the editing session. In either case, as you use the editor, the text is held in the system's memory in a storage area called a *buffer*. Using a buffer prevents you from directly changing the contents of a file until you decide to save the buffer. This is to your benefit if you decide you want to forget the changes you've made and start over.

As you make changes and additions to the text, these edits affect the text in the buffer—not in the file stored on disk. When you are satisfied with your edits, you issue a command to save the text. This command writes the changes to the file on the disk. Only then are the changes made permanent. You can save changes to disk as often as you like. You do not have to exit the editor when you save changes. This chapter shows you that there are several ways to exit the editor; some of those ways write the buffer to the text file on the disk.

The `vi` editor is said to be *interactive* because it interacts with you during the editing session. The editor communicates with you by displaying status messages, error messages, or sometimes nothing on the screen (in typical UNIX fashion). The last line on the screen, called the *status line*, holds the messages from UNIX. You also see the changes you make in the text on the screen.

You use the editor to modify, rearrange, delete, substitute, and search for text. You conduct these editing operations while using the editor in command mode. In several instances, a command is a single letter that corresponds to the first letter of an action's name. For example, `i` corresponds to the *insert* action and `r` is used when *replacing* a character.

Most commands operate on a single line or a range of lines of text. The lines are numbered from 1 (the top line) to the last line in the buffer. When you add or delete lines, the line numbers adjust automatically. A line's number is its *address* in the buffer. An *address range* is simply two addresses or line numbers separated by a comma. If you want to specify the range consisting of the third through the eighth line of the buffer, you use *3,8.*

The position of the *cursor* always indicates your current location in the editing buffer. Some of the commands you issue in command mode affect the character at the cursor position. Unless you move the cursor, changes take place at that position. Naturally, `vi` has several commands for moving the cursor through the edit buffer.

You know now that `vi` is a full-screen editor. You give `vi` commands to move the cursor to different positions in a file and you see the changes you make, as you make them. So `vi` has to be able to move to and modify the text on *your* terminal as well as on a host of other terminal types. It knows what terminal you are using and what its video capabilities are by checking the shell variable TERM. UNIX uses the TERM variable to determine your terminal's capabilities, such as underlining, reverse-video, screen-clearing method, function-key assignment, and color capability.

Troubleshooting

The `vi` *editor doesn't appear to be working correctly with your terminal or screen; you see "strange" characters.*

The TERM variable may not be set correctly. Another symptom of an improper terminal setup is that blocks of characters overwrite legible text. The $TERM expression gives the value of your current terminal setting. To check the value of TERM, enter **echo $TERM** and press <Return>. If you work at a terminal which is or emulates a vt100, this command should display the following result:

    vt100

If that isn't the case, set the value of TERM by entering the following commands:

```
TERM=vt100
export TERM
```

Your specific terminal type may be different than vt100; set TERM accordingly.

You start vi *but do not get the expected responses.*

Check to see whether your terminal is properly set up. Your terminal type is not the same as the name of your terminal; your terminal type must match one of the terminal types contained in the directory /usr/lib/terminfo. If you are not familiar with the terminfo directory, consult your system administrator.

Using *vi*

To start vi, you simply type its name at the shell prompt (command line). If you know the name of the file you want to create or edit, you can issue the vi command with the filename as an argument. For example, to create the file myfile with vi, enter **vi myfile**.

When vi becomes active, the terminal screen clears and a tilde character (~) appears on the left side of every screen line, except for the first. The ~ is the *empty-buffer* line flag. Following is a shortened version of what you should see on your screen (only five lines are listed to save space):

```
_
~
~
~
~
```

The cursor should be at the leftmost position of the first line (represented here as an underline). You will probably see 20 to 22 of the tilde characters at the left of the screen. If that's not the case, check the value of TERM (as described in the Troubleshooting box at the end of the preceding section) and perhaps talk with your system administrator.

When you see this display, you have successfully started vi; vi is in command mode, waiting for your first command.

Note

Unlike most word processing programs, vi starts in command mode. Before you start entering text, you must switch to input mode.

Looking at *vi*'s Two Modes

The vi editor operates in two modes: *command mode* and *input mode*. In command mode, vi interprets your keystrokes as commands; there are many vi commands. You can use commands to save a file, exit vi, move the cursor to various positions in a file, or modify, rearrange, delete, substitute, or search for text. If you enter a character as a command but the character is not a command, vi beeps. Don't worry; the beep is an audible indication for you to check what you are doing and correct any errors.

You can enter text in input mode (also called text-entry mode) by either *appending* after the cursor or *inserting* before the cursor. At the beginning of the line, this doesn't make much difference. To go from command mode to input mode, press one of the following keys:

              \<a>   To append text after the cursor
              \<i>   To insert text in front of the cursor

Use input mode only for entering text. Most word processing programs start in input mode, but vi doesn't. When you use a word processing program, you can type away, entering text; to issue a command, you have to use function keys or keys different than you use when typing normal text. vi doesn't work that way: you must go into input mode by pressing \<a> or \<i> before you start entering text and then explicitly press \<Esc> to return to command mode.

Creating Your First *vi* File

The best way to learn about vi is to use it. This section gives a step-by-step example of how to create a file using vi. In each step, you see an action to perform and then the necessary keystrokes. Don't be concerned with complete accuracy here. The example takes you through the motions and concepts of using vi to create a file, moving between command and input modes, and saving your results. If you run into difficulties, you can quit and start over by pressing \<Esc> one or two times; then type **:q!** and press \<Return>.

1. **Start** vi. Type **vi** and press \<Return>. You see the screen full of flush-left tildes.

2. **Go into input mode to place characters on the first line**. Press the \<a> key. *Do not press \<Return>*. Now you can append characters to the first line. You should *not* see the character a on the screen.

3. **Add lines of text to the buffer**. Type the following three lines, pressing \<Return> at the end of the first and second lines but not at the end of the third line:

```
Things to do today.
a. Practice vi.
b. Sort sales data and print the results.
```

You can use the <Backspace> key to correct mistakes on the line you are typing. Don't worry about being precise here: this example is for practice. You learn other ways to make changes in some of the later sections of this chapter.

4. **Go from input mode to command mode**. Press the <Esc> key. You can press <Esc> more than once without changing modes. You hear a *beep* from your system if you press <Esc> when you are already in command mode.

5. **Save your buffer in a file called** `vipract.1`. Type `:w vipract.1` and press <Return>. The characters `:w vipract.1` appear on the bottom line of the screen (the *status line*). The characters should *not* appear in the text. The `:w` command writes the buffer to the specified file. This command *saves* or *writes* the buffer to the file `vipract.1`.

6. **See your action confirmed on the status line**. You should see the following on the status line:

```
"vipract.1" [New File] 3 lines, 78 characters
```

This statement confirms that the file `vipract.1` has been created, is a new file, contains 3 lines and 78 characters. Your display may be different if you didn't type the information exactly as specified.

7. **Exit `vi`**. Type `:q` and press <Return>.

When you type `:q`, you are still in command mode and see these characters on the status line. When you press <Return>, however, `vi` terminates and you return to the login shell prompt.

Here is a synopsis of the steps you followed:

1.	Start `vi`	Type **`vi`** and press <Return>
2.	Go to input mode	Press <a>
3.	Enter the text	Type the text into the buffer
4.	Go to command mode	Press <Esc>
5.	Save buffer to file	Type `:w` *`filename`* and press <Return>
6.	Quit `vi`	Type `:q` and press <Return>

You use these steps, or variations of them, for all your editing tasks. Be sure that you can work through them before continuing.

Things To Remember about *vi*

- vi starts in command mode.

- To move from command mode to input mode, press either <a> (to append text) or <i> (to insert text).

- You add text when you are input mode.

- You give commands to vi only when you are in command mode.

- To move from input mode to command mode, press <Esc>.

- You give commands to vi to save a file and can quit only when you are in command mode.

Starting *vi* Using an Existing File

To edit or look at a file that already exists in your current directory, type **vi** followed by the filename and press <Return>. Try this with the file you created in the preceding section by entering the following command:

```
vi vipract.1
```

You see the following display (the number of lines shown here are fewer than you see on your screen):

```
Things to do today.
a. Practice vi.
b. Sort sales data and print the results.
~
~
~
"vipract.1" 3 lines, 78 characters
```

As before, tilde (~) characters appear on the far left of empty lines in the buffer. Look at the status line: it contains the name of the file you are editing and the number of lines and characters.

Troubleshooting

You type a filename that you know exists but vi *acts as if you are creating a new file.*

Not everyone is a perfect typist and you may possibly type the name of a file that doesn't exist in your current directory. Suppose that you type **vi vipract1.** and press <Return> but there is no file named vipract1. in your current directory. You still start vi, but vi acts as though you were creating a new file.

You try to edit a file but vi *displays a message about read permission denied and you see the shell prompt again.*

You have tried to edit a file you are not permitted to read. In addition, you can't edit a directory; that is, if you type **vi directory_name**, where **directory_name** is the name of a directory, vi informs you that you opened a directory and does not let you edit it. If you try to use vi with a file that is an executable program in binary, as opposed to ASCII, you'll see a screen full of strange (control) characters. It won't be something you can read and edit. vi expects files to be stored as lines.

You open a file in vi *but you see a message about line too long.*

You are trying to use vi on a data file that is just one long string of bytes.

You open a file in vi *but you some very strange characters on the screen.*

You may be using vi with a file produced by a word processor.

In all these cases, exit vi to return to your login shell prompt by pressing <Esc> to go to command mode and then typing **:q!** and pressing <Return>. *Using* **:q!** *ensures that you quit* vi *and make no changes to the existing file.*

Exiting *vi*

You can exit or quit vi in several ways. Remember that you must be in command mode to quit vi. To change to command mode, press <Esc>. (If you are already in command mode when you press <Esc>, you hear a harmless *beep* from the terminal.) Table 12.1 lists the commands you can use to exit vi.

Table 12.1: Ways To Quit or Exit *vi*

Command	Action
:q	Exit after making no changes to the buffer or exit after the buffer has been modified and saved to a file.
:q!	Exit and abandon all changes to the buffer since it was last saved to a file.
:wq	Write buffer to the working file and then exit.
:x	Same as :wq.
ZZ	Same as :wq.

As shown in the table, several keystrokes accomplish the same end. To demonstrate, use vi to edit the file vipract.1 created earlier in this chapter. To edit the file, type **vi vipract.1** and press <Return>. You see a display similar to this:

```
Things to do today.
a. Practice vi.
b. Sort sales data and print the results.
~
~
~
"vipract.1" 3 lines, 78 characters
```

The cursor is indicated by an underline character; when you first open the file, it is under the first character of the file, the *T* of *Things*. Because you haven't made any changes to the file since you opened it, you can exit by typing **:q** and pressing <Return>. You see the shell prompt. You can also type **:wq** to exit the file; if you do so, you see the following message before the shell prompt reappears:

```
"vipract.1" 3 lines, 78 characters
```

This message appears because vi first writes the buffer to the file vipract.1 and then exits.

Start vi again with the same file (type **vi vipract.1** and press <Return>). You see a display similar to this:

```
Things to do today.
a. Practice vi.
b. Sort sales data and print the results.
~
~
~
"vipract.1" 3 lines, 78 characters
```

Although vi starts you off in command mode, just to be sure, press <Esc>. Now press the <spacebar> enough times so that the cursor moves under the period following *today* in the first line. To replace that character with an exclamation mark, press <r> (for *replace*) and type an exclamation mark (**!**). The first line should now look like this:

```
Things to do today!
```

Because you have changed the buffer, vi won't let you exit unless you save the changes or explicitly give a command to quit without saving the changes. If you try to exit vi by typing **:q**, vi displays this message to remind you that you haven't written the file to disk since you changed it:

```
No write since last change (:quit! overrides)
```

To abandon the changes you have made to the file, quit by typing **:q!**. To save the changes, quit by typing **:wq** or any of the other equivalent forms (**ZZ** or **:x**).

> **Tip**
>
> vi doesn't keep backup copies of files. Once you type **:wq** and press <Return>, the original file is modified and can't be restored to its original state. You must make your own backup copies of vi files.

> **Caution**
>
> Use the :q! command sparingly. When you enter **:q!**, all the changes you have made to the file are lost.

Undoing a Command

In vi, you can "undo" your most recent action or change to the buffer—as long as you haven't saved that change to the disk file. You do this from command mode: press <u> (the lowercase letter) to undo the most recent change you made to the file. Suppose that you have inadvertently deleted a line of text, changed something you shouldn't have, or added some text incorrectly. Press <Esc> to change to command mode and then press <u>; things are back the way they were before the command that changed the buffer. Just remember that the undo command can undo only the latest action. Also, you can't use the undo command to undo writing something to a file.

Here is an example to demonstrate the use of the undo command. Start vi again with the file vipract.1: type **vi vipract.1** and press <Return>. You see a display similar to this:

```
Things to do today!
a. Practice vi.
b. Sort sales data and print the results.
~
~
~
"vipract.1" 3 lines, 78 characters
```

To add the phrase *for 60 minutes* between *vi* and the period on the second line, move to the second line by pressing <Return>. The cursor now appears under the first character of the second line. Now move the cursor to the period (.) after the *i* in *vi* by pressing the <spacebar> until the cursor moves to that location. Insert the phrase *for 60 minutes* by pressing <i> (the lowercase letter) to give the input command and then typing the characters of the phrase. Press <Esc> to return to command mode. Your screen should look like this:

```
Things to do today!
a. Practice vi for 60 minutes.
b. Sort sales data and print the results.
~
~
~
```

Is 60 minutes a good idea? Maybe not. To undo the change to the second line, make sure that you're in command mode (press <Esc>) and then press <u>. The second line of the file now looks like this:

```
a. Practice vi.
```

Then again, maybe it *was* a good idea to practice for 60 minutes. Press <u> again (you're already in command mode) and you see the phrase *for 60 minutes* reappear. Will you or won't you practice for that long? You decide. Use the undo command to undo the change (and undo the undo) as many times as you want. Even if you decide to leave the buffer in its original form, vi assumes that the buffer has changed and you must exit with either **:q!** (abandon changes) or **:wq** (save the changes).

If you decide to save the file with the changes, save it to another file. Enter **:w vipract.2** and press <Return>.

You can use the <Backspace> key to correct mistakes you make while typing a single line. Unfortunately, as you backspace, you erase all the characters you go back over.

Writing Files and Saving the Buffer

You have seen how to write the buffer to a file and quit vi. Sometimes, however, you want to save the buffer to a file without quitting vi. You should save the file regularly during an editing session. If the system goes down because of a crash or a power failure, you may lose your work if you haven't saved it recently. To save the buffer, issue the :w command from command mode. There are some variations to the steps you follow to save a file. The form of the write command you use depends on the case—of which there are four distinct ones. The following sections describe these cases; table 12.2 lists the variations of the write command.

Before you issue the write command, first press <Esc> to make sure that you are in command mode, if you are not already there. If you are already in command mode, you hear a harmless *beep*.

IV

UNIX Tools

Table 12:2: Commands To Save or Write a File	
Command	**Action**
:w	Write buffer to the file vi is editing.
:w filename	Write buffer to the named file.
:w! filename	Force vi to overwrite the existing file.

Saving a New File

If you started vi without specifying a filename, you must provide a filename if you want to save the file to disk. The write command you issue in this case has the following format:

```
:w filename
```

This command writes the buffer to the file *filename*. If the command was successful, you see the name of the file and the number of lines and characters in the file. If you specify the name of an existing file, an appropriate message appears on the status line:

```
File exits - use "w! filename" to overwrite.
```

This condition is described in "Overwriting an Existing File," later in this chapter.

Saving to the Current File

You may want to save the buffer to the file you are currently editing. For example, if you started vi with an existing file, made some changes to the file, and want to save the changes to the original file, you can simply enter this form of the write command:

```
:w
```

This command saves the buffer to the file you are currently working with (your *working file*). The status line tells you the name of the file and the number of lines and characters written to the file.

Tip

Save the changes you are making to a file regularly. Use the :w command frequently, at least every 15 minutes, during an edit session. You never know when the system might go down.

Saving as a New File

You may want to save the buffer to a new file—a file different than the one you originally started with. For example, if you started vi with the file vipract.1, made some changes to the file, and want to save the changes to a new file without losing the original vipract.1 file, you can save the file as a new file. Type this form of the write command to save the file with a new filename:

```
:w new_file
```

This form of the write command is essentially the same as the original form described in "Saving a New File," earlier in this chapter. The buffer is written to the file named *new_file*. If the command was successful, you see the name of the file and the number of lines and characters in the file. If you specify the name of an existing file, an appropriate message appears on the status line:

```
File exists - use "w! new_file" to overwrite.
```

The following section explains this scenario.

Overwriting an Existing File

If you try to save the buffer to an existing file different than the one you started with, you must explicitly indicate to vi that you want to overwrite or replace the existing file. If you specify an existing filename when you try to save the buffer, vi displays the following message:

```
File exists - use "w! new_file" to overwrite.
```

If you really want to save the buffer over the existing file, use this form of the write command:

```
:w! existing_file
```

In this syntax, *existing_file* is the name of the file you want to replace. Be careful: once you overwrite a file, you can't automatically bring it back to its original form.

Positioning the Cursor

When you edit text, you need to position the cursor where you want to insert additional text, delete text, correct mistakes, change words, or append text to the end of existing text. The commands you enter in command mode to select the spot you want are called *cursor-positioning commands*.

The Arrow Keys

You can use the arrow keys on many, but not all, systems to position the cursor. It's easy to see whether the arrow keys work: Start *vi* with an existing file and see what effects the arrow keys have. You may also be able to use the <Page Up> and <Page Down> keys.

> **Note**
>
> If you're running UnixWare on a PC, you can always use the arrow, <Page Up>, and <Page Down> keys to position the cursor.

Enter the following command to create a new file called vipract.3 that contains a list of the files and directories in the directory usr. You can use this file to experiment with cursor-positioning commands.

```
ls /usr > vipract.3
```

Once the file is created, start *vi* with the vipract.3 file (type **vi vipract.3** and press <Return>). Now try using the arrow keys and the <Page Up> and <Page Down> keys (if they are on your keyboard) to move around the editing buffer. If the keys appear to work well, you may want to use those keys for cursor positioning.

It may be the case that, although it appears that the cursor-positioning keys work, they are introducing strange characters into the file. To check whether the keys are entering characters instead of just moving the cursor, press <Esc> to be sure that you are in command mode and then enter **:q**. If *vi* allows you to quit and doesn't complain that the file was modified, everything is fine.

Here is one more check to see whether the cursor-positioning keys work. Start *vi* with the vipract.3 file. When the file appears, use the arrow keys to move the cursor somewhere near the middle on the third line. Insert the word *testing* at that position: give the insert-text command (press <i>) and type **testing**. Then press <Esc> to go back to command mode, type **:wq**, and press <Return>. Now open the file in *vi* again to look at the file one more time (type **vi vipract.3** and press <Return>). If you see the word *testing* where you expected it to be, you'll probably want to use the arrow keys to position the cursor.

> **Tip**
>
> In *vi*, you can clear the screen of spurious or unusual characters by pressing <Ctrl-l> (the <Ctrl> key and the lowercase letter <l>).

Other Cursor-Movement Keys

There are other ways to position the cursor in vi without using the arrow keys. You should become familiar with these methods in case you can't or don't want to use the arrow keys. This section also shows you some ways to position the cursor more efficiently than using the arrow keys.

When vi was developed, many terminals did not have arrow keys. Other keys were and still are used to position the cursor. Figure 12.1 shows how the <h>, <j>, <k>, and <l> keys can position the cursor. Why those keys? They are in a convenient position for touch-typists.

Fig. 12.1
Keyboard cursor-movement keys are in a convenient location for touch-typists.

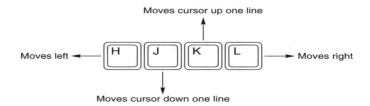

It takes a little practice to get comfortable with these keys, but some experienced vi users prefer these keys over the arrow keys.

Here are some other keys that move the cursor:

- Press the <spacebar> to move the cursor to the right one position.

- Press <Return> or <+> to move to the beginning of the next line. Note that using the <j> key to go down one line preserves your position in the line.

- Press the minus sign (<–>) to move to the beginning of the previous line. Note that using the <k> key to go up one line preserves your position in the line.

- Press <0> (zero) to move to the beginning of a line.

- Press <$> (the dollar sign) to move to the end of a line.

Some vi commands allow you to position the cursor relative to words on a line. A *word* is defined as a sequence of characters separated from other characters by spaces or usual punctuation symbols such as **.**, **?**, **,**, and **–**. These commands are given in table 12.3.

Command	Action
Table 12.3: Commands To Position the Cursor Relative to a Word	
w	Move forward one word.
b	Move to the beginning of the current word.
e	Move to the end of the current word.

The following example demonstrates some of these actions. Start vi and open the vipract.1 file by typing **vi vipract.1** and pressing <Return>. Now use any of the cursor-positioning commands just described to move the cursor, indicated by an underline character, to the *t* in the word *data* on the third line of the file. The third line looks like this:

```
    b. Sort sales data and print the results.
```

To move to the beginning of the next word, press <w>; the cursor is positioned under the *a* of the word *and*. To move to the end of that word, press <e>; the cursor is positioned under the *d* in *and*. To move to the beginning of that word, press <b>; the cursor is positioned under the *a* in *and* again.

You can move forward several words to the beginning of another word by typing a whole number before pressing <w>. For example, to move the cursor from its current position (under the *a* of the word *and*) to the beginning of the word three words forward (under the *r* of the word *results*), press <3><w>.

Likewise, you can move backwards four words by pressing <4><b>; you can move forward to the end of the second word by pressing <2><e>.

You can also use this whole-number technique with the keys <h>, <j>, <k>, <l>, <+>, and <–>. For example, press <1><5><j> to position the cursor down 15 lines. If there aren't 15 lines left in the buffer, you hear a *beep* and the cursor stays where it is.

Big-Movement Keys

You can quickly position the cursor to the top, middle, or bottom of the screen. In each case, the cursor appears at the beginning of the line.

■ Press <H> (<Shift-h>) to move to the first line of the screen. This is sometimes called the *home* position.

■ Press <M> (<Shift-m>) to move to the line in the middle of the lines currently displayed on the screen.

■ Press <L> (<Shift-l>) to move to the last line on the screen.

If you want to move through a file a screen at a time (which is more efficient than pressing <Return> or <j> 23 times), use commands that scroll through a file. The command <Ctrl-f> (press and hold the <Ctrl> key, press the <f> key, and then release both keys) moves you forward one screen. Table 12.4 uses the caret character (^) to indicate the Ctrl key.

Table 12.4: Scrolling through the Buffer	
Keystroke	**Action**
<^f>	Move forward one screen.
<^b>	Move backward one screen.

To move quickly to the last line of the file or buffer, press <G> (<Shift-g>). To move to the first line of the file, press <1><G> (press and release the number <1> and then press <Shift-g>). In fact, to move to a specific line in the buffer, type the line number before you press <G>. To move to line 35 of the file (if there is a line 35), press <3><5><Shift-g>.

Tip

Take a little time to practice positioning the cursor using the commands described in these last few sections. Remember that you must be in command mode for the cursor-positioning commands to work. Press <Esc> before you issue a cursor-positioning command.

Adding Text

To add text to the editing buffer, you must go from command mode to input or text-entry mode. Any usual text characters you type are then added to the buffer. If you press <Return> while you are in input mode, vi "opens," or adds, a line to the buffer. Before you start adding text, first position the cursor at the location you want to add text. Press <a> to go to input mode and append text *after* the cursor position. Press <i> to go to input mode and insert text *in front of* the cursor position. When you are done adding text, press <Esc> to go back to command mode.

Here are some examples. The position of the cursor is represented by an underline character. For each case, both a *before* and an *after* view is shown.

1. Example showing the use of <i> (the insert command) to add text.

Before: `This report is important.`

Press <i> to insert text in front of the word *important*, type **very<space>** and press <Esc>.

After: `This report is very_important.`

Note that the cursor is positioned under the last character you added (in this case, the space).

2. Example showing the use of <a> (the append command) to add text.

Before: `This report is important.`

Press <a> to append text after the word *is*, type **<space>very** and press <Esc>.

After: `This report is very important.`

Note again that the cursor is positioned under the last character you added (in this case, the *y* in *very*).

When you want to append text at the end of a line, you can position the cursor at the end of a line and press <a> (the lowercase letter); alternatively, you can position the cursor anywhere in the line and press <A> (<Shift-a>) to position the cursor at the end of the line, put you in input mode, and allow you to append text—all with one command. Likewise, you can move to the beginning of the current line and insert text at the beginning of a line by pressing <I> (<Shift-i>).

To add a line of text below or above the current line, you use the key <o> or <O>, respectively. Each "opens" a line in the buffer and allows you to add text. In the following two examples, you add a line to some existing text.

1. Example showing the use of <o> to insert lines below the current line.

Before: `All jobs complete`
              `please call`
              `if you have any questions.`

The cursor is on the second line. Press <o> to add a line or lines below that line. Now type the following lines:

`Lee Nashua <Return>`
`555-1837`

Press <Esc>.

After: All jobs complete
          please call
          Lee Nashua
          555-183<u>7</u>
          if you have any questions.

2. Example showing the use of <O> to insert lines above the current line.

Before: All jobs complete
          please call
          i<u>f</u> you have any questions.

The cursor is on the third line. Press <O> (<Shift-o>) to add a line or lines above that line. Now type the following lines:

          Lee Nashua <Return>
          555-1837

Press <Esc>.

After: All jobs complete
          please call
          Lee Nashua
          555-183<u>7</u>
          if you have any questions.

In both cases, when you press <Esc>, the cursor was positioned under the last character you typed (the 7 in the phone number). Although you added only two lines, you could have added more lines by pressing <Return> at the end of each line. Naturally, you could have added only one line by not pressing <Return> at all.

Table 12.5 summarizes the commands for adding text. Remember that you have to be in command mode to add text. Press <Esc> to be sure that you are in command mode.

Table 12.5: Commands To Add Text	
Keystroke	**Action**
<a>	Append text after the cursor position.
<A> (<Shift-a>)	Append text to the end of the current line.
<i>	Insert text in front of the cursor position.
<I> (<Shift-i>)	Insert text at the beginning of the current line
<o>	Open a line below the current line to add text.
<O> (<Shift-o>)	Open a line above the current line to add text.

IV

UNIX Tools

Deleting Text

Making corrections or modifications to a file may involve deleting text. You must be in command mode to delete characters. If you are in input mode when you type the delete-character commands, the letters of the commands appear as characters in the buffer file. If that should happen, press <Esc> to go to command mode and press <u> to "undo" the mistake.

With vi, you can delete a character, a word, a number of consecutive words, all the text to the end of a line, or an entire line. Because vi is a *visual* editor, the characters, words, or lines are removed from the screen as you delete them. Table 12.6 lists the delete commands and describes their actions. They all take effect from the current cursor position. Move the cursor to the character, word, or line you want to change and then issue the desired delete command. Practice using them to see their effect. You will find they are helpful in making corrections to files.

Table 12.6: Commands To Delete Text	
Keystroke	**Action**
<x>	Delete character at cursor position.
<d><w>	Delete from the cursor position in the current word to the beginning of the next word.
<d><$>	Delete from the cursor position to the end of the line.
<D> (<Shift-d>)	Same as d$: delete the remainder of the current line.
<d><d>	Delete the entire current line, regardless of cursor position in the line.

All these commands can be applied to several objects—characters, words, or lines—by typing a whole number before the command. This whole-number technique was introduced earlier in this chapter in the section on positioning the cursor. Here are some examples:

- Press <4><x> to delete four characters

- Press <3><d><w> to delete three words

- Press <8><d><d> to delete eight entire lines

You can also specify a range of lines to delete. You do that by pressing the colon (:), typing the two line numbers you want to delete (inclusive) separated by a comma, pressing <d>, and pressing <Return>. For example, to delete lines 12 through 36 (inclusive), type **:12,36d <Return>**.

When you delete two or more lines, the status line states how many lines were deleted. Remember that you can use <u> to undo the deletion.

Tip

To have vi display line numbers, press <Esc> to make sure that you are in command mode, type **:se number**, and press <Return>. To turn off the line numbers, type **:se nonumber** and press <Return>.

Changing and Replacing Text

Another editing task you are faced with often is changing text or replacing one text string with another (there isn't too much difference between the two operations). The *change* commands in vi allow you to change a word or the remainder of a line. In effect, you are replacing one word or the remainder of a line with another. You use the *replace* commands to replace or change a single character or sequence of characters. Table 12.7 summarizes the change and replace commands.

The changes take place relative to the position of the cursor. You must be in command mode before you can use these commands. Position the cursor at the location in the buffer file you want to correct and press <Esc> before using these commands. Because vi is *visual*, the changes are made to the buffer as you execute the commands. Each of these commands puts you into input mode. Except for when you use <r> to replace a single character, you must press <Esc> to finish making changes and return to command mode.

Table 12.7: The Change and Replace Commands	
Keystroke	**Action**
<r>	Replace a single character.
<R> (<Shift-r>)	Replace a sequence of characters.
<c><w>	Change the current word, from the cursor position to the end of the word.
<c><e>	Change the current word, from the cursor position to the end of the word (same as <c><w>).
<c><b>	Change the current word, from the beginning of the word to the character before the cursor position.
<c><$>	Change a line, from the cursor position to the end of the line.

Keystroke	Action
<C> (<Shift-c>)	Change a line, from the cursor position to the end of the line (same as <c><$>).
<c><c>	Change the entire line.

To change several words, use a whole number (representing the number of words to change) before pressing <c><w>.

Here are some examples of how to use the change and replace commands.

1. Example showing the use of <c><e> to change to the end of the word.

Before: `The report demonstraits thw,strengths of are apporach.`

The cursor is located at the point in the incorrectly spelled word at which corrections are to begin. To change the spelling, press <c><e>, type **tes**, and press <Esc>.

After: `The report demonstrates thw,strengths of are apporach.`

2. Example showing the use of <R> (<Shift-r>) to replace a sequence of characters.

Before: `The report demonstrates thw,strengths of are apporach.`

The cursor is located at the point in the incorrectly spelled word at which you want to start replacing characters. To correct *thw,* to *the<space>*, press <R> (<Shift-r>), type **e<space>**, and press <Esc>.

After: `The report demonstrates the_strengths of are apporach.`

3. Example showing the use of <c><w> to change text, beginning with the current word and continuing for two words.

Before: `The report demonstrates the strengths of are apporach.`

The cursor is positioned under the letter of the word where you want to begin changes. To fix the last two words on the line, press <2><c><w>, type **our approach**, and press <Esc>.

After: `The report demonstrates the strengths of our approach.`

Remember to press <Esc> after you make changes to the lines to go back to command mode.

Searching

Finding a word, a phrase, or a number in a file can be difficult if you have to read through each line yourself. Like most editors and word processors, vi has a command that allows you to search for a string of characters. You can search forward or backward from your current position in the buffer. You also can continue searching. vi starts searching from the beginning of the buffer file when it reaches the end. The commands for searching are summarized in table 12.8. In each case, vi searches for the string you specify, in the direction you specify, and positions the cursor at the beginning of the string.

Table 12.8: The Search Commands

Command	Action
/*string*	Search forward through the buffer for *string*.
?*string*	Search backward through the buffer for *string*.
<n>	Search again in the current direction.
<N> (<Shift-n>)	Search again in the opposite direction.

When you type the search command, it appears on the status line. To search forward for the string sales > 100K in a file, first make sure that you are in command mode and then enter this command:

```
/sales > 100K
```

This command appears on the status line. If the string is in the buffer, vi positions the cursor under the first *s* in the word *sales*. If the string is not in the buffer, vi displays the message Pattern not found on the status line. To search for another occurrence of the string, press <n>; vi either positions the cursor under the next occurrence of the string or, if there is no "next occurrence," the cursor does not move.

Troubleshooting

You typed a string you know exists in the file, but vi doesn't find it.

The most common cause for this error is that you typed the string incorrectly. vi (and computers in general) don't do a good job of thinking; vi has a terrible time figuring out what you really mean when you type something else. If you're looking for the string *vegi-burger* but you type **vigi-burger**, vi can't find what you want (unless you happened to misspell *vegi-burger* in the buffer and it matches the search string). Check the search string carefully before you press <Return>.

You search for a phrase that incorporates a punctuation mark and vi *returns some odd results.*

Searching in vi may not give you the results you want if you're looking for characters that are "special" to vi. For example, if you want to find a word you know is located at the end of a sentence (for example, the string *end.*), you must "escape" the period; to vi, the period means "any character," not "end of sentence." If you enter /**end.** and press <Return>, vi locates *ending,* the word *end* followed by a space, as well as *end* followed by a period. To find only *end* followed by a period, enter /**end\.** (slash *end* backslash period).

Searching in vi is also case sensitive. If you're looking for the word *Larry* in your buffer, enter /**Larry** and not /**larry**.

Copying, Cutting, and Pasting

When you delete or cut characters, words, lines, or a portion of a line, the deleted object is saved in what is called the *general-purpose buffer.* The name isn't too important; what *is* important is that you can *put* or *paste* the contents of that buffer anywhere in the text you're editing. You do that with the command <p> or <P>. The <p> command pastes the object to the *right of* or *after* the cursor position; the <P> (<Shift-p>) command pastes the object to the *left of* or *before* the cursor.

Here are some examples of cutting and pasting text:

1. Example showing the use of <p> to paste the contents of the general-purpose buffer after the cursor.

   Before: `Carefully carry these o̲ut instructions.`

   Delete the characters *out<space>* by pressing <d><w>. Now move the cursor to the space after the *y* in *carry* and press <p>.

   After: `Carefully carry out_these instructions.`

2. Example showing the use of <P> (<Shift-p>) to paste the contents of the general-purpose buffer in front of the cursor.

   Before: `Carefully carry t̲hese out instructions.`

   Delete the characters *these<space>* by pressing <d><w>. Now move the cursor to the first *i* in *instructions* and press <P> (<Shift-p>).

   After: `Carefully carry out these_instructions.`

> **Tip**
>
> To change the order of two characters, position the cursor under the first character and press <x><p>. Try it to change the word *tow* to the word *two*.

The preceding examples showed you how to paste after deleting text. But you don't have to delete before you can paste. You can use an operation called *yank* (which is the same as the copy operation in some word processors). The forms of the yank command are similar to the forms of the delete command. The idea is that you yank, or copy, a portion of text and then paste it somewhere else using the <p> or <P> command. Table 12.9 lists some of the yank commands (notice that most of the yank commands use the lowercase letter *y*).

Table 12.9: The Yank, or Copy Commands

Keystroke	Action
<y><w>	Yank from the cursor position in the current word to the beginning of the next word.
<y><$>	Yank from the cursor position to the end of the line.
<Y> (<Shift-y>)	Same as <y><$>: yank the remainder of current line.
<y><y>	Yank the entire current line.

All these commands can be applied to several objects—characters, words, or lines—by typing a whole number before the command.

To copy a sequence of four lines to another portion of the text, follow these steps:

1. Position the cursor at the beginning of the first of the four lines.

2. Press <4><y><y> to yank from the cursor to the end of the line four times. The buffer (what you see on the screen) is unchanged.

3. Position the cursor elsewhere in the text.

4. Press <p> to paste the yanked lines below the line holding the cursor.

Repeating Commands

Not only does vi keep the text just deleted or yanked for future use, it also stores the last command you used for future use. You can repeat the last command that changed the buffer by pressing the period (**.**).

Suppose that you have completed a report but think it would be a good idea to put two lines containing this text at key points in the report:

```
****** Please comment ******
****** On this section ******
```

To do that, follow these steps:

1. Position the cursor in the buffer file where you want to place these lines the first time.

2. Insert the lines: press <o> to open a line and type the two lines of asterisks and text.

3. Press <Esc> to be sure that you are in command mode.

4. As often as necessary, position the cursor to another section of the report and press the period (.) to insert these same two lines again and again.

Setting the *vi* Environment

The vi editor has several options you may or may not choose to use. Some of these options can be set on a system-wide basis by the system administrator. You can customize your environment with a number of options that are in effect whenever you start vi. Table 12.10 summarizes all the environment options you can set for vi. When setting environment options (as described in the next section) you can use either the abbreviation shown in the first column of the table or the full name of the option used in the second column.

Table 12.10: Environment Options for *vi*	
Abbr. Option	**Function**
ai	The autoindent, or ai, option indents each line to the same level as the one above. Useful for writing programs. The default is autoindent off.
ap	The autoprint, or ap, option prints the current line to the screen when the line is changed. The default is autoprint on.
eb	The errorbells, or eb, option causes the computer to beep when you introduce a command error. The default is errorbells off.
nu	The number, or nu, option displays line numbers when editing a file. The default is number off.

(continues)

Table 12.10 Continued	
Abbr. Option	**Function**
redraw	The redraw option keeps the screen up-to-date as changes occur. The default is redraw on.
report	The report option sets the size of an editing change that results in a message on the status line. For example, report=3 triggers a message when you delete three lines but not when less than three lines are deleted. The default is report=5.
sm	The showmatch, or sm, option shows a matching open parenthesis when the closing parenthesis is entered. This option is mainly useful for programmers writing program code. The default is showmatch off.
smd	The showmode, or smd, option displays INPUT, REPLACE, or CHANGE on the right side of the status line when the associated command is given. The default is showmode off.
warn	The warn option displays a warning message when an attempt is made to exit vi if the buffer has been changed and not saved to the disk file. The default is warn on.
wm=n	The wrapmargin, or wm option defines the right margin. In the syntax of this command, n is a whole number. If n is greater than 0, the command forces a carriage return so that no word is *n* or less characters from the right margin. For example, wm=5 instructs vi to wrap the line when a character occurs within five characters of the end of the line. Turn this option off by specifying wm=0. The default is wm=0 (off).
ws	The word search (called wrapscan on some systems) or ws, option wraps from the <eof> (end-of-file) character to the <bof> (beginning-of-file) character during a search. Default is word search on.

Using *set* To See and Set Options

To see the options currently set for your system, type **:set** (a colon and the word *set*) and press <Return> while in command mode in vi. The options currently set for this session of vi are displayed on the status line. The options displayed with the set command vary depending on the options set by default and by your particular implementation of vi. Here is an example of what you might see when you issue the set command:

```
autoprint errorbells redraw report=1 showmatch showmode term=vt100 wrapmargin=5
```

Note

Issuing the set command with no arguments results in a display of only the user-set options. You can abbreviate the set command as se. To set a number of options on the same line, use the se command and separate the options with a space, as in the following example:

```
:se ap eb redraw report=1 sm smd warn wm=5 ws
```

Notice that the first character is the colon (:) character; it has special meaning to vi.

To see the list of all possible options and their settings, type :set all and press <Return>. The options and their settings from table 12.10 are displayed.

Setting the *showmode* Option

One of the most used options is the showmode option. To learn about the showmode option, start vi again with the vipract.1 file (type **vi vipract.1** and press <Return>).

When vi executes, you see the text from your first vi session on the screen. In your first session, you may have noticed that there was no way to determine whether you were in input mode when you entered the text for this file. You can instruct vi to inform you when you are in input mode by using the showmode option.

The vi editor can cause real frustration when you don't know what mode you are in. The showmode option identifies the mode you are in. When showmode is set on, whenever you are in input mode, the mode displays in the lower corner of the screen.

When you set the showmode option, vi displays whatever type of input mode it is in: regular INPUT MODE, APPEND MODE, REPLACE 1 CHAR mode, and so on. To set showmode in vi, press <Esc> to be sure that you are in command mode and then enter :set showmode. Now go to input mode (press <i>). You should see the message INPUT MODE on the status line. Press <Esc> to go back to command mode. You may want to see what happens when you give the commands to replace or change text.

Here is another way to confirm that the showmode option is set: type the following commands:

```
:set showmode? <Return>
showmode
```

Setting Toggle Options

Any option that doesn't take a number argument is like toggle switch: it can be turned on or off. For example, as you learned in the preceding section, you set the showmode option as follows:

```
:se showmode
```

To turn the showmode option off, you simply add **no** in front of the option, as follows:

```
:se noshowmode
```

Changing Options for Every *vi* Session

Setting an option during a vi session sets that option only for the current session. You can customize your vi sessions by putting the set commands in a file named .exrc in your home directory. To see whether such a file exits, type the following commands:

```
cd <Return>
vi .exrc <Return>
```

The first command takes you to your home directory. The second starts vi using the file .exrc. If the file exists, it appears on the vi screen. If the file doesn't exist, vi lets you know it's a new file. The set commands in the .exrc file start with the word set but no colon (:). For example, the following line sets the options number and showmode:

```
set number showmode
```

> **Note**
>
> The .exrc file is read when you start vi. If you create it while you're in vi, you must restart vi to have the settings take effect.

The options you set and the values you give to some options depend on your preferences and the type of editing you will be doing. Experiment with some options or talk with more experienced users or your system administrator about vi options.

▶ Chapter 16, "Finding and Using Internet Resources," details how you can find programs, like text editors, on the Internet.

A Survey of Other Editors

You may have other text editors available on your UNIX system. Some are commercial and others are available free on the Internet or from other sources. Editors other than vi have been created because some users are uncomfortable with the two-mode (command and input) operation of vi. Some users are familiar with editors available on other systems and want to use the features of those editors when they move to UNIX. You should be aware of or familiar with some of these editors to match your working environment or personal tastes. However, as an experienced UNIX user, you should have some facility with vi.

A few dozen text editors are available for UNIX systems. This chapter mentions only four: UnixWare's Text Editor, emacs, joe (Joe's own editor), and pico.

The UnixWare Text Editor is a new approach for UNIX editors. It is a graphical text editor that works much like a word processor, although it still doesn't show underlining or other attributes on the screen. A discussion about editing on UNIX wouldn't be complete without mentioning emacs. The other editors are discussed as examples of some types of text editors available on UNIX systems. You may find that other editors are in use or popular on your system. Apologies to those who feel slighted that their favorite isn't mentioned here.

Looking at UnixWare's Text Editor

UnixWare (derived from UNIX System V Release 4.2) is based on a graphical Desktop. One of the graphical tools included is the Text Editor (see fig. 12.2).

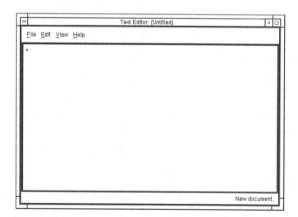

Fig. 12.2
The UnixWare Text Editor window.

The Text Editor is located in UnixWare's Accessories folder. After opening the Accessories folder, double-click on the Text Editor icon. When the Text Editor window opens, you can start typing to create a new file. To open an existing file, display the File menu by clicking on File at the top of the window. From the File menu, click on Open to display the Text Editor: Open dialog box. From there, you can select a file to open in a Text Editor window.

The Text Editor performs the same basic functions that vi does. For example, you can search for text in the file by using Find (located in the View menu). To move the cursor around the screen, you use the arrow keys and the <Page Up> and <Page Down> keys.

Unlike most UNIX utilities, UnixWare's utilities have online help available. To learn how all the Text Editor options work, use the online help.

Looking at *emacs*

The name *emacs* stands for Editor MACroS. The emacs editor is one of the most popular UNIX text editors and is used by almost as many users as vi. A full version of emacs is very large, taking up several megabytes of disk space. It is a full-featured editor, very powerful, and has been extended to be used for more than text editing. In some installations, you can use it to edit files, keep a calendar, work with electronic mail, manage files, read USENET or network news, create outlines, use it as a calculator, and so on. In some sense, emacs is a working environment that contains a text editor.

▶ The appendix lists sources for emacs, other editors, and utilities.

The emacs editor was created by Richard Stallman. The source code for emacs is essentially available for free. Richard Stallman is a founder and proponent of the Free Software Foundation and the GNU (GNU is Not UNIX) project. Stallman believes very strongly that all software should be free and that computer systems should be open for use by anyone. The fact that emacs is freely available matches his philosophy. Anyone can take it for his or her own use. Users are also encouraged to make modifications and share those changes with others.

The emacs editor is modeless: it doesn't have the two modes that vi does. That means that anything you type is put into the file buffer. To give the editor commands to save files, search for text, delete text, and so on, you must use other keys. In emacs, you use control characters (usually <Ctrl-x> and <Ctrl-c>) and the <Esc> key.

To start emacs, type **emacs** and press <Return>. You are presented with a blank screen with a status line at the bottom. This chapter doesn't discuss the key-strokes used in emacs other than to say that you can often get help by pressing <Ctrl-h><h> and that you use <Ctrl-x><Ctrl-c> to exit. Unlike vi, emacs has online help facilities. If emacs is available on your system, ask for some documentation or talk with a local expert.

The complete GNU emacs system is large but can be customized to match your local environment. Some smaller versions of emacs that are readily available are Freemacs, by Russell Nelson, and MicroEmacs, originally by Dave

Conroy. Some commercial versions of emacs are also available. Which of these you use depends on local policies and constraints. Because emacs is so popular, there is a large support network of emacs users.

Looking at *joe*

Joe's Own Editor, or joe, is a full-screen editor developed and maintained by Joseph H. Allen. It is available by anonymous ftp on the Internet. The joe editor is a small, modeless editor. You specify commands with keystrokes similar to those in the popular DOS editor, WordStar (joe is particularly popular with users who come from a DOS environment). It has online help and all the features you expect. It works only when your terminal is of type ANSI or VT100.

> **Note**
>
> Anonymous ftp is a special service that allows users to download files from a server without a password. On the server, anonymous ftp users have access only to the directory /usr/ftp/pub.

To start joe, type **joe** and press <Return>. You see an essentially blank screen with some status information. To get help, press <Ctrl-k><h>. The top 10 lines or so of the screen show all the necessary control-key combinations necessary to accomplish your work.

Looking at *pico*

The pico editor was developed at the University of Washington. Although it can be used on its own, it is part of the large pine mail system. The term *pico* stands for *PIne COmposer* (it is used as the editor for composing mail messages in pine). Like emacs and joe, pico is a modeless editor. When you start it, you are in input mode; you use control characters to move around the screen or perform other functions.

To start pico, type **pico** and press <Return>. You see a screen that allows you to enter text. You also see the following brief help at the bottom of the screen:

```
^G Get Help ^O Writeout ^R Read File ^Y Prev Page ^K Del Line ^C Cur Pos
^X Exit     ^J Justify  ^W Where Is  ^V Next Page ^U Undel Lin ^T To Spell
```

The caret (^) character indicates that you must press the <Ctrl> key to activate a function. For example, to delete a line, you press and hold the <Ctrl> key, press the <k> key, and then release them both.

The `pico` editor is good for those bothered by the two modes of `vi`. It isn't as powerful as `vi` or `emacs`, but it is good for many editing tasks.

Summary

This chapter introduced the standard UNIX full-screen text editor, `vi`. The best way to learn `vi` is by practice, experimentation, and talking with experienced users. The chapter also provided a brief survey of some other text editors, including UnixWare's Text Editor.

In the next chapter, you learn about using electronic mail on your system. You will see that it is convenient to know how to use a text editor like `vi` to create mail messages.

Chapter 13

Working with E-Mail

Electronic mail, or *e-mail*, seems to have taken the world by storm. Literally over ten million computer users worldwide have access to electronic mail. Your computer system is most likely shared by several users or is part of a network maintained by your organization. A number of commercial networks or Internet-access providers can provide you or your organization with access to electronic mail around the world. In any of these cases, you have the opportunity and necessity to use e-mail for personal and professional communications.

In this chapter, you learn the following:

■ How to send e-mail

■ How to read and reply to e-mail messages

■ How to delete, save, and print messages

Understanding E-Mail

Electronic mail, or *e-mail*, is a means for users on a single computer system or a network of systems to send and receive messages. You send a message to another person by using an e-mail program designed for that purpose. At a minimum, you provide the program with the address of the recipient and the message you want to send. The address includes the login name of the person who is to receive the mail. If that user is on another system in a network, the address also includes a means of identifying the target computer system. You either prepare the message while you are using your e-mail program or you prepare it beforehand using a text editor such as vi.

There are several advantages to using electronic mail:

- You can send reports, data, and documents that can reach their destination in a matter of seconds or minutes.

- You don't have to worry about interrupting someone when you send them a message; you aren't necessarily interrupted when you receive messages—that's handled by the computer system.

- You don't need to play phone-tag or make an appointment to communicate with someone.

- You can deal with the messages you receive at a convenient time.

- You can send electronic mail at times convenient for you.

When you send e-mail, it's up to the computer system to make the delivery, which can involve putting your message out on a network to be delivered at some other site. At this point, you say that the mail has been *sent*. Hopefully, soon after that, the message arrives at the recipient's machine. If both the sender and the receiver are on the same computer system, this all takes place on one machine. The e-mail system on the target computer verifies that the addressee exists and the message is added to a file that holds all the e-mail for that user (if no network is involved, the local computer system verifies the addressee). The mail-storage file is called the user's *system mailbox* and has the same name as the user who is receiving the mail. For example, if your login name is oliann, your system mailbox is the file named oliann in the directory /usr/mail. When the message has been "delivered" to the mailbox, you say the mail has been *received*. Figure 13.1 shows the relationship between sending and receiving e-mail.

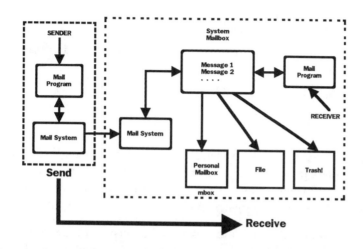

Fig. 13.1
Sending and
receiving e-mail.

IV

UNIX Tools

Does the Mail Always Get Through?

When you send e-mail, you may see a message on your screen that says Mail
Sent!. That means that the mail has been sent—not that it has been received or
delivered. Usually, you get e-mail in return if the e-mail system cannot deliver a
message.

There can be several reasons that e-mail may not go through. If mail is going out to a
network, the network address may be correct but the name of the user on that network may not be correct. Or perhaps the complete address is correct but because of
problems with permissions or quotas, the message could not be placed in the user's
system mailbox. In both of these cases, the mail was sent but was *undeliverable*.
Another scenario is that the e-mail was delivered but the user's mailbox was corrupted or destroyed. A final possibility is that the recipient ignores e-mail or does
not log in for several days, weeks, or more.

Your computer system notifies you when you have mail. When you read your
mail, you can treat it on a message-by-message basis. Some of the things you
can do with your mail are listed here:

- Delete individual messages after you read them—or without bothering
  to read them (using e-mail doesn't mean that you won't get junk-mail)

- Keep some messages in the system mailbox

- Keep some messages in a personal mailbox

- Keep other messages in individual files or folders

- Reply directly to the sender of a message

- Do a "group reply" to a group of users who all received the same message

- Forward mail to others

- Print your mail

It's up to you to manage your mail so that your mail doesn't take up any more file space than necessary. You really don't have to save every piece of e-mail you get. You'll also see that it is easier to read your incoming mail if you regularly delete or remove messages from your system mailbox.

UNIX typically comes with at least two mail programs you can use to work with e-mail: mail and mailx. UnixWare comes with a graphical mail program, which is discussed at the end of this chapter.

The program mail is primitive but usable. It does the job of sending or reading mail. The program mailx does everything mail does but is easier to use and has capabilities not present in mail. Some of the features mailx has that mail does not include the following:

- Makes it easier to manage and view your e-mail

- Makes it possible to include a Subject: header on e-mail you send

- Makes it possible to include a Cc: header for sending copies of e-mail to others

- Makes it possible to forward e-mail

- Makes it possible to set up mailing lists

This chapter shows examples of both mail and mailx. You see that mailx has more features and capabilities. Remember: everything you can do with mail you can also do with mailx.

Sending E-Mail

You can send e-mail to an individual, a group of individuals, or a mailing list. Just as when you want to send a paper letter, you must specify the address of the recipients with e-mail. Sometimes, you will compose or write a message while you are sending e-mail; at other times, you will send a prepared message; at times you may even send the output of a command or program with e-mail. When using mail or mailx, the message you send has to be a *text file*, that is, an ASCII file.

Regardless of how the message is prepared, you send mail by using a command of the following form:

```
mail address
```

or

```
mailx address
```

These commands start the mail system. You can then compose the mail message and send it to the specified *address*. In this syntax, *address* is the e-mail address of the person who is to receive the message. An address can have several different forms. To send e-mail to someone who has a login ID on the machine you are using, use the login ID of that person. For example, to send e-mail to someone on *your* system whose login name is anglee, enter the following command:

```
mail anglee
```

If anglee is on another system you can access through some network or collection of networks, you must include the name by which that system is known on the network. Suppose that anglee is the name of a user on a computer system whose network name is apples.startup.com. You can send e-mail by entering this command:

```
mail anglee@apples.startup.com
```

Or perhaps this command:

```
mail apples!anglee
```

The exact form of the address depends on the type of network being used and any local conventions or rules. Ask a local expert or your system administrator about the form of addresses on a network in your office or company.

To send the same message to several users, include each of their addresses on the line with the mail or mailx command, as in this example:

```
mailx oliver ernie lynn@apples.startup.com kacker tango!charlie!bigjr
```

Writing a Message while Sending E-Mail

Many users compose or write messages while they are sending e-mail. This is usually the quickest—but not the neatest—way to send mail. It's not neat because you have limited editing capabilities while composing your message. Generally, you can deal with only one line at a time. First you type the command to send e-mail and specify the address or addresses and press <Return>. Then you type the message, indicating that you're done by typing a period (.) on a line by itself. You can also use <Ctrl-d> to end the message. Here is an example of how to send e-mail to a user named lynn. Enter this command to start the mail system and specify the address of user lynn on your system:

```
mail lynn
```

Now type the message, pressing <Return> when you want to end a line. Here is a sample message that you may want to send to lynn; notice the use of <Return> to space the paragraphs of the message:

```
Lynn, <Return>
<Return>
Just wanted to tell you that I thought you did a great <Return>
job at the meeting yesterday! It seems as if we're <Return>
finally turning this problem around. <Return>
<Return>
Want to get together for lunch Thursday? <Return>
Give me a call.<Return>
ernie <Return>
. <Return>
```

When user lynn reads her e-mail, she'll see there is a message from you. However, she won't know what it's about until she reads it. It's a good idea to include a heading that states the subject of the e-mail: it makes your mail look better and is more efficient for the reader when he or she has many messages to select from. To include a subject header with a message, you have to use mailx. After you enter the mailx command with the address, mailx prints the line Subject: to prompt you for a subject header. At this prompt, you can type a subject or press <Return> if you don't want a subject header to appear with your mail. Following is an example (what you type is in bold):

```
mailx lynn <Return>
Subject: Congratulations! Lunch Thursday? <Return>
```

Now you can type the message to lynn (use the preceding sample message) but end it with <Ctrl-d> instead of a period. Remember that the <Ctrl-d> must be on a line by itself, just as the period must be on a line by itself. The computer responds by displaying EOT (which means *end of transmission*).

Canceling a Message

You can cancel a message while you're writing it, but you can't cancel it once it's sent. To cancel while you are writing a message, press whatever key is configured on your system as the interrupt key (usually either <Ctrl-c> or <Del>). When a message is canceled, it is saved in a file named dead.letter. You can delete this file or edit it later for another message. When you use mail, the message is canceled as soon as you press <Ctrl-c>. If you use mailx, you must press <Ctrl-c> twice to cancel (which is safer in case you press <Ctrl-c> or <Del> by mistake). After canceling your mail message, you see the command-line prompt. The following example shows how the cancel function works:

```
mailx lynn <Return>
Lynn, <Return>
<Return>
Just wanted to tell that I thought you did a great<Return>
job
```

At this point in the creation of the message, you press <Ctrl-c> or <Del>; the system responds with the message (Interrupt—one more to kill letter). At this point, you must decide whether you want to continue the letter or kill it. Suppose that you decide to continue; you just keep typing the text of the letter as follows:

```
at the meeting yesterday! It seems as if we're finally <Return>
turning this problem around. <Return>
<Return>
```

At this point, you decide to cancel the letter again, so you press <Ctrl-c> or <Del>. The system responds with (Interrupt—one more to kill letter). Because you want to kill the message, press <Ctrl-c> or <Del> a second time; mailx quits and you see the shell prompt.

Sending a Prepared Message

You may want to use a text editor such as vi to compose a message to be sent by electronic mail. If you use a text editor, you have the tools available to do things such as format the text and check your spelling. It doesn't matter what program you use to create the text as long as you end up with a text or ASCII file.

Suppose that the file you want to send is named report.txt and that the recipient's address is bigshot@turn.green.com. There are essentially three ways to send the file, as shown in the following list. You can use only the first two methods if you use mail because they use properties of your login shell. The following examples use both the mail and mailx commands; the mailx command accesses the subject heading differently than before. Here, the option -s is used and the string that serves as the subject heading is surrounded with quotation marks.

Here are the three methods you can use to send mail using a prepared message file called report.txt:

- **Use a pipe.** To send report.txt with the mail command, enter the following command:

```
cat report.txt ¦ mail bigshot@turn.green.com
```

To send the file with the `mailx` command and the `-s` option, enter this command:

```
cat report.txt ¦ mailx -s" Sales Report" bigshot@turn.green.com
```

■ **Redirect input.** To send `report.txt` with the `mail` command, enter the following command:

```
mail bigshot@turn.green.com < report.txt
```

To send the file with the `mailx` command and the `-s` option, enter this command:

```
mailx -s" Sales Report" bigshot@turn.green.com < report.txt
```

■ **Use ~r to include a file in a message.** To use `mailx` to send the file (using the default `Subject:` prompt), enter these commands:

```
mailx bigshot@turn.green.com <Return>
Subject: Sales Report<Return>
~r report.txt<Return>
~.<Return>
EOT
```

You see the system prompt after you complete any of these three methods—the result is the same in any case.

> **Note**
>
> In the third example, you use ~r to *read*, or include, the file `report.txt` in the e-mail message. This is an example of a *tilde command*. To use such commands, you precede a command with the tilde character (~) while you're reading or sending mail. You may find several other tilde commands useful; they are discussed at appropriate points in following sections.

Sending the Result of a Command or Program by E-Mail

◀ For more information about piping, refer to Chapter 10, "Understanding UNIX Shells."

If you run a command or program that produces results to the screen (known as `stdout`), you can pipe that output to a mail command. Suppose that you have some information in a file called `contrib.1st`, you use the command `sort` to sort it, and then you send the results to yourself (login name `imgood`) and `bigshot` (whom you've met earlier in this chapter). To do all that, enter the following command:

```
sort contrib.1st ¦ mailx -s "Sorted Contrib Info" imgood bigshot@turn.green.com
```

Reading Your Mail

Most UNIX systems notify you when you log in that you have e-mail. It's up to you to read and act on it. You can use either `mail` or `mailx` to read any mail you have. Because the `mailx` command gives you more control and more information about your mail, this section discusses that command. As you read your mail, the e-mail program marks a message as read. Depending on what commands you use and how you quit the e-mail program, the messages you have read are either kept in your system mailbox, `/usr/mail/$LOGNAME`, or in your login directory in the file named `mbox`.

Using *mail* To Read Mail

To read your mail with `mail`, type **mail** and press <Return>. Your current mail message is displayed. The entire message is displayed, regardless of its length. The details of the message are explained in the next section about using `mailx`. It's better to use `mailx` to read your mail because you have more control over what is displayed and how you can view it. To see the next message with `mail`, press <Return>.

Using *mailx* To Read Mail

To read your mail with `mailx`, type **mailx** and press <Return>. Suppose that your login name is `imgood`; you'll see a display similar to this (what you type is in bold):

```
mailx <Return>
mailx     Type ? for help.
"/usr/mail/imgood": 5 messages 2 new 1 unread
      1 sarah                     Wed Jan  5 09:17  15/363
      2 croster@turn.green.com    Thu Jan  6 10:18  26/657    Meeting on Friday
   U  3 wjones                    Fri Jan  7 08:09  32/900    Framistan Order
 > N  4 chendric                  Fri Jan  7 13:22  35/1277   Draft Report
   N  5 col.com!kackerma@ps.com   Sat Jan  8 13:21  76/3103   Excerpt from GREAT new UNI
?
```

Here are some things to note about the display:

- The first line identifies the program and says to type a question mark (?) for help.

- The second line indicates that `mailx` is reading your system mailbox, `/usr/mail/imgood`, and that you have five messages. Two have arrived since you last checked your mail, one appeared previously but you have not yet read it, and two messages have already been read.

■ The next five lines give information about your mail. Ignore the first few characters for now. Each line holds a message number, the address of the sender, the date the message was sent, the number of lines/number of characters in the message, and the subject (if one was given). Consider the following line:

```
2 croster@turn.green.com  Thu Jan  6 10:18  26/657  Meeting on Friday
```

This line indicates the message numbered 2 is from croster@turn.green.com—an address that indicates the message came to your machine from a network (mail from a local user is marked with just the user's login ID). The message was sent on Thursday, January 6, at 10:18; it consists of 26 lines and 657 characters. The subject is *Meeting on Friday*.

■ A message line starting with N indicates *new mail*—mail you didn't know about before.

■ A message line starting with U indicates *unread mail*—mail you know about but haven't yet read.

■ A message line without either N or U is mail you've read and saved in your system mailbox.

■ The greater-than character (>) on a message line marks the *current message*—the message you'll act on next.

■ The question mark (?) on the last line is the command prompt from mailx.

Reading the Current Message

The *current message* is the message marked by the greater-than character (>). To read that message, just press <Return>. If the current message is the one marked with the greater-than sign in the example in the preceding section, you see something similar to this:

```
Message 4:
From chendric Fri, Jan 7 13:22 EST 1994
Received: by your.system.com
Date: Fri, 7 Jan 1994 13:22:01 -0500
From: Carol Hendricks <chendric>
Return-Path: <chendric>
To: aborat, lynn, oackerm, imgood
Subject: Draft Report
Here is a draft of the report I intend to submit next week.
Please take a look at it and let me know your comments.
Thanks.
```

```
– – – – – – – Report Starts Here – – – – – – –
          Opportunities for Expansion
          Prepared by Carol Hendricks
Over the past 6 months, we've seen an indication of an increase in
the demand for our services. Current market trends indicate that
the demand will continue for at least 18 months and possibly
longer. The manager of our service staff states "We're up to our
necks in new customers and
:
```

The message is displayed one screen at a time. The colon (:) at the bottom of the screen tells you that the message won't fit on one screen. Press <Return> to see the next screenful of the message. Any time you see a colon, you can press <Return> to see the next screen or press <q> to quit viewing the message. When you have seen the last screen, you see EOF: (for *end of file*). Press <q> or <Return> to get back to the ? prompt. Notice that the greater-than character still points to the message you've just read. The message that *was* the current message is *still* the current message.

Some lines were displayed on the screen before the message itself began. This is the *header information*—which contains some useful information. Typically, header information includes the message number, who sent the message, when it was sent, the name of the system that received the message, the date the message was received, the "real name" of the sender as well as his or her login ID, the Return-Path, who the message was sent to, and the subject. All this is passed on with an e-mail message. The sender is always identified, making forgeries difficult. The real name that appears in the From: line is taken from a field from the sender's entry in the password file. The Return-Path or Reply-To information is used by the mail system if you generate a reply (as discussed later in this chapter). The To: line contains the address or list of addresses of the recipients of this message. (This sample message was a group message.) The Subject: line was provided by the sender.

Reading the Next Message

There are two ways to read the next message. By *next* is meant the message following the current message in your mailbox. You can press <Return> to display the next message or you can press <n> to see the next message. It becomes the current message after you read it. You read the next message in the same way you read the current message. After you read the last message in the list, you see the message At EOF.

Reading Any Message

All the messages in your mailbox are numbered. You can read messages in any order by typing the message number and pressing <Return> when you see the ? prompt. For example, to read message number 2, type **2** and press <Return> at the question mark. Message number 2 then becomes the current message.

Reading E-mail from Other Files

When you start `mail` or `mailx`, you read messages kept in your system mailbox, `/usr/mail/$LOGNAME`. Recall from Chapter 10, "Understanding UNIX Shells," that `LOGNAME` is the shell variable that holds your login name. If you log in as `imgood`, your mail is held in `/usr/mail/imgood`. You can read mail from other files that hold complete e-mail messages, that is, messages with the headers and text of the messages. Naturally, you must have read permission for those files.

To read messages from a file, type the command to start the e-mail program: type **-f** *filename* on the same line and press <Return>.

For example, to read the e-mail in the file `mbox`, enter this command:

```
mailx -f mbox
```

You can read the mail in that file in the same way you read e-mail from your system mailbox.

> **Note**
>
> The `mbox` file is located in your home directory and automatically contains messages you've already read but have not deleted. These messages are saved to `mbox` when you exit `mailx`.

Sending Mail while Reading

You can send e-mail while you are using the mail program to read your messages. You type **m** *address* and press <Return> when you see the ? prompt. Then follow the instructions given in the first part of this chapter for sending e-mail. For example, to send e-mail while using `mailx`, do the following:

1. Start the `mailx` program: Type **mailx** and press <Return>,

2. Read some messages or do other things, but at the ? prompt, type the following to send e-mail to a user whose login name is `ernie`:

   ```
   m ernie <Return>
   ```

3. At the prompt for a subject, type a subject heading:

   ```
   Subject: Game Time<Return>
   ```

4. Type the message and end it with a period on the last line, as in the following example:

```
Don't forget we're playing V-ball at 6:30<Return>
~.<Return>
```

The computer responds with the following lines:

```
EOT
?
```

5. Continue using `mailx`.

Printing Mail Messages

Using `mailx`, you can print the current message to a printer connected to your system. The way to do it is to first make the message you want to print the current message. Then type ¦ `lp` at the ? prompt and press <Return>. You are, in effect, piping the current message to the `lp` program.

To print a collection of messages, save them in a file and then print the file. Refer to "Filing and Saving Mail Messages," later in this chapter, for information on effective ways to save messages.

Quitting the Mail Program

As you read e-mail in a mailbox, you can read, skip, or delete messages. (You learn about deleting messages later in this chapter.) These actions don't take place in the mailbox itself but in a temporary copy of the mailbox. You can quit the e-mail program so that your mailbox is changed by your actions (the modified temporary copy replaces the original mailbox), or you can quit so that your mailbox is unchanged regardless of what you did during your e-mail session.

Quitting and Saving Changes

To quit either the `mail` or `mailx` program and save the changes that occur, press <q> and <Return> when you see the ? prompt. You see the shell prompt again. When you quit mail this way, messages you read but didn't delete are saved in a file named `mbox` in your home directory. If you use `mail` to read your mail, you see the shell prompt. If you use `mailx`, you see the shell prompt as well as other information, as explained in the following section.

Quitting and Saving Changes with *mailx*

Suppose that you use mailx to read your mail. Assume that your login name is imgood and your home directory is /home/imgood. When you type **mailx** and press <Return> to start the mailx program, you see the following screen of information:

```
mailx    Type ? for help.
"/usr/mail/imgood": 5 messages 2 new 1 unread
     1 sarah                    Wed Jan  5 09:17  15/363
     2 croster@turn.green.com   Thu Jan  6 10:18  26/657    Meeting on Friday
  U  3 wjones                   Fri Jan  7 08:09  32/900    Framistan Order
 > N  4 chendric                Fri Jan  7 13:22  35/1277   Draft Report
   N  5 col.com!kackerma@ps.com Sat Jan  8 13:21  76/3103   Excerpt from GREAT
?
```

Now suppose that you read the current message by pressing <Return> and then you read message 1 by typing **1** and pressing <Return> at the ? prompt. If you then press <q> and <Return> to quit, you see the following information:

```
     Saved 2 messages in /home/imgood/mbox
     Held 3 messages in /usr/mail/imgood
```

The two messages you read are saved in the file mbox in your home directory; the other three messages are saved in your system mailbox, /usr/mail/imgood. The messages that are put in mbox are *added* to that file. If you save messages like this often, mbox can grow quite large. You may want to print that file occasionally and delete it. You can also read the mail from that file as if it were your system mailbox, as described later in this chapter.

> **Note**
>
> You can read mail and indicate that the current message is to be kept in your system mailbox, /usr/mail/imgood, and not in the file mbox. To do this after you've read a message, type **pre** (for *preserve*) at the ? prompt and press <Return>.

Quitting and Not Saving Changes

The other way to quit either the mail or mailx program is to press <x> and <Return> at the ? prompt. When you do that, you *exit* the program with **no changes** to your system mailbox or any other file—as if you did not read your mail at all. You then see the shell prompt. You may want to exit the mail program in this way when you want to leave the program but save the mail in your system mailbox.

Getting Help

When you type the command to start your e-mail program, you see a ?
prompt. If you use `mail`, you see the ? prompt immediately. If you use `mailx`,
you see the prompt after a list of messages is displayed. The `mailx` program
tells you to type **?** for help. To get a list of commands and some information
about each command, type **?** and press <Return>. Although you may not use
all the commands listed, you can refer to the list when you need some help.

Getting Help with *mail*

To see help messages while you are using `mail`, type **?** and press <Return>.
You see a display similar to the following, which lists the commands you can
use from the ? prompt:

```
q               quit
x               exit without changing mail
p               print
s [file]        save (default mbox)
w [file]        same without header
-               print previous
d               delete
+               next (no delete)
m user          mail to user
! cmd           execute cmd
```

Although most of these commands are explained later in this chapter, here
are some things to note now:

- In each case, you can use the first letter of the command or type the
  entire command.

- Items in brackets [ ] are optional; you don't type the brackets as part of
  the command.

- The term *print* does not mean to print the message on a printer but to
  display the message on the screen.

- All commands apply to the current message.

Getting Help with *mailx*

To see help messages while you are using `mailx`, type **?** and press <Return>.
You see a display similar to the following.

```
mailx commands
print, type [msglist]   print messages
next                    goto and type next message
edit [msglist]          edit messages
from [msglist]          give header lines of messages
delete [msglist]        delete messages
```

```
undelete [msglist]      restore deleted messages
save [msglist] file     append messages to file
reply [message]         reply to message, including all recipients
Reply [msglist]         reply to the authors of the messages
preserve [msglist]      preserve messages in mailbox
mail user               mail to specific user
quit                    quit, preserving unread messages
xit                     quit, preserving all messages
header                  print page of active message headers
!                       shell escape
cd [directory]          chdir to directory or home if none given
list                    list all commands (no explanations)
top [msglist]           print top 5 lines of messages
z [-]                   display next [previous] page of 10 headers

[msglist] is optional and specifies messages by number, author,
subject, or type.
The default is the current message.
```

This listing shows you the commands you can use from the ? prompt. You can see that the list of commands available with mailx is more extensive than the list available with mail. Although some of these commands are explained in later sections of this chapter, here are some things to note right now:

■ In each case, you can use the first letter of the command or type the entire command.

■ Items in brackets [ ] are optional; you don't type the brackets as part of the command.

■ You can make the term *msglist* refer to all messages by using *. For example, to save all messages in a file named allmail, type **s * allmail** and press <Return>.

■ You can make the term *msglist* refer to a single message number. For example, to save message number 2 to a file named meeting, type **s 2 meeting** and press <Return>.

■ You can make the term *msglist* refer to a range of message numbers by separating the two message numbers by a hyphen (-). For example, 2-4 refers to messages numbered 2, 3, and 4. To save messages 2, 3, and 4 in a file named memos, type **s 2-4 memos** and press <Return>.

■ You can make the term *msglist* refer to mail from a specified user, that is, from the sender whose name you specify. For example, to save all the mail from a user named lynn in a file named lynn.mai, type **s lynn lynn.mai** and press <Return>.

- You can make the term *msglist* refer to mail dealing with a specified subject by specifying the text in the form /string. For example, to save all mail that has the word *report* in the subject line in a file named reports, type **s /report reports** and press <Return>.

- You can make the term *msglist* refer to a type of mail by specifying :*character*, where *character* is d for *deleted messages*, n for *new messages*, o for *old messages*, r for *read messages*, or u for *unread messages*. For example, to save all new mail in a file named today.mai, type **s :n today.mai** and press <Return>.

- The term *print* in the line print messages does not mean to print messages on a printer. It means to display the messages on the screen. To see all messages from a user named gfriend, for example, type **p gfriend** and press <Return>.

- The edit command is useful for modifying messages before forwarding them to someone else or saving them in a file.

- If you have so many messages that their headers can't be listed on one screen, use the command **z +** to see the next screenful of messages. Use **z-** to see the previous screenful of messages.

Filing and Saving Mail Messages

You will want to save some of the e-mail you receive. It's not practical to keep all your mail in your system mailbox for these reasons:

- You'll have too many messages to wade through whenever you want to read your mail.

- System administrators often put a limit on the size of your system mailbox. If you reach that limit, you may be prevented from receiving any new mail.

- Your mail won't be organized and it can be difficult to find important messages or all messages relating to a specific project or topic.

Earlier in this chapter, you learned that the messages you've read are saved (unless you say otherwise) in the file mbox. You also know that you can read these messages by typing **mailx -f mbox** and pressing <Return>. You can also read messages from other files by using the mailx -f option.

Saving Files with *mail*

There are two primary ways (with and without a header) to save the current message in a file when you are using mail. With both methods, you can specify a file to hold the message and the message is *added* to that file. If you don't specify a file, the message is added to the file mbox (your personal mailbox) in your home directory. If you use q to quit the mail program, the messages are removed from your system mailbox.

You use the s command to save a message with the headers intact (useful if you want to use your e-mail program to read the messages later). You use the w command to save a message without the header information (useful when you want to use only the text of the messages in a file that may be processed by some other program).

Tip

Always use w followed by a filename to save a message. Using the w command without a filename saves the messages to mbox without the header and either prevents you from reading messages from mbox or attaches the message to another mail message in mbox.

When you see the ? prompt, you can use any of the following methods to save a message:

- Type **s** to add the current message to mbox in your home directory.

- Type **s** *filename* to add the text of the current message to the file *filename*.

- Type **w** *filename* to add the text of the current message to the file *filename*.

Saving Files with *mailx*

You can explicitly save only a complete message (text and headers) to a file when you use mailx. You can specify a group of messages to save using the optional *msglist* parameter. The section "Getting Help with mailx," earlier in this chapter, gives the details of using *msglist* to save files.

You know that messages you have already read are automatically saved to mbox, unless you use the preserve command.

> **Tip**
>
> To keep messages in your mailbox after you've read them, use the preserve com-
> mand, pre. You can use this command with a message list (*msglist*). For example,
> to keep messages 3 through 6 in your mailbox after you've read them, type **pre 3-6**
> and press <Return> when you see the ? prompt.

It's a good idea to get in the habit of specifying a filename when you use the
save command, s. If you don't specify a filename, the current message is
added to the file mbox. If you include a *msglist* but don't specify a file, mailx
uses *msglist* as the name of the file to which it saves the current message. If
you use q to quit the e-mail program, the saved messages are removed from
your system mailbox.

Deleting Mail Messages

To delete a message from a file of messages you're reading, you use the d
command. If you quit the e-mail program using q, any messages you deleted
with the d command are removed from the file.

Deleting Messages with *mail*
When you use mail to read your e-mail, you can delete only the current message. Type **d** and press <Return> when you see the ? prompt. The current
message is removed from your mailbox. Unless you have saved it, it's gone
for good. For some messages, this is a very good idea.

Deleting and Undeleting Messages with *mailx*
You use the d or delete command to mark messages for deletion when you
use mailx to read your e-mail. If you then quit the program with q, the
marked messages are removed from your mailbox.

To delete the current message, type **d** and press <Return>. You can also
specify a message list (*msglist*). See "Getting Help with mailx," earlier in this
chapter, for details about using the *msglist* parameter. For example, to delete
all messages that have the string *Framistan Project* in their subject lines, type
d /Framistan Project and press <Return>.

If you mark a message or a group of messages to be deleted, you can change
your mind and undelete the message or messages using the u command.
You must use the u command before you enter **q** to quit. Once you enter **q**,
the messages are gone for good. Use the u or undelete command in the same
way you use d or delete.

> **Tip**
>
> To undelete all the messages you marked for deletion, type **u** * and press <Return> when you see the ? prompt.

Replying to Mail

To reply to e-mail, use the address specified in the Reply-To: header field. If that field isn't present, use the information in the Return-Path: header field. Following are partial headers of two messages; one has both header fields and the other has only the Return-Path: header field. The pertinent fields are in bold in each example.

Message 1:

```
From server@malte.abc.com Mon Nov  8 18:31 EST 1993
Received: from MALTE.ABC.COM by s850.mwc.edu with SMTP
Return-Path: <server@matle.ams.com>
Date: Mon, 8 Nov 93 18:17:15 -0500
Comment: From the DuJour List
Originator: dujour@mathe.abc.com
Errors-To: asap@can.org
Reply-To: <dujour@mathe.abc.com>
Sender: dujour@mathe.abc.com
```

Message 2:

```
From chendric Fri, Jan 7 13:22 EST 1994
Received: by your.system.com
Date: Fri, 7 Jan 1994 13:22:01 -0500
From: Carol Hendricks <chendric>
Return-Path: <chendric>
To: aborat, lynn, oackerm, imgood
Subject: Draft Report
```

To reply to the first message, use the Reply-To address dujour@mathe.abc.com. Note that the Reply-To and Return-Path fields are different. In the second example, use chendric to respond to the sender of the message.

> **Note**
>
> Always use the Reply-To address if included in the header because it represents the specific address of the sender. When the Reply-To address is not available, the Return-Path address usually provides an adequate address back to the sender.

Replying to Mail with *mailx*

You can let the mailx program determine the address to use to reply to an electronic mail message. To do this, use either of these commands:

R Addresses a reply to the sender of the message

r Addresses a reply to the sender and all recipients of an e-mail message

With either of these commands, you can use the *msglist* parameter as explained in "Getting Help with mailx," earlier in this chapter. Otherwise, the R or r command applies to the current message.

This section shows how to use these two commands by considering the following partial header, excerpted from a message from chendric, Carol Hendricks, in which she asks a group to comment on a draft of a report she has prepared:

```
From chendric Fri, Jan 7 13:22 EST 1994
Received: by your.system.com
Date: Fri, 7 Jan 1994 13:22:01 -0500
From: Carol Hendricks <chendric>
Return-Path: <chendric>
To: aborat, lynn, oackerm, imgood
Subject: Draft Report
```

To respond *only* to chendric, type **R** and press <Return> when you see the ? prompt. You see the following response:

```
To: chendric
Subject: Re: Draft Report
```

These lines tell you the reply is going to one person; the subject header indicates that the message is a reply to the one originally sent.

To make comments for *everyone on the distribution list* to see, type **r** and press <Return> when you see the ? prompt. You see the following response lines:

```
To: chendric, aborat, lynn, oackerm, imgood
Subject: Re: Draft Report
```

These lines tell you the reply is going to everyone on the original distribution list *and* the author. The subject header indicates that the message is a reply to the one originally sent.

From then on, you enter your message in the manner described in "Sending Mail," earlier in this chapter.

IV

UNIX Tools

Note

Be careful about using r to reply to a message. Whatever you send is sent to *everyone* who got a copy of the original message. It's a common mistake and is sometimes embarrassing.

Tip

Think about what you write and who will read your message before you send a reply. Being sarcastic or scathing doesn't work very well with e-mail. You usually end up sounding too strong and something like a bully. Using e-mail is not the same as talking with someone: you don't get a chance to see or hear their reactions and they don't get a chance to see or hear you, either. When you use e-mail, it's a lot easier and more effective to be polite and direct. You can see how easy it is to forward mail; after you send something to one person, you can never tell where the message will end up or how many people will see it. Think and be considerate.

Routing Mail to Others with *mailx*

Electronic mail is distributed by addresses. Tasks such as forwarding a message, sending copies (Cc:) of a message, creating aliases or simpler forms of addresses, and creating mailing lists all involve manipulating addresses. You don't have to do the manipulation directly. The mailx program has these capabilities built into it.

Forwarding Messages

To forward a message (actually, you're including the message with a message you compose), you must first start mailx in the same way as when you start it to read your messages. Then you use the m, r, or R command to send a message. As you compose your message, you use a tilde command, ~f, to forward one or several messages. The general form of the ~f command is ~f *msglist*. Refer to "Getting Help with mailx," earlier in this chapter, for more information about *msglist*. Here is a step-by-step example of how to forward a message:

1. Start mailx: type **mailx** and press <Return>. The system responds with the following:

```
mailx     Type ? for help.
"/usr/mail/imgood": 5 messages 2 new 1 unread
        1 sarah                      Wed Jan  5 09:17  15/363
        2 croster@turn.green.com     Thu Jan  6 10:18  26/657    Meeting on Friday
    U   3 wjones                     Fri Jan  7 08:09  32/900    Framistan Order
>   N   4 chendric                   Fri Jan  7 13:22  35/1277   Draft Report
    N   5 col.com!kackerma@ps.com    Sat Jan  8 13:21  76/3103   Excerpt from GREAT
?
```

2. Read message 5 by typing **5** and pressing <Return>. To conserve space, the text of that message isn't shown here (it is an excerpt from this book on UNIX). But suppose that you want to forward it to your friends with addresses sarah, anglee@hb.com, and netcong.com!parsley!lynn.

3. Use the m command to send mail to the addresses listed in step 2, type a subject, and type a beginning for your message. Here are the commands you enter to achieve this (what you type is in bold):

```
? m sarah anglee@hb.com netcong.com!parsley!lynn
Subject: Forwarding an excerpt from new Que UNIX book
Hi!
I'm forwarding an excerpt I came across from a new book by Que.
It's the Special Edition of Using UNIX. I'll be getting my own copy
tomorrow, Do you want me to pick up a copy for you too?
```

4. Use the command ~f to forward message number 5. Type **~f 5** and press <Return>. mailx responds with the following message:

```
Interpolating: 5
(continue)
```

5. The cursor is now under the word continue. You can continue with your mail message or end it by typing ~. and then pressing <Return>. The ? prompt appears.

Sending a Copy with *mailx*

You can send a copy of an e-mail message to one or more addresses by putting those addresses on what is known as the *Cc: list*. The Cc: list works as you expect it to: the mail is sent to the primary address or addresses (those in the To: header) and also to the address or addresses in the Cc: header. To include addresses in the Cc: list, use the tilde command ~c *address* while you are sending the message.

This example shows how to send a brief memo to a primary address (wjones) and a copy of it to yourself and another address (suppose that your address is imgood and the other user's address is ecarlst). You send one to yourself so that you have a copy of the memo. Follow these steps to add a Cc: list to the list of recipients:

1. Start `mailx` to send e-mail to the primary address, `wjones`, and give a subject header: enter these commands to achieve this (what you type is in bold):

```
$ mailx wjones <Return>
Subject: Memo - Sales Agreement with Framistan<Return>
```

2. Enter the text of the memo you want to send. For example, type the following:

```
TO:       William Jones
Date:     Jan 31, 1994
From:     Henry Charleston
RE:       Sales Agreement With Framistan Motors
On Thursday, January 29,1994, I held a meeting with the CEO
of Framistan Motors. We concluded and initialed a sales
agreement by which Framistan would purchase 10,000 units of
our thermo-embryonic carthurators. The agreement has been
forwarded to the appropriate parties in our organization
and we intend to formally complete the agreement within
two weeks.
```

3. Give the `~c` *address* command to add addresses to the Cc: list. For example, type the following to send copies to yourself (`imgood`) and to `ecarlst`:

```
~c ecarlst imgood
```

4. End it and send it: to end the message, type a tilde and period (`~.`) and then press <Return>. The `EOT` message appears, followed by the shell prompt.

When a message is sent this way, all the recipients can see the headers `To:` and `Cc:`. If someone replies to the message with the `R` or `r` command, he or she can expect the following results:

- With the `R` command, the reply is sent only to the author of the message.

- With the `r` command, the reply is sent to every address in the `To:` list and the `Cc:` list as well as to the author.

Tip

To review and possibly modify the headers on an outgoing message, type **~h** and press <Return> while you are composing the message. You are shown the headers one at a time and you can modify them.

You can customize mailx so that it always prompts you for a Cc: header in the same way it prompts you for the Subject: header. This is discussed in "Customizing Your mailx Environment," later in this chapter. Of course, you can keep from entering anything in the Cc: list by pressing <Return>.

Using Aliases and Mailing Lists

The mailx program, like most e-mail programs, allows you to create an alias for an address and a group alias for a list of addresses. You can treat the group alias as a mailing list. Having an alias for an individual address usually makes it easier to use the address because the alias is probably shorter and easier to remember.

You can set an individual or group alias for one mailx session by using the command alias or group from the ? prompt while you are reading your e-mail. To make the aliases more useful, put the aliases in a file named .mailrc in your home directory (as described in "Customizing Your mailx Environment," later in this chapter).

Following is an example of setting and using aliases with the mailx program:

1. Start mailx by typing **mailx** and pressing <Return>. After the headers are presented, you see the ? prompt:

```
mailx      Type ? for help.
"/usr/mail/imgood": 5 messages 2 new 1 unread
       1 sarah                     Wed Jan  5 09:17  15/363
       2 croster@turn.green.com    Thu Jan  6 10:18  26/657   Meeting on Friday
   U   3 wjones                    Fri Jan  7 08:09  32/900   Framistan Order
 > N   4 chendric                  Fri Jan  7 13:22  35/1277  Draft Report
   N   5 col.com!kackerma@ps.com   Sat Jan  8 13:21  76/3103  Excerpt from GREAT
   ?
```

2. Set up an individual alias: use the command alias followed by the alias for the address. The following example creates the alias ros for the address croster@turn.green.com:

```
alias ros crsoter@turn.green.com
```

3. Use the alias ros in an address; mailx expands it to its complete form. For example, you can enter the **m ros** command to start a message you want to mail to croster@turn.green.com.

4. Set up a group alias: use the command group followed by the alias for the addresses. The following example creates the alias friends and then forwards some mail to the group (what you type is in bold):

```
group friends chendric karlack abc.com!homebase!fran eca@xy.srt.edu
m friends
Subject: Excerpts from new UNIX book - get a copy!
~f 5
Interpolating: 5
~.
EOT
?
```

Customizing Your *mailx* Environment

You can customize your mailx environment by putting commands or set-environment variables in the file .mailrc in your home directory. The mailx program checks that file whenever you use the program. Quite a few environment variables and commands can be set in .mailrc. Check your local documentation for a list of all of them. Some of the commands mailx recognizes were given in "Getting Help with mailx," earlier in this chapter. This section describes the commands listed in table 13.1 and the environment variables listed in table 13.2.

You can set a system-wide environment by putting the commands or set variables in the file /usr/lib/mailx/mailx.rc. You can issue any of the commands in table 13.1 from the ? prompt any time you use mailx.

Table 13.1: *mailx* **Commands**

Command	Definition
#	Denotes a comment. No action is taken.
alias	Sets an individual alias. Used as alias *alias-name address*. Example: alias joe jroger@blackflag.net
group	Sets a group alias or mailing list. Used as group *alias-name address-list*. Example: group pirates jroger@blackflag.net bbow homebase!lead!bbeard
set	Sets an environment variable. Used as set *variable-name* or set *variable-name=string*. Examples: set askcc, set sign="Hank W, hwalton@mountain.top.org"

IV

UNIX Tools

Table 13.2: *mailx* Environment Variables

Variable	Definition
askcc	Prompts for the Cc: list after the message is entered. Default is noaskcc.
asksub	Prompts for the Subject: list before the message is entered. Enabled by default.
header	Prints header information on available messages when you start mailx. Enabled by default.
ignore	Ignores interrupt characters when you enter messages. This is useful if you have a "noisy" connection over some telephone or other communication lines. Default is noignore.
metoo	When you have your name in a group alias, a message is normally *not* sent to you. Setting this variable allows you to receive messages sent to a group alias that contains your address. Default is nometoo.
sign	Used with ~a to put a "signature" in an e-mail message. Sometimes thought of as an informal signature. For example, setting this variable to sign="Hank W, hwalton@mountain.top.org" places Hank W, hwalton@mountain.top.org in a message when you type **~a** and press <Return>.
Sign	Used with ~A to put a "signature" in an e-mail message. Sometimes thought of as a formal signature. For example, setting this variable to Sign="Dr. Henry J. Walton, hwalton@mountain.top.org" places Dr. Henry J. Walton, hwalton@mountain.top.org in a message when you type **~A** and press <Return>.

The following example sets up the file .mailrc so that you use the commands and environment variables listed in tables 13.1 and 13.2. The pound sign (#) is used to document the work. You can create this file using vi or any other editor that can produce a text or ASCII file.

```
# .mailrc file for H. Walton
# set variable so header summary is printed when starting mailx
set header
# make sure interrupts are NOT ignored
set noignore
# set variables so that prompts for Subject and Cc always appear
set asksub
set askcc
# set signatures
set sign="The Big HW,   hwalton@mountain.top.org"
set Sign="Dr. Henry J. Walton, hwalton@mountain.top.org"
# individual aliases
alias billy wbracksto
```

```
alias ham jhron@cucumber.abc.com
alias me hwalton@mountain.top.org
# group aliases, mailing list
group pirates jroger@blackflag.net bbow homebase!lead!bbeard
group research chendric jreynold eackerma uuport!farplace!consul
group framistan wjones imgood cornlo@framistan.org imgood
```

Place these statements in the .mailrc file. Now when you start mailx, these command statements are processed. Here is what you might see if you use the group alias research to send a message, use the alias me in the Cc: list, and use ~A for a signature (what you type is in bold):

```
$ mailx <Return>
mailx     Type ? for help.
"/usr/mail/hwalton": 5 messages 2 new 1 unread
      1 sarah                   Wed Jan  5 09:17  15/363
      2 croster@turn.green.com  Thu Jan  6 10:18  26/657   Meeting on Friday
   U  3 wjones                  Fri Jan  7 08:09  32/900   Framistan Order
 > N  4 chendric                Fri Jan  7 13:22  35/1277  Draft Report
   N  5 hombase!lead!bbeard     Sat Jan  8 10:21  76/3103  What's up?
? m research
Subject: Meeting Wednesday 1/18/94
Cc:  me wjones
We need to get together a week from Wednesday, January 18, 1994 to
discuss plans for the corporate meeting in May. I'll reserve Room D-12
for a meeting at 10:00 AM, Wednesday, January 18, 1994.
See you there.
~A
~.
EOT
? x
$
```

If you read that message, you see something such as this:

```
To: chendric, jreynold, eackerma, uuport!farplace!consul
Cc: hwalton, wjones
Subject: Meeting Wednesday 1/18/94
We need to get together a week from Wednesday, January 18, 1994 to
discuss plans for the corporate meeting in May. I'll reserve Room
D-12 for a meeting at 10:00 AM, Wednesday, January 18, 1994.
See you there.
Dr. Henry J. Walton, hwalton@mountain.top.org
```

Using UnixWare's Mail Utility

UnixWare provides a graphical utility for reading, managing, and sending mail. Figure 13.2 shows the main Mail window.

The Mail window contains four icons: Manager, Reader, Sender, and Alias Mgr. The following sections discuss how to use these functions.

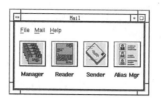

Fig. 13.2
The UnixWare
Mail window.

Using the Manager Window

From the Mail window, double-click on the Manager icon to display the Mail
Manager window (see fig. 13.3).

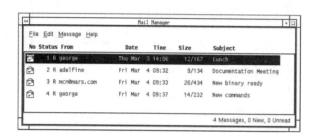

Fig. 13.3
The UnixWare
Mail Manager
window.

The Mail Manager window displays mail messages, each on its own line. The
menu options (menus are accessed by clicking on the appropriate word at the
top of the window) perform the same functions as those in `mailx` (discussed
earlier in this chapter), but you don't have to remember tilde commands.

- Use the File menu to open a file containing mail messages, save
  messages, print messages, and exit the Mail Manager window.

- Use the Edit menu to delete, undelete, select, or deselect messages.

- Use the Message menu to read, send, respond to, or forward mail
  messages.

- Use the Help menu to display online help for the Mail Manager
  window.

Using the Reader Window

From the Mail window, double-click on the Reader icon to display the Mail
Reader window (see fig. 13.4).

The Mail Reader window displays the header and body for one mail message.
There are five menus available from the top of the window:

- Use the File menu to open a file containing mail messages, save messages, print messages, access the Reader properties window, and exit the
  Mail Reader window.

■ Use the Edit menu to delete the message or select (or deselect) the entire body of the mail message.

■ Use the View menu to display the next or previous mail message.

■ Use the Message menu to open the Mail Manager window, reply to a message, or forward a message.

■ Use the Help menu to display online help for the Mail Reader window.

Fig. 13.4
The UnixWare
Mail Reader
window.

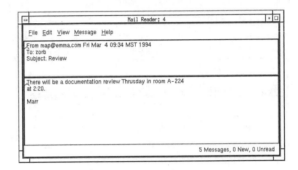

Using the Sender Window

From the Mail window, double-click on the Sender icon to display the Mail Sender window (see fig. 13.5).

Fig. 13.5
The UnixWare
Mail Sender
window.

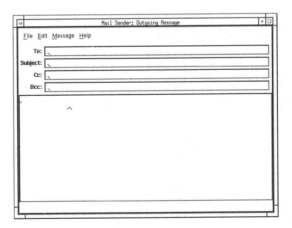

The Mail Sender window displays an empty screen so that you can compose a mail message. There are four menus available from the top of the window:

■ Use the Edit menu to cut, copy, and paste text in your message.
You can also undo changes and select the entire text of your message.

- Use the Message menu to send your message and insert aliases into the address of your message.

- Use the Help menu to display online help for the Mail Sender window.

Using the Alias Manager Window

From the Mail window, double-click on the Alias Mgr icon to display the Mail Alias Manager window (see fig. 13.6).

Fig. 13.6
The UnixWare
Mail Alias Manager
window.

The Mail Alias Manager window displays any aliases you have previously created. If no aliases exist, the center part of the window is blank. There are three menus available from the top of the window:

- Use the File menu to save and print your aliases and to exit the Mail Alias Manager window.

- Use the Edit menu to create new aliases and delete existing aliases.

- Use the Help menu to display online help for the Mail Alias Manager window.

Summary

This chapter provided an overview and tutorial introduction to using electronic mail, or e-mail. Using e-mail is an effective and efficient way to communicate with others on your system or other systems.

You send e-mail to another person by using their e-mail address. After you send mail, it is received by the computer system of the recipient. That system puts all the mail for a user in the user's system mailbox. Each user has a system mailbox, the file /usr/mail/$LOGNAME, where LOGNAME is the user's login name. Each user can save messages in specified files (messages are saved by default in a file named mbox in the recipient's login or home directory).

The next chapter looks at some other ways for remote communications or working on networked systems.

## Chapter 14

Using UNIX Remote Communications

There are a number of advantages to having your system networked or connected to other UNIX systems. On a network, you can exchange files, mail, and other information and distribute the work load, software functions, and specialized hardware among the systems on the network.

Looking at Kinds of Networks

One prevalent type of network on UNIX systems is a *UUCP network*. UUCP stands for UNIX-to-UNIX copy. Originally, UUCP was used to copy files between UNIX systems using the uucp command.

In a UUCP network, systems must be connected to each other while they exchange information. This is called a *point-to-point* network. The systems are usually connected over serial communication lines, either directly or through modems, although you also can connect systems over local area networks.

The primary advantage of a UUCP network is cost. The only special equipment required is a modem—cabling costs are minimal. The disadvantage is that transmission speed over the network is limited by the speed of serial connections, which are generally much slower than transmission speeds on other types of networks. In addition, files, mail, and so on are often put into a queue to be transferred to another system only once a day. However, UUCP networks have been in use for several years and have a well-established following.

This chapter explains how to do the following:

- Use commands on a UUCP network

- Use the rcp command for remote copying on the LAN

- Use commands to log in to remote systems

- Execute commands on other systems

- Use the UnixWare GUI to accomplish remote communications

The first part of this chapter covers how to use UUCP networks to exchange e-mail and copy files. You learn how to use the following commands:

uuname	Determine the UUCP network names of your system and the remote systems your system knows about
uuto	Copy files from your system to another
uupick	Manage files you received from uuto
uucp	General-purpose UNIX-to-UNIX copy program
uustat	Track and manage UUCP jobs
cu	Connect to another UNIX system using serial ports

Another type of network is a *broadcast* or *token-passing network.* In this model, all the networked systems monitor the traffic on the network. A system puts information out to the network with the address or name of the destination. All systems can see this but only the destination system accepts it. This sort of communication is prevalent on a *local area network,* or *LAN.*

The advantage to using a LAN is speed. Mail delivery or copying a file over a LAN seems instantaneous. You can distribute system loads, software, or specialized hardware by being able to execute commands or log in to remote systems. Again, there is no apparent delay. The disadvantage is cost and the limitations to the physical size of the network. You may have to purchase network hardware and install expensive cabling. Total coverage on a LAN may be only a few thousand meters; perhaps enough for an office building but not enough for a diverse organization.

The second half of this chapter explains some commands you use when working with TCP/IP utilities on a LAN:

rcp	Copy files from one system to another on the network
rlogin	Log in to a remote system from your current system
rsh	Start a shell on a remote system from your current system

Using UUCP

The most basic UNIX networking utility is a collection of commands and tables called UUCP (for *UNIX-to-UNIX Copy*). UUCP is actually a UNIX command, entered in lowercase letters at the command prompt. The name UUCP is a generalized name given to uucp and other basic networking commands.

When you see UUCP in this chapter, it refers to that collection of commands. UUCP has been available on UNIX systems for several years and enjoys a well-established following. Systems connected with UUCP communicate over serial communication lines, either through modems or direct connections.

There isn't any exotic networking software or hardware needed. The software is part of the usual UNIX distribution; connections are made through serial ports (ttys) or modems. Networks consist of individual computers connected to other individual computers. UUCP is an example of a *point-to-point* network because systems actually have to be connected to each other when they communicate with each other.

> **Tip**
>
> UUCP is usually set up to connect to remote systems over serial lines. However, starting with UNIX System V Release 3, you can configure UUCP to plug into any type of network that meets the AT&T Transport Interface specification. This includes the TCP/IP software that comes with UnixWare; this software lets you set up UUCP connections over LANs.

Transfers take place in both directions. You send and receive mail and copy files between systems. UUCP is useful for electronic mail, USENET news, and copying files. When a UUCP connection is made between systems, first one system sends all the files for the remote system and then it receives the files addressed to it.

Understanding UUCP

UUCP networks or connections are a cooperative venture between your system administrator and the administrator of another UNIX system. These administrators must configure both systems to communicate with each other. At your site, the administrator creates files and tables that contain the list of systems that can be accessed by UUCP and the list of systems permitted to contact your system. Your system administrator also configures and designates one or more ports to deal with UUCP. A system administrator at the remote system performs similar tasks. The administrator at either site establishes authorizations and permissions to provide capabilities for and security from remote systems.

Each system involved in UUCP must have a unique name. Using that system name with your login name (which is unique on your system) gives you an identity on the network. Suppose that your login name is cici and your system name is bradyb. Your UUCP address is bradyb!cici. If your system is connected by UUCP to a system named flints and you have a friend there whose login name is teresa, you can send mail to her using the address flints!teresa. The general form of an address in UUCP is as follows:

```
remote-system-name!target
```

More systems can be involved and they don't have to be directly connected to each other. Suppose that the system flints has a UUCP connection to another network named trinkle and you want to send mail or a file to a user named marsha on the system trinkle. You use the address flints!trinkle!marsha. A UUCP address with more than one exclamation mark (!) is called a *multi-hop address*.

There may be many sites between your system and the final destination; some large UUCP sites keep maps of connections between systems to minimize the number of system names in an address. You or your system administrator may find it useful to contact a local university or a commercial network to arrange for this sort of routing of UUCP requests. Figure 14.1 shows several systems connected by UUCP.

Fig. 14.1
A sample UUCP network.

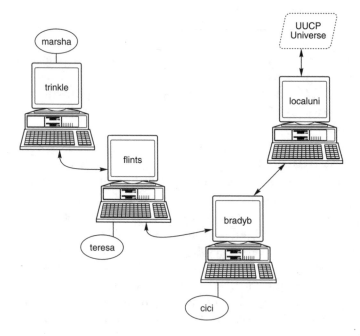

UUCP is often set up so that items are transferred to a remote site in batches. This is particularly true when UUCP connections use modems and when contacting the remote system means making a long-distance telephone call. It is also true if you can connect to several systems through only one port. This batching is called *spooling*, or *putting requests in a spool queue*. Spooling

IV

UNIX Tools

allows the administrator to reduce communication costs and arrange for systems to exchange information during off-peak times.

When you use the UUCP system, the software checks the destination address to be sure that the remote system can be contacted. Then the request or the information itself is put into the queue for transfer later. The address has the familiar form *remote-site-name!target*. Once the request or information arrives at the remote site, the UUCP software there examines the portion of the address after the first exclamation mark (!). If it contains another !, the information is put into a spool queue to be passed on to another remote site.

For example, if you send mail with UUCP to `flints!trinkle!marsha`, the information is first put into the UUCP spool queue for `flints` on your system. When it's transferred to `flints`, the software there issues the UUCP commands to send the information to `trinkle!marsha`. The information is put into a spool queue for the system `trinkle` and transferred at a specified time. If there are a number of system names, each separated by an exclamation mark (!), the message is passed along in this manner. This is called a *store and forward system*. Each system name in the address generally stores messages and then passes information along.

> **Note**
>
> If you are using the C shell (`csh`) as your login shell, you must put a slash (\) in front of the exclamation mark (!). The C shell gives the ! special treatment. If you use `csh`, you write a UUCP-style address as `cornflks\!cereal\!bowl`. You can also use this form if you use Bourne (`sh`) or Korn (`ksh`) as your login shell, although it is not necessary.

Finding Site Names

To communicate with other systems using UUCP, you must know your system's name on the network and the names of other systems. You find this information using the `uuname` command.

Finding the UUCP Name of Your Site

To find the UUCP name of your site or system, use the `uuname` command with the `-l` option. When you see the shell prompt, type **uuname -l** and press <Return>. If you were logged onto a system named `bradyb`, you would see the following (what you type is in bold):

```
$ uuname -l <Return>
bradyb
```

Finding the Names of Other Sites

To find the names of the other sites that UUCP knows about in your system, type **uuname** and press <Return>. You see a list of all the sites you can access directly through UUCP. Talk with your system administrator to add sites to the list. Here is an example on the hypothetical system used in previous examples (what you type is in bold):

```
$ uuname <Return>
flints
localuni
```

Using UUCP To Send Mail

▶ For more information about the Internet, refer to Part V of this book, "Using the Internet."

You don't have to change e-mail systems to send e-mail by UUCP. All you have to do is give an address in UUCP form. Electronic mail systems use tables of rules to look at an address and choose a way to send it. In this way, a mail system can decide whether to keep mail on the local system, send it to a system on a UUCP network, or perhaps route it through the Internet.

> **Note**
>
> UUCP and TCP/IP maintain different lists of systems that they can communicate with. It's possible to have the same system name in both lists because you can reach it from both networks. Mail chooses which network to use based on the order in which the networks are tested in the `/etc/mail/mailsurr` file.

A UUCP address has the general form *remote-site!target*. The portion *remote-site* is the name of a site UUCP knows about; *target* can be a user name or the general form of a UUCP address.

When you send mail using a UUCP address, it can take a long time before it's delivered. This is particularly true if your destination requires transfer through several remote sites. You're not only dealing with the schedule for sending UUCP files on your system, but you have to put up with schedules on other systems as well.

Sending Mail to UUCP Sites

In these next two examples, the file `report.txt` is sent. In the first case, it is sent to a user named `rangel` at the site `flints`, which is directly connected to your site by UUCP. You enter the following command to accomplish this transfer:

```
mailx -s "Confidential Report" flints!rangel < report.txt
```

In the second case, the file is sent to a user named `dhunte` at the site `trinkle`, which isn't connected to your site, but *is* in the UUCP network for the site `flints`. You enter this command to accomplish this transfer:

```
mailx -s "Confidential Report" flints!trinkle!dhunte < report.txt
```

Here are several things to note about these examples:

- In each case, the e-mail message is likely put into a spool queue that UUCP will manage.

- If the mail is sent out once a day from your site, it could be up to 24 hours before `rangel` at `flints` gets the report. If mail is sent out once a day from `flints` and your timing is bad, it could be up to 48 hours before the message is sent to `dhunte` at `trinkle`. You should hope that mail is not sent only once a week!

- In the second example, the mail (your report) is put into a spool queue for UUCP at the site `flints`. You can't count on mail being kept confidential there; it's not on your system and it's not on the system of the addressee.

Sending and Receiving Files with *uuto* and *uupick*

The UUCP software contains two programs you will find useful in sending files to remote systems and managing files sent from remote systems:

uuto	Sends one or more files *to* a remote system
uupick	Manages files sent to you *from* a remote system by uuto

Using *uuto* To Transfer Files to a Remote System

An easy way to copy one or more files from your system to a remote system is to use the command `uuto`. To use this command, type the command, the name of the file or files you are copying, and the UUCP address of the destination. To send copies of the files `report1` and `report2` to a user named `teresa` at the site `flints`, enter the following command:

```
uuto report1 report2 flints!teresa
```

Because the file transfer is handled by UUCP, the request to transfer the files is queued until the remote system is contacted. More than one file can be sent, but only one destination can be stated. The destination must be of the form *remote-site!user*. No multi-hop addresses are allowed.

The uuto command has two options:

-m   Sends mail to the sender and the recipient when the transfer is complete

-p   Copies the file to a spool directory before it is transferred

As you expect, there are advantages to using both of these options:

■ Using the -m option lets you know that the file or files have been sent and notifies the receiver of incoming mail.

■ Using the -p option has the effect of freezing the files. The files are sent to the remote site in the same shape they were in when you issued the command. Don't forget that there can be a delay of several hours from the time you issue the command to the time when the files are actually sent.

The following example uses the uuto command and the -m and -p options:

```
uuto -p -m memo flints
```

Once the remote copy completed successfully, you would receive a mail message that looks like the following:

```
REQUEST: trinkle!memo —> flints!~/receive/james/trinkle/ (james) (SYSTEM : flints)   copy succeeded
```

Using *uupick* To Manage Files Sent by *uuto*

Files sent to your site by someone using uuto are automatically put into the directory /usr/spool/uucppublic. That directory is set up so that anyone can write to it. All the files sent to you from a single site are grouped together. When a user at a remote site named flints sends you files by uuto, those files are stored in a directory named flints. (The full path name of the directory is /usr/spool/uucppublic/receive/*user*/flints, where *user* is replaced by your user name.)

Use the command uupick to browse through the files you receive by uuto. You run uupick by typing the command and pressing <Return>. If you don't have any files waiting, you see the shell prompt reappear. If you do have files waiting, you see something like this (what you type is in bold):

```
$ uupick <Return>
from system flints: play.lst ?
```

This message means that the file named play.lst has been received from the remote system flints. The ? is a prompt from the uupick program; you have several options for a response. You can move the file or the entire directory of files from that system to another location, skip the file and leave it there, display the file on the screen, or quit uupick. Table 14.1 lists the interactive commands you can use.

The following example moves all the files from flints to the directory Reports in your login directory and then quits (what you type is in bold):

```
$ uupick <Return>
from system flints: file report1 ?
a $HOME/Reports <Return>
from system bedrock: file little.peb ?
q <Return>
$ <Return>
```

Although the example doesn't explicitly state this, you can see that there are other files for you from at least one other remote system (file little.peb from the system named bedrock).

Table 14.1: *uupick* Interactive Commands

Command	Action
a [*dir*]	Moves all the files copied from the remote system to the named directory. The brackets indicate optional information (the brackets aren't part of the command). For example, a $HOME/Results copies files to the directory Results in your login directory. Use the a command by itself when you want to move the files to the current directory.
m [*dir*]	Similar to the a command except that only the current file is moved.
d	Deletes the current file.
p	Prints the current file to the screen. The file is displayed on your terminal. This command does not send the file to a printer.
q	Quits uupick.
*	Displays a summary of the available commands.
!*cmd*	Executes the shell command *cmd*. For example, if you want to check whether the file is already in the Results directory, use the command ls to list the names of the files in that directory: !ls $HOME/Reports.
<Return>	Goes to the next file.

Using *uucp* To Transfer Files

You can use the uuto program to copy one or more files from your system to a particular user on a remote system. The uuto program is a special case of the more general command uucp, which lets you copy files both *to* and *from* remote systems (remember that the acronym UUCP stands for *UNIX-to-UNIX CoPy*). The general form of the uucp command is as follows:

```
uucp [options] source destination
```

Both *source* and *destination* are names of files or directories, where one or both of the names include a UUCP-style address. The uucp command uses the same general form as the cp command used to copy files on a single computer. What's different here is that either *source* or *destination*, or both, can be on remote systems.

Just as with uuto, the destination address must be a system directly connected to yours. In other words, you can have only one exclamation mark (!) in the address.

Tip

The command uusend is available on some systems. You use it the same way you use uucp except that you can use multi-hop addresses. Check with your system administrator to see whether uusend is available at your site.

Note

The uuto command takes care of putting the files in the right places on the remote system. You really don't have any choice: with uuto, the destination is the UUCP address of a user. When you use uucp, however, you can be more general. More responsibility comes with this added opportunity. It's up to you to be sure that permissions are set so that anyone can read the source and that the UUCP system can write to the destination.

The *source* must be a file or directory that anyone can read; the *destination* must be a file or directory that can be written to by anyone. In a UUCP system, the directory /usr/spool/uucppublic has permissions set so that anyone can read from it and write to it. Because it is a directory and anyone can write to it, anyone can create a directory inside of it.

The uucp command gives you the capability to do the following:

- Copy files from your system to a remote system.
  your-system   →   *remote-system*

- Copy files from a remote system to your system.
  remote-system   →   *your-system*

IV

■ Copy files from one remote system to another remote system.

remote-system-A   →   *remote-system-B*

You can copy files *and* directories using uucp.

Using *uucp* To Copy Files to a Remote System

Suppose that you have a file named report1 you want to send to a colleague on the system whose UUCP name is flints. You must make sure that report1 can be read by anyone and you must specify that the destination is the name of a file or directory that can be written to by anyone.

To make sure that the permissions are set on report1 so that anyone can read it, enter the following command:

```
chmod a+r report1
```

This command gives all users read permission for report1. The UUCP system includes the directory /usr/spool/uucppublic which has permissions set so that anyone can write to it. You can use that for the destination address. When you see the shell prompt, type the complete uucp command and press <Return>:

```
uucp report1 flints!/usr/spool/uucppublic
```

The program checks that local permissions are correct and that the remote system (flints in this case) is recognized by your UUCP system. The shell prompt returns and uucp does the rest of its work in the background. Once the file is copied, it is available for anyone to read or change on the remote system.

The preceding command copies the file report1 to the system flints. Because /usr/spool/uucppublic is a directory, the file report1 becomes a file in that directory. To copy the file to a colleague whose login name is cici, put the file into a directory with that name, and make sure that both you and cici are sent mail when the file arrives, enter the following command:

```
uucp  -m -ncici report1 flints!/usr/spool/uucppublic/cici/
```

The options you can use with uucp are listed in table 14.2, later in this chapter. In this example, the option -m sends you mail when the copy is complete; the -n followed by your colleague's name sends cici mail when the copy arrives. The destination address ends with a / to indicate that the destination is a directory and should be created if it doesn't already exist.

◄ For more information on permissions and how to set them, refer to Chapter 7, "Understanding UNIX File and Directory Systems."

> **Tip**
>
> You can save some typing by using the tilde (~) to represent
> /usr/spool/uucppublic on a remote system. For example, type
> **uucp abc tucan!~/abc.cpy** and press <Return> to copy abc to the file
> /usr/spool/uucppublic/abc.cpy on the system named tucan.

> **Caution**
>
> Be careful to specify that you want to copy a file to a directory. If you type
> **uucp report1 flints!/usr/spool/uucppublic/cici** and the directory cici
> doesn't exist inside /usr/spool/uucppublic, cici is created as a *file*. That file will
> contain a copy of the file report1 from your system. To guarantee that the copy of
> report1 goes into a directory named cici and is in a file named report1, enter
> **uucp report1 flints!/usr/spool/uucppublic/cici/** (note the final slash).
> The uucp command then creates the directory cici if it doesn't already exist.

◀ Chapter 10, "Understanding UNIX Shells," describes the use of wild cards in the completion of filenames.

You can specify more than one file to copy. You can also use the shell's special characters for filename completion to specify a collection of files. For example, the following command copies all the files whose names start with the string rep:

```
uucp rep* flints!~/cici/
```

Using *uucp* To Copy Files from a Remote System

To copy files or directories from a remote system to your system, you list them in the *source* portion of the uucp command in much the same way as they were given in the *destination* portion in the preceding section.

For example, to copy the file report in the directory /tmp from the system flints to a file named report.flt on your system, enter the following command:

```
uucp flints!/tmp/report report.flt
```

Remember that, before you copy the file, you must set permissions so that anyone can write to the file report.flt. Make sure that the file exists and set its permissions so that any user can write to it: type **chmod a+w report.flt** and press <Return>. In this case, the report is copied into your directory. As an alternative, you can set the destination to a directory that anyone can write to such as /tmp or /usr/spool/uucppublic and not specify a filename. The name of the file on your system is the same (report) as it was on the remote system. For example, enter the following command to copy the `report` file from the `tmp` directory on `flints` to the `tmp` directory on your system; the file's name as it appears on your system is `report` by default:

```
uucp flints!/tmp/report /tmp
```

> **Note**
>
> Remember that, by default, you cannot read files from a remote system. Have the administrator on the remote system set up the `/etc/uucp/Permissions` file with additional permissions to allow you to read from the remote system or write to a directory other than `/usr/spool/uucppublic`.

If you use any special shell characters such as * or ? in *source* filenames on the remote system, you must enclose the *source* portion in quotation marks ("") to prevent those characters from being interpreted on your system. For example, to copy all files from a directory named `/usr/sales/reports` from the `flints` system to a directory named `flints.rep` in `/usr/spool/uucppublic` on your system, enter this command:

```
uucp "fints!/usr/sales/reports/*" ~uucp/flints.rep/
```

> **Tip**
>
> You can save yourself some typing by using ~uucp to represent the directory `/usr/spool/uucppublic` on your local system.

Using *uucp* To Copy Files from One Remote System to Another

To copy files from one remote system to another remote system, you use single-hop (only one !) names for the files in both the *source* and *destination* portions of the command. If you use the * or ? wild card, be sure that it is inside quotation marks so that the filenames are completed at the remote sites.

Suppose that you want to copy all the files in a directory named `/usr/sales/newprods` from the remote system `flints` to another remote system named `trinkle`. Enter the following command:

```
uucp "flints!/usr/sales/newprods/*" trinkle!~/flints/
```

This command causes a transfer of files from `flints` to `trinkle`. In effect, you're asking for uucp to be run on the `flints` system.

Using Options with *uucp*

Table 14.2 lists the options you can use with uucp.

Table 14.2: *uucp* Command Options	
Option	**Definition**
-c	Do not copy file to the spool directory. This is the default action.
-C	Copy the files to the spool directory so that the copies are the ones transferred.
-d	Create directories for the copy if they don't exist. This is the default action.
-f	Don't make directories when they don't exist.
-m	Send mail to the one who issued the uucp command when the copy is complete.
-n*user*	Send mail to *user* on the remote system when the copy is complete.
-s*file*	Instead of sending mail, put a message in *file* when the copy is complete.

The default actions are to *not* copy files to the spool area before they are transferred and to create directories as necessary. Suppose that you issue the following command:

```
uucp myfile faraway!~/friend/
```

Now suppose that you change myfile before it is sent. The new version of myfile is copied to /usr/spool/uucppublic/friend/myfile on the remote system. The directory friend is created on the remote system if it doesn't already exist.

You most likely want to copy the file to the spool area when you issue the uucp command because it may be some time before the file is actually copied. It's also a good idea to have uucp notify both you and the person receiving the file that the file has been copied. The following command uses the options to do just that:

```
uucp -C -m -nfriend myfile faraway!~/friend
```

Using *uustat*

You use the uustat command to find out about UUCP transfers that are queued and haven't taken place. You can also use uustat to cancel transfers before they take place.

Checking UUCP Transfers with *uustat*

To see which of your UUCP transfers are waiting to be completed, type **uustat** and press <Return>. Suppose that you enter the following command to copy the file myfile to the remote system flints and then check on that transfer operation with the uustat command:

```
$ uucp myfile flints!/~/friend <Return>
$ uustat <Return>
```

UNIX responds with something like this:

```
flintsN574d    01/16-12:25  S  flints  imgood 897 /usr/imgood/myfile
```

The first field holds the job ID flintsN574d; the next field holds the date the job was put into the UUCP queue; the S character notes that the file is being *sent*. The next few fields give the name of the remote system, who sent it (assuming that your login name is imgood), the size of the file in bytes, and the original location of the file.

To see *all* UUCP transfers, regardless of who issued them, type **uustat -a** and press <Return>.

Canceling a UUCP Request

The command uustat has an option, -k, which allows you to cancel a UUCP request. To use this option, you must know the job ID of the request you want to cancel. To do that, first enter **uustat** to see which jobs are queued:

```
$ uustat <Return>
flintsN574d    01/16-12:25  S  flints  imgood   897 /usr/imgood/myfile
vtlsN38bd      01/16-12:30  S  vtls    imgood 37920 /usr/sales/announce/products.new
```

To cancel the second UUCP request, enter the following command:

```
uustat -k vtlsN38bd
```

UNIX responds with the following message:

```
Job: vtlsN38bd successfully killed
```

Connecting to Other Systems Using *cu*

The cu command is part of the UUCP collection of software. It stands for *call UNIX*. You use the cu command when you need to spend a short time working on another system in your UUCP network. Your system administrator must set up certain files to allow you to use cu and contact some systems by name.

Using *cu* To Call Another System by Name

The cu command places a call to another computer system and allows you to log in to that system. If your administrator has set up things so that you can make contact with the system named trinkle, you call trinkle by entering the following command:

```
cu trinkle
```

After a short time, you should see a login prompt from the remote system named trinkle. Type your login and, when prompted, your password for the remote system.

Ending a *cu* Session

To terminate the connection you've made to a remote system, type a tilde followed by a period (~.) The name of your local system is displayed and the connection should be terminated.

Using *cu* To Call Another System Using a Phone Number

You can use cu to dial out through a modem to another system. This feature is advantageous when you need to contact a commercial network or service such as CompuServe or Lexis.

You also need to call another system with a phone number when your system administrator hasn't configured the UUCP system so that you can call another system on the network by its name. You should be sure that a modem is connected to one of the ports on the system. Your call is automatically directed to the modem if the administrator has configured it to dial out. Here's an example of using cu with a telephone number:

```
cu 9244311
```

Here are some tips when using cu and a phone number:

- You may be able to give only the phone number such as cu 5558761.

- You can include codes, for example a 9, to get an outside line: cu 9=5558761. Some business telephone systems have you dial a 9 to get an outside line. The equal sign (=) tells cu to wait for a second dial tone before dialing the rest of the numbers.

- You may have to specify the *baud rate*, or speed, of the modem and the port, or *line*, it uses. In this example, the speed is 2,400 baud and the port is tty04: cu -s1200 -l/dev/tty04 9=5558761.

Troubleshooting

You want to dial out with a phone number, but you also want to change some modem settings.

There may be times when you want to talk directly to the modem to set special modem features. Suppose that you have a Hayes-compatible modem connected to your COM1 port and you want to turn off auto-answering. Type **cu -l/dev/tty00** and press <Return> to set up a direct connection to the modem. When the modem responds with OK, type **ATS0=0** and press <Return>. While you're "talking" to the modem, try dialing out directly; for example, type **ATD5551212** and press <Return>. This is a good way to make sure that your modem is set up properly if you are having trouble with the cu command.

Using *rcp* for Remote Copying on the LAN

If your UNIX system is connected to a local area network, or LAN, you can use a whole new set of commands to work over the network. The most popular UNIX software to use over LANs is TCP/IP.

Using TCP/IP, you can copy files from one system to another using the rcp command. This command is similar to the cp command that enables you to copy files on a single system. The difference is that rcp lets you copy files among systems on your network. The general form of the rcp command is as follows:

```
rcp [options] source destination
```

The same rules apply to the *source* and *destination* options when you use rcp as when you use cp. You must have read permission on the source file and write permission on the destination file. If the destination file doesn't exist, rcp creates it for you, provided that you have permission to do so. Your system administrator sets up the systems on your network to allow you to copy files using rcp. One place to look for the names of systems on your network is the file /etc/hosts.

Remote Access and Security

If you have a login name on another system on your network, you can give yourself or others access to your files. In order to do that, you must create a file named .rhosts in your login directory on the other system. This file contains entries of the following form:

> *system-name*   *login-name*

For example:

> oregano   imgood

Once this file is in place, the user named imgood on oregano has a lot of power. He or she can copy files from your local system using rcp, execute commands on your system using rsh login, and log in to your system using rlogin from the system named oregano—all without supplying a password! The login name imgood must exist on the local system.

It is convenient to have .rhosts in your home directory. You can copy files using rcp and execute commands remotely. Before you create .rhosts, check with your system administrator: some don't allow users to create a .rhosts file because it creates a potential security risk. Following are some scenarios that show the risks:

Scenario 1: You inadvertently set the permissions on .rhosts so that anyone can write to it. That means anyone can change it. Someone changes it by adding a line with their system name and login name. Then they gain access to your directory and files, and they gain access to your system. Once they're in your system, they attack other security holes.

Scenario 2: Malicious hackers break into oregano and fool that system into thinking they are you, imgood. The hackers purposely look for a file named .rhosts. To make things convenient for yourself, you've included the names of all the systems you can access and your corresponding login names in that file. The hackers go from one system on your company's network to every system.

If you still want to create the file .rhosts, do the following:

1. Make a note of your current system's name. Suppose that it is thyme.

2. Log in to the other system.

3. Using vi or another text editor, add the following line to the .rhosts file in your login directory (suppose that your login name is imgood):

   > thyme imgood

4. Make sure that you are the only person who can read this file: type
   chmod 400 .rhosts and press <Return>.

5. Check to see that you're the only one who can read your login directory as well. Enter **ls -ld $HOME**. You see your directory name preceded by the permissions for that directory, as in this example:

drwx — x — x imgood ....

This line indicates that you're the only one who can read the directory. If you find that others can read this directory, talk with your system administrator and find out why others have read access to your directory.

You use the name of another system on your network as part of either the *source* or *destination* name. Suppose that oregano is the name of a system on your network and you want to copy the file spices to the file /tmp/spices.me on that system. You enter the following rcp command:

    rcp spices oregano:/tmp/spices.me

The shell prompt returns when the copy is complete. If you don't have permission to copy to that system or to that file, you see a message to that effect before the shell prompt is displayed. The shell prompt doesn't appear until the copy is complete. This is different than using UUCP where the copy is often put into a queue to be sent at a later time.

The command rcp gives you the capability to do the following:

■ Copy files from your system to another network system.
  your-system   →   *other-system*

■ Copy files from another network system to your system.
  other-system   →   *your-system*

■ Copy files from one network system to another network system.
  network-system-A   →   *network-system-B*

Copying a File from Your System with *rcp*

To copy a file from your system to another, use the name of the file you want to copy in place of *source*. The *destination* starts with the name of the other system on your network, followed by a colon (:), and finally the name of the directory or file on the other system.

The following three commands copy the file /etc/hosts from your system to another system named oregano. In the first case, the file is copied to the file /usr/tmp/hosts.etc:

    rcp /etc/hosts oregano:/usr/tmp/hosts.etc

In the second case, the file is copied to the directory /tmp on oregano. After the second statement is executed, the copy resides in /tmp/hosts:

```
rcp /etc/hosts oregano:/tmp
```

In the third case, the file is copied to your home directory on oregano. Naturally, you must have a login name on oregano:

```
rcp /etc/hosts oregano:
```

Copying Several Files from Your System with *rcp*

To copy several files, you can either list them individually or use the special shell characters * or ? to refer to a group of files.

In the next examples, several files are copied to the system oregano. In the first case, the files report1 and report2 are copied from the current directory to the directory /users/sales/reports:

```
rcp report1 report2 oregano:/users/sales/reports
```

In the second case, all files from the current directory whose names start with rep are copied to the directory /users/sales/reports/all:

```
$ rcp rep* oregano:/users/sales/reports/all
```

Copying Files from Another System to Your System with *rcp*

To copy one or more files from another system on the network to your system, list the remote files in the *source* portion of the rcp command. The *destination* is a file or a directory to which you have write permission.

The next two examples copy one or more files from the system named basil to your system. In the first case, the file /users/sales/reports/current is copied to the file sales.cur in your login directory:

```
rcp basil:/users/sales/reports/current sales.cur
```

In the second case, all files whose names contain the string rep in the directory /users/sales/data are copied to the directory sales/reports in the present directory:

```
rcp "basil:/users/sales/data/*rep*" sales/reports
```

> **Note**
>
> Notice that the special shell characters (two asterisks, *, in this case) are enclosed with quotation marks to prevent them from being expanded on the current system.

Copying Files from One Network System to Another Network System with *rcp*

To copy files from one system on your network to another, where neither of those systems is your own, you must give the names of the systems in both the *source* and *destination* portions of the command. In this example, a file named report in the directory /users/publications/drafts on the system named basil is copied to the directory /users/copyedit on the system named oregano:

```
rcp basil:/users/publications/drafts/report oregano:/users/copyedit
```

Using Options with *rcp*

There are two options you can use with rcp:

-p   Copies files and *preserves* permissions and time of last modification

-r   Copies a directory *recursively*; that is, it copies the directory and all its subdirectories

Using *-p* with *rcp*

Use the -p option when you want to preserve the permissions to the copied file or when you want the copy to have the same date as the original. Here is an example of the use of the -p option:

```
rcp -p special.txt oregano:/tmp/read.me
```

The files special.txt and /tmp/read.me on oregano have the same dates and same permissions as they did on your source system.

Using *-r* with *rcp*

The -r option is useful when you want to copy an entire directory and its subdirectories from one system to another. Suppose that you created a directory named Framistan that holds all the files relating to your account with Framistan Motors. Naturally, you've organized the files in Framistan into directories. To move the directory Framistan with all its files and subdirectories from the system named garlic to your login directory on the present system, enter the following command:

```
rcp -r garlic:/Framistan $HOME
```

> **Note**
>
> If permissions are closed off for any subdirectory from which you are trying to copy with rcp -r, nothing below that point in the directory structure is copied. For example, if you enter the command **rcp -r /home flints:/tmp**, any directory in /home for which you don't have permissions to read prevents you from copying any of the files or subdirectories beneath that directory.

Logging in to Remote Systems with *rlogin*

The rlogin command allows you to log in to another system on your network from your current system. This is a useful command when system loads or system functions must be distributed among several computer systems on a network. When you execute rlogin to log in to another system on your network, that system carries out your instructions. If your network administrator wants to restrict some programs or data to a single system, you can use rlogin to gain access to that system. If one system has a specialized input (digitizer) or output (high-resolution color) printer, for example, you can access those systems with rlogin.

The general form of the rlogin command is as follows:

```
rlogin host
```

In this syntax, *host* is the name of a system on your network. You use the file .rhosts to list the names of systems and users that are allowed to log in without giving a password.

Logging In and Logging Out with *rlogin*

To log in to another system on your network, you must know the name of the system. Check with your system administrator. Names of systems on the network may be kept in /etc/hosts.

In this next example, the remote system to log in to is named oregano, there is no .rhosts file, and your login name on oregano is the same as the login name on your current system.

When you type the **rlogin** command and press <Return>, you are prompted for a password by the system oregano. With the proper information in .rhosts on oregano, you wouldn't be asked for the password. Once you give the correct password, you see a prompt from your login shell on oregano.

To log out, type either **~.** (a tilde followed by period) or **exit**. You should use exit because this command is treated as a normal logout command by the remote system. If you use ~., you see a message like `Connection Closed`.

Once you log in to the remote system, it's just as if you were using a terminal or workstation directly connected to that remote system.

Using a Different Login Name with *rlogin*

You may want to log in to a network system from your current system using a login name that's different than your current login name. You can use `rlogin` to do this when your login name on another system is different than your current login name or you need to have the same capabilities of another user either on your system or on a network system.

To use a different login name, use the following form of the `rlogin` command:

```
rlogin remote-host -l login-name
```

Suppose that your current system's name is `basil` and your login name is `imgood`. To log in to the network system named `oregano` where your login name is `hotshot`, use this command:

```
rlogin oregano -l hotshot
```

To log in to the current system using the login name `demoacnt`, use this command:

```
rlogin basil -l demoacnt
```

Executing Commands on Other Systems with *rsh*

You use the `rsh` command to execute commands on remote systems on your network. The name stands for *remote shell*. Its general form is as follows:

```
rsh   remote-host command
```

Note

On some UNIX systems, the command `rsh` stands for *restricted shell*. It is used to start a shell that doesn't allow users to change directories or redirect output. Look for a command named `remsh` on your system if `rsh` is used in this way. For the remainder of this chapter, `rsh` denotes the *remote shell* command.

When you give the command `rsh`, a shell is started on a remote system. Use this command when you want to execute one or more commands on another system but don't necessarily want to log in to another system.

When you issue the `rsh` command, the following happens:

- You use the same shell on the remote system as your login shell.

- You don't execute the commands in your `.profile` file if you use the Bourne or Korn shell, or in `.login` if you use the C shell as your login shell.

- You can't execute any commands that expect input from the keyboard (such as `vi` or `more`) because the remote commands can't accept input from the keyboard. The input that comes from `stdin`, in this case the keyboard, is taken by `rsh` and *not* passed to the commands it executes.

- The output of commands is passed back to your home system.

In this next example, `rsh` is used to run the program, `chkstats`, which performs statistical analysis on the information in the file `sales.rpt`:

```
rsh oregano chkstats sales.rpt > stats
```

The shell prompt returns when the program terminates and the file `stats` is on the home system. Notice that the results of the `chkstats` program aren't put into a file on the remote `oregano` system.

Using *rsh* To Execute Multiple Commands

You can use `rsh` to execute several commands on the remote system, provided that the following are true:

- The commands are separated by semicolons (;)

- The string of commands is enclosed in quotation marks ("") or each semicolon is preceded by a backslash (\)

In the following example, the work is done on the system `rosemary`. The directory `/tmp/reports` is created, some files are copied into that directory, and that directory is copied back to the home system named `thyme`.

```
rsh rosemary "mkdir /tmp/reports; cp /users/sales/meetings/*
/tmp/reports; rcp -r /tmp/reports thyme:/tmp"
```

Using *rsh* with Pipes and I/O Redirection

The command `rsh` sends its output and error messages to the home system. In some cases, you may want the output to *stay* on the remote system, particularly when the work is done on a remote machine for the benefit of users on the remote system. You may also want to keep the output on the remote system if you want to take the results of a command and put it through a pipe on a remote system.

In this example, which you saw in the preceding section, the output, the file stats, was sent to the home system:

```
rsh oregano chkstats sales.rpt > stats
```

To keep the stats file on the remote system oregano, enclose the remote command in quotation marks, as in this version of the command:

```
rsh oregano "chkstats sales.rpt > stats"
```

You use the same technique to put the output of commands through a pipe. In the following example, the file research.dat is sorted, the results put into a file named rsrch.srt using the command tee, and then sent to be printed by the program lp. All this activity occurs on the remote system:

```
rsh oregano "sort research.dat ¦ tee rsrch.srt ¦lp"
```

This next sample command mails a copy of the sorted data to the user chendric. All this takes place on oregano:

```
rsh oregano "sort research.dat ¦ tee rsrch.srt ¦ mailx chendric"
```

Using Remote Communications from the GUI

The UnixWare version of UNIX provides graphical user interfaces to UUCP and TCP/IP. The Dialup Setup window lets you configure UUCP connections; the Internet Setup window lets you set up TCP/IP connections.

Once the administrator has configured the Dialup Setup and Internet Setup windows, you can use the lists of systems from these windows to communicate from the GUI. The Dialup Setup and Internet Setup windows are contained in the System Setup window (accessed by double-clicking on the System Setup icon in the UnixWare Desktop window).

Once you are in the System Setup window, double-click on the Dialup Setup or Internet Setup icon (the icon you choose depends on how the remote system you want to communicate with can be reached. Figures 14.2 and 14.3 show the Dialup Setup and Internet Setup windows.

Fig. 14.2
The UnixWare
Internet Setup
window.

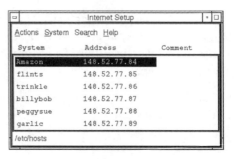

Fig. 14.3
The UnixWare
Dialup Setup
window.

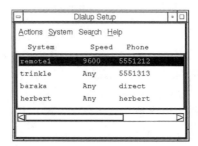

To communicate with the systems shown in the Dialup Setup or Internet Setup window, you must drag-and-drop the system you want to communicate with into one of your folders. With the mouse pointer on a system name in one of the two windows, press the left mouse button, drag the pointer to an open folder, and release the mouse button. An icon representing the remote system appears in the folder.

Once an icon for a remote system is placed in a folder, you can send files to the system or log in to that system. Here's how:

■ **Remote login.** Double-click on the remote system icon. A window opens, allowing you to log in to the remote system. (A remote system accessed from Dialup Setup uses the cu command to make the connection; one accessed from Internet Setup uses the rlogin command.)

■ **File copy**. Drag-and-drop a file from any folder window on the remote system icon. A window appears on the screen, asking you to select the recipient and the delivery method (UUCP or Internet). Click on Send to send the file.

You can select the delivery method only if the system is listed in both the Dialup Setup and Internet Setup windows. Otherwise, the method is selected for you. If you choose the Internet method, an additional text box appears, allowing you to request the remote directory to which the file is copied.

IV

UNIX Tools

Summary

The UUCP collection of software makes it possible to create an inexpensive, reliable, point-to-point network. UUCP can be used to send electronic mail and copy files between systems. With the UUCP system, you can copy files or directories to and from your local system; you can also copy files or directories from one remote system to another.

If your system is on a local area network, you can send mail and copy files at very high speeds. A number of commands are useful in communicating or working on LAN systems that use TCP/IP software.

If you use UnixWare or some other UNIX System V Release 4.2 system, both UUCP and TCP/IP have graphical user interfaces available. Using your mouse, you can copy files or log in to remote systems with great ease.

The next part of this book deals with the Internet. From a networking point of view, an *internet* is a collection of networks that can communicate with each other. The Internet is a good way to bring a collection of LANs together. The Internet is the world-wide collection of hundreds of thousands of networks that communicate with each other using the TCP/IP protocol.

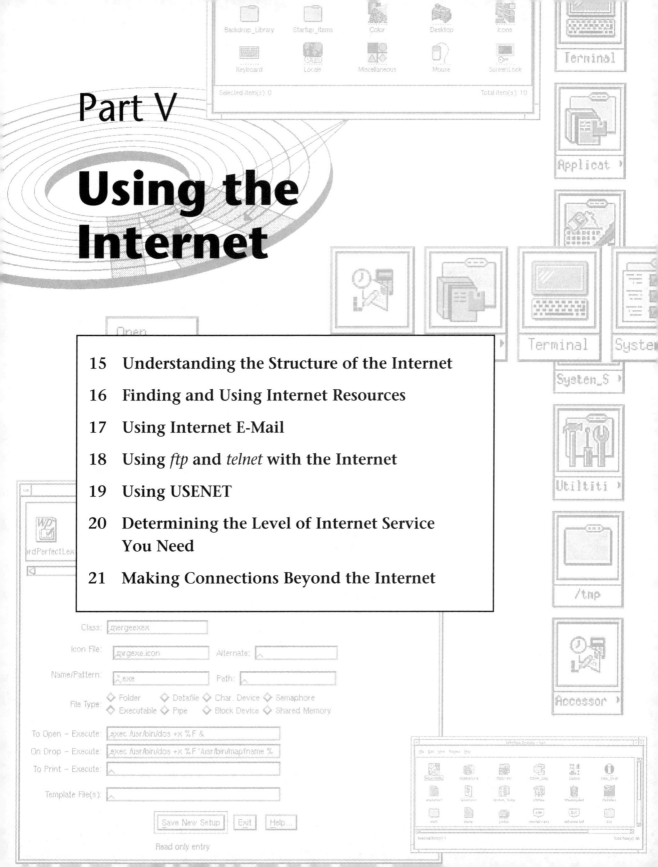

Part V

Using the Internet

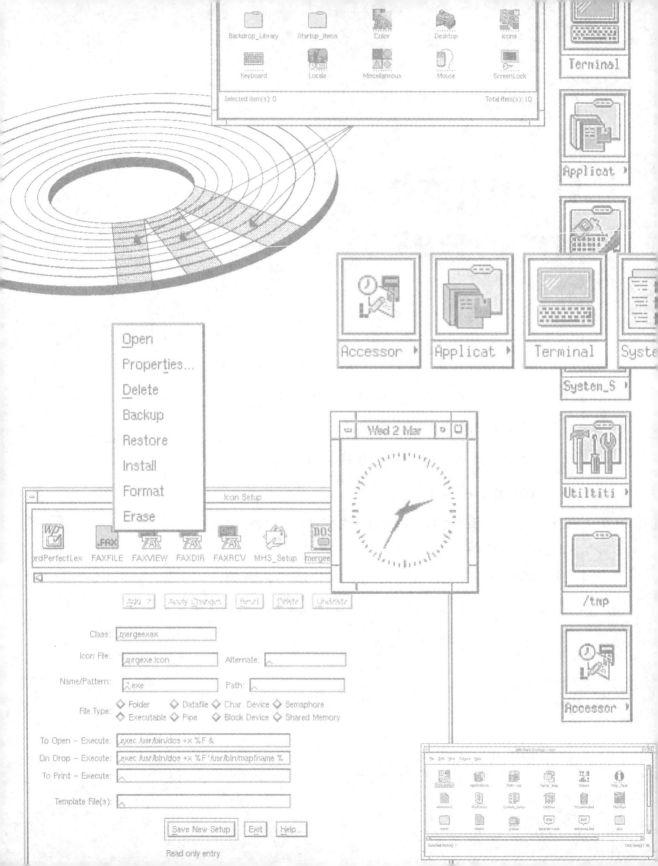

Chapter 15

Understanding the Structure of the Internet

Perhaps the hardest thing for a new user of the Internet to grasp is its incredibly non-uniform nature. Even its name, *the Internet*, sounds as though only one, massive network is connecting computing machines across streets or continents with equal ease and access. The fact that the software implementing the network struggles to make any differences between machines and connections invisible to you compounds this illusion.

A Dynamic Organization of Computers

In reality, the Internet is a tangled web of different machines in different networks with different users. Rather than settle down over time, the rate of growth and change in the Internet continues to increase. One way to describe the amorphous physical structure of the Internet is as a "cloud" of computers (see fig. 15.1), with the corresponding image of continuous melding and shifting over time.

Fig. 15.1

The Internet "cloud." Different computers and their users loosely joined to form a single, worldwide body.

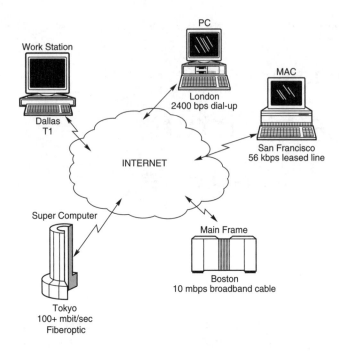

So how can the structure of such a dynamic organization be captured and explained? By taking a step back and analyzing what sort of structural information you would require to use the resources of the Internet effectively. For instance, do you really need to know where a certain computer is physically located, the network protocols in use, or the details of the file format for its operating system? Do you even want to know? Almost universally, the answers to these questions are *no.* You do need to be able to locate, identify, and exchange resources such as programs, data files, or computational capability. Fortunately, looking at the Internet from a functional rather than physical level reveals a much more organized—if not truly rigid—structure.

The participants in the Internet are a wide variety of machines, organizations, and individuals, all able to communicate and share information. The fundamental computing entities within this structure are called *hosts*, or *nodes*. Hosts may be massive, parallel processing supercomputers, data-processing mainframes, laboratory minicomputers, CAD system workstations, desktop PCs, or even laptops. These hosts are tied together through network connections that support data-transfer rates of from hundreds of bytes to hundreds of megabytes per second.

The hosts that comprise the Internet are collectively responsible for sending information to its intended destination, capturing and sorting incoming information, dispatching it to the proper recipient, forwarding data between hosts, and converting data formats and protocols (see fig. 15.2). To navigate within this structure successfully and confidently, you have to understand the basics of how a host operates and the services the host provides to make exchanging information a straightforward process.

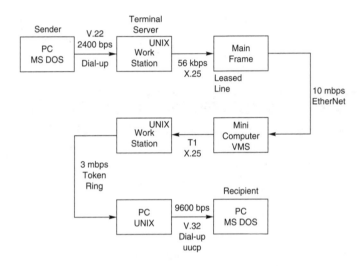

Fig. 15.2
An example of how several hosts cooperate to transfer a message across different networks until it reaches its final destination.

Obtaining an in-depth understanding of the configuration and operation of the Internet is a complex, challenging feat. Fortunately, you can safely ignore many details unless you are involved in network management or the oversight of a host. As a user, your interface to the Internet normally focuses on two structural areas: the name structure and the data storage structure.

The Name Structure

When you want to send a letter or make a phone call to someone, you need to know more than just that person's proper name. So it is when you send information through Internet. And just like a paper mailing address, an electronic address of an individual, computer, or organization on the Internet has several components. In Internet terminology, a name repre-sents any entity on the Internet, such as a user account, an executing software process, or a machine having one or many such accounts or processes.

To include as much information as possible in a succinct, consistent fashion, you create names by using a convention called the Domain Name System (DNS). The DNS defines a template for the structure of names. Names are constructed going left to right, and from the more narrow to the more broad in scope. A name consists of several elements or labels, each separated by a delimiter (an @ or . character). The general format for a name is as follows:

```
<account>@[subdomain].[subdomain].[...].<domain>
```

As you can see, several fields appear within a DNS name. An address that complies with this format contains a special ASCII string, called a *label*, that defines these fields. The significance of each field is detailed in the sections that follow.

> **Note**
>
> In the DNS syntax, *italic text* indicates that you shouldn't type the text literally, but that you should replace it with the appropriate information. Square brackets denote optional items. Don't type the brackets as part of a DNS name.

Labels

Labels must be no more than 63 characters long; start with a letter; end with a letter or digit; and contain only letters, digits, or the hyphen. Examples of legitimate labels follow:

```
blondie
DAGWOOD
r2d2
C3p0
six-pack
LONG12345678911234567892123456789312345678941234567 8
```

The following are examples of illegal labels:

```
endedwithhyphen-
2notstartedwithletter
spaces not allowed
no#othercharacters
```

Obviously, you could define some pretty hard-to-remember labels. As a practical matter, though, RFC 1032, "The Domain Administrators Guide," suggests that labels be kept to 12 characters or less to enhance human readability and memorization.

Domain Field

The domain for a name appears as its right-most label. Domains, one of the few well-specified and regulated areas, represent the top-most logical subdivisions of the Internet. Within the United States, each host on the Internet is assigned to one of the following domains based on its usage:

Domain	Description
gov	Non-military government affiliated
edu	Universities and other educational institutions
arpa	ARPANET members (largely obsolete now)
com	Commercial and industrial organizations
mil	Military
org	Other organizations, such as user groups
net	Network operations and service centers

Note

Many users initially confuse domains or subdomains with networks. This confusion is understandable because a subdomain consisting of only one network is often coincidentally true, especially for smaller organizations. But whereas a *network* is a grouping based on physical connectivity and the use of a similar communications protocol suite, a *domain* is a logical grouping that can contain multiple networks, entirely or partially. Thus, a host's domain hierarchy isn't necessarily dictated by its physical network (see fig. 15.3).

Outside the United States, each nation has a domain assigned to it that corresponds to its two-letter country code, as listed in table 15.1. These country codes are based on a document from the International Standards Organization (ISO), number 3166, which defines two-letter, three-letter, and numeric designations for each nation.

Fig. 15.3
Domains can encompass entire networks or only certain computers within a network.

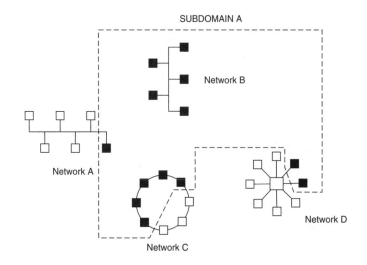

SUBDOMAIN A

Network B

Network A

Network C

Network D

Note

This list is updated occasionally as international events deem necessary. The list was particularly active before this printing because of the breakup of the former Soviet Union and the split of Czechoslovakia and Yugoslavia into new republics. The following table lists the international domains.

Table 15.1: International Domains

Country	Code
Afghanistan	AF
Albania	AL
Algeria	DZ
American Samoa	AS
Andorra	AD
Angola	AO
Anguilla	AI
Antarctica	AQ
Antigua and Barbuda	AG

Country	Code
Argentina	AR
Armenia	AM
Aruba	AW
Australia	AU
Austria	AT
Azerbaijan	AZ
Bahamas	BS
Bahrain	BH
Bangladesh	BD
Barbados	BB
Belarus	BY
Belgium	BE
Belize	BZ
Benin	BJ
Bermuda	BM
Bhutan	BT
Bolivia	BO
Bosnia Hercegovina	BA
Botswana	BW
Bouvet Island	BV
Brazil	BR
British Indian Ocean Territory	IO
Brunei Darussalam	BN
Bulgaria	BG
Burkina Faso (formerly Upper Volta)	BF

(continues)

Table 15.1 Continued	
Country	**Code**
Burundi	BI
Byelorussian SSR	BY
Cambodia	KH
Cameroon	CM
Canada	CA
Cape Verde	CV
Cayman Islands	KY
Central African Republic	CF
Chad	TD
Chile	CL
China	CN
Christmas Island	CX
Cocos (Keeling) Islands	CC
Colombia	CO
Comoros	KM
Congo	CG
Cook Island	CK
Costa Rica	CR
Cote d'Ivoire (Ivory Coast)	CI
Croatia (local name: Hrvatska)	HR
Cuba	CU
Cyprus	CY
Czech Republic	CZ
Denmark	DK
Djibouti	DJ
Dominica	DM

Country	Code
Dominican Republic	DO
East Timor	TP
Ecuador	EC
Egypt	EG
El Salvador	SV
Equatorial Guinea	GQ
Estonia	EE
Ethiopia	ET
Falkland Islands (Malvinas)	FK
Faroe Islands	FO
Fiji	FJ
Finland	FI
France	FR
French Guiana	GF
French Polynesia	PF
French Southern Territories	TF
Gabon	GA
Gambia	GM
Georgia (a former Soviet Republic)	GE
Germany	DE
Ghana	GH
Gibraltar	GI
Greece	GR
Greenland	GL
Grenada	GD
Guadeloupe	GP

(continues)

Table 15.1 Continued	
Country	**Code**
Guam	GU
Guatemala	GT
Guinea	GN
Guinea-Bissau	GW
Guyana	GY
Haiti	HT
Heard and McDonald Islands	HM
Honduras	HN
Hong Kong	HK
Hungary	HU
Iceland	IS
India	IN
Indonesia	ID
Iran, Islamic Republic of	IR
Iraq	IQ
Ireland	IE
Israel	IL
Italy	IT
Jamaica	JM
Japan	JP
Jordan	JO
Kazakhstan	KZ
Kenya	KE
Kiribati	KI
Korea, Democratic People's Republic of (North)	KP

Country	Code
Korea, Republic of (South)	KR
Kuwait	KW
Kyrgyzstan	KG
Lao People's Democratic Republic	LA
Latvia	LV
Lebanon	LB
Lesotho	LS
Liberia	LR
Libyan Arab Jamahiriya (Libya)	LY
Liechtenstein	LI
Lithuania	LT
Luxembourg	LU
Macau (Macao)	MO
Madagascar	MG
Malawi	MW
Malaysia	MY
Maldives	MV
Mali	ML
Malta	MT
Marshall Islands	MH
Martinique	MQ
Mauritania	MR
Mauritius	MU
Mexico	MX
Micronesia	FM
Moldova, Republic of	MD

V

Using the Internet

(continues)

Table 15.1 Continued	
Country	**Code**
Monaco	MC
Mongolia	MN
Montserrat	MS
Morocco	MA
Mozambique	MZ
Myanmar	MM
Namibia	NA
Nauru	NR
Nepal	NP
Netherlands	NL
Netherlands Antilles (Dutch West Indies)	AN
Neutral Zone	NT
New Caledonia	NC
New Zealand	NZ
Nicaragua	NI
Niger	NE
Nigeria	NG
Niue	NU
Norfolk Island	NF
Northern Mariana Islands	MP
Norway	NO
Oman	OM
Pakistan	PK
Palau	PW
Panama	PA

Country	Code
Papua New Guinea	PG
Paraguay	PY
Peru	PE
Philippines	PH
Pitcairn Island	PN
Poland	PL
Portugal	PT
Puerto Rico	PR
Qatar	QA
Reunion Island	RE
Romania	RO
Russian Federation	RU
Rwanda	RW
St. Helena	SH
St. Kitts and Nevis	KN
St. Lucia	LC
St. Pierre and Miquelon	PM
St. Vincent and the Grenadines	VC
Samoa	WS
San Marino	SM
Sao Tome and Principe	ST
Saudi Arabia	SA
Senegal	SN
Seychelles	SC
Sierra Leone	SL
Singapore	SG

(continues)

V

Using the Internet

Table 15.1 Continued

Country	Code
Slovakia (Slovak Republic)	SK
Slovenia	SI
Solomon Islands	SB
Somalia	SO
South Africa	ZA
Spain	ES
Sri Lanka	LK
Sudan	SD
Suriname	SR
Svalbard and Jan Mayen Islands	SJ
Swaziland	SZ
Sweden	SE
Switzerland	CH
Syrian Arab Republic (Syria)	SY
Taiwan, Province of China	TW
Tajikistan	TJ
Tanzania, United Republic of	TZ
Thailand	TH
Togo	TG
Tokelau	TK
Tonga	TO
Trinidad and Tobago	TT
Tunisia	TN
Turkey	TR

Country	Code
Turkmenistan	TM
Turks and Caicos Islands	TC
Tuvalu	TV
Uganda	UG
Ukrainian Soviet Socialist Republic (Ukraine)	UA
United Arab Emirates	AE
United Kingdom	GB
United States	US
Uruguay	UY
USSR (formerly)	SU
Uzbekistan	UZ
Vanuatu	VU
Vatican City State (Holy See)	VA
Venezuela	VE
Vietnam	VN
Virgin Islands (British)	VG
Virgin Islands (U.S.)	VI
Wallis and Fortuna Islands	WF
Western Sahara	EH
Yemen, Republic of	YE
Yugoslavia (formerly)	YU
Zaire	ZR
Zambia	ZM
Zimbabwe	ZW

V

Using the Internet

Subdomain Field

Being able to refer to a logical gathering of user names as one entity, such as the employees within a department or students within a class, is convenient. The DNS enables you to group names into subdomains for just such purposes. Usually a company, department, or other organization (such as a user group) will have several subdomains, such as that given in figure 15.4.

Fig. 15.4

An example sub-domain structure for an organization with several departments, and groups within each department. Each successively lower level of this hierarchy adds another subdomain field to the names of the users in that subdomain.

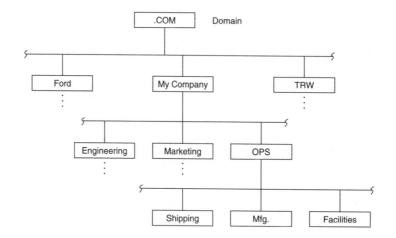

Developing groups of groups also may be handy, so subdomains can beget subdomains in a practically endless fashion, such as in the legitimate uses shown in figure 15.5.

Fig. 15.5

Examples of subdomains for groups within a company.

Each name has a limit to how long it can be. Because of the way the DNS encodes the name, that length depends on the number of labels in it. RFC 1035 specifies that a name can be no more than 255 bytes. Each label is coded as a length octet, followed by the characters of the label. The terminating octet of all names is the null (0) octet. Therefore, the total number of characters available for a name, excluding the delimiters, is as follows:

254 – (number of labels in name)

In reality, you typically run out of groupings before encountering this limit.

> **Note**
>
> RFC 1035, entitled "Domain names—implementation and specification," does not actually refer to a quantity called a *byte*, but instead to an *octet*, which is an equivalent eight-bit entity.

> **Note**
>
> It's troublesome for someone sending information to remember the address of a recipient that has lots of subdomains. One way around the problem of long names is for the host administrator to request that an *alias* be defined and registered for his host. An alias allows
> a user to replace the real name with a shorthand representation. The concept of an alias is discussed in more detail later in this chapter.

If you are sending a message to a user in your subdomain, you may find that specifying the entire name for that user is annoyingly tedious. But a machine powerful enough to be a part of the Internet is smart enough to assign a logical default to the parts of a name that aren't specified. If you don't specify a subdomain, the DNS assumes that you are referring to another user within your subdomain. So, in the earlier example, if Otto wanted to send an e-mail message to his buddy Joe in the same department, he would need to specify only this:

```
joe
```

V

Using the Internet

Similarly, if Otto sent e-mail to Rick in marketing, he could use the following, and `mycompany.com` would be assumed as the rest of the name:

```
rick@mkting
```

The hierarchical structure of the DNS enables your host to make such logical choices. To find a match for the name of the recipient of your message, your host works its way up the subdomain hierarchy until it finds the one that the sender and recipient share. It then moves down the hierarchy until it reaches the recipient. Although this seems trivial when sender and recipient names are located on one host, things quickly get more complicated when your local host has to begin traversing the Internet looking for the recipient. (This process is explained in more detail a little later in this chapter.)

User or Account Field

The left-most label defines the user or account and is separated from the remaining labels by an "at" symbol (@). The user label generally is chosen to reflect the real identity of the owner. So if Otto D. Smeadford has an account on a host, he would likely have a name with a user label something like one of these:

```
osmeadford
ods
ottos
smeadfordod
```

Although it isn't mandatory, having your user label reflect your real identity is a good idea because it facilitates the use of tools that another user can invoke to find your Internet name if he knows something about you.

Certain special functions also have user names. Many companies and organizations, for example, have a user name to which you can send mail to request that information be mailed back to you. If you wanted to get an overview of the Internet e-mail services provided by the Institute of Electrical and Electronics Engineers (IEEE) or the Association of Computing Machinery (ACM), you would e-mail your request to

```
info.email.services@ieee.org
```

or

```
Account-info@ACM.org
```

In these instances, the user label refers to an automated process that extracts the sender's name from the header of your e-mail message and mails the requested infor-mation back to your name. The contents of such messages are irrelevant and can be left blank. All that is of value is your name, which is included automatically in the message header.

You may have noticed something a little unexpected in one of the above names—specifically, the account label in `info.email.services@ieee.org`. The reason this is a legitimate name is that in its processing, the DNS effectively makes no distinction between an @ and a .(period). The @ is used as the delimiter after the account label to make it easier for humans to remember names.

IP Address

As you can see, the DNS provides a logical means for developing names and grouping them in meaningful ways. Hidden from view by the DNS, though, is a more primitive means of identification called the Internet Protocol (IP) address. Users rarely access this address, which is the underlying identifier used by the protocols that govern Internet information exchange. Your host converts DNS names to IP addresses before starting the routing process that gets your message to your intended recipient (see table 15.2 for some example IP addresses). The intervening machines and network software also use IP addresses as your message is passed along.

Table 15.2: Example IP Addresses and Their DNS Names

IP Address	DNS Name
16.1.0.2	gatekeeper.dec.com
128.89.1.178	nnsc.nsf.net
128.252.135.4	wuarchive.wustl.edu
130.127.8.1	hubcap.clemson.edu
192.112.36.5	nic.ddn.mil

V

Using the Internet

> **Note**
>
> Although addresses aren't case sensitive through the Internet, preserving the case of the name you communicate with is a good idea, for several reasons:
>
> ■ Many of your possible destinations for the information you send may not actually be on the Internet directly but are accessed indirectly through other network services such as CompuServe. Within these services, the specific software and protocols operating in that environment determine case sensitivity.
>
> ■ The RFCs that specify the naming conventions (1032-1035) require that case be maintained "just in case" a future implementation of the network software becomes case aware.

Similarities exist between an IP address for a host and a Social Security number for a human: a governing body assigns each to identify an entity uniquely, each is more machine-oriented than human-oriented, and each is rarely used as a means for reference during normal conversation. For IP addresses, the governing body is a member of the Internet Network Information Center (InterNIC) consortium; Network Solutions, Incorporated (NSI) of Herndon, Virginia, is the group within the consortium responsible for providing registration services. Technically, NSI assigns only a portion of the address (the network ID). The remaining portion (the host ID within that network) is assigned by those administering the network.

You don't often refer to your friends like "How's it going, 123-45-6789, dude?" do you? The creators of Internet realized that having to refer to hosts by their IP addresses would be just as cumbersome, and so the DNS developed as a much more suitable naming system for use by humans.

A host's IP address is a 32-bit value. Like a DNS name, the IP address also consists of fields, each separated by a period (.). For this reason, an IP address is sometimes referred to as a *dot address*. The number of octets in an IP address is fixed at four (8 bits per field), but the interpretation of the address varies based on the value of the first field. The address contains the host's network ID and host ID within the network. The value of the first field determines the length of each.

If the first octet has a value from 1 to 126, the IP address is class A format. In class A addresses, the network ID consists of the first octet, and the host ID uses the last three. This limits the number of nets to 126, but each net can have up to 16,777,214 hosts. Such addresses are limited to major service providers and participants.

Class B format addresses have a first octet range from 128 to 191 and use the first two octets for network IDs and the remaining two for host IDs. This gives 16,382 network ID values and 65,534 host IDs. Larger network organizations such as campus-wide systems for universities or larger businesses are assigned class B addresses.

Class C addresses have a first octet from 192 to 223, use the first three octets for the network ID and the last octet for the host ID. This class supports more than 2 million network IDs and only 254 host IDs for each net. This address class is typical for small networks or machines that aren't part of a local network.

Class D addresses have a first octet value of 224 to 239 and are used for *multicasting*, which is best described as broadcast by subscription. Multicasting allows a host to join or leave a multicast group dynamically. When a message is sent to a multicast address, all hosts in that group receive the message. This approach makes sending messages to groups of hosts easier and makes more efficient use of the available bandwidth.

Class E addresses, from 240 to 247, are reserved for future use.

Table 15.3 contains some real-world IP addresses for each class. In addition to the address classes, two special IP addresses are available. A message with its host ID set to all 1s indicates that the message is being broadcast to every host in the network. A host also may set the network ID to 0 if it wants to communicate on a network for which it doesn't know the actual net ID. In this instance, a net ID of 0 is interpreted to mean "this network I am on." The responses the host receives to these messages will include the actual network ID, so that it can update this information and begin using it in its messages.

V

Using the Internet

Table 15.3: Sample IP Addresses and Address Classes		
IP Address	**Net Owner**	**Address Class**
12.0.0.0	AT&T	A
128.5.0.0	Ford	B
128.30.0.0	MIT	B
192.112.59.0	Kellogg	C

Aliases

In reality, the names of many hosts are quite long and have many subdomains. Again, the problem of having the name be tractable to humans rears its head. Fortunately, a shorthand way is available to refer to a name—*aliasing*. By defining an alias, your host administrator can "promote" a host that may be at a fifth-level subdomain to appear as though it were at the second level. In this way, the host name myaccount@myhost.level4.level3.level2.com can be referenced as myaccount@myhostalias.com, which is a much easier name for your Internet partners to remember.

Although each host network connection can have only one IP address, by using aliases you can assign more than one name to the host address. One example of how you can use multiple names for a single host is to consider the situation in which two companies are sharing the same network (perhaps one is a wholly owned subsidiary of the other). Both companies would like to appear as independent organizations. By using aliases, a user account such as myaccount@smallfry.bigpotato.com can be referenced as myaccount@smallfry.com and myaccount@bigpotato.com.

> **Note**
>
> An alias can't be the same as another DNS name. Thus, if smallfry.com already exists, you will have to choose another alias.

Using an alias doesn't block any attempt to use your full DNS name. So in the preceding example, another member of your company who was aware of your full DNS name could use myaccount@smallfry.bigpotato.com without problems.

The Data Storage Structure

Now you can navigate through the naming structure of the Internet, but you also need to know how the data available on all those hosts is organized. You need a similar set of skills for navigating the data structures of the Internet.

File Structure

Fortunately, unlike the DNS, the data-storage organization on the Internet is more intuitive to most PC computer users. Although different operating systems implement the syntax of their file structures differently, almost all use some form of hierarchical tree-based structure of files and directories. An example file hierarchy is given in figure 15.6.

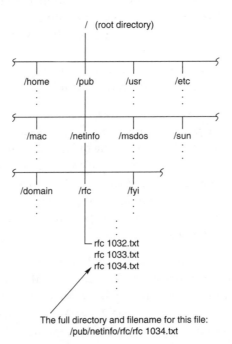

The full directory and filename for this file:
/pub/netinfo/rfc/rfc 1034.txt

Fig. 15.6
An example of a typical host file hierarchy. Each successive level of the hierarchy will add another field to the Location: field of an archie query for the files in that level.

You can use a tool called archie to locate files among the many ftp sites on the network. The following segment of output from an archie session shows some of the variation in syntax for directory and file names that you can find on the Internet. In this session, a search was performed for the file RFC1032.TXT, and two of the responses received were as follows:

```
Host maggie.telcom.arizona.edu     (128.196.128.233)
Last updated 06:26 16 Jul 1993
Location: /RFC.DIR;1/1000.DIR;1
FILE    -rwxrwx-w- 59 bytes 14:42  7 Apr 1988  RFC1032.TXT;1
```

and

```
Host nic.cerf.net    (192.102.249.3)
Last updated 05:56 17 Jul 1993
Location: /pub/infomagic_cd/doc/rfc
FILE    -r-xr-xr-x 28673 bytes 01:00 17 Feb 1992 rfc1032.txt
```

By examining the structure and syntax of the file specifications, an experienced user would assume that the first host, maggie.telcom.arizona.edu, most likely is running the VMS operating system, whereas nic.cerf.net is probably running UNIX. The syntax of the directory names given in the Location: field, as well as the filename syntax, give good clues. The overall impact from these differences is minor, though. You just as easily could ftp either file to your machine by specifying the filename in the proper form for the host of your choice.

One item that you may find a little confusing is *file links*. Some operating systems (such as UNIX) support the capability to add a file logically to a directory without actually having to copy the file's contents to the directory. Essentially, the linked filename acts as an alias, which points to the real file location. You can use a file link just as though it were any other filename, however, and the operating system will take care of getting or updating the information, wherever it really is.

Also, unlike PC operating systems, you don't have to be aware of which physical storage device you are accessing—that is, the files presented in a host's file hierarchy may reside on one hard disk or many, or perhaps other devices such as CD-ROMs. You don't have to be concerned with where the files are; the host's operating system worries about such things for you.

File Ownership and Access

One concept that PC users may not be familiar with is *file ownership*. Most PCs assume that they are being used primarily or exclusively by only one user. Their operating systems typically don't support identifying files as "owned" by a particular user, or limiting access to files based on who you are. This setup isn't so for larger machines—especially not for those connected to a network that allows access by users not associated in any way with the owning organization.

Most multiuser operating systems provide at least three levels of file access based on your relation to the file owner. If a file is assigned *read-only access*, you can view or copy the file. If you have *write* or *delete access*, you can erase, overwrite, or modify it. Finally, *execute access* allows you to run the file as an application.

Typically, the access level is specified for the types of user: the file owner, users belonging to the same previously defined group as the owner, and all other users. The example pictured in figure 15.7 shows how to interpret the access information provided from a directory listing.

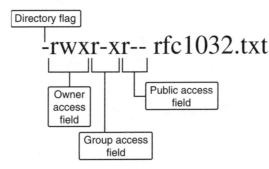

Fig. 15.7
The access level indicated in a directory listing.

As the figure shows, access level is indicated as follows:

Level	Description
r	Read access
w	Write/delete access
x	Execute access
d	Directory (in the directory flag)
–	Means no access available for that access type; in the directory flag, represents a file

V

Using the Internet

An Overview of DNS Operation

As mentioned in the introduction to this chapter, the process that a host must go through to transfer information from a sender to a recipient can be quite complex. Although you don't have to have an understanding of DNS operation, such an understanding does help you appreciate what a host does for you in locating the destination for your information. It's especially informative to be familiar with the concepts of name servers, name caches, resolvers, master files, and zones. These are the entities that point your message in the right direction and help get it there. A simple schematic diagram of DNS operation is given in figure 15.8. Besides, certainly you're a little bit curious, aren't you? Just a little?

Fig. 15.8
A schematic of DNS operation. Your host's resolver makes use of name servers and name caches to obtain the IP address for your recipient.

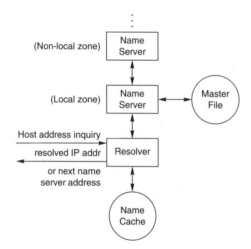

Name Server

In the earliest implementations of the Internet, each host had a file that contained all the information necessary to locate any other host on the Internet. This approach made finding another host and exchanging information simple for one host. Soon, however, the expanse and rate of change of the Internet meant that having such a complete picture of the Internet was impossible for every host. Before the current explosion of growth, such lists would become obsolete very quickly; the network traffic required to keep these lists up-to-date was becoming overwhelming.

To solve this problem, a more centralized approach was developed and implemented. In this approach, certain hosts are designated as *name* (or *domain*) *servers*. Name servers provide a means for getting the routing information and IP addresses for your destinations. Other hosts then need to know only the addresses of a name server or two to get the latest address information on a demand basis. Hosts listed with a name server are called *registered hosts* (the distinction between registered and unregistered hosts will be explained a little later in this section). Any registered host must have its name placed on at least two name servers; in case of host or network failure, an alternative means for getting the host routing information is available.

Resolver

The *resolver* is the software that operates on a host trying to determine where the specified address is. When you specify a destination for the data you are sending, the resolver queries the name servers it knows of to find the IP address of the reci-pient's host. Now your host knows who to send the data to, but in a network topology as diverse as that of the Internet, you could take literally thousands of routes to get the data there. The problem is analogous to planning a trip from New York to Los Angeles: knowing the ZIP code of your destination doesn't tell you anything about which highways to take. Fortunately, the name server also provides the resolver with the routing information it needs to point the data in the right direction.

To speed things up, the resolver keeps around a *name cache*. A name cache is a high-tech way of referring to a file that keeps the addresses resolved in the recent past. You can safely assume, based on statistical studies of network traffic, that if you send data to someone once, you likely will do so again soon. The name cache takes advantage of this assumption by avoiding the overhead of the name server query for recently resolved names.

Master Files

On every name server exists a database of all the registered hosts. This database, called the *master file*, is updated three times a week (Monday, Wednesday, and Friday) from the InterNIC and distributed to the name servers through the Internet itself. The name server uses the master file to look up zone, IP, and routing information to return to the inquiring host.

Zones

If only registered hosts participated in the network, the operation of the DNS would require only that a host's resolver find and query its name server. Not all hosts are registered, however. In fact, most aren't, and it's a good thing, too. You can imagine the headaches that would result from having to require that every host using the Internet be registered. Every time a computer within a company's network was added, removed, or transferred to a different network location, for example, the company would have to update its registration status.

To avoid this problem, the authority and responsibility for the domain name space is subdivided into zones, each with a registered host responsible for that portion of the name space. Within that portion of the name space, subdomains can be added or removed. For example, a registered host named `myzone.myprovider.com` would be responsible for the allocation and maintenance of the hosts and subdomains below it, such as `myhost.mysubdomain.myzone.myprovider.com`. One difference between a zone and a subdomain is that while unregistered hosts can also have subdomains, only the name space under a registered host can be designated a zone. As is true for subdomains, zones can exist within other zones.

Each name server is aware of other name servers responsible for the various zones, and if it receives a request for IP and routing information within a zone, it can contact that name server for information or direct its inquiring host to contact the appropriate zone name server. The former method is referred to as *recursive resolving* because one name server may call another, which in turn may call another, and so on, until the name is resolved. The latter method is called *nonrecursive resolving* because the inquiring host has to restart the resolving process with each new name server it's directed to.

Host Registration

As a user, you normally don't have to concern yourself with registering host names or aliases; your provider has taken care of that. If you are in the position of investigating what you need to do to register for your company or other organization, the following is provided to let you know what is involved.

You can obtain a domain questionnaire by using ftp to get the file `/templates/domain-template.txt` from host `ftp.rs.internic.net`. Fill out the questionnaire completely and return it through electronic mail to this address:

    HOSTMASTER@rs.internic.net

If your application is in order, getting registered should take about two weeks. You can check the status of your registration by telneting to `rs.internic.net` and following the instructions given in the login header.

A registered host may not be required by most purchasers of this book, so you should make certain that it is really necessary for the level of service you or your organization needs. When you are certain that you need to register a host, the best place to start the process is with your service provider. Service providers often can take care of registration for you and provide you with technical assistance on getting your network connection set up.

Finding and Verifying a Registered Host

If you need to locate a host or verify its registration, you can use an online utility called `whois` to accomplish this task. `whois` gives network address data and contact information such as administrator names, phone numbers, and postal addresses. If your Internet service provider has given you access to `whois`, you can use this command:

    whois *domain* *<domain name>* *<Return>*

Alternatively, you can telnet to `rs.internic.net` and log in as `whois`. At the `Whois:` prompt, type the name you want information on.

The reply from `whois` will supply the following information:

- The name and address of the organization "owning" the domain

- The name of the domain

- The domain's administrative, technical, and zone contacts

- The host names and network addresses of sites providing name service for the domain

You can use whois to get contact information for your host or others online, rather than have to find a business card, note, or wait for an e-mail reply from someone.

The following are some sample whois sessions:

```
Whois: unc.edu
University of North Carolina at Chapel Hill (UNC-DOM)
    Chapel Hill, NC 27514

    Domain Name: UNC.EDU

    Administrative Contact:
        Gogan, James P.   (JG452)  gogan@HERMES.OIT.UNC.EDU
        (919) 962-1621 (919) 962-0658 (FAX) (919) 962-5604
    Technical Contact, Zone Contact:
        Averett, Shava Nerad  (SNA) shava@HERMES.OIT.UNC.EDU
        (919) 962-1603 (919) 962-0658 (FAX) (919) 962-5604

    Record last updated on 27-May-93.

    Domain servers in listed order:

    NS.UNC.EDU                      152.2.21.1
    NS.BME.UNC.EDU                  152.2.100.1
    NCNOC.CONCERT.NET               192.101.21.1,128.109.193.1

Whois: nasa.gov
NASA Ames Research Center (NASA-DOM)
    Mail Stop 240-9
    Moffett Field, CA 94035

    Domain Name: NASA.GOV

    Administrative Contact, Technical Contact, Zone Contact:
        Medin, Milo  (MSM1)  MEDIN@NSIPO.NASA.GOV
        (415) 604-6440 (FTS) 464-6440

    Record last updated on 22-Feb-93.

    Domain servers in listed order:

    NS.NASA.GOV                     128.102.16.10, 192.52.195.10
    DFTSRV.GSFC.NASA.GOV            128.183.10.134
    JPL-MIL.JPL.NASA.GOV            128.149.1.101
    MX.NSI.NASA.GOV                 128.102.18.31

Whois: internic.net
Network Solutions, Inc. (INTERNIC-DOM)
    505 Huntmar Park Drive
    Herndon, VA 22070
```

```
Domain Name: INTERNIC.NET

Administrative Contact:
   Zalubski, John   (JZ7)   johnz@INTERNIC.NET
   (703) 742-4757
Technical Contact, Zone Contact:
   Kosters, Mark A.   (MAK21)   markk@INTERNIC.NET
   (703) 742-4795

Record last updated on 23-Mar-93.

Domain servers in listed order:

RS.INTERNIC.NET              198.41.0.5
IS.INTERNIC.NET              192.153.156.15
NOC.CERF.NET                 192.153.156.22
```

Whois: **ibm.com**
International Business Machines (IBM-DOM)

```
Domain Name: IBM.COM

Administrative Contact, Technical Contact, Zone Contact:
   Trio, Nicholas R.   (NRT1)   nrt@watson.ibm.com
   (914) 945-1850

Record last updated on 12-Dec-91.

Domain servers in listed order:

WATSON.IBM.COM               129.34.139.4
NS.AUSTIN.IBM.COM            192.35.232.34
```

Whois: **acm.org**
Association for Computing Machinery (ACM-DOM)
1515 Broadway
New York, NY 10036

```
Domain Name: ACM.ORG

Administrative Contact:
   Deblasi, Joe   (JD3017)   DEBLASI@ACM.ORG
   (212) 869-7440
Technical Contact, Zone Contact:
   Lemley, Bob   (BL162)   LEMLEY@ACM.ORG
   (817) 776-5695

Record last updated on 04-Jun-93.

Domain servers in listed order:

PASCAL.ACM.ORG               192.135.174.1
SESQUI.NET                   128.241.0.84
```

V

Using the Internet

Online Domain Information

Several text files are available online that provide information on Internet domains. The following online files, all available by ftp from `ftp.rs.internic.net`, contain pertinent domain information:

File	Description
/NETINFO/DOMAINS.TXT	A table of all top-level domains and the network addresses of the machines providing domain name service for them. This table is updated each time a new top-level domain is approved.
/NETINFO/DOMAIN-INFO.TXT	A concise list of all top-level and second-level domain names registered with the NIC. This list is updated monthly.
/NETINFO/DOMAIN-CONTACTS.TXT	A list of all the top-level and second-level domains, but also includes the administrative, technical, and zone contacts for each. This list is updated monthly.
/TEMPLATES/DOMAIN-TEMPLATE.TXT	The questionnaire to be completed before registering a top-level or second-level domain.

The Flow of Information from Host to Host

So far the process of moving information within a host or from one host to another has been taken for granted. You usually don't have to be concerned with the way in which data is moved through the Internet, but being familiar with the basic terminology and subsystems that are used helps.

Jumping across Network Boundaries

Because the Internet is a collection of smaller networks, any information you send or receive probably has to cross several networks to get to its destination (see fig. 15.9). Some network boundaries result from physical limitations such as the length of cabling over which an electronic signal can reliably be driven and received.

A problem with reliability arises when you connect greater numbers of hosts together within a single network. In many instances, a single failure of the network disrupts all communications for the entire net. A *bridge* is a device that isolates one physical section of the Internet from another, so that a failure at one place disrupts communications for only that portion of the Internet on the same side of the bridge as the failure. Bridges usually require that both segments of the network use the same physical-level connection, such as Ethernet or token ring.

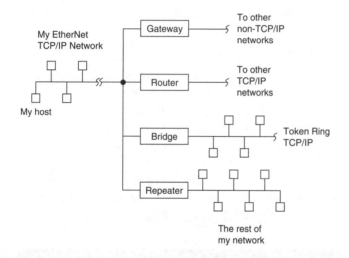

Fig. 15.9

As information traverses a network, it may encounter a variety of different hardware devices including repeaters, bridges, routers, and gateways.

> **Tip**
>
> You can use *repeaters* to extend the maximum effective extent of a network. You can think of a repeater as a simple amplifier that boosts the power of weak signals before sending them farther down the network.

If information is moving between two networks using the same protocol suite, such as TCP/IP, a *router* acts as the means for tying them together. A router has knowledge of the protocol suite and addresses associated with both networks, and monitors each for messages bound for the other. The router receives and forwards these messages between the networks. A router also may be able to connect networks with different physical-level interconnection schemes.

If two networks have dissimilar protocols, an interpreter called a *gateway* is required. Just like a human language interpreter, a gateway knows the protocol suites used by both networks it's serving to connect. A message bound for the other network is converted from its native protocol to that of the destination network. Typically, a gateway also performs the functions of a router.

Layers of Software

In this multilayer model of the software that implements TCP/IP (often called a TCP/IP stack because one layer "stacks" on another), an example of an application would be `ftp`, `telnet`, `archie`, `whois`, or any of the other tools and utilities you use to exploit the capabilities of the Internet. An application may also be any other program that makes use of TCP/IP to transfer data, such as a local area network (LAN) software package.

Applications interact with the next lower layer, TCP, through a series of special commands called *service primitives* that the TCP layer makes available to the application. A few of these primitives are listed in table 15.4. As you can see, TCP provides a high-level means for the applications to communicate with each other. For example, a connection with another host is established with the OPEN primitive. A major goal of TCP is to obscure the details of the connection from the application so that the application doesn't have to account for network-specific items such as transfer rates and data formatting.

Table 15.4: Typical TCP Primitives

Service Primitive	Summary Description
OPEN	Establishes connection to remote host
SEND	Sends data to remote host
DELIVER	Makes data available from remote host
CLOSE	Shuts down connection
STATUS	Provides status of connection

The IP layer in turn converts the service primitives of TCP into the low-level functions provided by the subnetwork layer, and vice versa. The

IP may segment the data from a TCP SEND primitive into a series of smaller messages. Lastly, the subnetwork layer is responsible for converting IP messages into a format suitable for the particular hardware and physical-level protocols being used to connect to the network. If your host is connected to a local network that uses a token-ring access control scheme, for example, the subnetwork interface will try to acquire a token so that it can send information. If, on the other hand, the connection is a dialup serial link, the subnetwork layer is responsible for tasks such as modem control (see fig. 15.10).

The goal of the TCP/IP stack approach is to limit and localize the changes that need to be made to accommodate different network configurations.

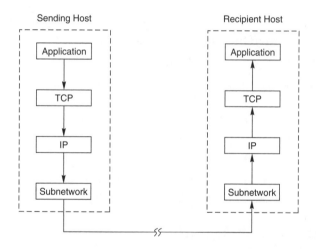

Fig. 15.10

Sample data flow between hosts through the TCP/IP stack. Information provided to an application such as ftp is processed through each layer of the stack until it's ultimately converted to a bitstream, which is transmitted to the recipient and reassembled.

Sharing the Interconnection Space

As many connections as are available throughout the Internet, efficient use of the available capacity (or *bandwidth*) of these connections is still a major issue. Even if you aren't paying the connection charges, you can rest assured that someone somewhere is. Try to keep these costs in mind when transferring information between hosts. Just because you can get a copy of an RFC from a host in Australia doesn't mean you should use it as your primary ftp site for RFCs if you live two blocks from a major university that can provide them.

Although it's an important Internet resource, usage of bandwidth still is not tightly regulated. Basically, if you don't make a true nuisance of yourself, no one will chase you down for an honest mistake or for an intercontinental transfer of a large quantity of data if done for a valid reason. Being wasteful is considered poor network etiquette, however, and you may receive a warning or even have your access terminated if you are a flagrant bandwidth hog. The goal of everyone using the Internet should be to use it efficiently.

The Host Administrator

Although most of your interaction with the Internet is electronic, a human element exists as well: your *host* (or system or network) *administrator* (HA). The HA is responsible for ensuring the reliable operation of your host within the proper usage guidelines established by the host owner and his or her service providers.

In your day-to-day use of the Internet, you shouldn't need any assistance from the HA. Please don't bother the HA with frivolous questions or as a way to get out of tracking down information on the Internet. One of the more embarrassing but frequent calls to an HA comes from users who have forgotten their passwords.

You can expect to require some assistance from your HA a few times, however, as explained in the following sections.

Establishing or Reconfiguring Accounts

When the HA sets up your account, he or she assigns you to a host and a subdomain. Sometimes, moving accounts from one host to another is necessary to help balance the computational and storage loads.

Controlling Service Access

Because of the incredible amount of information available and traffic through the Internet, the HA likely will place some limits on your access, such as limits on connect time, the number of connections, total file space available, or lockouts on features such as USENET. If you need additional space or access to a currently unavailable resource, ask your HA if your account access can be adjusted.

Handling Trouble

You need to contact the HA if any of the following occur:

- Access problems

- Possible security breaches

- Violations of the proper use limitations (for example, profane messages)

- Bugs or other problematic behavior of network software

- You suspect you have encountered a malevolent program (such as a virus) that poses a threat to the system or the network at large

Just be very sure that you have really found a problem in operation and not just committed "pilot error." Before contacting the HA, check to see whether other users on your host are experiencing the same problems. See whether others on the same network but different hosts are affected. The more information on the scope of the problem you can provide, the more quickly the HA will be able to track down and fix the problem.

Summary

Uncounted hours of some of the brightest minds in computer science and engineering have been put to the task of designing the structure and operation of the Internet. This chapter has touched only the surface of their remarkable results, but gives you the practical knowledge you need to make sense of what often seems to the newcomer a bewildering maze of computers, networks, and files. In the next chapter, you are taken on a guided tour of some of the useful resources available on the Internet as means of getting some hands-on experience exploring the structure of the Internet.

Chapter 16

Finding and Using Internet Resources

The Internet is certainly a valuable resource for obtaining information about virtually any field of inquiry. This chapter is dedicated to showing you how to find out more information about the Internet itself. The organizations that establish network policies are identified, and ways to obtain important documents pertaining to network operations are discussed. You easily can retrieve much of this documentation on-line through ftp. Even if you don't have access to ftp, you still can obtain much useful information by using e-mail.

Many sites on the network allow—some even encourage—network users to access their files, databases, or specialized software packages. This chapter identifies several of the major network nodes that maintain substantial amounts of information of value to network users. Two computer programs that provide tutorials in basic Internet concepts and operations are discussed as well.

CD-ROMs designed specifically for the Internet user community also are available. These CD-ROMs contain an enormous amount of information that would be time-consuming for you to locate or tedious to download from the network yourself. As such, the CD-ROMs could be very cost-effective purchases if you want more detailed information about the Internet than is within the scope of this book.

Keep in mind that the Internet is very dynamic and that descriptions of the major Internet sites, tutorial software, and CD-ROM offerings are subject to change over time. When using ftp to access files described in the text, always look for readme and index files to learn of new developments. Exploring directories containing files in which you are interested also is a good idea because they may have something else of interest to you.

> **Note**
>
> Portions of the text of this chapter were taken directly from public-domain information available through anonymous ftp. The sources for these passages are attributed.

Organizations that Set Internet Standards and Policies

No one owns the Internet or receives a portion of the fee your Internet service provider charges you. Rather, the Internet is a loose affiliation of smaller networks that have agreed to use common standards for communicating with each other. The communications protocols are standardized, but not their implementations. As long as the technical standards are met and acceptable use policies are observed, a local system can connect with the network and communicate with other systems.

An organization was established, however, for overseeing the creation, distribution, and updating of standards regarding the Internet. The Internet Society (ISOC) was formed in January 1992 as the umbrella organization given authority for all aspects of network administration. It is given "authority" by virtue of its members and other supporters; those members and supporters happen to include virtually the entire Internet user community in the United States.

ISOC also enjoys considerable support from European and other users outside the United States. Several major administrative bodies are part of ISOC, including the Internet Architecture Board (IAB), the Internet Engineering Task Force (IETF), and the Internet Research Task Force (IRTF).

The Internet Architecture Board (IAB) is concerned with overseeing development and evolution of network protocols. It has the authority to issue standards and allocate resources such as network addresses.

The Internet Engineering Task Force (IETF) is charged with developing the specifications that eventually will become standards, if approved by the IAB. It conducts regular meetings to discuss technical and operational problems that have been encountered or that likely will be experienced in the near future. The Internet Research Task Force (IRTF) considers longer-term issues than does the IETF. The IRTF focuses more on information science and networking technology than on establishing policies and standards.

The Internet Society (ISOC)

With the explosive growth in new systems connecting to the Internet, an international administrative body that determines and publishes technical, procedural, and operational standards and policies is essential. The Internet Society fills this role and is responsible for guiding the future development of the network as well. Its charter is as follows:

The Society is a non-profit organization operated for academic, educational, charitable and scientific purposes, such as the following:

- *To facilitate and support the technical evolution of the Internet as a research and education infrastructure and to stimulate involvement of the academic, scientific, and engineering communities, among others in the evolution of the Internet.*

- *To educate the academic and scientific communities and the public concerning the technology, use, and application of the Internet.*

- *To promote scientific and educational applications of Internet technology for the benefit of educational institutions at all grade levels, industry, and the public at large.*

- *To provide a forum for exploration of new Internet applications and to foster collaboration among organizations in their operation and use of the Internet.*

Individuals and organizations can join the Internet Society, although only individuals can vote.

ISOC publishes the *Internet Society News*, a quarterly newsletter, and conducts an annual conference (called INET) open to all members and other parties interested in various aspects of the Internet. It also sponsors workshops and symposiums from time to time on topics of current interest to the Internet community.

V

Using the Internet

Additional information about the Internet Society is available on-line through anonymous `ftp` to `nri.reston.va.us`. In directory `/isoc` you will find membership and other general information about ISOC as well as conference announcements. Under this directory are subdirectories containing the text of recent issues of the newsletter. For more information, you can contact the Internet Society as follows:

Internet Society
1895 Preston White Drive, Suite 100
Reston, VA 22091
Voice: (703) 648-9888
Fax: (703) 620-0913
E-mail: `isoc@isoc.org`

Internet Architecture Board (IAB)

The Internet Architecture Board (IAB) has authority to issue and update technical standards regarding Internet protocols. It doesn't have a role in day-to-day network operations. Originally founded in 1983 as the Internet Activities Board, its intent is to guide the evolution of the TCP/IP protocol suite and to provide research advice to the Internet community; it was placed under the Internet Society in June 1992. Its charter reads as follows:

The Internet Architecture Board (IAB) shall be constituted and shall operate as a technical advisory group of the Internet Society. Its responsibilities shall include:

■ *Expert and experienced oversight of the architecture of the worldwide multiprotocol Internet.*

■ *The editorial management and publication of the Request For Comments (RFC) document series, which constitutes the archival publication series for Internet Standards and related contributions by the Internet research and engineering community.*

■ *The development, review, and approval of Internet Standards, according to a well-defined and documented set of "Procedures for Internet Standardization." Internet Standards shall be published in the form of specifications as part of the RFC series.*

- *The provision of advice and guidance to the Board of Trustees and Officers of the Internet Society concerning technical, architectural, procedural, and (where appropriate) policy matters pertaining to the Internet and its enabling technologies.*

- *Representation of the interests of the Internet Society in liaison relationships with other organizations.*

The IAB holds meetings in person on a quarterly basis. Additional meetings may be conducted at intervening times by telephone, e-mail, and computer-mediated conferences. The minutes of meetings of the Internet Architecture Board are available on-line through anonymous ftp. Connect with host venera.isi.edu and look under /pub/IAB for text files containing the minutes of the most recent meetings.

Internet Engineering Task Force (IETF)

The information in this section was taken directly from material provided by the Internet Engineering Task Force (IETF):

The Internet Engineering Task Force (IETF) is the protocol engineering, development, and standardization arm of the IAB. The IETF began in January 1986 as a forum for technical coordination by contractors for the then U.S. Defense Advanced Research Projects Agency (DARPA) working on the ARPANET, U.S. Defense Data Network (DDN), and the Internet core gateway system. Since then, the IETF has grown into a large open international community of network designers, operators, vendors, and researchers concerned with the evolution of the Internet protocol architecture and the smooth operation of the Internet.

The IETF mission includes:

- *Identifying and proposing solutions to pressing operational and technical problems in the Internet*

- *Specifying the development (or usage) of protocols and the near-term architecture to solve such technical problems for the Internet*

- *Facilitating technology transfer from the Internet Research Task Force (IRTF) to the wider Internet community*

- *Providing a forum for the exchange of relevant information within the Internet community among vendors, users, researchers, agency contractors, and network managers*

Technical activity on any specific topic in the IETF is addressed within work-ing groups. All working groups are organized roughly by function into 10 technical areas. Each is led by one or more area director, who has primary responsibility for that one area of IETF activity. Together with the Chair of the IETF, these technical directors (plus the Director for Standards Proce-dures) compose the Internet Engineering Steering Group (IESG).

The IETF holds week-long meetings three times a year. These meetings are composed of working group sessions, technical presentations, network status reports, working group reporting, and an open IESG meeting. A Proceedings of each IETF meeting is published, which includes reports from each area, each working group, and each technical presentation. The Proceedings include a summary of all current standardization activities.

Meeting reports, charters (which include the working group mailing lists), and general information on current IETF activities are available on-line by way of anonymous `ftp` from several Internet hosts. Connect to `ds.internic.net` or `nri.reston.va.us` and look in the `/ietf` directory for information regarding the IETF and in directory `/iesg` for minutes of Internet Engineering Steering Group meetings.

Online Internet Documentation

As is appropriate for a worldwide electronic communications system, Internet Standards, reports, and other documents are available online. They are stored on many of the major network nodes that allow anonymous `ftp` access, although some sites may carry only a partial set of documents. To make those documents easily accessible to the widest possible audience, they are all stored as ASCII files. PostScript versions of some documents are available as well.

The Request For Comments (RFC) series of documents contains all approved Internet Standards, as well as many other documents de-signed to explain various aspects of the Internet. As of this writing, nearly 2,000 RFCs have been issued. Although most of the RFCs are technical in nature, some contain more general information, such as suggestions for selecting computer names (RFC 1178), answers to common questions (RFC 1206 and RFC 1207), and Internet growth statistics (RFC 1296). Although anyone can submit a document for consideration as a future RFC, the Internet Architecture Board (IAB) is responsible for approving all RFCs before they are issued.

The For Your Information (FYI) and Standards (STD) series of documents are subsets of the RFC series. The FYI series is concerned with issues at a more general level than most RFCs. FYI documents are good places to look for short, to-the-point answers to common, high-level questions about using the Internet.

The STD series, however, is devoted to descriptions of key technical issues. The purpose of this subseries of the RFC documents is to clearly identify those RFCs that describe approved network standards. An RFC can be included in the STD series only if it has completed the full process of approval for Standards required by the IAB.

The descriptions of the RFC, FYI, STD, Internet Monthly Report, and Internet Drafts are taken from FYI 4, "Answers to Commonly asked 'New Internet User' Questions."

RFC: Request For Comments Series

The *Request For Comments documents (RFCs)* are working notes of the Internet research and development community. A document in this series may be on essentially any topic related to computer communication, and may be anything from a meeting report to the specification of a standard. You can submit Requests For Comments to the RFC Editor (rfc-editor@isi.edu).

Most RFCs describe network protocols or services, often giving detailed procedures and formats for their implementation. Other RFCs report on the results of policy studies or summarize the work of technical committees or workshops. All RFCs are considered public domain unless explicitly marked otherwise.

Although RFCs aren't refereed publications, they do receive technical review from the task forces, individual technical experts, or the RFC Editor, as appropriate. Now, most Standards are published as RFCs, but not all RFCs specify standards.

Anyone can submit a document for publication as an RFC by way of e-mail to the RFC Editor. You can consult RFC 1111, "Instructions to RFC Authors," for further information. RFCs are accessible on-line through anonymous ftp at a number of sites, including nic.ddn.mil (directory /rfc), ftp.nisc.sri.com (directory /rfc), and nis.nsf.net (directory internet/documents/rfc).

V

Using the Internet

For a more complete list of RFC repositories, get the file /in-notes/rfc-retrieval.txt from host isi.edu (you can access this system through anonymous ftp). An index to the RFCs, arranged in descending order of RFC number, also will be in these directories. Two other indexes are available on some hosts: one arranged in alphabetical order by author, and one arranged in alphabetical order by title of the RFC.

After a document is assigned an RFC number and published, that RFC is never revised or reissued with the same number. Having the most recent version of a particular RFC is never in question. A protocol such as the File Transfer Protocol (ftp), however, may be improved and redocumented many times in several different RFCs. Verifying that you have the most recent RFC on a particular protocol is important. The "IAB Official Protocol Standards" memo (now RFC 1500) is the reference for determining the correct RFC corresponding to the current specification of each protocol.

FYI: For Your Information Series

For Your Information documents (FYIs) are a subset of the RFC series of on-line documents. FYI 1 states,

> The FYI series of notes is designed to provide Internet users with a central repository of information about any topics which relate to the Internet. FYI topics may range from historical memos to operational questions and are intended for a wide audience. Some FYIs will cater to beginners; others, meanwhile, will discuss more advanced topics.

In general, FYI documents tend to be oriented more toward general information, whereas RFCs are usually—but not always—more technically oriented.

FYI documents are assigned an FYI number and an RFC number. RFC 1325 ("Answers to Commonly asked 'New Internet User' Questions"), for example, also is denoted FYI 4; RFC 1207 ("Answers to Commonly asked 'Experienced Internet User' Questions") is the same document as FYI 7.

As with RFCs, if an FYI is ever updated, it is issued again with a new RFC number; however, its FYI number remains unchanged. This can be a little confusing at first, but the aim is to help users identify which FYI corresponds to a specific topic. For example, the document that today is designated FYI 4 will always be FYI 4, even though it may be updated several times and receive different RFC numbers during that process. At this writing, FYI 4 is RFC 1325; previously, it corresponded to RFC 1206, and before that, it was RFC 1177. Thus, you need to remember only the FYI number to find the proper document.

You can obtain FYIs in the same way as RFCs and from the same repositories. In general, look for an `fyi` directory at the same directory path level as the `rfc` directory. Also look for an index file in the `fyi` directory, which contains a complete listing of all FYI documents that have been issued to date.

STD: Standards Series

The newest subseries of RFCs are the *STDs (Standards)*. RFC 1311, which introduces this subseries, states that the intent of the STDs is to identify clearly RFCs that document Internet standards. An STD number will be assigned only to specifications that have completed the full process of standardization in the Internet.

Existing Internet Standards have been assigned STD numbers, which you can find in RFC 1311 and in the IAB Official Protocol Standards RFC (which is now RFC 1500). Like FYIs, after a Standard is assigned an STD number, that number won't change, even if the Standard is reworked, respecified, and later reissued with a new RFC number.

Note

Differentiating between a Standard and a document is important. Different RFC documents always have different RFC numbers; however, sometimes the complete specification for a Standard is contained in more than one RFC document. When this happens, each RFC document that is part of the specification for that Standard will carry the same STD number. The Domain Name System (DNS), for example, is specified by the combination of RFC 1034 and RFC 1035—therefore, both RFCs are labeled STD 13. Thus, you sometimes need to obtain several RFCs to have the complete Standard denoted by a single STD number.

Some hosts establish special directories that contain the STDs. Directory `internet/documents/std` on host `nis.nsf.net`, for example, contains the files `std13-rfc1034.txt` and `std13-rfc1035.txt`, which are the same as `rfc1034.txt` and `rfc1035.txt`, respectively. Thus, if you performed the `ftp` command `mget std13-*`, you would retrieve all the documents that comprise STD 13.

On the other hand, some hosts keep an index file for the STDs in the same directory that stores the RFCs. The file `std-index.txt` in the directory `/rfc` on host `ftp.nisc.sri.com`, for example, has a complete list of all STDs issued to date. The list of RFCs that comprise each STD is given in this file, and you must retrieve the specific RFC documents you need by using the RFC numbers.

IMR: Internet Monthly Reports

The *Internet Monthly Report (IMR)* communicates on-line to the Internet Research Group the accomplishments, milestones reached, or problems discovered by the participating organizations. Many organizations involved in the Internet provide monthly updates of their activities for inclusion in this report. The Internet Monthly Report is only for Internet information purposes.

You can receive the report on-line by joining the mailing list that distributes the report. To be added or deleted from the Internet Monthly Report list, send a request to `cooper@isi.edu`. Back issues of the report also are available via anonymous `ftp` from the `/internet/newsletters/internet.monthly.report` directory of the host `nis.nsf.net`. The file names are in the form `imryy-mm`.txt, where *yy* is the last two digits of the year and *mm* is the two digits for the month. The September 1993 report, for example, is in the file `imr93-09.txt`.

I-D: Internet Drafts

Internet Drafts (I-Ds) are the current working documents of the IETF. Internet Drafts are in a format very similar to that used for RFCs, with some key differences:

- Internet Drafts aren't RFCs or a numbered document series.

- The words `INTERNET-DRAFT` appear in place of `RFC` *XXXX* in the upper left corner.

- The document doesn't refer to itself as an RFC or as a draft RFC.

- An Internet Draft doesn't state or imply that it's a proposed standard. To do so conflicts with the role of the IAB, the RFC Editor, and the Internet Engineering Steering Group (IESG).

An Internet Drafts directory has been installed to make draft documents available for review and comment by the IETF members. These documents ultimately will be submitted to the IAB and the RFC Editor to be considered for publishing as RFCs. Several machines contain the Internet Drafts directories, as follows:

- NSFNET Network Service Center (NNSC): `nnsc.nsf.net`

- U.S. Defense Data Network Network Information Center (DDN NIC): `nic.ddn.mil`

- SRI, International Network Information Systems Center (SRI NISC): `ftp.nisc.sri.com`

To access on-line Internet Drafts, access one of these sites using anonymous `ftp` and go to directory `/internet-drafts`.

Major Internet Nodes You Can Access

Nearly 2,000 sites on the Internet allow their systems to be accessed through anonymous `ftp`. This section describes several of the more notable hosts that make available documents and software pertinent in using the Internet. Anyone can access these sites through anonymous `ftp` and retrieve, for example, the latest RFCs or an application form to join the Internet Society.

These sites are great places to begin experimenting with the Internet and, in particular, to learn about `ftp`. If you can use `ftp`, you can connect with one of these hosts, explore those directories open to the general public, and try retrieving some files. You will find no shortage of interesting files—in fact, you likely will be overwhelmed by the amount of information available at just these sites.

> **Note**
>
> Keep in mind the volatility of the network. The nature of the information these sites store is subject to change over time. Some of the file and directory names may change. You may even find that some day, one of these hosts no longer accepts anonymous `ftp` users, or that a host with one of these domain names is no longer attached to the Internet.

V

Using the Internet

Defense Data Network Network Information Center (DDN NIC)

Host Name: nic.ddn.mil

You can find the RFC and STD series of documents on this host under directories /rfc and /std, respectively. The directory /protocols also has the specifications of communications protocols authorized by the Department of Defense. Look in /templates for commonly used forms that you can fill out and send by e-mail to register, for example, a user in the whois database or a domain in the Domain Name System (DNS).

SRI, International Network Information Systems Center (SRI NISC)

Host Name: ftp.nisc.sri.com

In addition to maintaining a repository for all RFCs (directory /rfc) and FYIs (/fyi), this host also holds a number of other files containing general network information. Look in directories /netinfo and /introducing.the.internet for documents designed to help the novice Internet user become familiar with network resources and protocols. This site also maintains up-to-date reports and other information from the IETF (in /ietf) and IESG (/iesg). Internet Drafts are available in the directory /internet-drafts.

Merit Network, Inc. Network Information Center (Merit NIC)

Host Name: nic.merit.edu

Merit's Network Information Center host computer contains a wide array of information about the Internet, NSFNET, and MichNet. Directory /introducing.the.internet holds a number of documents oriented toward new Internet users.

Much information about the Internet is available in the sub-directories of /internet. Look in /internet/documents, for example, for RFC, STD, FYI, IETF, IESG, and Internet draft files. Also, Merit's A Cruise of the Internet (described later in this chapter) is available through this host, under /internet/resources.

SURAnet Network Information Center (SURAnet NIC)

Host Name: `ftp.sura.net`

SURAnet maintains its Network Information Center on this host under directory `/pub/nic`. Many documents available in this `ftp` archive are geared toward the new user of the Internet.

SURAnet has provided several how-to guides for network navigation tools such as `telnet`, `ftp`, and e-mail. These how-to guides are available in the directory `/network.service.guides`. The chapters of Richard Smith's e-mail-based introductory class are available in the `/training` directory. Also of interest is the SURAnet "Guide to Selected Internet Resources," which documents new and unique Internet resources. This document is in the file `infoguide.`*mm-yy*`.txt`, where *yy* is the last two digits of the year and *mm* is the two digits for the month of the most current dated version.

InterNIC Directory and Database Services

Host Name: `ds.internic.net`

This is a key site when it comes to storing documents generated by the major Internet administrative bodies. The RFC (directory `/rfc`), FYI (`/fyi`), and STD (`/std`) documents are available, as well as Internet Society (`/isoc`), IETF (`/ietf`), and IESG (`/iesg`) reports. Look in directory `/resource-guide` for ASCII text and PostScript versions of the Internet Resource Guide, a valuable compilation of facilities such as supercomputers, databases, libraries, or specialized programs on the Internet that are available to large numbers of users.

Corporation for National Research Initiatives (CNRI)

Host Name: `nri.reston.va.us`

This site maintains up-to-date documents pertaining to the Internet Society (ISOC) and several of its major components. Under directory `/isoc`, you can find ISOC membership information, announcements of INET conferences, and on-line files with the latest issues of the *Internet Society News* newsletter (in directory `/isoc/isoc_news`). Directory `/ietf` holds general information about the IETF and subdirectories containing reports by its various working groups. Look in directory `/iesg` for minutes of the most recent IESG meetings.

Mac Internet Tour Guide Visitors Center

Host Name: `ftp.farces.com`

This site, run by Arts & Farces, contains information and software helpful to Macintosh users. Look in directory `/pub/visitors-center/software` for the latest versions of Macintosh utilities, such as Eudora, MacTCP, TurboGopher, and Fetch. The directory `/pub/visitors-center/mac-internet-tour-guide` has a description of and order information for the book *The Mac Internet Tour Guide: Cruising the Internet the Easy Way* (described in greater detail later in this chapter).

Computer-Based Tutorials for Using the Internet

Given the millions of persons connected to the Internet, no wonder several computer-based tutorials have been developed to guide new users in exploring network resources. You can obtain, at no cost, the two programs described in this section through anonymous `ftp`. If you have the hardware and software required, these programs are worth trying. The program descriptions are based on information provided by the developers to the authors and are subject to change.

Merit's Cruise of the Internet

Merit Network, Inc. has produced a tutorial, called A Cruise of the Internet, that runs on an IBM PC or compatible under Windows 3.1. Your computer must be capable of displaying 640×480 pixels with 256 simultaneous colors. You also must be running Windows in Enhanced mode. A version also is available for the Macintosh II, LC, and Quadra computers. The Mac version requires 8-bit color and a color monitor (12 inches minimum), and you must be operating under System 6.0.5 or 7.x.

The tutorial briefly describes common Internet facilities, such as `ftp`, `telnet`, Gopher, `archie`, and WAIS. It also mentions several areas of special interest, such as supercomputing and space exploration, for which considerable information is available through the network.

To obtain A Cruise of the Internet, use anonymous `ftp` to connect to `nic.merit.edu` using `guest` as your password. If you want the DOS/Windows version, change to the `/internet/resources/cruise.dos` directory. If you have PKUNZIP, get the file `meritcrz.zip` (note that this requires that you use the binary `ftp` file transfer mode). This compressed file contains all the files you need to run the Internet Cruise. If you don't have PKUNZIP, get `meritcrz.txt` (an ASCII file) and `meritcrz.exe` (a binary file). The `meritcrz.txt` file has brief instructions for running the Cruise; `meritcrz.exe`, meanwhile, is the actual executable file for the program.

If you want the Macintosh version, change directory to `/internet/resources/cruise.mac`. Retrieve the `merit.cruise2.mac.readme` and `merit.cruise2.mac.hqx` files. You will need to use BinHex or StuffItLite to convert the `.hqx` file to a Mac executable form. The file `merit.cruise2.mac.readme` has brief instructions on configuring your computer and running the Cruise.

Alternatively, you can obtain a diskette containing the Cruise through postal mail. Send your name and address, specify which version you want to receive (DOS/Windows or Macintosh), and include a check or money order for $10 (payable to the University of Michigan) or your VISA/MasterCard number (including the expiration date and your signature) to the following address:

> Merit Network, Inc.
> Information Services
> 2901 Hubbard, Pod G
> Ann Arbor, MI 48105

The software will be sent to you on a 1.44M diskette. You can request additional information by sending e-mail to `cruise2feedback@merit.edu`.

NNSC's Internet Tour

For Macintosh users, the NSF Network Service Center (NNSC) has developed an Internet Tour in HyperCard 2 format for novice network users. It is intended to be a fun and easy way to learn about the Internet. The stack has basic information including history; sample e-mail, `ftp`, and `telnet` sessions; and a glossary. To run this stack, you need to have HyperCard 2 and System 6.0.5 or higher.

You can obtain the Internet Tour through anonymous ftp to `nnsc.nsf.net`. Go to the `internet-tour` directory and retrieve the files `Internet-Tour-README` and `Internet-Tour4.0.2.sit.hqx`. The readme file will give you information about the latest enhancements and changes to the software, as well as details on system requirements and configuration.

> **Note**
>
> The Internet Tour files have been compressed and saved as a StuffIt 1.5.1 archive, and converted to BinHex format. To use the files, you need to reverse this process by using the Macintosh application StuffIt 1.5.1 or StuffIt Classic.

You also can obtain Internet Tour by way of electronic mail. To do so, send a message to INFO-SERVER@nnsc.nsf.net. You don't need a subject field, but the text of your message must be in a special format (this is very important). You will receive the file split into messages small enough to pass through most gateways to the Internet. Use an editor to re-assemble the original file and transfer it to your Mac. The file Internet-Tour-README in directory internet-tour on host nnsc.nsf.net has a description of the required e-mail message format. If you can't access this file through ftp, try to retrieve it by using ftpmail (see Chapter 18, "Using ftp and telnet with the Internet").

Several Books and Periodicals of Special Interest

Many books have been written about the Internet; they range from short summaries of basic functions such as e-mail and network news to in-depth descriptions of specific aspects of the TCP/IP protocol suite. The following sections describe several books and periodicals that the authors feel, for one reason or another, are especially valuable to Internet users. Most of them are commonly available—your local computer bookstore or technical library will probably carry several of them.

The Whole Internet User's Guide & Catalog

Ed Krol; *The Whole Internet User's Guide & Catalog*; O'Reilly & Associates, Inc.; 1992.

This excellent book is oriented toward the general Internet user. Descriptions and explanations are crystal clear, and the coverage of most subjects is appropriate for the intended audience. Detailed information is given about how to use Internet tools such as `ftp`, `telnet`, and `archie`. The book also includes a 47-page Resource Catalog with brief descriptions of interesting items (covering dozens of topics) available through the Internet.

Internet: Getting Started

April Marine, Susan Kirkpatrick, Vivian Neou, and Carol Ward; *Internet: Getting Started*; PTR Prentice Hall, Inc.; 1993.

Another general-interest entry, this book contains very brief descriptions covering a large variety of Internet-related topics. As the title implies, it pays special attention to telling readers how they can receive value from connecting to the network, and then discusses follow-up topics, such as types of network connectivity and how to find a service provider. It also contains a number of useful tables and lists such as the RFC, FYI, and STD indexes; lists of major Internet service providers throughout the world; and a table showing the level of network connectivity available in every country.

Connecting to the Internet

Susan Estrada; *Connecting to the Internet: An O'Reilly Buyer's Guide*; O'Reilly & Associates, Inc.; 1993.

As the title implies, this short text focuses on issues pertaining to getting connected to the Internet. A wide range of options is explored, and lists of public dialup and dedicated line service providers are included. The book also leads you through the steps in establishing a network connection, from deciding which services and what level of system performance you require to evaluating specific providers. Facilities available through the network are only briefly mentioned, however, in the context of choosing the package of network services you need.

The Internet Companion

Tracy LaQuey with Jeanne C. Ryer; *The Internet Companion: A Beginner's Guide to Global Networking*; Addison-Wesley Publishing Company; 1993.

Oriented toward new Internet users—or nonusers wanting to know what the Internet can offer them—this short book is written in a

V

Using the Internet

high-level, descriptive fashion. The basic resources available through the network are discussed briefly, and a short list of network service providers is given.

The book is filled with interesting personal accounts of the experiences of actual Internet users, from computer simulations of real-world events (the Iraqi invasion of Kuwait) to a contest between a group of reference librarians and a WAIS user to see who could determine more quickly whether the Kremlin has a swimming pool.

The Matrix

John S. Quarterman; *The Matrix: Computer Networks and Conferencing Systems Worldwide*; Digital Press; 1990.

This comprehensive book discusses the worldwide matrix of computer networks in a very clear and thorough manner. Details about networks in every part of the world are given, including the protocols they use, interconnections they now have, and their plans for expansion. Valuable sections of the book are dedicated to a description of communication layers and protocols, a survey of international standard-setting organizations, and an in-depth discussion of legal issues in computer networking.

TCP/IP Network Administration

Craig Hunt; *TCP/IP Network Administration*; O'Reilly & Associates, Inc.; 1992.

If you now have or are considering a TCP/IP Internet connection, this book will provide you with information on all aspects of configuring and managing your network connection. The basic principles of TCP/IP are discussed, as are such considerations as obtaining an IP address and domain name, troubleshooting TCP/IP, and maintaining network security. Dialup IP—that is, SLIP and PPP—and dedicated connections also are described. This book is strongly oriented toward administrators of UNIX-based systems.

Using UUCP and Usenet

Grace Todino and Dale Dougherty; *Using UUCP and Usenet*; O'Reilly & Associates, Inc.; 1991.

This short book discusses the basic concepts of communicating through UUCP. The UUCP set of programs is described in detail, and many examples are provided that show how to perform common tasks. Differences between flavors of UNIX are identified. The fundamentals of using network news are discussed, and explanations of how to read and post news are given. A list of news groups is provided that contains their official names and a brief (single sentence) description of each one.

!%@:: A Directory of Electronic Mail Addressing and Networks

Donnalyn Frey and Rick Adams; *!%@:: A Directory of Electronic Mail Addressing and Networks*; O'Reilly & Associates, Inc.; 1993.

This book begins with an introduction to electronic mail message formats and addressing conventions. An exhaustive discussion of the major computer networks throughout the world then follows. A brief description is given of each network, with a list of the facilities it offers its users, the addressing format it uses, contact information, and a brief description of future network plans. Another third of the book contains a listing of the registered U.S. and international domain names.

The Mac Internet Tour Guide

Michael Fraase; *The Mac Internet Tour Guide: Cruising the Internet the Easy Way*; Ventana Press, Inc.; 1993.

As indicated by its title, this book is designed to help introduce the Macintosh community to the Internet. It contains discussions of electronic mail, `ftp`, `Gopher`, and other network facilities, as well as descriptions of commonly available Macintosh network-related software such as Eudora, MacTCP, Turbo-Gopher, and Fetch.

The most interesting aspect of this book is that it comes with a diskette containing the Macintosh utilities Fetch, StuffIt Expander, and Eudora. People who buy the book also are eligible for two free electronically distributed updates to the information in the book.

V

Using the Internet

Internet World **Magazine**

Internet World; Daniel P. Dern, editor-in-chief; published by Meckler.

Internet World magazine, published bimonthly, contains articles on areas of interest to the general Internet community. New network resources and publications are reviewed, and feature articles may include interviews with prominent Internet figures and overviews of specific network service providers. Contact Meckler for subscription information and a sample issue at

> *Internet World*
> Meckler Corporation
> 11 Ferry Lane West
> Westport, CT 06880
> **Voice:** (800) 635-5537
> **Fax:** (800) 858-3144
> **E-mail:** meckler@jvnc.net or ddern@world.std.com

Internet Society News **Newsletter**

The Internet Society publishes the *Internet Society News*, a quarterly newsletter that covers items of general interest to Internet users and providers. The text of these newsletters is also available on-line through anonymous ftp (see the earlier section "The Internet Society (ISOC)"). For more information, contact the Internet Society at

> Internet Society
> 1895 Preston White Drive, Suite 100
> Reston, VA 22091
> **Voice:** (703) 648-9888
> **Fax:** (703) 620-0913
> **E-mail:** isoc@isoc.org

CD-ROMs Useful to Internet Users

The Internet is a somewhat loose combination of an extremely large number of computer systems spread throughout the world. Several major sites act as repositories of useful network information. They usually carry the same core set of information files, but each also stores some unique files not carried by all the rest. Many other sites also carry files of value to the general network user community that aren't widely distributed.

Searching the Internet at large for files of interest to you can be time-consuming. Even if you are very familiar with the locations of key information files, loading them on your local computer can use a great deal of network connect time and storage on your local computer disk.

CD-ROM is an ideal medium for mass distribution of network information. With a capacity of more than 650MB, a CD-ROM can store as much data as 450 1.44MB diskettes. Furthermore, a CD-ROM can be manufactured so that it can be read on PC, Macintosh, and UNIX platforms.

With such a large amount of storage available, you also can store files without compression, thus eliminating the inconvenience of decompressing files, storing them on your local hard disk, and deleting them when you are done. You also don't have to worry if you have the correct decompression software installed on your local computer. This is especially troublesome if you want to access a file on your PC that has been compressed using the UNIX compress utility, for example.

> **Note**
>
> The descriptions in the following sections were taken from information provided to the authors by the sellers. This information is subject to change. If you are interested in these products, request the latest information about them directly from the firms themselves.

Atlantis Internet CD-ROM

Atlanta Innovation, Inc. offers a CD-ROM with a wide range of tools and information for accessing the Internet. This CD-ROM, called Atlantis, is updated regularly and features all the most widely used Internet documents, including the complete series of Requests For Comments (RFCs), For Your Information (FYIs), Namedroppers Forum, and Standards (STDs) documents.

The Atlantis CD-ROM also contains the latest on-line information from key groups involved in the design, maintenance, and expansion of the Internet, such as the Internet Society (ISOC), Internet Architecture Board (IAB), Internet Engineering Task Force (IETF), and Internet

Engineering Steering Group (IESG). Many other valuable lists of network providers and Internet services are included on the CD-ROM as well, thus saving you considerable time and effort in tracking down such information yourself.

The Atlantis CD-ROM contains a wealth of software acquired from the Internet in a single, easy-to-use package. Communications packages, demonstration software for Graphical User Interface (GUI) Internet interfaces, computer-based tutorials about the Internet, and many other utilities are provided to help you get the most from the Internet, whether you are a novice user or an experienced professional. Utilities and documents are provided for all the most common computing environments, including the DOS, Windows, Macintosh, and UNIX operating systems. The Atlantis CD-ROM is frequently updated to ensure that you have the most up-to-date software and most recent network-related documents.

The Atlantis CD-ROM sells for $39.95, plus a shipping and handling charge of $4.95. (For orders shipped outside the United States, shipping and handling charges are $9.95.) You will find an order card for the Atlantis CD-ROM in the back of this book. You also will find an ASCII file on the enclosed diskette by the name of CD-ORDER.TXT, which contains a printable order form for fax, e-mail, or postal mail orders. An annual subscription service is also available.

For more information about the Atlantis CD-ROM, contact Atlanta Innovation at the following address:

Atlanta Innovation, Inc.
P.O. Box 767849
Roswell, GA 30076
Voice: (800) 285-4680
Fax: (404) 640-8769
E-mail: cdrom-info@atlinv.com

SRI International Internet CD-ROM

The Network Information Center of SRI International sells The Internet CD-ROM, which offers comprehensive documentation on the fundamentals of TCP/IP networking. The price is $195 for delivery within the United States and $200 for shipments outside the United States.

This CD-ROM includes all the on-line Requests For Comments (RFCs); all on-line Internet Engineering Notes (IENs); For Your Information documents; the GOSIP specification; and other protocol, security, and informational files. Archives of technical mailing lists that discuss protocol implementation issues also are provided.

IFIND, an easy-to-use search program, is included on each disk. The search program works on UNIX and DOS systems and searches indexes made from all RFC, IEN, and FYI files, and all TCP-IP and Namedroppers mail messages. As a free bonus, the CD includes public domain source code related to TCP/IP networking for those who don't have direct access to Internet file-transfer capabilities.

For more information, contact SRI at

> SRI International, Room EJ291
> 333 Ravenswood Avenue
> Menlo Park, CA 94025
> **Voice:** (415) 859-3695 or (415) 859-6387
> **Fax:** (415) 859-6028
> **E-mail:** nisc@nisc.sri.com

InfoMagic Internet CD-ROMs

InfoMagic has produced several CD-ROM titles of interest to Internet users. The Standards CD-ROM ($40) is described as a comprehensive collection of U.S. and international communications standards and documentation. Included are the complete Internet Engineering Notes (IEN) and Request For Comments (RFC) series, Internet Engineering Task Force (IETF) and Internet Engineering Steering Group (IESG) meeting minutes, and the Network Resource Guide.

InfoMagic also offers the Internet Tools CD-ROM ($40), which the company calls a comprehensive collection of public domain networking tools and utilities. It contains a wide range of networking software, including SLIP and PPP implementations, SNMP packages, and KA9Q (TCP/IP for PCs). The USENET CD-ROM ($20) comes with assorted archives of the USENET news groups. It also includes the Frequently Asked Questions lists (FAQs) for many news groups.

You can find a brief description of these CD-ROMs and other offerings in file /isoc/cdrom.members on host nri.reston.va.us (you can connect using anonymous ftp). Discounts are available for members of the Internet Society. For more information, contact InfoMagic at these numbers:

Voice: (609) 683-5501
Fax: (609) 683-5502
E-mail: info@infomagic.com

Summary

As you can see from this chapter, you can obtain a great amount of information about the Internet on-line through the Internet itself. The major administrative bodies for the Internet maintain their protocol standards, meeting reports, and newsletters on Internet hosts. Many other organizations keep other documents and software available on-line to anonymous ftp users. You should explore a few of the Internet sites described in this chapter to see for yourself the tremendous volume of documents and software that are easily accessible through the network.

## Chapter 17

Using Internet E-Mail

Electronic mail is one of the major uses of the Internet, and certainly one of the easiest to take advantage of. Just as you can drop a letter in a postal box, you can electronically write, address, and send an e-mail message to someone. This chapter will give you the information you need to use this powerful tool.

What Is E-Mail?

E-mail (short for *electronic mail*) is a method of sending a message from a user on a computer to a recipient user on a destination host. This message is made up of a set of *header lines*, which tell the computer system how to deliver the message, and the *message body*, which can contain any text (such as an office memo or personal letter).

Historically, electronic mail has been one of the main uses of the Internet, and was one of its first applications. Early in the development of the Internet, computer users needed to send messages to other users; electronic mail applications were developed to make this communication possible. Electronic mail applications are now part of almost all computer systems on the Internet.

In general, two distinct sets of programs are used to handle e-mail. The first is called the *user agent*, which is the program that the user interacts with to compose outgoing mail, read incoming mail, and perform all the housekeeping chores necessary to deal with mail messages (such as deleting old mail or reorganizing the mail messages in a logical format).

The second set of programs, which users can't see operating, are the *mail delivery* programs. These programs are responsible for taking a mail message from the user agent program and delivering the mail message to the remote host. Mail delivery programs generally run as part of the underlying operating system on the originating and destination hosts; they are not run by users directly.

The format of electronic mail messages is specified in the Inter-net RFC (Request For Comments) number 822, available by way of anonymous ftp to `ds.internic.net` in directory `/rfc`. This RFC defines all the required headers and any optional parameters that you can use in mail messages. Read this RFC if you want to understand why certain information is required in your message.

> **Note**
>
> You don't need to read the RFCs that define what a mail message looks like (unless you are interested in knowing more about the mail standards), but you do need to make sure that your mail software follows these standards. Ask your software supplier to make sure.

If you want to interchange mail with other hosts on the Inter-net, the mail user program on your machine must generate mail messages that follow the RFC 822 standard. Most machines connected to the Internet also use mail transport programs that communicate by using the *Simple Mail Transport Protocol (SMTP)*, which is specified in RFC 821. This RFC defines the commands and options used by mailers that speak the SMTP protocol; you should read this RFC if you want to understand how the mail transport programs on the Internet operate.

This isn't to say that other mail transport mechanisms and mail formats aren't in use, but SMTP is the most widely used mail message transport protocol, and RFC 822 is the only common mail message interchange format accepted on the Internet.

The Format of an E-Mail Message

As mentioned earlier, an electronic mail message is composed of the mail headers and the message body. In general, the mail programs generate most of the mail headers automatically, but the user must specify some of the important information.

You can understand how the mail header information is used by thinking of an example out of a familiar situation: an office memo confirming receipt of a delivery.

```
To: David Smith, Shipping Department
CC: William Price, Purchasing Department
From: Roberta Page, Production
Date: April 1, 1993
Subject: Delivery of the widget shipment

Dave:
  I assume that we have received the widget shipment in its
entirety. If we have not, please inform me at once.

                Thanks,

                Roberta
```

The headers of a mail message appear at the top of the message and are separated from the message body by a blank line. Each header line starts with a keyword followed by a colon; for example, a valid header line is one starting with From:. Each header line can extend across several lines; wherever space can be allowed in a header line, you can use a carriage return followed by at least one space. The exact syntax of the header lines is fully defined in RFC 822, but summaries of the commonly used header lines follow.

Destination Header Lines

The headers of the mail message hold several different (and important) types of information. First of all, the address specification lines (or *destination lines*) give information that the mail programs use to deliver the message to the intended recipients. These header lines begin with any of the following key words: To:, Resent-To:, CC:, Resent-CC:, BCC:, or Resent-BCC:. The function of these lines is clear; they tell the system who is supposed to receive the message.

In the earlier office memo example, we see that two people are supposed to receive the memo: one specified by a To: address (David Smith) and one in a CC: address (William Price). The sample e-mail message would have header lines starting with To: and CC: and have the e-mail addresses of these two recipients.

All the destination lines specify an address (of the form *user@host*), with the To: address being the primary recipient(s) of the message. Addresses on any CC: line are the secondary recipients of the message (the primary recipients see these addresses), and addresses on any BCC: receive *blind carbon copies* (the primary recipients don't see that these people are receiving carbon copies) of the message.

The destination lines that begin with Resent- are treated the same as the equivalent lines without the Resent- part, but indicate that the mail message is being forwarded from another user who was the original recipient of the message.

For example, one of the recipients of the memo may want to forward the memo to one of his managers. With a paper memo, you could add a new recipient and just send a copy along; with an e-mail message, you would add a Resent-To: header with a new recipient address.

Originator Header Lines

The *originator headers* are those beginning with the key words From:, Sender:, Reply-To:, Resent-From:, Resent-Sender:, and Resent-Reply-To:. In the sample office memo earlier, there is only one originator (Roberta Page); if the memo was from a group of people, there could be many originators.

These header lines give information about the user who sent, or originated, the mail message. In general, the mail programs that users run generate these lines automatically, but the accuracy of the header information isn't guaranteed. It is quite possible for the sender to insert any information into these lines, so users shouldn't treat these originator lines as proof of who actually sent the message. (More information about *mail forging* is given later in this chapter.)

The From: line gives the primary (or only) author of the message. The mail programs should set this field to be the address of the person or program who caused the message to be sent. If this line isn't present, the Sender: line must be present.

The Sender: line also gives the primary person (or program) who sent the message. What makes the Sender: line different from the From: line is that Sender: is used when the sender of the message isn't the author of the message, or to indicate which author from among a group of authors actually sent the message. A mail message may be listed as from a particular user, for example, but may have been generated by an automatic program. In this case, the From:line designates the user, but the Sender: line designates the program that actually generated the message.

Again looking at the office memo, suppose that Roberta Page wrote the memo but had her secretary (Jim Short) actually send it out. In this case, the From: header line would have Roberta Page's address, but a Sender: line would give Jim Short's address.

The Reply-To: header line gives the mail address to which replies to this message should be addressed. Often, if the message is from a program or mailing list, the Reply-To: line indicates a person or list maintainer who should receive any replies. This way, users can reply to automatically generated messages without having to know the person associated with them.

As with the destination lines, the originator header lines that begin with Resent- indicate that the message was re-sent from a second user, who was the original recipient of the message. In the memo example, if William Price re-sent the message to one of his co-workers (for example, Carol Cage), a Resent-To: Carol Cage line and a Resent-From: William Price line would appear (using their e-mail addresses instead of their names, of course).

Other Mandatory Headers

Other header lines give information about the enclosed mail message. The Date: and Resent-Date: give the date and time that the message was sent (or re-sent). The date field is in the form of the current date followed by the time (in the local time zone or Greenwich Mean Time). The day of the week may be included before the date.

The Return-Path: line, automatically added by the final mail transport program, gives a definitive route back to the originating address. Often, you can use this line if the address given in the From: header isn't valid. This is as though the postal carrier stamped your home address on the outside of the envelope when he picked it up from your mail box; even if you didn't sign your letter on the inside, the recipient can still see who sent the message.

Other header lines are generated automatically by the mail delivery programs and record information about the mail delivery process. The Received header lines record the different machines that the mail message passed through during the delivery process. It is as though each post office that handled a letter would put a stamp on the outside, indicating where it had been.

Different parts of the Received headers give information about which host, mail program, and protocols were used in handling the mail message. This information can be extremely useful in debugging possible mail problems, but in most cases, you can ignore it.

Optional Mail Headers

According to RFC 822, mail programs may add other header lines for their own use, but the mail delivery programs don't require these headers. Some examples of these headers are as follows:

- Message-ID: and Resent-Message-ID:, which define a unique text string identifying the current message

- In-Reply-To: and References:, which refer to a message that this message is in reply to

- Keywords:, Subject:, and Comments:, which enable the user to insert text to identify the contents of the message body

- Encrypted:, which defines the program used to encrypt the message body and may optionally give an indication of the key used to encrypt the message

The user or the mail programs also may insert other headers, which the mail transport system will ignore. The user should be careful in using non-standard headers, however, because the mail transport programs may not understand them and may lose or misdirect your mail.

Addressing E-Mail Messages

The most difficult idea for new users of electronic mail to understand is mail addresses. A *mail address* is the way to specify the recipient of a mail message; every person who can receive mail messages on the Internet has a unique mail address. Using mail addresses isn't difficult, but the process of finding out the mail address of a person can be difficult.

User and Host Names

A mail address consists of two separate parts: the *host address* and the *user name*. These parts, separated by the at sign (@), make up a full mail address, such as postmaster@no-machine.com. In this example, the host address is no-machine.com and the user name is postmaster.

In most cases, the host address part of the mail address for a user is the name of the machine they use to connect to the Internet. As explained in Chapter 15, "Understanding the Structure of the Internet," the host address is a *fully qualified domain name*, which uniquely specifies the host on the Internet. The network administrator at the host's site assigns this host name.

The user name part of the electronic mail address is really an arbitrary string set by the systems administrator of the user's site. In most cases, it corresponds to the login name of the user, but some sites set up mail addresses that consists of the first and last name of the user.

> ### Note
>
> The user name field doesn't have to be associated with a real user. A site administrator can set up a *mail alias* that allows mail to a particular address to be delivered to a program (to retrieve files, for example) or to a mailing list. Both types of mail aliases are discussed later in this chapter.

Note that this type of mail address is the simplest form, although it is the one you usually encounter when communicating with users who are directly connected to the Internet. At times, though, you see more complicated address forms, especially when the user you are contacting is on some other network connected to but not a part of the Internet.

For example, mail for a user on another network (such as BIT-NET or UUCP networks) must go through a *gateway* machine that understands how to communicate between the Internet and the foreign network. Many times, to get mail to one of these users, you must manually tell the mail programs to contact this gateway machine.

Look at an example of this mail routing. Many machines not directly connected to the Internet use a protocol called *UUCP* (UNIX to UNIX Copy) to send mail and other information. If the administrator of one of these machines configured the machine to receive mail from the Internet, the host address for the machine usually ends in .uucp (for example, mail addresses for the machines look like user@machine.uucp).

The problem for Internet users is that the .uucp domain really doesn't exist for them—it simply indicates that mail should be sent through the gateway machine, which understands how to route the mail to the right place. So to send mail to a user in the .uucp domain, you usually

V

Using the Internet

must route the mail manually through the appropriate gateway machine. For example, if you receive mail from a user on a machine that is connected using UUCP, for example, the return address will be something like `uunet!host1!user`. This means that the mail goes through the machine `uunet`, then the machine `host1`, and then is delivered to the user (called simply `user` in this example). The gateway machine in this example is the leftmost machine in the address. In this case, the gateway machine is `uunet`, which on the Internet is called `uunet.uu.net`.

> **Note**
>
> Unfortunately, there is no central machine that you can use to route all mail to people on UUCP machines. The machine `uunet.uu.net` is one of the central hubs that connect the UUCP machines to the Internet, however, so it is a fairly common gateway.

So, in this case, you can address the mail by using an address of `host1!user@uunet.uu.net` (by removing the first part of the address and sending it manually through the `uunet` gateway), or even `user%host1.uucp@uunet.uu.net` (which is just a different way of writing the same address). While this process is somewhat complicated, your mail software often will generate the correct return address for you when you reply to a message.

Often, a user experienced on a network that needs special routing tells you explicitly how to reach him. You also can find information about how to route between the Internet and other networks by reading the `Updated_Inter-Network_Mail_Guide` file posted periodically to the news group `comp.mail.misc`, and also available by way of anonymous ftp to `rtfm.mit.edu` in the directory `/pub/usenet/comp.mail.misc`. (You can retrieve this also through ftpmail if you don't have direct ftp capabilities or access to USENET. ftpmail is discussed later in this chapter and also in Chapter 18, "Using *ftp* and *telnet* with the Internet.")

How To Find the E-Mail Address for a User

When you deal with electronic mail, one of the most common questions you hear is, *How do I find out the address for a user?* Often, this question isn't easy to answer due to the diverse nature of the Internet and the number of users connected to it. Just think how complicated trying to find out someone's postal address would be if no directories were available to list the information centrally! This is exactly the problem with finding electronic mail addresses: now very few central databases of mail addresses are on the Internet, and those that do exist list only a fraction of the people who can receive mail.

Even though very few central databases of electronic mail addresses exist, you can still use many resources to locate an address. The more information you have about the person you are looking for, however, the better the chance you have of locating that person on the Internet.

Some of the resources you can use to locate a user's address on the Internet are as follows:

- Direct contact with the person in question

- The Internet whois databases

- The USENET address server

- College and university address servers

Note

Don't distribute people's electronic mail addresses without their permission. Although you often can locate a person's address by looking in a public database, you shouldn't distribute that person's address widely (to a large mailing list, for example) without asking that person first. The user in question may not know that his or her address is publicly available, or that user simply may not want his or her electronic mail box flooded with unwanted mail. (As electronic junk mail becomes more prevalent, distribution of an e-mail address becomes an open invitation for a flood of electronic junk mail.)

Direct Contact

Because of the lack of databases of e-mail addresses, quite often the easiest way to discover the mail address for a particular user is to ask that person directly. If you have some other contact with a user (for example, a business card or postal address), you often can simply call or write the user in question and ask if he or she has a valid electronic mail address. In fact, many companies with Internet connections now print their e-mail addresses right on their business cards.

Alternatively, if you have seen a netnews post from a user and you want to send electronic mail to that user, you can often examine the headers of the netnews post to determine the return address for the user. This information usually is given in the From: or Reply-To: header lines in the post, or the user may include an e-mail address in his *signature*—text included automatically at the end of his post. See Chapter 19, "Using USENET," for more information about news posts.

The *whois* Databases

Originally, the whois databases were set up to register the host and network administrators at the various sites on the Internet. These databases have been expanded to include other people as well, including people who are not administrators. Two different sites now run major whois databases: nic.ddn.mil and whois.internic.net.

> **Note**
>
> The databases are referred to as the whois databases because many of the original systems on the Internet had a command called whois that would connect to this database and automatically look up the information you wanted. This command is still part of many systems on the Internet.

These two databases contain similar information, but for different parts of the Internet. The database at the site nic.ddn.mil contains information only on machines that are part of the Department of Defense military network, while the database at the site whois.internic.net contains information on the rest of the Internet.

For each of these databases, you can find information such as the names and addresses (electronic and postal) for the administrators who run a particular domain, or part of the Internet. You can find information about individual sites on the Internet, sometimes including which machines at that site are connected to the Internet and who uses them.

To use the whois databases, you can telnet to the whois server machine and run the command whois after you are connected. The whois command allows you to ask for information about a user, host machine, or network. You can use the command whois host ds.internic.net, for example, and receive information about the address of the machine, the administrator of the machine, and some of the users of the machine that are registered with the whois service.

The search keywords that the `whois` server supports are `domain`, `network`, `host`, `gateway`, `organization`, or `group`. `whois` searches that don't specify a keyword are assumed to be searching for a user name.

If you can't telnet directly to the `whois` server, you also can use the database by sending electronic mail to the address `whois@whois.internic.net` (or `service@nic.ddn.mil` for military addresses). If you send a message with `help` in the message body, you will receive more information about the mail server.

You also can access the `whois` database by using a *Gopher* client to connect to the two machines. Some computer systems (most UNIX systems, for example) also have a local `whois` command that connects automatically to the central `whois` database and does a query for you. Check with your local site administrator to see if such a command is available on your system.

The `whois` database is a valuable resource for finding out information about sites on the Internet. Because all networks must be registered with the network registration services and must provide the name of a person to contact for the network, you have a very good chance of finding out a contact name for a particular network. On the other hand, many users or hosts aren't in the `whois` database, so you aren't as likely to find information about individual users there.

Other sites on the Internet run local `whois` servers to provide information about their local users. Unfortunately, finding out exactly which sites do so is difficult, unless you ask administrators there. One list of sites that run `whois` servers is available by way of anonymous ftp to the site `sipb.mit.edu` in the file `/pub/whois/whois-servers.list`. See Chapter 18, "Using *ftp* and *telnet* with the Internet," for more information about how to use anonymous `ftp`.

USENET Addresses Server

If the person you are looking for posts articles on netnews, finding out an address for that person is possible by using the USENET addresses server. This database server, run on the machine `rtfm.mit.edu`, scans all USENET posts and stores the addresses it finds in a central database.

To ask the server for an address, send an electronic mail message to the address `mail-server@rtfm.mit.edu` with a message of the form `send usenet-addresses/`*string* in the message body. You should replace

V

Using the Internet

string with a list of words to search for. For example, if you were look-ing for the address of the user mjohnson, you could send the request send usenet-addresses/mjohnson.

The server will send a mail message back to you with all the addresses that match any words you specify. You should include in the search string items that will help identify the user in question, such as the user's first and last name, and possibly the site that person may post from.

Because the database search matches any of the words you gave, you may get quite a few addresses in response. The server will return only a maximum of 40 addresses, however, so if you get 40 addresses back and the address you want isn't among them, you should eliminate some of the words to reduce the number of matches.

The USENET addresses database is also available through WAIS, on the machines rtfm.mit.edu and cedar.cic.net. On both machines, the database is called usenet-addresses and can be reached on port 210. For more information about USENET and netnews posts, see Chapter 19, "Using USENET."

Looking Up Addresses at Colleges and Universities

If the person you are looking for is a student or employee of a college or university, you may be able to find out information about the elec-tronic mail addresses by looking in the *College Email Addresses* postings in the news group soc.college.

This set of articles gives the electronic mail address policies for many universities and colleges across the country, and can often give enough information so that you can look up a particular user at that site.

You can retrieve these articles by looking in the soc.college netnews group (see Chapter 19, "Using USENET," for more information about reading news groups), or by anonymous ftp to rtfm.mit.edu in the directory /pub/usenet/soc.college. The articles are the ones starting with the name *FAQ:College-Email-Addresses*.

Other Tools and Techniques for Finding Addresses

You can use many other tools and techniques to look up electronic mail addresses, and more of these tools and techniques are being introduced every day.

Many companies run central servers to provide mail addresses for their employees, and even some countries have mail address servers (called *white pages* or *X.500 servers*). These servers are set up quite like a telephone directory, and the information in them is divided into small pieces called *organizations*. An organization is like a single phone book, while the X.500 server is like a whole library of phone books.

One way to locate and use these servers is to use Gopher and WAIS clients. Many of these servers are advertised through these services, and you can browse around different sites without having to know which sites actually offer the services. If you know the name of the site where the person is (the college or university, or the company they work for), you can use a Gopher or WAIS client to look for a server at that site and get information about users there.

Gopher and WAIS are very valuable tools that can help you find an incredible amount of information about the Internet as a whole, and users on the Internet in particular.

Other services available for finding information about mail addresses, such as *netfind* and the *Knowbot Information Service*, are described in the `finding-addresses` Frequently Asked Questions post. You can find this post in the net-news group `comp.mail.misc`, and you can retrieve the file by way of anonymous ftp to `rtfm.mit.edu` in directory `/pub/usenet/comp.mail.misc`.

If you know the site where a user is but can't find out any information about the user name to use, you can ask the postmaster at that site for help. Every site on the Internet is required to have a mail address called `postmaster`, which is set up to be a person who can answer questions about the site. So you can send mail to the address postmaster at the site in question, and at least be reasonably sure that you will get an answer.

V

Using the Internet

When you contact the postmaster at a site, you need to remember a few things. First of all, be specific about the user you are looking for, and be polite! The user who is designated as postmaster is quite often a systems administrator, and almost always very busy. Answering mail probably isn't something that is high on his priority list, so you should be patient. You probably will get a response within a few days. That said, almost every postmaster on Internet sites takes the job seriously and will make every effort to find the information for you.

As a last resort, you can post a message to the news group `soc.net-people` and ask for the electronic mail address for the person. Because this is like advertising in the *New York Times*, asking if anyone has an address for your old college roommate, you should try this only when all other attempts—including calling the person in question— have failed. You should be as specific as possible when identifying the person, and you probably shouldn't get your hopes up too high. If all the aforementioned techniques have been tried and failed, the readers of `soc.net-people` probably won't have much better luck. For information about posting to news groups, see Chapter 19, "Using USENET."

Determining the Host Address

Most of the techniques given so far assume that you know at least a little about the site where a user is. If you don't know even this information, you probably won't be able to find the electronic mail address for the person. However, if you know something about the person (such as where they work or go to school), you often can deduce the site name for that person.

First, you need to determine the domain part of the address. As described in Chapter 15, "Understanding the Structure of the Internet," host names are made up of words separated by periods. For example, the name `charon.mit.edu` is a valid host name. The parts of the name go from the least specific at the right side (the `edu` part, called the *domain*) to the most specific at the left (`charon` in the preceding host name).

You can deduce the domain of the person's site if you know what type of institution he or she is at. For example, if the person is at a university, that person probably will have an `edu` domain. If the person works at a company, the domain probably will be `com`. Similarly, if the person lives in a foreign country, the domain will be the one associated with that country (for example, fr is the domain for France).

After you determine the domain, you need to find the site name. This name is often related in some way to the institu-tion the person is affiliated with. For example, if the user is at Stanford University, the site name is stanford.edu. In other cases, acronyms are used. For ex-ample, the site name for Carnegie Mellon University in Pittsburgh is cmu.edu. These two examples show the most common ways that do-mains are named.

The WHOIS databases described so far are a very good way to look up these domain names. If you connect to the appropriate server, you can find all sites that match a search string. For example, you can use a command such as whois carnegie and search through the results until you find the entry for Carnegie Mellon University. This entry reveals that their domain name is cmu.edu. Another example is to use the com-mand whois international business to find out that the site name for International Business Machines is (not surprisingly) ibm.com.

Getting Access to Electronic Mail

Now that you have read a little about the format of electronic mail messages and discovered how to find out how to address those mes-sages, it is time to discuss how to get access to electronic mail.

When you try to get access to e-mail, the first consideration is what level of service you want to have. Although setting up and configuring electronic mail servers and applications isn't especially difficult, it may require some understanding of networking and operating systems. Fortunately, several ways of getting access to electronic mail don't require any administration on your part at all.

Public Access Sites

If you don't have a specific need to have electronic mail running di-rectly on your local machine, the easiest way to get access to it is to use one of many *public access sites* available on the Internet. These public access sites are machines connected to the Internet that provide ac-counts on a commercial basis. Almost all these systems provide elec-tronic mail; many also provide access to netnews and other Internet services, such as Gopher and ftp. The fees charged by these sites vary widely; some don't have a usage fee, others charge a small fee to cover their costs. Some are commercial providers that have levels of service running from inexpensive to quite expensive.

The advantage of using a public access site is that you don't need to worry about setting up and maintaining an electronic mail system; someone already has done it for you. All you need to do is log in to the machine (usually by way of telnet from your local machine) and use the local mailer to send your mail.

The disadvantages of using such as public access site is that you have no say (usually) about the configuration of the mail system. You must use the software the site administrators provide, and you must observe whatever policies they maintain concerning the content of electronic mail (such as prohibitions on commercial use). Also, because you often are using terminal emulation software, the software you run to send mail usually isn't graphical in nature. Given the number and variety of public access sites, however, these usually aren't problems—you can often find a site that suits your needs.

> ### Note
>
> Explaining exactly the use you will make of the public access machine account when you apply for it is always best. Although cen-sorship is almost unheard of on the Internet, some public-access machines do have restrictions on commercial use (such as receiving orders for merchandise) or material offensive to minors. You are much better off talking about your needs in advance rather than have the administrators of the machine "discover" your possible abuse of their policies later on.

After you decide to use a public-access site, several resources are available to help find one. To locate a public-access site, consult the lists provided on the disk included with this book in the file PDIAL.TXT. The PDIAL document is updated as the maintainer gets information about new public-access sites. It is kept at an ftp site (identified within the file) on the Internet and posted regularly to certain news groups, which also are identified in the file.

After you have the names of sites that may be able to provide the news access you need, you should contact the administrators at that site (given as the contact for information in the listings) to determine the features of the mail system on that machine. You need to ask about the following:

■ *What mail programs are available to compose and send mail?* Most of these programs will be terminal oriented (that is, they don't have a graphical user interface), and several do have help features built in. Common mail interfaces are Elm, Pine, and MH, although many others exist. Some examples of the different mail interfaces used on public-access sites are discussed later in this chapter.

■ *How much disk space is allocated to store user mail?* If you expect to receive large amounts of mail (you want to subscribe to several mailing lists, for example), you want to make sure that the system has sufficient disk space available to store it, and that you won't go over whatever amount is allocated to you. Some of the more active mailing lists can send you several megabytes of mail per week!

■ *What are the system policies regarding the content of electronic mail messages?* Also, can the systems administrators examine users' mail at will, or are there policies against it? You want to make sure that both you and they are comfortable with what you will be doing, and how they run the system.

Off-Line Mail Readers

An *off-line mail reading system* is another way to get access to electronic mail without having to administer the actual mail delivery programs on your local machine. Off-line mail systems use a local communications program to connect to a remote system or service. In general, you read your existing mail and compose new mail messages when you aren't connected to the remote machine; you connect periodically to send any new mail and to receive any mail that is waiting on the mail server machine.

This type of setup is more efficient than connecting to a remote machine and performing your mail tasks online. Because reading and composing mail are time-consuming tasks, you can save the connect time on the remote system (which often costs money!) by doing those tasks on your local machine.

Many different organizations offer off-line mail (and NETNEWS) services. Most of these organizations now have Windows-compatible programs that provide a simple-to-use interface to the remote system, as well as easy-to-understand tools for managing your local mail (reading, filing, and sorting your mail messages, for example). Some of these organizations also feature other on-line services, such as an interactive "chat" service or file downloading capabilities.

> **Note**
>
> An *interactive chat program* allows you to talk to several people at once. These other people can be on the same machine you are on, or they can be on a machine anywhere else on the Internet.

Examples of these off-line mail services include Computer Witchcraft, Inc., which offers a system called WinNET Mail (which also offers netnews capability—see the chapter on netnews for more information about this part of their service), and General Videotex Corporation, which offers a service called BIX. BIX, accessible through a program called BIXnav, offers on-line chat programs and other services. Some examples of these programs are given later in this chapter.

If your system is running DOS only (that is, not Microsoft Windows), an off-line mail service from PSI (Performance Systems, Inc.) can be used to send and receive mail. This system, available in a DOS and a Windows version, has options to read and send mail, as well as read USENET news and retrieve files.

Setting up a Local Mail System

Setting up a mail system on your local machine isn't an easy task. Some experience with computer networking and the operating systems that are running on your systems will be required to make the mail programs run correctly. You also may have to buy some additional computer systems to act as mail gateway machines. Also, someone at your site must be designated as the postmaster and should monitor the mail system to make sure that it continues to work as expected.

To decide what mail software is appropriate to your site, you will first have to review what existing software your mail programs will have to work with. If, for example, you have existing mail software, and you simply want to be able to communicate with mailers on the rest of the Internet, you will have to run significantly different software than you would if you don't have any existing software.

The simplest type of mail system to set up is a stand-alone mail system. In this case, you have a single machine that communicates with the rest of the Internet. This type of system is simple, because you have only to set up and maintain a single computer system and mail programs.

To communicate with the majority of machines on the Inter-net, the mail system you run must be able to speak the Simple Mail Transport Protocol to communicate with the remote mail system. If you also want to receive your incoming mail on your local machine, it should also run an SMTP server that can accept mail from other Internet machines.

One option for sending and receiving mail on your local machine is PC-Eudora. This software is available by way of anonymous ftp to `ftp.qualcomm.com`. It uses the SMTP protocol to send mail to a remote server machine (usually, your Internet service provider will have a machine you can route mail through), but uses a different protocol called the *Post Office Protocol Version 3* (POP3) to receive mail. This configuration requires that you have a second machine to receive your mail and run the POP3 server.

> **Note**
>
> The Post Office Protocol is a way to have your electronic mail sent to a central machine and to allow you to pick up the messages on your personal machine whenever you want. A program on your local machine connects to the central mail machine and copies in any mail you have waiting.

Another option for a single machine to send and receive electronic mail is a commercial product called SelectMail from Sun Microsystems Inc. This product—available in Microsoft Windows and MS-DOS versions—supports SMTP for sending mail and requires a POP server for receiving mail. Many other mail programs run on stand-alone machines; check with your computer system or software vendor to see what they have available.

Integrating with Existing Networks

If you already have some networking systems running at your site, your choices of electronic mail systems are very different and will depend on what you already are running.

If, for example, you already are running an internal network of computers with a product such as Microsoft Mail or Lotus Notes, you probably will want to buy a product that allows these systems to send mail through the SMTP protocol to the rest of the Internet. These products are available from the vendor from whom you bought your existing mail products. Third-party products that interface these systems to normal Internet mail systems also may be available.

If you are running a Novell network on your local system but don't have a mail system already, several inexpensive products can give you e-mail access. One mail system that uses the Novell MHS system to send mail locally is called Pegasus Mail. This system is available by way of anonymous ftp to `ftp.uu.net` in the file `/systems/ibmpc/msdos/simtel20/novell/pmail235.zip`.

Although Pegasus Mail can be used to send mail between systems on your local Novell network, you will need a gateway system to send mail to other Internet sites using SMTP. One such gateway product is called XGate, which is a share-ware product available by way of anonymous ftp at the site `wuarchive.wustl.edu` in the file `/systems/novell/lan/xgate140.zip`. XGate must run on a separate dedicated personal computer system on your Novell network.

XGate is a MHS to SMTP gateway, but it also requires an SMTP agent to handle the actual transmission of the mail. Two such products are available, XSMTP and Charon. XSMTP is a shareware product available from ftp Software (but usually is included in the shareware version of XGate), and Charon is a freely available software product of Clarkson University. Charon is available by way of anonymous ftp to `sun.soe.clarkson.edu` in the file `/pub/cutcp/charon.zip`.

Configuring XGate with XSMTP or Charon is beyond the scope of this chapter, but documentation is included with the packages. Because these are shareware products, you can obtain them and experiment with them before paying the registration fee. The main cost of these packages is the expense of operating a separate gateway machine for the XGate software. XSMTP runs on the same machine as XGate, but Charon also requires a separate computer system to run on.

Examples of Different Mail Systems

This section shows examples of several different mail systems that you can use, on your own system or on a remote service provider. The first examples are of character-oriented interfaces, Pine and MH, which you can use if you are using a public access site as your mail server. Later examples are from different off-line mail readers that run on your PC.

Examples of the Pine Mail System

The Pine mail system is a simple screen-oriented interface to sending electronic mail. This system is often used on public- access sites, because it is easy to use and includes on-screen help for novice users. If your public-access site has the Pine mail system available, you will normally use the command pine to run the program after you log in to the public-access system.

When you first run Pine, you will see the main menu screen, which gives you the commands that are available. The main menu screen is shown in figure 17.1.

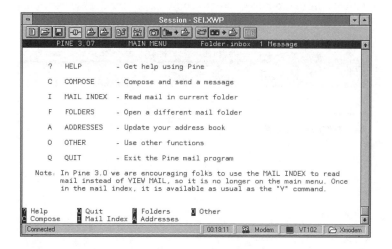

Fig. 17.1

The Pine Mailer main screen, which shows the main commands available and how to get help.

The I command will give you a list of the new mail messages that you have received, and allows you to select the message you want to view. At this point, you can use the V command to view a message, as shown in figure 17.2.

Fig. 17.2
The Pine View
Message screen.

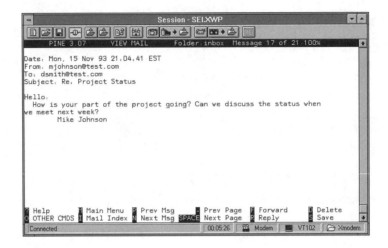

Other Pine commands enable you to move a message into a different *folder*. For example, you may have a folder for all mail from your boss, or different folders for mail relating to different projects you are working on. This way, you can organize your mail for easy access. You can also, of course, delete mail messages when you no longer need them.

The Pine c command allows you to compose, or send, new mail messages. An example of the compose screen is given in figure 17.3.

Fig. 17.3
The Pine Compose
Message screen.

Examples of the MH System

The MH mail system is another common mail system you may encounter on a public access system, especially if that system runs the UNIX operating system. MH is a *command-line* oriented mail system—you issue MH commands at the operating system prompt.

MH, available for many different operating systems, can be obtained by way of anonymous ftp to the site `ftp.uu.net` in the directory `/mail/mh`. MH is made up of many commands that enable you to read, send, or manipulate your mail messages. MH also includes the idea of mail "folders," where you can keep mail messages that are related in some way.

Examples of commonly used MH commands are as follows:

Command	Description
inc	Reads your system mail file into your inbox, which is the default folder created the first time you ran an MH command. Messages in your inbox (or any other folder, really) are numbered, and MH keeps track of the current message for you.
show	Displays your current message.
next	Moves to the next message in your folder and displays it.
prev	Moves to the previous message in your folder and displays it.
scan	Displays the headers of the messages in your folder. You can specify a range, or list, of the messages you want to look at.
comp	Allows you to compose a message to send to someone.
rmm	Removes the current message (or the one you specify).
repl	Replies to the current message.
refile	Lets you move a mail message into another folder.

V

Using the Internet

Quite a few other MH commands manipulate messages or folders. MH is a very flexible mail system, and it works even when you don't have a graphical environment available.

Examples of the WinNET Mail System

WinNET Mail is an off-line mail system that allows you to read and compose mail messages while not connected to the service provider; you can then call the provider to actually deliver your mail (and receive new mail messages if any exist). WinNET Mail, a Microsoft Windows application, is a product of Computer Witchcraft, Inc. The WinNET Mail system consists of the main user interface program, the communications module that contacts the server system to transfer your incoming and out-going mail, and several support programs. (WinNET Mail is included on the disk accompanying this book.)

When you start up WinNET Mail, you will see your main mail folder, which lists all the messages you now have received. This screen has icons that you can use to move among the mail messages, compose new mail, reply to or forward a mail message, or move a mail message to another folder. This mail screen is shown in figure 17.4.

You can read a mail message by double-clicking the line for that message. A second window comes up, displaying the message you selected. You can have many different windows with different mail messages displayed, as shown in figure 17.5.

To send a new mail message, click the Compose icon, which brings up the Mail Composition Editor to edit your outgoing mail message. After you edit your mail message to your satisfaction, you can send the mail message by clicking the Done button. This queues your mail message on your local disk, where it waits until you connect to the server machine. Figure 17.6 shows the Mail Composition Editor window.

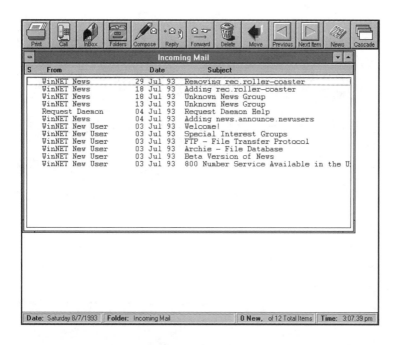

Fig. 17.4
The WinNET Mail
main screen.

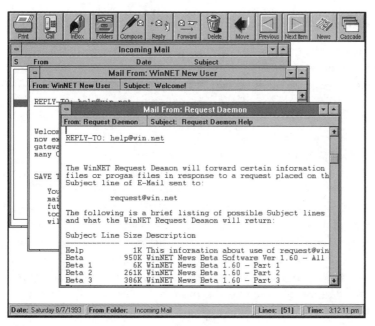

Fig. 17.5
Reading mail in
WinNET Mail.

Fig. 17.6
The WinNET Mail
Mail Composition
Editor window.

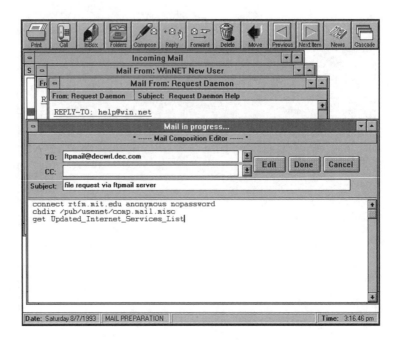

Using Electronic Mail

When you have access to electronic mail, you have access to most of the resources of the Internet. Of course, the primary use of e-mail is to send messages to other individual users on the Internet. You can do many other things with electronic mail, however, as described in the following sections.

Mailing Lists

Early in the development of the Internet, a problem was encountered with electronic mail: people with a common interest wanted to distribute mail messages to a group of people. One way to send these mail messages was to send around the addresses of everyone in the group. Each person would then address his or her mail message to everyone on the list of people. The problems with this idea soon became obvious: everyone had to have the same list of names, and adding or removing people from the list was hard to do. Everyone on the list also had to be able to get mail to everyone else on the list.

From these early attempts at group communications, the current concept of a *mailing list* evolved. Rather than each person in a group have the address of everyone in the group, one person at a central site keeps track of who is on the list. The mail administrator at this central machine then sets up a mailing address for the list. Mail sent to this address is redistributed (usually by way of some intermediate software) to everyone on the list. Usually, a second address is set up to deal with requests to the list administrator, which enables people to communicate with the person maintaining the list without explicitly knowing who that person is.

The advantages of the central mailing list are obvious. With only one copy of the addresses, who is on the list is never in question. Because a central person maintains the mailing list, no confusion exists about who is supposed to keep track of additions or deletions to the list. Also, only the central site needs to be able to contact every address on the list; the other sites need to be able to contact only the central site.

The centrally maintained mailing list has a few disadvantages, however. If the central site is unavailable (because of a hardware failure or a network problem, for example), the entire mailing list is unavailable. Also, if the maintainer of the list goes on vacation or is simply busy, it may be hard to be added to or removed from the list.

Most mailing lists are set up to send out automatically all messages submitted to the list. These lists usually are called *mail reflectors*, as everything sent in is reflected out to the entire list. This type of list works well for low-volume lists or those where little controversy exists. Other types of lists exist to deal with unusual situations.

Moderated Mailing Lists

One of these types is the *moderated* list. With this list, submissions to the list are mailed to the list maintainer, or *moderator*. This person reviews the message, and if it meets his or her criteria for acceptance, it is then sent out to the rest of the list. Usually, the list moderator weeds out messages that are off-topic for the list or those that contain objectionable material. This type of list works well for topics that may be controversial, or where a particular user often disrupts the list with objectionable material.

Although the moderator has absolute control over the messages that flow through the list, in almost every case, his job simply is to keep the topics discussed on the list relevant to the charter of the list. The moderator of the list almost always publishes the criteria he uses for selecting the articles, but these are in fact approved by the people who subscribe to the list.

There have been cases where the moderator of a mailing list has refused to allow certain topics or posts from legitimate users to pass to the list; such censorship is relatively rare, however. Ultimately, the only recourse the readers of the list have to deal with an objectionable moderator is to start another mailing list.

Mailing List Digests

In cases where a very high volume of messages exists, the list may be set up to condense the messages. In this case, submissions to the list are accumulated and then sent out in one large message, called a *digest*. This reduces the load on the central site, because one large message is easier to process than a great deal of little messages. Usually with the mailing lists, the digests are sent out at regular intervals (daily or hourly, for example).

Finding Mailing Lists

Mailing lists exist on almost every topic imaginable. Any time a group of people have a common interest, a mailing list usually is set up so that these people can communicate. Because of the dynamic nature of the Internet, these mailing lists have a tendency to begin and grow quickly, and then decline and disappear as the need or interest declines. Some mailing lists last a few months to deal with a particular problem or interest; others have lasted for many years.

You can find a list of publicly available mailing lists posted periodically in the news group `news.announce.newusers`. The list (in five separate files) is also available by way of anonymous ftp to `rtfm.mit.edu` in directory `/pub/usenet/news.announce.newusers` in files starting with the name `Publicly_Accessible_Mailing_Lists`.

This file is updated frequently by the list maintainer, Stephanie da Silva (who you can reach through e-mail at the address `arielle@taronga.com`), but the information may be out of date. You should contact the individual list maintainers to see whether the list still exists and what the topics covered by the list are.

Mailing List Etiquette

To join a mailing list, or to talk to the maintainer of the list, you should always send mail to the "request" address listed for the mailing list. In most cases, the address for submitting requests to the list maintainer is the same as the address for submissions to the list, but with `-request` added on the end.

Note

Please don't send your requests to the entire list; this will greatly annoy the people who subscribe to the list and probably won't get you the information you want.

For example, if the mailing list address for submissions is `network-talk@some.machine.com`, the address for the list maintainer is usually `network-talk-request@some.machine.com`.

After you are on the list, remember that every message you send to the list will be re-sent to everyone on the list. If you are simply agreeing with another list message, you probably should respond just to the person who originated the message. Also, if you send in a request for information to the list, a usual practice is to send in a summary of the responses to your question after a reasonable period of time.

If the list is moderated, the moderator may reject one of your submissions, for any of several reasons. Someone else recently may have asked your question (in which case the moderator often supplies you with an answer), or your question may be one that causes long and prolonged arguments in the list (in which case the moderator probably will explain the trouble it causes). In any case, you often can reword your request or ask the moderator how to get the information you need. Don't simply argue with the moderator about why the message was rejected; the moderator's job is to keep the list on topic and the people on the list happy.

Sending Non-Text Data

Most of the time, your mail messages contain only printable characters (called *ASCII data*). In some cases, however, you will want to send binary data in a mail message. This binary data may be an executable program file, sound or graphic file, or any of a number of binary formats. Because the mail transport programs in use today were designed to handle printable (ASCII) data only, you must take some special measures to make sure that your binary data gets through correctly.

The first step you must take to transmit binary data in a mail message is to translate the binary into ASCII. This step usually is done with a command such as uuencode, which encodes the binary data as a series of printable ASCII characters. Most UNIX systems have the uuencode program available on it as a standard system program. Versions of uuencode are available for other systems; you should use archie to find a version for your system.

After you use uuencode to translate your binary file into ASCII data, you can include it in your mail message. You should note, however, that if the encoded file is longer than about 1,000 lines, you should split the data into several parts by using a text editor or some other tool. These parts can be enclosed in separate mail messages.

When you send encoded binary data, always include information in the messages that tell the remote user what the data was originally. You also should include information on what method was used to encode the data, and information about which part of a multipart message this one is (for example, you can say that this message is part two of five total parts). This information allows the remote user to take the message, assemble the different parts if the file was split up, and then decode the file (using the uudecode program) into its original binary form. If everything worked correctly, the destination user will have an exact copy of the original binary file.

Multimedia Electronic Mail

As outlined earlier in the section on sending non-text data, the process of sending binary data through the normal mail channels is a somewhat complicated one. Many possible locations exist where a slight error will cause the file extracted on the remote side to be wrong, often in a subtle way. Multimedia electronic mail is designed to simplify the process of sending binary data and extracting the data on the receiving side.

A multimedia electronic mail system automatically encodes binary data to send along with a mail message and automatically decodes and processes binary data in incoming mail messages. For example, you can send a binary file containing a voice message along with a normal mail message. The receiving mail program automatically plays this sound file when the mail is received. Because the process is automatic (and handled by the mail programs themselves), the user doesn't have to be concerned with the details of the process. Of course, if the computer system the user is on can't deal with the binary data (it doesn't have a speaker for playing the sound file, for example), the user is simply notified that the binary data exists.

Multimedia is a relatively new idea, and the details of the exact format of the messages are still in the process of being worked out. As this book is being written, the standards for multimedia electronic mail are being finalized, and mail systems that implement these standards are being written. A few mail systems that implement multimedia e-mail are already available: the "meta-mail" package from AT&T Bell Laboratories is one. You can retrieve the "metamail" package by way of anonymous ftp to the site `ftp.uu.net` in the directory `/networking/mail/metamail`. It is also available from many other sites around the Internet.

Retrieving Files Using Electronic Mail

Although the primary means of retrieving files on the Internet is by use of the ftp file transfer program, sometimes this isn't the best way to get access to files. Many sites on the Internet don't have the direct Internet connection that ftp requires, or their Internet connection may be over a slow line, making the ftp transfer too slow to be practical.

In any case, many more sites have access to electronic mail than can use the ftp program directly. The logical question, then, is whether you can retrieve files using electronic mail. The answer is *yes*—several ways exist for retrieving files using only e-mail.

The way that the ftp-by-mail servers (commonly called *ftpmail servers*) work is that a mail message containing a file retrieval command is sent to the server mail address. On some ftpmail servers, the command must be in the `Subject:` header; on others, the command must be in the message body.

> **Note**
>
> Almost every ftpmail server supports a help command. You should always try this command first to determine what commands the ftpmail server expects. Most of the time, if you give the server a command it doesn't recognize, it will send you back a mail message telling you how to get help.

As an example, you can look at one ftpmail server provided at the site `decwrl.dec.com`. You can use this server by sending mail to the address `ftpmail@decwrl.dec.com`. Sending a message with the word `help` in the message body returns the commands that the server understands. This server is unusual in that it supports a `connect` command that allows you to connect to any ftp server on the Internet and retrieve files. Most ftpmail servers let you retrieve files only on the machine they are run on.

In this case, if you wanted to retrieve the file /pub/test.message on the machine some.machine.com, you can use the following commands to the decwrl ftpmail server to get it:

```
connect some.machine.com anonymous anypassword
chdir /pub
get test.message
```

The first line tells the server to connect to the machine that has the file, using the user name anonymous and the password *anypassword*. The server is then told to change to the directory /pub and then to get the file test.message. This file will be mailed to you.

This ftpmail server has many other options, and other servers have other commands.

> **Note**
>
> The ftpmail server at decwrl.dec.com is provided as a service to the Internet community, and it shouldn't be abused. Try to limit your use of the server to hours late at night, and don't retrieve many files through it, because it will overload the machine quickly.

Other Services by Electronic Mail

Many other services are available on the Internet by way of electronic mail, and more are being added every day. You can access a list of these services (as well as other Internet services) through anonymous ftp to rtfm.mit.edu in file /pub/usenet/alt.internet.services/Updated_Internet_Services_List.

This list also is posted to the news group alt.internet.services at least monthly.

Here is a sampling of services offered on the Internet by way of electronic mail:

- *An archie lookup service* is available via e-mail to addresses archie@archie.rutgers.edu and archie@archie.sura.net. If you send a message with help in the body, the server will give you a list of commands available.

■ *An IP address resolver service* is available by mailing to the address resolve@cs.widener.edu. You can look up the address for a machine or network by sending the phrase site *hostname* in the message body; replace *hostname* with the name of the machine or network you want to look up.

■ *A* whois *service* is available by mailing to the address service@rs.internic.net. You should send a message with the subject help to get the list of commands available. Also, if you send a message with the subject send RFC-*XXXX*.TXT (where you replace the *XXXX* with the RFC number you want), the server will send the appropriate RFC file to you.

As you can see, many services can be reached with only electronic mail—if you read the appropriate news groups and read the lists (and experiment a little!), you can find a wealth of information on the Internet.

Common Problems with Electronic Mail

As with any other Internet function, electronic mail has its own set of problems and pitfalls. This section deals with some of the most common ones, and gives tips on how to get around the problems.

> **Note**
>
> Because the configuration of mail systems differs widely, this section can't deal with problems in configuring the mail programs in detail; only the broadest solutions for problems will be discussed.

Most mail systems do an amazingly good job of delivering mail to the various sites on the Internet. When mail is sent out, the user-level mail programs place your outgoing mail message into some kind of queue for the mail delivery program to act on. Generally, the mail delivery program is run at intervals (once an hour is common; sometimes more frequently, depending on the configuration). When the mail delivery program runs, it tries to connect to the remote computer and deliver the mail message.

V

Using the Internet

If the attempt to deliver the mail fails, one of two things can happen. If the mail delivery program encounters what it believes is a temporary error condition (the remote machine appears to be down, for example), the outgoing mail message will be placed back in the queue for another attempt later on. The number of times the mail delivery program will try to send the message varies, but quite often the message will be held for a day before the message is returned in a mail message to the user with an indication of the error encountered.

If the mail delivery program encounters what it believes is a fatal error condition (the user address wasn't valid or the remote machine couldn't be located), the program immediately returns a mail message, indicating the failure to the sender with the error.

> **Note**
>
> The error message sent when a mail message fails is often called a *bounce message*, because the message bounced back to the sender rather than get to its destination. You may often hear the lament, "My mail bounced again!"

In either case, the result is that the mail message is returned to the sender. The error message (which is actually a mail message sent to the original sender of the message) lists the reason the message failed, and almost always includes the entire original message so that you can figure out the message that failed. Because error messages are generated automatically by the mail transport programs, the reasons why a message failed are often hard to understand.

Mail errors can occur for many different reasons, many of which are out of the control of the person sending the original message. The following sections talk about some common problems and how to resolve them.

Mail Addressing Problems

Mail addressing problems are the most common problems that users of electronic mail run into. These problems usually are in-dicated by error messages such as User unknown or Host unknown from the mail transport programs. Often, the Host unknown error messages are sent by your local mail transport program, indicating that it couldn't find the remote host. The mail transport program on the remote machine usually re-turns User unknown errors; that mail transport program is the only one that knows whether the user name is valid.

> **Tip**
>
> Try resending your mail message to see whether the problem has corrected itself. Resending the mail message often can prevent hours of fruitless searching for a problem that no longer exists.

Because mail addresses are often non-intuitive and hard to type, the first thing you should check is the spelling of the user name or host name (depending on the error received). For example, check to make sure that you didn't confuse the number 0 with the letter O or the number 1 with the letter l. Mail addresses are case insensitive, so it doesn't matter if letters are in uppercase or lowercase.

If this is the first time you have sent mail to this address, you should go through the process listed earlier in this section for finding out a person's electronic mail address to verify that the address you have is correct. If the host name you have is incorrect, you can check the WHOIS database to determine a valid host name, for example. If the host name you have is correct, but the user name is invalid, you can often send mail to the postmaster address at the host to ask for a valid user name.

If, however, you sent mail to this address before without difficulty, and this time it failed, several possible problems exist. First of all, the condition that caused the failure may be temporary. The remote network or host may have been unavailable due to a hardware failure, or a configuration problem may have caused the user name to be temporarily invalid.

Other problems may have happened to cause an address that previously worked to stop working. If the user name is returned as invalid, the user possibly is no longer at that host. A student user may have graduated (or left the school), which caused that person's account to stop working. Similarly, an employee of a company may have left, or the host the user was on may have been removed from service or been renamed to something else. Quite often, only by sending mail to the postmaster for the site in question can you find out this type of information.

Mail Configuration Problems

Sometimes you will receive an error message that indicates a mail configuration problem. These errors are usually some of the more cryptic ones, such as No permission to write or No such file or directory. In these cases, you must first determine whether the error came from your local mail delivery program, or the one on the remote machine. You can determine this information by examining the mail error message itself. The sender of the message is usually the mail program (sometimes called *mail daemon*) from the system that found the error.

In general, these conditions can be corrected only by the mail administrator on the machine in question, so you should notify the postmaster at the site where the error has been found. When reporting a mail problem to the postmaster, you always should include the error message you received, with as much detail as you can. You don't need to include any of the text of the original message you sent, however; in most cases, the postmaster needs to see only the headers of the messages.

> **Note**
>
> If the mail configuration is incorrect enough to cause mail to be returned, the mail to the postmaster possibly may be returned also. In this case, you can try to find a telephone number for the administrator of the machine (by using the whois database, for example) and contact the administrator that way (if the problem is urgent). Or you can wait and hope the administrator notices the problem and fixes it.

Unwanted Mail Messages

As electronic mail becomes more prevalent, receiving unwanted mail messages becomes more common. Unwanted e-mail can be anything from a "business opportunity" from someone you don't know (electronic junk mail) to harassing or threatening mail. Dealing with this problem is often difficult because of the lack of control on the Internet.

Most of the unwanted electronic mail is of the junk mail variety. This type of message, while annoying, is generally the easiest to ignore. The main problem with electronic junk mail is that if you are paying for your Internet access, you are probably paying for each junk mail message you receive. Some ways of dealing with these messages are as follows:

- Delete the mail message.

- Send a mail message back to the sender, asking him or her not to do it again.

- Send a mail message to the sender's postmaster, asking him or her to get the person to stop.

- Send a mail message to the administrator of the system that provides the sender with Internet access, asking them to cut off the person's account.

Naturally, you should start at the top of the list and work down, depending on how many messages you get from the person.

If you receive harassing or threatening electronic mail from a person, you should treat it seriously—as seriously as a threat in a postal letter. The first thing to do is to bring it to the attention of your local postmaster or systems administrator. This person should be able to examine the message and determine whether it's a hoax or forgery.

If your local administrator or postmaster thinks the problem is serious, you should involve your local police in the matter. One main problem with this approach is that in many cases, the local police don't have experience in dealing with electronic mail, so you may have to educate them in this matter.

Mail Security Issues

Although receiving and sending electronic mail messages usually doesn't cause security problems, users and administrators must be aware of several issues when dealing with electronic mail.

First of all, the programs that deliver mail to users are generally run as a system-level program, one that has access to write or modify almost any system file. The system administrator should make sure that the mail delivery programs don't have any bugs or loopholes that may enable a remote user to overwrite important system files. In fact, one of the ways that the famous Internet Worm got into systems was by exploiting a debugging feature of a common mail delivery program.

A remote user also can cause system problems, perhaps inadvertently,

V

Using the Internet

by sending enough mail to a user to fill up the disk the mail is stored on. Or a misconfigured mail program can cause a mail "loop," where a single message is routed through a series of machines forever, with the message getting a little larger each time. This can cause a severe load on the machines and networks the message is looping on.

Forging of Mail Messages

Forging mail messages is another security issue that users need to be aware of. When they receive a electronic mail message, most users believe that the message is from who it says it is from. But this may not necessarily be the case. Because the mail delivery programs generally have no way to verify the contents of the mail message headers or message body, those programs simply pass along the information to the recipient.

In fact, the sender of a mail message can put anything he or she wants into the message headers and body. A knowledgeable user can cause a mail message to appear to be from whomever he or she wants, and only a close examination of the mail headers can point to a possible forgery. One of the main ways to detect a mail forgery is to examine the Received By: header lines to see which hosts the message has passed through. If these lines do not match the host name indicated by the originator header lines, the message may be a forgery.

Although the exact mechanism of forging mail messages is beyond the scope of this book—and is to be discouraged in any case—users should be skeptical of the contents of electronic mail. For example, if you receive a mail message claiming to be from your system's administrator telling you to change your password to something suggested in the message, contact your administrator to verify that the message is valid.

> **Caution**
>
> The preceding example isn't just an example; computer system intruders regularly use this trick to break into systems.

In fact, if you receive any suspicious mail, you should talk to your administrator; the potential damage caused by someone breaking into the system is well worth a few minutes looking over a suspicious mail message. As you gain more familiarity with electronic mail, you will soon be able to tell what mail is normal and what is not.

Mail Message Authentication and Privacy

Another issue related to mail message forging is mail message authentication. Several mechanisms have been proposed to deal with the problem of mail forging by allowing the user to determine the real originator of the mail message. These mechanisms generally use some kind of digital signature to encrypt the message; the receiver can get the sender's decryption key and therefore determine that the presumed sender was the actual sender of the message.

Considerable work is going on in the Internet community to develop standards for allowing electronic mail to be secure. The primary one, called *Privacy Enhanced Mail* (PEM), is described in Internet RFCs 1421 through 1424. Mail programs that fully im-plement PEM aren't generally available, but one implementation of a subset of PEM is called RIPEM.

RIPEM is publicly available, but it depends on the public key encryption mechanism written by RSA Data Security Inc. You can get the RIPEM code and information about RSA by way of anonymous ftp to rsa.com in the directory /rsaref; read the README file there for more information about the RSA algorithms.

The other side of the encryption problem is that of mail privacy. Although electronic mail is generally private, in many cases a mail message has been read by unintended parties, intentionally or unintentionally. Common causes of this problem include the following:

- The sender misaddressed the message. The message was sent to another user (or, even worse, is posted to a public bulletin board system).

- An error occurred in the mail delivery program, causing the message to be sent to someone else, probably the postmaster at the source or destination machine.

- A system administrator was trying to find the cause of a mail delivery problem and read the user's mail files.

- A person who can read mail files was being nosy and read the user's mail files.

In any case, the best way to go is to assume that mail messages can be read by anyone at any time. You shouldn't say anything in an electronic mail message that would cause you embarrassment, legal problems, or worse.

In fact, if you talk to any experienced postmaster or systems adminis-trator, you always can find an example of a personal message being misaddressed and winding up on a public USENET group or electronic bulletin board. Also, sending a private message to a public mailing list is very easy (remember to check the destination address when replying to a mail message from a mailing list). It is very embarrassing when someone's job performance review is posted on the company elec-tronic bulletin board!

The use of PEM-based mail products, however, can provide some relief from this problem by encrypting the mail message so that only the intended reader can actually read the message.

Summary

Electronic mail is one of the great conveniences of the Internet. The capability to send a message instantly to anyone on the global Internet is one of the main reasons for getting access to the Internet. After you decide the level of mail service you require and what programs you need to get the service set up,
you can begin to take advantage of this remarkable service.

With a little experience in finding people's electronic addresses and how to send mail to the various networks connected to the Internet, communicating electronically becomes easy. And the mailing lists and services available via e-mail provide a wealth of information.

## Chapter 18

Using *ftp* and *telnet* with the Internet

In Chapter 17, "Using Internet E-Mail," you saw how to send and receive electronic mail. Although e-mail is a powerful communications tool, it isn't truly interactive. Two-way communications using electronic mail consists of sending someone an e-mail message, waiting for it to reach its destination, waiting for your addressee to become aware of your mail message and read it, and, finally, waiting to receive a reply. This process is like playing "telephone tag"—communicating with people only through their telephone answering machines instead of directly speaking with them on the phone.

Internet itself has the capability for interactive communications. Many service providers allow you to connect with remote computers in such a way that you can interactively examine directory contents, change directories, upload or download files, or even run programs on remote computers. Furthermore, you can do these things almost as easily on the remote computer as you can on your local computer. Not all service providers offer this interactive Internet access, however. Ask whether your provider supports *ftp* (File Transfer Protocol) or *telnet*, the main topics of this chapter. If not, you still can access files noninteractively through *ftpmail*, which also is described in this chapter.

The theme of this chapter is how to access resources of remote computers interactively through the Internet. Some of the procedures show how to transfer text and binary files using ftp and how to log in to a remote computer using telnet. The programs ftp and telnet ask you for the user name and password of your account on the remote computer.

However, many computers have guest accounts for ftp users called *anonymous* accounts, which are available to the general public.

> **Note**
>
> No single standard set of commands exists for ftp or telnet. The command set and issues such as case-sensitivity can vary from system to system. In this chapter, a common UNIX implementation is described. It is the implementation you are most likely to encounter, although there is even some variance in ftp and telnet across UNIX systems. UNIX is case-sensitive, so you must enter commands and file names with this in mind.

Using ftp To Access Files of Remote Network Computers

Many computers on the Internet support *ftp* (File Transfer Protocol) access, a simple way for you to interactively examine their file directories and exchange files with them. You need the following to use ftp:

■ An account with an Internet service provider that allows you to use ftp to connect with remote computers.

> **Note**
>
> Your provider doesn't need to allow other network computers to access its files using ftp.

■ The name of the system on the network that has the files you want to obtain, or on which you want to place files. In other words, because you want to use ftp to access files on a remote computer, you need to know the name of the system containing the files in which you are interested. For remote systems containing many files, you also should try to know beforehand in which directories the files you want reside.

■ A valid user name and password to use on the remote computer. Many remote computers that you encounter, however, allow *anonymous ftp*, where you use the user name anonymous (see the following section on anonymous ftp).

> **Tip**
>
> This book has several real-life examples that include specific file and host names. To obtain a list of file names (and their hosts) for a specific topic, use a navigational aid such as archie.

The ftp program is designed specifically to simplify file access between network computers. You may move from directory to directory on a remote computer, examine the contents of its individual directories, transfer files from the remote computer to your computer, and put files from your local computer onto the remote computer.

> **Note**
>
> You can't use ftp to perform non-file-oriented operations on a remote computer. For example, ftp has commands to rename and delete files on the remote computer, but you can't run programs on the remote machine.

Be aware that no single standard way exists to implement ftp. The ftp program you run on one computer may appear (and behave) differently than the one you run on a different computer. UNIX implementations of ftp are very similar, however, although differences do exist. You may find that the version of ftp offered by your provider varies significantly from that described in this chapter. Before using ftp for the first time on an unfamiliar system, you first should examine the command structure of that particular version of ftp. Furthermore, you may encounter remote computers that don't process ftp commands in a manner compatible with your local computer's ftp program. Incompatibilities rarely are experienced these days and shouldn't be a problem when connecting with major sites offering anonymous ftp access.

Now, tremendous growth is occurring in the amount and types of information available through ftp, with much of it accessible through anonymous ftp. Many government agencies, educational institutions, and other organizations make databases and other information available to ftp users.

For example, the Association for Computing Machinery (ACM), the society for computer professionals, has established an anonymous ftp server that rapidly and easily can provide information of use to its members. The ACM has the advance program and registration forms for its SIGGRAPH (special interest group for computer graphics) conference available through anonymous ftp to `siggraph.org`.

Of course, ftp is extremely useful for transmitting data rapidly between sites that are working jointly on projects. Using ftp eliminates many of the usual considerations, including the following, in transferring files between computers:

- You don't need to worry about requiring both computers to be able to use the same types of floppy disks or tapes to transfer files. An astronomical observatory in Chile, for example, could transmit new digital images to an astronomer in Georgia in minutes using ftp. The two facilities could be using different types of computer systems, and many megabytes of image data could exist, yet the ftp servers on the two systems would handle all these issues without human intervention.

- You can transmit large files as is; you don't have to break up a file into several smaller files because the larger file won't fit on a single floppy disk.

Your Internet service provider may not make ftp access available to you. In this case, you may use a facility called *ftpmail* to get files from remote computers. File retrieval through ftpmail can be quite tedious, and your file access has several significant limitations. However, ftpmail does provide you with an automated method to retrieve files and requires only that you be able to send and receive electronic mail over the Internet. The ftpmail facility is discussed in more detail later in this chapter.

Anonymous ftp

When you try to connect to a remote computer using ftp, you are asked for a user name and password. Many facilities have information that they want to allow people without accounts on their computers to be able to access. These common types of connections, called *anonymous ftp*, mean simply that you enter anonymous as the user name.

The system gives you instructions regarding what to enter as the password. Often, you are asked to enter your Internet e-mail address for the password.

Allowing essentially anyone in the world to access one's computer involves some amount of risk. Therefore, when you establish an anonymous ftp connection with a system, you likely will have significantly restricted access, compared with someone using a personal account on that computer. You should expect to be able to see only files and directories that the systems administrator considers appropriate for unlimited distribution (again, this literally means to anyone anywhere in the world). Also, you may not be able to place any of your files on the remote computer. This restriction is to keep anonymous users from consuming the system's disk storage and to prevent the system from being used for unauthorized purposes.

> **Note**
>
> Anonymous ftp is a great way to explore remote computers on the Internet. Thousands of sites, spanning a tremendous diversity of topics, accept anonymous ftp users. Try connecting to some of the major sites described in Chapter 16, "Finding and Using Internet Resources," as a starting point for your own personal exploration of Internet resources available through anonymous ftp.

A Sample ftp Session

The following example illustrates how easy using ftp is to get files from remote computers. In it, ftp connects to the Network Information Center (NIC) and retrieves several Internet Request For Comments (RFC) documents. A quick search is made for a master index to the RFCs (which is found and retrieved). Then, files containing RFC 1206 (entitled *Answers to Commonly asked "New Internet User" Questions*) and RFC 1207 (entitled *Answers to Commonly asked "Experienced Internet User" Questions*) are accessed.

First, the ftp program is invoked and directed to connect the local computer with the NIC, whose Internet node name is nic.ddn.mil. Because you don't have an individual account on this system, the anonymous account is used.

```
atlinv.com> ftp nic.ddn.mil
Connected to nic.ddn.mil.
220-*****Welcome to the Network Information Center*****
      *****Login with username "anonymous" and password "guest"
      *****You may change directories to the following:
       ddn-news           - DDN Management Bulletins
       domain             - Root Domain Zone Files
       iesg               - IETF Steering Group
       ietf               - Internet Engineering Task Force
       internet-drafts    - Internet Drafts
       netinfo            - NIC Information Files
       netprog            - Guest Software (ex. whois.c)
       protocols          - TCP-IP & OSI Documents
       rfc                - RFC Repository
       scc                - DDN Security Bulletins
       std                - Internet Protocol Standards
220 And more!
Name (nic.ddn.mil:kb): anonymous
331 Guest login ok, send "guest" as password.
Password:
230 Guest login ok, access restrictions apply.
```

Note that **guest** was entered as the password (as the remote computer had requested), although the password didn't appear on-screen.

The welcome message indicated that RFC documents are stored in the rfc directory on this system. Therefore, the cd command in the following listing is used to set the default directory to rfc. Having an index to all the many RFCs would be handy. Such a file, if it exists in the rfc directory, likely will have a name like index or Index. Therefore, the dir

command is used to make a listing of all files matching the pattern
ndex. (The two * wild-card characters used in this fashion mean that
any file name with the contiguous characters *ndex* is a match.)

> **Note**
>
> Entering the dir command without an argument produces a listing of the
> contents of the entire directory. Because (for this directory) this listing likely
> will occupy more than a thousand lines on-screen, a more restrictive directory
> listing was specified.

```
ftp> cd rfc
250 CWD command successful.
ftp> dir *ndex*
200 PORT command successful.
150 Opening ASCII mode data connection for /bin/ls.
-r--r--r--  1 postel   1     6254 May 27 15:14 fyi-index.txt
-rw-r--r--  1 postel   1   181249 Jun 10 19:31 rfc-index.txt
226 Transfer complete.
remote: *ndex*
138 bytes received in 0.87 seconds (0.16 Kbytes/s)
```

This strategy for finding an index to the on-line RFCs was successful,
having found the file rfc-index.txt. This file is retrieved simply by
using the get command, shown in the following listing. Because this is
a text file, the file transfer type doesn't need to be changed because, by
default, it's set to ascii (see the ascii and binary commands later in
this chapter for further discussion of this issue).

```
ftp> get rfc-index.txt
200 PORT command successful.
150 Opening ASCII mode data connection for rfc-index.txt
(181249 bytes).
226 Transfer complete.
local: rfc-index.txt remote: rfc-index.txt
185823 bytes received in 5e+02 seconds (0.36 Kbytes/s)
```

Now you can obtain both of the desired RFCs by using the mget command, which prompts the user before retrieving each file to verify that
it should be transferred. The user responds with y at each prompt, as
shown in the following listing, thereby causing the transfer to occur.
Note that if the prompt command had been executed previously, this
prompting would have been disabled.

```
ftp> mget rfc1206.txt rfc1207.txt
mget rfc1206.txt? y
200 PORT command successful.
150 Opening ASCII mode data connection for rfc1206.txt (70685
bytes).
```

V

Using the Internet

```
226 Transfer complete.
local: rfc1206.txt remote: rfc1206.txt
72479 bytes received in 1.5e+02 seconds (0.48 Kbytes/s)
mget rfc1207.txt? y
200 PORT command successful.
150 Opening ASCII mode data connection for rfc1207.txt (32543
bytes).
226 Transfer complete.
local: rfc1207.txt remote: rfc1207.txt
33385 bytes received in 72 seconds (0.45 Kbytes/s)
```

Finally, the ftp session is terminated and control is returned to the local computer (shown as follows). Three new files now should be in the default directory on the local computer.

```
ftp> bye
221 Goodbye.
atlinv.com>
```

Summary of ftp Commands

This section partitions the ftp commands into groups of commands related by the functions they perform. No single standard exists for defining the ftp commands—they may vary from system to system. The commands described in the following sections are the ones you likely will find in UNIX implementations of ftp. Fortunately, ftp on other systems usually closely resembles the UNIX implementations, especially regarding the most commonly used commands.

Strictly speaking, the ftp program you run is actually a user interface to a low-level set of commands called the *File Transfer Protocol Service Commands*. This lower-level command set is standardized (see RFC 959), but few ftp user interfaces exploit the full capability of entire command set.

In the following descriptions, the full command syntax is given. Anything you enter literally (such as the command name) is represented in a special typeface—for example, `get`. Command arguments that you must supply are *italicized*. Optional arguments are enclosed in [brackets]. For example, the syntax

```
get remote_file_name [local_file_name]
```

indicates that you type the word `get`, followed by the name of the file you want to retrieve from the remote system, followed (optionally) by the name you want this file to have on your local computer.

> **Note**
>
> Do not actually type the brackets when entering your ftp command line.

Starting an ftp Session

Syntax: `ftp [-div] [remote_host]`

Entering `ftp` followed by the name of a remote computer causes ftp to try to establish a connection with that computer. If no computer name is given, ftp starts its command interpreter and responds with a prompt such as `ftp>`.

> **Note**
>
> You can establish a connection later in the session through use of the open command.

The optional flags may differ for different implementations of ftp, but common ones are as follows:

    `-d`   Turn on debug mode (see ftp `debug` command)

    `-i`   Turn off interactive prompting for multiple file transfers (see ftp `prompt` command)

    `-v`   Turn on verbose mode (see ftp `verbose` command)

You can terminate ftp by executing the `bye` or `quit` commands.

Getting Help on ftp Commands

Commands: `help, ?`

Syntax: `help [command]`
                     `? [command]`

The `help` and `?` commands perform identical functions. If `help` or `?` is entered without a valid ftp command, a brief listing of all the available ftp commands, such as the following, is printed on-screen:

```
ftp> help
Commands may be abbreviated.  Commands are:
```

!	cr	ls	prompt	runique
$	delete	macdef	proxy	send
account	debug	mdelete	sendport	status
append	dir	mdir	put	struct
ascii	disconnect	mget	pwd	sunique
bell	form	mkdir	quit	tenex
binary	get	mls	quote	trace
bye	glob	mode	recv	type
case	hash	mput	remotehelp	user
cd	help	nmap	rename	verbose
cdup	image	ntrans	reset	?
close	lcd	open	rmdir	

If a valid ftp command follows help or ?, a brief (usually one line) description of that command is given.

Establishing and Terminating an ftp Connection

Commands: open
close
disconnect
bye
quit

These commands establish and terminate ftp sessions with remote computers. You can connect with a sequence of sites by using the open and close commands. When you are finished with all your ftp accesses, you can use the bye command to exit ftp.

Establishing an ftp Connection to a Remote Computer

Syntax: open remote_host

The open command attempts to establish a connection with the indicated remote computer. If you want to connect with only a single site while running ftp, you don't need to use the open command. Instead, you can specify the site name on the command line invoking ftp. To end the connection, use the close or bye command.

Ending an ftp Connection to a Remote Computer

Syntax: close
disconnect

The close and disconnect commands are identical; they terminate the connection with the remote host. Because they don't terminate ftp, you can establish another connection by using the open command.

Terminating the ftp Program

Syntax: bye
                quit

The bye and quit commands are synonymous. They close the current connection, if one is open, and then terminate the ftp program.

Changing Directories and Examining Their Contents

Commands: cd
               cdup
               pwd
               dir
               ls

These commands enable you to move about the directory structure on the remote computer and list the files contained within a directory. You can change the default directory on the local computer through the lcd command, which is discussed in more detail later in the section "Executing Commands on the Local Computer in an ftp Session."

Changing the Directory on the Remote Computer

Syntax: cd *new_directory*

cd changes the default directory on the remote computer to *new_directory*.

Moving to the Parent Directory on the Remote Computer

Syntax: cdup

The cdup command changes the default directory on the remote computer to the parent of the current directory. If the remote computer is UNIX-based, for example, cdup is equivalent to the cd .. command.

Showing the Current Directory's Name on the Remote Computer

Syntax: pwd

The pwd command shows the name of the current default directory on the remote computer.

V

Using the Internet

Showing a Full Directory Listing on the Remote Computer

Syntax: dir [*directory*] [*local_file*]

The dir command produces a full listing of the contents of the indicated directory on the remote computer. The optional *directory* argument may contain wild cards in the syntax supported by the remote computer. If *directory* isn't specified, a listing of the current working directory on the remote computer is given.

If you specify a *local_file*, the listing is placed in a file of that name on the local host. Otherwise, the directory listing is printed to your screen.

Using dir produces a "full" directory listing, meaning that information such as owner, date, size, and protections are given for each file. The remote computer determines the actual set of listed information. For example, the command dir *ndex* may produce the following listing:

```
-r--r--r-- 1 postel    1   6254 May 27 15:14 fyi-index.txt
-rw-r--r-- 1 postel    1 181249 Jun 10 19:31 rfc-index.txt
```

Showing a Brief Directory Listing on the Remote Computer

Syntax: ls [*directory*] [*local_file*]

The ls command is identical to dir, except that ls produces a "brief" listing of the directory contents—only the file names are given. For example, the command ls *ndex* may generate the following output:

```
fyi-index.txt
rfc-index.txt
```

Getting Files from a Remote Computer

Commands: get
                 mget
                 recv

You can retrieve individual files by using the get command and multiple files with the mget command. Make sure that the file transfer type you are using matches the types of the files you are actually transferring. The default type is ASCII but can be changed through the ascii (for printable files) and binary (for graphics, executable, ZIP, and other non-printable files) commands. You can abort a file transfer by typing the terminal interrupt key (usually <Ctrl-c>).

Often you encounter files that are stored in a compressed form. Remember that you have to use a binary transfer to retrieve them. You usually can tell these files by their file extension. A file with the extension Z was most likely compressed with the UNIX compress utility. To restore the original file, use the UNIX uncompress program. Files ending in .zip were compressed using the utility PKZIP and can be decompressed with PKUNZIP. This compression scheme is the most widely used for PCs. For Macintosh users, the most common compression programs are BinHex 4.0 (extension hqx) and StuffIt (extension sit). Information services like CompuServe often carry decompression programs for these file formats.

> **Note**
>
> The recv command is identical to the get command but may be considered obsolete. Its use is not encouraged.

Retrieving a Single File from the Remote Computer

Syntax: get *remote_file_name [local_file_name]*
recv *remote_file_name [local_file_name]*

The get and recv commands are identical; they retrieve the single file named *remote_file_name* from the remote computer and copy it to your local machine. If you don't specify a *local_file_name*, the copied file is given the same name on your local computer as it had on the remote computer (or at least as closely as possible, if *remote_file_name* isn't a valid file name on your computer). If you specify - in the *local_file_name* field, the file is printed on-screen.

Retrieving Multiple Files from the Remote Computer

Syntax: mget *remote_file_names*

The mget command retrieves multiple files from the remote computer and copies them to your local machine. The argument *remote_file_names* may be a list of file names and may use wild-card characters. Use the syntax of the remote computer for specifying wild cards and file name lists. If you don't want to be prompted before each file is retrieved, issue a prompt command before you issue the mget command.

V

Using the Internet

Putting Files on a Remote Computer

Commands: put

                  mput

                  send

Individual files are written to a remote computer using the put command. The mput command transfers multiple files from your local computer to the remote computer. You must set the file transfer type properly for the type of files you want to transfer. ASCII is the default type but may be changed by the ascii or binary commands. You can abort a file transfer by typing the terminal interrupt key (usually <Ctrl-c>).

> **Note**
>
> The send command is identical to the put command but may be considered obsolete. Its use is not encouraged.

Writing a Single File to the Remote Computer

Syntax: put *local_file_name [remote_file_name]*

             send *local_file_name [remote_file_name]*

The put and send commands are synonyms. They write the single file *local_file_name* on your computer to the remote computer. If *remote_file_name* is specified, the transferred file is given this name on the remote computer. If *remote_file_name* isn't specified, the transferred file keeps the same name as on your local machine (or at least as close to the original name as possible, if *local_file_name* isn't a valid file name on the remote computer).

Writing Multiple Files to the Remote Computer

Syntax: mput *local_file_names*

The mput command writes multiple files from the local computer to the remote computer. The argument *local_file_names* may contain wild cards and file lists in the syntax of the local computer. If you don't want to be prompted before each file is transferred, use the prompt command.

Selecting the File Transfer Mode

Commands: ascii

binary

The file transfer mode *must* match the type of file being transferred. If it doesn't, the transferred files almost certainly will be totally useless. When ftp is started, by default it begins in ASCII mode.

> **Note**
>
> Examples of ASCII and binary files are given in their respective sections.

Setting File Transfer Mode to ASCII

Syntax: ascii

This command indicates that subsequent file transfers will be comprised solely of printable ASCII characters. Examples of such files are text files, programming language source files, and PostScript files. Using the binary command changes the file transfer mode from ASCII to binary.

Setting File Transfer Mode to Binary

Syntax: binary

By specifying the binary command, you indicate that subsequent file transfers will involve only files that should be transmitted exactly as is (that is, without carriage control conversion) between the remote and host computers. Examples of such files are most word processor files (such as WordPerfect and Microsoft Word), executable programs, compressed files (such as PKZIP or UNIX compress), and most backup files (such as UNIX tar).

The ascii command changes the file transfer mode from binary to ASCII.

Deleting Files on a Remote Computer

Commands: delete
                  mdelete

You can delete an individual file on the remote computer by using the delete command. To remove multiple files, use mdelete.

> **Note**
>
> You must have delete privilege on the remote computer for files you want to delete.

Deleting a Single File on the Remote Computer

Syntax: delete *remote_file_name*

The delete command deletes the *remote_file_name* on the remote computer. For this command to succeed, you must have sufficient privilege to delete this file on the remote computer.

Deleting Multiple Files on the Remote Computer

Syntax: mdelete *remote_file_names*

Use the mdelete command to delete the indicated files on the remote computer. The *remote_file_names* argument may contain wild cards in the syntax of the remote computer. This command won't succeed unless you have sufficient privilege to delete these files on the remote computer.

Getting Status Information

Commands: status
                  bell
                  hash
                  prompt
                  verbose

These five commands can help you monitor the progress of your file transfers or your ftp session in general. Your ftp implementation probably has more modes than those mentioned here, so look at your documentation for additional information.

Getting Overall Status Information
Syntax: status

The status command prints information concerning the current state of the ftp session to your screen. In particular, the values of binary-valued mode flags that the user can set are displayed. An example output from the status command follows:

```
ftp> status
Connected to nic.ddn.mil.
No proxy connection.
Mode: stream; Type: ascii; Form: non-print; Structure: file
Verbose: on; Bell: off; Prompting: on; Globbing: on
Store unique: off; Receive unique: off
Case: off; CR stripping: on
Ntrans: off
Nmap: off
Hash mark printing: off; Use of PORT cmds: on
```

Ringing the Bell after Completion of Each File Transfer
Syntax: bell

The bell command toggles a mode flag that indicates whether the bell (beep) should be sounded at the completion of each file transfer command.

Printing # after Each Data Block Is Transferred
Syntax: hash

The hash command toggles a mode flag specifying whether the # character should be printed on-screen after each data block is transferred. By using this command, you can verify that your transfer is proceeding and, if you can determine the data block size through your documentation or experimentation, calculate what percentage of your transfer has completed.

Toggle Prompting for Multiple File Transfers
Syntax: prompt

By default, the mget and mput commands (discussed earlier) ask you to confirm each file to be transferred. The prompt command toggles the mode flag controlling this. Using the prompt command before an mget, for example, instructs mget not to ask you before it retrieves each file. Executing prompt again means that mget would now prompt you before transferring each file.

Toggling Verbose Mode
Syntax: `verbose`

In verbose mode, all responses from the ftp server are displayed, as well as the data transfer statistics for file transfers. The `verbose` command toggles the use of this mode.

Executing Commands on the Local Computer in an ftp Session
Commands: `lcd`
`!`

Often, you will want to execute commands on your local computer without ending your ftp session. You may want to change directories, get a directory listing, or examine the contents of a file on the local computer. The `lcd` command changes your local working directory; the `!` command executes a system command on your local machine.

Changing the Directory on the Local Computer
Syntax: `lcd [new_directory]`

`lcd` changes the default directory on the local computer to `new_directory`. If you don't specify `new_directory`, the user's home directory is used.

Executing a Command on the Local Host
Syntax: `! [command]`

The specified command is executed on your local computer. If no command is given, an interactive shell is started on the local host. To get back to ftp, exit the shell as you normally would for a local host shell.

Non-Interactive ftp through E-Mail

Unfortunately, many users who can send and receive electronic mail through the Internet don't have access to ftp. If you fall under this category, you can use a facility called *ftpmail* to receive files from remote computers through e-mail. Although using ftpmail involves numerous restrictions and limitations, it is a simple, automated way to obtain files.

> **Note**
>
> The first thing to do if you want to try ftpmail is to get the help document describing how to use it. You can have this document mailed electronically to you by sending an e-mail message to `ftpmail@decwrl.dec.com` with the single word `help` in the body of the message. You should receive a brief description of the ftpmail command set and notes regarding the proper usage and limitations of ftpmail.

To use ftpmail, send to `ftpmail@decwrl.dec.com` an e-mail message in which each line in the body of the message contains an ftpmail command (described in later sections). The subject of your message appears in the subject field of the replies you receive from the ftpmail server. When the server receives your request, you then receive an immediate reply verifying receipt of your ftpmail request, indicating any errors in processing your request, and indicating the number of ftpmail requests ahead of yours. When your request is actually processed, you receive an e-mail message containing a log of the ftp session the ftpmail server conducted to fulfill your request. Thus, for every ftpmail e-mail message you send, you receive two status e-mail messages, plus the e-mail messages containing the files you are trying to get.

Capabilities and Limitations of ftpmail

The ftpmail facility isn't ftp. Its command set is different and much less capable than that of ftp. You can't send files to other users using ftpmail—you can only receive them. You also can't change directories more than once. Furthermore, you can't get more than 10 files from a single ftpmail request.

ftpmail also can be quite slow. The documentation states that you should receive the results of your ftpmail session in approximately one day; however, it could take considerably longer. Also, if an error occurs in processing your request, you have to resubmit it, thus incurring an additional cycle of delay.

The limitations of Internet electronic mail also greatly hamper ftpmail. Internet e-mail was designed to carry relatively short packets of ASCII data. Thus, ftpmail will easily retrieve small printable ASCII files. You must convert binary—that is, non-ASCII—data into some kind of ASCII representation before mailing it. ftpmail offers two ways to do so: uuencode format and btoa format. Programs that encode and decode files using these formats are commonly available for UNIX-based computers and for PC and Macintosh computers. (CompuServe should have programs that perform these operations.)

A more annoying aspect of Internet e-mail is the limitation in message length. Commonly, messages are limited to no more than 64,000 characters. You must split files longer than the maximum length of an e-mail message into multiple files and transmit them separately. You can specify the maximum characters to be transmitted in a single e-mail message (by using the chunksize command), but the maximum message size which ftpmail can use is 100,000 characters. Many RFCs, for example, are larger than 100,000 characters; ftpmail would have to send them through multiple e-mail messages. Binary files often exceed this limit.

ftpmail does support two types of data compression: compress and compact. The compress compression type uses Lempel-Ziv encoding; compact, on the other hand, uses adaptive Huffman coding. Decoding programs called uncompress and uncompact are commonly available on UNIX-based computers and also can be found for PC and Macintosh systems. These compression techniques are especially useful in reducing the number of mail messages into which a large binary file must be broken.

> **Note**
>
> If you compress or compact a file, you must transmit it as a binary file, even if the original file is ASCII.

A Sample ftpmail Request

The following example illustrates how to retrieve a single file using ftpmail. Like the example ftp session detailed earlier in this chapter, this ftpmail request causes the document RFC 1206 to be mailed to you. Because the file containing this document is larger than 64,000 characters, it is divided into two sections, which are sent in two separate e-mail messages.

Your request is mailed to ftpmail@decwrl.dec.com. You can use anything you want in the subject field of the message, but it should remind you of the particular file retrievals you are performing in this ftpmail request. In this example, an appropriate subject would be *Get RFC1206 from the NIC.* The body of the message is as follows:

```
connect nic.ddn.mil
chdir rfc
get rfc1206.txt
quit
```

After you send this message, you receive confirmation from the ftpmail server that your request has been placed on the queue. When processing is complete, you receive three additional mail messages: a log of the ftp session ftpmail conducted to fulfill your request and two messages containing portions of the file rfc1206.txt. You must combine these two pieces to re-create the complete document but, because the original is an ASCII file, you easily can concatenate the two parts using a text editor.

Summary of ftpmail Commands

ftpmail commands are simpler to use than their corresponding ftp commands, and fewer of them exist. The commands are described briefly in table 18.1, but you should refer to the ftpmail help message for further information.

Table 18.1: ftpmail Commands	
Command Syntax	**Description**
reply *your_address*	The string *your_address* is used as the e-mail address to which all responses will be sent. If the request doesn't con-tain a reply command, the responses are sent to your address as indicated in your requesting e-mail message.
connect [*hostname* [*username* [*password* [*account*]]]]	This command specifies the name of the host and the user information to use when connecting with that host. A command in the form connect *hostname* will try to establish an anony-mous ftp connection on the system *hostname.*
ascii	Use this command when retrieved files are printable ASCII.

(continues)

Table 18.1 Continued

Command Syntax	Description
binary	Use this command when retrieved files aren't printable ASCII. Examples of binary files are compressed files, executable files, and graphics files.
chdir *new_directory*	The argument *new_directory* is selected as the default file directory. You can have at most one chdir command in a single ftpmail request.
compress	Use this command to perform Lempel-Ziv encoding before transmitting the file. You have to decode the files you receive.
compact	Use this command to perform adaptive Huffman encoding before transmitting the file. You have to decode the files you receive.
uuencode	Mail binary files using the uuencode format. You have to unformat the files you receive.
btoa	Mail binary files using the btoa format. You have to unformat the files you receive.
chunksize *max_size*	Use this command to break files into portions no larger than *max_size* characters. The default for *max_size* is 64,000, and it can't be larger than 100,000.
ls *[directory]* or dir *[directory]*	Either command lists the contents of the indicated *directory*. If *directory* isn't specified, the command lists the contents of the current default directory.
get *file_name*	This command retrieves and mails the indicated file. You can issue no more than 10 get commands within a single ftpmail request.
quit	Use quit to end the ftpmail session. Any further lines in your requesting e-mail message are discarded.

Typical Problems Encountered with ftp

This section describes problems frequently encountered when trying to use ftp. Even if you aren't experiencing any difficulties now, you probably should scan this section to become familiar with common pitfalls. Almost all new ftp users ask themselves at least one of these questions while gaining experience with ftp. Although you can figure out the recommended solutions to each of the following situations from the information given in this chapter, having a short list of the most frequently asked questions is often convenient.

Problem: I don't have a password on the remote computer I want to access.

Recommendation: Try using anonymous ftp (see the earlier "Anonymous ftp" section). If the remote computer maintains information of general use to Internet users, it may accept anonymous users. If not, you have to obtain an account through the systems manager of the system you want to access.

Problem: I transferred a program/image file/ZIP file from a remote computer but it won't execute/can't display correctly/won't UNZIP properly.

Recommendation: You must specify a binary transfer for all non-ASCII files. Examples of binary files include executable programs, object code, graphics files, and compressed files (created, for example, by PKZIP or UNIX compress). Non-ASCII files that are transmitted without previously using the `binary` ftp command do not transfer correctly.

Problem: I want to get several files, but doing a `get` command for each one is very tedious.

Recommendation: The ftp command `mget` retrieves multiple files. Furthermore, it accepts wild-card characters in the file name specification. Even if you want to transfer only a single file, `mget` is often more convenient than `get` if the file name is long.

Problem: The remote computer has many files and directories—I'm not sure where the files I want are located.

Recommendation: After you connect with the remote system, look for index, help, and readme files in the directories you examine. Note that the file names are likely to be case-sensitive and not restricted to some arbitrary length. Issuing the command `dir *ndex*`, for example, lists the files `index`, `Index`, and `Index-public-files`, but doesn't list the file `INDEX`.

Problem: I want to transfer files using ftp, but my Internet provider doesn't allow me to have interactive Internet access.

Recommendation: You can use ftpmail to retrieve files in a noninteractive manner. The commands of ftpmail are different than those of ftp, and ftpmail has significant limitations compared with ftp. Otherwise, many remote computers have servers that can send you specific files through e-mail. RFCs and FYIs, for example, can be retrieved through the RFC-Info service, and you can request the instructions for ftpmail by sending an e-mail message to `ftpmail@decwrl.dec.com` with the single word `help` in the body of the message.

Problem: I want to look at the contents of a file without having to transfer it to my local computer.

Recommendation: Often, you aren't sure whether a file contains the information you desire. Other times, you need only a very specific piece of information from a file and don't need to transfer it to your local computer. The command

```
get remote_file_name -
```

prints the file contents on your computer screen. Unfortunately, it prints the entire file. On UNIX systems you can use the command

```
get remote_file_name - "| more"
```

which pipes the output through the `more` filter, or

```
get remote_file_name - "| grep string"
```

which sends lines of the file having only the character string *string*.

Problem: I am retrieving a large file; how can I tell that the transfer is proceeding?

Recommendation: Use the hash command before beginning your file transfer. This command causes the # character to be printed on your screen after each data block transfer.

The documentation for your system's implementation of ftp may state the size in bytes of a single data block. If so, you can calculate the number of bytes transferred at a particular time from the number of # characters appearing on-screen.

Logging in to Remote Network Computers Using *telnet*

The *telnet* facility allows you to execute commands on a remote host as though you were logged in locally. Like ftp, you need to know the name of the computer you want to access and have a valid user name and password for that computer.

Unlike ftp, telnet has no common analog to anonymous ftp. Although many remote sites allow guest logins, no convention exists on the user name and password a guest may use. Furthermore, guest logins aren't nearly as common as anonymous ftp accounts. This makes sense because a remote site is more likely to want you to be able to access certain files than for you to be able to execute software on it.

In essence, a telnet session allows you the same capabilities on the host computer you would have if you were logged in locally under the same account. A common situation, however, is for telnet users to run a special operating environment shell that restricts their actions. This shell is especially common for guest accounts under telnet.

The NASA Marshall Space Flight Center, for example, allows telnet access to the host spacelink.msfc.nasa.gov for persons interested in space technology. If you don't now have an account on this system, enter newuser as the user name and password. The system then allows you to set up an account for yourself by choosing a user name and password for future logins.

V

Using the Internet

> **Tip**
>
> This particular NASA system is designed to provide easy access to educators, journalists, and other persons seeking information about space exploration.

Although your telnet session is actually running software directly on this host, you will be running a program that prevents you from accessing the general capabilities of that computer. Specifically, you will be running a menu-driven system whose main menu is as follows:

```
NASA Spacelink Main Menu
1.    Log Off NASA Spacelink
2.    NASA Spacelink Overview
3.    Current NASA News
4.    Aeronautics
5.    Space Exploration: Before the Shuttle
6.    Space Exploration: The Shuttle and Beyond
7.    NASA and its Centers
8.    NASA Educational Services
9.    Instructional Materials
10.   Space Program Spinoffs/Technology Transfer
Enter an option number, 'G' for GO TO, ? for HELP, or
     press RETURN to redisplay menu...
```

As you can see, this operating environment prevents you from exploring the file system of the remote computer and running any unauthorized programs. In this case, you enter the number corresponding to the category in which you are interested. Any other responses are invalid.

Another common use of telnet is for users to be able to log in to their computers from remote locations. In this case, users enter their own user names and passwords and, therefore, have the same user privileges they would have when logged in without using telnet. Usually, the only losses in capability are slower access and having to use a terminal-type environment rather than a window-type environment (if that was available on the host). Thus, users away from the office can read their own e-mail, edit files, or run programs off their own computer. Public computers with telnet access are becoming more common at professional conferences so that attendees can keep in touch with their organizations.

Summary of *telnet* Commands

Like ftp, no single standard is available for defining the telnet command set; the commands may vary from system to system. This section describes commands commonly found in UNIX implementations of telnet. Quite likely you will need to use only a handful of the total telnet commands.

Command	Description
open	Establishes a telnet connection with a remote host
close	Terminates a telnet connection
quit	Closes the current (if any) telnet connection and terminates telnet
z	Suspends telnet so that commands can be executed on the local computer
?	Obtains help on using telnet commands

Furthermore, because you can specify the host name as a command-line argument when invoking telnet, and because the quit command closes the current connection, you don't need to use the open and close commands unless you want to contact several hosts without terminating telnet.

> **Note**
>
> To learn about telnet's specific command set and capabilities, refer to the documentation for your particular implementation of telnet.

Most versions of telnet support two modes of operation: character and line. Character mode—the preferred mode of operation—sends each character to the remote computer as it is typed. Character mode is usually the default mode. In line mode, all characters are echoed and edited locally, and a line is transmitted only when it is completed. The main difference to a telnet user is that typed lines are edited locally (using the local computer's line editing capabilities) in line mode and are edited under control of the remote computer in character mode.

V

Using the Internet

Normally during a telnet session, your local computer acts as though it were a terminal connected to the remote computer. You temporarily can escape from interaction with the remote computer by entering the telnet escape character, which normally is the ^] (Ctrl+right bracket) character. The telnet escape character may vary from system to system; you can tell telnet that you want to use a specific escape character with the set escape command. When the escape character is entered, telnet enters its command mode, and you see a prompt such as telnet> on-screen. In this mode, lines you type are interpreted as telnet commands. To leave telnet command mode, enter a carriage return at the telnet prompt (that is, a blank line).

Note

The telnet escape character shouldn't be confused with the ASCII escape character (ESC).

In the following descriptions, the full command syntax is given. Anything entered literally (such as a command name) is represented in computer-like type—for example, mode. Command arguments that you must supply are *italicized*. Optional arguments are inside [brackets]. For example, the syntax

    open *remote_host*

indicates that you type the word open, followed by the name of the remote computer with which you want to establish a connection. The syntax

    ? [*command*]

specifies that you can enter ? by itself or ? followed by the name of a telnet command.

Starting a *telnet* Session

Syntax: telnet [*remote_host*]

Entering telnet on the command line of your local computer begins a telnet session. If the name of a remote host follows the word telnet, Internet tries to establish a connection to that computer. Otherwise, telnet begins in its command mode with no connection established.

> **Note**
>
> Some implementations of telnet have additional command-line options defined.

Establishing a Connection with a Remote Computer

Syntax: open *remote_host*

The open command attempts to establish a connection with the specified remote computer. Executing an open command isn't necessary if telnet had been invoked with the name of a remote host and the connection was successful.

Ending a *telnet* Session

Syntax: close

The close command terminates the connection with the remote computer and returns to telnet command mode. You now can make another connection to a remote computer by using the open command.

Exiting *telnet*

Syntax: quit

The quit command closes any open connection and terminates telnet. If you now are connected, you will be disconnected from the remote computer, and your local computer will regain process control.

Suspending *telnet*

Syntax: z

The z command temporarily suspends telnet so that you can enter commands on your local computer.

> **Note**
>
> This command isn't available on all implementations of telnet—not even all UNIX implementations. Consult the documentation for your particular version of telnet to determine whether the z command is available and, if so, how to unsuspend telnet after a z command.

V

Using the Internet

Obtaining Help on Using *telnet* Commands

Syntax: `? [command]`

Use `?` to obtain a brief description (usually one line per command) of the telnet command set available to you. Enter `?` followed by the name of a telnet command to get a brief description of that command and any options it may have.

Selecting Character or Line Mode

Syntax: `mode type`

Most implementations of telnet can transmit to the remote computer in character-by-character or line-by-line mode. If `type` is specified as `line`, characters are transmitted only when the line they are on is complete. If `type` is `character`, each character is sent to the remote host as it is typed.

Showing the Current Status of a *telnet* Session

Syntax: `status`

The `status` command shows the current state of telnet—including whether line mode or character mode is now in use—and may show the current escape character.

Sending One or More Special Character Sequences to the Remote Host

Syntax: `send argument1 [argument2 [...]]`

You can use the `send` command to send special telnet command sequences to the remote computer. Use `send ?` to obtain information about the specific command sequences supported.

Showing the Settings of One or More *telnet* Variables

Syntax: `display [argument1 argument2 ...]`

telnet uses a number of variables to store internal states and other information. Most likely, the only one of interest to you is the `escape` variable, which specifies the character that causes telnet to enter command mode.

Entering `display` with no arguments lists the current values of all telnet variables. Entering `display` followed by a valid telnet variable shows the value of that particular variable. You can change variables through the `set`, `unset`, and `toggle` commands.

Setting the Value of a *telnet* Variable

Syntax: `set telnet_variable value`

You can use the `set` command to change the value of a telnet variable. The command `set ?` gives a brief description of the telnet variables that you can change through the `set` command. The only one likely to be of interest to you is the `escape` variable, which specifies the character that causes telnet to enter command mode. For a binary-valued variable, the value `off` disables the action associated with the variable.

> **Tip**
>
> You can examine the current settings of variables by using the `display` command.

Unsetting the Value of a *telnet* Variable

Syntax: `unset telnet_variable`

You can use the `unset` command to set binary-valued telnet variables to false and turn their associated functions off. You can use the `display` command to show the current values of telnet variables.

The `unset` command isn't available on all telnet implementations. Use `unset ?` to obtain a brief description of the telnet variables that you can change with the `unset` command.

Toggling the Value of a *telnet* Variable

Syntax: `toggle telnet_flag`

The `toggle` command toggles binary-valued flags that control how telnet responds to events. Use `toggle ?` to get a brief listing of the flags that you can alter through the `toggle` command. You can use the `display` command to show the current values of these flags.

V

Using the Internet

Summary

The ftp and telnet facilities are the most important interactive Internet utilities. With ftp, you can transfer ASCII and binary files of unlimited size across the network. Many hundreds of hosts accept anonymous ftp users, which means that you can have easy access to several million files. You can log in to remote computers using telnet and use them just as though you were logged in locally. You also can connect to sites offering publicly available navigational aids such as archie, Gopher, and WAIS through telnet.

Chapter 19

Using USENET

One of the things that the Internet is probably best known for is USENET. What is USENET? USENET (short for *users' network*) is notactually a part of the Internet, but it uses the Internet to propagate itself. USENET is made up of all the machines that receive network news groups, which are something like computer discussion groups or forums. People who have access to these news groups can read messages, post messages, and reply to a particular poster, among other things. This chapter explains the general concepts behind USENET, including how network news works, some common interfaces to USENET, and network news history.

What Is the Network News?

The network news (commonly referred to as *netnews*) is a mechanism for broadcasting messages, called *articles*, from your local host to a large number of hosts across the world. The transport mechanism used is called *store and forward*, which means that each host that receives a netnews article stores it locally and then forwards, or *feeds*, it to other hosts that are part of the USENET network. Because a single host may feed the article to any number of other hosts, who then may feed it to additional hosts, this mechanism ensures that each article can reach a very large number of hosts (and readers) in a very short period of time.

On each individual host, the netnews system is split into two distinct systems. The first system is for receiving articles, storing them, and forwarding them to other sites. You probably don't need to worry about this system unless you directly receive a news feed at your site. The second system allows local users to read articles and post new articles (this system commonly is called a *news reader*). These two systems are distinct and are treated separately in this chapter.

The Structure of Netnews

This section talks about the different news groups, how they are organized, and how to determine what topics are discussed in each group. Before you can make effective use of the information available in news groups, you should understand how to locate the appropriate group and how to contribute to that group.

News Group Organization

Each article posted to netnews is placed into one or more *news groups*. Each group is a place in netnews where conversations about a particular topic occur. News groups have names made up of several components, separated by periods. For example, a valid news group name would be `comp.sys.ibm.pc.games`. The name's different components tell you something about the topic of discussion in the group, with the left-most name component being the most general (`comp` stands for computer-related topics), and the right-most name component being the most specific (`games` indicates that only games are discussed in the group). Taken as a whole, the group `comp.sys.ibm.pc.games` discusses games running on IBM personal computers.

The most general of the name components are the so-called "top-level" names, or *hierarchies*. These hierarchies are well established, and new top-level hierarchies are created very rarely. The most commonly used hierarchies include the following:

Hierarchy	Designates
`comp`	Computer-related topics
`rec`	Recreational topics
`sci`	Topics related to sciences
`soc`	Topics related to social issues
`news`	Topics related to the operation and administration of a netnews system
`talk`	Conversational topics, often controversial
`misc`	Miscellaneous topics not covered elsewhere

In addition to these standard top-level hierarchies, quite a few other news group hierarchies exist. Many of these other hierarchies relate either to a specific topic or a local geographic area. For example, here are a few of these alternative hierarchies:

Hierarchy	Designates
alt	An alternative hierarchy with relaxed rules for new group creation
vmsnet	A hierarchy devoted to systems running the VMS operating system from Digital Equipment Corporation
bionet	A hierarchy devoted to biological sciences
k12	A hierarchy devoted to education in grades kindergarten through 12

You can use the information presented so far to locate the news groups that hold the information you are interested in. In addition, your local news system may have a copy of a news groups file, which has a one-line description of each news group. You should ask your local news administrator to see whether a copy is available. If you cannot locate one, you can get a copy using anonymous ftp to the machine `ftp.uu.net` and retrieving the file `/archive/uunet-info/news groups`. This file lists almost all the groups carried by USENET sites around the world; your local site probably does not carry all these groups.

◀ See Chapter 18, "Using *ftp* and *telnet* with the Internet," for more information about how to use anonymous ftp.

Contributing to a News Group

Although a newcomer to netnews may know the definite set of topics discussed by each news group, the newcomer may have difficulty understanding a group's background and how the people who read that news group are expected to behave. You can picture netnews with its many news groups as a building with a large number of rooms, each of which is identified only by a name on the door. In some of these rooms, you find a small number of people politely discussing a topic of mutual interest while others quietly listen. In other rooms, you find a large crowd with everyone shouting out their opinions and paying no attention to anyone else in the room. Both of these types of news groups, and many other types in between, can be found in netnews.

V

Using the Internet

Although this topic is discussed in further detail in the later section dealing with the culture of netnews, for now you should realize that you need to learn about the history of each individual news group before joining in the discussion (called *posting to the group*). Some topics may be discussed frequently (or just recently), and the group participants may not want to talk about them again. Other topics may be the cause of protracted arguments (called *flame wars*) and probably won't make you popular with group regulars.

> **Note**
>
> You should read the introductory information contained in the group news.announce.newusers before posting to any group on netnews. It contains valuable information about how USENET works and how to post effectively. Information about the history of USENET, posting etiquette, and writing style are also available in this group. See the sections "Subscribing to News Groups" and "Reading News Articles" for information on how to read news.announce.newusers.

News Distributions

In addition to news group names, netnews also involves the idea of *news article distribution*. A distribution is a keyword (such as "us" or "local") that can be placed in a news article. The article distribution controls which machines can receive an article posted to a news group. Distributions generally are associated with a geographic area and are used to ensure that an article is received only by machines in that geographic area. The news administrator for each site determines which distributions that site will accept from other USENET sites.

Why would you want to limit the distribution of an article? Many articles are not of interest to people across the entire USENET. For example, not many people reading news in California are interested in buying a car you have for sale in New Jersey. Similarly, if you are posting an announcement for a meeting of a local organization, people outside your immediate community probably won't be interested. And, bear in mind, posting a message worldwide can cost the network hundreds, even thousands, of dollars.

You limit the distribution of your news article by including a `Distribution:` line in the headers of the message. Often, this distribution header is generated automatically by your news posting mechanism (using a default value provided by your news administrator); you can edit this value if it is not appropriate. If the distribution header is not included automatically, you may be able to include it manually by editing the headers of your post. The format of this header line is the word `Distribution:`, followed by a space (after the colon), and then a value that identifies the distribution you want for your article. See the section "Posting an Original Article" for more information about how to post.

Commonly used distribution values follow:

Value	Identifies This Distribution
local	By convention, the article won't leave your local news machine; often used for groups that are private to your organization.
pa	The posting will be propagated to all machines in the state of Pennsylvania; all states in the United States have their own distribution code (that is the same as the state's postal code), and other countries often have distribution codes for the state or province level.
us	This article will be propagated to all machines in the United States; other countries have their own distribution code, and it is generally the same as their postal country code.
na	The article will be propagated to all machines in North America.

By default, if no distribution header is included in the article, the article propagates to all machines receiving the groups the article is posted to—including machines worldwide.

Many other distributions exist for local cities and regions. You should consult the periodic postings in the group news.announce.newusers for the valid news distributions in your area. The section "Reading News Articles" gives more information about how to read a particular group.

The Process of Reading and Posting News

This section discusses the basic steps necessary for reading and posting news articles. In addition, you learn formatting and content guidelines to be used when composing articles. Examples of some specific net-news interfaces are given later in the section "Examples of News Readers."

Subscribing to News Groups

To read news, you first need to decide to which groups you want to subscribe. Most news readers provide you with a way to view all the available news groups. Some, like the WinNET Mail system, mail you a list of the available news groups. Other systems, such as PSILink, auto-matically download the list to your system when you first connect and keep a local list on your machine that is updated automatically each time you call in to your account. See the section "Examples of News Readers" for more information about specific news readers.

You can determine from the news group's name or the news group's file (discussed in the section "News Group Organization") whether it may be of interest to you. You then subscribe to the groups you are interested in joining. Your news reader software explains in detail how you subscribe to a news group. In most cases, subscribing involves marking the news groups so that the news reader knows to save and/or show you articles from this group automatically, whenever you read news. After you subscribe to a news group, you see any new messages that have been posted to that group. You can unsubscribe from a group if you find that it doesn't interest you.

Reading News Articles

After subscribing to a news group, you are ready to begin reading ar-ticles. Your news reader may display each article one at a time sequen-tially, or it may display a list of the subjects and authors and allow you to pick which articles you want to see displayed. Some news readers are *threaded*, which means that they display sequential listings of articles grouped by topic, rather than a sequential listing of all articles in the news group.

When you display an article, you see information at the top of the article about what news group(s) it was posted to, who posted it, and what subject the article discusses. Other information also may be listed at the top of the article, such as the organization the sender works for, keywords related to the main topic of articles (some news readers allow you to search for keywords), a short summary of the article, and possibly a few other things that you may not care about. In most news readers, after you display an article, you aren't shown that article again (only new messages are shown). The article continues to exist in the group for a while, but you may have difficulty going back to it.

Posting a Follow-Up Article

After reading an article, you may decide that you want to add something to the discussion, or comment about the author's viewpoint. If you think that your comments may be of general interest to everyone who reads the news group, most news readers allow you to post a follow-up article. When you give the follow-up command, your news reader creates a blank message with a header that contains the name of the news group, your return address, and a subject line that is the same as that of the original article, but with Re: attached to the front of it. See the discussions of individual news readers in the "Examples of News Readers" section for examples of follow-up commands.

Some news readers automatically include in the follow-up article the text of the original article, and some give you the option of including it or not. If you are going to include the original text, you should remove any of the text that is not relevant to the point you want to make. This editing makes the follow-up article easier to read and saves network resources.

Replying to an Article with E-Mail

If your comments are intended only for the author of the article, most news readers enable you to compose a mail message directly to the author. When you use the command in your news reader to reply to the message, the news reader uses the information in the article to generate a mail message to the author of the article. Some news readers also enable you to include text from the article automatically in the e-mail message. The news reader then displays an editor that enables you to edit the mail message. After you have finished editing the message, the mail message is sent to the author of the news article, using your computer system's electronic mail system.

◀ See Chapter 17, "Using Internet E-Mail," for more information about electronic mail.

V

Using the Internet

Posting an Original Article

If you want to post an article on a completely new subject, use your news reader's Post command. This command asks you to identify what news groups you want to post to and the subject of your article, and then puts you into an editor to allow you to compose your article. After you finish editing, you simply exit the editor and use your news reader's Send command. Most news readers have a provision for aborting a message if you decide not to send it. The store-and-forward systems, like WinNET Mail or PSILink, place your news post into a queue on your local system, where it waits for you to connect to your account on the central computer system. Some of these systems allow you to edit and delete messages that are in the queue if you've not connected to the system yet. When you are connected, the messages you have composed are no longer on your system and cannot be edited or deleted.

Guidelines for Composing Your Article

When you compose a news article, you should keep a number of things in mind. Try to make your subject relatively brief, but descriptive. For example, "Information needed" is too short, but "Information needed about the best way to test for out-of-bounds errors" is too long. A better subject would be something like "Question about error testing." Also, you need to follow a number of formatting guidelines when composing your article, to make it easier to read. Here are a few guidelines:

- Use text characters only. Control characters do odd things to different types of displays.

- Keep your line length under 80 characters (the maximum line length of some displays).

- Break up your text into medium-size paragraphs with blank lines between them. This format is much easier to read than long, solid blocks of text.

- Use mixed case, because text in all uppercase is hard to read and is generally used for emphasis in your message. A message in all uppercase is considered "shouting" and should be avoided.

In addition to the above guidelines for how you format the text of your article, you should follow some guidelines concerning the content of your article. Most of these guidelines involve common courtesy towards USENET readers and authors:

- Commercial advertising is not permitted on netnews groups (but advertising personal items of interest to other members of the group usually is permitted). Some forms of advertising do occur on netnews groups, but a blatant advertisement posted to inappropriate groups is frowned on and won't gather much support for the advertiser. A separate hierarchy (called `biz`) was created specifically to allow companies to form groups for their products. Also, the group `comp.newprod` contains postings for new-product announcements.

- Try to keep the length of individual articles to 1,000 lines or less. Longer articles can break some older news transport mechanisms.

- Postings of binary files (files that contain control characters in addition to text) should be encoded using a program such as uuencode, because current news transport mechanisms don't pass binary data correctly. (Many news readers make provisions to use uuencode automatically when you send a binary file.) In addition, post binary files only to those groups that accept them.

- Posting an e-mail message without the sender's permission is greatly frowned on and may in fact violate copyright restrictions. If you have any question about the legality of posting the mail message, you should contact the author first.

- When you quote someone else's article, indicate the quoted material with some character in the left-hand column—most news readers use the greater-than sign (>) as the standard indicator of quoted material.

- Posting large amounts of information (usually binary files) is frowned on. Because netnews is transmitted by a store-and-forward mechanism, every article you post costs people around the world some amount of money for its reception and transmission.

V

Using the Internet

In the case of sites that still use UUCP links to transmit and receive news, the telephone charges for netnews transmission can
be considerable (especially overseas, where phone charges are
much higher than in the United States). Statistics that indicate
which people and sites have posted the largest number of articles
each month, and which news groups are most popular, are
posted to the group news.groups.

■ If you are posting information that some people may not want to
read (like the plot of a new movie, or something that might be
offensive to some people) use the rot13 format command to
encrypt the text. Most news readers have commands to encrypt
text into rot13 format and to decode encrypted text so that it can
be read.

Your Signature

When you post an article or a follow-up to an article, your news reader
software may not generate a proper return e-mail address in the From:
line of your article. Even if you have a valid return address in your
headers, and your article is requesting or giving information about
your local area, people who are reading your article may not recognize
your site name or know where that local area is. So it's a good idea to
include a signature at the bottom of your message that contains a valid
return e-mail address and, at least, the geographical area that you are
posting from, if not a complete identification of the organization with
which you are affiliated.

Many people put a favorite quote or a picture made out of text characters in their signature. Most news reader systems, however, suggest that
you limit your signature to a maximum length of four lines, to avoid
wasting network resources on unnecessary information. With most
news readers, after you set up your signature, the news reader automatically appends that signature to each article that you post. On
UNIX, for example, you can have a .signature file in your home directory that is appended automatically to your news posts.

The Culture of USENET

As with any large group of people (estimates indicate that well over
a million people are USENET users), USENET has a unique culture
that you should become familiar with before beginning to read (and

certainly post to!) news groups. Just as you would not join a conversation before understanding what is being talked about, you should not post to a news group before you understand the culture of USENET. As a USENET user, you can make better use of the information available and encounter fewer problems if you have a good idea of how USENET works.

First, USENET is made up of all the machines that receive network news groups. These machines, and the users on those machines who read and post articles, make up a very diverse community. Netnews reaches the United States, Canada, and most of the rest of the world. As a result of this international span, every article you post on USENET may be read by someone in virtually any part of the world. You can't assume, therefore, that everyone who reads your article speaks English as a native language or shares your cultural background.

USENET also reaches many different kinds of sites. Because the Internet initially was a research and educational network (and still is, to a great extent), many sites receiving netnews are educational institutions. Since the Internet has become more diverse, however, the number of commercial, governmental, and private sites receiving netnews has increased.

Even though USENET reaches thousands of sites and many thousands of readers, no central authority controls USENET. No central group or organization dictates which groups are carried by a site. In fact, there is no way that a particular person or site can impose rules or restrictions on how other sites run USENET. This lack of central authority always confuses new netnews readers, who have a hard time adapting to the idea that USENET has no central authority to run things or complain to; the local site administrator is the only authority, and he or she can control only that site.

So, if no central authority controls USENET, how does it continue to run and grow? Even though USENET has no hard and fast laws and no authority to enforce laws (if they did exist), USENET is run by cooperation between sites, and a set of customs and conventions that have grown up during the years that USENET has existed. In addition, the opinions of certain people are respected by a large number of site administrators. These respected individuals have gained authority by expressing reasonable opinions over a number of years; quite often, they have contributed considerable time to USENET, either writing and maintaining the netnews software or administering netnews sites.

V

Using the Internet

USENET, therefore, represents a diverse, multicultural community. It is significantly different than any other group, both in its diversity and its size. Rather than be guided by laws or some governing body, it is run according to the customs, conventions, and opinions of respected members of the community. Given this loose organization, it is amazing that USENET has managed to grow, and indeed flourish. The continued existence of USENET is a tribute to the cooperation of the people using it.

The Culture of a Particular News Group

As USENET in general has a culture associated with it, so each individual group has its own particular culture. As discussed earlier, a group can be polite and friendly, easily welcoming new users, and patiently explaining what has gone on in the past. Other groups can be decidedly unfriendly, with opinions flying rapidly and no regard for newcomers.

In general, groups in the "serious" hierarchies such as comp, news, and sci are more likely to place emphasis on discussing facts rather than opinions. Groups in these hierarchies often are less likely to tolerate the expression of opinions that lack supporting facts, and they generally are more tolerant of newcomers who are willing to listen to "reason."

On the other hand, groups in the soc and rec hierarchies are more oriented toward opinions on topics and are thus more likely to be argumentative. People in these groups are likely to listen to the opinions of a newcomer. But if you join one of these groups and express your opinions, be prepared to receive other people's opinions in return—opinions that may not be the same as yours!

Finally, groups in the talk and misc hierarchies definitely tend toward inflammatory topics, such as politics and abortion. Discussions in many of these groups often generate much more heat than light (discussions often referred to as having a low "signal-to-noise ratio"), and you are wise to tread lightly when entering these groups for the first time. Expressing a strong opinion in one of these groups will certainly elicit a strong response, and you should be prepared for negative reactions to your posts. Although you will not (and in fact cannot) be forbidden to post to a group, you may find other readers of a group ignoring your posts (if they hold differing opinions), or responding negatively (or abusively) to your posts, either in follow-up posts or by electronic mail directly to you.

And, although anyone can post to most of the news groups, some news groups are "moderated." In a moderated news group, before articles can be posted, they must be approved by a person who is the moderator of the group. All articles are sent to the moderator, who decides whether the content of each article is appropriate to the topic and tone of the group. If the article meets the moderator's approval, the moderator then posts the article to the news group. Moderated news groups tend to have few problems with abusive and/or inappropriate postings. Most news readers automatically send to the moderator all articles posted to a moderated group. Your news-reading software usually informs you if a group is moderated, and the news groups file (discussed earlier in the section "News Group Organization") also indicates whether a group is moderated.

Getting To Know a News Group

So, how do you know the culture of a news group when you first begin reading the articles in it? The answer is that you don't. And you shouldn't make any assumptions about the group before understanding its culture.

The best way to understand the culture of a group, and netnews in general, is to read it for a while. Before you post an article to a group, it's a good idea to read the group for at least a month before attempting a post; read it longer if you don't have any pressing questions.

Read the Frequently Asked Questions Lists

Some groups maintain a list of frequently asked questions (called a *FAQ*), which the groups post periodically (generally once a month). Always read a group's FAQ before posting any questions to the group. Quite often, your question has been asked before (possibly many times), and asking it again won't generate any new information.

All the FAQ postings for netnews groups are available for anonymous ftp to the site `rtfm.mit.edu`. These postings really are a wealth of information about numerous topics, and are well worth reading. The FAQs also are posted to the groups `news.answers`, `comp.answers`, `soc.answers`, and so on.

After you have read a news group for a while, you begin to get a feeling for its culture. You learn to recognize the group's common topics (and those that cause the most problems!), the regular posters to the group

V

Using the Internet

(including the most and least respected), and how new users are treated. At this point, you have the background information necessary to "live" in the group.

Problems with News Group Discussions

The most important thing to remember when posting to a news group is that no matter how hard you try, you can't please everyone reading your articles. The number of people reading netnews is just too large, and the USENET community too diverse, for you to expect everyone involved to share your opinions. Even if you post a simple request for information ina polite news group, you are likely to receive mail from people either asking for you to forward the same information to them (called "me too" messages) or complaining that your message was inappropriate for the group you picked. On the other hand, you will almost always receive an answer to your question, and the chances are good that the answer will be correct. The USENET community contains experts on almost every field.

One serious problem with holding discussions in a news group is that you may experience long propagation delays between the time you post your article and the time it gets to the many user sites. If you're directly connected to the Internet, your post will be available on many other directly connected sites within a few hours. Because some sites still use UUCP to transfer their news, and many overseas sites get their news in batches only a few times a day, several days may pass before all netnews sites receive your article.

Similarly, replies to your article may take several days to reach your site. What may happen, then, is that the news group contains your original article, replies to your article, replies to the replies, and so on. These articles appear in the news group in a more or less random order and may take many days to die out (depending on how much discussion your article generates), as people in distant parts of USENET finally get your article and respond to it. You may find that in a discussion with many replies, the topic is still being discussed long after most of the people in the news group are tired of the subject!

Netiquette

Netiquette is a term that refers to common netnews etiquette. Enforcing any particular code of behavior on posters to a news group is almost impossible (see the section "Dealing with Problem Users" for more information). However, most people voluntarily follow the many rules of common courtesy that exist in the USENET community. And, when you post an article, remember that you don't know who may be reading your post, including your boss, your spouse, or a future employer! The section "Guidelines for Composing Your Articles" discusses the content and form of your article this section addresses the tone of your article and how people may react to it.

When you are composing an article, make sure to word your post carefully so that it accurately communicates your thoughts. With the lack of immediate feedback from your reader, and the absence of your voice inflection, tone, and physical indicators (facial expressions, hand gestures, and so on), the intent of your message easily can be misunderstood. Also, your message may be read by someone who is not a native speaker of your language, or who doesn't understand your culture. Your message may be reaching hundreds of thousands—or even millions—of readers, many of whom are in places with which you've never dreamed of holding communication. And when communicating on USENET, you cannot quickly correct a misunderstanding by your reader.

Don't post *flames*, articles that are personal attacks on another poster or tirades about a topic. Although flaming is accepted (and even encouraged) in some groups, members of most groups lose respect for someone who does it frequently. Before you take offense at an article, have an e-mail discussion with the author to clarify that individual's position; you may have misunderstood what the author was trying to say. When you get angry after reading an article, don't respond immediately. If you're still angry after you investigate to uncover any misunderstanding on your part, think carefully about how you best can respond.

When you read an article, read all the replies to that article before you post your reply. Someone else may have already replied with the same point that you were going to make. It just wastes time and computer resources for you to post the same response. Due to delays in receiving replies, of course, multiple replies do get posted; you may post your reply and later receive one that makes the same point.

Finally, try to avoid lengthy conversations over netnews with a particular individual. You and another reader may share opinions on an issue or have widely opposing ones. After a few messages about the topic go back and forth, however, you should move the conversation to personal electronic mail.

Expressing Emotions without Visual Cues

One of the main problems in communicating with people over netnews is that you aren't talking with them face to face. Your netnews communications lack the many visual cues that you use to express feelings and emotions, and, as a result, their meanings can be misinterpreted.

You can draw on a number of commonly used conventions to try to put some of the more physical aspects of communication into articles. Shouting is indicated with all uppercase letters (for example, THAT IS NOT TRUE!). You can emphasize a phrase by enclosing it with asterisks (for example, *do this step first*).

Another way to indicate emotions in your messages is to use commonly understood symbols (often called *emoticons*, or *smileys* after their main use). For example, to indicate that you are making a joke, you can use :-). (Hint: Look at the symbol sideways!) Here are a few of the most common emoticons:

Emoticon	Description
:-)	Smiley (happy) face
:-(	Sad face
;-)	Winking
:-0	Surprise (or shouting)
8-)	Wide-eyed smile
:->	Sarcastic smile
:-{)	Smiley with mustache

These examples are only a few of the many emoticons you can use to express feeling. You can, of course, simply write that you are joking in your post, which prevents any misunderstanding!

Always remember, however, that the best way to avoid misunderstandings is to express yourself as clearly and concisely as possible in your messages. Your readers will know nothing about you other than what they learn from reading your postings. Rather than assume that the reader of your post will know when you are joking or being sarcastic, you should tell them explicitly. Humor can be indicated by spelling out the intended physical clue in angle brackets (for example, <grin>).

Using Abbreviations in Your Articles

In addition to the emoticons, you will find that news articles often contain abbreviations for commonly used phrases. Some of the more common abbreviations are IMHO, which means *In My Humble* (or *Honest*) *Opinion*; BTW, for *By The Way*; FYI, which means *For Your Information*; OTOH, which stands for *On The Other Hand*; and FWIW, which means *For What It's Worth*. You can also abbreviate <grin> with <g>. You probably will come across other abbreviations as you read news articles; the meanings of most of them are obvious from their context in the message. Abbreviations are a way to save space and network resources by reducing the number of characters in an article.

Dealing with Problem Users

Eventually, you will have a problem with another user on USENET. Someone may send you abusive mail concerning a post you made, or a person may disrupt a news group with repeated, unwelcomed posts. Occasionally, someone posts a message that appears to be from another person (called *forging* a post). Even more rarely, problems such as death threats or other forms of harassment are reported.

The first thing to try as a means of dealing with problem users is to ignore them. If a person is posting articles that annoy you, just don't respond to those posts. Many news readers support a feature called a *kill file*. This feature automatically removes (kills) articles specified by criteria you set. The kill file feature enables you to kill all posts from a particular user, posts that regard a particular subject, or that meet any other criteria. Check the documentation on your news reading software to see Whether it supports such a mechanism. Using the kill feature of your software is often very effective in reducing the amount of annoyance generated by netnews.

If the problem user is going further than simply posting annoying articles (such as sending harassing e-mail), you can try to contact the administrators at the user's site. See Chapter 17, "Using Internet E-Mail," on how to contact the administrator at a user's site.

How Do You Access USENET?

Two common methods exist for individual PC users to gain access to USENET. The first of these methods is through a store-and-forward system, which enables you to read and compose news articles on your PC and connect to an Internet provider only when you want to receive or send your news and e-mail. Alternatively, you can connect on-line through a terminal interface to an account on an Internet provider's host. In either case, you don't have to worry about setting up a mechanism on your PC to manage news groups. The Internet provider does all the news group management and sends you (or gives you access to) the news articles that are of interest to you. Most Internet providers give you information about how to use the particular news reader that they supply.

In some cases, users may want to receive an actual local news feed. Information on using and receiving a local news feed appears later in this chapter, in the "How To Receive Netnews" section.

Examples of News Readers

This section discusses examples of a number of different news readers that you may encounter from your Internet provider. This section outlines common news reader features and provides examples of some of their commands.

Common News Reader Features

Some news readers give you the option of ignoring certain threads (articles with the same subject), ignoring posts from certain people, marking articles as unread (so that you see the header of these articles the next time you read the group), marking an entire thread as read, or marking an entire group as read. This last option is valuable if you return from vacation, for example, and find a large number of articles in a news group, and you don't have time to read them all. You can use the "catch up" feature to discard the unread articles. You can then start reading new articles as they appear.

Expiring Articles

Because of the huge volume of messages that arrive daily for all the thousands of news groups, most news group managers "expire" articles after a certain period of time. After an article is expired, you can't call it up again on USENET, so you may want to save articles that are of particular interest to you to a permanent file on your local disk. Even if you are getting the news articles downloaded to your local disk by the provider, you probably need to save interesting articles to a separate file, because the provider's news group reader needs to delete articles occasionally to keep your disk from filling up.

The rn News Reader

The rn news reader commonly is available on UNIX hosts. You may need to use this news reader if you are connected through a terminal interface directly to your Internet provider's UNIX host. To use rn, you can give the command rn followed by the name(s) of the news group(s) you want to read. Or, if you have used rn's subscription feature, you can just give the rn command by itself, because rn keeps a file in your account of all the groups you have subscribed to.

> **Note**
>
> The trn news reader has the same commands as the rn news reader, but it groups articles into threads. The rn reader displays articles in the order they are received on your news system.

After you give the rn command, you see a list of the news groups you specified with information about how many new messages are in each group. The rn news reader then cycles through this list of news groups and asks, for each group, whether you want to read the new articles. As a rule, you answer by pressing y to read the group immediately, or n to go on to the next group in the cycle. Alternatively, you can press p to return to the previous group, or q to quit reading news.

The rn news reader enables you to read new articles sequentially, in the order they appear in the news group. It displays as much of the current article as fits on your screen, and it displays a command line at the bottom of the screen. You can perform a number of different functions in rn by entering single-character commands. Table 19.1 lists the most common commands. The h command gives help at every prompt.

V

Using the Internet

Table 19.1: rn News Reader Commands

Command	Action
<space>	Display the next page of the current article
n	Go to the next unread article
N	Go to the next article, read or unread
P	Go to the previous unread article
p	Go to the previous article, read or unread
b	Back up one page
M	Mark this article as unread
k	Mark as read all articles with the current subject (kill a subject)
r	Reply to the author through e-mail
R	Reply to the author through e-mail, quoting the article
f	Post a follow-up article to the news group
F	Post a follow-up article quoting the article
s*file*	Save the current article to *file*
w*file*	Save the current article minus headers to *file*

The rn news reader is complex and powerful (if not very user-friendly). For more information on using rn, refer to the UNIX manual page (type man rn at your UNIX prompt). And be aware that rn doesn't enable you to post new articles (only follow-ups). If you use this news reader and want to post a new article, you can use the postnews command, which prompts you to indicate your article's subject and the name of the news group to which you want to post the article. The command then puts you in an editor where you can compose your article. When you exit the editor, you have the option of sending or aborting the article.

The tin News Reader

The tin news reader is screen oriented and much more user-friendly than rn. The tin news reader enables you to subscribe to groups and post new articles directly. Further, tin is a *threaded* news reader, which means that it organizes articles both in sequence and by topic; thus, you don't have to go through a sequential listing of all articles in the news group if you are interested only in those articles pertaining to a specific topic.

When you start tin (by using the `tin` command), it displays all the news groups to which you have subscribed (like rn, it keeps track of your news groups in a file). You see an on-screen list of those news groups and the number of new articles in each group to which you have subscribed. You can use the up- and down-arrow keys to move to the group that you want to read; then press Enter to read that group, or u to unsubscribe from that group. Other commands allow you to search for a group by name, move a group to a different place in the group list (so you can put your most frequently read groups first), or subscribe to a group that is not already in your list of read groups.

Table 19.2 lists some tin news reader commands and their actions.

Table 19.2: tin News Reader Commands

Command	Action
<Enter>	Read the current article
N	Move to the next article
n	Move to the next threaded group of articles
P	Move to the previous article
p	Move to the previous threaded group of articles
K	Kill and mark as read the entire current thread
w	Post an article to the current group of articles
q	Return to the news group selection screen
Q	Quit tin

The tin news reader has many more commands for selecting, viewing, or deleting articles. On-screen help is available at all times, and the h command gives you a description of all available commands. You also can view the UNIX manual page for the tin program by using the man tin command at the UNIX prompt.

The WinNET Mail News Reader

The WinNET Mail news reader (available from Computer Witchcraft, Inc.) is an example of an "off-line" news reading service that enables you to receive news (and mail) destined for your site. WinNET Mail is a Microsoft Windows program that connects through a modem on your computer to the WinNET Mail central computer. Using that connection, WinNET Mail downloads the news and mail for your site onto your local disk. After transferring all the files, the program disconnects, enabling you to read your news and mail without running up expensive phone bills. Because the program uses the Windows interface, reading and posting news on WinNET Mail is very easy.

Chapter 17, "Using Internet E-Mail," discusses the procedures for reading and sending mail with WinNET Mail, but the mail and news parts of the program are very similar. The WinNET Mail program starts up in mail reading mode. If you click the News icon on the startup screen (on the button bar), the Usenet News Group Folders window shown in figure 19.1 appears.

Fig. 19.1
The WinNET Mail News Group Folders window.

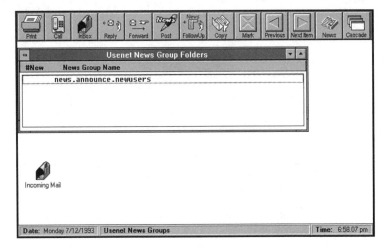

After you are in the Usenet News Group Folders window, you can see the news that has arrived in a news group by double-clicking the name of the news group in the News Group Name column. For example, you double-click the news.announce.newusers line to read the articles in that group. This opens a new window with the list of articles that you have received in that group, as shown in figure 19.2.

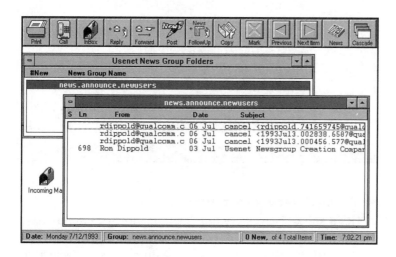

Fig. 19.2
The articles available in a news group.

This screen shows that four articles have arrived in the news group news.announce.newusers. To read a news article, double-click the line that contains that article's name. So, for example, if you want to read the last article in the group (from Ron Dippold), double-click that line. The article then appears in a new window, as shown in figure 19.3.

You can click the Next Item icon in the button bar at the top of the WinNET Mail screen to move to the next article; click the Previous icon to move to the previous article. Other icons enable you to print, move an article to another folder, or post and delete news articles. You subscribe to a new news group by using the Subscription item on the News menu. This item displays a dialog box that asks you for the group to subscribe to. When you register your WinNET Mail account, you receive instructions (through electronic mail) for using the system that include lists of available news groups. More information about the program is also available through the on-line Windows help.

V

Using the Internet

Fig. 19.3

The news article window.

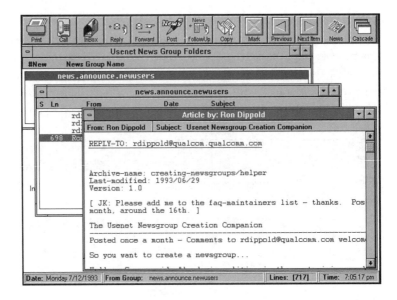

The PSILink News Reader

The PSILink software (available from Performance Systems International, Inc.) is another example of an off-line news reader. The software connects to the PSI news server to retrieve the articles available in the groups you have subscribed to. The PSILink software is available in DOS and Windows versions (both versions operate in much the same way). When you enter the PSILink DOS version, you see the main screen, as shown in figure 19.4.

Fig. 19.4

The PSILink main screen.

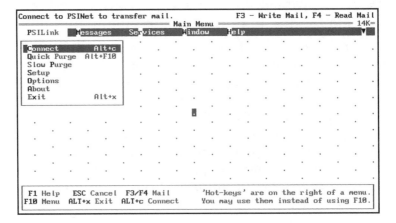

You can activate menus and issue commands to the PSILink software by choosing menus and menu items either with the mouse or by pressing Alt plus the highlighted letters for the items. For example, you activate the Messages menu by clicking it or by pressing <Alt-m>.

To subscribe to news groups, for example, you choose Messages followed by Subscribe To News. This choice brings up a list of all available groups. This very large list, a portion of which is shown in figure 19.5, is transmitted to your system the first time you connect to the PSI server. You can scroll through this list and choose the groups in which you are interested. Pressing the space bar subscribes (or unsubscribes) to the current news group, and you can search for a particular group by using the s command.

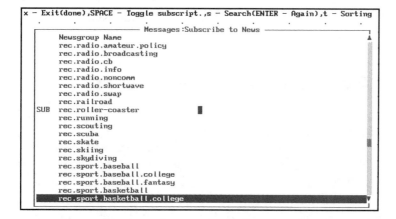

Fig. 19.5
The PSILink news subscription screen.

Reading news in PSILink is exactly the same as reading mail. You use the Read Mail/News menu item under the Messages menu to bring up the list of available mail and news folders. Press Enter to read the news or mail available in the selected folder; the Next and Prev menu items move around the available folders and messages.

You post news with the Write News option in the Messages menu. Choosing Write News brings up the New Messages screen, shown in figure 19.6. This screen prompts you to enter the name of the news group to which you want to post the article and to indicate the subject of the message. You then can edit the article and post it to the group. The File menu allows you to send or cancel the article, and the Header menu allows you to change one of the header lines. The Edit menu allows you to cut and paste and perform other edits on your message.

Fig. 19.6

The PSILink New
Messages screen.

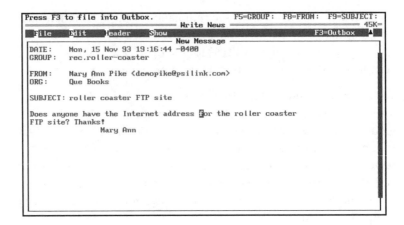

More information about the PSILink software is available in the program's on-line documentation and the printed manuals.

A Brief History of Netnews

Although computer bulletin boards, where users can post a message for
many people to read, have been popular almost from the beginning of
the computer age, the idea of sending messages from a local bulletin
board to a similar board on another machine wasn't explored until the
early 1980s. Electronic mailing lists enabled a user to send a single
message to a number of other users, but this practice wasted resources
because every user that wanted to read the article had to receive a private copy of the article. Thus, if you had 20 people on a system who
were also on a mailing list, the system received 20 copies of each message sent to the list. It is more efficient, however, if a single copy of the
message is placed where each of the 20 users can read it, which is what
a bulletin board system does.

News Transport Systems

In early 1980, computer programmers at Duke University and the University of North Carolina set up a rudimentary system to forward messages between their two systems. Using a UNIX Version 7 utility called
UUCP (UNIX to UNIX Copy), the system transmitted, through modems and phone lines, articles posted to a local news group to the
other machine.

This news transport system was presented at the 1980 summer Usenix (a professional organization of UNIX users) conference, where it generated a small amount of interest in the UNIX community. With a few improvements, the system was released to the public domain and was called "A news" (as the first version of the netnews system). Although it was slow, the message transport system worked. The system's authors expected it to handle only about 10 messages per day to a few news groups.

Soon, a few more computers were linked into this UUCP network, and the flow of articles increased. The early success of the A release of the news article transport system soon pointed up its failings, and a complete rewrite of the software was begun at the University of California at Berkeley. This release, known as "B news," was made available in 1982. B news was designed to handle a large number of news groups and articles, and it remained the standard for many years. The final version of B news was released in late 1986, and the system has been stable since then.

The UUCP system soon became too slow to handle the amount of articles it was called on to handle, and the phone calls were often expensive. With advancements in the development of the Internet, many people realized that it should be used to transmit news articles. In 1986, a program to implement NNTP (Network News Transport Protocol) was written, and that program became the standard for the transmission of netnews articles across the Internet. NNTP is defined by the Internet RFC 977. (RFC stands for Request For Comment, an Internet standard.)

With the advent of NNTP, the already fast growth of netnews exploded. The B news release, although relatively robust and well used, became too slow to handle the flow of news. In 1987, Henry Spencer of the University of Toronto released the "C news" version of the netnews transport mechanism. This release featured increased speed, reliability, and configurability, and quickly became the standard in use on the Internet.

As of this writing, several other systems also are used to transmit netnews articles, such as Waffle and Fido BBS (a network of PC systems that communicate through telephone lines) and INN (Internet News), which is similar in use to C news. These systems, although not as

V

Using the Internet

widely used as C news, perform the same function of transmitting news articles between machines. In a later section, this chapter discusses the operation of some of the available PC-based news transport systems.

News Reader Systems

Although the news transport mechanism has changed to reflect the increase in volume of news, relatively few transport systems have been in use. On the other hand, the number of news reader systems has been greater, to reflect different user needs and tastes. Some news readers are easy to learn and use, although others have very complex interfaces but allow users to sort through large numbers of articles quickly.

While an in-depth description of the many news readers currently available is beyond the scope of this book, the features of many of the readers are similar. Because this book is oriented toward users with PC systems, this chapter discusses some of the news readers available for that platform.

With the original B news release came a very simple news reader, called *vnews*. The sections "The rn News Reader" and "The tin News Reader" earlier in this chapter discuss two other popular news readers in detail. Another popular news reader is trn (a threaded version of rn). These programs all can be compiled and run on many different platforms, are available at no cost on the Internet, and are actively supported by their authors.

All of these news readers allow users to read and post articles, and many allow users to follow "threads" of conversations (articles that are related to the same topic). Other features in popular news readers are discussed in the section "Examples of News Readers."

News Group Creation

One of the most frequently asked questions about netnews is: How are new news groups created? This topic is one of the most central to the administration of netnews; in fact, quite a lot of the history of netnews is tied to the process of creating news groups.

How Groups Used To Be Created

When the bulk of the netnews traffic was being carried by the UUCP method of transmission, most people who carried net- news had to pay telephone charges to receive and transmit news. When the amount of traffic was small, these charges weren't excessive; but as netnews be-came popular, these telephone charges were a burden on sites.

Some central sites (such as Duke, the University of Toronto, and others) imported the news hierarchies into a certain area and then distributed them to local sites. Many of these central sites could absorb the tele-phone charges because the benefits of receiving the news transmissions at their site was worth the cost. However, because these sites (called the *backbone*) essentially were providing a service to the rest of the net free of charge, they held a certain authority over the process of creating news groups. In fact, if these backbone sites refused to carry a certain group, it was impossible to get that group to a large number of users.

So although the UUCP transport mechanism was still carrying the majority of news, the group of administrators at these backbone sites (sometimes called the *backbone cabal*) were the final authority on news group creation. Users and administrators would propose a news group publicly, and the administrators of the backbone sites would raise any objections that they had to the group. If no one objected to the pro-posed news group, the group was created on the backbone sites, and everyone on the netnews network (called USENET) began receiving the group.

Although the backbone cabal was an effective way to control the cre-ation and deletion of news groups (and in fact created the current main hierarchies in the so-called *great renaming* of the mid-1980s), many people in the netnews community wanted a more liberal approach to the creation of news groups.

One way of dealing with the strict rules for news group creation in the main news hierarchies was the creation of the `alt` hierarchy. Initially proposed by Brian Reid at the Digital Equipment Corporation, the `alt` hierarchy has very liberal rules for the creation of new groups; literally anyone with the capability to post an article to the news system can create a new group under the `alt` hierarchy. You should note, however, that although the `alt` hierarchy has some groups that are carried by a majority of netnews sites, most `alt` groups are carried by few news sites worldwide.

In the end, it wasn't the objections of users or some political process that caused the end of the backbone cabal. It was, instead, the growth of the use of the NNTP transport mechanism that reduced, and finally ended, the influence of the backbone administrators. Sites that used the NNTP transport could receive their news from literally any other site on the Internet (instead of the local UUCP backbone site). If the local site refused to carry a particular news group, the chances were that, somewhere on the Internet, you could find a site that would feed the desired group to you.

How Groups Are Created Now

The current news group creation mechanism came into being to replace the influence of the backbone administrators. The current mechanism for creating news groups is described fully in periodic postings to the news group news.announce.newusers, but the process (in brief) is as follows:

1. The group's name and a brief description of the topics it is ex-pected to cover are posted to the news.announce.newgroups group (as well as to any news groups with topics related to the new group). This proposal is called a "call for discussion" (often abbrevi-ated CFD) and is expected to generate discussion about the validity and usefulness of the new group.

2. Following a two-week discussion period, if no serious objections to the name and charter of the new group are raised, a "call for votes" (often abbreviated CFV) is posted to the same news groups as above. In this call for votes, the electronic mail address for the "vote taker" (who is supposed to be an independent, nonpartisan person) is given. The vote taker collects the names of people voting for and against the news group proposal. During the vot-ing process, the vote taker periodically posts the names of the people who have voted on the proposal (but not how they voted) so that people can verify that their vote has been received. The vote taker is explicitly forbidden from publishing the current number of votes for or against the group proposal.

3. After the two-week vote process is completed, the vote taker an-nounces the results of the vote. To pass, the news group proposal must receive at least 100 votes in favor of the group; the proposal must receive at least 100 more Yes votes than No votes; and the Yes votes must be at least two-thirds of the total votes. If all these criteria are met, the group is approved and, after a one-week waiting period, is created.

The important thing to remember about the process of creating a news group is that the group must be accepted by a legitimate vote. Even when a majority of the votes is for the new group proposal, if the news administrators on the various machines receiving netnews feel that the group is not legitimate, they will not carry the group on their machine. For all the democratic appearances of the above process, the local news administrator is free to do what he/she wants with his/her site's machine. One of the facts of life in netnews is that you generally cannot control someone else.

Why You Shouldn't Create a News Group

One final note on creating a news group. One of the most common mistakes made by new readers of netnews is to try to create a news group before understanding the process and culture of netnews. A new user often begins reading netnews, discovers that a group covering his or her favorite topic is not available, and immediately proposes the creation of such a group. This kind of proposal is almost certain to fail because the group proposed probably does not have sufficient interest to gather the required number of Yes votes.

New readers of netnews should read the material in the groups `news.announce.newusers` and follow the discussion in groups such as `news.groups` (which often discusses the creation, deletion, and renaming of news groups) for at least six months before trying to propose a new group. If you cannot wait that long, you should at least get someone who has read netnews for an extended period of time to make the actual new group proposal. If you don't do this, your new group proposal will probably not be well received, and ultimately the group will probably not be created.

How To Receive Netnews

If you want to receive netnews on your personal machine, or a central machine at your organization, you need to learn how to manage netnews. The first thing that you must decide before getting access to netnews is what level of service you want to receive. Because the reception of netnews on a local machine can require significant resources (depending on the number and type of news groups you want to receive), you may decide on one of several options that don't require you to dedicate local resources to netnews in order to read the news.

The resources required to have netnews on a local system vary with the number of groups received locally, but in general, you need a machine with enough disk space and CPU power to handle a large amount of traffic. At this writing, a full feed of the main hierarchies (including the alt hierarchy) averages almost 80M of data per day. So, if you want to keep a week's worth of news articles on your system, you need more than 500M of local disk storage, plus a few megabytes for storage of the news binaries and sources.

Similarly, you need a CPU that can handle this amount of traffic moving into your system. A personal computer with an 80386 or 80486 processor is necessary to handle the load of a fairly large number of groups.

As you can see, getting a local feed of more than a few groups is not something to be undertaken lightly. Fortunately, other ways of getting access to netnews exist that don't require significant local resources.

Public-Access News Sites

If your site is one at which only a few people want to have access to netnews, and you don't need to have control over the length of time a particular news article is available on a system (how long until an article *expires*), you may want to get access to netnews on one of many public access machines around the country.

For a monthly fee, you can get an account on a public access machine. These systems, called *public-access sites*, are connected to the Internet and may provide services such as electronic mail, netnews feeds, ftp, or other Internet services to their customers. Often, these sites are set up to allow people who do not have direct Internet access to dial in via a modem and connect to their site. If you already have an Internet connection, you don't need to use a modem, but instead you can simply telnet to the remote machine and log in.

These public-access sites are available around the country, and you should pick the one which gives you the best service for your money. If your primary need is simply netnews access, you should pick a site that receives the groups you're interested in and keeps the groups on-disk for an amount of time acceptable to you. Generally, you should require the site to keep the groups you require on-disk for at least four days so you can skip reading the news over an extended weekend without missing any articles.

Another item you should consider when picking a public-access site is the site's reputation. Because any posts you make to a news group display the public-access site from which they originate, you should try to find a site that has a professional reputation—one that won't cause people to discount your posts. Try to find a site that allows you to customize your outgoing posts so that the organization name and return mail address listed in the article headers reflect your actual organization and Internet mail address (rather than the public access site). This arrangement enables you to receive replies to your post at your regular mail address, if you choose.

To locate a public-access site, consult the lists provided on the disk included with this book in the file PDIAL.TXT. The PDIAL document is updated as the maintainer gets information about new public-access sites. The file is kept at an ftp site (identified within the file) on the Internet and is posted regularly to certain news groups that also are identified in the file. After you have the names of sites that may be able to provide the news access you need, you can contact the administrators (given as the contact for information in the listings) at those sites to determine their news policies and features.

Remotely Reading News with NNTP

You may have a few problems reading news at a public-access computer. For example, if you want to keep a news article around for future reference, you probably need to transfer it to your local site by using the ftp program (discussed in Chapter 8, "Using ftp and telnet"). Further, you may not like the news readers available on the remote site, and you generally have to pay a per-hour fee for the time you spend reading news (which can be a significant amount, given the amount of news available!).

If you have only a few people at your site who want to read news, and you don't want to use a public-access site to read news, another option available to you is to set up a local news reader that accesses the news stored on a remote machine. These news readers use the NNTP protocol (the same one used to transfer news between sites that feed each other) to retrieve individual articles that you want to read. The rn and tin news readers can be set up to use the NNTP protocol to read articles; most other popular news readers have this capability also.

The advantage of using an NNTP-based news reader is that you have control over the news reading interface you use—you can pick the news reader that suits your tastes. In addition, because the news reader is running on your local machine, any articles you save for future reference are stored locally. You don't need to devote large amounts of computer resources to receive a local news feed.

One disadvantage of using the NNTP-based readers is that you transfer the articles you want in real time. Network congestion, the load on the remote machine, and other factors can slow the transfer of articles to your news reader and can result in slower responses than reading the news off of a local disk.

Getting access to a system that supports NNTP-based reading is similar to finding a public-access site. Your choices are somewhat broader, however, because you require only an NNTP connection and don't require a login account on the remote machine. Many of the same public-access sites that allow news reading also allow NNTP access to their news. Also, commercial news providers such as UUNET and PSI provide NNTP-based news access. To locate such a site, consult the public-access site list (PDIAL.TXT) included on the disk provided with this book.

Also, local universities and even some commercial sites allow NNTP-based readers; check around in your local area for such sites.

Getting a Limited Number of Groups through Electronic Mail

Quite often, the people at your site don't require a full netnews feed to receive the groups whose articles they want to read. If the total number of requested groups is small, and few articles are posted in those groups, receiving the news groups via electronic mail is often easier than the normal netnews transport mechanisms.

To receive the news articles via electronic mail, your site should need to receive less than 5M of information per day (or a few hundred articles). If your site receives more than this amount of information, you may find it more efficient to use the normal news transport mechanisms that are designed to handle a large flow of articles. Also, news reader programs are somewhat more efficient at presenting news articles in a logical, readable format than most electronic mail reading programs.

That said, you can set up an electronic mail-based news feed by contacting the same type of sites as listed above. Because an electronic mail-based feed is not a "normal" type of news feed, however, you may have better luck contacting some of the commercial news providers, such as UUNET, because they are accustomed to setting up these types of feeds. Any of the public-access sites, however, may be willing to set up an e-mail feed; you can contact the administrators at these sites for availability and prices of such a feed.

In addition to getting someone to feed you news via electronic mail, you need a mechanism that enables you to post messages to news groups via electronic mail. The site that provides you with a feed may set up such an e-mail-based posting mechanism (usually done with mail aliases), but if the site is unwilling to set it up, several sites are on the Internet that provide mail-to-news gateways.

One of these mail-to-news gateways is at the machine `decwrl.dec.com`; you can post to a group such as `news.admin.misc` by sending a message to `news.admin.misc.usenet@decwrl.dec.com` (in effect, you use the netnews group name with `.usenet` appended to it as the user name for the mail). Other gateways exist at the machines `pws.bull.com` and `news.cs.indiana.edu` (using addresses such as `news.admin.misc`), and at the machine `cs.utexas.edu` (using addresses such as `news-admin-misc`). The news group `news.admin.misc` is also a good place to ask for advice in setting up your news feed or locating someone to feed you news.

Because these sites may restrict gateway access to users at their site, or the gateway may be turned off at any time, you should always check with the administrators at the individual sites before using their gateway. You generally can contact the news administrator at a netnews site by sending electronic mail to the address `usenet` or `netnews` at the site. Don't post large amounts of news through these gateways, however, as these large postings place a burden on the remote site; if people abuse these gateways, they will be turned off.

V

Using the Internet

Getting a Full or Partial News Feed from NNTP

Only a few reasons support a decision to receive your news feed locally; these reasons outweigh the costs of necessary hardware and administrative time. Some of these reasons follow:

- You want to control how long groups are kept on-line.

- You want to control fully which groups you have access to.

- You want to create groups that are local to your site only (perhaps containing proprietary information).

- You want to be able to provide news feeds to other sites.

If you have made the decision to receive more than a few news groups locally, you probably are going to be using one of the NNTP-based transport mechanisms. These mechanisms are the only ones in widespread use carrying news over the Internet and are designed to carry a large volume of news efficiently. Given this, make your choice of news transport systems based on the operating system you want to run on your news machine.

UNIX-Based News Transport Mechanisms

Most of the news transport systems in wide use on the Internet are written based on the UNIX operating system. Although setting up and running a UNIX system may seem intimidating to people who are accustomed to the DOS world, several inexpensive (even free) versions of UNIX are available for the PC platform. The initial trouble in setting up the single UNIX machine often pays for itself many times over by allowing the use of an efficient, well-tested news transport system.

Of course, after you have the single news transport machine set up, the rest of your local system can read the news from the UNIX machine, either by having the news area on a Novell network disk (or by some other network disk scheme such as PC-NFS), or by using an NNTP-based reader, as described earlier in the section "Remotely Reading News with NNTP."

The popular C news transport mechanism compiles and runs on systems running SCO UNIX as well as many other variants of UNIX for the PC platform. The C news release is currently available from its archive site cs.toronto.edu via anonymous ftp. After you retrieve and extract the release files, the on-line instructions lead you through the building process. Help for setting up a C news system is available from the system's authors and several netnews groups.

The recently released INN (InterNet News) transport system also can compile and run under SCO UNIX. INN is available at the site `ftp.uu.net` and also has full on-line instructions for building and setting up the feed.

After you build your news transport mechanism and test it with local posts, you have to find someone to feed you news via NNTP. As already described, local universities, public-access sites, and commercial netnews providers are all possible NNTP-based news feed sources. You also can post a message to `news.admin.misc` asking for a local feed, using one of the mail-to-news gateways described earlier.

When setting up an NNTP-based feed, you need to tell the remote site your machine name and Internet address, plus the news groups or hierarchies that you want to receive. The remote site then configures their NNTP feed program to contact your site at regular intervals and transfer the news to your machine. Similarly, you need to set up your outgoing transmission program to feed any posts your users have made locally to your feed site so that your posts can be transmitted to the rest of the world.

During the initial few days of receiving a news feed, you should monitor the news system closely to make sure that it is working correctly. You also should monitor the programs that remove old news from your system (called *expiration programs*) to make sure that your disk doesn't fill up.

DOS-Based News Transport Mechanisms

A couple of options are available to you if you must run your news transport mechanism under DOS. Basically, these systems are bulletin board systems that have functions to receive, send, and read news and mail.

One system in fairly wide use for receiving news is Waffle, a shareware product available on the Internet through anonymous ftp to the site `halcyon.com` in the file `/pub/waffle/waffle/waf165.zip`. Waffle is a bulletin board system that offers news reception and reading, as well as electronic mail, conferencing, and other features commonly found on bulletin boards. If you don't need the full functionality of a bulletin board system, you can use only the parts of Waffle that you need.

The details of setting up a Waffle system are beyond the scope of this book, but the ZIP file contains complete instructions on installing, configuring, and operating the Waffle functions. Additional assistance is available via electronic mail to the author Tom Dell (dell@vox.darkside.com) and in the netnews group comp.bbs.waffle. The "frequently asked questions" file posted monthly to comp.bbs.waffle gives a good overview of the Waffle system and is also available via anonymous ftp to rtfm.mit.edu in the file /pub/usenet/comp.bbs.waffle/W_F_A_Q_(F).

Further, many additional packages have been written to work with Waffle to provide more functionality (such as different editors, news or mail readers, or gateways to other BBS systems). These packages also are available on the Internet via anonymous ftp to halycon.com in the directory /pub/waffle.

Waffle was designed to receive and transmit news and mail through a telephone link using the UUCP protocol; but by getting the optional file waf165nn.zip (for the current version), you can receive news via the NNTP protocol. This package is limited in regard to which network adapter cards and network software it supports, so make sure that your hardware and software are supported before trying to set up an NNTP-based Waffle news site.

Other PC-based bulletin board systems that also receive and send netnews (as well as mail) exist, but these are all based on modems and UUCP transfers of data. Systems such as Fido, Wildcat, and other BBS systems are available through the Internet.

Summary

USENET is a relatively simple system for sending messages to thousands of others who are interested in the message's topic. Most of the members of the USENET community are friendly and helpful, but some others are adversarial and downright malicious. But the latter group of people are in the minority, and USENET tends to reflect the composition of the societies who have access to it.

USENET can be an amazing resource. It allows you (relatively) quick access to thousands of people who have the same interests as you do. You can post a request for information and, within a few days, receive replies from all over the world. Something that may have taken you weeks or even months to discover can be found within hours or days by tapping that vast resource of experts who make up the USENET community. We're all experts on something, whether it's astronomy, gardening, or child raising. Everyone can contribute to the success of the USENET community.

V

Using the Internet

Chapter 20

Determining the Level of Internet Service You Need

The previous chapters have shown you many services available through the Internet. Many firms offer some type of Internet access; the options they offer span the spectrum of possible service levels. Some offer only an electronic mail gateway, whereas others provide true interactive Internet access through a T3 (44.746 Mbps) link. As a result, Internet services have a broad price range. You already may have a computer account that enables you to send and receive electronic mail, access network news, and run ftp and telnet, for example, without incurring any charges. But at the other extreme, you may need to provide Internet access to a large number of users divided into several groups. Such an arrangement may cost tens of thousands of dollars a year in Internet access fees alone. And high-volume network usage implies a commitment of substantial computer, facility, and personnel resources, just to manage your organization's network access.

This chapter will help you determine the level of service you need from your Internet service provider. It prepares you for several of the subsequent chapters in this book by exploring the issues involved in choosing levels of service and by giving numerous examples of the service requirements of various types of users.

▶ Chapter 21, "Making Connections Beyond the Internet," provides an in-depth examination of Internet access through popular information services such as CompuServe and MCI Mail.

Deciding Which Internet Services You Need

As the earlier chapters of this book show, the Internet is rich in resources, and the growth of its capabilities is explosive. You must decide, however, which services are essential to your networking needs. If all you really need is an electronic mail address and you plan to check your mail only once or twice a day, you don't need to pay for a more expensive service that also enables you to run ftp.

You probably will have to compromise when choosing a service provider. Ideally, you may like to maintain a 24-hour-a-day connection, but perhaps you can't justify the fee of several hundred dollars per month for such service. You may find, however, that you obtain satisfactory results for $20 to $30 a month from a dialup service that you check once an hour to check for new electronic mail messages.

> **Note**
>
> Changing network service providers is relatively easy. Because providers realize this fact, they compete vigorously for your business. Expect to see more services at the same, or even lower, prices.

Electronic Mail

Electronic mail is the most fundamental service offered; essentially all providers include it in their service packages. You need to answer two questions before deciding on your e-mail service:

- How quickly do you need to be notified of new incoming e-mail?

- Do you need multiple, independent e-mail addresses?

If you maintain a continuous connection to the network, you are notified immediately of incoming mail. Otherwise, you must access the network to check for new mail. Periodically checking for new events is called *polling*. You may find that polling your provider enables you to respond satisfactorily to new mail. Just make sure that you can poll as often as you like! You may find that connecting to your provider during certain times of the day is difficult, or that the connection fees are expensive for this method of access.

Many network providers give you one e-mail address and set up a single mail folder per account. If multiple users access the account, they share the e-mail address, and all their mail is placed in the same folder. Thus, they can read and reply to each other's mail. This state of affairs can be confusing, even with a small number of users sharing an account. And an individual user may want to have several independent e-mail addresses as well, to distinguish between mail messages (separating personal mail from business mail, for example). Users also may want to set up separate addresses for different projects or activities.

Of course, remaining on-line while composing or reading mail messages isn't actually necessary. You can do this work at your leisure on your local computer, thus reducing connect-time fees (if you are charged in this manner). Furthermore, simple operations such as downloading your e-mail can be automated to reduce further the actual time you are connected to your provider. Many common communications packages (such as PROCOMM PLUS) allow you to write *scripts*—programs to control your communications sessions—to do this and other straightforward, commonly used procedures. Service providers like the idea that you do not tie up a communications line while examining and responding to your e-mail. CompuServe, for example, offers its CompuServe Information Manager, which can retrieve your mail and then immediately disconnect you from the network.

Network News

Most providers offer USENET and other news feeds to their users. If you want to have access to network news, you need to consider two main issues:

- Your provider needs to carry the news groups in which you want to participate. Your provider may not receive each one of the several thousand news groups available, because they cumulatively generate around 90M of news every day. Investigate the news feeds carried by potential providers; if a provider of interest doesn't carry a news group you want to follow, ask whether it can be added to the daily feed.

- Estimate the resource cost for accessing your news groups. Remember that you can spend a great deal of time just reading the news, and use a significant amount of disk space or connection time in accessing it. Loading a large amount of news each day to your computer over a 2,400 bps connection, for example, could be quite expensive.

Although you may be tempted to participate in many news groups, only a few of them will be of use to you on a regular basis. Most providers that carry network news make changing the news groups you receive easy. Thus, you can try out a news group for a while and then drop it when it's no longer of interest to you.

Interactive Access to Remote Computers

If you want to use ftp and telnet, you need interactive access to the Internet. The main issue for you to consider before choosing this level of service (offered by many providers) is the cost of connect time. Because you are connected to the network during your entire interactive session, you can incur large expenses if you are charged for connect time. Try to plan your accesses off-line as much as possible and disconnect from the network whenever you pause for more than a few minutes (to examine downloaded files on your local computer, for example).

If you plan to transfer frequently large amounts of data using ftp, make sure that the data rate of your network connection is cost effective. A 14.4 Kbps connection, for example, can transfer data six times faster than a 2,400 bps connection. Compression schemes such as V.42*bis* also can increase the effective transfer rate by as much as a factor of four.

Network Navigation Aids

Navigation aids such as archie, Gopher, and WAIS are invaluable when you need to locate network resources. You can use all these tools—and others as well—by way of publicly accessible telnet accounts. If you can connect to remote computers using telnet, you can use these common navigation aids.

Many service providers install one or more of these programs on their local systems; these locally installed tools are sometimes more responsive. Your provider also may offer a version of your favorite tool with a more advanced user interface.

Real-Time Textual Chatting

Real-time interactive character-based communications is commonly available to Internet users with interactive access. Many providers offer facilities such as *talk* and *Internet Relay Chat (IRC)*. If you plan to use these features often, you need to consider two major issues:

■ As with ftp and telnet, you must remain connected to the network for the duration of each chatting session. Compare the cost
of chatting through the Internet to other means of communicating, such as telephone calls or e-mail. Unlike ftp usage, chatting
is a very low data rate activity; faster connections don't improve
performance significantly.

■ As with electronic mail, you must be connected to the network to
be aware that someone wants to chat with you. And you can't
effectively poll your service provider (as you can with e-mail) to
monitor requests to chat. Statistically speaking, the person trying
to reach you almost certainly will give up before you respond.
That means you must have a continuous network connection if
you want people to be able to initiate requests to chat with you
at any time of day.

Teleconferencing over the Internet

You can transfer audio and video data in real time through the network, but these processes require an extremely high-speed connection.
Note that the complete path between all the teleconferencing sites
must support an adequate data transfer rate. Generally speaking, such
support is now too expensive for individuals and small organizations
to justify.

Although most network teleconferencing capabilities are experimental
at this time, interest in them is growing, especially in the business
community. Transfers of real-time audio through the network are
likely to become more common in the near future. But to become a
viable alternative, real-time audio teleconferencing has to be cost-
competitive with conference telephone calls and fax communications.

Allowing Network Users To Access Your Computer

You may want to allow outside users to establish ftp and/or telnet
connections to your local system. You may want members of your
organization who are traveling, for example, to be able to access
your local computer from another location that is connected to the
Internet. You also may want to make a resource such as a database
or specialized software package available to outsiders through the
network.

If you want to allow users to access your computer from the Internet, you must set up a server on your local system and connect it to the network as an Internet host. In such a case, you probably want a continuous connection and need a fast communications link to support the anticipated volume of network traffic. For security reasons, if you plan to allow unregistered network users to access your system (through anonymous ftp, for example), you should set up a dedicated system for this purpose. If possible, this system normally shouldn't be connected to other computers in your facility.

You Already May Have Internet Access and Not Know It

Many people can obtain Internet access easily, without any cost to themselves, through their schools or workplaces. Professional societies, especially in fields involving computers, are beginning to offer some Internet-related services to their members. Local users' groups in your area also may offer some type of Internet connection for a small fee, or for free. Of course, you must observe some restrictions on your Internet usage when using accounts obtained through such organizations.

You may find that accessing the network through such an account provides you with all the Internet services you need. And even if connections such as these don't handle your full Internet requirements, you can use them to learn more about the network and to experiment with the services provided. Your initial Internet connection will help you acquire information about other service providers and currently available hardware and software for accessing the network.

Educational Institutions

If you are a student at a large university, chances are good that you already have a computer account through which you can send and receive electronic mail and run ftp and telnet. You may have no idea that this account exists. Many colleges and universities automatically set up accounts for all new students, regardless of their majors. Such accounts also may be established for part-time and non-degree-seeking students. Many colleges provide each student with an individual account on their central computer system to facilitate course registration, allow access to the library's on-line databases, and handle electronic mail within the university community.

Contact the manager of your educational institution's central computer facility for information concerning the availability of computer accounts, the level of Internet access they provide, and their acceptable use policies. Also ask faculty members (your academic advisor, for example) and the administrator of your department's computer facility (if one exists). If you obtain an account through an educational institution, remember that its acceptable use policy almost certainly prohibits for-profit use and extensive use for private or personal business. These prohibitions are imposed by the NSFNET backbone, through which most educational institutions receive their Internet access.

Employers

Commercial activity on the Internet has been increasing steadily and now comprises more than half the traffic on the network. The critical mass of network participants has been reached; justifying the costs of Internet access now is easy for many businesses. If you use a computer that's connected to other computers at work, ask the systems administrator if the local network can access the Internet. If it can, you may find that you can send and receive electronic mail but can't run interactive applications such as ftp or telnet. If you want more extensive network privileges, ask your company's computer systems administrator if you can have a special account that allows you interactive Internet access.

Although you may think a business would encourage its employees to use the rich resources on the Internet—after all, large universities do—commercial institutions can be very restrictive concerning network access for a number of reasons. If you use your employer's Internet connection, keep in mind the considerations discussed in the following paragraphs. Otherwise, you may find your network privileges revoked and your job in peril. The bottom line is to act like a respectful guest when using your employer's Internet connection for non-job-related purposes.

Businesses are very sensitive to security issues. The process of connecting their computers to a world-wide network with millions of users in dozens of countries carries some risks. Employees easily can send sensitive information to persons outside the company—intentionally or by accident or negligence. Employers also worry about reduced productivity caused by employees using the Internet connection for personal uses during their work time. Non-work-related Internet activity (receiving large USENET news feeds, for example) also can place a significant load on the employer's computing facility, decreasing network performance for genuine work-related access. Always remember that your employer may be monitoring your networking activities; never assume any privacy when sending or receiving messages or files by way of an employer's computer.

Professional Societies

Some professional societies are experimenting with offering their members Internet-related services. The most common of these is an e-mail forwarding service. The Institute of Electrical and Electronic Engineers (IEEE), for example, the principal electrical engineering professional society in the United States, offers its members a permanent e-mail address of the form *xxx.yyy*@ieee.org, where *xxx.yyy* uniquely identifies the member within the domain ieee.org. The IEEE allows you to keep this address as long as you are a member of its organization.

The IEEE, however, doesn't store your e-mail messages—you must provide the electronic mail handler at ieee.org with an e-mail forwarding address. All mail sent to your permanent e-mail address *xxx.yyy*@ieee.org is forwarded to another e-mail address, which you are free to change from time to time. The advantage of such a scheme is that you have a permanent e-mail address that remains the same, even if you change employers, choose a different Internet service provider, or move to a different part of the country (or even the world).

Your professional society may provide additional Internet services in addition to forwarding your e-mail. For instance, the Association for Computing Machinery (ACM), the principal society for computer professionals in the United States, offers two types of accounts: a mail forwarding account and a full service account. The full service account provides electronic mail, network news, and Internet tools such as ftp, telnet, archie, and Gopher.

Keep in mind that these services are new for most societies and are therefore subject to rapid change. You also should review the acceptable use policy for Internet access through your professional society's connection. You may find significant restrictions (for example, no for-profit activities allowed) that severely limit its usefulness to you. Such policies often are due to the professional society receiving its network connection through NSFNET. But you may feel that a permanent e-mail address is valuable to you, especially when it's provided at an extremely low charge (or even at no cost at all).

Local Users' Groups

Some associations established in your community may allow you to access the Internet through their members' connections. The services offered are usually electronic mail and network news through a UUCP connection. Such groups, if they exist in your local area, are usually composed of volunteers dedicated to promoting Internet awareness and experimentation.

The Atlanta Regional Network Organization (ARNO), for example, offers this kind of service to the greater metropolitan Atlanta area. ARNO describes itself in the following terms (taken from information provided by ARNO):

- A volunteer group of interconnected local hub systems that provide non-Internet sites with UUCP network connectivity to the Internet and other sites

- A means to provide UUCP connectivity to the rapidly growing small-system community (including Waffle and UUPC users)

- A central contact point where requests for UUCP connection may be sent (so that new systems don't have to search for a site that will provide them with a UUCP connection)

- A means to provide netnews feeds for those sites wanting this service

- A way to provide domain registration to the atl.ga.us domain for all who want it (and get rid of those long "bang" path e-mail addresses)

ARNO is *neither* of the following things:

- An attempt to compete with any commercial enterprise that provides UNIX access

- A UNIX support group or UNIX education group (those facilities are available elsewhere)

You can obtain this information as well as additional information about ARNO by sending an e-mail message to arno-post@mathcs.emory.edu or arno-post@gatech.edu.

You may have to do some hunting to determine whether a similar group can provide you with network access. Ask the computer facilities managers at local colleges and universities (and other experienced network users in your area) about such organizations.

Often no fee or a token charge is assessed for connections obtained in this manner. Be forewarned, however, that their service reliability can vary from good to unacceptable, and reaching someone may be difficult if you experience problems or have questions. Of course, faulting this type of provider is difficult if your connection is provided at no cost to you.

Types of Internet Service Providers

Now that you are aware of the services you can obtain through the Internet, you are prepared to investigate the ways Internet services are typically packaged. You aren't likely to find exactly what you want for the price you are willing to pay. But you almost certainly can find a provider in your price range that offers the set of essential services you need. Keep in mind that changing from one service provider to a more suitable one is generally easy. Your Internet service easily can evolve with your networking needs.

BBS, UUCP, and Other Polled Services

Providers such as these don't offer interactive Internet access. Electronic mail and (in some cases) network news are the only Internet services available. These providers may offer other non-Internet-related services, however. The cost depends on the total package of services available and the profit orientation of the system owner. Prices for these providers typically range from no charge to around $30 per month.

Such a provider generally operates in one of two ways. In the first method, the host system is set up so that you log in using a modem and a terminal (or a computer running a terminal emulation package, such as PROCOMM PLUS from Datastorm Technologies or Microsoft Windows Terminal). After logging in, you enter commands to accomplish your tasks (such as instructing the system to show you new mail received since your last connection). After you finish a session, you disconnect from the host. All your transactions occur when you are connected to the host.

In the second method of operation, your local computer runs software such as Waffle (developed by Darkside International), which acts as a network server. It buffers all outgoing traffic, such as electronic mail messages originating from your computer. When your computer connects with the host computer, it sends all outgoing traffic to the host and receives any incoming traffic in a batch. The connection is terminated immediately after all traffic is exchanged. Your computer then stores any traffic it received from the host for you to review at a later time. Check with your system administrator to see what software you need to connect with a specific provider and how much it will cost (you may not be charged).

Online Services and Terminal Servers

These service providers offer the quickest and easiest way for you to establish an Internet connection. Essentially, you are given an account with a single electronic mail address on their computer system. Services such as CompuServe and Delphi enable you to sign up by telephone (by voice or modem). You don't even need a computer to access the network through these providers—you need only a terminal with a modem.

> **Note**
>
> You must pay long-distance charges unless your dialup provider has a local phone number in your area or a toll-free 800 number.

If you use your computer to access these services, the only software you need is a terminal emulation package. Low-cost graphical user interface (GUI) software is now available from some providers, and additional providers are expected to offer GUI front-ends to their systems in the near future.

This class of service provider can be subdivided further into two basic types. The only Internet access offered by the first type, exemplified by CompuServe and MCI Mail, is electronic mail. Of course, such providers typically offer many more non-Internet-related services that you may find valuable. The cost of service can depend to a great extent on the total package of services provided. You also may find that your charge for connect time depends on the speed of your modem. For purposes of comparison, CompuServe's standard service costs $8.95 per

V

Using the Internet

month, which includes $9 worth of free electronic mail (at the time of this writing). Sending or reading an Internet message normally costs 15 cents for the first 7,500 characters and 5 cents for each additional 2,500 characters. With this pricing structure, you can send or receive up to 60 Internet mail messages containing no more than 7,500 characters (approximately up to three pages in length) every month for $8.95.

The second type—Delphi, CRL, or Netcom, for example—provides interactive access to the Internet and allows subscribers to run ftp, telnet, navigational aids, and other facilities. Again, these providers offer additional services, such as databases and software archives, that may interest you. They usually charge a fixed monthly fee or else accrue charges on a connect-time basis. Charges to typical users are usually in the range of $10 to $20 per month.

> **Note**
>
> Even though you basically are logging in to one of your service pro-vider's computers, you may be presented with a specialized user interface rather than enter the native operating environment. Such interfaces sometimes are provided as a service to you, to make performing network operations easier. They also are provided to enhance system security by preventing you from using the full set of commands and resources available through the operating system.

The *Public Dialup Internet Access List (PDIAL)*, compiled by Peter Kaminski, lists providers offering inexpensive public access to the Internet through an ordinary phone line using your regular modem and computer. PDIAL lists only providers directly connected to the Internet. This document is included on the disk accompanying this book.

SLIP and PPP Service

When you use an on-line service to access the Internet, you basically are given an account on a computer that's connected to the network. You log in to your provider's system by way of an ordinary telephone line to perform your Internet transac-tions. *Serial Line Internet Protocol (SLIP)* and *Point-to-Point Protocol (PPP)*, on the other hand, enable you to connect your computer directly to the Internet using an ordinary telephone line. Your computer, in turn, can be connected to other computers on your local network, thus permitting all these computers to have direct Internet access. This class of service is often called *dialup IP*.

With SLIP and PPP connections, you can use the full range of Internet services. The relatively slow speed of your communications link and the number and duration of your network connections impose the only restrictions.

You don't want to use a dialup IP connection with anything slower than a 9,600 bps modem. The slow communications link limits the number of computers you can use through a single dialup IP connection. If most of your local computers perform light, infrequent Internet accesses, they generate little network traffic. SLIP and PPP are generally considered suitable for connecting a single computer or a very small local network to the Internet.

> **Note**
>
> You don't need to maintain a continuous connection to the Internet. You can disconnect from the network whenever you want. Because you likely won't be charged for connect time when using SLIP or PPP, the main reason you may choose to operate in this fashion is to avoid dedicating a phone line to your Internet access. You also may want to access your connection from multiple locations, such as your home and office.

These connections are considerably more expensive than the connections offered by the providers discussed previously. You can expect to pay $150 to $300 per month for your Internet connection alone. Also, you must obtain dialup IP software to run on your local computer (at an approximate cost of $300 to $600). Also consider that, although not required, you may want to dedicate a phone line—and even a complete computer system—to the task of handling your Internet communications.

Dedicated Connections

If dialup IP is inadequate for your direct Internet connection needs, you can obtain a connection through a high-speed dedicated communications link. But if you do so, be prepared to spend a substantial amount of money and to make a major commitment to maintaining your connection. Available speeds range from 56 Kbps through nearly

V

Using the Internet

45 Mbps. Expect to pay roughly $1,000 to $1,500 per month for a 56 Kbps connection and approximately $3,000 to $4,000 per month for a T1 connection (1.544 Mbps).

Your connection fees usually include the network router, customer support, and field service on all equipment provided. Furthermore, most service providers help you set up your site and register your network with the DDN Network Information Center.

With a dedicated connection, you can connect essentially as many computers to the network as you like. You have a 24-hour-a-day presence on Internet and can use any services the network provides. The main limitation in this case, again, is the speed of your communications link.

> **Note**
>
> Obviously, only organizations with a substantial amount of Internet traffic can justify the expense of this type of network connection. Typically, large organizations with a large base of network users utilize dedicated connections.

Determining the Network Performance You Need

Now that you have some ideas concerning which package of network capabilities you want, you must consider the level of performance you need from your connection. An organization that wants to connect many individual users obviously places a greater burden on the connection than a single user making short, infrequent accesses.

A multiuser organization may be able to justify a more costly connection, because the extra expense is distributed among more users. Network performance is usually equated with response time, which obviously is affected by the maximum data transfer rate your connection supports and by the amount of network traffic you expect. You also need to consider how well your connection can handle the number of your users having access to the network.

Who Will Use Your Internet Connection?

In general, Internet connections take one of two forms. Your connection can be a domain or a user account on a host in someone else's domain. In the first case, you can set up multiple user accounts (and subdomains, if you like) off your domain. Individual users can have their own private e-mail addresses and mail folders. You can monitor network usage by individual users. You can even establish subdomains to correspond to groups of users within your organization. Also, you may find that setting up certain e-mail addresses that automatically reply to incoming mail with informational messages is useful.

In the second case, you appear to the Internet as an individual user on someone else's host. Essentially, you have a single account on a computer that has an Internet connection. All mail sent to your account is placed in the same incoming mail folder. If several persons use the account, each user can read and reply to any incoming electronic mail messages. This may cause difficulties, even if only a few people share the account. With a single user account, you can't break down network usage by individual. Further, you may find that only one person is allowed to use the account at a time.

> **Note**
>
> You should monitor each user's on-line time to determine the amount and type of use he or she is giving the network. On-line time can be addictive and—if used for personal endeavors—expensive to your company.

What Data Transfer Rate Will Work for You?

Before choosing your network connection, you need to determine how many persons will be allowed Internet access, how many of them likely will use the network at the same time, and how much network traffic will be generated on average. You need to estimate the peak usage. You also should have an idea of how much delay in response time is acceptable. The particular services you choose partly determine these issues.

At present, network data rates can be grouped into two main categories: those supported by ordinary telephone lines, and those available through dedicated, high-speed connections. Low-cost modems capable of transferring 14,400 bps over ordinary telephone lines are readily

V

Using the Internet

available. Compression schemes such as V.42*bis* can increase the effective transfer rate by as much as a factor of four. Faster modems, although relatively expensive, are already available; even faster ones are being developed. You may find, however, that some network service providers support only dialup speeds up to 9,600 bps (or even 2,400 bps) and don't support data compression.

Dedicated connections, on the other hand, can offer rates from 56 Kbps to 44.746 Mbps (for T3 links). Unless you have a high-speed dedicated communications link, you can't use the high-end interactive network services such as teleconferencing. Most users can't justify the cost of such a link just to send real-time audio and video through the network. The two most likely reasons why you would need high data-transfer rates are as follows:

- You are servicing a large number of simultaneous interactive users

- You are receiving and transmitting massive amounts of data in items such as news feeds and large ftp transfers

If you can restrict these activities to times of days when few users are accessing the network, you may do fine with an ordinary telephone line connection. Note that you can transfer a megabyte of data in less than 12 minutes with a 14,400 bps rate.

How Often and How Long Will You Connect to the Network?

You need to consider three main issues concerning the number and length of your network connections:

- *Connect-time fees.* If your service provider charges you for connect time, maintaining a connection for more than a few hours per day, on average, is relatively expensive. If you need extended network connection time, you can cut costs by finding a provider that charges a flat monthly rate.

- *User access conflicts.* If you share your account with other users and your service provider doesn't allow multiple simultaneous logins using the same account, the persons sharing the account may have to wait long periods of time before they can connect. If access conflict is frequently a problem, you may want to set up an additional account or two.

■ *Continuous connection.* You obviously can't be aware that you have new mail or that someone wants to chat with you over the Internet unless you are connected. A continuous connection enables you to receive instant notification of incoming mail. The less frequently you connect, the less responsive you are to correspondence conducted through the network.

Many people find that they need to connect to the network only infrequently. You may determine, for example, that your network needs are limited to electronic mail and an occasional ftp transfer or Gopher access. Checking for new mail several times a day may be okay in your situation. In this case, you don't need to be connected to the network constantly; a provider that charges on a connect-time basis may be a good choice. If you want to be notified immediately when incoming mail is received, on the other hand, your local host must maintain a continuous Internet connection.

What Systems Administration Burdens Can You Handle?

You can access the Internet interactively without even having a computer at your location. You can use such on-line services as Delphi with just a computer terminal, a modem, and your home telephone line. At the other extreme, you can set up a dedicated computer for network activity with a dedicated communications link to an Internet provider.

The larger the facility, the larger the burdens of systems administration will be. Dedicated resources must be managed and maintained; security and reliability issues must be addressed. Sometimes a service interruption can be a serious condition (depending on your network usage). If so, you may need to maintain multiple systems with active, independent network connections to ensure continuous service.

The cost of a dedicated facility and staff for managing network access can surpass the access fees charged by your provider and the expense of your communications link combined. Estimating the costs—including money and hassle—of connecting to the network is important. To determine the amount of system supervision necessary in your case, consider the impact of two conditions on the organization:

■ A temporary loss of network connection

■ A security violation involving your network connection

The network connection could be interrupted due to equipment failure, pauses for routine maintenance and system upgrades, or a problem with your service provider. A security breach could arise from the actions of someone at your facility or from unauthorized access of your local system by someone on the network.

After you consider all these issues, you will have to determine the number of persons needed to manage your network connection and the expertise required of them. Remember to include staff for non-business hours, weekends, and holidays if you need coverage during these periods. Also, you may need more than one connection to the Internet to provide redundancy.

Evaluating a Specific Provider

Although evaluating the packages of services an individual provider offers is relatively easy, assessing issues such as system reliability, customer service, effective system speed, and ease of access is much more difficult. The explosive growth in Internet usage has placed many providers in the position of being overwhelmed, in effect, by their own success. User activity quickly can outgrow the providers' system capacity, resulting in poor performance.

Unfortunately, an access provider (especially a BBS or dialup service) with a user base too large for its computer or personnel resources—at least, with respect to providing Internet access—is common. This condition occurs for two primary reasons:

■ Internet users usually need to access the network several times a day. Depending on your needs, you may want to poll your provider to check for new e-mail messages as rarely as once a day or as often as once every 15 minutes. Your provider may not have enough inbound phone lines to allow its users this frequency of access.

■ Your provider's access to the network may be inadequate. Remember that your provider must, in turn, have a service provider that connects it to the network. Your service provider's network connection may use a data rate that can't support network traffic properly. In fact, the bottleneck you experience when using the network may not be directly due to your provider—another system in the connection between you and the network may be causing the problem.

If you are a commercial Internet user, you likely have low tolerance for poor system performance. You probably conduct critical communications with clients, vendors, and colleagues by sending e-mail through the Internet. If so, you depend on your service provider to be continually available to you. Business users of dialup services, for example, expect to connect to the network nearly every time on the first attempt. After logging in, they expect their transactions to be processed with essentially no system delays. They want data to be transferred at rates approaching the maximum rates supported by their modems. If they have questions about setting up their equipment for accessing the network, or about the use of network services, they expect help to be readily available.

At a minimum level, these expectations mean that an adequate number of knowledgeable customer service representatives must be available by phone during normal business hours. Also, questions or requests for assistance made outside business hours should receive prompt responses. Generally speaking, a commercial user should avoid obtaining network access through an organization that doesn't consider providing such a service to be an important revenue-generating activity. In other words, a free or cheap connection is no bargain if it is undependable.

Use the following three methods to evaluate a network service provider:

1. Find out whether the provider also offers non-Internet-related services. If so, try to determine whether providing Internet access is considered a primary function or whether it's just a bonus offering added to the provider's mainstream business.

   Also, try to ascertain whether you fit one of the user profiles for the system. You can expect better service from an organization dedicated to providing Internet access to users like you. Someone who wants an Internet connection for commercial purposes, for example, may be disappointed by the service provided through a BBS used mainly for playing computer games.

2. Talk to other users about their experiences with a particular pro-
    vider. You might even use an on-line forum where other users
    discuss problems and make suggestions for system improve-
    ments. Again, look for comments from users with needs similar
    to yours.

3. Some providers offer free trial periods during which you can
    explore their services. Such offers can take the form of a certain
    amount of free connect time or a usage credit for a specific mon-
    etary amount.

    If available, a trial period is clearly the best way to determine
    whether the provider can meet your needs. Make sure that you
    understand the complete terms of the trial period before begin-
    ning, and that you can cancel the service without further obliga-
    tion at any time.

Summary

For most potential Internet users, the main decision is whether you
require interactive access to the network. If not, you may find the access you need through a service such as CompuServe, WinNET Mail, or
a UUCP connection. These service types can be very cost-effective ways
to use electronic mail, and many such providers also offer USENET
news feeds.

If this type of service doesn't satisfy your needs, shell accounts and
low-cost SLIP/PPP connections are available that provide interactive
access to the Internet. From such an account you will be able to use
ftp, telnet, and navigational aids such as Gopher, in addition to accessing e-mail and network news.

Organizations that need to connect a large number of users may need
to establish a dedicated network connection. This undertaking is fairly
expensive; such a connection also implies a significant administrative
burden.

Fortunately, changing Internet service providers is fairly easy. Many
firms offer some type of Internet access. If your organization outgrows
its connection, you should have no difficulty finding a provider that
can provide the service you require.

Chapter 21

Making Connections Beyond the Internet

The Internet isn't a single unified entity, but a patchwork of thousands of interconnected smaller networks. Many of these networks were developed to support the on-line services, corporate communications networks, and research consortia that proliferated in the 1980s. Although the Internet existed at that time, it still was used primarily as a tool for network research and for communications between universities, research institutes, and government-affiliated organizations. Restrictions governing much of the network infrastructure prevented effective commercial use.

Most on-line services targeted owners of early PCs as their main market. Because modem transfer rates ran between 300 and 1,200 bps and PC disk space was limited, the idea of Internet connectivity for PCs seemed unrealistic at best. Of course, computer technology has progressed at a tremendous pace since those early days. Modems operating at 14.4 kbps are commonplace, and high-performance PCs now rival low-end workstations in computational power and disk capacity.

In recent years, high-powered computing platforms placed in network environments have become commonplace (even for smaller schools and businesses). During that time, many individual users came to appreciate the advantages of e-mail and file transfer through the local network, and many gained their first access to the Internet through their local system. As more users came to appreciate the advantages of an Internet connection, they also began to expect that any communications service they used would provide such global connectivity.

Today, every major on-line service provides a gateway to the Internet for e-mail exchanges. Some even support file transfer and other services for their customers.

Unfortunately, communicating with a member of one of these other networks isn't as simple as you may think. Although the physical and protocol-level connections may exist for moving data from one network to another, many application details are unique to each network. One of the most frustrating things about moving your e-mail to or from these other networks is that they aren't required to conform to the Domain Name System (DNS) naming schemes explained in Chapter 15, "Understanding the Structure of the Internet."

The Internetwork Cross-Reference

This chapter provides an internetwork addressing cross-reference—in other words, it provides a means for translating the addresses of one network type to an Internet name, and vice versa. It doesn't cross-reference every network's address to every other network; to do so would probably take several volumes. Instead, only the most popular networks and messaging services are listed here.

Getting the Cross-Reference from the Internet

This cross-reference is based in part on *The Inter-Network Mail Guide*, which is compiled and posted periodically by Scott Yanoff (yanoff@csd4.csd.uwm.edu). You can get the list by way of anonymous ftp (described in Chapter 18, "Using *ftp* and *telnet* with the Internet") from csd4.csd.uwm.edu, or you can use the finger utility on Mr. Yanoff's account name to get information about other ways of acquiring it.

If you need a more detailed and well-presented list in print, O'Reilly and Associates, Inc. publishes a book by Donnalyn Frey and Rick Adams titled *!%@:: A Directory of Electronic Mail Addressing and Networks*. The 1993 edition of this text gives feature and address information for more than 180 research, educational, and commercial networks. It also provides a comprehensive list of U.S. and international subdomains and their owning organizations. The subdomain list can be very useful for finding the network subdomain associated with a known company or organization.

Using This Chapter's Network Cross-Reference

The cross-reference is organized in alphabetical order by network name. Each entry in the list briefly describes the capabilities of the network and explains how to send e-mail to and from these networks. Conversion to and from the Internet DNS is given if needed, along with any limitations or restrictions you should know about.

In this chapter, the address formats that you use with each network service appear in computer-like typeface, such as `user@attmail.com`. Placeholders—that is, phrases you need to replace with the actual name—are `italicized`.

America Online

America Online is a commercial on-line service based in the United States that provides e-mail, forums, and file archives. Dialup access is available through Public Data Networks (PDNs) such as Sprintnet, so most users can log in with a local call. America Online uses proprietary software available for PC and Macintosh platforms.

It now provides only mail gateway service to the Internet.

Sending an e-mail message to an Internet name from America Online is simple. Merely address your message to the DNS name of the recipient—`recip@subdomain.domain`, for example—when you compose it.

To send e-mail to America Online users, you must convert their account names to DNS-compliant names by removing spaces and entering all characters in lowercase. Then add the America Online domain—`aol.com`—to each name. To send a message to the America Online account of `John Q`, for example, address the message to `johnq@aol.com`.

> **Note**
>
> When you send mail to an America Online account, the content of your mail is limited in two ways:
>
> - Messages are truncated to a maximum length of 32K characters.
>
> - Non-printable characters are translated into spaces.

V

Using the Internet

AppleLink

Apple Computer employees and organizations, dealers, developers, and users use the AppleLink information service. AppleLink is managed and operated on contract with General Electric Information Services (providers of GEnie). It provides e-mail, file archives, and on-line technical support for Apple and participating third-party products.

AppleLink supports an e-mail gateway to the Internet. To send e-mail to an Internet DNS name from AppleLink, add the string `@internet#` to the name. The address for an e-mail message to *dnsuser@sub.domain*, for example, would be as follows:

```
dnsuser@sub.domain@internet#
```

> **Note**
>
> The address of an outbound message from AppleLink must be less than 35 characters. The AppleLink/Internet e-mail gateway supports transfers of up to 4M long, thus allowing mail transfer of uuencoded binary files.

To send mail from Internet to an AppleLink user, simply add the address of the gateway to the user's name. To send mail to *alinkuser*, for example, address your message to *alinkuser*`@applelink.apple.com`.

AT&TMail

AT&TMail was developed initially to fulfill the business communications needs of AT&T. Since its inception, however, it has integrated other customers and services, including the former Western Union EasyLink service. AT&TMail provides e-mail, file transfer, BBS, and fax services.

To send e-mail to an Internet name such as *dnsuser@sub.domain*, address your message to `internet!`*sub.domain*`!`*dnsuser*.

To convert an AT&TMail user account name to a DNS name, simply connect the gateway name to the user name with an `@`. To send e-mail to *attmailuser*, for example, address the message to *attmailuser*`@attmail.com`.

EasyLink accounts are referenced by 8-digit numbers that start with 62—`62123456`, for example. To send mail to an EasyLink account, use `eln.attmail.com` to represent the gateway.

BITNET

BITNET is a global network of commercial organizations, research institutes, and universities. E-mail and file transfer services are available between BITNET and the Internet. BITNET user names are formatted as follows:

```
USER@NODE
```

Several gateways between Internet and BITNET are available. Two of the better known are `cunyvm.cuny.edu` and `mitvma.mit.edu`.

> **Tip**
>
> To obtain a list of organizations within the BITNET, subscribe to `listserv@bitnic.educom.edu` or ftp to `bitnic.educom.edu`.

The means for sending e-mail from BITNET to the Internet vary depending on the mail program running at the BITNET host. First, try addressing mail to the DNS name itself—*dnsuser@sub.domain*, for example. If that doesn't work, try addressing mail to *dnsuser%sub.domain@gateway*, replacing *gateway* with an actual BITNET gateway name such as `cunyvm.cuny.edu`.

To send e-mail from the Internet to *BITUSER@BITSITE*, address your mail to *bituser%bitsite*.`bitnet@gateway`, replacing *gateway* with the correct BITNET gateway name.

BIX

BYTE magazine created BIX—the Byte Information eXchange—to provide an on-line service oriented to its technically adept readership. BIX maintains an Internet gateway and has recently begun to offer access to Internet features such as ftp and telnet.

To send e-mail from BIX to Internet name *dnsuser@sub.domain*, address your message to `INTERNET:`*dnsuser@sub.domain*.

To send e-mail to a BIX user such as *bixuser*, address your message to *bixuser*`@bix.com`.

Calvacom (France)

Calvacom is a commercial messaging service provided within France.

To send e-mail from Calvacom to an Internet DNS name such as *dnsuser@sub.domain*, address your message to `EM/`*dnsuser@sub.domain*.

To send e-mail to a Calvacom user such as *caluser*, address your message to *caluser*@calvacom.fr.

> **Note**
>
> Message lengths are limited to 100,000 characters.

CompuServe

CompuServe is the largest and best-known on-line service provider in the United States. Dialup access of 1,200, 2,400, and 9,600 bps is available by way of a local call in most U.S. cities. Many forums available cover various discussion topics; a number of vendors such as Microsoft, Borland, and Lotus also offer technical support information.

A CompuServe account name consists of two numeric fields separated by a comma, such as 71234,1234.

CompuServe provides global public access to e-mail, forum, file transfer, and on-line chat services. Now, only an e-mail gateway is provided to the Internet, although connecting to Compu-Serve via telnet is possible. This method of connecting doesn't circumvent the fees charged with normal access, however.

To send e-mail to the Internet DNS name dnsuser@sub.domain from CompuServe, address your message to

```
INTERNET: dnsuser@sub.domain
```

CompuServe supports individual and organizational accounts. How you address your Internet e-mail depends on the account type of the CompuServe recipient. To send e-mail to an individual account, simply replace the comma in the address by a period and add the gateway name. To send e-mail to Compu-Serve user 71234,5677, for example, address your message to 71234.5677@CompuServe.com.

For a CompuServe organizational account of the form *organization*:*department*:*csuser*, address your e-mail to *csuser*@*department*.*organization*.CompuServe.com.

> **Note**
>
> The *department* field may not be present for some organizational accounts.

Connect

Connect is a professional information network, providing e-mail and file archive services. Connect maintains an e-mail gateway to the Internet.

To send e-mail from Connect to the Internet DNS name *dnsuser@sub.domain*, address your message to DASN and enter **"*dnsuser@sub.domain*"@DASN** as the first line of your message.

To send e-mail to a Connect user such as *CONUSER*, address your message to *CONUSER*@connectinc.com.

DFN (Germany)

DFN is the *Deutsches ForschungsNetz* (German Science Network), a large, X.400-based network connecting universities and research institutions. Some of its sites are also EARN/BITNET sites.

To send e-mail from DFN to an Internet DNS name such as *dnsuser@sub.domain*, try addressing your message to the DNS name directly. Another option you can try is BITNET style addressing, using *dnsuser%sub.domain@gateway* (replacing *gateway* with the address of a BITNET gateway).

How you address a DFN user depends on whether the user's host is connected by way of X.400 or EARN. To send e-mail to an X.400-based user such as *dfnxuser*, address your message to *dfnxuser@sub.domain*.dbp.de. For an EARN-based user such as *earnuser.earnsite*, send your message to *earnuser@earnsite*.bitnet.

> **Note**
>
> An address conversion program is available by telnet to sirius.dfn.de. Log in as adressen with no password. Address conversion is also available through e-mail by sending a message whose body contains the addresses to be converted (one per line) to
>
>   C=DE; ADMD=DBP; PRMD=dfn; S=adrserv
>
> from DFN or
>
>   adrserv@dfn.dbp.de
>
> from the Internet.

V

Using the Internet

EARN

EARN is the European Academic and Research Network. EARN connects universities and research institutes throughout Europe, the Middle East, and Africa. EARN uses BITNET style addressing—*EARNUSER@EARNSITE*.

> **Note**
>
> Network traffic within EARN is subject to an acceptable use policy forbidding commercial use.

The means for sending e-mail from EARN to the Internet vary, depending on the mail program running at the EARN host. First, try addressing your mail to the DNS name itself—*dnsuser@sub.domain*, for example. If that doesn't work, address mail to *dnsuser%sub.domain@gateway*, replacing *gateway* with a BITNET gateway name such as cunyvm.cuny.edu.

To send e-mail from the Internet to EARN user *EARNUSER@EARNSITE*, address your mail to *earnuser%earn.bitnet@gateway*, replacing *gateway* with a BITNET gateway name.

EASYnet

EASYnet is a network service operated by Digital Equipment Corporation (DEC). EASYnet now connects more than 100,000 computers worldwide, using a variety of connection protocols including DECnet and TCP/IP.

EASYnet provides e-mail, file transfer, USENET news, remote logins, and conferencing services.

The form of address to use when sending e-mail to the Internet from EASYnet depends on the operating system and software running on your host:

- Within the VMS operating system using DECnet mail, address your message to nm%DECWRL::"*user@domain*".

- From within Ultrix, address your message to *user%domain*@decwrl.dec.com.

- From within All-In-1, use *user@domain* @Internet.

> **Note**
>
> Notice the space between *domain* and the second @ symbol in the All-In-1 address form.

Sending e-mail to an EASYnet user also depends on the address form of the recipient. To send mail to *EASYHOST*::*EASYUSER*, for example, use the DNS name *easyuser*@*easyhost*.enet.dec.com. To send mail to an All-In-1 address such as John Public@AI1SITE, address your message to John.Public@AI1SITE.MTS.DEC.COM.

Envoy (Canada)

Envoy is an X.400-based commercial messaging service provided by Telecom Canada. Envoy provides an e-mail gateway to the Internet.

To send e-mail from Envoy to Internet name *dnsuser*@*sub.domain*, address your message to

```
[RFC822="user(a)sub.domain"]INTERNET/TELEMAIL/US
```

> **Note**
>
> You may need to convert some characters of your address. For @, use (a), as shown in the preceding example. Also convert ! characters to (b) and blanks to (u).

To send e-mail to an Envoy user, send your message by way of UUCPnet to uunet.uu.net!att!attmail!mhs!envoy!*envoyuser*.

EUnet

EUnet is a consortium of 25 national service providers of European network connectivity. One top-level domain is provided for each nation:

Domain	Country
at	Austria
be	Belgium
bg	Bulgaria

(continues)

V

Using the Internet

Domain	Country
ch	Switzerland
cz	Czech Republic
de	Germany
dk	Denmark
eg	Egypt
es	Spain
fi	Finland
fr	France
gb	Great Britain
gr	Greece
hu	Hungary
ie	Ireland
is	Iceland
it	Italy
lu	Luxembourg
nl	Netherlands
no	Norway
pt	Portugal
si	Slovenia
sk	Slovakia
su	Former Soviet Union
tn	Tunisia

EUnet uses Internet-style addresses.

FIDOnet

FIDOnet is a public network of bulletin board systems (BBSs). FIDOnet hosts consist of widely differing operating systems and platforms, including UNIX, DOS, Windows, Macintosh, Amiga, Atari, and others.

FIDOnet provides e-mail, file transfer, forum, and USENET services. Because the particular capabilities of each site depend on the BBS administrator (called a *system operator*, or *sysop*), not all services are available at all sites.

> ### Tip
>
> To obtain information on FIDOnet sites and network organization, send mail to `Hostmaster@f1.n1.z31.fidonet.org`.

FIDOnet addressing is based on a hierarchical organization of zones, networks, and nodes. The zone, network, and node fields are all numeric values. The general address form looks like the following:

```
firstname lastname@zone:net/node
```

A sample address, then, may be `john public@1:10/100`.

FIDOnet also hosts a number of *virtual* networks such as K12net, a network for educators dealing with topics of educational interest.

To send e-mail from FIDOnet to an Internet DNS name such as *dnsuser@sub.domain*, address your message to

```
dnsuser@sub.domain ON 1:1/31
```

To construct an Internet DNS name for a FIDOnet user, use the following template:

```
first.last@f<node>.n<net>.z<zone>.fidonet.org
```

To send e-mail to FIDOnet user `john public@1:2/3`, for example, address your message to `john.public@f3.n2.z1.fidonet.org`.

GEnie

GEnie is an on-line service provided by General Electric Information Services. GEnie provides e-mail, forums, file archives, and fax services to its customers. GEnie maintains an Internet e-mail gateway.

To send e-mail to an Internet name such as *dnsuser@sub.domain*, address your message to *dnsuser@sub.domain*@INET#.

To send e-mail to a GEnie user, such as *geuser*, address your message to *geuser*@genie.geis.com.

GeoNet Mailbox Services, GmbH

GeoNet is a commercial messaging service. GeoNet addresses have the form *user@host*, where *host* is geo1 (for Europe), geo2 (United Kingdom), or geo4 (US).

To send e-mail to Internet name *dnsuser@sub.domain*, address your message to DASN and enter *dnsuser@sub.domain*!*subject* as the subject line of the message.

To send e-mail to a GeoNet user such as *geouser@geohost*, address your message to *geouser@geohost*.geomail.org.

Gold-400 (United Kingdom)

Gold-400 is an X.400-based commercial messaging service operated by British Telecom.

To send e-mail to an Internet DNS name such as *dnsuser@sub.domain*, address your message to

/DD.RFC-822=*dnsuser*(a)*sub.domain*/O=uknet/PRMD=uk.ac/ADMD=gold 400/C=GB/

> **Note**
>
> You may need to convert some characters of your address. For @, use (a), as shown in the preceding address. Also convert ! characters to (b), % characters to (p), and " characters to (q).

To send e-mail to a Gold-400 user such as John Q. Public at JohnsOrg, address your message to

john.q.public@JohnsOrg.prmd.gold-400.gb

gsfcmail

Gfscmail is the in-house e-mail system for NASA's Goddard Space Flight Center.

V

Using the Internet

> **Tip**
>
> For help concerning interactions with gsfcmail, phone (800) 858-9947.

To send e-mail to Internet name *dnsuser@sub.domain*, address your mail to

```
(SITE:SMTPMAIL,ID:<dnsuser(a)sub.domain>)
```

or to

```
(C:USA,A:TELEMAIL,P:SMTPMAIL,ID:<dnsuser(a)sub.domain>)
```

Alternatively, you can send your message to POSTMAN and enter

```
To: dnsuser@sub.domain
```

as the first line of the message.

To send e-mail to a gsfcmail user such as *gsfcuser*, address your mail to *gsfcuser*@gsfcmail.nasa.gov.

IBM VNET

VNET is a network of mainframe computers using the Network Job Entry (NJE) protocols. VNET maintains an Internet e-mail gateway.

To send e-mail to Internet name *dnsuser@sub.domain*, address your message to the DNS name directly.

To send e-mail to a VNET user such as *vnetuser*, address your message to *vnetuser@vmnode.ibm_subdomain*.ibm.com.

> **Note**
>
> VNET provides an e-mail whois name/address service. To look up *vnetname*'s address, for example, send a message including the line whois *vnetname* to nic@vnet.ibm.com.

Keylink (Australia)

Keylink is an X.400-based commercial messaging service provided by Telecom Australia.

To send e-mail to John Q. Public with an Internet DNS name such as jpublic@*sub.domain*, address your message to

```
(C:au, A:telememo, P:oz.au, "RFC-822":"John
Public<jpublic(a)domain>")
```

> **Note**
>
> You may need to convert some characters of your address. For @, use (a), as shown in the preceding address. Also convert ! characters to (b), % characters to (p), and " characters to (q).

To send e-mail to Keylink user John Public of JohnsOrg, address your message to John.Public@JohnsOrg.telememo.au.

MCI Mail

MCI Mail is a commercial messaging service that provides an e-mail gateway to the Internet.

MCI Mail addresses consist of a user name and ID. The user name is sufficient for addressing, provided that it is unique. If it isn't unique, you must use the ID also. An example of an MCI Mail address is John Public (123-4567).

MCI Mail offers e-mail and telex to its customers. No file transfer or other network services are provided.

To send e-mail to John Q. Public with an Internet DNS name such as *dnsuser@sub.domain*, address your message by entering the following information at the mail composer prompts:

```
To: John Public (EMS)
EMS: INTERNET
Mbx: dnsuser@sub.domain
```

To send e-mail to an MCI Mail user such as *mci_user* with ID 123-4567, address your message to *mci_user*@mcimail.com if *mci_user* is unique; use *mci_user*/1234567@mcimail.com otherwise. (Note the conversion of a space in the name to an underscore.)

NASA Mail

NASA Mail is an enterprise wide messaging system for the National Aeronautics and Space Administration.

To send e-mail to Internet name *dnsuser*@*sub.domain*, address your message to (site:smtpmail,id:<*user*(a)*domain*>).

To send e-mail to a NASA Mail user such as *nasauser*, address your message to *nasauser*@nasamail.nasa.gov.

> **Note**
>
> You can get help with NASA Mail by phoning (205) 544-1771 or (800) 858-9947.

Prodigy

Prodigy, one of the newest on-line services, was the result of a cooperative effort by Sears and IBM. From its introduction, Prodigy has been targeted at a more casual computer user audience than most other on-line services.

Prodigy uses proprietary software that provides a graphical user interface (GUI) for its users. This software is available for PC and Macintosh platforms.

To send e-mail to a Prodigy user from the Internet, address your message to *userid*@prodigy.com, replacing *userid* with the user ID that Prodigy assigned to the recipient.

Prodigy users also can send e-mail to other Internet addresses, but they must have a software package called Mail Manager (which is available only for IBM-compatible PC users). To send e-mail to an Internet address, simply use the appropriate DNS name.

Relcom

Relcom provides network connectivity to the former Soviet Union. Relcom provides top-level domains for the following nations:

Domain Name	Country
by	Byelorussia
ee	Estonia
ge	Georgia

(continues)

Domain Name	Country
lt	Lithuania
lv	Latvia
su	Former Soviet Union
ua	Ukraine

Relcom uses Internet-style addressing.

SprintMail

SprintMail is an X.400-based messaging service. Dialup access to SprintMail is available through Public Data Networks (PDNs) such as Sprintnet, so most users can log in with a local call.

SprintMail provides e-mail, BBS, file transfer, telex, and fax services to its customers. It maintains an Internet e-mail gateway.

To send e-mail to Internet name *dnsuser@sub.domain*, address your message to

`(C:USA,A:TELEMAIL,P:INTERNET,"RFC 822":<dnsuser(a)sub.domain>) DEL`

Note that the @ in the name has been converted to (a).

To send e-mail to a SprintMail user such as `John Public` at `JohnsOrg`, address your message to `john_public@JohnsOrg.Sprint.com`.

> **Note**
>
> You can get help with SprintMail within the United States by calling (800) 336-0437 and pressing 2 on a Touch-Tone phone.

UUCPnet

UUCP (UNIX-to-UNIX Copy program) is a means for transferring data between machines, usually over a serial line or modem connection. UUNET is an organization that provides networked UUCP connections. UUCPnet uses *bang path* addressing, which reverses the order of DNS address fields and uses ! (referred to in UNIXdom as a *bang* symbol) rather than . as the field separator.

UUNET provides a gateway between UUCPnet and Internet.

To send e-mail to an Internet DNS name such as *dnsuser@sub.domain*, address your message to *uunet!domain!sub!dnsuser*. To send e-mail to a UUCPnet user such as *uunet!domain!sub!uucpuser*, address your message to *uucpuser%sub.domain@UUCP*.

Summary

As you can see from this chapter, most of the larger networks around the world have some type of connectivity with the Internet. Electronic mail can, in general, be sent between these networks and Internet hosts, and some networks also support file transfers as well.

In the future, you can expect many of these networks to adopt Internet-style e-mail addresses. As the number of Internet hosts continues to increase rapidly, many will also provide to their users a way to access the Internet interactively. In fact, some networks probably will switch to the TCP/IP protocol suite to ensure compatibility with other networks and allow for future growth.

V

Using the Internet

Part VI

Working with Applications

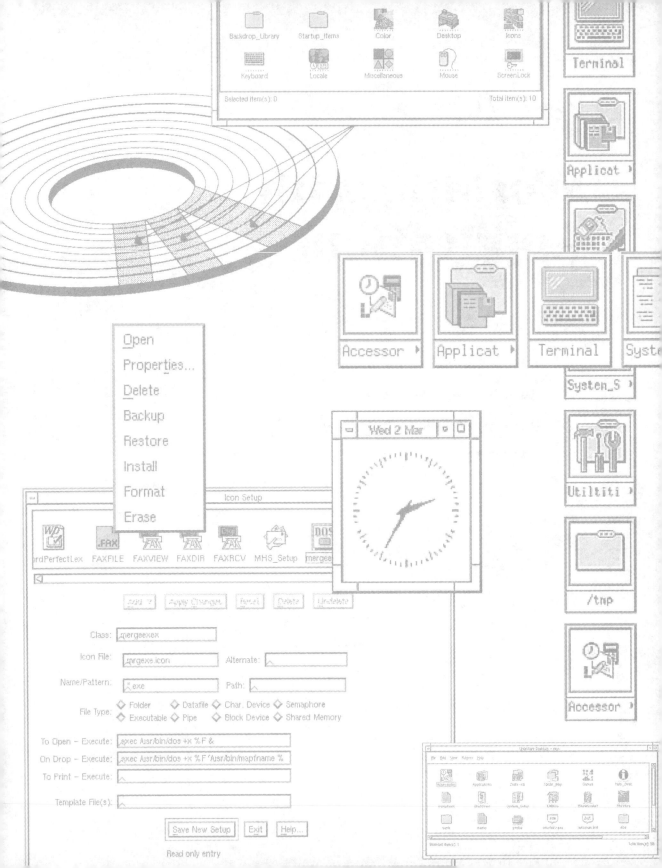

Backdrop_Library   Startup_Items   Color   Desktop   Icons

Keyboard   Locale   Miscellaneous   Mouse   ScreenLock

Selected item(s): 0   Total item(s): 10

Terminal

Applicat ▶

Open
Properties...
Delete
Backup
Restore
Install
Format
Erase

Accessor ▶   Applicat ▶   Terminal   Syste

System_S ▶

Utiltiti ▶

Icon Setup

WordPerfectLex   FAXFILE   FAXVIEW   FAXDIR   FAXRCV   MHS_Setup   mergee

Add ▼   Apply Changes   Reset   Delete   Undelete

Wed 2 Mar

/tmp

Accessor ▶

Class: mergeexex

Icon File: mrgexe.icon   Alternate:

Name/Pattern: *.exe   Path:

File Type: ◇ Folder   ◇ Datafile ◇ Char. Device ◇ Semaphore
             ◇ Executable ◇ Pipe   ◇ Block Device ◇ Shared Memory

To Open – Execute: exec /usr/bin/dos +x %F &

On Drop – Execute: exec /usr/bin/dos +x %F '/usr/bin/mapfname %

To Print – Execute:

Template File(s):

Save New Setup   Exit   Help...

Read only entry

Chapter 22

Loading UNIX Applications

UNIX systems initially contain only a core set of utilities and data files. The *system administrator* or a *superuser* (both of which have special operating privileges) install additional commands, user application programs, and various data files as required. The administrative process of installing new programs is often referred to as *loading programs*.

The word *loading* means copying the associated program files onto the system's hard disk and *configuring* the application (assigning resources) for proper operation on a specific system. The *configuration* of a program instructs it which device drivers to use to access those peripherals. *Device drivers* are small software components of the basic UNIX operating system core (the *kernel*) that control the CPU in routing input to and receiving output from system peripherals.

Most brands of UNIX ease the installation process by including a command to start the installation; AT&T's UNIX System V, Release 3 (SVR3) uses the `installpkg` command. SCO UNIX uses the `custom` command for installing applications. A graphical installation interface, Application Setup, is provided with UnixWare 1.1 (UNIX version SVR4.2), the successor to AT&T's UNIX. Most of these installation interfaces can unravel software packages that come in various archive formats, such as `tar`, `cpio`, and `pkgadd` formats.

Most application programs, with the exception of very simple ones, require a particular UNIX version and release number to install and run properly. On large systems, an administrator usually installs applications because most users don't have access to the tape or floppy drives. Administrative permission is also often needed to install components of the applications into

This chapter covers the following topics:

- Terms you need to know to understand UNIX application installation

- How to install large-scale, multiuser applications

- How to install smaller personal productivity applications

system directories. Components may include shared libraries, utilities, and devices that need to go into directories a normal user can't access.

By using graphical interface such as the one that comes with UnixWare, a PC owner running UNIX can install applications without any special knowledge of the UNIX system. This makes installation more acceptable for users who are used to installing personal productivity applications in DOS or Windows.

Key Terms Used in This Chapter

As you may have surmised if you read the introduction to this chapter, the installation of applications involves an expanded vocabulary. Table 22.1 lists some terms and their definitions with which you should be familiar.

Table 22.1: Application Installation Terms	
Term	**Definition**
superuser	The highest privileged user on the system. Also called the *root user*.
system administrator	The person in charge of keeping the UNIX system optimized and properly running. He or she has superuser privileges and can install new software onto the system. Others may also have superuser privileges (there is no restriction on the number of superusers).
loading applications	The initial installation or update of a program for a UNIX system. The process usually requires superuser privileges and access to the computer's tape or floppy disk drive.
version	Application software is typically written to be compatible with a particular version of UNIX (System V or BSD).
release	Associated with a particular version of UNIX is a release number. The latest version of UNIX System V is Release 4.2. SCO's UNIX is based on System V Release 3.2. The first part of the release number (the number to the left of the decimal point) represents a major release of new features; the second part (the part to the right of the decimal point) represents point releases that make corrections and minor enhancements to major releases. (For example, Release 3.0 was a major release and 3.1 and 3.2 were point releases.)
configuring	The act of setting up an application to work with your particular operating system. Configuring can include setting up the application for many users to use, putting it in accessible directories, or sharing it with the network.

Loading Major Applications

Installing, or *loading*, a major program onto a UNIX system is more complicated than installing a similar program on a single-tasking operating system
such as DOS or Apple Macintosh System 7. The multiuser nature of UNIX
means that any application on the system sometimes receives simultaneous
calls for access. A popular UNIX program, like one used for word processing
or a spreadsheet application, can run several copies of itself in RAM all day
long.

To further complicate installation, most application programs, with the exception of very simple ones, require configuration to your specific system
before they can be used. It is up to the system administrator or other
superuser installing the software to identify users and users' configurations
to an application's initialization tables.

For example, one user may have only an older character-based terminal while
another has a fancy new X-Windows terminal. The superuser must make sure
that the application responds correctly to the older terminal, sending only
characters (that is, letters and numbers) and that the X-Windows terminal
receives full advantage of the application's colors and graphics.

The system administrator manages the system and has the responsibility of
keeping it optimized (all programs up to current versions, proper user accounts assigned, and so forth). Superusers, which include the system administrator, are those persons having special privileges that allow them to run any
program on the system or access any file. Both the system administrator and
all superusers are discussed in greater detail in the following section.

As already stated, loading a program onto a UNIX system is more complicated than doing so on single-user operating systems. The superuser installing
an application may have to create new directories to house the files associated with this program. Some software packages call for the configuring or
reconfiguring of system devices, such as mice or terminals. Although the end
user worries only about learning the new program's features and operating
commands, the superuser must make sure that system resources are properly
allocated, configured, and maintained for this program (while, of course, not
screwing up any already installed applications).

VI

Working with Applications

The superuser also decides and implements who can use the new application. He or she accomplishes this by setting permissions so that only a certain user or group of users have access to the program (this topic is covered later in this chapter).

Understanding the loading of software onto a UNIX system first requires a basic knowledge of the responsibilities and privileges of the system administrator and superusers.

Understanding the System Administrator and Superusers

If you use DOS or the Macintosh's single-user operating system, you are your own system administrator. You install and run your applications. It is your responsibility to keep a current backup of files, maintain a proper amount of free space on the hard disk, make sure that the system runs optimally through memory management and other means, and do everything else required in the administration of an efficient and productive system.

On a traditional UNIX system, running on a mini-computer or mainframe with many users, someone is usually assigned to handle the administrative load. This person, called the *system administrator*, supports all other users on the system in their daily work by taking on the responsibility for backups, file-system maintenance, and all the other little things that go into keeping the system running at its best. The following list briefly summarizes what the system administrator does:

- Starts and stops the system, as needed

- Makes sure that there is enough free disk space and that file systems are free from error

- Tunes the system so that the maximum number of users have access to the system's hardware and software resources and so that the system operates as fast and as efficiently as possible

- Protects the system from unauthorized entry and destructive actions (a process called *system security*)

- Sets up connections to other computer systems (a process called *networking*)

- Sets up or closes user accounts on the system

- Works with vendors of software and hardware and those who have training or other support contracts for the system

- Installs, mounts, and troubleshoots terminals, printers, disk drives, and other pieces of both system and peripheral hardware

- Loads (installs) and maintains programs, including new application programs, operating system updates, and software-maintenance corrections

The more users on a system, the greater the workload of the system administrator. Some system administrators create a staff or otherwise alleviate their load by giving one or more other users *superuser* status. Superusers, to the system, have essentially the same rights and privileges of the system administrator—that is, they have access to all files, directories, and programs. They assist the administrator by helping maintain the system and, along with other administrative tasks, can load new programs as required.

A superuser also can assign users to do specific administrative tasks. For example, the uucp login can handle configuration for serial communications and the lp login has permission to set up printing. These logins are prevented from having other superuser privileges, however.

Superusers on Smaller Systems

The positions of system administrator and superuser are best handled by having separate accounts for these functions. In most smaller UNIX systems, neither of these are full-time positions. If you are a system administrator or superuser on such a system, you should log in using a regular user account when you are not performing system-related maintenance.

A standard user does not have all the privileges of a superuser—privileges that might be dangerous if, in the course of normal work, an accidental command is entered that has disastrous results. If something requiring superuser powers comes up, you can log out of the standard user account and log back on under your superuser account.

Another option, if you have the correct password, is to use the su command, available on many versions of UNIX. Entering **su** at the shell prompt causes the system to ask for a password. If you enter the correct password, the system recognizes you as a superuser until you exit back to regular user status. Yet another way is to use the login command, which allows you to become another user. Assuming that you have a superuser account, access it with the login command; when finished performing administrative duties, type **exit** to return to your regular user account, already in progress.

VI

Working with Applications

Installing Software

Most versions of UNIX assist the system administrator or superuser in maintaining the system in general and in loading software specifically. The graphical user interface in Novell's UnixWare 1.1 is a good example of the help that the various versions of UNIX now offer all users.

As Novell's literature emphasizes, the UnixWare GUI eliminates the need for users to remember and enter complex UNIX command syntax. By using simple point-and-click and drag-and-drop mouse operations, users can launch applications, select actions from pull-down menus, connect to networks, manage and print files, send electronic mail, and seek online help information. UnixWare's GUI is based on X-Windows and lets the user choose between either Motif or OPEN LOOK interfaces. A comprehensive online hypertext system offers help when and where it is needed.

This ease-of-use extends to the system administrator or superuser. UnixWare provides easy access to powerful UNIX administration capabilities. Activities such as reliable backup and recovery, security, user account management and configuration, and system-resource control are a seamless part of the UnixWare GUI. This latter item, system-resource control, includes the loading of new applications, the modifying of existing programs, and the updating of system software.

Other UNIX versions also provide software tools for loading new software and modifying that which is already installed. A common method in UNIX SVR3 and SVR4 is the sysadm menu. The choices on this menu and associated submenus give the system administrator a fast way to load new applications. Although this menu is also a feature of the popular SCO UNIX for the Intel platform and of that UNIX's predecessor, XENIX, future sysadm development has been abandoned in UNIX System V (see figs. 22.1 and 22.2).

Fig. 22.1
The main (opening) screen of a sysadm menu.

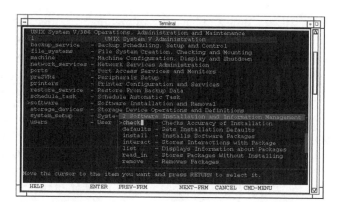

Fig. 22.2

The submenu of a sysadm program, which allows the administrator to load new software.

In the more recent versions of AT&T UNIX, now superseded by Novell's UnixWare but still extant in many thousands of installations, you choose the software option on the sysadm menu. This gives you access to tools for the installation, modification, or removal of programs from the system. Other UNIX sysadm menus work the same (with minor changes in names of submenus and tools).

Other versions of UNIX have simpler arrangements but require more effort on the part of the superuser because he or she must remember specific commands instead of making choices from a menu. Some installations of AT&T UNIX (again, using it as an example because of its wide installed base) call for use of these manual commands.

The installpkg command loads a new program onto the system, removepkg takes software off the system, and displaypkg shows a list of applications currently installed. Some systems also have a runpkg command, which allows you to *sometimes* run a program from floppy disk for a temporary installation or evaluation. This command may or may not work, depending on the system resources required. In other words, a full installation may be required before the program runs.

SCO XENIX—another old but widely installed version of UNIX—offers the custom command. Although later versions of XENIX sport the sysadm menu, they also have the custom command, which accesses an installation script. A superuser without access to the sysadm menu can still install software using custom.

Installing software using menus or commands is outwardly a relatively simple task; to the system itself, however, the task is complex. Applications for single-user operating systems, such as DOS programs, usually run only one

VI

Working with Applications

copy of themselves at a time and have no competing programs. In even a simple UNIX installation with only one user logged on, literally hundreds of processes can be running at the same time. Multiply this activity by several users all running programs—including some users who utilize the same *application*—and complexity increases dramatically.

The UNIX operating system excels at juggling a multitude of processes, programs, users, and peripherals simultaneously. To live in a UNIX environment, an application must be properly loaded. An ill-behaved application, or one improperly installed, can cause a system crash (when a process or program goes wild and locks the CPU, causing it to lose control of all the currently running programs). The system shuts down, all users are kicked off, and their programs are interrupted. There is often much wailing and gnashing of teeth from frustrated persons in the midst of some complicated task.

As the one loading a new application, it is the responsibility of the system administrator or superuser to make sure that the application is compatible with the system and to test the application after it is installed.

Looking for Supported Software

All the techniques for installing software presented in the preceding section predisposes that the software package you're loading is supported for the brand of UNIX system you use. The term *supported* means that the software developer has adhered to the installation scheme or schemes built into that brand of UNIX and that the system's loading programs, such as `installpkg`, recognize the format and installation instructions of the application. If this is so, the software package can be installed, removed, or updated using existing system aids.

Unsupported software is more difficult to use; it requires a great deal more manipulation—assuming that you can make it work at all. Normally, you do not have to worry about that problem because good system administrators make sure that programs are compatible with the system before purchasing them.

UnixWare and other SVR4.2 systems include support for UNIX applications originally produced for other UNIX system implementations. For example, UnixWare can run most SCO UNIX applications. Likewise, it can install applications in formats other than the `installpkg` format, such as `pkgadd`, `cpio`, `custom`, and `tar` formats.

> **Tip**
>
> Programs developed on your system, using UNIX's excellent programming environment, are compatible with your system from the start. Loading the program is usually a simple matter of finding the binary in the /bin directory and setting permissions properly. A good programmer does that for you and gives you the documentation explaining how the program works.

Reviewing File Permissions

Setting permissions for a supported software application usually occurs automatically during installation. The installation script that comes with your application usually installs each file with the proper ownership and permissions. Only if something goes wrong and a user who should be able to access the program cannot do so are you required to find the directory the application was copied to and check the permissions.

Typically, the executable file that you run to start the application is installed with permissions that let any user run the file; however, only the superuser can delete or overwrite it. The application is usually installed in a directory that has read and execute permissions, but no write permissions.

Solving Problems

A well-written and well-supported application loads onto your system with minimal requests for information from you. It sets permissions properly so that all you have to do is test the program and inform your users that the application is now available. This is often done through news bulletins or electronic mail.

◀ Chapter 13, "Working with E-mail," explains how to send messages to other users.

But things can and do go wrong in the loading of programs and their subsequent operation (or nonoperation). For whatever reason, if the program does not complete the loading process or fails to operate correctly after installation, it is your responsibility to determine *why* and fix the problem.

If a program does not load completely, your troubleshooting efforts often require no more than reading the documentation supplied with the application and looking for a list of exceptions or problems and their solutions. The system manuals are often also useful.

However, no one expects you to possess expertise and familiarity with the scores of applications various people in your company or institution may require. Occasionally, you'll require outside help. Your next step in

VI

Working with Applications

troubleshooting a problem involves contacting the application developer. Most software companies have support personnel who are familiar with installation problems and who can point you in the right direction with only one phone call.

Most larger systems also have contracts with companies that support the system's hardware and software. The trick is to determine which is causing your problem—equipment or program—and call the appropriate contractor.

Updating Applications

Your responsibility does not end after the application is loaded and available to the users that need it. Large application programs contain thousands of steps and are quite complex. Mistakes happen in the programming process, whether through error or because the programmers failed to anticipate your system's exact hardware or software configuration; the result is a conflict or other type of malfunction in operation.

In such cases, once a fix is supplied, you must load it onto your system. Sometimes, you may have to reload the entire application (or rather, a new and corrected version of the application). More often, you have to work with only a small correction program, called a *patch*. Still, you should be familiar with your system's way of accomplishing updates. Usually, all this is handled on the sysadm menu, making your life easier.

Good software applications are not static. Developers keep improving them, adding more features, and fine-tuning operation. From time to time, you may receive *updates* for applications on the system. Updates are like error patches, but are usually more extensive. Loading updates onto the system adds the new features to the application.

Large computer vendors usually have forums on online services, such as CompuServe, to keep you abreast of the latest updates and patches to their products. For example, to access Novell's forum on CompuServe, type **GO UNIVEL** to get the latest information on updates and problems related to UnixWare.

Removing Applications

If an application is superseded by another, better, package or is no longer used by any user on the system, removing it is a good idea. Disk space is always precious; you certainly don't want old, unused programs to hog space required by new applications.

The sysadm menu or its equivalent provides the removal procedure. Removal, like installation, of a program on a UNIX system is more complicated than for single-user operating systems. It is sometimes not enough just to erase the application's files and remove its directory. Drivers and other software connections must be disconnected to avoid future problems. Follow your system's removal procedure. Usually, however, the removal process deletes the files and devices it created.

Loading Small Applications

With the growing popularity of UnixWare and other PC-based UNIX systems, tasks like installing software is becoming more common for end users. Application vendors have responded by making more personal productivity applications available to UNIX users and by designing those applications to be easy to install and use.

In UnixWare and other SVR4.2 systems, the Desktop GUI provides a graphical means of installing applications so that a non-expert UNIX user can install the applications they need. The graphical interface for installing in UnixWare is the Application Setup window.

Because the Application Setup window recognizes many of the different formats a PC-based UNIX application can come in (`custom`, `tar`, `pkgadd`, and so on), you can try to use it for any UNIX application you have. It is recommended, however, that you read the documentation before you try to install software. Sometimes, there are special requirements or procedures for installing an application.

To use the Application Setup window to install an application in UnixWare, do the following:

1. Double-click on the Application Setup icon in the System Setup folder. The system catalogs the applications installed on your system and displays them on the Application Setup window, as shown in figure 22.3.

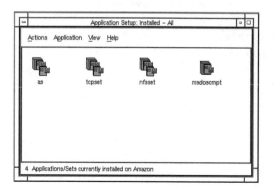

Fig. 22.3
The UnixWare Application Setup window, showing all currently installed applications.

2. Insert the medium on which the application was distributed into the appropriate drive on your computer (floppy, tape, or CD-ROM).

3. Click on View, click on Uninstalled Applns, and then click on the medium containing the application. The system catalogs the applications you can install from that medium. (Sometimes, an application consists of several installable packages on the same medium. For example, a word processor may have a font package and a utilities package in addition to the basic word processing application.)

4. Click on the icon for the application you want to install.

5. Click on Application and then click on Install. A Terminal window opens and the installation procedure for that application displays any questions it needs to complete the installation. When the installation is complete, a message appears telling you it was successful or responding with an error message.

Summary

This chapter acquainted you with loading application programs onto a UNIX system. UNIX systems initially have only the core operating system and utility programs. On large UNIX systems, applications must be loaded (installed) onto the system by someone having special system privileges, such as the system administrator or a superuser.

Because applications on UNIX must be set up to access the system's resources (through device drivers) and for multiuser operation, they require a loading procedure for proper installation. The system administrator must also correctly set permissions before users can access and use the application.

With the advent of the UnixWare Desktop GUI and the increased number of personal productivity applications available for UNIX, installation of applications is becoming a more common activity for average users. The Application Setup window in UnixWare provides a simplified interface for UNIX application installation.

But what if the program you want to use on the system is a DOS application? The next chapter introduces you to running DOS programs on a UNIX system.

Chapter 23

Running DOS Applications

If UNIX is so wonderful, why even mention DOS? After all, interest in UNIX as an operating system for personal computers grows at a rapid rate in the computer industry and among end users. Who needs DOS?

With apologies to the aficionados of UNIX, Macintosh, and other operating systems, MS-DOS has become the standard in desktop computing. This admittedly limited and awkward single-user system rules the computing world through the sheer force of numbers. Tens of millions of DOS installations—exceeding the installed UNIX base by a factor of many times—ensures that the DOS market has immense clout in the hearts, eyes, and pocketbooks of software developers.

Because of the MS-DOS/IBM PC-compatible dominance in the marketplace, the majority of computer resources and individual experience is often DOS based. Moving over to UNIX makes a lot of sense in the long run, but how do you maintain your investment of time and money in DOS? Having all the advantages of UNIX and the ability to run DOS applications at the same time would be the best of both worlds. A UNIX system administrator can and should expect requests from users for DOS applications. Luckily, those are not impossible dreams because you *can* run DOS programs on a UNIX system. In fact, UnixWare from Novell comes with DOS emulation built in. You just click on an icon to start a DOS or Windows session.

The answer is *DOS-under-UNIX*, and that's what this chapter is about. Using a technique called *software emulation*, your UNIX operating system creates a DOS environment which, to an application, looks just like an IBM-compatible personal computer. Through the magic and power of UNIX, you can have several of these DOS sessions running at once, and your fellow users on the system can also run DOS sessions.

Here's an exciting concept that may bring the power of UNIX home to you: If you have UNIX installed on a computer based on the Intel Pentium, 486, or 386 microprocessor, you can run several sessions of DOS at once. This is an excellent example of the real power of UNIX; using the exact same hardware on which DOS can do only one thing at a time, UNIX allows you to perform many jobs simultaneously.

Key Terms Used in This Chapter

An understanding of several new terms will help your comprehension of this chapter. Table 23.1 lists some terms and their definitions with which you should be familiar.

Table 23.1: DOS Application-Installation-Related Terms	
Term	**Definition**
MS-DOS	The Microsoft Disk Operating System, a single-user operating system primarily used on IBM PC-compatible personal computers; by numbers, it is currently the predominant operating system in the world. Note that PC DOS and Novell DOS are also available versions of DOS. PC DOS, available from IBM, is essentially the same as MS-DOS. Novell DOS, on the other hand, was developed separately from Microsoft's version. Novell DOS has its roots in DR-DOS (developed by Digital Research). Digital Research was purchased by Novell and the product name was changed. For the purposes of this chapter, the term *DOS* refers generically to any of these products. When necessary to distinguish between products, the full product name is used.
software emulation	A program that creates a complete operating system environment using software only. In this chapter, it specifically means fooling a DOS application into thinking it is running on an IBM-compatible personal computer that uses DOS.

Term	Definition
DOS-under-UNIX	DOS environments emulated on a UNIX system.
virtual PC	DOS sessions running under UNIX. The simultaneous sessions may exist by means of software only, but to applications, they look like real computers, hence the use of *virtual* (computers that do not really exist but whose existence is implied to the applications being run within those environments).
Intel family	The Pentium, 80486, 80386, 80286, 8088, and 8086 CPUs.

Understanding and Using DOS-under-UNIX

DOS applications are almost ubiquitous. As a system administrator or a regular user, you will face the need or desire to run DOS programs on your UNIX system on occasion. If your duties include that of the administrator, your responsibilities include providing DOS capabilities to other users—and accomplishing the performance tuning, memory management, and device sharing installation and maintenance necessary for efficient DOS emulation (although some say that efficient DOS operation is an oxymoron).

Software that does DOS emulation is now available for most versions of UNIX, even those for CPUs other than the Intel family. But, as you read in the following sections, it's easier to implement DOS emulation on an Intel-made CPU because DOS is designed for those CPUs. However, DOS emulations exist for various RISC chips as well.

This chapter is concerned with *emulation*, or the fooling of DOS applications into thinking they really are running on DOS. The big trend these days in the DOS world is toward Microsoft Windows applications. Windows is a Graphical User Interface (GUI) that overlays DOS.

Windows is designed for ease of use and also provides display, printing, file management, and other services to the applications it supports. Most of the truly useful applications under not just DOS but in all of computerdom will

VI

Working with Applications

soon be Windows applications. Like it or not, such is the force of the current marketplace. Other factors like Windows NT, the new operating system from Microsoft that does not require DOS to run and that supports existing Windows applications, only reinforce this fact of life.

Most DOS emulators for UNIX can also be made to run Windows. In that case, Windows is also being emulated. In effect, you then have three operating systems in layers: UNIX emulating DOS which, in turn, is running Windows. Even on fast UNIX systems, this can result in a slow response time. The way around this slowness is Wabi: Windows Application Binary Interface, announced by SunSoft and UNIX System Laboratories (USL) in May 1993, just before USL sold the rights to UNIX to Novell. Wabi is software that lets both Solaris (Sun's version of UNIX on SPARC and Intel processors) and UNIX System V Release 4 and Release 4.2 run Windows 3.x applications without requiring either DOS or Windows code. Other software developers are beginning to offer similar software that can run Windows applications on UNIX systems without needing DOS or Windows at all. Wabi (a trademark of SunSoft) and similar programs are covered in the next chapter, "Running Windows Applications."

Looking at DOS Emulations on Sun Systems

Sun is a leading maker of UNIX workstations. Like Hewlett-Packard, DEC Alpha, IBM RS6000, and other popular and powerful workstations, Sun systems now use RISC (Reduced Instruction Set Computing) chips. These chips are usually faster and have greater capacity than the Intel family of chips (Pentiums, 80486s, 80386s, and so on) found in IBM-compatible personal computers. Sun workstations are popular and widespread in larger UNIX installations and as stand-alone workstations for engineering, publishing, and other CPU-intensive jobs. They are good examples when you are looking at DOS emulation on non-Intel machines.

It should be noted again that DOS emulation is easier on Intel chips because DOS was created for that chip and only runs on the Intel family in its native installations. Although Sun systems and other RISC-based versions of UNIX can and do emulate DOS and run DOS and Windows applications, the Intel chip does it better, even when that Intel chip is running DOS-under-UNIX. Sun and other manufacturers also offer a hardware solution: plug-in circuit boards that have an Intel chip used for DOS emulation.

Actually, Sun has several DOS-under-UNIX solutions. As Sun describes it, their SunSelect SunPC product family lets you run thousands of the leading MS-DOS and Microsoft Windows applications, plus your in-house applications, on the SPARC workstation. SunPC products eliminate the need to switch between the workstation and a PC to get your job done. In fact, SunPC products integrate MS-DOS and Windows applications with your UNIX environment, letting you copy and paste text between DOS and UNIX windows, access network printers and CD drives from the SunPC window, and share the UNIX file system—all for easy interoperation and reduced costs.

Sun says the SunPC product family gives you the flexibility to choose the level of power and functionality you need. By itself, SunPC software gives you the power of a complete 286 PC; you can run MS-DOS and Microsoft Windows applications that require lots of memory and take advantage of SunPC 80287 floating-point emulation. With its VGA graphics capabilities, SunPC software gives you the benefit of running your applications in a high-resolution color window.

You can get even more PC power with the addition of a SunPC Accelerator SBus card. The SunPC Accelerator SX, with its powerful 16 MHz 486SX CPU and custom acceleration circuitry, is ideal for running Microsoft Windows and applications that require high-performance or SuperVGA graphics. Alternatively, choose the 25 MHz SunPC Accelerator DX, the most powerful 486 SBus accelerator available for SunPC software, for even higher performance, built-in floating-point acceleration, and SuperVGA graphics.

SunPC software has an OPEN LOOK graphical user interface, making your system easy to configure: you change printer settings, memory size, or video mode by simply pointing and clicking on pull-down menus. And with the SunPC floating license, any user on your network can take advantage of the power and functionality of SunPC software.

Sun emphasizes that without a hardware accelerator card, SunPC software emulates an 80286 processor. Applications that run acceptably on an 80286 or 80386SX PC also perform satisfactorily in a SunPC software session. If you are running character-based DOS applications, and occasionally use Windows 3.x, a SunPC may suit your needs without an accelerator card. By installing SunPC 80486SX 16 MHz or 80486DX 25 MHz accelerator cards, you replace the software-based 80286 emulation with hardware-based 486SX emulation—a noticeable performance improvement.

VI

Working with Applications

Other types of DOS emulation solutions are available for other brands of RISC-based workstations (see your hardware vendor for options). But if your UNIX system is based on the Intel family of microprocessors (as more and more are these days), DOS emulation is even easier.

Looking at DOS Emulations on the Intel Platform

Various versions of UNIX for the Intel platform (IBM PC-compatible computers) have charged into the arena and are jousting for supremacy against other contenders for the desktop crown over the mortally wounded body of a dying DOS. Will the winner be one of the UNIX versions or OS/2 or Windows NT or some new operating system technology yet to be revealed (such as the IBM/Apple-sponsored consortium of Taligent)? Or will the desktop market simply becomes less of the DOS/Windows monolith it is now as competition increases?

As it stands, UNIX has a good advantage in that it is already a long-proven and powerful multitasking, multiuser, 32-bit operating system. To this head start, add its capability of running popular DOS and Windows applications, and you see that UNIX has a real chance of winning the race for the desktop. All the best-selling versions of UNIX for the Intel microprocessors offer DOS emulation. UnixWare from Novell, SCO UNIX and OpenDesktop products, Steven Jobs' NeXTStep, Sun's Solaris (available in both RISC and Intel versions), and others are ready to replace DOS on your PC while still giving you the option of running your DOS and Windows applications.

Emulating DOS on an Intel microprocessor has built-in design advantages because of the design of the CPU. By using a *protected mode* of the Intel chip, an independent environment can be set up for any application, including an operating system. The software is thus fooled into thinking it is running its own 8086 or 80286 Intel-CPU computer. Depending on the amount of memory available, a number of these *virtual PC* sessions can run simultaneously. Expanded memory (EMS) is even available to the DOS applications that call for it.

Several software DOS emulators are now available for Intel-platform versions of UNIX, including Insignia Software's SoftPC, Locus Computing Corporation's Merge 386 (included with UnixWare), and Phoenix Technologies' VP/ix. Your UNIX vendor may offer you one of these emulators under a different name (a "house" brand), but these three are the main vendors.

All these DOS emulators work well as long as your DOS application is well behaved. Unfortunately, some DOS programs are not. The memory and device handling applications that are part of DOS (and that are the reason so many people are looking for an alternative operating system) are the cause of a lot of compatibility problems. Frustrated DOS application programmers have pushed DOS to the limit and considerably beyond, doing several ingenious but nonstandard things to obtain even more performance from a balky operating system. Some of these things blow the mind of an emulator.

Lotus 1-2-3, the popular DOS spreadsheet, is a good example. Lotus 1-2-3 Release 3.1 really extends and pushes DOS hard. It probably will crash under most DOS emulators. Any other DOS application that accesses devices directly can also create problems. Trying to connect to a NetWare server under a DOS emulator brings nasty surprises. Running Windows 3.1 in enhanced mode also causes crashes. In both cases, the software fights with UNIX for direct control of the processor. These conflicts tend to shut down the system—at times, dramatically and emphatically.

Device Drivers

UNIX *device drivers* have been introduced in previous chapters. These small programs instruct the UNIX operating system in routing peripheral input and output. Drivers are an integral design feature of UNIX; a proper driver must be installed before the system sees and uses any device. This often causes problems in DOS emulation. There are many hundreds of peripherals and little in the way of real standards. Making operational all your disks, network devices, mice, and so forth can be time consuming. It is up to the system administrator or, in the case of a single-user system, the end user to find and install the right driver for a particular piece of hardware. A good starting point is the manufacturer of the peripheral.

Caution
Many inexpensive peripherals are designed to work only on a single-user DOS machine; no UNIX driver is available for them. Check before you buy.

The driver situation is improving. Most versions of UNIX for the Intel platform now come with a number of standard drivers for various types of disks, Logitech and Microsoft mice, network interface cards, tape drives, and multiport adapter boards.

VI

Working with Applications

The Virtual PC

Intel did a good job designing the 80386 microprocessor chip; it was a quantum leap over the 80286. The 80486 and Pentium chips that followed are not as great a jump, but continue the tradition of desktop power that allowed DOS, despite its many shortcomings, to become the dominant operating system today.

The virtual, or protected, mode of the 80386 and higher Intel chips makes it easy for an Intel-based UNIX to run many DOS sessions at once while, it must be emphasized, still providing regular UNIX service for all those users not using DOS. In this, UNIX has an advantage over IBM's OS/2 (a competing multitasking system, albeit one designed for just a single user): OS/2 doesn't support the virtual mode and, thus, is restricted to running only one DOS session at a time. The term *protected mode* means that the virtual PC is not affected by the CPU running other virtual PCs as well as performing other unrelated tasks simultaneously.

An 80386 in protected mode has considerable power. The internal architecture of the CPU in this mode is 32 bits, which allows the addressing of up to 4 gigabytes of memory. The chip can easily handle large programs and vast amounts of data. Protected mode also provides memory management and the virtual 8086 modes that ease DOS emulation under UNIX.

The virtual 8086 mode "fools" DOS applications into thinking they are running on a standard 8086-based personal computer. However, the much more powerful 80386, 80486, or Pentium is really running things behind the scenes. For example, DOS character-based programs write characters to the display screen addresses of the PC under normal, single-user operation. In 8086 virtual mode, the DOS application writes to the same addresses (and thus sees no differences) but the 80386 or higher CPU decides where and when to send those characters. The output can be routed, for example, to a terminal on the system or a DOS window on an X-Windows console.

In other words, the regular single-minded control of all hardware that DOS programs have is modified into standard input and output that the UNIX operating system fits into its multitasking, multiuser scheme. Again, this is possible under total software emulation on non-Intel platforms, but the Intel family of microprocessors makes it faster with the hardware-assisted boost of the virtual 8086 mode.

Reality always intrudes, even on UNIX systems. Use of the virtual 8086 mode and the number of sessions depends somewhat (but not totally) on system hardware limitations. For example, if you are running an Intel-based UNIX on a 80486 computer with only 8 megabytes of memory, it is possible for the operating system to use the top 4 megabytes of memory to set up four independent virtual 8086 DOS environments. Each session is isolated so that a DOS application behaving badly in one session cannot corrupt any of the others. UNIX sees those sessions as just four more of the many tasks and processes it is currently running. Now for some magic: as far as UNIX is concerned, the DOS sessions are only other tasks to which it allocates CPU time slices in rotation with all the other currently active processes. Like other processes, if the working memory becomes full, it swaps memory contents on and off of the hard disk. This cybernetic sleight of hand means that complete virtual 8086 DOS environments can swap back and forth to disk, allowing the system to run more sessions than it has actual physical memory for! Of course, the more disk swapping the system does, the slower its overall operation. Still, the potential far exceeds that of a single-user system on the exact same hardware.

The two leading DOS emulation software packages for Intel-based versions of UNIX—Merge 386 and VP/ix—both set up virtual 8086 environments to imitate as closely as possible the hardware and software parameters of an ordinary IBM-compatible personal computer running DOS. This fools most DOS applications because they see the BIOS and screen buffer at the addresses they expect to see them. Interrupts and other services work as expected, and the communications ports are apparently in the proper place (even though UNIX may be using another device entirely).

Although DOS emulation using the virtual 8086 mode is convincing to the vast majority of DOS applications, no current DOS emulator can completely imitate all facets of a PC's hardware and software. Applications that depend on precise timing (something that multitasking systems using CPU time-slicing features are a bit lax on) tend to bomb. Overall, however, DOS emulation provides a worthwhile added dimension to any UNIX system because of the sheer pervasiveness of significant DOS applications.

Merge 386/486 for UNIX

Merge 386/486 for UNIX (included with UnixWare and shown in fig. 23.1) is one of the two leading DOS emulators for UNIX on the Intel platform (VP/ix is the other). Over 300,000 of these packages have been sold. Merge requires a minimum of 1MB of RAM and 5MB of disk storage space. The current version was released in 1993. Merge is made by Lotus Computing Corporation in Inglewood, California.

Fig. 23.1
Two DOS sessions
running under
Merge, shown on
the UnixWare
Desktop.

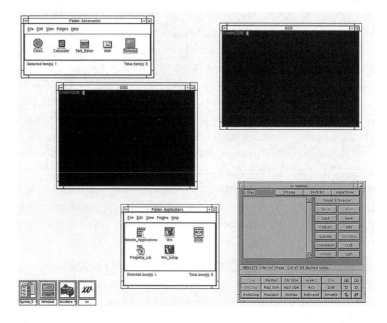

Merge is a flexible way to implement DOS emulation on your UNIX for Intel system. Of course, you will want to make sure that Merge supports your specific brand of UNIX. Extensive documentation is supplied with the package and you should expect to do some heavy reading. Merge's flexibility means that it requires some work to properly configure and tune it for efficient operation on your system.

Merge 386/486 allows you to run most DOS commands from UNIX and most UNIX commands from DOS. As its name implies, it *merges* the two operating systems, letting you install new software that is accessible to both operating systems. You can even create pipes for data from one system to the other. Merge, by default, uses the UNIX file system. Any DOS partitions on your hard disk are available only to DOS software running under Merge.

Merge 386/486 has a multiscreen feature that allows a user on the system console to switch from one session to another. Terminal users are limited to only one session of DOS at a time, but the console user can have several simultaneous DOS and UNIX sessions, with convenient switching between those sessions. With UnixWare, you can have multiple DOS and Windows sessions on the Desktop, running alongside UNIX applications.

There are numerous options for fine-tuning the performance of Merge 386/486. These options allow you to specify the amount of memory, the default console screen type, how printers operate, and the configuration of other devices including mice. CONFIG.SYS and AUTOEXEC.BAT files can be set up for the entire system or for each individual user. Other options, such as one that forces DOS applications that poll the keyboard to sleep when not in use, speed general system efficiency.

VP/ix

The other major DOS emulation software for Intel-based versions of UNIX is VP/ix. VP/ix was developed as a joint venture of Interactive Systems Corporation and Phoenix Technologies (a leading manufacturer of BIOS chips for IBM-compatible PCs). This program runs most DOS applications, supports VGA graphics as well as EMS, and handles the SunRiver high-speed, high-resolution graphics terminal, which allows several users to simultaneously use DOS (or UNIX) graphics software. VP/ix is available as an add-on package directly from several UNIX vendors, including SCO and Sun.

Each VP/ix session requires approximately 1MB of memory, in addition to whatever amount of RAM is used by the UNIX system itself (usually about 2MB on an Intel platform). UNIX uses disk swapping to run more tasks than can fit into memory at once. With disk swapping, a computer with 4MB of memory can run five simultaneous VP/ix sessions in addition to UNIX itself. Again, once the memory load is heavy enough to require disk swapping, you will notice some loss in overall system speed. For better performance, you should increase your system RAM to 8MB or even 16MB.

VP/ix allows you to install and run Microsoft Windows, as well as most major DOS and Windows applications. If you are the system administrator or a superuser, you can configure and tune VP/ix for each user. Like Merge 386/486, VP/ix comes with copious documentation; as with Merge, you'll need it.

Understanding Memory Management for DOS Emulation

The single greatest pain connected with DOS is memory management. By design, DOS has a 640KB limitation on working memory. In the early 80s, when the first IBM PCs came with only 64KB of RAM, the 640KB limit was thought to be far in excess of the maximum that would ever be needed. Today, many single programs take up more than 640KB, much less run in that cramped space.

VI

Working with Applications

Extended and expanded (EMS) memory systems for DOS were developed in desperate attempts to overcome the infamous 640KB wall. Companies like the manufacturers of QEMM and 386Max have become rich supplying utilities that eke out a few more precious kilobytes of working memory. Despite the fact that your DOS-based machine may have 16MB of working memory, it takes some real programming magic to access all but 640KB of that memory.

UNIX does not have a 640KB limitation. As you saw earlier in this chapter, UNIX and OS/2 operate your PC's microprocessor in protected mode, using all your system's extended memory with the necessary memory management built in to access 4 gigabytes (4,000 megabytes) of memory—a lot more than 640KB.

UNIX's wonderful memory management carries over to the implementation of DOS-emulation sessions. You don't have to worry about loading applications high or loading TSR (Terminate and Stay Resident) programs; under UNIX's multitasking environment, all processes are essentially TSRs.

This does not mean all your memory-management problems disappear when you switch to UNIX. The UNIX operating system is big and requires a lot more RAM and disk resources from PCs. Nor does running DOS applications under a DOS emulator become any less of a pain. Along with emulating the DOS environment for the application, you must emulate EMS and the other DOS memory-management techniques so that the application is fooled into running.

DOS emulation is a memory hog regardless of the emulation package you use. It requires at least 1MB per session, on top of the UNIX operating system's need for another 2MB.

A good system administrator figures out the typical number of DOS sessions that users run on the system and makes sure that there is enough memory to handle the demand. Memory prices tend to go up and down; when they are down, consider adding another 8MB or 16MB to your system. The more RAM, the faster a multitasking system works.

Tip

In a system that uses Merge 386/486, VP/ix, Sun's SoftPC, or any other DOS emulator, the system administrator should tune and configure the system for the least amount of memory possible for each session. Being a memory miser with DOS emulation speeds up the overall system. Specific configuration and tuning tricks are covered in the documentation of your DOS emulation package.

Summary

This chapter gave you the basics about running DOS applications under UNIX. UNIX is a superior operating system to DOS but, because of the economics of the market, many more applications are available for DOS than for UNIX. Luckily, you can run many DOS applications on a UNIX system by using DOS-emulation software. Such software creates a virtual PC that fools DOS applications into running as if they were on a stand-alone personal computer.

You can emulate DOS only in software, so that non-Intel versions of UNIX can run DOS applications. Software emulation of DOS is slower than accessing the protected mode of Intel CPUs and getting a hardware boost in speed. Several workstation manufacturers, such as Sun, offer plug-in boards that have Intel microprocessors to accelerate DOS emulation.

Merge 386/486 and VP/ix are the two leading DOS emulators for versions of UNIX running on the Intel family of CPUs. Memory management is crucial for keeping a UNIX system running efficiently. You must configure and fine-tune DOS-emulation software so that it uses the least amount of memory possible.

Although you can run Microsoft Windows and its applications with DOS-emulation packages, they run much faster if a Wabi-type program runs Windows application packages directly, bypassing DOS emulation entirely. The next chapter covers that and the other ways in which you can run Windows software on a UNIX system.

VI

Working with Applications

Chapter 24

Running Windows Applications

"A thermonuclear desktop war," is what Scott McNealy, CEO of Sun Microsystems, called it in his keynote speech at Uniforum '92. He was describing UNIX's competition with OS/2, Windows NT, and other operating systems for the desktop computer market.

As you know, DOS and the IBM-compatible personal computer have created an immense market. Tens of millions of people who never even thought about computers before now find the machines indispensable. But the very market DOS created is its undoing; the basic design of this single-user system limits it. Once computers became the necessity they now are, people started demanding more and more from them. And DOS is folding under the pressure. UNIX vendors, IBM with OS/2, and even Microsoft, whose creature DOS is, vie to replace it on the desktop.

One hurdle to overcome in replacing DOS is the many thousands of popular and useful applications that run on DOS and its Graphical User Interface (GUI), Windows. People may bemoan the shortcomings of DOS and Windows, but they want their applications, the programs that make computers an indispensable part of the workplace. As a system administrator, one way you have of getting people to start using the UNIX system to its full advantage is by letting them bring their favorite DOS and Windows applications along with them.

In this chapter, you learn the following:

- Terms relating to UNIX-over-Windows

- Using UNIX-over-Windows

- Running Windows with DOS emulation

VI

Working with Applications

Key Terms Used in This Chapter

An understanding of several new terms will help your comprehension of this chapter. Table 24.1 lists some terms and definitions with which you should be familiar.

Table 24.1: Windows Application-Installation-Related Terms	
Term	**Definition**
Microsoft Windows	The GUI from Microsoft, the developer of DOS. Windows runs on top of DOS; a number of exceptionally useful applications have been developed for it.
Windows application	A program developed to run in the Microsoft Windows GUI environment. Windows provides printer, display, file management, and other services for applications, making them smaller, more economical to develop, and consistent in operation with other Windows applications, simplifying the user's learning curve.
GUI	Graphical User Interface, an environment like Microsoft Windows and the UNIX-based X-Windows that uses graphic elements such as icons and mouse-type pointing devices to make the operation of programs easier. The GUI concept was developed first by Xerox and was made famous on the Apple Macintosh.
Windows-over-UNIX	The process by which Windows application programs are run on a UNIX system without having either Windows or DOS present.
Wabi	Windows Application Binary Interface (the capitalization of *Wabi* is correct, even though the word is an acronym). A software method from Sun Microsystems' SunSelect division that allows implementation of Windows-over-UNIX by running Windows applications without running Windows.

Understanding UNIX-over-Windows

Sun Microsystems launched the first strike in the "thermonuclear desktop war" with Wabi (pronounced *wah-be*), the Windows Application Binary Interface. Microsoft retaliated almost simultaneously by giving its blessing to SoftWindows, a similar Windows-over-UNIX package under development by Insignia Solutions of Mountain View, California. These two products offer solutions for running Windows applications on UNIX systems: Windows applications run on UNIX as direct binaries, without the high system overhead that the combination of a DOS emulator and native Windows requires to fool a program into thinking it is on a DOS system running Windows.

> **Note**
>
> Although the Wabi and SoftWindows methods of running Windows applications are best, this chapter also explains how to run Windows applications in an emulated DOS environment. On some systems, this latter option may be the only option for the time being.

The job of running Windows applications on a UNIX operating system is challenging. The Windows environment must be duplicated on what is most often a non-Intel CPU. Because the Windows program was developed and coded for an Intel-family chip, such as an 80486 or 80386, it sends the Intel machine instructions and expects similar binary strings in return. The Wabi or SoftWindows program has the horribly complex task of translating these instructions "on the fly" so that the application thinks it is running in the Windows environment on an Intel machine.

Further complicating the task is the GUI problem. Windows applications can now display on the UNIX system's X-Windows-based GUI. X-Windows screens require modification in order to look like standard Microsoft Windows screens.

And all of this must be done fast enough so that users see their Windows applications running at an acceptable speed (even though Windows itself is often no speed demon). Running Windows applications on UNIX without the overhead of DOS emulation and Windows itself is the most efficient method. It is, however, a technology still under development. As this book goes to press, Sun's Wabi is certified for only 13 Windows applications. SoftWindows runs more applications, but neither can handle *all* of the many thousands of Windows software packages now available. An additional problem is that your version of UNIX may not yet be supported by Wabi, SoftWindows, or any similar program.

While solutions are evolving, you may have to run DOS emulation and Windows in order to execute Windows applications. The following sections first cover running of Windows applications on UNIX without emulating DOS or Windows and then using of DOS emulation to implement Windows on a UNIX system.

VI

Working with Applications

Wabi

Wabi lets you launch Microsoft Windows 3.1 applications and display them on UNIX workstations just like standard X-Windows applications. Wabi works under version 2.0 and higher of the Solaris operating system (Sun's version of UNIX) for both the Sun SPARCstation and any Intel platform running Solaris. Wabi versions for other CPUs and operating systems are under development.

According to Sun, Wabi 1.0 is largely self contained but does not yet include native support for advanced Windows features such as DDE, OLE, the online help viewer, or any support for the multimedia parts of the Windows API or networking APIs (such as WinSock and NetBIOS). Only two qualified applications (of the 13 approved as this book goes to press) require that Microsoft Windows be installed for the application to run under Wabi: Borland Paradox for Windows and Microsoft PowerPoint 3.0.

> ### Note
>
> If Wabi is Windows, why do you have to install "real Windows" to get some applications (like PowerPoint and Paradox) to run under Wabi? Sun emphasizes that this is just a temporary requirement with Wabi 1.0. Wabi 1.0 has a few holes in it; the easiest way to fill them in the short term is to merge it with "real Windows." Later versions of Wabi will not have the requirement to install "real Windows" to run these applications. Sun says there are not many other benefits to installing "real Windows" on a system that has Wabi.

Several Windows applications, such as WinTach, use routines to find out what kind of hardware they're running on. Wabi knows and intercepts all these common routines. In every case, Sun says, Wabi returns "reasonable lies" to the application. Wabi always makes the application think it's running on an 80386 chip.

Windows-based applications care about only two possibilities: an 80286 chip implies standard mode and an 80386, 80486, or Pentium chip implies enhanced mode. Once Wabi reports an 80386 CPU, the application knows that it can use all the enhanced-mode features it wants to use. If Wabi reported an 80486 or Pentium chip, there would be no further performance or functionality gains.

Versions of Wabi are available for many different types of hardware: SPARC, PA-RISC, Power PC, Intel, and so on. Wabi obviously can't return the "truth" about the hardware in every case (lots of Windows applications wouldn't know what to do if they discovered they were running on a SPARC CPU).

Therefore, Wabi always returns what it is simulating rather than what it is actually running on. And Wabi always simulates an Intel enhanced-mode chip: an 80386.

> **Note**
>
> Wabi doesn't make exceptions when it actually runs on real Intel hardware. Wabi always returns what it's simulating, even if the simulation is simply passing Intel instructions through to a real Intel 80386, 80486, or Pentium CPU.

Sun stresses that there are two important points to remember about Wabi:

- Wabi's behavior gives applications permission to use enhanced-mode extensions.

- Wabi's always reporting that it is running on an 80386 rather than on an 80486 or Pentium has no impact on performance or functionality of the Windows applications.

> **The Inside Story on Wabi**
>
> Unlike its competitor, SoftWindows, Wabi runs Windows applications in enhanced mode. It translates Windows system calls "on the fly" into standard X-Windows and UNIX system service calls. Wabi contains no licensed code from Microsoft. All the Dynamic Link Libraries (DLLs) Wabi uses are based on the Windows ABI (Application Binary Interface) specification and written in a way that does not violate copyrights and patents held by Microsoft. SoftWindows, by the way, uses licensed code from Microsoft.

At the time of this writing, Wabi is still a new product. Although the next few months will see improved versions of the product and the certification of more Windows applications, Wabi is currently somewhat limited. However, Wabi can run several major and useful Windows applications on a Sun work-station, including Microsoft Excel for Windows (spreadsheet), Microsoft Word for Windows (word processor), CorelDRAW! (illustration package), and PageMaker (desktop publishing). Sun has already announced that Wabi 2.0 will support seven more major Windows applications.

SoftWindows

At the time this book went to press, Insignia's SoftWindows runs many more DOS and Windows applications than Sun's Wabi. Sun has gone head-to-head with Microsoft Windows and is implementing Wabi without benefit of help from Microsoft. Insignia, on the other hand, has licensed code from Microsoft and has Microsoft's "blessing" (for what that may be worth).

Although SoftWindows runs a lot more Windows applications than Wabi, those applications can run only in standard mode (SoftWindows 2.0 will include support for enhanced mode). Network support is stronger in SoftWindows as well. Insignia's SoftNode software is included with SoftWindows, allowing connection to NetWare networks. SoftWindows also supports TCP/IP and NFS through Novell's LAN WorkPlace for DOS, although you have to pay extra for this feature.

◀ For more information about SoftPC, the DOS-emulation product, see Chapter 23, "Running DOS Applications."

Insignia also makes the SoftPC DOS emulation product. On-screen, SoftWindows resembles SoftPC running Windows but SoftWindows provides a significant increase in the speed at which Windows applications run because it uses neither DOS nor Windows emulation.

Reviewers—such as Jason Levitt, writing in the December 6, 1993 issue of *Open Systems Today*—have nice things to say about SoftWindows. As Levitt points out, Insignia's licensing of DOS and Windows code from Microsoft, in addition to the company's years of experience in developing DOS-emulation products for UNIX, has paid off, at least in the early going. SoftWindows performs "much better" at any job requiring "compute-intensive and disk I/O-intensive tasks" than Wabi.

This is not to say that SoftWindows is totally superior to Wabi. Using Microsoft code, as SoftWindows does, can also be a disadvantage. Wabi does better than SoftWindows right now at tasks involving screen input/output because Wabi's screen calls are translated directly to X-Windows calls. Display under Wabi is faster than display under SoftWindows because SoftWindows uses an 80286 emulator before passing the calls to X-Windows.

Insignia has announced that SoftWindows 2.0 will bring screen I/O to the same speed or faster than Wabi's screen I/O. Another interesting feature for SoftWindows 2.0 is that it will give the user the choice of either the standard Microsoft Windows look-and-feel for applications or that of the Motif/X-Windows look. For those not used to Windows who want to run the many unique Windows applications in a familiar environment, this latter choice may be very nice.

Other Windows-under-UNIX Products

The concept of running Windows applications without Windows is definitely one whose time has come. In addition to SunSelect and Insignia, other companies are working on "Wabi-type" software packages. There is even a *free* package in the works by hackers on the Internet to run under linux.

Linux is a UNIX clone for 386/486-based PCs written from scratch by Linus Torvalds with assistance from a loosely-knit team of hackers from around the world. Linux is available free for the downloading from many sources on the Internet.

According to the linux FAQ (Frequently Asked Questions, a text file available on the Internet), linux has all the features you expect in a modern, fully fledged version of UNIX, including true multitasking, virtual memory, shared libraries, demand loading, shared copy-on-write executables, proper memory management, and TCP/IP networking. It does, however, require a considerable knowledge in UNIX programming to compile and install on your system.

The "Wabi project" for linux, according to information posted on the Internet, is an attempt to write something with functionality similar to the Wabi developed by Sun. The name *Wabi* was chosen in haste at the outset of the linux project (and is trademarked by Sun); anything that comes out of the linux project will undoubtedly have a different name.

> **Note**
>
> The Windows binary will run directly in the linux product; there will be no need for machine-level emulation of the instructions. Sun has reported better performance with their version of Wabi than is actually achieved under MS-Windows; the same result is theoretically possible under linux.

The linux "Wabi project" started as a result of discussions on `comp.os.linux` (an Internet discussion group) in early June 1993. Once something is ready for public consumption, it will be uploaded to a publicly visible directory. The final product will almost certainly be under the GNU Public License (or GPL for short).

Running Windows with DOS Emulation

The first part of this chapter is concerned with ways of running Windows applications without Windows. As you know, DOS applications run on UNIX with the aid of a DOS-emulation package. Windows runs over DOS and so is classified as a DOS application. A number of versions of UNIX provide Windows support in this manner. Novell's new UNIX, UnixWare, is a good example of a UNIX version that can run Windows applications through a DOS-emulation package (see fig. 24.1).

VI

Working with Applications

Fig. 24.1
Microsoft Word
for Windows
running on
UnixWare.

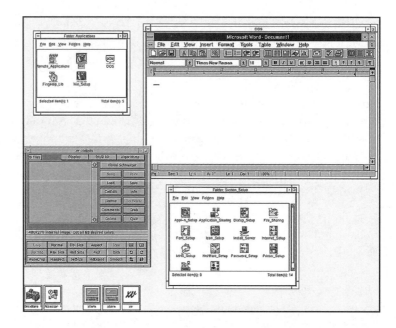

According to Novell, UnixWare protects investments in existing software by offering support for DOS applications and Windows 3.0 and 3.1. Users must provide a licensed copy of Windows. DR-DOS 6.0 is included with UnixWare. UnixWare supports Windows and DOS under X-Windows, unlimited Microsoft Windows and DOS sessions on the console, VGA support, and support for running Windows and DOS sessions on the Desktop alongside UNIX applications or in full-screen mode (as on a DOS-only system).

The two major DOS-emulation packages introduced in the preceding chapter—Merge 386/486 and VP/ix—both let you install and run Windows as a DOS application. Again, emulating DOS and running Windows "normally" causes applications to run slower than they would under a Wabi-type package. And UnixWare's Merge doesn't support enhanced-mode applications such as FrameMaker. Only applications that run in Windows standard mode are supported.

Insignia, who makes SoftWindows and SoftPC for several workstation vendors (you looked at Sun's version of SoftPC in the last chapter), recently released its SoftPC 3.0 for UNIX DOS emulator. SoftPC 3.0 supports super VGA graphics and protected-mode Windows applications. Various reviewers have reported that the package approximates the speed of a 386SX machine running a DOS application when the package is implemented on a Sun SPARCstation. Insignia claims that the speed of execution approaches an 80486 on faster workstations like the HP series 700.

Actually, SoftPC 3.0 is reputed to run Windows and Windows applications faster than Windows under DOS. This is accomplished by means of a special driver for X-Windows that Insignia codeveloped with Microsoft. In fact, Microsoft has obtained the rights to use Insignia's code in future versions of its Windows NT operating system.

In general, the considerations detailed in Chapter 23, "Running DOS Applications," also apply to implementing Windows under DOS emulation on a UNIX system.

Regardless of whether you decide to use a Wabi-type package, to implement Windows under DOS emulation, or to use a combination of both on your system, the effort almost certainly is worth it. Windows has conquered the desktop; because of the economic pressure from tens of millions of users, Windows applications predominate in the business world today. You need the ability to meld UNIX's multitasking, multiuser power with the convenience of relatively cheap and plentiful Windows and DOS applications. When you do so, your system has the best of two worlds and you have enhanced productivity and flexibility.

Summary

There two methods of running Windows applications on a UNIX system: using a Wabi-type program that runs Windows binaries without Windows or DOS, and running Windows with a DOS-emulation program.

Sun's Wabi runs Windows applications without Windows by translating Intel calls to X-Windows and UNIX system service calls on the fly. Although Wabi can run Windows applications in enhanced mode, it is currently limited in the number of Windows applications it supports. Later versions will run more applications. Insignia's SoftWindows currently runs more Windows applications than Wabi does but only in standard Windows mode. The next version of SoftWindows will support enhanced mode. Other versions of Wabi-type programs are being developed, including a "free" version by the hackers who are implementing linux. Because most DOS-emulation programs can run the Windows environment, they can also run Windows applications.

Regardless of the method you use to run Windows applications on a UNIX system, you enhance the system's productivity and flexibility when you add Windows applications to your repertoire of UNIX applications.

Part VII of this book, "UNIX Networking," looks at networking in a UNIX environment.

VI

Working with Applications

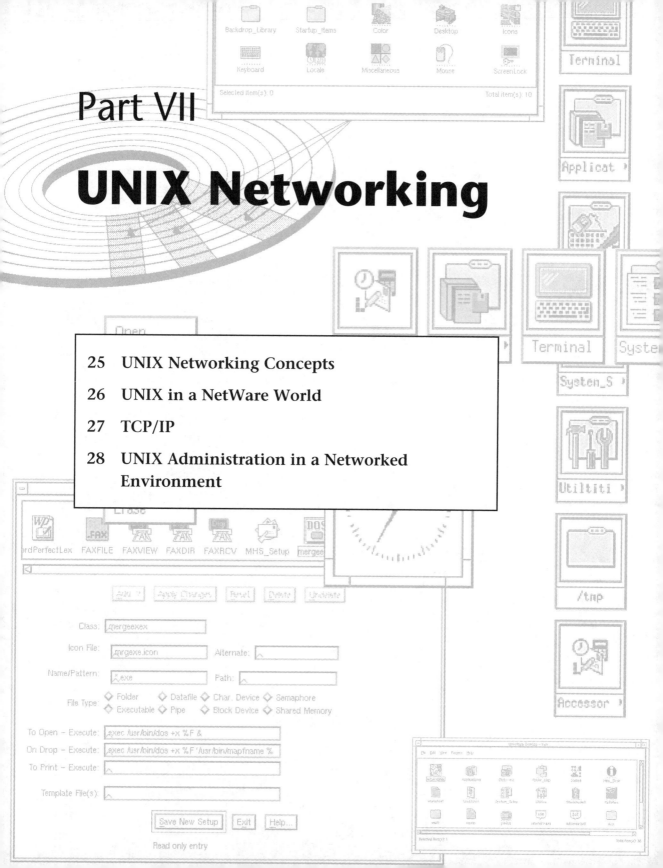

Part VII

UNIX Networking

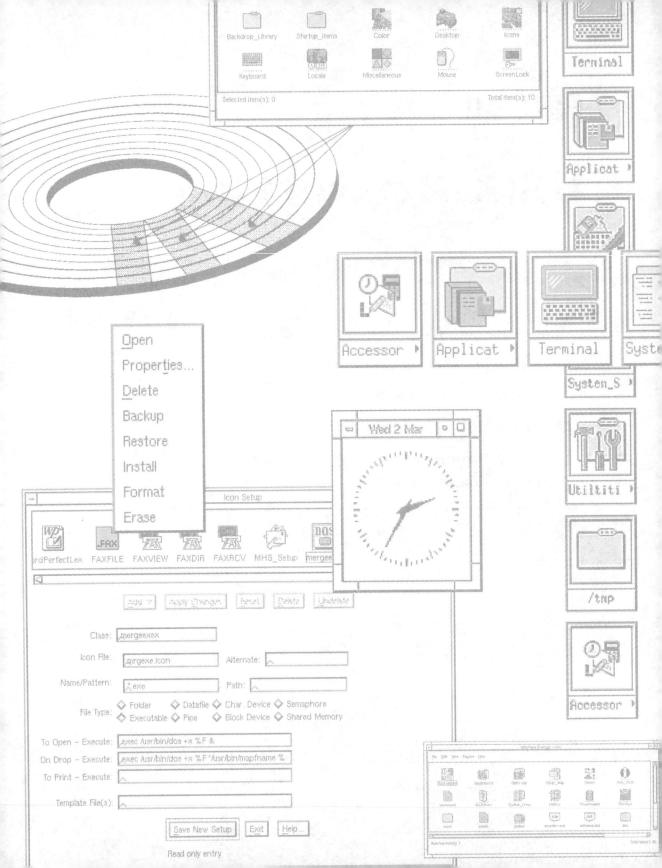

Backdrop_Library   Startup_items   Color   Desktop   Icons

Keyboard   Locale   Miscellaneous   Mouse   ScreenLock

Selected item(s): 0   Total item(s): 10

Terminal

Applicat ▶

Accessor ▶   Applicat ▶   Terminal   Syst

System_S ▶

Open
Properties...
Delete
Backup
Restore
Install
Format
Erase

Icon Setup

Utiltiti ▶

Wed 2 Mar

/tmp

rdPerfectLex FAXFILE FAXVIEW FAXDIR FAXRCV MHS_Setup mergee

Add ?   Apply Changes   Reset   Delete   Undelete

Accessor ▶

Class: _mergeexex

Icon File: _mrgexe.icon   Alternate:

Name/Pattern: _*.exe   Path:

File Type: ◇ Folder   ◇ Datafile ◇ Char. Device ◇ Semaphore
              ◇ Executable ◇ Pipe   ◇ Block Device ◇ Shared Memory

To Open – Execute: _exec /usr/bin/dos +x %F &

On Drop – Execute: _exec /usr/bin/dos +x %F '/usr/bin/mapfname %

To Print – Execute:

Template File(s):

Save New Setup   Exit   Help...

Read only entry

Chapter 25

UNIX Networking Concepts

Networks are becoming a more and more important part of many information systems. The need to share information such as databases and resources such as printers makes networks an integral part of many computing environments.

This chapter provides a look at the terms used in computer networking, followed by a technical discussion of the most common networking protocols encountered in UNIX. Finally, there is a discussion of the various devices used in internetworking.

In this chapter, you learn the following:

- Basic networking concepts

- Popular features of the TCP/IP protocols that let you share information among UNIX systems

- How to access and use the Internet

- How your system reaches other systems on the Internet

What Is Networking?

▶ Chapter 27,
"TCP/IP,"
describes the
TCP/IP
protocol.

A *network* is a collection of computer systems that communicate with each other in a cooperative manner. Although these systems need not run the same operating system, they do need to communicate with each other using a common *protocol* (a "language," or set of rules). In the UNIX world, this common protocol is most often TCP/IP.

In the UNIX environment, most processing is done on the UNIX host itself. So why the need to communicate with other machines? Very often, information you seek is not available locally. Suppose that you need to work with a sales database that someone at another location in your company has created. If you obtain a copy of that database locally, the two copies can easily get out of sync and out of date. If you could access the original database on the other host *transparently*, life would be easy. Transparent access of remote files is one of the many reasons why networking is becoming popular and important today.

> **Note**
>
> In the TCP/IP world, each computer is called a *host*. Your workstation is also known as a host in TCP/IP or UNIX terminology.

To have a basic understanding of how networks function, you must know some networking buzz words. First are two communication models: the Open Systems Interconnection (OSI) model and the Department of Defense (DoD), or the Internet, model.

Open Systems Interconnection Model

Many different types of computers are used today. These systems differ in operating system, CPU, network interfaces, and many other variables. These differences make the problem of communication between diverse computer systems nontrivial. In 1977, the International Organization for Standardization (ISO) created a subcommittee to develop data communication standards to promote multivendor interoperability. The result is the Open Systems Interconnection (OSI) model.

The OSI model does not specify any communication standards or protocols; instead, it provides guidelines that communication tasks follow.

> **Note**
>
> It is important to understand that the OSI model is simply a model—a framework—that specifies the functions to be performed. It does not detail *how* these functions are performed. ISO, however, does certify specific protocols that meet OSI standards for parts of the OSI model. For example, the CCITT X.25 protocol is accepted by ISO as an implementation that provides most of the services of the Network Layer of the OSI model.

To simplify matters, the ISO subcommittee took the "divide-and-conquer" approach. By dividing the complex communication process into smaller subtasks, the problem becomes more manageable and each subtask can be optimized individually. The OSI model is divided into seven layers:

1. Physical

2. Data Link

3. Network

4. Transport

5. Session

6. Presentation

7. Application

> **Tip**
>
> One easy way to remember the order of the layers (from the top down) is by making a sentence from the first letters of the layer names: All People Seem To Need Data Processing.

Each layer is assigned a specific set of functions. Each layer uses the services of the layer underneath it and provides services to the layer above it. For example, the Network layer makes use of services from the Data Link layer and provides network-related services to the Transport layer.

Following are explanations of the services offered at each layer:

Layer	Description
Physical layer (Layer 1)	This layer provides the physical connection between a computer system and the network. It specifies connector and pin assignments, voltage levels, and so on.
Data Link layer (Layer 2)	This layer "packages" and "unpackages" data for transmission. It forms the information into frames. A *frame* represents the exact structure of the data physically transmitted across the wire or other medium.
Network layer (Layer 3)	Provides routing of data through the network.
Transport layer (Layer 4)	Provides sequencing and acknowledgment of transmission.
Session layer (Layer 5)	Establishes and terminates communication links.
Presentation layer (Layer 6)	Does data conversion and ensures that data is exchanged in a universal format.
Application layer (Layer 7)	Provides an interface to the application that a user executes; a "gateway" between user applications and the network communication process.

Note

The concept of a layer making use of services and providing services to its adjacent layers is simple. Consider how a company operates: the secretary provides secretarial services to the president (the next layer up) to write a memo. The secretary uses the services of a messenger (the next layer down) to deliver the message. By separating these services, the secretary (application) doesn't have to know how the message is actually carried to its recipient. That way the secretary (application) doesn't have to know everything about how to get a message to the recipient. It merely has to ask the messenger (network) to deliver it. With the addition of a standard messenger service, many secretaries can send memos in this way.

Caution

Do not confuse the Application layer with application programs you execute on the computer. Remember that the Application layer is part of the OSI model that does not specify *how* the interface between a user and the communication pathway happens; an application program is a specific implementation of this interface. A real application typically does Application, Session, and Presentation layer services and leaves Transport, Network, Data Link, and Physical layer services to the network.

Each layer communicates with its peer in other computers. For example, Layer 3 in one system communicates with Layer 3 in another computer system.

When information is passed from one layer down to the next, a *header* is added to the data to indicate where the information is coming from and going to. The header-plus-data block of information from one layer becomes the data for the next. For example, when Layer 4 passes data to Layer 3, it adds its own header. When Layer 3 passes the information to Layer 2, it considers the header-plus-data from Layer 4 as data and adds its own header before passing that combination down.

In each layer, the information units are given different names (see table 25.1). Therefore, by knowing the terms used to reference the data, you know which layer of the model is being discussed.

Table 25.1: Terms Used by OSI Layers To Refer to Information Units	
OSI Layer	**Information Unit Name**
Application	Message
Transport	Segment
Network	Datagram
Data Link	Frame (also called packet)
Physical	Bit

Before the advent of the OSI model, the US Department of Defense defined its own networking model, known as the DoD model (and almost always called the Internet). The DoD model is closely related to the TCP/IP suite of protocols, as explained in the following section.

Department of Defense Model

The US Department of Defense (DoD) networking model was established in the mid-60s, much earlier than the OSI model. The DoD model defines a four-layer networking model. Each layer of the model specifies a set of communication protocols. This set of protocols are collectively known as the TCP/IP protocol suite or, more correctly, the Internet protocol suite. Today, the Internet protocol suite consists of hundreds of protocols. The most common and important ones are discussed in the next section, "Understanding UNIX Networking Protocols."

Although the DoD model predates the OSI model by over 10 years and has only four layers instead of the seven in OSI, some meaningful comparisons can be drawn between the two models (see fig. 25.1):

■ The Process/Application layer in the DoD model corresponds to the top three layers of the OSI model. The Process/Application layer provides specific application interfaces between two computer systems.

■ The Host-to-Host layer in the DoD model maps to the Transport layer of the OSI Model. The Host-to-Host layer is responsible for establishing and maintaining connections.

■ The Internet layer in the DoD model maps to the Network layer of the OSI Model. The Internet layer is responsible for routing packets between different networks and systems.

■ The Network Access layer in the DoD model corresponds to the bottom two layers in the OSI model. The Network Access layer specifies the physical characteristics of the physical connection between networks.

Fig. 25.1
A comparison of layers in the OSI and DoD models.

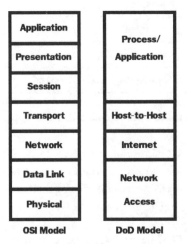

Associated with each layer is a protocol that outlines how specific networking functions behave. The next section takes an in-depth look at some of the most common protocols.

Understanding UNIX Networking Protocols

The TCP/IP protocol suite used in UNIX networking consists of well over one hundred protocols. The specification of each protocol is defined by one or more "Requests for Comments" (RFCs). These RFCs are public documents you can obtain from a number of sources. RFCs describe how to use, as well as how to implement, TCP/IP networks.

> **Note**
>
> If you have access to the Internet, you can obtain RFCs from a number of depositories, including the famous host named NIC.DDN.MIL (IP address 192.67.67.20). For a list of all available RFCs, retrieve RFC-INDEX.TXT.

Figure 25.2 shows a list of the most common protocols used in UNIX networking. Each of them is discussed in detail in the following sections, starting from the top down.

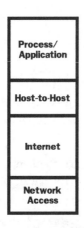
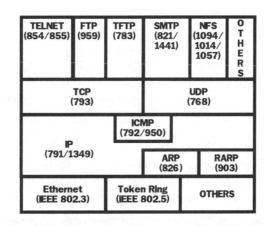

Fig. 25.2
Common protocols used in UNIX networking (shown with the corresponding RFC, or standards, numbers).

Process/Application Layer Protocols

At the very top layer of the DoD model is the Process/Application layer. Protocols at this layer provide services such as terminal emulation (TELNET), file transfer (FTP), electronic mail (SMTP), file sharing (NFS), and network management (SNMP) to name but a few.

Each protocol in this layer is made up of two components: a client program and a server program.

In UNIX terminology, the server program is often referred to as the *daemon program*, or simply the daemon. The daemon runs as a background process on the server. The executable file usually ends with the letter *d* to mark it as a daemon. For example, the daemon program for the TELNET process (discussed below) is called `telnetd` (see fig. 25.3).

Fig. 25.3

The client/server communication path.

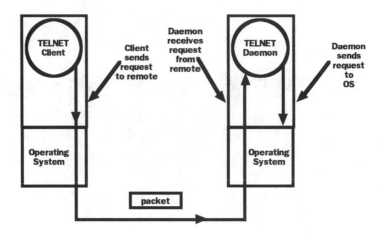

TELNET

The TELNET protocol provides the remote host with a virtual terminal connection to another host, as though there were a direct physical connection. Because UNIX implements devices as drivers, each TELNET session uses a virtual network drivers known as *pseudo ttys*. Pseudo ttys is transparent to applications and users. Users appear to be sitting at a terminal directly connected to the remote host, even though the remote host may be thousands of miles away.

Many client software products implement the TELNET protocol in an executable file also called `telnet`. In most cases, to invoke your terminal emulator, you simply execute this program. However, depending on the developer of the software, this may not always be the case.

> ### Tip
>
> Many applications require you to use a specific terminal model to take advantage of certain keys or display attributes. Your TELNET software (not the protocol) may not support your existing terminal type. Fortunately, many UNIX applications work with the VT100 terminal type, which almost all TELNET software supports.

The TELNET protocol is defined in RFCs 854 and 855.

FTP and TFTP

There are two file-transfer protocols available: the File Transfer Protocol (FTP, defined in RFC 959) and the Trivial File Transfer Protocol (TFTP, defined in RFC 783).

File transfers using FTP require you to be an authorized user on the remote host; such transfers are subject to the security imposed by the operating system on the user. The user interface program is usually called `ftp`. Using FTP, you can do the following:

- List directories and files

- Send binary or text files

- Retrieve binary or text files

Many sites on the Internet provide a service called *anonymous ftp* that allows users to access remote sites without having an authorized user ID and password. The general login ID is `anonymous`; by convention, the password is `guest` (or no password, should you chose not to use one). If the site does not ask you to use `guest` for a password, it is customary to use your e-mail address as the password instead. This gives that site's administrator some idea of where the users are from.

As mentioned earlier, RFCs can be obtained from the Internet host `NIC.DDN.MIL`. You can use anonymous ftp to retrieve these files. A sample FTP session to grab RFC 959 is shown in figure 25.4.

```
$ ftp nic.ddn.mil
JAY.SUNNYBROOK.UTORONTO.CA MultiNet FTP user process 3.2(106)
Connection opened (Assuming 8-bit connections)
<*****Welcome to the DOD Network Information Center*****
<     *****Login with username "anonymous" and password "guest"
<     *****You may change directories to the following:
<     domain            - Root Domain Zone Files
<     gosip             - DOD GOSIP Registration and Information
<     netinfo           - NIC Information Files
<     protocols         - TCP-IP & OSI Documents
<     rfc               - RFC Repository
<     scc               - DDN Security Bulletins
<     std               - Internet Protocol Standards
<And more!
NIC.DDN.MIL>user anonymous
<Guest login ok, access restrictions apply.
NIC.DDN.MIL>cd rfc
<CWD command successful.
NIC.DDN.MIL>get rfc959.txt rfc959.txt
<Opening ASCII mode data connection for rfc959.txt (147316 bytes).
NIC.DDN.MIL>bye
Bye!
FTP>exit
```

Fig. 25.4
A sample FTP session used to retrieve RFC 959.

TFTP does not require a user password. You simply must know the name of the host, the location of the file, and the exact filename you want to retrieve. Without this information, you cannot obtain a file using TFTP.

TFTP retransmits the *entire* file if there be a transmission error. On the other hand, FTP provides a "smart" transfer protocol; if, during transfer, one of the frames is lost or damaged, FTP retransmits the single frame, not the whole file. Because of this extra error correction safeguard, FTP has more overhead than TFTP.

> **Note**
>
> It is common for users to use FTP for regular file transfers. TFTP is used mostly by automated procedures, such as a router getting firmware update information or a smart hub getting management information.

SMTP

One of the most common services provided by networks is electronic mail (e-mail). E-mail is usually implemented differently than protocols like TELNET or FTP. The remote site need not be up and running in order to send e-mail. E-mail messages are usually stored and then forwarded when the link between the systems is available. Therefore, you use a front-end program (called the *agent*) to compose and read your mail messages. A back-end program (called the *transport engine*) stores and delivers mail.

The Simple Mail Transfer Protocol (SMTP, defined by RFCs 821 and 1441) is used to transport messages between two hosts. The message format is defined by the Standard for the Format of ARPA Internet Text Messages (defined by RFC 822). Fortunately, as the user, you do not have to worry about the specific formatting. Formatting is taken care of by the front-end program.

Each UNIX system comes with a mail front-end; the executable is usually called `mail` or `mailx`. Your site may choose to implement a different front-end; consult your system administrator. Many different front-ends are available—some free and some commercial software.

NFS

Network File System (NFS) was first developed by Sun Microsystems. NFS is made up of three protocols:

■ Network File System (NFS)

■ eXternal Data Representation (XDR)

■ Remote Procedure Call (RPC)

> **Note**
>
> Strictly speaking, NFS is a protocol suite, much like TCP/IP. It is not a single protocol like FTP, for example.

Unlike TELNET and FTP, NFS (defined by RFC 1094) is a "transparent" protocol as far as the end users are concerned. NFS is designed to share file systems between dissimilar machines, such as a PC running DOS and a UNIX host. The NFS server (the machine with the files to be shared) makes its file system appear to be part of the client machine's local computer environment. For example, a PC running TCP/IP and NFS client software may use drive D as the hard drive on a remote UNIX host. To access files from this drive, the PC user gives the standard DOS COPY command. All files appear as local to the user.

> ### Note
>
> As part of NFS security, the host system's security is enforced through the use of user and group IDs. If the user does not have write permission to a given directory, he or she does not have write permission to that directory with NFS.

To provide transparency between dissimilar systems, the eXternal Data Representation protocol (XDR, defined by RFC 1014) allows for the description and encoding of data in a machine-independent format. Continuing with the preceding example, when the PC reads a file from drive D, the UNIX machine first converts the file contents into XDR format before transmitting the file to the PC. After receiving this file, the PC converts it to PC format (see fig. 25.5).

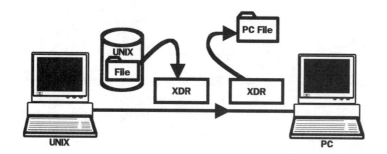

Fig. 25.5
Data transmission using the eXternal Data Representation protocol (XDR).

How does the client (the PC in the example) know that it needs to ask the UNIX host for the file? This is where Remote Procedure Call (RPC, defined in RFC 1057) comes in. Part of RPC is a "redirector" piece that decides whether the request can be serviced locally or must be processed by the remote host (see fig. 25.6).

Remote Procedure Call (RPC) is not limited to NFS. Other RPC implementations are not related to NFS. However, the Remote Procedure Call defined by RFC 1057 is specific to NFS.

With NFS, users can access files residing on remote host machines transparently, without having to learn any new commands, as they do when using FTP or TELNET.

Fig. 25.6
The workings of
the Remote
Procedure Call
protocol.

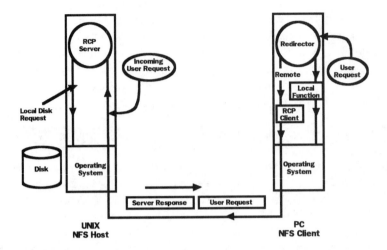

Two common terms used in NFS are these:

Exports	A file system available for sharing to client machines. For example, if you want to make your /usr file system available to remote NFS clients, export /usr.
Mount points	These identify where on the local file system the remote file system will start. For example, by specifying a mount point of /u/home, the remote file system shows up as subdirectories under /u/home on your system.

Caution

If you have any directories under your mount point (/u/home in the preceding example), you will lose access to them. However, the subdirectories are not deleted,
simply hidden. You have access to them again when you dismount the remote file
system.

SNMP

In order to obtain information from and issue instructions to other devices and systems, the Simple Network Management Protocol (SNMP, defined by RFC 1157) is used. Just like the other upper-layer protocols discussed in the preceding sections, SNMP uses a client piece (called a *management console*) and a server portion (called an *agent*).

The agent can reside on any TCP/IP device, such as a host, router, or wiring hub. The information you can obtain from the agent's database is known as the Management Information Base (MIB). It is up to the management console to query the agent for information. The agent does not automatically report data to the console unless that data is an error condition. Error conditions in SNMP are called *traps*.

Currently, there are two standard MIBs in use: MIB I (defined by RFC 1356) and MIB II (defined by RFC 1450). MIB I contains about 114 objects (variables), such as device uptime and number of interfaces installed in the device. MIB II contains all MIB I objects plus some extensions for a total of about 172 objects. Originally, the MIBs were designed to manage IP routers. However, MIBs now sometimes contain extensions to include other devices such as smart wiring hubs. Figure 25.7 shows a sample screen of a DOS-based SNMP manager console (LWPCON from Novell's LAN WorkPlace for DOS 4.1) looking at a MIB I agent.

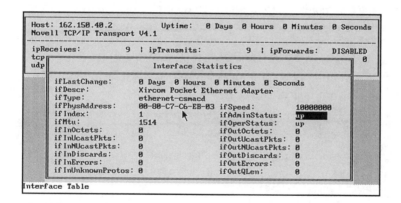

Fig. 25.7

A sample SNMP management console displaying some MIB I information.

A new standard MIB, called RMON (Remote MONitoring) is being ratified by the Internet community. RMON is not an extension to MIB II like MIB II was an extension of MIB I. RMON is designed to provide monitoring information such as average cable utilization, number of frames on the wire, and so on.

There are two additional categories of MIBs: experimental MIB and private (or enterprise) MIB. Experimental MIBs contain important information about aspects of the network not contained by one of the standard MIBs. Once an experimental MIB has been approved by the Internet community, it is recognized as one of the standard MIBs.

Enterprise or private MIBs are specific to individual companies for collecting information from their own network devices. For example, SynOptics sells a private MIB for its manageable hubs. Private MIBs usually provide specific data not available through standard MIBs.

> **Note**
>
> A new version of SNMP, called simply SNMP II, is currently under ratification by the Internet standards body. SNMP II provides enhanced security, among other features.

Associated with each SNMP message or query is a "community" name or password. A community name in SNMP is an ASCII string of up to 32 characters. There are three communities in SNMP:

- *Monitor Community.* Management console messages containing this name can only read the MIB data.

- *Control Community.* Management console messages containing this name can read and modify the MIB data.

- *Trap Community.* Trap messages containing this name are accepted by the management console also set to the same name.

For example, if you want to browse the MIB variable of a TCP/IP device, you must set your monitor community name to that used by the TCP/IP device. If the names do not match, you cannot read the MIB.

> **Caution**
>
> Community names can contain any characters except for <space>, <Tab>, open square bracket ([), equal sign (=), colon (:), semicolon (;), or the pound sign (#). Community names are also case sensitive.

In general, community names provide a simple and unsecured method of accessing MIB information. SNMP II will address the security shortcoming.

Host-to-Host Layer Protocols

Two protocols are defined in the Host-to-Host layer of the DoD model: the Transmission Control Protocol (TCP) and the User Datagram Protocol (UDP).

These protocols are designed to ensure the safe transmission of data between two hosts. A look at how these protocols work provides some insight about why two protocols are defined.

TCP

In network communications, there are basically two types of communication delivery mechanisms between two machines:

- Connection-oriented, guaranteed delivery

- Connectionless, nonguaranteed delivery

Connection-oriented delivery means that a logical connection is first established between the two systems before any data is transmitted. At the same time, each transmission is acknowledged to ensure data integrity. Connectionless delivery means a "best attempt" delivery. No logical link must first be established and no acknowledgment of delivery is needed. Connectionless delivery is a faster transmission method because there is less overhead. Because of the lack of checking, the higher-layer protocol must verify that the data is transmitted and received correctly.

> **Note**
>
> Consider the difference between making a telephone call and making a radio call. To make a telephone call, you must first dial the desired telephone number and wait for the connection to complete before you can communicate with the other party; usually after you say something at one end, the other party acknowledges by saying "okay." This is connection-oriented, guaranteed delivery.
>
> When you make a radio call (say, using a CB), you simply pick up the microphone and transmit. No prior connection to your calling party is made. And you do not know whether the other party received your call unless they send a reply message back. This is an example of a connectionless, nonguaranteed delivery.

The Transmission Control Protocol (TCP, defined by RFC 793) is designed to be a connection-oriented, guaranteed delivery protocol. The following items are included as part of TCP header information:

- **Source and destination "ports"** to identify which upper-layer protocol the data comes from and goes to.

- **Sequence number** to ensure that the packets arrive in the correct order.

- **Acknowledgment number** to acknowledge the total number of packets received.

Each upper-layer protocol is assigned a unique ("well-known") port number so that TCP knows which protocol stack to hand off the data to. For example, TELNET is assigned a port number of 23 (decimal).

The upper-layer protocol decides whether it wants to use the services provided by TCP. For example, TELNET, FTP, and SMTP all use TCP's services.

> **Note**
>
> Together, TCP and IP (IP is discussed later in this chapter) are by far the best-known protocol in the Internet protocol suite. It is common to use the term TCP/IP for this suite of protocols.

UDP

The User Datagram Protocol (UDP, defined by RFC 768) is a connectionless, nonguaranteed delivery protocol. It simply accepts and transports the information passed down from the upper-layer protocol. No error checking, correction, or acknowledgment is done by UDP; these tasks are left totally to the upper-layer protocol.

Because there is no established connection in UDP, each packet of information must carry with it its own address information. These types of packets are referred to as *datagrams*.

When compared to TCP, UDP's header information is very simple. It only has four fields:

- Source port
- Destination port
- Length
- Checksum

Because it is much faster to use UDP than TCP, many upper-layer protocols use UDP as the transport method of choice. For example, TFTP and NFS use UDP. Because UDP does no error correction, TFTP retransmits the whole file if an error is encountered. TFTP cannot recover by retransmitting the bad frame (because it has no idea which frame was bad); FTP can determine which was the bad frame because FTP uses TCP (with error checking) instead of UDP.

Internet Layer Protocols

A number of protocols function at the Internet layer. Among them are the Internet Protocol (IP), the Internet Control Message Protocol (ICMP), the

Address Resolution Protocol (ARP), and the Reverse Address Resolution Protocol (RARP). The function of each of these protocols is discussed in the following sections.

IP

The Internet Protocol (IP, defined by RFCs 791 and 1349) provides datagram services between TCP/IP hosts. It is also responsible for routing packets and performing fragmentation and reassembly of datagrams when necessary.

> **Note**
>
> IP is the transport protocol of TCP/IP and can be compared to IPX in the NetWare environment.

IP provides a connectionless, nonguaranteed delivery of datagrams across the network. This means that data is sent without establishing a prior logical connection. No acknowledgment is required. Connectionless delivery gives a faster data flow but is not reliable. However, if TCP is used as the Host-to-Host layer protocol, error correction is taken care of. If UDP is used as the Host-to-Host layer protocol, the upper-layer protocols must handle error detection and recovery. There is no need for IP to duplicate the effort.

Because one of IP's functions is to find a route for the datagram in order to get it to the other host, IP headers contain information such as the source and destination IP addresses. *IP addresses* are software addresses assigned by the network administrator. In the case of Internet, IP addresses are assigned and regulated by `NIC.DDN.MIL` (Network Information Center).

▶ Details about IP addressing are presented in Chapter 27, "TCP/IP."

> **Note**
>
> Part of the IP address identifies the IP network (a *software* address). The IP address is divided into two portions: the network part and the host part. Think of the network part as the street name and the host part as the number on the house.

ICMP

The Internet Control Message Protocol (ICMP, defined by RFCs 792 and 950) is used mainly by routers and hosts to send error messages or control information to other routers or hosts.

For example, if a router finds that, instead of using its own connection to another network, there is a better path (router) for a host to communicate with another host, the router sends an ICMP message to the host to inform the host of the alternate route. Another common use of ICMP messages is for a host to test whether another host is reachable—the equivalent of the `ping` command.

ARP

Each Network Interface Card (NIC) has a unique hardware address. If an NIC is to recognize that a frame is addressed to it, the frame must contain the NIC's *hardware address* in its header. So far, all the way from the topmost protocol layer down, only software (IP) addresses have been used. The hardware address information is obtained with the aid of the Address Resolution Protocol (ARP, defined by RFC 826).

Each host has an ARP table that contains the IP (software) address to NIC (hardware) address mapping. If the information is not in its table, the host broadcasts an ARP request that asks, for example, "Who is 162.1.4.56?" The host with that particular IP address replies "Here I am! My NIC address is 08-00-20-11-22-33."

> **Note**
>
> ARP requests go out as broadcast messages; all TCP/IP devices on the *local* network hear it. Only the device with the appropriate IP address responds to the request. This broadcast/reply process is transparent to the user.

RARP

Each TCP/IP host must be assigned a unique IP (software) address. If you have many TCP/IP devices, it is difficult to manage. When you need to change an IP address, you must change that IP address on each individual machine. Reverse Address Resolution Protocol (RARP, defined by RFC 903) allows you to manage these IP addresses centrally.

ARP looks for a hardware address based on a given IP address. RARP works in the other direction: given a hardware address, RARP looks for the IP address.

You must maintain the table of IP-NIC hardware address on a system assigned as an RARP server.

> **Caution**
>
> The drawback of using an RARP server is the need to keep the database that maps IP and hardware addresses up to date with any changes in hardware.

Network Access Layer Protocols

The lowest protocol layer in the TCP/IP suite provides the physical connection for the network. The specifications used in this layer include those of the Institute of Electrical and Electronics Engineers' (IEEE) 802 standards and industry standards:

- IEEE 802.3 for Ethernet: 10Base5 (thick coax), 10Base2 (thin coax), 10BaseT (twisted-pair).

- IEEE 802.5 for Token Ring: 4/16 Mbps over shielded and unshielded twisted-pair.

- Fiber Distributed Data Interface (FDDI).

- Datapoint ARCnet.

These physical-layer specifications define both the physical wires used for transmission and the electrical impulses sent across the wire. The standards used in the Network Access layer are common across all networking implementations, regardless whether the network is for UNIX or another networking operating system.

Part of the Network Access layer's header information is the hardware address of the device sending the information (the source address) and the hardware address of the device the information is intended for (the destination address). These hardware addresses are used by certain internetworking devices, such as a bridge. Internetworking devices are discussed in the following section.

> **Note**
>
> As an analogy, consider the network as a city block and the hardware address as the street number on a given street.
>
> Very often, hardware addresses are referred to as MAC (Media Access Control) addresses.

When you must communicate with another TCP/IP device, you have to specify its IP address (its street name and the house number); ARP looks up the corresponding hardware address (street number) if it is not already in the host ARP table. With this information, the two devices can communicate with each other.

Internetworking

Over time, your network will grow and expand. You may need to exchange data with other networks (such as the Internet) or segment your network to reduce the amount of traffic and improve performance. The next sections look at ways to connect networks, also referred to as "internetworking." The terms *bridge*, *router*, and *gateway* are often used incorrectly; the next sections clarify these terms with respect to the OSI model and discuss when they should be employed.

Repeater

Working at the Physical layer of the OSI model is the *repeater* device. When electrical signals travel across a medium, they attenuate (or fade) as a function of distance traveled. A repeater simply reconditions the signal (bits) and retransmits it. It does not care about any addressing information. Repeaters are transparent to protocols.

> **Note**
>
> Repeaters cannot be used to connect segments of different topologies, such as Ethernet to ARCnet. However, repeaters can be used to connect segments of the same topology with different media, such as Ethernet fiber to coax Ethernet.

Repeaters extend the distance limit of your network segment—and nothing more. Sometimes, repeaters are used as signal splitters (for example, Ethernet multiport repeaters). Because repeaters do not do any filtering, they do not slow down your network.

Bridge

A *bridge* operates at the Data Link layer of the OSI model (see fig. 25.8). As Data Link layer devices, bridges have access to hardware address information. Using this information, a bridge can filter network traffic based on source and destination hardware addresses.

A bridge keeps track of the hardware addresses for each network segment it is connected to. When the bridge sees a frame from Pluto going to Donald, it knows (from its internal table) that both hosts are on the same segment (both are listed under Interface A) and the bridge ignores the frame. However, if Pluto sends a frame to Mickey, and the bridge knows that Mickey is on the other segment (Interface B), the bridge makes a copy of the frame and transmits it to segment B.

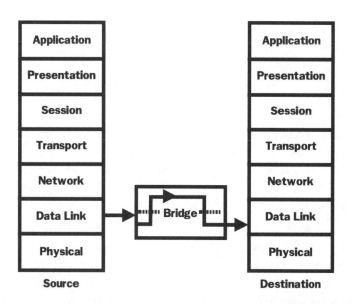

Fig. 25.8
A bridge, shown in an OSI model.

Tip

A bridge forwards frames destined for a different segment. Therefore, bridges are often used to cut down, or segment, traffic on a heavy network.

Like repeaters, bridges are transparent to protocols. Bridges can also be used to extend the distance of a segment because bridges also perform the function of a repeater. This type of bridge is usually known as a *transparent bridge* (also known as a *spanning tree* or *learning bridge*). *Source routing bridges*, another type of bridge, are found primarily in IBM Token Ring networks. In TCP/IP-based networks, transparent bridges are most dominant.

Bridges can connect segments of similar topology, such as Ethernet to Ethernet. They also can connect segments of different media, such as coax cable to fiber. Some manufactures produce *translational bridges* that connect Ethernet with Token Ring (the IBM 8209 bridge, for example).

Tip

If you must connect segments of different topology, use a router (see the next section).

In most cases, users are not aware of the presence of a bridge. However, if users must cross a bridge to get to their destination, they may notice a slight slowdown because the bridge looks up addresses for each frame forwarded. A typical bridge can forward frames at a rate of 10,000 frames/second.

Router

A *router* operates at the Network layer of the OSI model. That means it has access to the network (software) address information. Each interface on the router must be assigned a network address. Therefore, routers are *protocol dependent*. Typically, if a router encounters a protocol it does not support, it drops the frame.

Suppose that you have TCP/IP, IPX, and AppleTalk on your network, but your router supports only TCP/IP. This means none of your IPX or AppleTalk devices can communicate with other IPX or AppleTalk devices located on the other side of the router. This arrangement may be useful in isolating traffic by protocol (as compared to using a bridge to isolate traffic by hardware address).

> **Note**
>
> Unlike a bridge that sees every frame on the segment, a router sees the frame only if the frame is addressed to the router.

A router is much more intelligent than a bridge in that it can determine the *best* path for a frame to reach its destination. The path may change depending on a number of variables, such as segment utilization (if a link becomes congested, the router picks a different path) and availability of the link (if the more direct path is unavailable because of a downed line, the router reroutes using the next-best path).

Because a router has to do a lot more work than a bridge, the throughput for a router is lower than that for a bridge. A typical router can process about 8,000 frames/second.

Because a router deals with network (software) addresses, it has no idea whether a frame came from Ethernet or Token Ring. Therefore, it is a perfect device for connecting different topologies.

Brouter

The preceding section mentioned that routers are protocol dependent. Frames with unknown (unsupported) protocols are dropped. Sometimes, this is not a desirable situation.

In such cases, you may be able to configure your router to route certain protocols and bridge unsupported protocols. Because a router operates at the Network layer of the OSI model, it has access to the Data Link layer services (where a bridge operates). This type of router is known as a *brouter* (bridging router).

> **Note**
>
> Not all routers can also function as a bridge. Most hardware-based routers are brouters; software-based routers usually do not have the capability to act as a bridge.

Gateway

A *gateway* is a device that translates between protocols of different network architectures, such as TCP/IP and SNA. Like routers, gateways are protocol specific. In addition, gateways tend to support only certain upper-layer protocols, such as terminal emulation. For example, if you want to exchange both terminal emulation and electronic mail between two hosts that use different protocols, you may need two separate gateways.

Because a gateway must translate most, if not all, protocol layers, it operates over the entire seven layers of the OSI model.

Looking at an IP Routing Example

This section applies the concepts from the preceding sections to help you understand how routing is performed on an IP network.

1. A user initiates a `telnet` command on host `Donald`. The following can be used: `telnet 143.2.5.9`. (In this example, 143.2.5.9 is an example of an IP address.)

2. Because TELNET uses TCP services, an IP header is added to the TCP message that contains the connection request. The header contains `143.2.5.9` as the destination IP address and `129.1.1.5` as the source IP address (see fig. 25.9).

3. Because `Mickey` is located on a different IP network than `Donald` (`129.1.1.0` vs. `143.2.5.0`), a router is required.

4. If `Mickey` does not have the hardware address of the router in its ARP table, it issues an ARP request to obtain it.

5. The hardware address of the router is used as the destination MAC address; the hardware address of `Donald` is used as the source MAC address (see fig. 25.10). The resulting frame is sent directly to the router.

Fig. 25.9
The IP datagram
for the case study.

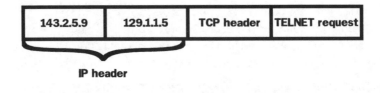

Fig. 25.10
The data frame
sent to the router.

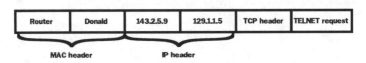

6. The router receives the frame and examines the IP information. The router notes that it can reach host Mickey directly because they are on the same IP network. The router then creates a new frame, with the same IP header information, but a different MAC header.

7. If the router does not have the hardware address of Mickey in its ARP table, it issues an ARP request to obtain it.

8. The hardware address of the router is used as the source MAC address; the hardware address of Donald is used as the destination MAC address (see fig. 25.11). The resulting frame is sent directly to Mickey.

Fig. 25.11
The data frame
received from the
router.

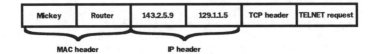

Mickey uses the same process to send replies back to Donald for the TELNET request.

Summary

This chapter discussed some of the terms used in computer networking and presented a technical discussion of the most common networking protocols encountered in UNIX. A discussion of the various devices used in internetworking and a simple case study on how routing is performed on an IP network finished off the chapter.

Chapter 26

UNIX in a NetWare World

Of all the networks installed around the world, Novell, Inc.'s NetWare is probably the second-largest installed base—the largest installed base is TCP/IP (the Internet). Among local area networks (LANs) in the business community, NetWare has, by far, the largest installed base in the world. Today, more and more people find they need to integrate UNIX with NetWare.

This chapter focuses on some of the specific needs people have in integrating UNIX and NetWare; it also explains some of the available ways of meeting those needs. The chapter first identifies the services to be shared. Then it gives specific examples of ways these objectives can be achieved using Novell software products and other third-party solutions.

Integrating UNIX and NetWare Services

As a company grows, departments within a large organization often choose different computer platforms, each selecting the one that addresses its specific needs. For example, the word processing department may use DOS PCs on a NetWare network, while the engineering and accounting departments use UNIX minicomputers. Yet all these departments need to share information and, sometimes, applications. This need for sharing information creates a number of common objectives in UNIX-to-NetWare connectivity:

■ NetWare users need to have access to UNIX printers.

■ NetWare users need to have terminal sessions on UNIX hosts—no dumb terminals on their desks.

In this chapter, you learn about the following:

■ Integrating UNIX and NetWare services

■ Connecting NetWare clients to UNIX servers

■ Connecting UNIX clients to NetWare servers

- NetWare users want *transparent* file access to UNIX hosts.

- NetWare users want simple file-transfer capability to and from UNIX hosts.

- Low-memory overhead on PCs is required in supporting multiple protocols (TCP/IP and IPX).

- UNIX users need DOS command-line and Windows support.

- UNIX users need to have access to NetWare printers.

- UNIX users need to run some DOS applications but do not want both a terminal and a PC on their desks.

- UNIX users want *transparent* file access to NetWare servers.

- UNIX users want simple file-transfer capability to and from NetWare servers.

> **Note**
>
> The TCP/IP protocol stack is available on many platforms, such as Digital VAXes and IBM mainframes; therefore, many of the products discussed in this chapter can be applied in connecting *any* TCP/IP hosts with PCs. They are not limited to connecting only NetWare and UNIX systems.

Connecting NetWare Clients to UNIX Servers

This section addresses the first five objectives just listed—how best to connect NetWare (PC) clients to UNIX hosts.

The first two solutions, LAN WorkPlace and NFS Client, do not require you to have a NetWare server. Therefore, they can be employed if you have other local area network operating systems, as long as you can use Novell's Open Data-Link Interface (ODI) drivers. The third option, NFS Gateway, is a set of NetWare Loadable Modules (NLMs) that must be installed on a NetWare server.

LAN WorkPlace for DOS

LAN WorkPlace for DOS (LWP) from Novell provides media-independent TCP/IP protocol stacks and services for both DOS and Windows users (see fig. 26.1). Because LWP uses Novell's ODI driver to communicate with the network card, it supports a variety of topologies, including (but not limited to) Ethernet, Token Ring, and ARCnet. In general, any type of network interface card that has a corresponding ODI driver can be used.

> **Note**
>
> The Open Data-Link Interface (ODI) driver allows multiple protocols to share a single network interface card. Think of it as a "protocol multiplexer" for the network card.

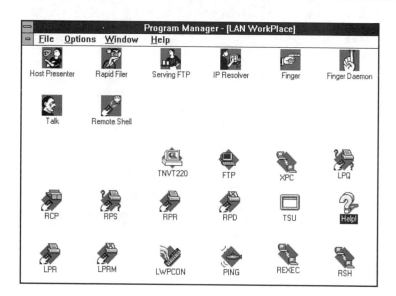

Fig. 26.1
LAN WorkPlace for DOS utilities.

LWP provides DOS and Windows clients with a wide variety of TCP/IP services such as the following:

- TELNET terminal-emulation services to UNIX hosts by way of TNVT220 (DOS) or Host Presenter (Windows)

- FTP file-transfer client capability by way of FTP (DOS) or Rapid Filer (Windows)

- FTP file-transfer server capability by way of FTPD (DOS) or Serving FTP (Windows)

- TFTP file-transfer client and server capability by way of TFTP and TFTPD (DOS only)

- Access to remote UNIX printers through the LPR protocol

- User capability to submit remote command execution requests to UNIX hosts with the R-utilities (such as rsh)

> **Note**
>
> You do not need to have a NetWare server in order to use LAN WorkPlace for DOS. All the necessary ODI drivers (except, perhaps, the specific driver for your network card) is shipped with the product.

The TNVT220 and Host Presenter emulator allow a PC user to emulate a DEC VT220, VT100, or VT52 terminal in DOS and Windows environments, respectively. If you prefer to use a third-party terminal emulator and are using LWP's TELNET stack, LWP provides a TELNET Session Utility (TSU) for that purpose (see fig. 26.2).

Fig. 26.2
The TELNET
Session Utility
(TSU).

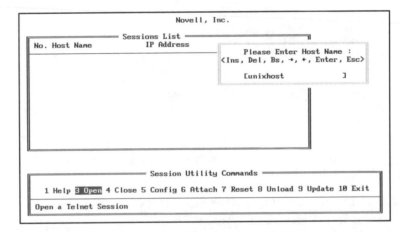

> **Note**
>
> In order to use a third-party terminal emulator with TSU, you need to ensure that it supports Novell's TELNET Application Programming Interface (TelAPI). One such emulator is MS-KERMIT from Columbia University.

A number of different file-transfer options are available. You can use the FTP or TFTP client modules from the workstation to transfer files to and from UNIX hosts, or you can use the daemon modules (FTPD or TFTPD) to allow other TCP/IP hosts to transfer files to and from *your* workstation.

> ### Tip
>
> To make your workstation an FTP server, use Serving FTP, the Windows utility. The DOS version of Serving FTP lets you take advantage of the multitasking capability of Windows without dedicating a workstation for the task.

> ### Caution
>
> Before you set your machine up as an FTP or TFTP server, spend some time and consider any security issues involved. If you do not want *everyone* to be able to access your server, set up the FTPDUSER.LOG file. Check your LWP documentation for details.

Using a line printer protocol such as LPR, you can submit a file for printing from the command line. For example, to print the file USERCH01.DOC, you would enter **LPR USERCH01.DOC**. (This does not address the need for printing from a DOS application directly to a UNIX printer; that is addressed in the next section.)

If your UNIX host has the remote shell daemon (rshd) running, you can submit print jobs using the rpr command. You can also use the rsh command to execute some UNIX commands on the remote host and have the result sent back to your workstation.

LAN WorkPlace for DOS is licensed on a per-workstation basis. You must install it on each workstation that requires TCP/IP services. This arrangement makes management of files and upgrades difficult. If you have a NetWare server, there is an alternative: LAN WorkGroup for DOS.

> ### Note
>
> LAN WorkPlace is also available for the OS/2 platform. LAN WorkPlace for OS/2 v3.0 supports OS/2 v2.1.

LAN WorkGroup for DOS

LAN WorkGroup for DOS (LWG) provides TCP/IP services, just like LAN WorkPlace for DOS does, for DOS/Windows workstations to remote UNIX hosts. However, you must have a NetWare server in order to install this product because part of LWG is a set of NetWare Loadable Modules (NLMs).

LWG has two advantages over LWP:

■ All LWG files, including utilities such as Host Presenter (a Windows-based TELNET emulator), are installed on the NetWare server (see fig. 26.3). This arrangement provides central management as well as control for who has access to software.

Fig. 26.3
LAN WorkGroup files are installed on the NetWare server.

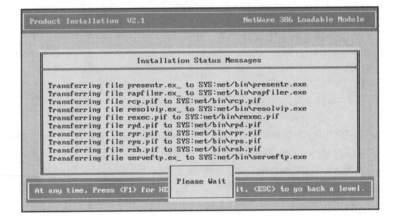

■ The LWG server can act as a BOOTP server (see fig. 26.4). The BOOTP server allows the LWG server to assign IP addresses to workstations centrally. As a result, you can administer IP addresses centrally.

Fig. 26.4
LAN WorkGroup can act as a BOOTP server by automatically assigning IP addresses to clients.

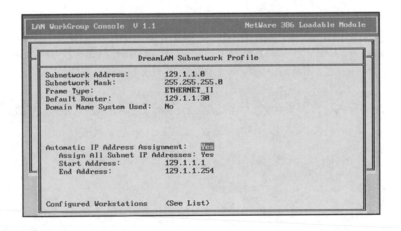

> **Caution**
>
> The drawback of using LAN WorkGroup instead of LAN WorkPlace is that when the NetWare server is not available, workstation clients have no access to any of the TCP/IP services.

The IP address assignment can be done either automatically on a first-come, first-served basis, or you can predefine which workstation has which IP address. In a way, BOOTP provides a similar function to RARP in that you use the hardware address to obtain an IP address. However, RARP cannot assign IP addresses dynamically as BOOTP can.

XPC

LAN WorkPlace/WorkGroup v4.1 is shipped with an interesting utility called XPC. XPC is a Terminate-and-Stay-Resident (TSR) DOS program that turns a PC workstation into an X-server. XPC allows remote PCs to run TELNET sessions (VT100 or VT220 emulation) and X-servers to run character-based DOS applications. The capability provided by XPC is similar to that provided by remote control programs such as CloseUp or Norton pcAnywhere, except that XPC does it over TCP/IP using the TELNET protocol.

If you have a NetWare LAN, the printing-to-UNIX solution provided by LWP/LWG is not very convenient or efficient because it can print files only from the command line and not directly from DOS applications. The addition of NFS Client for LWP helps in this area, as well as in file access to UNIX.

NFS Client

The NFS Client for LWP (called NFS Client for short) from Novell is an add-on product for the LAN WorkPlace and LAN WorkGroup family. By making use of the NFS Client NET USE command, PC workstations can do the following things:

- Execute DOS applications stored on an NFS server.

- Redirect print jobs from the PC workstation to a UNIX host.

- Have *transparent* file access on an NFS server.

- Support file and record locking on an NFS server.

Using the TELNET protocol (which LWP and LWG provide to PC workstations to access a UNIX host), users must utilize the UNIX commands and CPU of the UNIX host. With NFS Client, on the other hand, the operating system running on the host (where the files are located) does not make any difference to the PC workstation user, as long as the NFS protocol suite is supported.

Authentication. NFS Client requires an "authentication server." The Remote Procedure Call (RPC) protocol in the NFS protocol suite requires that every request from an NFS client be accompanied by a user identification (UID) and group identification (GID) to ascertain the client security permissions on the NFS host. Because DOS does not make use of UID and GID, some authentication server must provide that information on behalf of the DOS-based NFS clients.

Most UNIX systems come with a daemon called PCNFSD. This daemon is provided by Sun Microsystems to authenticate PC-NFS clients. The DOS NFS client must first "register" with PCNFSD, using a valid user name and password; then PCNFSD provides the corresponding UID and GID.

> **Tip**
>
> NFS Client is shipped with the C source code for an authentication program, LWPNFSD, that can be compiled and run on a UNIX host, if your NFS host does not have PCNFSD. You can have LWPNFSD and PCNFSD running concurrently without conflict.
>
> The source code has been tested with Berkeley BSD, SunOS, AT&T System III, AT&T System V, Silicon Graphics, Santa Cruz Operations (SCO), and IBM AIX UNIX systems.

> **Note**
>
> If you have a Network Information Service (NIS) server on your network, you can use it as the authentication server. NIS was formally known as Yellow Pages.

Windows Driver. A Windows driver is provided with NFS Client. If you load it under the Disk menu using File Manager, a PC has a Network Connection option that enables linking and unlinking of NFS drives (see fig. 26.5).

NET LINK. Using NET LINK commands, you can easily redirect LPT outputs from your workstation to a UNIX printer. Most PC applications require no special configuration to work with NFS Client.

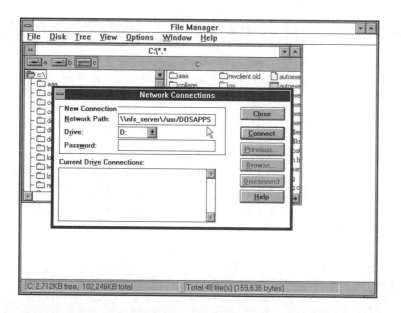

Fig. 26.5
The Network
Connection
option from
the File Manager
icon, Disk menu.

Tip

For best results, if your application allows you to specify an output printing device, select LPT?.DAT (where ? = 1, 2, or 3) as the destination port.

From within Windows, you must specify LPT?.OS2 or COM?.OS2 under the Printer Control Panel to print over the network.

Because of DOS's file-naming limitation (8 characters for the filename and 3 characters for the extension), NFS Client provides a mapping scheme to convert UNIX filenames (which, depending on your version of UNIX, can be up to 255 characters long) to the DOS format. The rules are these:

■ All characters are converted to uppercase.

■ Invalid characters (in DOS) are replaced with a caret (^) symbol.

■ Filenames are truncated to the DOS format.

■ To ensure uniqueness, a random sequence of characters may be appended after a tilde (~) character at the end of the filename. For example, the UNIX file named test is mapped to TEST; the file .longfilename is mapped to ^LONGFIL.~AA.

> **Tip**
>
> If you have many UNIX files with long names, you can easily get confused when viewing them from the NFS Client side. Fortunately, NFS Client provides a DOS utility called LS.EXE that displays both the original UNIX name and the converted DOS name.

Although NFS Client for LAN WorkPlace can provide NetWare workstations with access to UNIX hosts, it requires dual protocols (IP and IPX) on each of the workstations needing that access. Management and updates to these drivers can become tedious. A much better solution is to use the NetWare NFS Gateway product discussed next.

NetWare NFS Gateway

Instead of having to load the TCP/IP protocol stack and NFS Client for LAN WorkPlace on each NetWare workstation to access the file system on UNIX hosts, you can use the NetWare NFS Gateway.

> **Note**
>
> The NetWare NFS Gateway is a set of NLMs that provide TCP/IP connectivity and NFS services between NetWare clients and NFS hosts. The NFS Gateway mounts a remote NFS exported file system as a NetWare volume. Therefore, NetWare clients simply need to "map" to this NetWare volume using the standard MAP command to be able to work with files stored on the remote NFS server using standard DOS and NetWare commands.

With NetWare NFS Gateway, none of the workstations run TCP/IP and NFS; therefore, the NetWare server running the NFS Gateway has to translate NetWare Core Protocol (NCP) requests from NetWare workstations into NFS RPC protocols before sending the requests on to the NFS host.

Any replies from the NFS server go first to the NFS Gateway, which translates them into NCP replies before sending them back to the originating workstation.

Because the workstation's request goes to the NFS Gateway first, the NetWare server does a trustee-assignment check before deciding whether the request should be passed on. In essence, two security checks are made: one by NetWare and one by NFS (UNIX).

Because NetWare's security system is far more comprehensive than what is available in UNIX, this dual system allows a tighter level of security than NFS alone can provide.

> **Note**
>
> The security is always adjusted so that the user has the least access as viewed by either NetWare or UNIX. For example, if the NFS permissions for a directory are read and write but NetWare allows only read and file scan, the user has only read permissions for that directory. By the same logic, if NFS allows only read permissions for a directory but NetWare allows read and write permissions, the user has only read permissions for the directory—the lowest common access allowed.

One drawback of the NFS Gateway solution, compared with NFS Client for LAN WorkPlace, is that the Gateway product does not provide remote printer sharing. You need additional products, such as FLeX/IP (discussed in the next section), for such capabilities.

Just as NFS Client requires an authentication server, NFS Gateway requires such a server as well. You can either use an NIS server to provide UID and GID information, or you can use database files stored locally on the NFS Gateway.

Connecting UNIX Clients to NetWare Servers

This part of the chapter addresses the last five objectives listed at the beginning of this chapter—allowing UNIX users to access resources on NetWare servers.

The two Novell solutions presented in the following sections address the issues of sharing file and print resources between UNIX and NetWare servers, as well as allowing UNIX clients access to DOS applications.

> **Note**
>
> None of the products described in the following sections allow a UNIX, NFS, or TCP/IP host to log on to a NetWare server using the TELNET protocol. No TELNET daemon is currently available for NetWare servers.

NetWare NFS and NetWare FLeX/IP

NetWare NFS is a collection of NLMs, much like the NFS Gateway product described in the previous section. However, NetWare NFS provides exactly the opposite function: it makes NetWare volumes available for NFS mounting by NFS clients. In other words, UNIX (NFS) clients can have transparent file access to NetWare files.

In this case, the client workstations can supply UID and GID information (but not NetWare username information); an authentication server is not required. However, as part of the NLM configuration steps, you need to specify how UNIX UIDs and GIDs are to be mapped into NetWare users and groups (see figs. 26.6 and 26.7).

Fig. 26.6

Mapping UNIX UIDs to NetWare users.

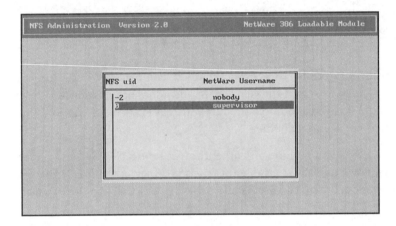

Fig. 26.7

Mapping UNIX GIDs to NetWare groups.

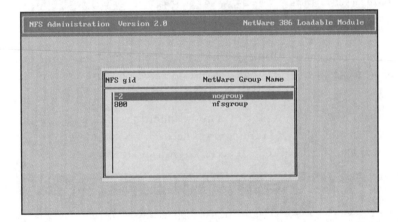

These mappings must be maintained manually. One way to do this is to edit them using NFSADMIN.NLM. Alternatively, you can directly edit the files NFSUSERS and NFSGROUP located in SYS:ETC on the NetWare NFS server.

In addition to providing services as an NFS server, NetWare NFS also includes the following services (see fig. 26.8):

■ File Transfer Protocol (FTP) server

■ UNIX-to-NetWare print service (LPD)

- NetWare-to-UNIX print gateway (LPR)

- Lock Manager daemon (LOCKD)

- Status daemon (STATD)

- Remote X-Windows console

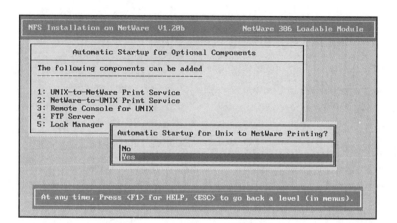

Fig. 26.8
Services available with NetWare NFS.

The FTP server implemented by NetWare NFS software is fully RFC 959 compliant. You can use any FTP client to transfer text and binary files to and from the NetWare FTP server.

> **Note**
>
> Anonymous ftp is supported by the NetWare FTP server. However, you must manually create a NetWare user called ANONYMOUS.

Normally, FTP clients can access files only on a host that has the FTP daemon running. However, the NetWare FTP daemon allows you to access other NetWare servers that do not have the FTP NLM running. And those servers need not be running TCP/IP either. Therefore, you do not need to purchase and install FTP NLM for each and every server on your network.

To access a NetWare server without the FTP daemon NLM running, you first need to establish an FTP session on a NetWare FTP server. The username *and* password you use must also exist on the remote NetWare server. This is the only requirement.

> **Caution**
>
> FTP clients do not take up licensed NetWare connections on your NetWare FTP server because they are TCP connections. However, in accessing a remote NetWare server without an FTP server running, a licensed connection is used on the remote server.

To access the remote server, you change directories to get to the other host:

```
cd //remote_server_name/volume/directory
```

The Line Printer Daemon protocol (LPD, defined by RFC 1179) is probably the most commonly implemented remote printing protocol between UNIX hosts. It can be compared to the NPRINT and CAPTURE commands in NetWare.

LPD allows UNIX clients to submit print jobs transparently to any print queues on a NetWare server—and thus to any NetWare printers servicing those queues. UNIX print jobs are spooled to NetWare print queues, which are then serviced by NetWare print servers.

To facilitate printing from NetWare to UNIX printers, NetWare NFS supports the LPR (Line PRinter) protocol—the client portion of the LPD protocol. Using this LPR gateway, DOS, OS/2, and Macintosh clients on a NetWare server can print transparently to a UNIX printer. Because the submission of print jobs to UNIX is handled by the NetWare server, no TCP/IP protocol is needed on the client workstations.

It is important for an NFS server to track the status of file and record locks. However, this functionality is not part of the NFS protocol and additional NLMs are required. The LOCKD (Lock Manager daemon) is used to enforce file-locking and record-locking on the NetWare NFS server. It makes use of NetWare's built-in file-locking and record-locking services. The STATD (Status Monitor daemon) is used to reestablish file locks after an NFS server crash.

X-Windows is available on many UNIX hosts today. It provides a windowing graphical environment that many users find friendly. Novell provides an XCONSOLE.NLM module, which is a remote console program for X-Windows servers. To use XCONSOLE instead of RCONSOLE, you load XCONSOLE.NLM instead of RSPX.NLM on the NetWare server console.

> **Tip**
>
> You can have both RSPX.NLM and XCONSOLE.NLM loaded on the NetWare server. This way, you can manage the console using either RCONSOLE over IPX/SPX or X-Windows over TCP/IP.

If you do not require the NFS server module but do need bidirectional printing capabilities, NetWare FLeX/IP is what you want. FLeX/IP contains the same set of software NLM modules as NetWare NFS, except for the NFS portion.

The FLeX/IP solution is perfect for sites that require bidirectional printing and need only occasional nontransparent file transfer.

UnixWare

A few years ago, Novell entered a joint venture with UNIX Systems Laboratories (USL), created a new company called Univel, and developed UnixWare. UnixWare is based on AT&T System V Release 4.2 (SVR4.2). In early 1993, Novell purchased USL; therefore, UnixWare is now a Novell product.

UnixWare is available in two versions: Personal Edition (PE) and Application Server (AS). Built into UnixWare is the IPX transport support. You can use either PE or AS at a regular IPX workstation and log on to a NetWare server. This arrangement gives you the flexibility of running UNIX-based applications or DOS-based applications (through its DOS session support). At the same time, TCP/IP and NFS support is packaged with Application Server.

> **Note**
>
> UnixWare Personal Edition can support two concurrent users. Realistically, however, it is designed to support only one power user.

UnixWare has the following features:

- Virtual DOS sessions with access up to 8MB of expanded (EMS) memory

- Built-in Message Handing System (MHS) for electronic mail exchange with other MHS systems

- Built-in IPX protocol stack

- Novell Virtual Terminal (NVT) protocol stack for accessing a UnixWare host from IPX workstations

- Remote application sharing between UnixWare hosts

- Bidirectional printing between UnixWare host and NetWare server (using IPX)

- TCP/IP and NFS support

- X-Windows support

The X-Windows implementation in UnixWare is X11-R5, with backward compatibility provided for X11-R4. The Graphical User Interface (GUI) provided by UnixWare is called MoOLIT. It is based on the Motif and OPEN LOOK window managers. However, those who prefer the HP OpenView interface can configure the window to look at OpenView instead.

UnixWare is binary compatible with System V, meaning that any software for System V on an Intel platform will run on UnixWare without recompiling. Lotus 1-2-3 for UNIX is an example of this truth.

Although software-development tools, such as a C compiler, are not shipped with UnixWare, you can download the GNU C compiler from the UnixWare forum on CompuServe. Many GNU tools are now available for UnixWare.

> **Note**
>
> Richard Stallman, a UNIX guru and hacker, started the Free Software Foundation (FSF). He has created a comprehensive, completely free set of UNIX applications to support his belief that all software should be free to individuals. His software is distributed under the name GNU, which stands for *GNU is Not UNIX*.

The current shipping version of UnixWare is 1.1.

> **Tip**
>
> Free upgrades from UnixWare 1.0 to 1.1 are being shipped to all registered owners. If you purchased and registered UnixWare 1.0 before April 1, 1994, you are entitled to the free upgrade. This offer applies to both the Personal Edition and Application Server. For your upgrade, call (800) 457-1767.

Other UNIX-to-NetWare Networking Options

This part of the chapter presents some non-Novell solutions available to connect NetWare clients to UNIX hosts and to connect UNIX clients to NetWare servers.

NOVIX

NOVIX for NetWare from Firefox Communications is a NetWare-to-TCP/IP gateway that runs either as a Value Added Process (VAP) or an NLM on a NetWare server or router. No TCP/IP protocol stack is required on the client workstations.

> **Note**
>
> Because the ROUTEGEN router does not support multiple protocols over the same network interface card, you must install a second network card to use NOVIX.

By using LAN WorkPlace for NOVIX, which Firefox licensed from Novell, NOVIX users can print directly from UNIX to NetWare print queues, which can each have different IP addresses and port numbers. If you are short on IP addresses, you can configure a *single* IP address to be shared; alternatively, you can assign multiple addresses to clients through the use of configuration tables.

> **Tip**
>
> For fault tolerance, you can set up multiple NOVIX servers. NOVIX client software can automatically reroute connections should the primary NOVIX server be unavailable.

You can reach Firefox Communications at Firefox Communications, P.O. Box 8165, Kirkland, WA 98034-0165; (206) 827-9066.

Ipswitch

Ipswitch, Inc. has available a set of NetWare-to-TCP/IP solutions that complements some of the Novell products already discussed:

- *Piper/IP* provides a full range of DOS-based TCP/IP utilities (both client and server) for file transfer, terminal emulation, mail, backup, NFS, and more. The R-utilities are also included. Piper/IP provides a TCP/IP protocol stack that can take as little as 6KB of conventional memory (if you have memory above 1MB).

- *Catipult* is an OS/2-based NetWare-to-TCP/IP gateway solution. By using Novell's OS/2 requester, you can use any supported network interface card for the gateway. No special hardware is required. A full set of DOS-based TCP/IP utilities (client and server) is provided.

- *Vantage/IP* is a TCP/IP software product for OS/2 with a complete set of OS/2 (and DOS for OS/2's DOS session) client and server applications, including NFS.

- *Merq* is an NFS client for Novell's LAN WorkPlace for OS/2. Merq provides the equivalent functionality to an OS/2 version of LAN WorkPlace as does the NFS client for LWP to the DOS version of LWP (as discussed earlier in this chapter).

Of particular interest is Catipult's NetWare-to-TCP/IP gateway product. It is similar to NOVIX for NetWare in that no TCP/IP protocol is required at the PC client workstations. In this case, however, the IPX-to-TCP/IP transport protocol translation happens on the OS/2 gateway machine (instead of on the NetWare server). Using the TELNET daemon program running on the Catipult gateway, you can "telnet" from a UNIX host into any of the PCs. This freedom allows UNIX users to run certain DOS-based applications and makes remote troubleshooting easier.

> **Tip**
>
> Catipult requires only *one* IP address to support up to 300 Catipult users, an important consideration for sites short on IP addresses.

For more information about Catipult and other Ipswitch products, contact Ipswitch, Inc., 333 North Ave., Wakefield, MA 01880, Internet: `support@ipswitch.com`; (617) 246-1150.

SoftNet Client

Puzzle Systems Corporation's SoftNet Client software allows users of HP9000, Silicon Graphics, and Sun SPARC UNIX hosts to function as full NetWare clients and directly access NetWare servers. UNIX users can log in to and mount NetWare server volumes without the need for an NFS daemon on the NetWare server.

Puzzle Systems can be reached at Puzzle Systems Corporation, 16360 Monterey Road, Suite 250, Morgan Hill, CA 95037, Internet: `jal@puzzle.com`; (408) 779-9909.

NetWare for UNIX

NetWare for UNIX, formally known as Portable NetWare, is an implementation of NetWare 3.11 on a non-Intel platform. Novell licensed NetWare to a number of vendors including (but not limited to) Data General, Digital Equipment Corporation, and IBM.

NetWare for UNIX is implemented as a process (daemon) running under the operating system of the host machine, such as UNIX. Because each client NetWare request must first be passed to the NetWare daemon before it is translated into a UNIX request, performance is an issue. In general, the performance of NetWare for UNIX is about that of native NetWare running on an Intel 80386 33-MHz platform.

> **Caution**
>
> You should not consider using NetWare for UNIX as your primary file server. It is, however, perfectly fine as a file-sharing solution between UNIX and NetWare users.

Under NetWare for UNIX, a user can be a pure NetWare user, a pure UNIX user, or a hybrid user.

Part of NetWare for UNIX is the NVT protocol, which allows PC workstations to "telnet" into the UNIX host without the need for a TCP/IP protocol stack on the client. NVT uses IPX as a transport protocol.

Novell is working on the next generation of NetWare for UNIX called Processor Independent NetWare (PIN). Under this implementation, NetWare will run as the native operating system instead of as a daemon under the host's operating system.

PopTerm/NVT

In order to "telnet" into a host with the NVT server (for example, a UnixWare host or a UNIX host running NetWare for UNIX), you need a DOS terminal emulator that supports INT14. Among the emulators available, PopTerm/NVT from Rational Data Systems, Inc. is probably the most popular.

Unlike other terminal emulators (which need to load the NVT protocol separately), PopTerm/NVT has the NVT protocol built in. Yet it is still small enough to be loaded as a TSR in high memory. It lets you establish multiple sessions on different hosts simultaneously; this means that you can have quick access to multiple hosts by pressing a hotkey. Windows support is also available.

> **Note**
>
> At the time of this writing, Rational Data Systems is beta-testing a new version of PopTerm that supports both the NVT and TCP/IP protocols. Novell's LAN WorkPlace TCP/IP transport will be included.

Rational Data Systems, Inc. is also a Novell-authorized porting house for NetWare for UNIX. For more information, contact Rational Data Systems, Inc., 11 Pimentel Court, Novato, CA 94949, Internet: melissa@rds.com; (415) 382-8400.

Summary

The first section of this chapter examined some of the NetWare products that can help you connect NetWare clients to UNIX hosts. By using LAN WorkPlace or LAN WorkGroup, you can have dual protocols (TCP/IP and IPX) on the workstation and access remote UNIX hosts using TELNET or FTP. However, these products do not provide transparent file sharing between NetWare workstations and remote UNIX hosts, nor do they provide transparent remote printer access. With the NFS Client for LAN WorkPlace add-on, you do have transparent file sharing and remote printer sharing. However, you still run dual protocols on the workstation. With the NetWare NFS Gateway product, you need only a single protocol (IPX) on the client workstation, and you still have transparent file sharing capability. However, printer sharing is not available without additional software.

The second section of the chapter considered products that help you connect UNIX clients to NetWare servers, including LAN WorkPlace for DOS, LAN WorkGroup for DOS, XPC, and NFS Client.

The last section of the chapter presented some third-party UNIX-NetWare connectivity solutions.

Chapter 27
TCP/IP

The suite of widely used protocols known as Transmission Control Protocol/ Internet Protocol (TCP/IP) has become increasingly important as national networks such as the Internet and the proposed information highway depend on it for their communications.

TCP/IP sprouted from initial development as a government-sponsored project to widespread use today, connecting networks of all sizes. Recognized for its ability to enable communication among dissimilar machines, it is found on virtually all workstations, minicomputers, and mainframes. This chapter describes the origins and language of TCP/IP, its addressing and naming conventions, and concepts fundamental to the creation of the Internet.

History of TCP/IP

In the mid-1970s, the U.S. Department of Defense (DOD) recognized an electronic communication problem developing within their organization. Communicating the ever-increasing volume of electronic information among DOD staff, research labs, universities, and contractors had hit a major obstacle. The various entities had computer systems from different computer manufacturers, running different operating systems and using different networking topologies and protocols. How could information be shared?

The Advanced Research Projects Agency (ARPA) was assigned to resolve the problem of dealing with different networking equipment and topologies. ARPA formed an alliance with universities and computer manufacturers to develop communication standards. This alliance specified and built a four-node network that is the foundation of today's Internet. During the 1970s,

This chapter covers the following:

- Understanding TCP/IP and Internet terms

- Connecting TCP/IP protocol suites— and their components

- Assigning and using TCP/IP addresses

- Breaking logical networks into smaller, physical networks

- Putting together a computer network to form a TCP/IP network this network migrated to a new, core protocol design that became the basis for TCP/IP.

◀ More complete descriptions of the Internet are contained in Chapter 15, "Understanding the Structure of the Internet," Chapter 16, "Finding and Using Internet Resources," and Chapter 25, "UNIX Networking Concepts."

The mention of TCP/IP requires a brief introduction to the Internet. The Internet connects hundreds of thousands of computers. Nodes include universities, many major corporations, and research labs in the United States and abroad. It is a repository for millions of shareware programs, news on any topic, public forums and information exchanges, and e-mail. Another feature is remote login to any computer system on the network using the TELNET protocol. Because of the number of systems that are interconnected, massive computer resources can be shared, allowing large programs to be executed on remote systems.

Internet Terminology

The Internet protocol suite is composed of many related protocols based on the foundation formed by TCP and IP. In order to clarify the relationship of these components, table 27.1 provides some definitions and notations.

Table 27.1: Networking Terms	
Term	**Definition**
datagram	Used interchangeably with the words *data packet* or *network message* to identify a unit of information that is exchanged.
DNS	Domain Name Service. A service provided by one or more computers in a network to help in locating a path to a desired node. This saves every system on a network from having to keep a list of every system it wants to talk to. Used by mail gateways.
GOSIP	Government Open System Interconnection Profile. A collection of OSI protocols used in United States government computer networks and projects.
Internet	A computer network based on TCP/IP and related protocols. A public network interconnecting business, universities, government facilities, and research centers.
FTAM	File Transfer, Access, and Management. A file transfer and management protocol as specified by OSI.
FTP	File Transfer Protocol. A protocol that allows file transfer between systems.
IP	Internet Protocol. A protocol responsible for transporting datagrams across the Internet.

Term	Definition
NFS	Network File System. A network virtual disk system that allows a client computer to mount remote file systems and directories. Originally developed by Sun Microsystems.
NIC	Network Information Center. Responsible for administering the Internet, TCP/IP address, and network names.
OSI	Open System Interconnection. The ISO standard model for defining data communication.
RFC	Request for Comments. The documentation maintained by the NIC relating to Internet protocols, addressing, routing, configuration, and other related Internet topics.
RIP	Routing Information Protocol. Used to exchange information between routers.
RMON	Remote MONitor. A remote network monitor that enables the collection of information about network traffic.
RPC	Remote Procedure Call. Allows procedures to be executed on a server.
SMTP	Simple Mail Transfer Protocol. Used to transfer electronic mail between systems.
SNMP	Simple Network Management Protocol. A protocol used to manage remote network devices and to collect information from remote devices related to configuration, errors, and alarms.
TCP	Transmission Control Protocol. The protocol between a pair of applications responsible for reliable, connection-oriented data transmission.
TELNET	The protocol used to establish remote terminal connections.
UDP	User DATAGRAM Protocol. A connectionless protocol used to transfer data between agents.
VT	Virtual Terminal. A method for using TELNET to log in to remote systems through the network.

VII

UNIX Networking

Looking at the TCP/IP Protocol Stack

The TCP/IP protocol stack represents a network architecture that is similar to the ISO OSI networking model. Figure 27.1 shows the mapping of TCP/IP layers onto the ISO protocol stack.

Fig. 27.1

OSI and TCP/IP
comparison.

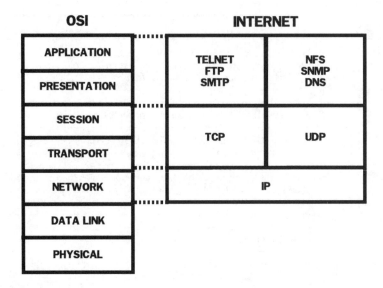

Chapter 25, "UNIX Networking Concepts," contains a complete description of the OSI protocol stack. TCP/IP doesn't make as fine distinctions between the top layers of the protocol stack. The top three OSI layers are roughly equivalent to the Internet Process protocols. Some examples of process protocols are TELNET, FTP, SMTP, NFS, SNMP, and DNS.

The Transport layer of the OSI model is responsible for reliable data delivery. In the Internet protocol stack, this corresponds to the host-to-host protocols. Examples of these are TCP and UDP. TCP is used to translate variable-length messages from upper-layer protocols and provides the necessary acknowledgment and connection-oriented flow control between remote systems.

UDP is similar to TCP except that it is not connection-oriented and does not acknowledge data receipt. UDP only receives messages and passes them along to the upper-level protocols. Because UDP does not have any of the overhead related to TCP, it provides a much more efficient interface for such actions as remote disk services.

The Internet Protocol (IP) is responsible for connectionless communications between systems. It maps onto the OSI model at part of the Network layer. The Network layer of the OSI model is responsible for moving information around the network. This is accomplished by examining the Network layer address. This address determines the systems and the path to send the message.

IP provides the same functionality as the Network layer and helps to get the messages between systems—but it does not guarantee the delivery of these messages. IP may also fragment the messages into chunks and then reassemble them at the destination. Each of the fragments may take a different network path between systems. If the fragments arrive out of order, IP reassembles the packets into the correct sequence at the destination.

IP Addresses

The Internet Protocol requires that an address be assigned to every device on the network. This address is known as the *IP address* and is organized as a series of four octets. Each octet defines a unique address, with part of the address representing a network (and optionally a subnetwork) and part representing a particular node on the network.

◀ To better understand IP addressing, see Chapter 15, "Understanding the Structure of the Internet."

Several addresses have special meanings on the Internet:

- An address starting with a zero references the local node within its current network. For example, 0.0.0.23 references workstation 23 on the current network. Address 0.0.0.0 references the current workstation.

- The loopback address, 127, is important in troubleshooting and network diagnoses. The network address 127.0.0.0 is the local loopback inside a workstation.

- The ALL address is represented by turning on *all* bits, giving a value of 255. Therefore, 192.18.255.255 sends a message to all nodes on network 192.18; similarly, 255.255.255.255 sends a message to every node on the Internet. These addresses are important in use for multicast messages and service announcements.

> **Caution**
>
> It is important that when assigning node numbers to your workstations you do not use 0, 127, or 255.

IP Address Classes

The IP addresses are assigned in ranges referred to as *classes*, depending on the application and the size of an organization. The three most common classes are A, B, and C. These three classes represent the number of locally assignable bits available for the local network. Table 27.2 shows the relationships among the different address classes, the available number of nodes, and the initial address settings.

Table 27.2: IP Address Classes			
Class	**Available Nodes**	**Initial Bits**	**Starting Address**
A	2^{24}=167772	0xxx	0-127
B	2^{16}=65536	10xx	128-191
C	2^{8}=256	110x	192-223
D		1110	224-239
E		1111	240-255

Class A addresses are used for very large networks or collections of related networks. All educational facilities are grouped under a class A address. Class B addresses are used for large networks having more than 256 nodes (but less than 65,536 nodes). Class C addresses are used by most organizations. It is a better idea for an organization to get several class C addresses because the number of class B addresses are limited. Class D is reserved for multicast messages on the network, and class E is reserved for experimentation and development.

Obtaining IP Addresses

The administration of Internet addresses is through the Network Information Center (NIC):

> DDN Network Information Center
> 14200 Park Meadow Drive
> Suite 200
> Chantilly, VA 22021
> 1-800-365-3642
> 1-703-802-4535

It is a good idea to contact the NIC to obtain a unique IP address for your network. This prevents you from having to change all of your node addresses in the future should you decide to connect to the Internet, and allows for network management within your organization because you have a preallocated set of unique addresses that can be distributed to your computer systems. Getting a unique IP address for your network also prevents the duplication of node addresses and the assignment of addresses outside the range at which your systems can communicate.

The information to be provided to the NIC must be typed and in a certain order. The following is the order and information required:

1. The name of the governmental body sponsoring your connection to the Internet. If your network will not be connected, this information is not required. The name of the sponsoring organization and the name, title, mailing address, phone number, net mailbox, and NIC handle of the contact person.

   The format is as follows:

   1a) Sponsoring organization

   1b) Contact name

   1c) Contact title

   1d) Postal mailing address

   1e) Phone number

   1f) Net mailbox

   1g) NIC handle (if one is available)

2. The NIC handle name, title, mailing address, phone number, and organization of the technical point of contact. This is the information relating to your organization.

   2a) NIC handle if available

   2b) Your name

   2c) Your title

   2d) Postal mailing address

   2e) Phone number

   2f) E-mail address of organization if applicable

3. The name of your network. This is usually the company name up to twelve characters.

   3) Network name

4. The network geographic location and the responsible organization.

   4a) Postal address of main network site

   4b) Name of organization

5. This item is for DOD or military request only. This is for connection to NSFNET.

> 5a) Should MILNET announce your network on NSFNET?

> 5b) Is there an alternate connection to NSFNET?

> 5c) If there is an alternate connection to NSFNET, should MILNET be a backup?

6. Make an estimation of the number of nodes on the network.

> 6a) At time the network is installed

> 6b) Number of connections in one year

> 6c) Number of connections in two years

> 6d) Number of connections in five years

7. This is where you can try to convince the NIC that you need a class B network number. Unless you have compelling reasons to need a class B address, class C addresses will be assigned.

   What class should you request? Most of us have the notion that we should get what we need for today and the future; although this is not a bad idea, only a limited number of addresses are available. If you have 520 nodes to connect, do not think that you need a class B address. You should obtain 3 class C addresses, for a total of 768 nodes, and then expand in the future as needs dictate by obtaining more class C addresses.

8. Define the type of network, such as educational, research, commercial, defense, or government (nondefense).

9. Purpose of network. This is where you explain what the network will be used for.

After the required information has been submitted to the NIC, it takes about two weeks to obtain your addresses. This information is provided in detail in a document called `netinfo/internet-number-template.txt` that can be obtained from sites that also contain RFCs. The following section describes how to obtain RFCs.

Obtaining RFCs

In addition to assigning addresses, the NIC can provide other information of value. It is a repository for all technical documentation related to the Internet. It has a collection of documents that describe all the associated protocols, routing methodologies, network management guidelines, and methods for using different networking technologies.

RFC stands for *Request for Comments*. RFCs can be obtained from the Internet by using the FTP protocol to connect to several different repositories. At the time this book was written, the following centers have Internet RFCs:

```
FTP.CONCERT.NET

FTP.NISC.SRI.COM

NIC.DDN.MIL

NIS.NSF.NET

NISC.JVNC.NET

SRC.DOC.IC.AC.UK

VENERA.ISI.EDU

WUARCHIVE.WUSTL.EDU
```

Table 27.3 provides a listing of the pertinent RFCs for establishing a network. Some of these documents go into great detail about how the different protocols function and the underlying specifications and theory. Others are more general and provide key information that can be useful to a network manager. At a minimum, an Internet network manager should know where these documents are located and how to obtain them. They provide information that can help in planning and growing an organization's network.

◀ Further details on obtaining RFCs from the Internet are found in Chapter 16, "Finding and Using Internet Resources."

Table 27.3: RFCs of Interest

RFC Name	Description
RFC791.txt	Internet Protocol DARPA Internet Program Protocol Specification
RFC792.txt	Internet Control Message Protocol
RFC793.txt	Transmission Control Protocol DARPA Internet Program Protocol Specification
RFC950.txt	Internet Standard Subnetting Procedure
RFC1058.txt	Routing Information Protocol
RFC1178.txt	Choosing a Name for Your Computer

(continues)

Table 27.3 Continued	
RFC Name	**Description**
RFC1180.txt	A TCP/IP Tutorial
RFC1208.txt	A Glossary of Networking Terms
RFC1219.txt	On the Assignment of Subnet Numbers
RFC1234.txt	Tunneling IPX Traffic through IP Networks

Network Naming

The naming of network nodes requires some planning. When selecting names, keep network management and user acceptance in mind. Many organizations have network naming standards. If your organization has such standards in place, it is best to follow them to prevent confusion. If not, there is plenty of room for imagination. Computer and network names can be a simple as naming the workstations after the users, such as Diane, Beth, or John.

If you have many similar computers, numbering them (for example, PC1, PC2, . . . , PC128) may be appropriate. Naming must be done in a way that gives unique names to computer systems. Do not name a computer `thecomputerinthenorthoffice` and expect users not to complain. After all, even the system administrator must type the names of computers from time to time. Avoid names like `oiiomfw932kk`. Although such a name may prevent network intruders from connecting to your computer, it may also prevent you from connecting to your workstation.

Names that are distinctive and follow a theme work well, helping the coordination of future expansion and giving the users a sense of connection with their machines. After all, it is a lot easier to have a good relationship with a machine called `sparky` than a machine called `0F1284`.

Remember the following points when selecting a naming scheme:

1. Keep names simple and short—six to eight characters at most. Although the Internet Protocol allows names up to 255 characters long, avoid lengthy names. (Each label can be up to 63 characters in length. Each part of a period-separated full domain name for a node is a label.)

2. Consider using a theme like stars, flowers, or colors, unless other naming standards are required at your site.

3. Do not begin the name with digits.

4. Do not user special characters in the name.

5. Do not duplicate names.

6. Be consistent in your naming policy.

If these guidelines are followed, a successful naming methodology can be established.

Internet names are representative of the organizations and the functionality of the systems within the network. Following are examples of names that can be used.

```
spanky.engineering.mycompany.com
nic.ddn.mil
```

The following names are difficult to use or remember:

```
thisismyworkstation.thelongwindeddepartment.longcompnam.com
n34556nx.,m3422.mycompany.com
```

The last listed name could be encoded information about a workstation in room 345 on network 56 with network executive functions, but this type of naming is usually considered poor practice because it can lead to confusion and misdirected messages.

Internet names allow you to reference a user on a particular node. For example, the following name can be used to send electronic mail to the user on a particular node:

```
Eddie@PC28.Programming.mycompany.com
```

NIC Naming Tree

The NIC maintains a network naming tree. This tree is used to group like organizations under similar branches of the tree. Figure 27.2 shows the naming tree. Major organizations are grouped under similar branches. This is the source for Internet labels like com, edu, and gov that are seen in Internet names.

VII

UNIX Networking

Fig. 27.2
The NIC naming
tree.

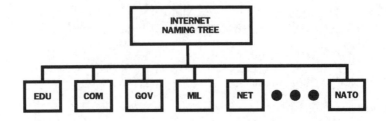

Table 27.4 shows some of the common leaf names and definitions for the
NIC tree. There are many other leaves under the tree, but the table shows the
most common.

Table 27.4: Common NIC Names	
Name	**Type of Organizations**
edu	Educational facilities (such as universities and colleges)
com	Commercial (most corporations)
gov	United States nonmilitary government bodies (White House, Department of Agriculture)
mil	Military (military users and their contractors)
net	Internet network management and administration

Subnetworks

Subnetting is the process of dividing a large logical network into smaller physical networks. Reasons for dividing a network may include electrical limitations of the networking technology, a desire to segment for simplicity by
putting a separate network on each floor of a building (or in each department
or for each application), or a need for remote locations connected with a
high-speed line.

The resulting networks are smaller chunks of the whole and are easier to
manage. Smaller subnets communicate among one another through gateways
and routers. Also, within an organization there may be several subnetworks
that are physically on the same network. This may be done to logically divide
the network functions into workgroups.

The individual subnets are a division of the whole. Suppose that a class B network is divided into 64 separate subnets. To accomplish this, the IP address is viewed in two parts, network and hosts (see fig. 27.3). The network part becomes the assigned IP address and the subnet bits. These bits are in essence removed from the host's part. The assigned number of bits for a class B network is 16, and the subnet part adds an additional 6 bits, for a total of 22 bits to distinguish the subnetwork. This division results in 64 networks with 1024 nodes in each. The network part can be larger or smaller, depending on the number of networks desired or the number of nodes per network.

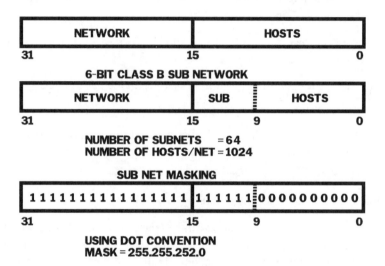

Fig. 27.3
Class B subnetwork masking.

Subnet Masks

Setting a subnet mask is a matter of determining where the network address ends and the host address begins. The subnet mask contains all 1s in the network field and 0 in the host field.

Suppose that a class C network is composed of the following:

```
N = network
H = Host
NNNNNNNN.NNNNNNNN.NNNNNNNN.HHHHHHHH
```

Each position represents a single bit out of the 32-bit address space. If this class C network is to be divided into four class C networks, the pattern would resemble the following:

```
NNNNNNNN.NNNNNNNN.NNNNNNNN.NNHHHHHH
```

The subnet mask would then look like this:

```
11111111.11111111.11111111.11000000
```

If this address is written in base-ten dot notation, the subnet mask is 255.255.255.192. This mask is used to communicate among nodes on all subnetworks within this particular network.

If three bits are taken from the host field, eight networks can be formed, and the resulting network mask would be as follows:

```
11111111.11111111.11111111.11100000
```

The subnet mask is 255.255.255.224. Each of the eight networks would have 29 nodes because five address bits are available. (It would be 32 except that all 1s, all 0s, and 127 are not legal addresses.)

This concept can be extended to class B and class A networks. The only difference is that the remaining fields are 0 (zero).

Consider a class B network. The address space is divided as follows:

```
NNNNNNNN.NNNNNNNN.HHHHHHHH.HHHHHHHH
```

If two bits are taken from the host field and added to the network part, the following subnet mask is used:

```
11111111.11111111.11000000.00000000
```

The mask is written as 255.255.192.0.

The bits needed for the subnet mask can be taken from any of the bit positions within the host field—but this leads to complex subnet masks and address exclusions. This should be avoided if at all possible.

Routing

Routing is a method of transferring information between networks. A router works at the Network layer of network protocols. There are several different means by which data may be routed. The one implemented for an Internet network is the Routing Internet Protocol (RIP).

Routing Information Protocol (RIP)

Information about routing can be obtained from several RFCs. At this writing, there are 21 different RFCs about routing. The one of most interest to network managers is RFC 1058, Routing Information Protocol (RIP). This RFC is dated June, 1988, and discusses the protocol in detail.

The RIP is designed to be used in small- to medium-sized networks and is based on Xerox Network Systems (XNS) routing protocols. RIP determines a message route by using a distance-vector routing algorithm. This algorithm assumes that each path is assigned a cost. This cost can be representative of network throughput, type of line, or desirability of the path. The protocol then determines the lowest cost path over which to transmit the message.

How a Routing Protocol Works

In order to maintain a list of hops to adjacent nodes, an RIP router keeps a routing table in the router or computer memory. This table is updated at 30-second intervals with information from neighboring routers. The information is used to recalculate the lowest cost path between systems. Each router on a network sends out, or advertises, and receives routing information.

The routing protocol is limited in the distance a message can be routed. Each router can route a message only to a cost of 16. If the message sent out on a wire costs more than 16, the host is deemed unreachable. Cost is a method of assigning values to different paths through the network and is a way of ensuring an efficient route to a destination when there is more than one way to get there.

When a network break occurs, the routers must relearn least-cost paths. This takes time and can result in messages being transmitted at higher cost for a period of time. When a node goes down, all routers must readjust their respective routing tables. During this time, messages can be lost in the network. After a period of time, the routers are resynched and routing continues.

Router crashes are also a concern. In the event of a crash, adjacent routers update their adjacency to a crashed router in 180 seconds. After that period of time, if no routing information is received from the crashed router, that path is removed from the local router's database.

The RIP does not manage routing distances, just cost. Because of this, the RIP may not use the shortest physical path between two points. Work and modifications have been made to the protocols to help correct this problem. A new routing protocol being developed and tested is Open Shortest Path First (OSPF). This protocol has begun to gain acceptance and use. Currently, NetWare implements RIP.

Network Segmentation

Internet networks are divided into segments for a variety of reasons. Some of these reasons are related to the underlying networking technologies. Others are related to geographical locations. Some of the best reasons to isolate network segments are based on network usage. If a lot of traffic in a network is between a few nodes, it is best to isolate those nodes. This isolation drops the usage and provides a more responsive network to the other network users.

Other reasons to segment are to change networking technologies or to communicate between different networking technologies. For example, an office area may be running Token Ring, and the shop floor area may be running Ethernet. Each has a distinct function. The office may require Token Ring to communicate with an AS/400. The shop floor may have Ethernet to allow shop floor controllers and computers to communicate. The shop floor information then may be uploaded to the office network for order tracking. The connection between the technologies is usually through routers. The routers forward only information that must be exchanged from one network to the other. This information can then be shared between nodes on the respective networks.

Excessive use of routers in a network can become a burden to the network, outweighing their benefits. The use of a router is of little benefit if all the nodes on one network must get to all the nodes on another network and vice versa. In this instance, the advantages of routing would be diminished because of the overhead in the routing protocols. In that kind of situation, a bridge is a better alternative.

A bridge allows all information from two networks to be shared. The access is at the Physical layer and not at the Network layer, so address translation and routing overhead are not incurred. A bridge allows all information, including system broadcast messages, to be transmitted. If two networks rarely share information, a router is a better choice; otherwise, a bridge is the proper choice.

Setting Up Internet Networks

The design and configuration of an Internet network are similar to the design of any computer network. It includes many types of nodes, including workstations, servers, printers, mainframes, routers, bridges, gateways, print servers, and terminals. The Internet requires that each device have a unique IP address. A device can have more than one address, depending on its function, but at least one address is required for communication with the other devices.

Types of Connections

A TCP/IP network can consist of several systems connected to a local area network or hundreds of systems with connections to thousands of systems on the Internet. Each organization can create the type of network appropriate for their needs.

Figure 27.4 shows a simple network. This network consists of several workstations and a file server. Each station on the network is assigned the network address of 194.62.23. Each device is assigned an individual node address. This network is typical of most departments within a company or even a small office. There is room to connect printers and more workstations to the network. The network has no provisions for connections to other local or wide area networks.

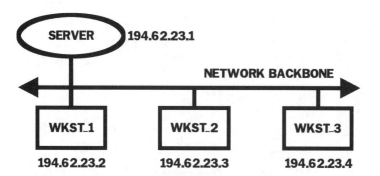

Fig. 27.4
A simple network.

The network in figure 27.5 is more complex. It includes three separate networks interconnected through a combination of routers and servers. Each of the workstations and computers on each segment may or may not be isolated from using information on one of the other two networks. This is a characteristic of the subnet mask and security enabled on the servers and routers.

Information from one network is routed to one of the other networks on an as-needed basis. This type of configuration is typical of most large corporate networks. It may be chosen based on physical-length limitations of the underlying network technology or individual network loading. One or more of the networks may experience high traffic that must be distributed across several networks.

Router 1 between networks 1 and 2 provides for routing information between the two networks. If server 1 connecting networks 2 and 3 has routing enabled, information from network 3 to network 2 is routed. Also, information can be routed from network 3 to network 2 by means of server 1 and from network 2 to network 1 by means of router 1. Server 1, connecting networks 2 and 3, has two IP addresses—one IP address on network 2 and another address on network 3. The same is true for router 1, with addresses on network 2 and network 1.

Consider a situation in which there is a lot of Internet network traffic between network 3 and network 1. In this case, it may be worthwhile to place an additional router between network 1 and network 3. The additional router can eliminate some of the routing overhead on server 1 and allow information to be passed between networks when server 1 is down.

Fig. 27.5
A more complex
network.

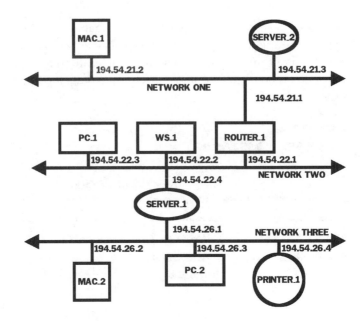

The additional router can add a level of fault tolerance to the network. This
fault tolerance is based on the fact that information can still be routed to
network 2 from network 3 even when server 1 is down. The path between
network 3 and network 2 would be through network 1 and router 1. The
addition of router 2 is shown in figure 27.6.

Fig. 27.6
Adding a second
router for fault
tolerance.

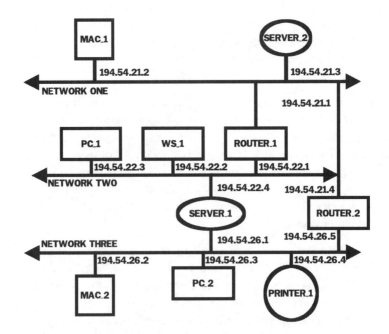

The fault tolerance of a network improves its integrity and can be of particular importance in certain applications. If time-critical information must be shared between two networks, an alternative path should be provided between the networks. This could be provided through the use of additional routers. Because these paths may be indirect (through a third network), a configuration parameter should be used.

This parameter is usually referred to as *network cost*. The cost of a hop can be increased by increasing the value a packet takes across a network path. The default preferred path is the low-cost path; the alternative path is the high-cost path. This arrangement prevents information from being routed over the high-cost path on a regular basis.

Figure 27.6 shows an additional router added between network 1 and network 3. The desired path for information from network 3 to network 2 is through server 1. Because router 2 connects network 3 and network 1, information can be routed between those two networks. Also because router 2 is between network 1 and network 2, information is routed through that path. Information from network 3 that is bound for network 2 can go over one of the two paths: either through server 1 or through router 2 and router 1. The latter is not the preferred path because information can be routed directly over server 1. Therefore, a higher cost is assigned to the path of router 2 and router 1 from network 2. This type of path analysis must be performed in a multiple segment network.

Choosing a Networking Configuration

The physical media used by an Internet network can be almost any network technology in current use. Internet network traffic is not limited to Ethernet, ARCnet, or Token Ring. It can travel over asynchronous RS 232, T1 lines and through frame-relay. Whatever networking topology is selected for the network, the configuration, installation, and operation rules associated with that networking technology must be followed.

Keep in mind the bandwidth that an application requires. Many applications require megabytes of data to be transferred, so bandwidth becomes a prime consideration. Another consideration is the physical location of the network. If all nodes are in the same building, a single LAN can be used. However, if the networks are located across town, a T1 connection may be needed. If the nodes are located in different geographical locations, a frame-relay or a packet-switched network can be used.

In laying out a network, you must consider the type of information to be carried over the network, the physical location, and network loading. To help determine the capacity of the network, examine the type of workstations, servers, and applications.

If diskless workstations are used in a network, a higher network load is placed on the network for each node. The reason for this is that each remote diskless workstation requires all operating system code to be downloaded through the network. Because all applications and utilities as well as data files are stored remotely, every action on that workstation requires network access.

Also of concern is the amount of NFS traffic that will occur on the network. NFS provides remote virtual disk services, so information retrieved and stored on these remote disks will constantly be used on the network.

Other considerations are large graphical images, swapping and page files used for virtual memory, distributed database applications, printer traffic, and terminal traffic. These are all considerations in any network, but the designers and users of PC LANs do not usually have to contend with them. When a network is connected into a general user community, all aspects of the networking environment come into play.

Other items to be examined are the need for dial-up and remote access. If this access is related to terminal and screen traffic, a serial port from an existing system may suffice. If a Serial Line IP (SLIP) connection is made, you must consider how much overhead it will impose on the network when users are loading software utilities, programs, and databases over the phone lines. This is of concern because IP is not limited to a high-speed link like Novell IPX and other networking protocols.

Network Configuration Guidelines

A network must be designed based on guidelines and rules. Some questions to consider when planning a network include the following:

- How will the network be used today?

- How will the network be used next year and the year after?

- What applications are going to be used on the network?

- Will workgroups within the organization require networking resources in the future?

- What types and numbers of workstations will be on the network?

- How many servers, minicomputers, and other hosts will be on the network?

- What other network devices, such as printers and plotters, will be on the network?

- Will shared disk arrays and optical jukeboxes be necessary?

- Will management of the network be centralized?

- Will the network be connected to the Internet or other corporate networks, or will it be the basis for a wide area network?

- . What other protocols will utilize the networking technology (IPX, DECNET, LAT, OSI protocols, and TCP/IP)?

- Where will critical data be interchanged (determine several different paths)?

- How will the network grow and change?

After all these questions have been addressed, the network can be defined. The number of nodes indicates how many class C address spaces are needed or if a class B is needed.

Connection to remote facilities should also be addressed. The load can be distributed across multiple network segments. Common access defines the division point to isolate as much network traffic as possible to individual network segments. Try to minimize the traffic that has to go across networks. For example, if you have two systems that exchange a lot of information and hops across three networks are required for them to communicate, consider moving the systems to the same network.

Determine the best networking topology to meet the requirements specified in the network analysis. To allow for growth in the network, the best approach is to determine the maximum load and develop a network in which that load is at a minimum.

Routers and Bridges

Special-purpose devices are used to provide connections between networks and systems. Sometimes the terms *gateway* and *router* are used interchangeably. Strictly speaking, the term *gateway* describes a system that sends messages between different types of networks; a *router* sends messages between networks of the same type.

In this text, the term *router* is routinely used to describe any device that takes messages from one network and passes them through to another network. The router contains enough intelligence to know whether the message received must be forwarded to another network or a router.

Routers operate at the Network layer and are usually associated with a protocol like IP or IPX. Most routers that route IPX traffic can route IP traffic as well. The router is used to connect multiple local and wide area networks. It provides a method of sharing data between networks. Also, because a router works at the Network layer, it can help reduce broadcast traffic.

If one network uses a lot of different protocols and another network only uses IP, a router that routes only IP messages is needed if those two networks are to communicate. The router prevents messages from being placed on a network that cannot manage them.

Bridges, on the other hand, can be used to interconnect local and wide area networks; they share information regardless of protocol. A bridge allows two interconnected networks to have many different protocols on them at the same time. The messages forwarded by a bridge usually do not contain any further routing information. The messages are usually left undisturbed.

One drawback of bridges is that all network broadcast and multicast messages from all interconnected networks are seen on all legs connected by a bridge. This results in a lot of overhead related to network update messages. Additionally, a bridge forwards messages only to network addresses on the other side of the bridge, but it can forward all network protocols and broadcast messages.

Note

Use bridges only if multiple protocol packets are to be shared. Otherwise, a router is a better choice because it helps reduce network overhead.

Routers and bridges are used to share information between networks. The appropriateness of each is determined by networking requirements, the protocols involved, network capacity, and user demands. The proper selection of components can help a network operate efficiently, allow for future growth, and help ensure continued reliability.

Summary

Using TCP/IP and related Internet protocols in a network allows for growth and expandability. As the number of computer vendors migrating their systems from proprietary protocols to open communication protocols increases, the need for TCP/IP also increases. Internet Protocols and the suite of related protocols provide the same network services provided by proprietary network schemes in the past. Virtual disk support, network printing, remote booting, routing, and virtual terminal support are offered throughout the Internet Protocol suite.

Applications emerging today and in the future require many different computer systems to share information and programs. Whether these systems are across the hall or across the world, the Internet Protocols can help the information to be shared in a reliable and efficient manner.

The Internet Protocol suite provides for the connection of more than four billion computers. This wide address space has been divided into smaller address segments to help manage addressing and networks. The Internet Protocol suite has been in existence for more than 20 years and continues to expand in functionality.

In the future, there may be a formal convergence of OSI and Internet Protocols. This is being initiated by the U.S. government's adoption of GOSIP (Government OSI Protocol). Networking technology continues to grow and change to meet the needs of the networking community.

## Chapter 28

UNIX Administration in a Networked Environment

A UNIX network usually takes the form of many computers, large and small, tied together over directly connected wires or common telephone lines. Administering the network is usually the task of a person or persons located at one of the sites in the network.

Most people can learn UNIX and administer a network. Although it would be nice to find a qualified person right away, such people are somewhat rare—and usually well paid. However, even people with limited or no background in computers can learn how to administer a corporate UNIX computer.

This chapter takes a common-sense approach to system administration in a networked environment. It is reasonable to expect one administrator, properly prepared and using the tools outlined in this chapter, to be able to administer a handful of systems at a single location.

Using the graphical tools provided in UnixWare or another SVR4.2 system, you can administer a small network of systems with very little expertise. Using features like the Internet Setup and Dialup Setup windows, you can configure a basic network by clicking on icons and filling in forms.

This chapter covers the following topics:

- Setting up and maintaining a UNIX network

- Accessing your system and supporting users' needs

- Understanding the network hardware you can use to connect to your UNIX system

- Considering security issues

Defining the Role of the Network Administrator

Any time you have more than a few UNIX systems connected in a network, you should probably have a dedicated network administrator. Some expertise is needed to decide how systems are connected (LANs or modems), the level of security needed, and how shared peripherals (printers, tape backups, and so on) are distributed. On a day-to-day basis, the administrator maintains lists of system name, network addresses, and user access, and generally makes sure that the network is running properly.

Corporations with networks of 50 to 100 computers can afford to have several administrators with extensive training in selected topics. This can be a necessity if you have complex printing needs, for example. Printers and printing, as an administrative topic, can require extensive knowledge of specific printers and how to interface that equipment to UNIX.

Hardware and Software Issues

If, as a UNIX system administrator, you are required to choose the networking software and hardware for the computers under your control, there are several things you should consider. As with most things in life, you will primarily be balancing what you need with what you can afford.

If your UNIX systems are close together in the same building, a local area network is a low-cost, high-speed means of networking your computers. Put an Ethernet board in each UNIX system and use TCP/IP as the networking software. (TCP/IP comes with many UNIX systems.)

To connect over greater distances, you can use modems for lower-speed transmissions and UUCP as the software to connect the systems. (Most UNIX systems come with UUCP.) For higher speeds over long distances, you can get leased lines from the telephone company.

Don't buy just any old networking hardware. Although many off-the-shelf networking hardware products come with drivers needed to make them work with DOS, the same isn't true with UNIX. As a result, most UNIX systems have many standard networking drivers built in. Check which drivers are supported before you make your purchases.

There are many reliable accounting, word processing, spreadsheet, and database programs available for UNIX. Many of these are integrated with networking products. Check with the product's vendor to see what networking products are required to use it in a networked environment.

Even applications that are not integrated with networking products can be used in a network environment. For example, you can install an application on a UNIX system and have many users from other computers use the application by running the remote execution commands (rsh and uux) built into UNIX. Or you can share an application by remotely mounting the file system that contains the application and then running it from the local system.

Common Networking Administrative Tasks

Administration of a network takes on several dimensions. Most networks don't just occur; they typically evolve. In the ideal situation, the administrators are involved with the purchase of the computers and software so that they know what will be expected of them as administrators and what the users will be getting.

Setting Up the System

Network software should be installed and ready to connect on-site. If you are using fiber optics, Ethernet, or direct wiring for this part of your network, it is a good idea to have the continuity tests completed. If you are using telephone lines, have them tested. Wiring and terminals for users should also be tested and ready. Installation *should* be "plug-and-play," but it never is. There are always connection problems.

The advantage you have when you buy a computer for a situation in which the operating system is not yet installed is that you can set up file systems to accommodate your specific needs. You must know what software is going on the computer, the number of users who will be using the system, and the intensity of their usage.

When the system is fully functional, the application software should be installed. Software on a UNIX computer is often more complex than on a single-user system, so anticipate that it will take time to install, tune, and make the software fully operational. This task can take from a couple of hours to several days, or longer.

> **Tip**
>
> You have invested time and money in setting up the network to this point. Back up the configuration files you have set up immediately.

You are now ready to start adding users to the system, even though you are still not on-site. Add a few key people's logins to the system and put in a common startup password such as *temp01*. This provides some initial security, and will give you a chance to get key people onto the system and operational right away when you install the system.

After installation, the computer should be brought up on the network. Be sure that you can communicate from any point in the network to any other node. Test communications by moving large and small files from one computer to another. Electronic mail should be directed to and from other nodes in the network. All computers must "know" this new computer in the network. This means both the /etc/uucp/Systems file and the /etc/hosts file must have the new system identified. Some UNIX versions have other files that must be set up; the specifics of each system are outlined in your manuals.

Handling Peripherals

Printers can be a major issue to an administrator. Monitoring and maintaining printers is a significant task and can take a lot of an administrator's time. Understanding the spooling of print jobs, the interface tools, and equipment peculiarities requires time and patience.

Modems are the cheapest way to link a network that spans long distances. Modems and common uucp are tools that can make it practical for a small staff to administer many computers. However, as with printers, there are some problems with modems that will require time to get running right. Choose one or two brand names and really learn the idiosyncrasies.

Monitoring the System

When the installation is completed, you can set up UNIX tools to monitor this new system. The acctcom and sar commands should be implemented, and the administrator(s) should start getting a feel for how the system is performing.

Monitoring running systems in a network is ongoing, but if you are not constantly adding peripherals or software, the administrative load should stabilize after a while. Occasionally, something will fail, or "tweaking" may be necessary. A good administrator will learn to determine whether the problem is hardware-related or software-related.

Coping with Software Upgrades

Some software companies are constantly updating their software. The good news may be that a bug is fixed. The bad news may be that each system in the network has to be updated. Expect a new challenge with each update.

The best advice is not to put all new versions on your systems but to test the upgrade or patch on one noncritical system. When you are sure that the new version is okay, upgrade the other systems. A good administrator will learn how to install these patches or new versions without going to the other sites in the network. This sounds impossible at first, but you will find that many UNIX tools facilitate this.

Training the Administrator

Training in most organizations is very "hit or miss." Perhaps the person has some computer background in some computer topic, but there is little done to formally train that person to administer the system. Administration requires attention and a solid knowledge of the following topics:

- *UNIX design and usage.* The administrator has to have a thorough understanding of redirection, pipes, background processing, and so on.

- *The vi editor.* The vi editor is on virtually every credible UNIX computer put out over the last 10 years. Many people criticize it, and many people substitute other editors for their own use, but it is advisable to have an administrator learn and become proficient in the use of vi.

- *Shell script programming.* Many of the key programs used to administer UNIX are written in shell script language and may require modification for your specific needs. Many of the tools outlined in this chapter require knowledge of how to put together and use a shell program. Some people recommend that you use the C shell or the Korn shell (both have merit). You should, however, stay with the common Bourne shell until you master this shell language. Also, all the shell programs written by the UNIX creators are written in the Bourne shell.

- *Communications.* Communications training is generally not very good as of this writing. The uucp, described in this chapter, is sometimes taught, but only in generic terms. This protocol should be taught in a laboratory environment and with the many options available. Attend classes, or at least buy manuals on the subject, but accept that you will be spending much time experimenting.

- *UNIX conventions.* UNIX conventions are not taught or even mentioned in many UNIX classes, and you will probably have to pick them up by observing as you go through training. An example will help explain this point: The bin directories are where binary source programs are generally located. You can put your programs in lib (library) directories, and UNIX operates with them located there. Understanding and following standard UNIX industry conventions like these can save time in finding and fixing problems.

Several reputable companies, perhaps including the company from which you bought your computer, offer training on all of these topics. Some vendors who sell the UNIX operating systems offer classes on selected topics. There are training courses through various academic institutions and even through correspondence courses.

Training is best done in small pieces. You should take a course, and then come back and use what you learned right away on your network. UNIX has an elaborate set of tools that will probably never be completely mastered, but you have to know where to find information in manuals.

Managing Users

UNIX lets you add and manage the permissions users have to the resources on your system. Once you connect to a network, the potential access to your system grows beyond your list of users. Now you not only have to deal with your users, but you also must decide which systems (and which users from those systems) can connect to your system. Then you must decide what they can do once they are connected.

TCP/IP and UUCP, which come with most UNIX systems, let you create access lists of systems that can connect to yours. Both networking applications also let you decide which users can access your system (for remote login, file transfer, and remote execution).

Adding Users

Everyone who uses your system should have his or her own user account, protected by a password. As a network administrator, it is your job to add users with an eye toward the entire network environment.

Most systems require the user's name to be at least three letters and, by tradition, in all lowercase letters. In larger corporate environments, the letters are usually the initials of the person. Thus, John J. Smith is jjs. On smaller networks, you may want to go with just plain john. If you have two Johns on a node computer, you could have johns for John Smith and johnd for John Doe.

Because you are managing a group of systems on the network, you should think of maintaining a list of users across all your systems. So, if John Doe needs a login on your UNIX systems named mars, jupiter, and venus, give him the same user name (johnd) and same user ID (for example, 102) on all three systems. When John Doe wants to share data between these systems, the task is much easier if this information matches across the systems.

In UnixWare and other SVR4.2 systems, you add users with the User Setup window in the graphical user interface. This sets up users so that they can immediately log in to their own graphical interface in which they can select the way icons are laid out, colors are presented, and mouse actions work.

For nongraphical users and those who need to log in only from remote systems, you can add a user who is set up to use UNIX from the standard command-line interface. To add a nongraphical user, type the following commands to create a user with root permission:

```
useradd -m username
passwd username
```

This adds the user *username* to your system and creates a home directory for that user in /home/*username*. The second command (passwd *username*) lets you set a password for *username* that the user can use the first time he or she logs in.

Computer users who work together on a task or series of tasks can be configured to be part of a UNIX group. When you add a new user, you can also add that user to one or more groups. Each group has a name and a number, also referred to as the group ID (GID). Group names, GIDs, and the users assigned to each group are listed in the /etc/group file. You can examine the groups by typing the following:

```
cat /etc/group
```

Here is a typical result:

```
root::0:
other::1:root,daemon
bin::2:bin,daemon
sys::3:bin,sys,adm
adm::4:adm,daemon,listen
uucp::5:uucp,nuucp,ntum,epi,sbcs,zeno,mtech3,ars,stet,sps
mail::7:
asg::8:asg
network::10:network
sysinfo::11:sysinfo,dos
daemon::12:daemon
terminal::15:
cron::16:cron
audit::17:audit
lp::18:lp
backup::19:
mem::20:
auth::21:auth
mmdf::22:mmdf
sysadmin::23:
nogroup::28:nouser
group::50:ingres,george,pat,ntum,epi,sbcs,chul,ryan
gma:*:100:george,mlm,pat,dad,tel
assoc:*:101:ann,chul,ryan,dfx,tel
```

The group line `assoc` reads like this: The group ID (GID) is 101, and users `ann`, `chul`, `ryan`, `dfx`, and `tel` are part of the group.

Once the user is identified on the computer and a group is assigned, the person is ready to access the system. You must assign the user a password. Later sections of this chapter deal with assigning permissions. You may want to assign a `umask` for individual users. You can put a `umask` in either the `/etc /profile` file (thus affecting all users) or in a `.profile` file in the user's home directory. Following are a few sample lines from an actual `.profile` file:

```
# cd /u/ann <Return>
# cat .profile <Return>
umask 002
  DOSPATH=/usr/vpix/dosbin:$HOME/vpix/xenixbin:.
  PATH=$PATH:$DOSPATH
  DFPRINTER==eps
  export DOSPATH PATH DFPRINTER
  exec dskmgma gma
  exit
```

In this example, a `umask` of 002 means that any file created by `ann` will have read and write permission for her, and for anyone else in the group `assoc`. Anyone else will only have read permissions. For a further explanation of `umask`, check your manuals. Suffice it to say that `umask` is very important for making sure that only certain people can access a file. The following is an example:

```
# >/tmp/file <Return>
# ls -l /tmp/file <Return>
  -rw-r--r-- 1 ann   assoc 0 Feb 17 17:21 /tmp/file
```

In this example, creating a file `/tmp/file` automatically makes it readable and writable by the owner `ann`. It is readable by anyone in the `assoc` group, and anyone else who has a valid login on the system.

Moving Users

A quick method of adding a new user to a system is to copy information from a system on which the user currently has a login. Here's one way it can be done.

A user with the user name `georgew` and user ID 102 wants a new login in the system named `mars`. You go to the system named `venus` (where `georgew` already has a login). You copy the lines from the `/etc/passwd` and `/etc/shadow` files on `venus` that list `georgew` and put those lines into the same files on `mars`. Then copy all configuration files (`.profile`, `.kshrs`, and so on) from `georgew`'s home directory (probably `/home/georgew`) on `venus` to the same directory on `mars`. Immediately, `georgew` can log in to the new system (using his same old password) with his shell environment the same as it was on his old system.

> **Note**
>
> Some UNIX systems warn against editing the /etc/passwd and /etc/shadow files directly. Although many administrators do it anyway, it is usually safer to add users with whatever interface is provided (such as the useradd command or the User Setup icon in the UnixWare GUI).

Users on one system can be moved to other home directories, or they can share their home directory. Some systems permit you to go directly into the /etc/passwd directory and just change homes, UIDs, or GIDs. It is a good idea to read your system's documentation to make sure that you do it right. The point here is that you can make many modifications to particular items for any user.

Deleting Users

Most systems have system administration tools to handle adding or deleting users. UnixWare and other SVR4.2 systems use the userdel command or the User Setup window for deleting users. Both methods give you the option of removing the user's directories when you delete the user's account.

If an employee is terminated for any reason, it is a good idea to change the password for that account immediately. This gives you time to go through the user's files before you delete them.

Configuring Peripherals

By networking your computers, you can save money on computer peripherals. You can attach a printer to one system and open access to users from all other systems on your network. Instead of having each computer do its own backup, you can have a more expensive tape drive back up all systems on the network. Likewise, you can share other peripheral devices such as CD-ROM drives, modems, fax machines, scanners and plotters, to name a few.

Printers

Printing is one of the basic UNIX services that was designed to operate in a networked environment. Once a remote UNIX printer is configured, a user from any system on the network can send print jobs to it without needing to know the system to which it's connected (although it does help to know where the printer is so that you can pick up your print job).

◀ Setting up a UNIX system printer is described in Chapter 9, "Printing."

When you add the UNIX printer, you can define remote systems that can have access to that printer. Suppose that you're on a UNIX system and you want to provide access to the other system's printer from your system. If you are using UnixWare, here's how you would set up your system from the GUI so that you could print on the remote system's printer:

1. Double-click on the Printer Setup icon in the System Setup folder.

2. Click on Printer, click on New, and click on Remote UNIX Printer. The Printer Setup: Add Remote UNIX System Printer window appears.

3. Fill in the printer name (the name you want to use locally for the printer), the type of printer (Epson, HP, and so on), the name of the remote system, and the name of the remote printer. Then click on System V or BSD (depending on what kind of print spooler is running on the remote system).

4. Click on Add. The remote printer is added to your system and is accessible for printing for your users.

If you are using a UNIX System V system but don't have a GUI, you must identify the remote system associated with the printer from the command line by using the lpsystem command.

Communications

Most UNIX systems come with one or both of the following communications packages: UUCP and TCP/IP. UnixWare comes with both of these packages and provides interfaces to them from both the command line and the GUI.

The advantages of using UUCP for all your communication needs are numerous. This tool is generic; when you use it, you can expect the oldest version of UNIX on the simplest of computers to work with the most sophisticated large version of the operating system running on your network. Despite what you may have heard, UUCP is reliable if it is installed and maintained properly. UUCP is the most popular UNIX method for modem communications.

TCP/IP is the primary method of communicating from UNIX systems to the Internet. It's also the best method for communications between UNIX systems on a LAN. Many of the advanced UNIX networking services, including NFS (for sharing file systems over the network) and remote printing, require a TCP/IP connection.

UUCP makes use of several files that normally must be modified in the /etc/uucp directory. If you are using the Dialup Setup window from the GUI, these files are updated automatically. Otherwise, you can modify these files as the root user from the command line.

The first is a file called Systems. Following is an example of a line from the Systems file:

```
mars Any ACU Any 5551212 "" \r\d "" \r\d in:—in: nuucp word: xyz
```

This entry identifies the remote system as mars. The next word, Any, says that your system can use any devices of the type ACU (Automatic Call Unit) to connect to mars. The second Any says to use any baud rate (line speed) supported by the local and remote modem. The 5551212 is the telephone number for the remote system's modem.

The rest of the information is used when your system calls the remote system to transfer a file. The quotation marks and \r\d say that, once you get a response from the remote system, send a few carriage returns. Then, if your system sees the characters in: (the last part of the word *Login:*), it responds by typing nuucp. After that, if your system sees the word word: (the last part of the word *Password:*), send the nuucp login's password xyz (or whatever the nuucp password is on the remote system).

The next file is the Devices file. Following is an example of a Devices file entry:

```
ACU tty00,M - Any hayes
```

The tag from the Systems file relates to the tag in the Devices file (in this case, ACU). The ACU here is connected to the COM1 port on the PC (/dev/tty00). The M lets the process connect to this device without waiting for a carrier signal. The word Any says to use any supported baud rate. The final entry, hayes, says that the modem is a Hayes modem. The hayes entry is defined in the Dialers file, examined next.

```
hayes=,-, "" \M\dAT\r\c OK\r ATDT\T\r\c CONNECT \r\m\c
```

This entry defines the "chat script" used to connect to the modem and dial the telephone number. First, however, the codes for "wait for a secondary dial tone" (=) and "pause" (-) are defined as a comma (,) for the modem. When your system tries to call on the modem, it sends the characters AT; the modem responds OK. Then your system asks to dial a number (with the characters ATDT) and replaces \T with the telephone number of the remote system. When the modem responds CONNECT, your system starts the communication with the remote system.

You need one more file to effectively use uucp: the Permissions file. As an administrator, you must understand what is happening in this file. By default, there is only one line in the Permissions file: LOGNAME=nuucp. This tells your systems that systems can only transfer files to your system with uucp using the nuucp login.

The following are examples of lines from a Permissions file you may want to create:

```
......
LOGNAME=nuucp:imc:irn:off:rcwr:spare:arg:dic \
SENDFILES=yes REQUEST=yes \
READ=/ WRITE=/ \
COMMANDS=ALL
MACHINE=iac:geo:gmap:sbcs:gdp:gma:epi \
READ=/ WRITE=/ \
COMMANDS=ALL
......
```

The computer on which this Permissions file is located is open for use and abuse. Note that if remote computer imc communicates with this computer, it can read and write to the root file system (/). Although the COMMANDS line says ALL, in reality most systems cannot perform all the commands. The administrator should specify who can do what on your computer—and what directories they can use. This is partly a security issue and partly an administration issue.

The line in the preceding file that begins with MACHINE specifies which computers can be called over uucp and the permissions your users have while using uucp.

Optimizing UNIX Performance

UNIX was designed to handle as large a user load as the hardware can support. The basic design has been refined over the last 20 years. DOS users are amazed when they see a 486 EISA bus computer with 16MB of random access memory and a large hard disk compile a C program with UNIX in half the time it takes on a DOS computer. The computer can do this at the same time that several people are using the word processor and others are using a database application.

Choosing the Right Hardware

You should start designing your network by buying more computer power than you will need and then keeping the system under control. If some of the people using the system are writing complex programs, make sure that you accommodate them by having a substantial computer for them to compile on.

If some users are using common database software, make sure that you have very fast disks—and use some of the RAID software that is becoming popular (see the next section for details on RAID). If you can't afford RAID, and if you have more than one hard drive, you should at least split your applications and data between different disks.

Tuning System Performance

RAID stands for Redundant Array of Inexpensive Disks. Using RAID plus caching controllers results in more throughput than upgrading from a 486 to a Pentium Intel processor. Most speed problems in UNIX revolve around I/O, not CPU issues. For example, the military has been using a 386 to handle 20 to 40 users for over three years. The secret has been high-speed disks, splitting the load between the disks, and a caching controller.

RAID is important to your company because you can gain significant improvements in performance on a computer with a minimum investment. By "striping" several disks (RAID level 0) and upgrading your disk controller, you can cut average I/O access time from perhaps 12 milliseconds for an "unstriped" disk to about three milliseconds if you "stripe" four 12-millisecond disks.

However, chasing a two-percent improvement in performance on a computer can take much of an administrator's time. The result is similar to running a race car at its maximum speed: You spend a lot of time with the car in the shop. You can't be constantly bringing down a 30-user system while you retune parameters.

Setting the Sticky Bit

As with so many features in UNIX, the tools for speed tuning are there, but it takes time to analyze what parameter to change—and then to carefully note the changes you see. If you have a slow computer, you have to find out what is happening. But to try to "tweak" another 10 percent from a computer that is performing well is impractical.

There is one exception. If you have an application that is used extensively on your system, you can put a *sticky bit* on the source program. On a program, a sticky bit is a special permission bit that causes UNIX to keep a copy of the program in the swap area of the hard disk. Doing this makes repeated usage occur much faster than if the computer has to find the program by looking down each branch in a path.

> **Note**
>
> Shell scripts have many UNIX programs spawned from what may appear to be a simple program. Using the `acctcom` command can give you clues about what programs are being used repeatedly.

To set a sticky bit, use the following command:

```
chmod +t dfcomp dfrun
```

If you then run an `ls` command, you should see a result like this:

```
# ls -l <Return>
total 1218
-r-xr-xr-x 1 root  sys 46304  Mar 27  1993 dfauto
-r-xr-xr-T 1 root  sys 81136  Mar 27  1993 dfcomp
-r-xr-xr-x 1 root  sys 43988  Mar 27  1993 dfedit
-r-xr-xr-x 1 root  sys 68364  Mar 27  1993 dffile
-r-xr-xr-x 1 root  sys 65064  Mar 27  1993 dfindex
-r-xr-xr-x 1 root  sys 37612  Mar 27  1993 dfpack
-r-xr-xr-x 1 root  sys 94900  Mar 27  1993 dfquery
-r-xr-xr-T 1 root  sys 114944 Mar 27  1993 dfrun
-r-xr-xr-x 1 root  sys 57500  Mar 27  1993 dfsetup
```

Note the T in the final portion of the permission field for `dfcomp` and `dfrun`. This indicates that the file is a sticky-bit program.

Altering Internal Parameters

UNIX has an array of internal kernel parameters that can be changed to meet your business needs. The `ulimit` is a good example. You can set a kernel parameter that makes it impossible for a user to create a file over a prescribed limit. This is less of an issue with the current large-capacity disks than it was a few years ago.

You can list your system's tunable parameters and the value for each by typing **/usr/sbin/sysdef** as root user from a command line. Following is a partial example of the output from `sysdef` on a UnixWare system:

```
*
* i386 Kernel Configuration
*
*
* Tunable Parameters
*
   100  number of buffer headers allocated at a time (NBUF)
  1024  maximum kilobytes for buffer cache (BUFHWM)
   250  entries in callout table (NCALL)
   200  entries in proc table (NPROC)
```

The values of these parameters depend on your particular UNIX system configuration. It is strongly recommended that you read the manuals that come with your UNIX system for descriptions of these tunable parameters before you attempt to change them.

If you do change the tunable parameters, understand that there are trade-offs. If you increase the number of files a user can have open, you may run out of RAM and severely affect performance.

When a UNIX computer runs out of room in memory, it swaps jobs to the disk and brings the jobs back into memory when memory is free. Swapping is a high-overhead activity that generally occurs at the busiest time of the day. If you run the sar program with the -w option (sar -w), you can see the system swapping jobs in and out of the swap area on the disk. The following is a typical result:

```
gma gma 3.2 2 i386  02/17/94
 00:00:05 swpin/s bswin/s swpot/s bswot/s pswch/s
01:00:10  0.010.1  0.010.1  48
02:00:03  0.010.1  0.020.2  37
03:00:01  0.010.1  0.000.09
......
07:00:02  0.141.1  0.151.2  22
08:00:01  0.060.5  0.030.2  23
08:20:03  0.252.0  0.322.6  20
08:40:01  0.020.1  0.000.0  10
......
15:00:00  0.010.1  0.000.0  10
15:20:06  0.272.2  0.342.7  18
15:40:00  0.020.2  0.000.0  11
16:00:01  0.010.1  0.000.0  11
16:20:03  0.040.3  0.000.0  11
16:40:02  0.534.2  0.433.4  30
17:00:01  0.110.9  0.120.9  33
......
Average0.060.5  0.060.4  20
```

On this computer, note the sw for *swap* in the preceding listing. This is an example of a computer in need of more RAM. Also note that the swapping is heaviest at the busiest times of the business day, which further slows the computer's performance.

> **Tip**
>
> Document all kernel changes on any system in your network. You should keep track of why the change was made, the parameter that was changed, and any consequences noted after the change.

Developing a Secure System

Along with power comes responsibility. UNIX's power to share information, processing resources, and peripherals, if not handled carefully, can leave your system open to abuse. Your job is to set up system security so that only the right users and systems can connect to yours and that even they can use only the parts of your computer you want to share.

Controlling the Root

The root login is reserved for your administrators. The person who logs in as the root has the power to erase any file, restrict use by any person on the network, and quite literally cause havoc among users. That is the downside of the picture. UNIX was designed to give the person having root access the tools to do his or her job better than in other environments.

Many proprietary operating systems have blockages established by the creators to avoid accidental damage to files and other operating factors on the system. The people who created UNIX took a different attitude toward the administrator. You will find tools that permit you to connect almost any computer device. You will find software that monitors the performance of the computer. You can create an endless array of software and adapt to just about any business environment.

Additionally, you can force your users to do only specified things on the computer, or you can give them limited rights until they grow in their knowledge. The root user, the administrator, has the power to do these things.

Caution

Because access to the root is so important, some companies restrict use to a select few—but *every* administrator must have permission to use the root login. Access to the root must be controlled, but not to the exclusion of those who are to monitor and keep the network operational.

When UNIX was created, it was decided there would be several administrative activities assigned to different people. There was an lp (line printer) administrator, a uucp administrator, and more.

Daily Routines for the Computer

Many UNIX systems are up and on the network all the time. Electronic mail can come and go at any time of the day or night. System backups can run at off hours, deep into the night. Insomniac programmers can get up and write code in the middle of the night.

A wise administration staff should make backups automatically in the early morning hours without disturbing the users of the system during the business day. These after-business hours also represent the ideal time to pull back files that have meaningful statistics about the running of the system. Files such as those produced by the sar (System Activity Report) command can be brought back and examined by the administration staff to see what has been happening on the networked computers. Excessive swap activity on a node computer, for example, points out the need for more RAM on the computer.

Bringing Down the System

If you notice that the system performance has slowed significantly or that your hard disks are becoming used up quickly, you probably want to reboot your computer.

Many functions are performed in shutdown sequence, and several checks are made of the system when it is brought down and rebooted. First, all counters are cleared and the system reinitializes all the programs running in the background.

The program fsck is automatically initiated on most UNIX systems if corruption has occurred on the system. This program is a powerful tool, which the system uses frequently when booting up. Some UNIX systems with many large disk drives take several minutes to boot because UNIX is doing a silent check of all of the file systems. The latest UNIX systems, however, only do a file-system check if they detect a problem.

The fsck command should be run any time corruption is believed to have occurred. Tell the users to exit the file system you want to check, and bring the system down to single-user mode. Then unmount the file system (using the umount command) and run the fsck command.

This command can detect many possible problems. In general, when UNIX asks if a problem should be fixed, your response should be *yes*.

You can bring down most UNIX computers remotely. First, connect over your network to the node computer. Most UNIX systems, by default, won't let you log in as root over the network. So you must log in as another user and then obtain root permissions (using the su command).

You can use the command /etc/shutdown to bring down the computer, whether you are on the console or logged in remotely. The disadvantage of shutting down over the network is that you won't be able to see all the shutdown messages displayed at the console and your login session is killed before the shutdown process is complete. Also, once you shut down the system, you can't start it up again, except from the console. (Obviously, you can't remotely log in to a system that is down.)

Usually, it you are shutting down a system remotely, you shut it down to the reboot state (init state 6). This state, supported on most computer hardware, brings your system all the way down and then restarts it. Here's an example of using the shutdown command to reboot a UNIX system (either from the console or from a remote login).

```
shutdown -g5 -y -i6
```

In this example, the shutdown command alerts the users that the system is coming down and gives them a grace period of five minutes (-g5) to finish their work and get off. (You can change that grace period as you like.) The -y option tells UNIX not to prompt you to confirm that you want to shut down. The -i6 option says to shut down to initialization state 6 (initialization state 6 is the reboot state). With this command, the system goes all the way down and then comes back up (if the hardware supports it). You can change -i6 to -i0 (zero) if you want to simply shut down the system without rebooting.

If you ran shutdown from a remote system, keep trying to log in over the network to find out whether the system has come back up. Or you can call someone who can get to the computer's console.

Working Smart

After you gain experience with UNIX, you find you can do many things with existing UNIX tools. You can write a shell script executed from cron that performs a series of steps at a prescribed time of day. You can begin to see why UNIX has become so popular with people who are administering large networks.

Some UNIX commands can make a small administrative staff very productive and extend its effectiveness. Suppose that you need to run a command on a computer at a specific time, just once. You have determined that disk space on one of the computers in the network is diminishing rapidly. Suppose that you run the following command:

```
find / -type f -mtime -3 -size +50 -print
```

This command means the following: search from the root directory through all directories looking for a file (-type f) that has been modified or changed in the last three days (-mtime -3) and is more than 50 blocks in size. This command searches through thousands of files on the average system. It takes time and puts a strain on the computer. You should make the computer do this search during the lunch hour and transmit back the results. Here is how this task could be completed on the remote system:

```
at noon
find / -type f -mtime -3 -size +50 -print¦mail georgew@vforge
Cntrl D
job 759294600.a at Sat Jan 22 12:00:00 CST 1994
```

The at command knows what noon is and will execute the find command at noon today. The results of the command will be mailed to georgew, the administrator at vforge. The at command has an array of optional times outlined in the manuals; its date can be a future date or time. The Cntrl D symbolizes pressing the <Ctrl-d> keys on your keyboard. This is normally a termination sequence in UNIX.

The at command along with cron extends your capabilities to administer many computers without being on-site. But there is yet another command to help: the uux command. The uux command enables you to route a command to a distant networked computer and then return the results of the command. The advantage of uux is that you don't have to go through logging in on the distant computer to get a command executed. On your local computer, you type the following:

```
uux "site2!/etc/dfspace >vforge!/tmp/info.fr.vforge"
```

This example checks the disk space (/etc/dfspace) on the remote system named site2 and sends the dfspace output to the file /tmp/info.fr.vforge on the system named vforge. The reason uux can be difficult to administer is that the /etc/uucp/Permissions file must be configured to allow uux to work on the remote system. By default, all remote uux requests are rejected.

Security Issues

UNIX security is perhaps the best in the industry; it is so good that most government requests for computers include UNIX as a requirement. UNIX System V Release 4.1 includes features designed specifically to meet advanced government security requirements.

Traditionally, UNIX has had excellent security tools, but because there are so many ways to use and access the system, you must be diligent to protect it. Passwords can be left blank, or the root login can be open to all. There are times and places where this is appropriate. If you have a closely knit group working on a common project, all working in the same room not readily accessible to others, it may be appropriate to have no security.

Modems and Hackers

Allowing access from a common modem, similar to those that people have at home, can permit someone to "hack" into the system and destroy important data. As a result, many companies insist that the computer have elaborate security mechanisms—which can make these computers almost impossible to work with. Some companies put a dial-back option on the computer so that you must dial the computer and then wait for a return call before you can interact with the system.

Most of the time, a traditional UNIX approach is recommended. Make sure that all your user logins have passwords. Restrict the systems that can connect to your system. Keep permissions closed on sensitive files. Be careful of set UID bit programs (those that give the user who runs the program the permission to run as another user). Most break-ins occur because someone left the door open.

Passwords

Most password-assignment programs on major computers check to make sure that you have chosen a password that will be difficult to guess. It is good practice to talk to each user about passwords and encourage the construction of good passwords. New users should assign their own, if possible.

A good password is one you can remember but is somewhat obscure to others. The name of the dog you had while you were growing up might be a good starting point, but then alter it with numerals, spaces, capital letters, or other characters. The name *curly* could be `curly07`, or `c rly7`. By giving users some suggestions like this one, you can help them pick good passwords.

Don't use the names of family members. They're too easy to guess. Also, use different passwords on different systems, so that someone who gets into one of your systems won't get into all of them.

> **Note**
>
> Ultimately, security is a problem with people rather than systems. You cannot allow passwords to be etched in the wall near a terminal or have DOS computers with root passwords embedded in communication programs.

Idle Terminals

Users should log off or use some kind of terminal lock program when they leave at the end of the day. Most UNIX systems have a program, sometimes called `idleout`, that shuts down terminals left on beyond a prescribed length of time. Most programs like `idleout` have a time limit. The following is an example of how this program works:

```
idleout 2:30
```

In this case, any person who hasn't used the terminal in the last two hours and 30 minutes is forced out of the system. An `idleout` limit will irritate some users more than just about any other restriction. Therefore, recommend that your users use a standard screen-lock program (such as the Screenlock program in the Preferences folder in UnixWare). A screen-lock program locks your screen and runs a pattern on it to prevent the screen from burning in. To unlock your screen, you simply type your password and resume your work.

Enforcing Security

Security in defense firms is clearly understood. Companies that have highly sensitive products in the design cycle understand the need for security. But employees in a small distributor of plumbing parts may have a hard time understanding what everybody is so concerned about. Security in this example is not an issue until you can't figure out who removed a file that included a key proposal.

Employees should have a quick lesson about the sensitivity of data on your computer. A business has a significant investment in the data on the computer. Loss of data can be a distraction, or it can mean chaos. Employees who are unwilling to participate in securing a computer should understand that this can be cause for dismissal.

Handling Security Breaches

Security on a computer can require a little detective work. For example, look at the following:

```
# who -u <Return>
root    tty02   Jan 21 08:35   old    15677 Ofc #2
martha ttym1d  Jan 20 13:20   .       591  Payroll #1
ted     ttyp0   Jan 21 08:36   8:25   15763 Warehouse
margo   ttyp2   Jan 21 07:05   9:45   15761 CEO Ofc
root    ttyp4   Jan 21 08:36   .      15767 Modem #1
# date <Return>
Fri Jan 21 19:18:21 CST 1994
```

Suppose that you know that `martha` left the office at 5 p.m. Has someone found her password, or did she leave the terminal on when she left? You can see that she logged in at 13:20 today. It is now 19:18, and somebody is active on the system using her login. Do you dispatch security?

Let's try another situation. You are routinely checking the acctcom and you see that charlie is logged in to the system. But charlie was fired two weeks ago. The following is what you see:

```
# acctcom <Return>
COMMAND                       START      END      REAL CPU  MEAN
NAME     USER    TTYNAME TIME       TIME     (SECS)   (SECS) SIZE(K)
 - - - - - - - - - -
 - - - - - - - - - -   <-- many routine listings
 - - - - - - - - - -
rm      charlie   ?     07:26:00  07:26:00  0.09     0.02  6.25
ls      charlie   ?     07:26:04  07:26:04  0.09     0.02  6.25
cat     charlie   ?     07:26:04  07:26:04  0.40     0.08  1.56
sh      charlie   ?     07:26:04  07:26:04  0.68     0.07  1.79
sh      charlie   ?     07:26:04  07:26:04  0.79     0.08 10.31
rm      charlie   ?     07:26:06  07:26:06  0.05     0.03  4.17
sh      charlie   ?     07:26:06  07:26:06  0.13     0.05 16.60
dfrun   charlie   ?     07:26:00  07:26:05  5.69     0.39  0.32
sh      charlie   ?     07:26:00  07:26:05  5.84     0.04  3.13
sh      charlie   ?     07:26:00  07:26:05  5.98     0.03  4.17
```

When an employee leaves, for whatever reason, personnel should contact the computer staff to retire the login. It appears that charlie is in the computer and running some applications. This is a little deceptive; note that there is a question mark in the ttyname column. No one is on the system. This is either something Charlie had in his cron file or an at job he queued before he was terminated.

UNIX provides the means to protect a file or a directory. If you try the following command sequence, you can get a feel for this protection feature:

```
# cd /u/dflib <Return>
# ls -al <Return>
total 1458
  drwxrwxrwx   2 dfx    assoc  1824 Jan 21 10:02 .
  drwxrwxrwx  20 pat    root    368 Jan 13 14:37 ..
  - - -x- -x- - -   1 dfx    assoc   295 Jul 13  1993 age
  -rw-rw-rw-   1 dfx    assoc   136 Oct 08  1992 append
  -rw-rw-rw-   1 dfx    assoc  2739 Jan 06  1993 at
  -r- - - - - - - -   2 dfx    assoc   282 Oct 08  1992 bank
  -rw-rw-rw-   1 dfx    assoc   150 Feb 20  1993 compressed
  -rw-rw-r- -   1 dfx    assoc   212 Oct 28  1992 console
  -rw-rw-r- -   1 dfx    assoc   134 Oct 29  1992 console1
  -rw-rw-r- -   1 dfx    assoc    22 Oct 29  1992 console2
  -rw-r- - - -   1 dfx    assoc   129 Dec 29  1992 copyright
  -rw-r- -r- -   1 root   other   126 Jan 17 22:23 date.check
  -rw-rw-rw-   1 dfx    assoc   447 Oct 08  1992 days
  drw- - - - - - -   1 dfx    assoc    13 Jan 16 11:13 tmp
  -rw-r- -r- -  23 dfx    assoc   169 Dec 08 07:41 unit
  -rw-r- -r- -   1 dfx    assoc  4279 Apr 22  1992 util.mac
  -rw-rw-rw-   1 dfx    assoc   679 Dec 03 15:27 vendor
  -rw-rw-rw-   1 dfx    assoc   120 Apr 02  1993 year.episc3
```

The first command changed to the `/u/dflib` directory. The next command, `ls -al` (*list specific* with the options *all* items in *long* format), provides details about what is in the directory, the permissions for each file, and the associations for the files.

For an administrator, the task becomes apparent. If you are the chief security officer for the network, how can you be sure that files and directories are adequately secured? Fortunately, there are many tools to help you, such as `umask`, `cron`, and UNIX itself.

Permissions seems to be a significant source of worry for most administrators. New administrators typically tighten up permissions and then field calls from people saying they can't gain access to a file they need or they can't execute a program on the system. After a while, these administrators loosen up the permissions so that anybody can do anything. The balancing act of securing the computer while permitting the proper people the tools to do their job is sometimes frustrating.

Backups

Few issues that the typical UNIX administrator deals with are as important as the backup or archiving of a system. An administrator can lose his or her job or a company can literally fail because of the loss of valuable data. The disk or disks on a computer are electromechanical devices, and they *will* fail at some time.

Most new hard disks are rated at around 150,000 hours mean time between failures—more than five years! But the mean time statistic can be deceptive. Your disk could fail at the 50,000 hour mark, or it might last for more than 10 years (highly unlikely). You are gambling if you only occasionally back up your systems, and you take an even greater chance if you aren't checking your backup tapes.

First, you have to make some decisions about the frequency of backup, reuse of media, and storage requirements. And the method of backup and integrity checks should give you absolute assurance that the data will be there when the system crashes.

The simplest scheme for backing up your system is rotational. Following are the requirements for each system in the network:

- Do one full backup of the system at the time you install the computer or at the time you change operating system versions. Follow the manufacturer's recommendation and follow up with an integrity check of the data.

This backup tape should be stored off-site, perhaps in the administrator's home. A heat-resistant vault may be fine. Take some time to make sure that this decision makes sense and you are sure that a fire or other catastrophe will not permanently disable your organization. When you do the backup, your computer system should be in a quiet state, with no users on the system.

- Do a full backup of each system at least once every month. This backup is done like the first backup, but can be done while there is activity on the system. Some people say you should have all files closed at the time you do this backup, but most system files are restorable with only minor damage. If you attempt to do this backup on a totally quiet system, you or someone will be working some pretty odd hours to stay out of the way of your users. Additionally, you will have the following incremental backup to fill gaps. Rotate these tapes over a six-month period; in other words, January's backup will be overwritten with July's data.

- Back up every day the dynamic files or data altered since yesterday. If you back up your dynamic files, you are probably backing up your inventory files, customer files, and other files that change daily. These directories are usually easily identified; backing them up gives you the reassurance that your employees will not have to do massive updating if today is the day the disk fails. This can be a little more of a gamble than an incremental backup.

  If you change a file that is not in the daily backup path, that file is not backed up until the next full backup. The advantage here is that you are doing very few full backups (full backups take a lot of time). This plan is the one that is easiest to live with, especially in a networked environment.

- You can do what is called an *incremental backup* if you do a weekly full backup. For example, suppose that you do a full backup on each Friday at 3 P.M. All other days of the week, the computer backs up only files that have changed since the weekly backup was done. If you restore after using this plan, you would probably rebuild your system after the hardware is repaired and restore the full backup from the tape media. You then reload each day's incremental backup media in the order the backups were made.

  If your system was fully backed up on Friday and you did an incremental backup on Monday, Tuesday, and Wednesday, and the disk crashed on Thursday, you would start with the full backup from Friday. After this is loaded, you load the Monday, Tuesday, and Wednesday tapes.

If the system crashes at 11 A.M. on Thursday, you lose only the work from Thursday morning.

Backing up files is normally done using one of two utilities on UNIX. Regardless of which command you use, you should use it consistently throughout the network. This decision, although seemingly not very important, can assure administrators that the tape created on one computer in the network can be read on another computer.

Many people like the `tar` command (*tape archive*) because of its simplicity. This command can be as simple as entering the following commands:

```
cd /u/my.files
tar -cvf /dev/rmt/c0s0 *
```

The first command, `cd` (change directory), puts you into the subdirectory you want to back up. The second command does the tape archive. It creates a new volume on the tape (`-c`); is verbose (`-v`, telling you what it is putting on the tape); and, finally, copies from the device (`-f`), or in this case to the device `/dev/rmt/c0s0`. The * represents all files in that directory and its subdirectories.

The second backup option is the `cpio` command. This command gives you greater control and options in the archiving process. This command is generally preferred.

```
find /home/georgew -depth -print¦cpio -ocv > /dev/rmt/c0s0
```

This command is a little more cryptic but very effective. The `find` command goes to your home directory and prints all of the files in the directory and its subdirectories. These files are then piped to the `cpio` command. The `ocv` means output, provide header information in ASCII format, and be verbose in telling what is going on the tape. The > sign means that the destination is the `/dev/rmt/c0s0` device.

After you have selected the backup tool you want to use, the next task is to provide a backup program on each computer that ensures that the backup is done reliably each night (or whenever the backup is used). The following program is used extensively and can ensure you of a good backup:

```
# Prompt user to put bu tape in drive -- 'bu'  - SCO Unix
#
# Written : June 6, 1988  By : G.W.Mayleben
# Revised : October 28, 1993 By : George
#
tape reten           # Step 1 - retention the tape
if [ "$?" != "0" ]   # Has this been successful?
then                 # If retention fails mail georgew a message
echo "
```

```
Backup failed...tape not installed! ('uname -n') 'date'
Install and do manual backup!"¦mail georgew@vforge
exit                   # Stop execution of this program
else                   # Successful retention - Step 2 cpio to tape
  find /u/my.files -depth -print¦cpio -ocv >/dev/rct0
  if [ $? != "0" ]
  then                 # cpio fails - notify georgew
  echo "
  Backup totally failed...Check tape quality! ('uname -n') 'date
  Replace tape and re-run manually!"¦mail georgew@vforge
  exit                 # Notify georgew of failure and exit program
  else                 # Step 3 - Verify what is on the tape
  cpio -ict </dev/rct0 >/dev/null 2>&1
  if [ $? != "0" ]
  then                 # If verification fails
  echo "
  Verification failed...Check on tape quality! ('uname -n') 'date'
  Replace tape and re-run manually!"¦mail georgew@vforge
  else                 # SUCCESS
  echo "
  Complete backup DONE and verified on 'date' ('uname -n')
  Put in tape for today."¦mail georgew@vforge
  fi
  fi
  fi
  exit 0
```

There are several things to note in this program. First, the program begins
with an explanation of what the program does. Second, dates are provided
about when the program was created and last modified. Third, explanations
are included in the program. As an administrator, you may forget details
about why programs were created and whether they should be thrown out.

There is one other item to note in this program. Any program you write that
is critical to the running of the network should have a mail-notification step.
Some people don't like the clutter that seems to occur when you have 20
computers all notifying you that the backup occurred properly, but paying
attention to these messages can permit you to sleep well at night.

UNIX uses electronic mail extensively to notify the administrative staff of
problems or successes. You will normally find a uucp, lp, adm, mmdf, sys, and
root mailbox on your system. Because you will probably not have an lp or
uucp administrator in your company, it is a good idea to have a forwarding
message to a single mailbox that is always read on your administrator's computer. The following message should be put in each of the /usr/spool/mail
adm, lp, uucp, mmdf, and sys mail files:

```
Forward to georgew@vforge
```

The message must have the exact words Forward to, or the forwarding will
fail. Experiment and be absolutely sure that your systems function properly.

Summary

Administering systems on a network multiplies the task of administering a UNIX system that is not networked. Instead of managing just your users, you also manage the use of your system by users from other systems.

Many of the administrative tasks can be automated. For example, you can run scripts to monitor disk space, back up files, and check the activities of remote users.

Standard UNIX security features—passwords, file permissions, and controlled system access lists—are sufficient for securing most systems in a networked environment. Versions of UNIX that meet more stringent government security requirements, however, are also available.

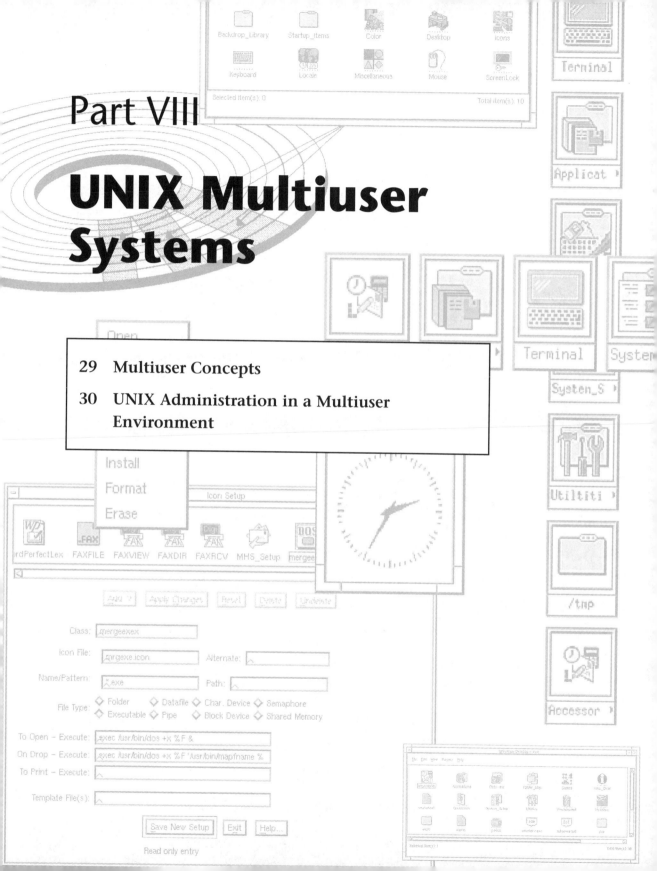

Part VIII

UNIX Multiuser Systems

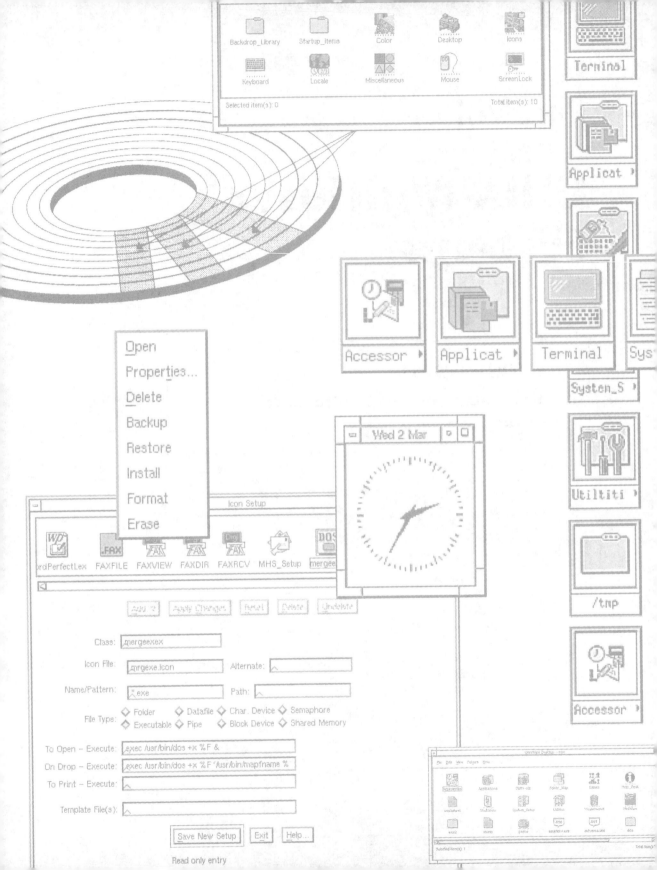

Backdrop_Library   Startup_Items   Color   Desktop   Icons

Keyboard   Locale   Miscellaneous   Mouse   ScreenLock

Selected item(s): 0   Total item(s): 10

Terminal

Applicat ▸

Open
Properties...
Delete
Backup
Restore
Install
Format
Erase

Accessor ▸   Applicat ▸   Terminal   Sys

System_S ▸

Utiltiti ▸

Wed 2 Mar

Icon Setup

rdPerfectLex   FAXFILE   FAXVIEW   FAXDIR   FAXRCV   MHS_Setup   mergee

/tmp

Add ?   Apply Changes   Reset   Delete   Undelete

Class: mergeexex

Icon File: mrgexe.Icon   Alternate:

Name/Pattern: *.exe   Path:

File Type: ◇ Folder   ◇ Datafile ◇ Char. Device ◇ Semaphore
            ◇ Executable ◇ Pipe   ◇ Block Device ◇ Shared Memory

To Open – Execute: exec /usr/bin/dos +x %F &

On Drop – Execute: exec /usr/bin/dos +x %F '/usr/bin/mapfname %

To Print – Execute:

Template File(s):

Save New Setup   Exit   Help ...

Read only entry

Accessor ▸

Chapter 29

Multiuser Concepts

A multiuser system employs two main concepts: multitasking and multiuser services. UNIX has the apparent ability to execute multiple tasks concurrently, transparent to the user. For example, you can read your e-mail while compiling a program.

Each task, whether it's a simple command you enter on the command line or a complex application, starts one or more processes. Everything running on a UNIX system is associated with a process. What makes UNIX multitasking is its ability to run many processes simultaneously. See Chapter 11, "Managing Multiple Processes," for a detailed discussion on processes.

There are many ways you can connect to a computer running UNIX (referred to as a *server*). You can use either a terminal or a computer; you can be located physically near the server, connected with a cable, or you can be on the other side of the planet connected with high-speed data lines or ordinary phone lines. Whether you're using a terminal or computer and how you are connected to the server determines whether the computer's resources are considered to be distributed or centralized.

A single-user computer operating system, such as DOS, is designed to be used by a single user at a time. All the processing is done on one computer which has sole access to resources such as printers, storage, and processing. Multiuser systems use the centralized and distributed processing models to accommodate many users simultaneously. In a *centralized processing environment*, many users (large systems can have hundreds of users) access the resources of one computer: storage, printer, memory, and processing. In the *distributed environment*, processing can occur on the user's own workstation,

In this chapter, you learn the following:

- Concepts of centralized processing

- Elements of centralized processing

- Concepts of distributed processing

- Elements of distributed processing

VIII

UNIX Multiuser Systems

and the central processor is used to distribute applications and data. Printers and storage can be either connected to the user's workstation or to the main server.

Understanding Centralized Processing Systems

As technology in the 1950s and 1960s advanced, operating systems began to allow multiple users to share resources from separate terminals. Two users could, in a batch processing sequence, execute two sets of instructions while sharing a processor, storage, and output.

With the advent of a switched telephone network, computers began to use telephone resources to extend computer resources geographically. With this model, each processor used communications-processing resources to connect with remote terminals. This created a need for better ways for computers and terminals to communicate. The result was the development of front-end processing for communications tasks and the centralized processing system.

Until personal computers became inexpensive, powerful, and ubiquitous, most UNIX systems used the centralized processing model. With centralized processing, mainframe computers handled all the processing. Users connected to the mainframe shared its resources. This model is used less and less today, although it's still appropriate for computing sites in which users are separated geographically.

For example, your bank may have one main processing center, yet all of the bank's branches can access the data center, regardless of their location. On each user's desk is a terminal, including a keyboard, a monitor, and a direct connection to the mainframe so that it can access the centralized resources: processing, printing, and storage (see fig. 29.1). The centralized processing model is usually made up of many elements, such as the server, front-end processors, terminals, modems, and multiport adapters.

As a user requests data, the request is processed by the computer in the bank's main office. Results of the processing are sent back to the terminal in the branch office. All data is processed and stored by the mainframe computer.

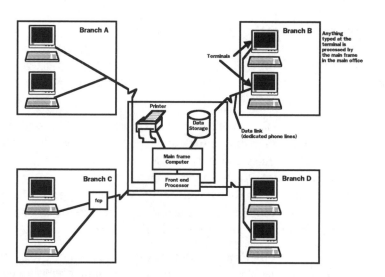

Fig. 29.1
The centralized
processing model.

Elements of the Centralized Processing Model

To make the centralized computing model work, you need many elements, including the server, front-end processors, terminals, modems, and multiport adapters.

A *server* can be defined as any computer set up to share its resources (processing power, storage, printers, and so on). For example, you can use an IBM-compatible personal computer as a server as long as it has enough hard disk space and RAM.

A *front-end processor* connects the communication channels and the server. It handles the details of communication so that the server is free to process its data.

There are two popular types of *terminals* used today: dumb terminals and smart terminals.

Traditionally, UNIX was used with *dumb terminals*, which have a keyboard, monitor, and nothing else. The most important thing to realize about dumb terminals is that they have no local processing power. The communications port on the terminal is connected, either directly or through a modem, to the server. When you type on a dumb terminal, each keystroke is transmitted to the server, where it is processed.

Smart terminals can complete minimal processing at the local site. Cash registers and other point-of-sale devices are examples, as are the familiar automated teller machines (ATMs). The local device stores the transaction request and transmits the entire request instead of transmitting each keystroke as does a dumb terminal.

To connect your terminal to a telephone line, you use a *modem*. Modems translate the digital signals of terminals and computers into analog signals required by telephone lines. Modems are always used in pairs. The first one connects your terminal to the telephone line; the second connects the server to the telephone line. To make the connection, you dial out on the terminal. When the modem on the other end (the one connected to the server) answers, your terminal can communicate with the server.

To expand the number of ports available to which users can connect, you install a *multiport adapter*. For example, a personal computer typically has only two serial ports: COM1 and COM2. If you want to use a PC as a server for more than two users, you need more ports. The multiport adapter, in this case, consists of a card that you install inside the computer, a small box with eight or more connectors, and a cable that connects the box and the card. Software is supplied with the adapter to permit the added connectors to act like additional serial ports.

Understanding Distributed Processing Systems

In distributed processing, the terminal is replaced by a workstation, which is itself a computer, usually running either DOS or UNIX. Programs can be located and run from either the server or your workstation. Similarly, files can be located on either system. If you process a file on your workstation, you store it on the server so that others can access it. You can print either on local printers connected to your workstation or on printers connected to the server.

With workstations in common use, your bank probably uses a distributed processing system instead of the centralized system described in the preceding section. Figure 29.2 shows the same bank with a distributed processing system.

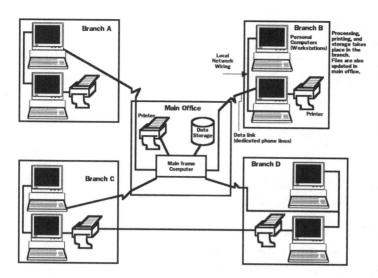

Fig. 29.2
The distributed
processing model.

Elements of the Distributed Processing Model

Distributed processing uses file servers, workstations, network interface cards, hubs, repeaters, bridges, routers, and gateways. The *file server* is usually based on an Intel 386, 486, or Pentium microprocessor. The purpose of the file server is to distribute files and segments of programs to workstations, to print from a central location, and to control flow on the connection between workstations. More than 90 percent of processing occurs at the workstation level, leaving 5 to 10 percent of the load at the file server for administrative tasks. The following sections describe the elements of distributed processing.

Workstations

Besides being used as a file server, you can use a personal computer (with an Intel 386, 486, or Pentium CPU) as a workstation. The minimum configuration is 512KB of RAM to load the network workstation shell (today, most personal computers are equipped with 2MB to 4MB of RAM). Generally, resources should be applied to the workstation level, where most of the processing occurs. The amount of additional resources depends on the type of tasks you plan on doing. For example, word processing programs takes minimal resources (hard drive, RAM, quality of monitor) as compared graphics-intensive tasks, such as multimedia and computer-aided-design (CAD) programs. For applications involving CAD, you want very large hard disks (1 gigabyte or more), lots of RAM (16MB, 32MB, or even 64MB), and high-resolution monitors and video cards (1280×1024 or higher). You may even want a tape drive for backup and a CD-ROM drive for loading large applications.

Network Interface Cards

A Network Interface Card (NIC) attaches to a slot on the motherboard and is the physical link between the microcomputer and the cabling for the network. For example, a popular Ethernet NIC is the 3COM 3C509. Network interface cards are generally available for either coaxial or twisted-pair cabling.

Hubs

The hub serves as a connecting point for coaxial cables and can be either passive or active. A *passive hub* usually has four connectors. An *active hub* usually has eight ports and amplifies or relays the signal.

Repeaters

Repeaters amplify or regenerate the signal over the network so that you can extend the normal distance limitations for network cabling.

Bridges

Use a bridge when you need to connect two similar network types together.

Routers

Routers are used in large, complex networks in which there are many paths for networks signals to travel to the same destination. The router determines and sends the signal along the most effective route.

Gateways

Use a gateway when you need to connect dissimilar network types together. The gateway performs the necessary protocol conversions so that the two networks can communicate.

Looking at Topologies

Topology refers to how workstations and file servers are connected together in a network. The names of various topologies are derived from the pattern the cables make after you connect the various terminals, workstations, and file servers. The most common topologies include star, bus, and ring. When more than one topology is used in a network, it is referred to as a hybrid network.

Star Topology

The star topology is connected in such a way that all workstations are connected to a central file server or hub (see fig. 29.3). You can have either passive or active hubs in this scheme.

A passive hub is simply a connecting point for the workstations. An active hub also offers amplification of the signal. AT&T's Starlan is an example of a network using star topology.

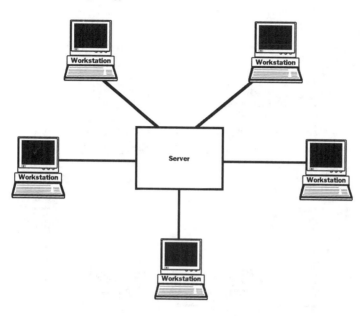

Fig. 29.3
All workstations connected to a central file server in a star topology.

VIII

UNIX Multiuser Systems

Bus Topology

In a bus topology (see fig. 29.4), all workstations and file servers share a common pathway. They are, in fact, connected directly together. The bus topology is the foundation for Ethernet and Token Bus.

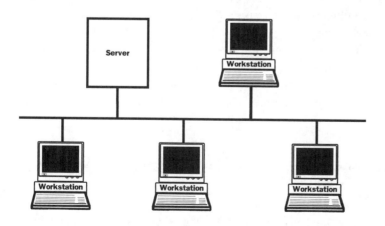

Fig. 29.4
All workstations and file servers share a common pathway in a bus topology.

Ring Topology

A ring topology looks like a wagon wheel without the hub (see fig. 29.5). The server is connected to the workstations in bus fashion; however, the last items along the network are connected together to make a closed loop. Ring topologies use a repeater, which IBM refers to as a Multistation Access Unit (MAU). IBM's Token Ring network is an example of a ring topology.

Fig. 29.5

A ring topology has the server connected to the workstations in bus fashion.

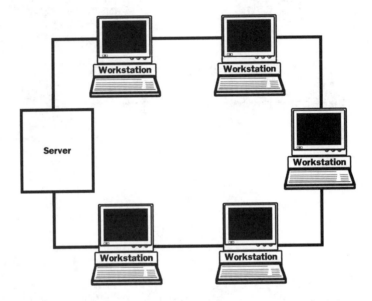

Hybrid Topology

In the 1970s and 1980s, firms with decentralized purchasing experienced the growth of different topologies on their network. For example, the accounting department used a bus network; the purchasing department installed token-ring machines; manufacturing used an Ethernet bus; and administration relied on mainframe technology. This combination of networks planted the seeds for enterprise computing and *hybrid* wide-area networks. The integration of these networks linked dissimilar topologies such as rings, stars, and buses.

Understanding the Client/Server Model

The result of the development of distributed processing is the *client/server model*. Today, UNIX is frequently used in this model as either the client, the server, or both.

To illustrate a client/server setup, assume that several UNIX workstations (these are the *clients*; make them 66 MHz, 486 PCs running UnixWare—the latest standard version of UNIX from Novell) are connected in a bus topology to a server (a high-end Pentium PC with several gigabytes of disk space, also running UnixWare). Because this server is used by a documentation group, it has FrameMaker installed on it with a floating license for 10 people. Up to 10 clients can access and run FrameMaker at the same time (as the department's needs grow, additional floating licenses can be added). The server has directories for each client in which important files can be stored and backed up with the server's nightly backup. The server also has directories from which clients can share files. Connected to the server is a fast laser printer everyone can access, and a tape drive suitable for backing up the large hard disks. In addition, several of the clients have their own, slower, less-expensive laser printers connected locally.

> **Note**
>
> The server in this example is a PC running UnixWare—just like the clients' PCs, although the server is more powerful. There's no reason why the server can't act like a client at times, and share resources with the clients. In other words, any UNIX system can be both a client and a server.

VII

UNIX Multiuser Systems

Summary

In this chapter, you learned about multiuser systems and how, through centralized and distributed processing, many users are connected to and can use a server simultaneously.

In a centralized processing model, you can use front-end processors, terminals, modems, and multiport adapters. In a distributed processing model, you can use workstations, network interface cards, hubs, repeaters, bridges, routers, and gateways.

Network topologies, including star, bus, ring, and hybrid, and the client/server model were also described.

Chapter 30

UNIX Administration in a Multiuser Environment

A UNIX system should have one or more people designated as the system administrator to manage the system and oversee its performance. The system administrator has the responsibility to see that the system is functioning properly, to know who to call if things can't be fixed locally, and to know how to provide software and hardware facilities to current and new users.

A UNIX system requires initial configuration and continuous attention to ensure that the system remains effective, trustworthy, and efficient for all users. The system administrator is the person responsible for attending to the UNIX system's needs. This chapter discusses some of the major tasks and issues confronting a system administrator in a multiuser environment. If you are a system administrator, you'll find this material immediately pertinent. If you are a user, it may help you to know about some of the jobs that an administrator tackles and the issues that are faced when making resource allocations and policies.

Looking at the Importance of Proper Administration

All UNIX systems are different in one way or another, and each is unique in the way it must be administered. Your administrative duties vary, based on, among other things, the number of users you manage, the kinds of peripherals attached to the computer (printers, tape drives, and so on), networking connections, and the level of security you require.

The following topics are covered in this chapter:

- Why UNIX administration is needed

- How to add users and passwords to a system and manage them

- How to configure modems, terminals, and other devices

- How to develop a plan for backing up the files on your system

- Considerations for shutting down your UNIX system

The manuals supplied with UNIX are the system administrator's guide to the system. However, the overview of UNIX system administration given in this chapter provides you with some additional perspective.

> **Note**
>
> The commands used in this chapter are available on any UNIX system that uses UNIX System V Release 4.2 (SVR4.2), including UnixWare. The techniques and issues apply to any UNIX system.

A UNIX system administrator, either alone or with a support staff, must provide a secure, efficient, and reliable environment for system users. The administrator has the power and responsibility to establish and maintain a system that provides effective and dependable service. In a multiuser environment, a number of competing purposes and priorities exist. The admin-istrator exercises the power and responsibility necessary to provide a well-functioning system.

The delegation of administrative responsibilities varies from system to sys-tem. On large systems, system administration tasks can be divided among several people. Some small systems do not even require a full-time admin-istrator; such systems simply designate a certain user to act as system administrator. If you work in a networked environment, your system may be administered over the network by a network administrator.

Each UNIX system has a single user who can perform virtually any operation he or she wants on the computer. This user is called the *superuser*. The superuser has a special login name, called *root*. The user named *root* is logged to the root directory of the file system when he or she logs on to the system.

The system administrator logs in as the superuser to perform privileged work. For normal system work, the system administrator logs in as an ordinary user. The superuser's login—root—is used for limited, special purposes only. The number of users who can log on as root should be kept to a minimum (at most two or three). When any person logs on to the system as root, that per-son is the superuser and has absolute privilege on the system. With this privi-lege, the superuser can change the attributes of any file, stop the system, start the system, make backups of the system's data, and perform many other tasks.

The administrator must be aware of many of the technical aspects of the computer system. Also, the administrator must be aware of the needs of the users as well as the primary purpose of the system. Any computer system is a finite resource; policies regarding its use must be established and enforced. The administrator thus has a technical and policy role to play. That role, combined with the power to perform virtually any possible action, requires a responsible, skillful, and diplomatic person in the role of administrator.

> **Note**
>
> With UnixWare and UNIX SVR4.2, the *system owner* concept was introduced. An owner is a special user (who has whatever name you choose) with the permissions to do many administrative tasks through the GUI. As a result, tasks such as configuring printing, adding users, and installing applications no longer require you to use shell commands and have root permissions to do basic administration.

Common Administrative Tasks

The precise job description of the system administrator often depends on the local organization. As system administrator, you may find yourself involved in a wide variety of activities, from setting policy to installing software to moving furniture. However, there are a number of tasks that all system administrators have to either perform or manage:

- *Manage users.* Adding users, deleting users, and modifying users' capabilities and privileges.

- *Configure devices.* Making available and sharing devices such as printers, terminals, modems, tape drives, and so on.

- *Make backups.* Making copies of files and storing the backups for possible restoration if the system's files are lost or damaged. This also includes determining schedules for backups.

- *Shut down the system.* Shutting down the system in an orderly manner to avoid inconsistencies in the file system.

- *Train users.* Providing or obtaining effective training for users so that they can use the system effectively and efficiently.

- *Secure the system.* Providing a secure environment. Users need to be protected from interfering with each other through accidental or deliberate actions.

- *Log system changes.* Keeping a log book to record any significant activity concerning the system.

- *Advise users.* Acting as the "local expert" to aid the system's ordinary users.

VIII

UNIX Multiuser Systems

About Administrative Interfaces

UNIX System V Release 4.2 (UnixWare) provides a GUI for performing basic system administration tasks. By double-clicking the mouse on an icon in the UnixWare System Setup folder, you can open windows relating to printing, networking, user, and password administration.

Earlier versions of UNIX include different programs for accomplishing the main system administration duties. These include sysadmsh on XENIX systems, sam on HP-UX systems, and SMIT on AIX systems. UNIX SVR4.0 includes the FACE utility and OA&M (Operation, Administration & Maintenance) to assist in system administration.

Administrative personnel use these systems to initiate tasks rather than issuing UNIX commands that initiate the same tasks. The UnixWare GUI offers a mouse-driven, fully graphical interface. The sysadm, FACE, and OA&M programs present, on the administrator's screen, menus of items from which you can select.

To many administrators, graphical and menu-driven presentations are easier to use than standard UNIX commands. A typical system administrator must have a broad knowledge of UNIX to administer a system effectively. Wide-ranging administrative commands can be difficult to remember, and administrative programs relieve the administrator from the burden of remembering esoteric command names.

You'll want to use a simpler administrative interface when you're sure it's reliable and you don't want to go through or know all the details involved. You probably will not want to use it if you have to repeat the same task several times; you'll want some more direct and efficient way of doing things.

Everything that can be done with these administrative interfaces can be done with individual commands. In many cases, however, particularly when you are getting started, you'll find that it's to your advantage to use these other administrative interfaces.

Understanding User Management

The system administrator is in charge of managing users. This involves adding users so that they can log in to the system, setting user privileges, assigning users to certain directories and groups, and deleting users when it is necessary.

Working with Users

Every user should have a unique login name. This makes it possible to identify each user and avoids problems of one person deleting another's files. Furthermore, each user must have a password. About the only exception to this is when there is only one user on a system and the system has absolutely no connection by modem or network to any other computer. When there is no real reason for a person to have access to your system, you must make sure that he or she cannot log in. That person's login name should be removed, along with any files that don't have to be kept around any more.

Adding a User

When you add a user, the result is an entry for the user in the file /etc/ password. That entry has this form:

login_name:encrypted_password:user_ID:group_ID:user_information:login_directory:login_shell

In this syntax, fields are separated by colons (:). The fields are these:

Field	Description
login_name	Name used to log in.
encrypted_password	The password required to authenticate the user; the primary line of defense against security violations. For security reasons, most UNIX systems put an x in this field and store the password in the /etc/shadow file.
user_ID	A unique number the operating system uses to identify the user.
group_ID	A unique number or name used to identify the primary group for this user. A user can change to other groups if permitted by the administrator.
user_information	A description of the user, such as the user's name or title.
login_directory	The user's home directory (where the user ends up after logging in).
login_shell	The shell the user uses when he or she logs in (for example, /usr/bin/ksh, if using the Korn shell).

You can use the command useradd to create or add a user to your system. This makes the entry, except for the password, in the password file. You'll use the command passwd for that. Some of these items have default values or values you can set that will apply to users you create when you use the command.

Note

Don't add a user with the useradd command if you want that user to be able to use the UnixWare GUI. Use the User Setup window instead. The useradd command doesn't create the user environment needed to start the GUI automatically when the user logs in. See "Adding Users with the GUI," later in this chapter, for further information.

The useradd command also copies the files in the directory /etc/skel into the user's home directory. The directory /etc/skel should contain files you want every user to have. These typically include "personal" configuration files such as .profile for Bourne or Korn shell users, .login for C shell users, .mailrc if users are using mail or mailx for e-mail, .exrc for users using vi as an editor, and so on. You can also specify supplementary group IDs so that a user can switch groups as necessary.

Table 30.1 lists the options you can use with the command useradd.

Table 30.1: Options To Use with the *useradd* Command

Option	Meaning
-u *UID*	Make *UID* the user ID number of the user. There is no default value. If this isn't specified, the next available number above the highest number currently assigned is used.
-g *group*	Make the *group* the user's primary group instead of the default value. The value for *group* must be either the name or group ID number of an existing group.
-c *info*	Put *info* in the user information field. If *info* contains blanks, enclose it in quotation marks. Colons (:) aren't permitted. For example, -c "Typ User, Research Group". There is no default value. If this isn't specified, the user information field is left blank.
-d *dir*	Make *dir* the login or home directory for the user instead of the default. Specify a full path, such as /users/tuser rather than just tuser.
-s *shell*	Make *shell* the user's login shell. This must be specified as a full path name such as /usr/bin/ksh.
-G *group*	Make the *group* the user's supplementary group, so that the user can use the newgrp command with the group(s) listed here. There is no default value. The value for *group* must be the group ID of an existing group. If you must specify more than one, separate them with commas. For example, -G 21,31.

Option	Meaning
-k *dir*	Copy the file from the directory *dir* into the user's login directory. This option is useful for giving a user an initial .profile file and other files that serve as resources for various commands. The default value is /etc/skel.

You can set default values for useradd by using the command defadm in the following form:

```
defadm useradd parameter=value
```

The parameters you use must be specified with full path names and are these:

Parameter	Definition
SHELL=*shell*	The login shell
HOMEDIR=*dir*	The login or home directory
SKELDIR=*dir*	The skeleton directory
GROUPID=*group*	The primary group

For example, if you want future users to be members of the group sales, whose group ID number is 21, type the following command and press <Return>:

```
defadm useradd GROUPID=21
```

To add a user name tuser with home directory /users/tuser, type the following command and press <Return>:

```
useradd -d /users/tuser -c "Typical User" tuser
```

This creates an entry in the password file something like this:

```
tuser:*:123:21:Typical User:/users/tuser:/usr/bin/ksh
```

The exact values depend on the defaults for useradd. In any case, with these commands you have the following:

- The user's login name is tuser.

- The * in the password field means that the user cannot log in until a password is set.

- The user ID number is 123.

- The group ID is 21.

VIII

UNIX Multiuser Systems

- The user's "real name" is Typical User.

- The home or login directory is set to /users/tuser.

- The login shell is /usr/bin/sh, which is evidently the current default value.

When the command is executed, the home directory is created, the files are copied from /etc/skel to that directory, the file /etc/group (which keeps track of group memberships) is modified to include tuser in the specified group(s), and tuser is made the owner of the login directory and the files it contains.

Setting User Passwords

You set a user's password using the command passwd. The system administrator should set a password for each user added to the system. Users can change their passwords when they log in. Use passwd as follows:

1. Type the command and the login name (for example, **passwd tuser**) and press <Return>.

2. You are prompted to enter a password for the user. Type the password and press <Return>; you won't see the password on the screen:

   New password: *newpassword* <Return>

3. You are prompted to type the password again. Type the password again and press <Return>.

   Re-enter new password: *newpassword* <Return>

The password is encrypted and put into the file /etc/passwd (or /etc/shadow if your system uses a shadow password file). Because each user must be able to read the file /etc/passwd, for the sake of security some systems have created another file, /etc/shadow, that can be read only by the root user and that contains the encrypted passwords.

It is important that you take the time to enter passwords that follow the rules for the choice of a password:

- Passwords should be at least 6 and preferably 8 characters long.

- Passwords should contain all of the following: uppercase letters, lower-case letters, punctuation symbols, and numerals.

When you're adding a number of users, you'll be tempted to enter short, easy passwords. Don't fall for it! Good passwords are your first line of defense against intruders. Be sure to tell your users why you've assigned that type of password.

You can also specify that users change their passwords after a certain number of days. You do this by issuing the following command:

```
passwd -x number_of_days user_name
```

It's a good idea to have passwords changed regularly, but remember to educate system users about the choice of good passwords.

After a user is assigned a password, the file entry looks something like this:

```
tuser:Zoie.89&^0gW*:123:21:Typical User:/users/tuser:/usr/bin/ksh
```

The second field is the password—not as it was typed but in encrypted form.

Note

Users occasionally forget their passwords. It isn't possible for a system administrator to tell someone her or his password. However, you can change a user's password by using the `passwd` command. Have a procedure in place to deal with this situation, and let your users know about it.

Note

For more information about choosing passwords for better security, read the "System Security" section, later in this chapter.

Removing a User

There are several different degrees of user removal. Removing a user from the system need not be a final, irrevocable act. Here are some possibilities.

- **Remove only the ability to log in.** This is useful if the user will be away for a while and will need to be reinstated some time in the future. The user's directory, files, and group information are kept intact. Edit the file where passwords are kept, either `/etc/passwd` or `/etc/shadow`, and put a * in the second field of the user's entry, as follows:

```
tuser:*:123:21:Typical User:/users/tuser:/usr/bin/ksh
```

■ **Remove the user from the password file but keep the user's files on the system.** This is useful if the files are used by others. Delete the user's entry from the password file or files. You can do this by using an editor or by using the command userdel *login_name*. You then can change the ownership and location of the deleted user's files using the commands chown and mv.

■ **Remove the user from the password file and remove all files the user owns.** This is the ultimate and complete form of deleting a user. You must delete the user's entry from the password file and delete the user's files from the system. You can do this using the find command:

```
find users-home-directory -exec rm {} \;
```

Then remove the directory with rmdir *users-home-directory* and remove the appropriate entry from the password file or files. Another way to do all this is to use the -r option with the command userdel. For example, userdel -r tuser.

Changing User Attributes

A user's needs, status, and assignments often change. These changes are often reflected in either the password or group file. It may be that a user is assigned to another project and needs access to the files of another group. To modify a user's attributes, use the command usermod. The options with this command include some of those available with useradd (-u*UID*, -g*group*, -C*info*, -d*dir*, -s*shell*, -G*group*, -k*shell*). Two additional options are these:

-l   Change a user's login name

-m   Move the user's home or login directory to the directory specified with the -d option

In this example, user tuser's login name is changed to typuser, is added to the group frstan98, and has the home directory changed and moved to /research/typuser:

```
usermod -l typuser -d /research/typuser -m -G frstan98 tuser
```

The changes take effect the next time the user logs in.

Working with Groups

Each user is a member of a group. You can give different types of groups different capabilities or privileges. For example, it is reasonable to give users of a group that uses the system for analysis of a company's sales data access to a different set of files than a group of users whose main function is researching new products.

The password file contains information for a single user. Information about groups is kept in the file /etc/group. Here is a sample entry:

```
sales::21:tuser, jdreiss, staplr
```

The group name is sales, the group ID number is 21, and the members are tuser, jdreiss, and staplr. Files and directories have permission associated with them for the owner, group, and others. A user can be a member of more than one group, and you can change group memberships.

Adding a Group

You create a new group by either editing the file /etc/group directly or using the command groupadd. To create a new group named sales, type the following command and press <Return>:

```
groupadd sales
```

The group is added and has a unique group ID number associated with it. If you want to assign the group ID number yourself, use groupadd with the -g option, as in this example:

```
groupadd -g 21 sales
```

You still must give a name to the group. You can add users to this group using useradd or usermod.

Deleting a Group

You delete a group by using an editor to modify the file /etc/group or by using the command groupdel. Type the command followed by the name of the group to be removed. To delete the group sales, for example, type the following command and press <Return>:

```
groupdel sales
```

VIII

UNIX Multiuser Systems

Modifying Group Attributes

Over time, you may want to change the group ID number associated with a group if that group number is to be used for another purpose. To do that, type the following command and press <Return>:

```
groupmod -g new-group-id-number group-name
```

To change the name of group without changing its membership, type the following command and press <Return>:

```
groupmod -n new-group-name old-group-name
```

Suppose that you have a group of users working on a project identified as xf345 but now they are working together on the project frstan98. To change the group, type the following command and press <Return>:

```
groupmod -n frstan98 xf345
```

Adding Users with UnixWare's Graphical Desktop

Although the useradd command is provided with UnixWare, the User Setup window (shown in fig. 30.1), located in the System Setup folder on the Desktop, is a much more intuitive way of adding users. You *must* use the User Setup window instead of the useradd command if you want to add a graphical user (one that can automatically start with the Desktop after logging in).

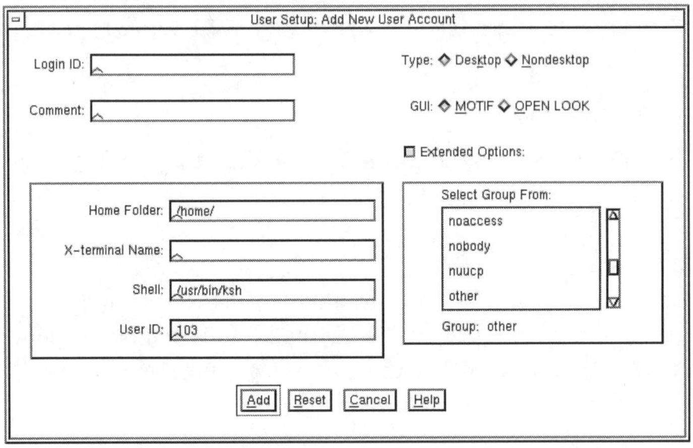

Fig. 30.1
The User Setup window.

To add a graphical user using the Desktop, do the following:

1. In the Desktop window, double-click on the System Setup icon. The System Setup folder opens.

2. In the System Setup folder, double-click on the User Setup icon. The User Setup window opens.

3. Enter the user's login ID in the Login ID text box. If the user has an established login ID on a network, use the same login ID here to avoid problems when the user tries to communicate between systems.

4. Next to the Type option, click on Desktop (the default; it should already be selected).

5. Enter the user's real name or other information in the Comment text box. This data is for information purposes only and is not used by the system.

6. Next to the GUI option, click on MOTIF (the default; it should already be selected).

7. Click on Extended Options. The User Setup window expands.

8. Look at the Home Folder text box, in which /home/ is shown. Unless you want the home directory somewhere else on the system, don't enter anything here. UnixWare automatically creates a directory in /home with the same name as the login ID. If you want the user's home directory in another directory, you *must* enter the full path, including the login ID. For example, to create a home directory for user spike in /home2, enter **/home2/spike** in the Home Folder text box.

9. Enter the X-terminal's name in the X-terminal Name text box only if the user is logging in from an X-terminal. If the user will be using the computer's monitor and keyboard or a dumb terminal for logging in, leave this text box blank.

10. Enter the type of shell the user wants to use in the Shell text box. The Korn shell (ksh) does not come with the Personal Edition version of UnixWare. However, if the user wants the functionality of ksh, enter **/usr/bin/wksh** in the Shell text box. This installs the Windowing Korn shell, a superset of ksh.

11. If the user has an established user ID on other systems in a network, enter that number in the User ID text box. Having the same user ID on all systems that the user logs in to avoids problems in communicating between systems.

12. Select the group the user belongs to from the Select Group From box.

13. Click on Add. A window appears, confirming that you want to create this user account. Click on Yes. The Password Manager window appears. Enter a temporary password for the user. After the account is created, be sure that the user changes his or her password.

VIII

UNIX Multiuser Systems

Working with Serial Devices— Terminals and Modems

Attaching terminals, modems, and other serial devices to your computer is one of the most cost-effective ways to use your UNIX system. With one computer and a few inexpensive pieces of hardware, you can outfit a small business with a terminal on every desk and modem connections to the outside world.

Under SVR4, special files are in /dev/term/*dd* (where *dd* is the terminal line or port number). Other System V special files are in /dev/tty*dd*. (Actually, /dev/term and /dev/tty devices are linked together.) Terminals are serial devices usually connected by a serial connector to the appropriate physical port.

Characteristics for specific terminals are stored in subdirectories of /usr/lib/terminfo. Each file there gives characteristics of the specific terminal. For example, the entry for a VT100 terminal is in /usr/lib/terminfo/v/vt100. These files contain information about a terminal (for example, the number of lines, columns, and character sequences required to do things such as clear the screen or move the cursor to the home position).

Adding a Serial Device

To add any terminal or modem, you must physically connect it to the computer. Begin by identifying the locations of the ports on the computer system; they correspond to the special files in the directory /dev. On an SVR4 system, the device files are in /dev/term and have names corresponding to port numbers such as 0, 00, 01, 12, or some other one-digit or two-digit number. On a PC, the COM1 port is /dev/tty00 and COM2 is /dev/tty01.

The connection is made with a serial cable. You need a cable that's properly wired with the proper connectors. Use one that came with your system or have one made that matches the specifications for your system.

You must know the type of terminal (such as VT100) you're connecting so that you can use the proper file in /usr/lib/terminfo. You also need to know the maximum device speed (such as 9,600 baud).

Modifying Configuration Files

Once the serial device is connected, you're ready to make or modify the entries in the appropriate configuration files. The required modifications differ in different versions of System V.

Configuration Under Older Versions of System V

Under versions of System V before Release 4, the file `/etc/gettydefs` contains definitions for generic serial lines. Consider the following entry in that file:

```
4800#B4800 CLOCAL#B4800 SANE CLOCAL#login: #9600
```

This entry specifies a 4,800-baud line, locally connected (CLOCAL), with standard terminal characteristics (SANE). The login prompt is set to `login:` and the final #9600 indicates that if the baud rate doesn't match, a line in the file whose first entry is 9600 should be checked. That way, you can set a "hunt sequence" for a device to find the proper baud rate it needs to communicate with your system. The entry for 9,600 might be as follows, indicating that no other line is tried:

```
9600#B9600 CLOCAL#B9600 SANE CLOCAL#login: #9600
```

For modem lines, you can include an HUPCL directive, which indicates "hang up on close":

```
m2400#B2400#B2400 SANE HUPCL#login: #m4800
m4800#B4800#B4800 SANE HUPCL#login: #m9600
```

These entries correspond to entries in the file `/etc/inittab` that are used to initialize the terminal. A sample entry is shown here:

```
t2:234:respawn:/etc/getty tty2 9600
```

When the system attempts to run level 2, 3, or 4, the terminal on `/dev/tty2` is initialized using the 9600 entry from `/etc/gettydefs`.

Configuration Under System V Release 4

The configuration of a serial device is somewhat different on systems that use UNIX SVR4. Instead of individual `getty` processes for each terminal line, a server process `ttymon` is used. The server is always running; it's started as part of the normal boot process.

> **Note**
>
> Setting up `ttymon` processes and related components is complicated. Use this section to gain an understanding of how the port monitor mechanism works in UNIX. Then use the sysadm menus or the Dialup Setup window in the UnixWare GUI to actually configure the `ttymon` port monitor.

VIII

UNIX Multiuser Systems

Instead of using the file /etc/gettydefs, the file /etc/ttydefs is used by ttymon. You add an entry to /etc/ttydefs using the command sttydefs. The main options for sttydefs are these:

Option	Description
-a	Label for entry
-b	Autobaud detect for that line
-i	Initial flags, set on line before login is executed
-f	Final flags, set on line after login is executed
-n	Label to be used to set up the next field in the hunt sequence

Using these options, your entry would resemble the following:

```
sttydefs -a 2400 -n 4800 -i"2400 CLOCAL" -f"2400 CLOCAL SANE"
```

If you're setting up a modem line, use HUPCL instead of CLOCAL, as follows:

```
sttydefs -a m2400 -n 4800 -i"2400 HUPCL" -f"2400 HUPCL SANE"
```

Check the man page entry for termio(7) to see the flags that can be set for line characteristics. To find a man page on the termio command, type **man termio** and press <Return>. If you have a GUI, check the Fingertip Librarian icon for the termio entry.

You use sttydefs -r *ttylabel* to remove an entry from ttydefs, like this:

```
sttydefs -r m2400
```

Be careful. If the deleted entry was part of a hunt group, the entries in that group must be modified. (A *hunt group* is a series of ttydef entries that are tried, one after another, until one that works is found. Usually, each entry in a hunt group represents a different baud rate.)

Now you have to access the port monitor system to add terminal lines. This is designed to be very general for all sorts of services—serial lines, network connections, and so on. In fact, it's so general that it's very complicated. Your best bet is to use a system administration menu system, or the Dialup Setup window in the UnixWare GUI, to add terminals or modems at this point.

The following command adds a terminal connected to /dev/term/00s (usually com1) to the port monitor ttymon; the baud rate is specified as 9,600:

```
$ pmadm -a -p ttymon -s 00s -i root -f u -v 'ttyadm -V' \
-m "`ttyadm -d /dev/term/00s -l 9600 -s /usr/bin/login \
-m ldterm -p \" login: \"'"
```

This is all one command. The characters \ at the end of the first two lines indicate that the command continues to the next line. The single apostrophe (') indicates that the output of the `ttyadm` command is to be used as input to this command. Here's the command explained in more detail:

`pmadm -a`	Adds a port to be controlled by ttymon
`-p ttymon`	Names the specific port controller
`-s 00s`	Name of port
`-i root`	The service (/usr/bin/login) is run as root
`-f u`	Creates a wtmp entry for the port
`-v 'ttyadm -V'`	Yields the version number of the port administration file

The rest of the command essentially puts /dev/term/00s under the control of `ttymon`. The initial speed of the port is 9,600 baud. The program /usr/bin/login runs, waiting for a response; when it senses activity, it displays the `login:` prompt.

Working with Printers

Printers are a computer system's hardest working output devices. Printed material—or "hard copy"—usually is a variety of information that appears in a variety of formats. UNIX system printers print everything from inventory lists to address labels and bar-code labels. For high-volume output, most systems employ dot-matrix printers or high-speed line and page printers. For high-quality output, many systems rely on laser and ink-jet printers. Nearly all UNIX systems use at least one printer; most larger systems have multiple printers.

◀ Configuring and working with printers is described in Chapter 9, "Printing."

In the multitasking/multiuser environment of UNIX, it is quite possible that more than one program will attempt to send output to the same printer at the same time. Of course, a printer can accept output from only one program at a time. So that users do not have to wait until the printer is finished with the current job before they can submit their own print job, UNIX employs a print-queuing mechanism. This printer queue is managed by a program called `lpadmin`.

VIII

UNIX Multiuser Systems

Each printer is associated with a print queue that has a unique name and is called a *destination*. Users send requests to a destination. You can associate more than one printer with one destination, called a *device class* (useful when you have similar printing devices). Users can send a print request to the printer class and have output produced on whichever printer in that class is free. Suppose that you have two similar laser printers and one is currently busy. If the printers are in the same class, when you send the request to the class (rather than the destination), the print job is sent to the printer that is least busy.

The command lp is used to send a request to a destination. The request is put into a queue for the printer(s) associated with the destination. The files to be printed are not necessarily put into the queue, only the request. When the printer is free, the file is printed.

Performing System Backups

Various kinds of problems can result in loss of data. Files get accidentally removed or there is a hardware failure or important information stored in files is no longer available. Users should feel confident that, in such cases, they can access a timely backup of the "lost" files.

Your company's future—and your future with your company—may depend on making those backup files available. At times like these, you and others will be thankful that you've taken the time and effort to copy files to some sort of media according to a regular, rigorous, and well-documented schedule. Backing up files isn't very glamorous, but no administrator can ignore the process.

There are several issues to consider in backing up a system:

- **Full or incremental backups**. A *full backup* copies every file. Is it necessary to do that every day? A full backup usually requires a good deal of time and enough media that can hold all the files on the system. An *incremental backup* copies the files that have changed since the last full backup.

- **File systems to back up**. Naturally, active file systems must be backed up regularly. Others can be backed up less frequently. Be sure that you have copies of all the file systems and that they are current.

- **Types of backup media**. Depending on the devices on your system, you may be able to use 9-track tape, 1/4 inch cartridge tape, 4mm or 8mm DAT tapes, or floppy disks. Each has advantages over the other in terms of sheer bulk, amount of information they can store, and cost for devices and media. Choose the backup media to fit your budget, remembering that the least expensive media may be the most time-consuming.

- **Effect of backups on users**. Performing a backup operation increases the load on a system. Will that be an unreasonable burden on users? Also, files that are changed during the backup process may not be backed up. This can merely be an inconvenience or a very important consideration if you're backing up an active database. Should you perform backups when the system is quiet?

- **Commands to use for backups**. There are some relatively simple, time-honored commands for creating backups such as `tar` and `cpio`. Are they sufficient? Should you use a system administrator's menuing system to schedule and perform backups?

- **Documentation of the backed up files**. You must label all backed-up material so that you can use it to recover files when necessary. Some procedures and commands allow you to prepare a table of contents or list of the material that has been backed up.

From an administrator's view, the file system should be backed up according to some automated process with as little operator intervention as possible. It should also be done when the system is relatively quiet so that the backup is as complete as possible. This consideration must be balanced with convenience and costs. Should an operator or administrator have to stay until midnight on Friday to perform a full backup? Is it worth $3,000 for a DAT tape drive so that the entire system can be backed up automatically at 3 A.M. with no operator intervention?

Consider the alternatives, determine the true costs, and make a decision or recommend a course of action. It's generally a lot cheaper and always easier to restore well-managed backup information than to have to recreate it or do without it.

VIII

UNIX Multiuser Systems

Considering Backup Tips

The purpose of performing backups is to be able to restore individual files or complete file systems. Whatever you do about backups should be focused on that central purpose.

Set up a backup plan. Include the files to be backed up, how often they'll be backed up, and document how the files are to be restored. Let all users know the backup schedule and how they can request restoration of files. Be sure to stick with the plan.

Be sure to verify your backups. This could include reading a table of contents from the backup medium after it has been stored or restoring an arbitrary file from the medium. Remember that it is possible for the backup media—disk or tape—to have a flaw.

Make backups so that files can be restored anywhere on the file system or on another computer system. Use backup or archive utilities which create archives that can be used on other UNIX computer systems.

Be sure to label all media—tapes, disks, whatever—used in a backup. If you have to use multiple items, be sure that they are numbered sequentially and dated. You must be able to find the file or files you need.

Plan for a disaster. Have copies of the files on your system so that the entire system can be restored in a reasonable amount of time. Store copies of backup tapes or disks off site.

Plan to reevaluate your backup procedures periodically to be sure that they're meeting your needs.

Planning a Backup Schedule

It's important to come up with a backup schedule that meets your needs and that makes it possible to restore recent copies of files. After you decide on a schedule, stick to it!

The ideal situation is be able to restore any file at any time. Taken to an extreme, that's not possible, but you ought to be able to restore files on a daily basis. To do this, you use a combination of complete and incremental backups. A *complete backup* is one that contains every file on the system. An *incremental backup* is one that contains files that have changed since the last backup. Incremental backups can be at different levels—incremental to the last complete backup or incremental to the last incremental backup. It's convenient to think of backups as occurring at different levels:

level 0   Complete backup

level 1   Incremental to the last complete backup

level 2   Incremental to the last level 1 backup

Here are some sample schedules.

- **Full backup one day, incremental other days:**

  Day 1   Level 0, complete backup

  Day 2   Level 1, incremental backup

  Day 3   Level 1, incremental backup

  Day 4   Level 1, incremental backup

  Day 5   Level 1, incremental backup

  If you create and save an index of each of these backups, you should need only one day's backup to restore an individual file. You'll need only two days' backup (day 1 and another day's) to completely restore the system.

- **Full backup once a month, weekly incremental, and daily incremental.** This example is built around Tuesday but could be any fixed day of the week.

  First Tuesday   Level 0, complete backup

  Any Other Tuesday   Level 1, incremental backup

  Any Other Day   Level 2, incremental backup

  To restore an individual file under this schedule, you may need the complete backup (if the file wasn't changed during the month) or the level 1 backup (if the file was changed the previous week but not this week) or the level 2 backup (if the file was changed this week). This schedule is more complex than the previous example, but takes less time per day performing backups.

VIII

UNIX Multiuser Systems

Performing Backups and Restoring Files

Several different utilities are available for backing up and restoring files in a UNIX system. Some are simple and straightforward; others are more complex. The simple methods have their limitations. Choose one that meets your needs.

A good way to start is by using a system administrator's menu such as sysadm or the OA&M (Operations, Administration, and Management) package installed on your system. UNIX SVR4 contains a sophisticated backup and restore system called bkrs or *extended backup and restore service*. You can access this service through either of the menu systems.

Because backing up and restoring files is very important, there are a number of available software systems dedicated to that task. The following sections present three of them:

Command	Description
tar	Tape archive utility available on every UNIX system; easy to use, limited to saving files on only one tape or disk
cpio	General-purpose utility for copying files; available on every UNIX system; easy to use, more robust than tar, and can use several tapes or disks
backup and restore	System V basic backup utilities; easy to use and sufficient for many systems

Using *tar*

The UNIX tar utility was originally designed to create a tape archive (to copy files or directories to tape and then to extract or restore files from the archive). You can use it to copy to any device. It has several advantages:

- It is relatively simple to use.

- It is reliable and stable.

- Its archives can be read on any UNIX system.

It also has a couple of disadvantages:

- The archive must reside on one disk or tape, which means that if a portion of the media fails—from a bad sector on a disk or bad block on a tape, for example—the entire backup may be lost.

- On its own, it can perform only complete backups. If you want to do incremental backups, you have to do a little shell programming.

Some of the commonly used options for `tar` are as follows:

Option	Description
c	Create an archive either on the default device (given in /etc/default/tar) or on the device specified by the f option.
x	Extract or restore files from the archive that is either on the default device on the device specified by the f option.
f *device*	Create the archive or read the archive from *device* specified in /dev, such as /dev/rmt/c0s0.
v	Verbose mode. Create an index of all files stored or extracted on stdout.

Consider some examples of the use of `tar` in backing up and restoring files. The following command copies the directory /usr2 to the standard backup device:

```
tar c /usr2
```

The following command also archives the directory /usr2:

```
tar cvf /dev/rmt/c0s0 /usr2 > usr2indx
```

In this case, the f option specifies that the archive is created on the device /dev/rmt/c0s0. The v option indicates verbose mode, and a list of files copied is redirected to usr2indx. It is a good idea to take a look at that file to see what was copied.

The following example uses the command `find` to create a list of all files that have been modified in the last day:

```
find /usr2 -mtime -1 -type f > bkuplst; tar cv 'cat bkuplst'
```

To use the list as input to the `tar` command, place the command `cat bkuplst` in backquotes (backward, single quotation marks: `cat bkuplst`).

The following command restores the file /usr2/ernie/chap31.txt from the default device (note that you have to give the complete filename to restore it):

```
tar xv /usr2/ernie/chap31.txt
```

> **Tip**
>
> Any of these commands can be automated by putting them in root's cron file. For example, the following entry in the root's cron file performs a backup of /usr2 every day at 1:30 AM:
>
> ```
> 30 01 * * * tar cv /usr2
> ```

See the man page for tar for a complete description of the options you can use with this command.

Using *cpio*

The UNIX cpio utility is a general-purpose command for copying file archives. You can use it to create backups using the -o option or to restore files using the -i option. It takes its input from standard in and sends its output to standard out.

Advantages of cpio are these:

- It can back up any set of files.

- It can back up special files.

- It stores information in a more efficient manner than tar.

- It can be used to back up information to several tapes or disks.

- It skips bad sectors or bad blocks when restoring data.

- Its backups can be restored on any UNIX system.

To perform incremental backups, you do have to do some shell programming.

Here are some of the commonly used options for cpio:

Option	Description
-o	Copy out. Create an archive on standard out.
-B	Block input or output at 5120 blocks per record. Useful for efficient storage on magnetic tape.
-i	Copy in. Extract files from standard input (assumed to be the result of a copy out action of cpio).
-t	Creates a table of contents of the input.

Consider some examples of use of `cpio` in backing up and restoring files. The following command copies the files in the directory `/usr2` to device `/dev/rmt/c0s0`:

```
ls /usr2 ¦ cpio -o > /dev/rmt/c0s0
```

The following example extracts the files on the device `/dev/rmt/c0s0` and creates an index the file `bkup.indx`:

```
cpio -it < /dev/rmt/c0s0 > bkup.indx
```

The following example uses the command `find` to create a list of all files on `/usr2` that have been modified in the last day:

```
find /usr2 -mtime 1 -type f -print ¦ cpio -oB > /dev/rmt/c0s0
```

The output of that command is piped to `cpio`, which creates an archive on `/dev/rmt/c0s0` where the data is stored in 5120 bytes per record.

The following command restores from the device `/dev/rmt/c0s0` the file `/usr2/ernie/chap31.txt`:

```
echo "/usr2/ernie/chap31.txt" ¦ cpio -i < /dev/rmt/c0s0
```

Note

You must give the complete filename to restore it with `cpio`.

Tip

Any of these commands can be automated by putting them in root's `cron` file. For example, the following entry in the root's `cron` file performs a backup of `/usr2` every day at 1:30 AM:

```
30 01 * * * ls /usr2 ¦ cpio -o > /dev/rmt/c0s0
```

See the man page for `cpio` for a complete description of the options you can use with this command.

Using *backup* and *restore*

The commands `backup` and `restore` are part of the basic backup services of SVR4. They can be used for complete or incremental backups. Table 30.2 gives the options you can use with the command `backup`.

VII

UNIX Multiuser Systems

Table 30.2   Options To Use with the *backup* Command

Option	Action
-h	Show when last complete and incremental backups were performed. (This option only gives information about when backups were done; it doesn't perform a backup.)
-w	Perform a complete backup.
-p	Perform an incremental backup. (Only files that have changed since the last complete backup are saved.)
-f *files*	Back up files given in the *files* list. (You can use the shell's meta or special characters as wild cards. The list given in *files* must be enclosed in quotation marks.)
-u *user*	Back up the home directory of the user specified by *user*. (This can one or more users. If all is used, all home directories are backed up.)
-d *device*	Give the *device* for the backup. (If none is specified, backups are done to /dev/rdsk/f0.)
-T	Perform backup to a tape device. (This is required when the device specified with the -d option is a tape device.)

You can list files or directories to be backed up by putting them in the file /etc/Backup. Directories to be ignored can be specified in the file /etc/Ignore. For example, you can put the name /usr2/sales/data in the file /etc/Backup to ensure that it will be backed up. To keep the directory /tmp from being backed up, put /tmp in the file /etc/Ignore.

Consider some examples of performing backups using the command backup. The following command performs a complete backup to the standard backup device:

```
backup -w
```

The following command makes a complete backup to the tape device /dev/rmt/c0s0:

```
backup -T -w -d /dev/rmt/c0s0
```

The following command performs a partial or incremental backup to the tape device /dev/rmt/c0s0:

```
backup -T -p -d /dev/rmt/c0s0
```

The following command backs up the files in the directory /usr/local to the tape device /dev/rmt/c0s0:

```
backup -T -f "/usr/local/*" -d /dev/rmt/c0s0
```

Tip

Any of these commands can be automated by putting them in root's `cron` file. For example, the following entry in root's `cron` file performs a backup of the entire file system every day at 1:30 AM:

```
30 01 * * * backup -T -p -d /dev/rmt/0h
```

You use the command `restore` to restore files that were backed up using the command `backup`. Its general form is as follows:

```
restore options pattern
```

In this syntax, `pattern` is a list of files or shell expressions for the files to be restored. Table 30.3 gives some of the options you can use with `restore`.

Table 30.3: Options To Use with the *restore* Command

Option	Action
`-i`	Get the index file from the medium. (This shows the names of the files that are on the backup. No files are restored.)
`-w`	Perform a complete restore.
`-O`	Overwrite any existing files. (If this option isn't given, the existing files are not overwritten from the backup medium.)
`-W device`	Give the `device` from which files are to be restored. (If none is specified, the restore is taken from `/dev/rdsk/f0`—the diskette device.)
`-T`	Perform restore from a tape device named with the `-W` option.

Consider some examples that use the `restore` command. The following command performs a complete restore of the files on the device `/dev/rdsk/f1` (existing files are not restored):

```
restore -w -W /dev/rdsk/f1
```

The following example performs a complete restore of the files on the tape device `/dev/rmt/c0s0` (any existing files are overwritten, replaced by the versions on the backup medium):

```
restore -T -w -O -W /dev/rmt/c0s0
```

VIII

UNIX Multiuser Systems

The following command restores all the files backed up whose names end with `.dat` from the directory `/usr2/ernie` (existing files aren't overwritten or changed):

```
restore -T -W /dev/rmt/c0s0 "/usr2/ernie/*.dat"
```

See the man pages for `backup` and `restore` for a complete list of options to use with these commands.

Training

You need to take advantage of training for yourself, the administrator, your staff if you have one, and the users of the system. Managing and using a UNIX system can be a complex task. Everyone involved should be informed concerning proper use of and changes to the computer system. Budget for the proper training for you and your staff. It is money well spent.

System Administrator Training

Administering any system can be a complex and demanding task. Formal instruction gives you the opportunity to communicate with an expert or other system administrators who have faced similar challenges. It also gives you the chance to create a network of other administrators or experts you can call when problems arise. Training can be very costly, but it's usually worth the expense.

You need to be well versed in all the aspects of system administration. Many of these concerns are addressed in the manuals that came with your system— but they may not be written in a manner or style you're comfortable with. The place to start is with a basic system administration course offered by your system vendor or manufacturer. If that's not available, consider getting some training from a local user group or enrolling in a workshop at a conference. After that, get training in specific areas such as system security, optimizing system resources, and the use of specialized systems and devices.

User Training

Users also benefit from training. They can find better and more efficient ways to carry on their work. Training also exposes them to expert advice on ways to take advantage of the capabilities of their system. As they become more informed, they develop their own expertise and confidence. You'll find that they can handle their own problems better after some training. It can relieve some of their frustration and lighten your load as well.

Beginning users benefit from an introductory UNIX course or training session to give them an overview of the system they're working with. After that, they will probably need training in areas more specific to their work. This might include shell programming or use of specific systems such as accounting or database development. Tailor the details to their needs or assignments. Some of this training can be in-house, provided by you or your staff. The better users are informed about the system they are working with, the more productive they will be.

Implementing a Training Program

A variety of sources exists for training courses and materials, including classes off site and on site, video and audio tapes, and self-paced materials. Talk to other users of systems similar to yours to find out what training opportunities they have found most beneficial.

At a minimum, plan for the following training:

- Introductory or basic system administration relevant to your specific system for yourself either before or soon after your system is installed

- Introductory or basic system administration relevant to your specific system for all members of your staff

- Specialized system administration at least once a year for yourself and all members of your staff

When you become well versed about your system, you can begin to offer or recommend training sessions for your users. Be sure that all new users have some sort of training or information about the computer system they will use. You and your staff ought to offer in-house courses, training, or training materials for all users on a regular basis. Match these offerings with needs and work schedules. It's also a good idea to survey users to see what topics they feel are most important. Be sure to offer regularly scheduled (perhaps once a month) introductory courses or sessions about basic system use plus specialized courses on topics such as the following:

- System security

- Working with UNIX files

- Electronic mail

- Using an editor

- Shell programming

VIII

UNIX Multiuser Systems

Speak with users' supervisors about the need to provide for training. Try to make them aware of the costs involved in terms of time away from primary tasks, costs for the training sessions or materials, and the expected increase in productivity.

Be sure to plan for an appropriate setting for training. Try to provide for or reserve well-lit, comfortable rooms for some sessions and also some facilities where they can immediately try or experiment with topics. Users benefit most from hands-on training.

As you see the needs of users expressed in the types of questions they have about using the computer system, develop some training materials of your own. These can include useful tip sheets, a list of frequently asked questions with stock answers, and materials you have found useful. See that each user gets a copy of the materials you create to help them with their daily tasks. You'll also find it useful to be able to recommend training materials available from external sources.

Shutting Down the System

UNIX systems should be shut down in an orderly manner. A UNIX system is always working, so keep these things in mind as you plan a shut-down:

- A number of background processes or daemons are always running.

- An active system usually has a number of open files. These can be files used by an individual or groups.

- If you are running any sort of database, it's possible that the database itself is open and being modified.

- The UNIX file system is implemented in such a way that changed files or directories aren't always written immediately to a disk or other medium. They are held in main memory and written to the disk at later times to improve the efficiency of access to a disk. (Delays to the recording of changes are only for several seconds or fractions of a second.)

If you just "pull the plug," turn off the power, or hit a reset button, you run the risk of damaging files or directories in such a manner that internal tables aren't consistent with the actual contents of a disk. Although UNIX SVR4.2 uses the Veritas file system and so has reduced the risk of losing data (see "Shutting Down from the UnixWare Desktop," later in this chapter), shutting down properly is still recommended.

To halt the system in an orderly manner, you use the command shutdown.

Using *shutdown*

The command `shutdown` puts the system in a state so that no new processes are started and any running processes are stopped. It brings the system to a point from which you can safely turn off the power or reboot the machine. The `shutdown` command can be run only by the root user and must be run from the root directory. Before you use it, make sure that no job is printing and that file transfers to other systems have been completed. If interrupted, those operations are restarted when the system comes back up.

The `shutdown` command must be run from the root directory. To change to the root directory, use this command:

```
cd /
```

The command `shutdown` has three options:

`-gseconds`	Give *seconds* "grace period" before all processes are terminated. (For example, to specify a grace period of 5 minutes, use `-g 300`).
`-ilevel`	Specify the run-level of the system after `shutdown` does its work. (The *level* option can be 0 to turn off the power, 1 or S for single-user mode, 5 for a firmware state, and 6 to reboot after shutdown.)
`-y`	Answer yes to any questions `shutdown` asks.

The grace period allows users to complete their work. No processes are killed until the grace period has expired.

To shut down the system in five minutes and put it in single-user state so that there is no activity except your own, type the following command and press <Return>:

```
shutdown -g300 -iS
```

To shut down the system in 90 seconds and immediately reboot, type the following command and press <Return>:

```
shutdown -g90 -i6
```

In either case, you see some messages from the system about its killing processes and going to the state you specified.

Shutting Down from the UnixWare Desktop

In the past, when a UNIX system was suddenly brought down (turned off) by a power failure, someone tripping over the power cord (this *has* happened), or by someone just turning off the power switch, there was a more-than-likely chance that files were destroyed. Not so with UnixWare.

UnixWare employs the Veritas file system (vxfs) which is fairly bulletproof. The authors have yet to lose files from turning off the power on a running UnixWare system. However, it is still not recommended that you turn off your UnixWare system as you would a DOS system.

Another benefit of vxfs is that UnixWare doesn't perform the time-consuming file-system check of past UNIX versions. The vxfs system allows UnixWare to boot relatively quickly for a UNIX system.

To shut down UnixWare, do the following:

1. In the Desktop window, double-click on the Shutdown icon (see fig. 30.2). The Shutdown window opens, as shown in figure 30.3.

Fig. 30.2
The Shutdown icon.

Fig. 30.3
The Shutdown window.

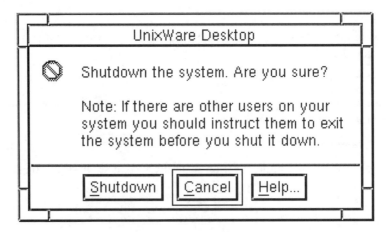

2. In the Shutdown window, click on Shutdown. The Desktop Session window opens (see fig. 30.4).

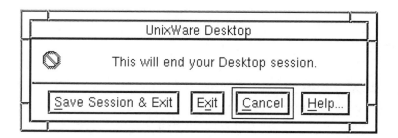

Fig. 30.4
The Desktop
Session window.

3. In the Desktop Session window, click on Save Session & Exit if you want to save the positions of the open windows on your Desktop. Click on Exit if you don't want to save your configuration.

4. The system shuts down and you'll see a prompt to press <Ctrl-Alt-Del> to reboot the system. Press those keys simultaneously to reboot the system. Otherwise, turn off your system's power to totally shut down your system.

Understanding System Security

Unless your system is locked in a closet, you are the only one with a key, and you keep the key on a chain around your neck at all times, you should be concerned about system security. That really is no joke. If there are multiple users, if the system is connected to the outside world by modems or a network, or if there are times when the system is not attended, there are real risks that someone may gain unauthorized access to it.

Sometimes, unauthorized access is benign—but it can still be unnerving. If someone takes the time to gain access to your system, it's likely that he or she has the skill to copy information you want to keep confidential, make unauthorized use of your system's resources, and modify or delete information.

In most organizations, the system administrator has the responsibility for system security. You don't have to be paranoid about it, but you should be aware of the risks and be able to take steps to keep your system secure. Be assertive and professional when addressing security issues.

The security issues discussed in the following sections are these:

- Physical security

- Password security

- Login security

- File security

- Security threats

Physical Security

Make sure that your system and associated components are physically secure. Some systems and devices are small enough to be carried away. Here are some steps you can take to improve the physical security at your installation:

- Don't leave a system, tape drives, disk drives, terminals, or workstations unattended for a prolonged period of time. It's a good idea to have some restrictions regarding access to the room or rooms that house your primary system and associated tape and disk drives. A lock on the door goes a long way in providing security. An unauthorized person can remove backup media—disks or tapes—from an unlocked area.

- Don't leave the system console or other terminal device logged in as root and unattended. If someone knows the system, he or she can easily give themselves root privileges, modify important software, or remove information from the system.

- Educate system users about physical security risks. Encourage them to report any unauthorized activity they may witness. Feel free to courteously challenge someone you don't recognize who is using the system.

- If possible, don't keep sensitive information on systems that have modem or network connections.

- Keep backups in a secure area and limit access to that area.

Password Security

The first line of defense against unauthorized access to a system is passwords. This section describes some steps you can take to keep passwords secure.

The root password is special. Anyone who knows it can access anything on your system and perhaps other systems to which yours is connected through a network. Change the root password often, choose it wisely, and keep it secure. It's best committed to memory. In most organizations, it's a good idea for two people to know it but not any more than that.

Choosing Passwords

Passwords ought to be at least six characters long; only the first eight characters in any password are recognized. It's not too difficult to write a program that can attempt to guess a password. The longer the password, the more time it takes for a password-guessing program to be successful.

Choose a password that isn't a word. One thing people sometimes do in guessing passwords is to try words in a dictionary to gain access to your login account. Choose a password that isn't your name, your login name, or the name of a child, spouse, or pet.

Include both uppercase and lowercase letters, punctuation symbols (but not # or @), and numerals in your password. This makes for more possibilities for a password-guessing program to check.

Following are some good examples of passwords:

```
Sta$^671p
mAr..67op
eaG7651!
```

Choose a password you or a user will remember. One point to make is that the password should be *remembered*. It shouldn't be written down, anywhere!

Password Aging

The system administrator can require that users change their passwords regularly. This is called *password aging*. If someone gains access by guessing a password, their access to the system is limited in the future to the time when the password changes. A disadvantage of changing passwords is that users have to choose new passwords—and they may not be as conscientious as they ought to about choosing good passwords.

You invoke password aging by use of the passwd command. You can do this when you assign a password or at any time. The passwd command has following options:

Option	Description
-x *days*	*days* is the maximum number of days the password is valid. The user is forced to change passwords within that many days.
-n *days*	*days* is the minimum number of days between password changes. The user cannot change passwords for that many days. This may prevent others from changing a user's password.
-w *days*	*days* is the number of days' warning a user gets before having to change passwords.

VII

UNIX Multiuser Systems

To require that a user named `ernie` must change passwords within 30 days, cannot change passwords for 3 days, and will get 7 days' warning, the command is as follows:

```
passwd -x 30 -n 3 -w 7 ernie
```

To lock a password, make the value of days after `-n` greater than that after `-x` (this allows the user to continue logging in, but allows only the root to change the password):

```
passwd -x 1 -n 3 ernie
```

To turn off aging, set the value after `-x` to negative 1 (-1):

```
passwd -x -1 ernie
```

You can also force a user to change passwords the next time he or she logs in by using the `-f` option with the `passwd` command:

```
passwd -f ernie
```

Secondary Passwords

You can require users to enter a secondary, or dial-up, password in order to access the system. This is particularly useful on devices such as modems, but secondary passwords can be set on any port.

To set up secondary passwords, first list the ports that will be affected in the file `/etc/dialups`. For example, to set up a dial-up password on `/dev/term/01s`, put the following line in the file `/etc/dialups`:

```
/dev/term/01s
```

Then enter login programs and encrypted passwords in the `/etc/d_passwd` file. To require a dial-up password, put the following lines into the `/etc/d_passwd` file:

```
/usr/bin/csh:encrypted-password
/usr/bin/ksh:encrypted-password
/usr/bin/sh:encrypted-password
```

Finally, create an *encrypted-password* by following these steps:

1. Create a temporary user by issuing the `useradd temporary` command.

2. Give `temporary` a password by issuing the `passwd temporary` command.

3. Copy the entry from the password file to another file by using the `grep temporary /etc/shadow > temp.pwd` command.

4. Delete the user `temporary` by issuing the `userdel temporary` command.

5. Use `vi` or some other editor to edit the file `/etc/d_passwd`, read in the file `temp.pwd`, and place the encrypted password in the proper positions of `/etc/d_passwd`.

6. Delete `temp.pwd` by issuing the `rm temp.pwd` command.

The final step is to notify authorized users of the dial-up password. Users must enter this password before they get the standard login prompt. Because you use this password to restrict access, you probably will want to change it regularly.

Login Security

There are several things you can do to protect against unauthorized attempts to log in to the system, including the following:

- Limit the number of incorrect attempts to log in.

- Lock login entries of unused logins.

- Remove login names for unused logins.

- Deactivate a login name.

- Set expiration dates for login names.

- Log login attempts.

- Record use of the command `su`.

Limiting the Number of Incorrect Attempts To Log In

By default, users are permitted five attempts to log in with a specific login name. After that, access is denied. UNIX counts the number of times users try to answer the `Password:` prompt. You can change this to another value by setting the `MAXTRIES` or `LOGFAILURES` parameter to another value. These can be set in the file `/etc/default/login`.

To limit a user to three unsuccessful login attempts, add the following line to the file `/etc/default/login`:

```
MAXTRIES=3
```

VII

UNIX Multiuser Systems

Locking Login Names for Unused Logins

If you know a user who is no longer with your organization or whose login is no longer needed, you can lock that login so that it can't be used. To do this, use the command passwd with the option -l. For example, to lock the login for the user ernie, enter the following command:

```
passwd -l ernie
```

To unlock the login, the superuser must use the passwd command for ernie.

Deactivating a Login Name

If a login name won't be used any more, you can use the command userdel to delete the login name. For example, to remove the login name ernie, use the following command:

```
userdel ernie
```

To deactivate a login name if the user hasn't used it for a number of days, use the command usermod -f *number-of-days login-name*. For example, to deactivate the login name ernie if it hasn't been used for seven days, use this command:

```
usermod -f 7 ernie
```

You can reactivate it by entering this command:

```
usermod -f 0 ernie
```

Setting Expiration Dates for Login Names

Use the useradd command to set expiration dates for users. This is useful in situations in which you want to grant temporary access to your system. Suppose that the company has hired a consultant who needs access to your system until June 12, 1994. When you create the user (named consltnt), use the following command:

```
useradd -e 06/12/94 consltnt
```

The date can be changed, extended, or shortened, by using the command usermod. For example, to extend the login until July 23, 1994, use the following command:

```
usermod -e 08/23/94 consltnt
```

Logging Login Attempts

You can set up a log file to keep track of all login names attempted by any user who fails after five unsuccessful tries. If the user succeeds in five or fewer tries, nothing is recorded.

To set this up, create the file /var/adm/loginlog. This file can become quite large in a small amount of time, so be sure to monitor it regularly, trimming its size as necessary.

Follow these steps to create and use the login log file:

1. Create the login log file:

   > /var/adm/loginlog

2. Set proper permissions for the file:

   chmod 700 /var/adm/loginlog

3. Change the group ownership to sys and the user ownership to root:

   chgrp sys /var/adm/loginlog
   chown root /var/adm/loginlog

Recording Use of the *su* Command

When users use the command su, they can become the root or another user. They must know the password of the user to which they are changing. For example, for a user to set his or her user ID to that of user ernie, the command is as follows:

   su ernie

The user is then prompted for the password associated with the login ID ernie.

To change to root, the command is as follows:

   su root

The user is then prompted for the root password.

All attempts at using su are automatically logged in the file /var/adm/sulog. Examine this file periodically to check on this sort of activity.

Security Threats

You can monitor your system for security threats. To determine who is using your system and the type of work they are doing, use the command ps with the option -ef. Be wary of jobs that seem to be running a very long time or users who seem to be using more resources than normal. These can be indications that a login has been compromised and an unauthorized user is running a program to guess passwords.

◀ For more details about the ps command, see Chapter 14, "Using UNIX Remote Communications."

VIII

UNIX Multiuser Systems

Summary

This chapter has dealt with a number of issues involved with administering a multiuser UNIX system. Besides supporting the users who have logins to your system, the system administrator must configure printers, add terminals, and generally maintain the security of the system.

Proper training and planning are essential to the successful administration of your system. To protect your system's data, you must set up reliable backup schedules. To secure your system, you must make sure that your system's users understand the need for password protection and maintaining file protection.

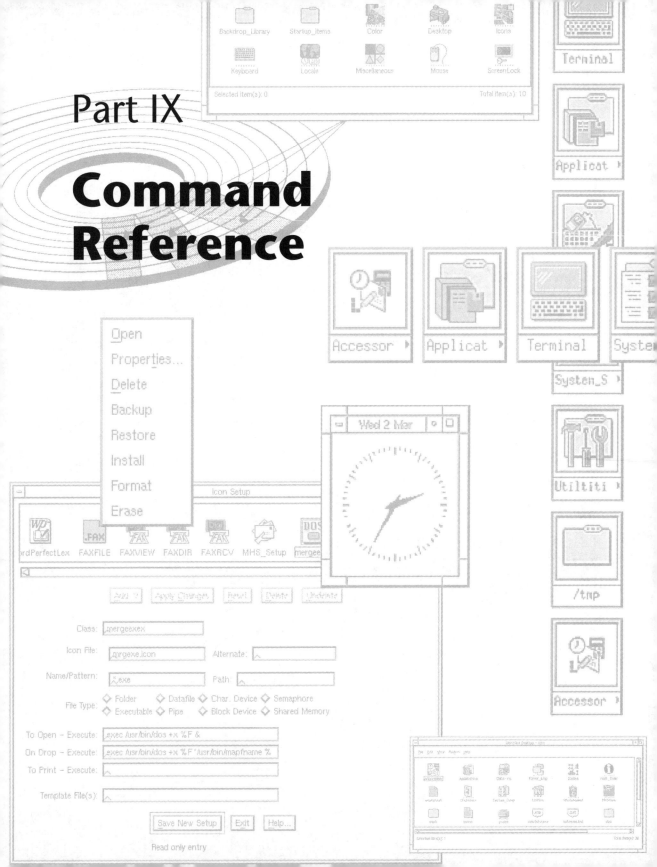

Part IX

Command Reference

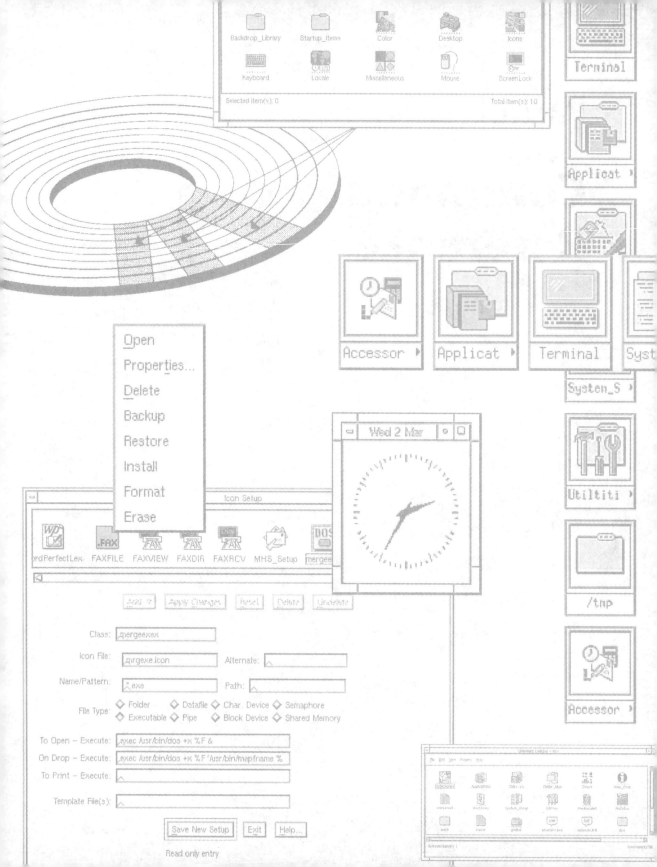

Backdrop_Library Startup_Items Color Desktop Icons

Keyboard Locale Miscellaneous Mouse ScreenLock

Selected item(s): 0   Total item(s): 10

Terminal

Applicat ▶

Open
Properties...
Delete
Backup
Restore
Install
Format
Erase

Accessor ▶   Applicat ▶   Terminal   Syst

System_S ▶

Utiltiti

Wed 2 Mar

Icon Setup

WordPerfectLex .FAX FAXVIEW FAXDIR FAXRCV MHS_Setup mergee
                FAXFILE

Add ?   Apply Changes   Reset   Delete   Undelete

Class: mergeexex

Icon File: mrgexe.icon   Alternate:

Name/Pattern: *.exe   Path:

File Type: ◇ Folder   ◇ Datafile ◇ Char. Device ◇ Semaphore
            ◇ Executable ◇ Pipe   ◇ Block Device ◇ Shared Memory

To Open – Execute: exec /usr/bin/dos +x %F &

On Drop – Execute: exec /usr/bin/dos +x %F '/usr/bin/mapfname %

To Print – Execute:

Template File(s):

        Save New Setup   Exit   Help...

                Read only entry

/tmp

Accessor ▶

Command Reference

This command reference is provided as a means of covering some of the more common commands you may use in the UNIX environment. This is not meant to be an exhaustive listing. After the command is listed, it is described as to what function it fulfills or why you would want to use the command. Following this is a syntax line. The syntax line shows what "format" you have to use to type in the command. For example:

```
cp source dest
```

In this example cp is the command; source and dest are arguments.

When parts of the command are enclosed in square brackets [ ], it means that the enclosed text is optional and does not have to be supplied for the command to do something. Words in the syntax in italics are decriptions of arguments you need to supply. After the syntax, is a detailed description of what each element of the command means and its effect on the command. A notes section is provided to explain various facets of the command and things to look out for, or basic premises needed to be done. A messages section is provided to show you what would happen if the command was misused and what those messages are. This is followed by the examples section that demonstrates how to use the command in some real-world situations. Finally the example section is followed by a cross-reference of related commands.

assign

assign designates a device to a particular user and restricts access to other users. On many systems the devices are publicly accessible, and such assignments are not necessary. On security conscience systems, device assignment can enhance the level of security for users who work with sensitive data.

Syntax

```
assign [flags] device
deassign [flags] device
```

Argument or Option	Description
device	The name of the assigned device.

Flags

Argument or Option	Description
-d	Duplicates the action of deassign.
-v	Displays the devices that are assigned or unassigned.
-u	Performs error-checking; no assignment is made.

Rules

The user who wants to be assigned the device is the user who invokes the command. In a sense, the command is misnamed because no one assigns anything; a user must request the device assignment.

The system-defined user, asg, owns all assignable devices. On the first invocation of assign, the operating system builds the file /etc/atab. This file contains a list of assignable devices and designated users.

To add a device to the list of assignable devices, simply make asg the owner of the device. To remove a device from the list, make the owner something other than asg, for example, bin. To activate these changes, deassign all devices, delete the /etc/atab file, and reassign the devices.

A *raw device* acts as a blank sheet of paper so that you can provide your structure or none at all. The raw device is automatically assigned and may not be asked for separately. An error message is produced if you try to request the raw device separately.

Message

```
can't assign device
```

The device isn't in the assignable device table or you requested the assignment of a raw device.

Examples

```
assign fd096
```

Assigns the current user the raw floppy disk and the block device.

```
deassign fd096
```

The user relinquishes device ownership.

at

Schedules jobs to execute at a later time. batch runs the command with a lower priority at a point when system utilization is lower—it may run immediately and it may run later; depending on the system load.

Syntax

```
at -qqueue time

at -l job-ids

at -r job-ids

batch
```

Argument or Option	Description
-qqueue	An optional queue designation may be specified. *queue* may be any letter between a and z, and the queue is defined as discussed under queuedefs(F) in the manual page. a is the default.
time	This is the time when the job starts. The format of *time* is highly flexible, and is divided into three basic parts: *time*, *date*, and *increment*.

	time	This may be 1, 2, or 4 digits. If 1 or 2 digits are used, this is interpreted as hours (at 1, at 10). If 4 digits are used, this means hours and minutes; a colon also may be used (at 0815, or at 8:15). The suffix am and pm may be used, otherwise a 24-hour clock is assumed. noon, midnight, and now also are acceptable.
	date	This can be a month name followed by a day number and an optional year number preceded by a comma:

at 9:00am Dec 25

at 9:00 Dec 25, 1992

It also can be a day spelled out or abbreviated:

at 9:00 Friday

at 9:00 Fri

Special days are today and tomorrow. today is the default.

(continues)

IX

Command Reference

Argument or Option	Description
increment	Enables you to state an increment of the given time/date as *+n* units. Units may be *minutes, hours, days, weeks, months,* or *years.* The singular also is acceptable. *next* may be used to mean the same as +1.
-l *job-ids*	Lists the currently scheduled jobs. The list may be limited to specific job ids. When no *job-id* is specified all jobs are listed. If you are not the super user, only your jobs are listed.
-r *job-ids*	Removes the specified *job ids* from the queue. Unless you are the super user, you may remove only your own jobs.

Notes

at takes all of its commands from standard input. Therefore, the commands are piped to it, redirected to it, or entered interactively.

at returns a job id when it is invoked. This id may then be used as the *job-id*(s) parameter described previously.

Only those users specified in the file /usr/lib/cron/at.allow are allowed to schedule jobs. If this file doesn't exist, then the file /usr/lib/cron/at.deny holds the list of users who can't use at.

If the time specified is less than the current time then the next occurrence of the time is used. For example, if at noon is used and it is 1:00 p.m., the next day is used.

The standard output and standard error of the commands executed are mailed to the user via UNIX e-mail.

Message

```
at: bad date specification
```

You have entered a time for the execution to take place that is not formatted properly.

Examples

```
at noon <doit
```

Runs the commands found in the file `doit` at noon.

```
at noon Wed next week <doit
```

Runs the commands at noon on Wednesday of next week.

```
at 8:00 Dec 15 <mail-cards
```

Here is the file `mail-cards` that contains a list of commands to mail some electronic Christmas cards.

```
batch
date
find / -name "*.old" -print
```

This is an example of interactively entering commands executed by batch. To end this list of commands, type Ctrl-d. at may be used interactively as well. In this example, you are going to `batch` a search for files ending with the characters `.old`.

See also

cron, date, find, mail

awk

awk, a very powerful scripting programming language, is useful when generating reports from text-based files. awk supplements the file processing capabilities of the shells: sh, csh, and ksh. You can process files based on pattern matches of certain fields. awk also gives you C-like structured programming constructs and a printf command much like that of C. These capabilities allow for fairly straight-forward programming and robust formatting of output.

The power of awk is beyond the scope of this discussion. Several good books are available on awk programming.

Syntax

```
awk [ -Ffldsep ] [ [-e] '¦" awk_code '¦" ] ...\
[ -f  awk_code_filename ] ... [ [ -v ] var=init_val ... ] [ filelist ]
```

IX

Command Reference

Flags

Argument or Option	Description
-F*fldsep*	An optional field separator. *fldsep* may be a regular expression, a single character, or a *t* to mean the tab character. The default field separator is white space (spaces and tab characters). The awk variable FS may also be used to control the field separator in the awk code.
-e '¦"*awk_code* '¦"	An optional script of awk code. The *awk_code* is the actual script to run. It may be enclosed in either single (') or double (") quotation marks. Use one or the other depending on how you want the shell (sh) to interpret the *awk_code*. Single quotation marks do not allow shell interpretation. Double quotation marks allow you to pass shell environment variables to the scripts. The -e is optional. You may chain several of these *awk_code* instances on the command line. Each instance is appended to the last and executed as the complete program.
-f *awk_code_filename*	An optional file name holding awk code. You may specify several of these on the command line. The contents of the files are concatenated and executed as the complete program.
-v *var=init_val*	Allows you to specify an initial value for a variable used in your awk code. You may specify several values on the command line.
filelist	An optional list of files for the awk script (program) to manipulate. If no file is specified, awk assumes its input is the standard input.

Rules

Awk code has this general form:

> *pattern*   { *action* }

This form may be repeated several times. That is, you may have more than one *pattern* { *action* } combination.

Argument or Option	Description
pattern	This is the pattern to match. Awk reads each record of the input file list and compares it to the pattern specified here. If no pattern is specified the associated action is always performed. Two special patterns are BEGIN and END. BEGIN is executed once on script entry, and END is executed just before script exits. Patterns may be any valid regular expression.

Argument or Option	Description	
	Regular expressions	
	/*expr*/	Scans the current record for the expression's *expr*. If a match is found, the associated action is performed.
	expr	Tests the expression *expr*. If the expression is true, the associated action is performed.
	expr1 && *expr2*	Both expressions *expr1* and *expr2* must be true for the associated action to be performed.
	expr1 ¦¦ *expr2*	If either expression *expr1* or *expr2* is true, the associated action is performed.
	(*expr*)	Allows for grouping of expressions.
	!*expr*	Negates the expression such that if the expression is not true, the associated action is performed.
	beg_expr, *end_expr*	Matches all records between the first expression *beg_expr* and the last expression *end_expr*.
	Operators	
	<	Less than
	<=	Less than or equal to
	>	Greater than
	>=	Greater than or equal to
	==	Equal to
	!=	Not equal to.
{ *action* }	This is the action performed when the pattern is matched. Each action block must be enclosed in braces. Each action statement is terminated with a semicolon (;). Action statements may consist of built-in functions, flow control statements (if, while, do, and for), input functions, and output statements.	

Flow control

while (*test_expr*) *statement*

As long as the expression *test_expr* is true, *statement* is executed.

(continues)

Argument or Option	Description
	if (*test_expr*) *statement1* [else *statement2*]
	The expression *test_expr* is tested, if true *statement1* is executed, otherwise if the optional else clause is present, *statement2* is executed.
	for (*init_expr* ; *test_expr* ; *increment_expr*) *statement*
	On entry to the for loop, the expression *init_expr* is evaluated. This expression is only evaluated once in the for loop. The expression *test_expr* is evaluated then, and if true, *statement* is executed. After *statement* is executed, the expression *increment_expr* is evaluated, and the expression *test_expr* is evaluated. If *test_expr* is true, then the process starts over.
	do *statement* while (*test_expr*)
	This is like the while statement, except that *statement* is executed at least once before the expression *test_expr* is evaluated.
break	Used with the looping flow control statements: for, while, and do. break is a controlled "go to" statement. It allows you to force the looping to stop as if the *test_expr* were no longer true, and execution continues.
continue	Used with the looping flow control statements: for, while, and do. continue is a controlled "go to" statement. It allows you to stop processing the current iteration of the loop and return control to the beginning of the loop.
next	Causes the next input record to be read and control is passed back to the first *pattern* statement of the entire script.
exit	Causes execution to go straight to the END statement. If no END statement is present, execution is halted.
Operators (in order of precedence)	
$	Field indicator ($1 means field one, $2 means field two, $*n* means field *n*, $0 means the whole record)
++ --	Increment and decrement
^	Exponential

!			Logical negation
+	–		Unary plus and unary minus
*	/	%	Multiply, divide, and modulo
+	–		Addition and subtraction
(no op)			No operation specified is an implied concatenation of strings. Strings are concatenated simply by juxtaposition.
< > !=	<= >= ==		Logical relations (less than, less than or equal to, greater than, greater than or equal to, not equal to, and equals, respectively)
~	!~		Regular expression match, negated regular expression match.
in			Array membership
&&			Logical and
¦¦			Logical or
? :			Conditional expression
= -= /= ^=	+= *= %=		Assignment (equals, add to and set equals, subtract from and set equals, multiply by and set equals, divide by and set equals, modulo and set equals, and raise to the power of and set equals, respectively). These are borrowed from the C programming language.

The conditional expression

test_expr ? *true_expr* : *false_expr*

The expression *test_expr* is evaluated. If it is non-empty and non-zero, then the expression *true_expr* is executed, otherwise the expression *false_expr* is executed.

Output

print *expr1* , *expr2* , ..., *expr(n)*

print prints the arguments (expressions) given. Each placement of a comma (,) indicates where print places the output field separator. The end of the record is written with the record separator. When commas are omitted they are concatenated and assumed to be the same field. Assuming an output field separator of a colon (:), consider the following two examples.

(continues)

IX

Command Reference

```
print hello, how, are, you,?
                                    hello:how:are:you:?
```

```
print hello how, are you? hello how:are you?
```

```
printf ( format , expr1 , expr2 , ..., expr(n) )
```

printf in awk follows the same rules as the printf(S) routine in the C programming language. Where print assumed the output field and record separators, printf prints how it is formatted based on the format, *format*. *format* consists of a string specifying where numbers, strings, hard-coded text, and special strings should go.

Valid format operators are

%c	A character
%d	A decimal integer
%e	Scientific notation in the form of $[-]d.ddddd\mathrm{E}[+-]dd$
%f	Scientific notation in the form of $[-]ddd.ddddd$
%g	The shorter of %e or %f
%o	An unsigned octal number
%s	A string
%x	An unsigned hexadecimal number
%%	An actual percent sign
\n	A newline
\b	A backspace
\f	A form-feed
\r	A carriage return
\t	A tab
\ddd	An octal value of *ddd*

Variables

awk allows you to define your own variables. Notice from the operators table that fields are designated using the dollar sign ($). However, unlike the shell that used the dollar sign for variables, awk doesn't. Variables are simply referenced by their names. For example, to add all numbers in field 5, you can use the variable *mysum* as in this example, *mysum* += $5 . Notice that to reference field 5, the dollar sign is needed, but the variable *mysum* is simply the word "mysum," with no special syntax.

The preceding is a basic discussion of awk. Some areas not covered are special input processing, predefined variables, some built-in functions, and array processing.

Note

awk supports the concept of associative arrays. Typically an *array* is a process of storing multiple values; each value is indexed by a number. An *associative array* allows you to store values based on the value of a string or a number; the string becomes the index.

Examples

Suppose you have a church group that periodically likes to visit. People are randomly picked to go to a house called the host. Some of the older members can't handle children in their houses, or maybe their houses are just too small, and some don't feel comfortable having anyone come to their houses, but enjoy visiting others. To control this you maintain a database with people from the church with the following fields.

```
:Bontrager, Bob & Harriet:2:0:y:12:y:10
 !         !                   ! ! !  ! ! !
 !         !                   ! ! !  ! ! !->last w/ group
 !         !                   ! ! !  ! ! ->can take kids
 !         !                   ! ! !  ! !->max take
 !         !                   ! ! !->  will host
 !         !                   ! !->number of children in family
 !         !                   !->number of adults in family
 !         !->name of family
 !->indicator that will be host this time, normally blank
```

To get an orderly printout of this, write the following awk script:

```
awk -F: '
BEGIN {
printf("Name                    Adults Kids Will-be-host Max-take Kids-Ok
last_with\n\n");
}
{
if ($5 == "y")                              # test if they will be a host or not
   {
   HOST="yes";                          # set output value of HOST variable to "yes"
   hosting++                                # increment the hosting variable count by 1
   max_take_tot+=$6                 # add to the total number all hosts can take
   }
else
   HOST="no";                             # if not a host then set HOST variable to "no"
if ($7 == "y")                                  # test if they can take kids, and
                                                       # set KIDS appropriately
```

```
    KIDS="yes";
else
    KIDS="no";
printf("%-30s%5d%5d        %-5s       %5d   %-5s  %5s\n", $2,$3,$4,HOST,$6,KIDS,$8);
                              # print the formated output
n_adults+=$3;                                    # add up the total number of adults
n_kids+=$4;                                       # add up the total number of kids
}
END {
printf("\nTotal                          %5d%5d%22d\n", n_adults, n_kids,
(max_take_tot / hosting));
                              # print the totals and the average number of people
needed at each host
}
' <data
```

Running the following awk script on the sample data set:

```
:Bontrager, Bob & Harriet:2:0:y:12:y:10
:Bontrager, Fritz & Chris:2:1:y:12:y:11
:Bontreger, Gene & Alma:2:0:y:12:y:1
:Bontreger, Randy & Janis:2:2:y:12:y:6
:Bontreger, Omar & Mary Alice:2:0:y:12:y:2
:Byers, Daryl & Janet:2:2:y:15:y:7
:Chupp, Harvey & Carolyn:2:0:y:12:y:8
:Freed, Lowell:2:5:y:14:y:10
:Fry, Ezra:2:0:y:10:y:1
:Fry, Olen & Lucy:2:0:n:0:n:5
:Gerber, Walter & Anna:2:0:y:10:y:2
:Guth, Ron & Caryl:1:0:y:25:y:6
:Hochstedler, Cal & Linda:2:3:y:15:y:2
:Hochstedler, Lamar:2:0:y:15:y:2
:Hochstetler, Gene & Beth:2:0:y:10:y:1
:Hochstetler, Lonnie & Shirley:2:0:y:12:y:6
:Hostetler, Bud:2:0:y:10:y:3
:Hostetler, Doug & Dee:2:1:n:0:n:1
:Hostetler, Jim:2:2:y:10:y:3
:Hostetler, Merv & Margaret:2:0:y:12:y:4
:Hostetler, Richard:2:0:y:10:y:6
```

will produce the following:

Name	Adults	Kids	Will-be-host	Max-take	Kids-Ok	last_with
Bontrager, Bob & Harriet	2	0	yes	12	yes	10
Bontrager, Fritz & Chris	2	1	yes	12	yes	11
Bontreger, Gene & Alma	2	0	yes	12	yes	1
Bontreger, Randy & Janis	2	2	yes	12	yes	6
Bontreger, Omar & Mary Alice	2	0	yes	12	yes	2
Byers, Daryl & Janet	2	2	yes	15	yes	7
Chupp, Harvey & Carolyn	2	0	yes	12	yes	8
Freed, Lowell	2	5	yes	14	yes	10
Fry, Ezra	2	0	yes	10	yes	1
Fry, Olen & Lucy	2	0	no	0	no	5
Gerber, Walter & Anna	2	0	yes	10	yes	2
Guth, Ron & Caryl	1	0	yes	25	yes	6
Hochstedler, Cal & Linda	2	3	yes	15	yes	2

Hochstedler, Lamar	2	0	yes	15	yes	2
Hochstetler, Gene & Beth	2	0	yes	10	yes	1
Hochstetler, Lonnie & Shirley	2	0	yes	12	yes	6
Hostetler, Bud	2	0	yes	10	yes	3
Hostetler, Doug & Dee	2	1	no	0	no	1
Hostetler, Jim	2	2	yes	10	yes	3
Hostetler, Merv & Margaret	2	0	yes	12	yes	4
Hostetler, Richard	2	0	yes	10	yes	6
Total	41	16		12		

The preceding example doesn't use pattern matching. You can modify it as follows to print out any of the Frys.

```
awk -F: '
BEGIN {
printf("Name                        Adults Kids Will-be-host Max-take Kids-Ok
last_with\n\n");
}
 /Fry/ {                     #only look for the names with Fry
if ($5 == "y")              # test if they will be a host or not
   {
   HOST="yes";              # set output value of HOST variable to "yes"
   hosting++                                # increment the hosting variable count by 1
   max_take_tot+=$6         # add to the total number all hosts can take
   }
else
   HOST="no";               # if not a host then set HOST variable to "no"
if ($7 == "y")              # test if they can take kids, and set KIDS appropriately.
   KIDS="yes";
else
   KIDS="no";
printf("%-30s%5d%5d    %-5s      %5d  %-5s  %5s\n", $2,$3,$4,HOST,$6,KIDS,$8);
                    # print the formated output
n_adults+=$3;                       # add up the total number of adults
n_kids+=$4;                         # add up the total number of kids
}
END {
printf("\nTotal                   %5d%5d%22d\n", n_adults, n_kids, (max_take_tot / hosting));
                    # print the totals and the average number of people
                    # needed at each host

}
' <data
```

results in the following:

```
Name                                 Adults Kids Will-be-host Max-take Kids-Ok last_with

Fry, Ezra                              2    0     yes            10      yes       1
Fry, Olen & Lucy                       2    0     no              0      no        5

Total                                  4    0                    10
```

See also

ed, sed, sh, ksh, csh, cut, paste, grep

banner

banner produces an "enlarged" version of the arguments passed to it. As many as 10 characters may be specified. These characters are then enlarged using a series of asterisks (*). The output of banner is the standard output.

Syntax

banner *strings*

Argument or Option	Description
strings	The list of 10 character strings to create a banner. Each string, if separated by a space, creates a banner on successive lines. Two strings may be enclosed in quotation marks ("), which causes banner to place the strings on the same line.

Note

The lp spooler uses banner to print the banner page, typically passing banner the login id of the user requesting the printout.

Examples

banner hello

Produces the word hello in a larger format to the standard output.

banner "My Banner" ¦ lp

Prints My Banner on the default printer.

basename

Extracts the file name portion of a path name. You can also strip off trailing characters or extensions.

Syntax

```
basename pathname extension
```

Argument or Option	Description
pathname	The path name of the file of which you want the basename.
extension	The extension or suffix to strip off.

Examples

```
basename /usr/acct/frank
```

The result displayed on the standard output is frank.

```
basename /usr/acct/frank/bowling.wk3 .wk3
```

The result displayed on the standard output is bowling. Notice how the characters .wk3 are stripped from the output.

Tip

Suppose you copy Frank's home directory to Pete's and then discover that you shouldn't have. Because you can't delete all of Pete's home directory, you have to delete each file one at a time. When used with the shell's output assignment operator ('), basename is a powerful tool when writing shell scripts. The following deletes all files found in Frank's home directory from Pete's home directory:

```
for i in /usr/acct/frank/*
do
rm /usr/acct/pete/'basename $i'
done
```

See also

dirname

batch

See at.

bc

bc is a calculator program offering not only the ease of simple math operations, but also a programming language similar to C in construct. bc is particularly useful for base conversions. For a complete list of operators and structures consult the User's Reference supplied with your system or the on-line man pages.

Syntax:

```
bc -c -l filelist
```

Argument or Option	Description
-c	Normally, bc acts as a preprocessor for the dc (desk calculator). This option sends the "compiled" output to the standard output instead of dc.
-l	Enables access to the math library that includes the trigonometric and logarithmic functions.
filelist	The list of files containing bc functions to be executed. After executing the list of files bc reads from the standard input. This enables you to load the functions with which you have to work from a set of files and then to interactively call on these functions.

Examples

The following example multiplies 40 times 512. The result (20480) is displayed on the next line.

```
bc
40*512
20480
^D
```

The next several examples are base conversions from one number system to another. In each of these, the word ibase refers to the input base, and the word obase refers to the output base.

Converts the base 16 (hex) number 1B to its decimal equivalent.

```
bc
ibase=16
1B
27
^D
```

The following example converts from base 16 to base 2 (binary).

```
bc
ibase=16
obase=2
1B
11011
^D
```

This example sets the scaling to 4 decimals and calculates the result of 2 divided by 3.

```
bc
scale=4
2/3
.6666
^D
```

Message

```
cannot open input file on line 1, badfilename
```

You supplied bc with a file name that it cannot open.

See also

dc

bdiff

Runs diff on files that are too large for it. bdiff breaks up the two files for comparison into smaller chunks. The output is merged and the line numbers adjusted as if diff had been run directly.

Syntax

```
bdiff file1 file2 lines -s
```

Argument or Option	Description
file1	The first file used in the comparison. If a dash (-) is used then standard input is read.
file2	The second file used in the comparison. If a dash (-) is used then standard input is read.
lines	The number of lines to send to diff at a time. The default is 3500.
-s	Suppresses the printing of bdiff diagnostics. This does not stop the printing of diff diagnostics, however.

Rule

Because the file is broken up into pieces, `bdiff` may not be able to find a minimum number of differences.

Messages

```
ERROR: arg counter(bd1)
```

You didn't supply `bdiff` with the right number of arguments.

```
ERROR: 'filename' non-existent( (ut4)
```

The file name you supplied `bdiff` doesn't exist.

Example

```
bdiff letter-to-mom letter-to-mom.old
```

Passes the two files to `diff` for comparison after breaking them up into 3500 line pieces. (These were presumably very long letters.)

See also

diff, split

cal

`cal` displays a calendar on the standard output. The output is small. One year takes less than one 8 1/2-by-11-inch sheet of paper. This can be useful when you have to quickly compare several years or want to find out on what day of the week a particular date occurs.

Syntax

```
cal month year
```

Argument or Option	Description
month	May be a number between 1 and 12, or enough letters to represent a unique month. (J is not enough to distinguish January, June, and July.) The default is the current month.
year	May be any number between 1 and 9999. The default is the current year. All four numbers of the year must be specified. That is, 92 refers to the year 92, not 1992.

Note

When no arguments are given, the current month plus the previous and the next are displayed along with the current date and time.

Messages

```
cal: bad year 0
```

Tells you the year 0 cannot be printed. The year must be between 1 and 9999.

```
cal: non-unique month name Ma
```

Here you supplied only the letters Ma, and cal can't determine if you wanted May or March.

Examples

```
cal
```

Shows the current month plus the previous month and the next month.

```
cal 1960
```

Shows the calendar for the year 1960.

```
cal 10 1994
```

Shows the month of October for 1994.

calendar

Produces a to-do list by reading the file calendar in your current directory.

Syntax

```
calendar -
```

Argument or Option	Description
- (hyphen)	When this argument is given, calendar looks in every user's home directory for the file calendar and mails them the results.

Rules

To be mailed a "to-do" list, you have to have a file called calendar created in your home directory. In this file you can list one-line entries containing the date that the task or appointment is on. You may specify multiple lines for the same task. Each line, however, must contain the date or that line is not mailed.

`calendar` accepts the following date formats:

```
12/25/91
Dec 25 1991
Dec 25
```

However, `25 Dec` is not acceptable.

`calendar` mails you the lines found in the `calendar` file one day before the date and on the date. Friday is considered to be one date before Monday. No similar adjustment is made for holidays.

The `calendar` file must have public read permissions for the `calendar` utility to be able to access the information.

Tip

You can make this process automatic by adding the following line to your `crontab` for root:

```
0 1 * * * calendar -
```

This way, each day at 1:00 a.m. `calendar` runs—searching each user's home directory and mailing them their appointments.

Example

```
calendar
```

Gives you a list of the tasks and appointments in your `calendar` file.

See also

cron, mail

cancel

Cancels a print request generated by the `lp` spooler.

Syntax

```
cancel request-ids
cancel printer
```

Argument or Option	Description
request-ids	This is a list of `lp` spooler request ids. The `lp` spooler assigns a unique id to each print request. To list the request id use `lpstat`.
printer	The name of the printer to which print requests go. If a printer name is specified, then the job currently printing is canceled.

Notes

Unless you are the super user or an `lp` administrator, you may cancel only the jobs you have requested.

If the job is currently printing, a message regarding its termination is printed on the paper. Also, if a print request is canceled by someone other than yourself, you are informed by system mail as to who canceled the job and what request id was canceled.

Messages

```
cancel: "bad-id" is not a request id or a printer
```

You have tried to cancel a print request that doesn't exist or have given `cancel` a bad printer name.

```
cancel: request "bad-id" is non-existent
```

You have given `cancel` an id that doesn't exist.

Examples

```
cancel frontdsk-107
```

Cancels the print request that is going to the `frontdsk` printer.

```
cancel frontdsk
```

Cancels the currently printing job on the `frontdsk` printer.

Note

If the job you want to cancel is currently printing, the termination message is printed and the next job begins to print immediately. The paper does not advance to the top of form. A good practice to adopt is to first disable the printer; this stops the printing of the current request and stops printing all jobs on that printer until it is enabled again. You can then cancel the request, realign the printer to the top of the form, and then enable the printer.

See also

lp, lpstat, disable, enable

cat

Concatenates files. This is sometimes used to display a file.

Syntax

```
cat [flags] filelist
```

Argument or Option	Description
`filelist`	This is an optional list of files to concatenate. If no files are specified or a dash (-) is specified, the standard input is read.

Flags

Argument or Option	Description
`-s`	Suppresses messages about unreadable files.
`-u`	Causes the output to be unbuffered.
`-v`	Displays the control characters with a caret (^) before the character that was used to generate the character (for example, an end-of-text, 04, displays as ^D). Characters above octal 0177—the Del character—are displayed with an `M-` in front of the character that has a high bit set to generate the character. Tabs and formfeeds are not affected by this option.
`-t`	Valid only with the `-v` option, this causes the tabs and formfeeds to be displayed in the `-v` format as well.
`-e`	Valid only with the `-v` option; newlines are preceded by the dollar sign ($).

Note

An output file name must not be the same as any of the input names unless it is a special file.

Messages

```
cat: illegal option -- -badoption
```

You invoked `cat` with an option other than those listed previously. *-badoption* is replaced with the option you specified.

```
cat: cannot open badfile
```

You invoked `cat` with a file name that can't be opened.

```
cat: input filename is output
```

You specified an output file name that was used in the input (for example, `cat myfile hisfile >myfile`).

Examples

```
cat letter-to-dad
```

Concatenates `letter-to-dad` with nothing and sends the output to the screen.

```
cat letter-to-dad signature >send.let
```

Appends the file `signature` to `letter-to-dad` and creates a new file called `send.let`.

Note

`cat` is a powerful, yet simple utility that I have used to capture the printout from an old machine for which no other suitable media exchange existed. I merely plugged the serial cable into the appropriate port and typed something similar to this: `cat </dev/tty1a >my-file`. This allowed my UNIX machine to be the "printer" for the old machine and logged the output to the file `myfile`.

See also

echo, pr, pg, more, cp

cd

Changes the current working directory.

Syntax

```
cd dirname
```

Argument or Option	Description
dirname	Changes to an optional directory name. If no directory is specified, the user is returned to his home directory.

Note

You must have execute permissions on the directory to which you wish to change.

Messages

> *baddir*: bad directory

You have specified a directory that doesn't exist.

> cd */dir*?

If you type a directory to change to and misspell the directory name, cd prompts you with what it thought you might have meant. */dir* is replaced with the directory cd thinks you mean. Any response not starting with an *n* is assumed to be yes, thus simply pressing return accepts the prompt.

See also

> pwd, sh, chmod, ls

checkmail

checkmail reports the status of mail you sent that hasn't reached its destination.

Syntax

> checkmail -a -f

When invoked with no arguments, checkmail shows the subject of messages and shows the addresses that did not receive them.

Argument or Option	Description
-a	Causes both delivered and undelivered addresses to appear on the report. Depending on the system configuration, the delivered addresses may not be accessible due to the mail system cleaning up after itself.
-f	The "fast" mode that suppresses the printing of the subject line. Only the addresses appear on the report.

Note

If mail remains in the queue, it is usually because a host is down.

See also

mail

chgrp

Changes the group ownership of a file.

Syntax

```
chgrp group filelist
```

Argument or Option	Description
group	The group to change to. This may either be the numerical value of the group id, or the name as found in the file /etc/group.
filelist	A space-separated list of files of which to change the group ownership.

Note

You may not change the group ownership of a file unless you are the owner of the file or the super user.

Messages

```
chgrp: unknown group: badgroupid
```

You entered a group id that doesn't exist; *badgroupid* is substituted with the bad group id you supplied.

```
badfile: no such file or directory
```

You supplied chgrp with a file name that doesn't exist.

Example

```
chgrp sales /usr/salesstuff/*
```

Changes all the files found in the sales stuff directory to the group ownership of sales.

See also

chown, chmod

IX

Command Reference

chmod

Changes the mode of files. The mode of a file controls the access permissions associated with that file. UNIX has three levels of security: ownership, group access, and everyone else. Within these three levels are three permissions: read, write, and execute. On standard files the read permission means you are able to look at the contents of that file, the write permission enables you to modify the file, and the execute permission means you can execute it. Directories behave only slightly differently. The read permission enables you to view the contents of the directory—an `ls` command works. The write permission enables you to create new files in the directory and to delete files from the directory. Finally the execute permission means you can change to the directory—the `cd` command works.

Syntax

```
chmod mode filelist

chmod level action permission filelist
```

There are two formats. The first is less complicated but requires knowledge of the valid numbers to set the various permissions. It is the "absolute" method. It sets the permissions at all levels. The second format is more complicated but lets you use symbols to specify the permissions, and they are specified incrementally. This is the "relative" method because you can add or remove permissions.

Argument or Option	Description
filelist	Lists the files affected by the `chmod` command.
mode	The numeric mode, in octal, of the permissions this file has for all levels. Each octal number sets a bit in the mode field stored in the i-node table of the file system. Adding the numbers together sets the combination of the permissions. The permissions at the user/owner, group, and other/world levels all follow the same pattern. An additional level controls some special handling. The mode is in the following form: SUGO, where S=special, U=user/owner, G=group, and O=others/world. Each number may be any from the following table (consult the user's reference provided with your system for the Special meaning of the numbers as they differ from the U, G, and O meanings).

Argument or Option	Description		
		Value	**Permission**
		0	None!
		1	Execute
		2	Read
		4	Write
level	The level affected by the rest of the command. It can be any character listed in the following table:		
		Code	**Meaning**
		u	The user/owner of the file
		g	The group level
		o	Others or the world level
		a	All of levels. Default if nothing for *level* is specified.
action	Specifies what action takes place on the mode of the file. It can be any character listed in the following table:		
		Code	**Meaning**
		+	Adds the permission
		-	Removes the permission
		=	Sets the permission to only what is specified.
permission	The permission to apply to the file. It can be one or more listed in the following table:		
		Code	**Permission granted**
		r	read
		w	write
		x	execute

Message

```
chmod: ERROR: invalid mode
```

You didn't specify the mode correctly. Check each portion of the command again. The second form of the command must use the rules described previously. You may have typed the wrong thing.

Examples

```
chmod 777 letter-to-dad
```

Enables `letter-to-dad` to have all permissions at all levels. Notice how the "special" level isn't specified; this is an implied 0 and no special permissions are granted. The execute permission, in this case, is nonsense; however, it demonstrates the use of the 7 to mean all possible permissions.

```
chmod 644 letter-to-dad
```

Allows everyone to read `letter-to-dad`, but only the owner can change it.

```
chmod a+w letter-to-dad
```

Adds the write permission to the letter for everyone.

Removes both read and write permissions at both the group and other levels.

```
chmod o=r letter-to-dad
```

Sets the other level to allow reading only. All other permissions at this level are taken away.

See also

umask, ls

chown

Enables you to change the ownership of the file. In a sense, you are giving the file to someone else.

Syntax

```
chown user filelist
```

Argument or Option	Description
user	May be a numerical user id or a valid user name as found in the /etc/passwd file.
filelist	The space-separated list of files of which to reassign the ownership.

Note

The ownership of the file can be changed only by the owner or the super user. However, if you are the owner of a file and you assign that file to another user, you can't change your mind and reassign it to yourself because you are no longer the owner.

Messages

```
badfile: No such file or directory
```

You specified a file in *filelist* that doesn't exist; *badfile* is substituted with the file you specified.

```
chown: unknown userid baduserid
```

You used a user name not found in /etc/passwd. *baduserid* is substituted with the user name you specified.

Example

```
chown pete/usr/acct/pete/*
```

This example changes all the files found in pete's home directory to the ownership of pete.

See also

chgrp

clear

Clears the screen, or if you are working at a hard copy terminal, this command formfeeds the paper.

Syntax

```
clear term
```

Argument or Option	Description
term	If not specified, the environment variable TERM is used. Must match a valid entry in the file /etc /termcap.

Note

The cl termcap type can be defined in the /etc/termcap file. If not, a series of newlines is sent.

Example

```
clear
```

Clears the screen and leaves the prompt in the upper left corner.

See also

echo

cmp

Compares two files.

Syntax

```
cmp -l -s file1 file2
```

Argument or Option	Description
file1	A valid file name or the dash (-) to have cmp read from the standard input.
file2	A valid file name.
-l	Causes cmp to list the offset (in decimal form) of the files where a difference occurs, and to list the differing bytes (in octal form).
-s	Tells cmp not to produce output. cmp sets only an exit status (0=no differences, 1=the files are different, and 2=inaccessible or missing file).

Messages

```
cmp: EOF on file
```

One file is shorter than the other. *file* becomes the name of the shorter file.

```
cmp: cannot open file
```

Access to the file is not possible, the file may not exist, or you don't have read permission. *file* becomes the file you specified to open.

Example

```
cmp letter-to-mom letter.save
```

Compares the letter (letter-to-mom) with a letter named (letter.save).

Note

The cmp command is best suited for binary files; diff is better suited for text files. If you want to know only if two files are identical and don't care why they are different, cmp works fine.

See also

diff, diff3, sdiff, comm

comm

comm finds common lines in two sorted files. The command generates three columns of information: the lines found only in the first file, those found only in the second file, and the lines found in both files.

Syntax

comm [*flags*] *file1 file2*

Argument or Option	Description
file1	The first file to use in the comparison. You can specify the dash (-) if you want comm to read the standard input.
file2	The second file to use in the comparison.

Flags

Argument or Option	Description
-1	Doesn't produce the first column.
-2	Doesn't produce the second column.
-3	Doesn't produce the third column.

Message

comm: cannot open *badfilename*

You gave comm a file name that doesn't exist or that you don't have permission to read. *badfilename* becomes the file name you specified to open.

Examples

```
ls /usr/sue >sue.dir
ls /usr/frank >frank.dir
comm sue.dir frank.dir
```

Stores the directory listings of files found in two users' accounts. If frank and sue work on files with similar names, you can find out what the files have in common. (dircmp is actually a better tool for this task—for example, dircmp /usr/sue/usr/frank).

```
comm -12 sue.dir frank.dir
```

Uses the same directory listings as in the previous command. In this example, output is limited to those files that have something in common.

See also

diff, sdiff, sort, uniq, cmp, dircmp

compress

compress allows you to compress or reduce the amount of disk space a file uses. Sometimes you have files in your directories that you don't need to access often but that you don't want to remove. You can use compress to make these files smaller, and make room for other files. Compressing files also reduces the amount of time it takes to send them across a modem.

Syntax

```
compress [-cdfFqv ] file-list

uncompress [ -fqc ] file-list

zcat file-list
```

Argument or Option	Description
file-list	A space-separated list of files to compress/uncompress.

Flags

Argument or Option	Description
c	Writes the result of compress/uncompress to standard output without altering the original file. Allows compress and uncompress to be used as a filter in a pipeline.

Argument or Option	Description
d	Decompresses the file and expands it to its original size. It makes compress behave like uncompress.
f	Forces the output file to be overwritten even if it already exists. Normally, compress creates a file with a .Z suffix. Without this flag set, if a file already exists with a .Z suffix, you are prompted to overwrite the files. This flag forces the file to be overwritten without a need for your response.
F	Forces the output file to be written even if no file savings take place. Normally compress does not create a file with the .Z suffix unless compression actually saves space. This flag forces creation of a .Z suffix file even though no savings take place.
q	Quiet mode. The opposite of -v; nothing displays except error messages.
v	Verbose mode. Displays the name of the file being compressed and the percentage of compression. When used with uncompress, only the file name displays.

Rules

compress cannot compress files with links; if you attempt to do so you get an error message. If you compress a file with a symbolic link, the link is broken, and you end up with a compressed copy of the file; the pointer no longer exists to the original file.

If no file is specified on the command line, then the standard input is used. This, along with the -c flag, allows compress to be easily integrated into a pipeline of commands.

Normally compress creates a file with the suffix of .Z when the -c option is not specified. These files retain the ownership and permissions of the original file. When you use the -c flag, the file created has your default permissions and you are the owner of the file.

When passing *file-list* to uncompress and zcat, the .Z suffix is assumed. For example, if you compress the file letter_dad, you end up with a file called: letter_dad.Z. When you want to uncompress this file, you need only type: uncompress letter_dad. uncompress looks for a file with the .Z suffix.

IX

Command Reference

Messages

```
hello: No such file or directory
```

You attempted to compress a file named `hello` that doesn't exist.

```
ben: Compression: -2.22% -- file unchanged
data: Compression: 41.20% -- replaced with data.Z
print: Compression: 29.09% -- replaced with print.Z
tst: Compression: -14.63% -- file unchanged
```

An example of using the `-v` flag. Note how the files `ben` and `tst` do not result in a file savings; the original file remains intact. The `-F` flag wasn't used.

```
ben.Z: No such file or directory
```

You attempted to uncompress a file called `ben.Z` but it does not exist.

```
data:   -- has 1 other links: unchanged
```

You attempted to compress a file called `data` and this file had a link to some other file.

```
data.Z: already has .Z suffix -- no change
```

You attempted to compress a file (`data.Z`) which already had the `.Z` suffix.

Examples

```
compress *
```

Compresses everything in the current directory.

```
uncompress *.Z
```

Uncompresses everything with a `.Z` suffix.

```
zcat *.Z
```

Uncompresses and displays the contents of all files with a `.Z` suffix and leaves the original file intact.

See also

pack, pcat, unpack, cat

copy

Copies files or entire directory structures, keeping the same ownership, permissions, and modification times.

Syntax

```
copy [flags] sources destination
```

Argument or Option	Description
sources	A space-separated list of files or directories to be copied.
destination	The directory or file to which to copy.

Flags

Argument or Option	Description
-a	Asks for confirmation before each copy. Any response beginning with a *y* is assumed to be a yes; any other response is assumed to be a no.
-l	Uses links instead of copies whenever possible. This is not possible with directories. (This option, if links are possible, is significantly faster because copies of the data are not made.) See Chapter 6 for more information on links.
-n	Copies the file only if it is new. If the destination file already exists, then the copy isn't performed.
-o	Keeps the original owner and group ownerships of the copied files. Otherwise, the file's owner and group become the user who is running the copy procedure.
-m	When the files are copied, they keep their modification times; otherwise, they are set to the time of the copy.
-r	This recursively traverses directories, copying each file and directory encountered.
-v	Displays the files copied by copy.

Message

```
copy: cannot open badfilename
```

You tried to copy a file that doesn't exist or you don't have permission to read; *badfilename* is substituted with the name you supplied.

Examples

```
copy * /tmp/temp
```

Copies all the files in the current directory to the /tmp/temp directory. It also copies the first files found in any subdirectories into the current directory.

(For example, suppose the current directory has a subdirectory called play and in the play subdirectory there is a file called rules and a directory called games. The file rules is copied, but the contents of games are not; you must use the -r flag to copy the subdirectory's contents.)

```
copy -r . /tmp/temp
```

Recursively copies the current directory to the directory /tmp/temp. A duplicate of the directory structures is made.

Caution

The documentation provided in the user's reference provided with the system states that entire file system may be copied. In the general sense this is not true. When you have files in a file system, links may be created within the file system, and links are not preserved across file systems. If copy were used to move a file system then the links are lost. The following cpio command, however, preserves the links:

```
find . -depth -print ¦ cpio -pamdlv /my-new-filesystem
```

Copies all files found in the current directory to the new file system.

See also

cp, ln, cpio, mv

cp

Copies files. You may copy one file to another file, or a list of files to a directory.

Syntax

```
cp source-file dest-file
```

```
cp source-list dest-directory
```

Argument or Option	Description
source-file	The file to copy.
dest-file	The destination name. This may be a directory name, as well, in which case the source file name is used as the name and the file is placed in this directory.
source-list	A space-separated list of files to copy.
dest-directory	The destination directory.

Examples

```
cp letter-to-dad letter.save
```

Copies letter-to-dad to a file called letter.save.

```
cp letter* /old-letters
```

Copies all the files starting with the word letter to a directory called old-letters.

Caution

No verification is done of a file of the same name already existing in the destination. Therefore, if you aren't careful, you can end up overwriting a file in the destination you need.

See also

rm, copy, ln, mv

cpio

cpio stands for *copy in out*. It is useful not only for making backups, but also for moving files around the file system.

Syntax

```
cpio -o [flags]

cpio -i [flags] filelist

cpio -p [flags] dirname
```

Argument or Option	Description
-o	Creates the archive. You are generating the output. cpio accepts its list of files to backup from the standard input.
-i	Copies in from a previously created archive (that is, the -o option).
-p	Accepts a list of files from the standard input and passes them to the specified directory. Useful for copying entire directory structures on the file system.
filelist	A space-separated list of files to extract from the archive. May contain wild cards. The wild cards supported are the same as the simple regular expression expansion provided by the shell (sh).

(continues)

IX

Command Reference

Argument or Option	Description
	! means not
	? matches a single character
	* matches any number of characters
	[] matches the set of characters specified between the brackets
	If you use wild cards, enclose *filelist* in quotation marks ("); otherwise, the shell expands these wild cards and not cpio. A weakness of another archiver, tar, is that it doesn't support wild cards; it has to rely on the shell for wild-card expansion to generate a list of files.
dirname	The destination directory for the files given cpio with the -p option.

Flags

Argument or Option	Description
-B	Signifies a blocking factor of 5,120 bytes per record. Used with the -o and -i options and only when sending the output to, or reading the input from, a character special device (for example, tape, or floppy).
-C*buff-size*	Functionally equivalent to -B, but allows you to specify the buffer size to use. *buff-size* is normally the number of bytes. When used with the -K option, *buff-size* is interpreted as a multiple of 1,024 bytes or 1K.
-a	Reset the access times of the files after the copy is completed. If used with -1, the files with links are not affected. Used with -o or -i.
-c	Creates and reads the header information in the archive in an ASCII character format. This creates headers readable on other platforms. For example, you can move an archive created on an X86 Intel-based machine to a 68X Motorola-based machine. Used with -o or -i.
-d	Creates the directories as needed. If the directories don't exist, cpio creates them. Used with -p or -i.
-b	Reverses the order of bytes within a word. -b is used with the -i option only.
-f	Enables you to change the interpretation of *filelist*. Normally *filelist* is a list of files to extract. When the -f option is used, *filelist* is the list of files not to extract. Used with -i.

Argument or Option	Description
-K *volsize*	Specifies the size of the source or destination volume. *volsize* is a number representing the size in kilobytes. Useful when reading or writing to removable media (for example, tapes or floppy disks) as you are prompted to insert the next one.
-l	Links files rather than copying them, if possible. Used with -p.
-m	Retains the modification times of the files as found in the archive. Normally the modification times change to the current time. This has no effect on directories. Used with -i and -p.
-r	Renames the files in *filelist*. You are prompted for each file in *filelist* for the new name. If none is given, the file is skipped. Used with -o or -i.
-t	Prints a list of the files in the archive. Used with -i.
-u	Extracts the files from the archive unconditionally. Normally cpio only extracts the file from the archive if the file in the archive has a newer modification time than the one on the file system. Used with -p or -i.
-v	Signifies verbose mode. Tells cpio to give status reporting on what it is doing. Used with -i.

Message

The message you are most likely to see is a usage clause showing you the necessary syntax to use cpio. If you get this message, you probably forgot to provide an option that was needed. Check your command line again.

Examples

```
ls ¦ cpio -oBc >/dev/rdsk/5h
```

Lists the current directory, passing the list through the pipeline to cpio. cpio uses the input from the pipeline as its list of files to copy. It copies this list of files to the standard output with a blocking factor of 5120 and the header information is written in a portable ASCII format. This output is then redirected to the character special device /dev/rdsk/5h (a high-density 5 1/4-inch floppy disk).

```
cpio -iBcdm "*.ltr" </dev/rdsk/5h
```

Extracts only the files ending in .ltr from the floppy disk, placing them in the current directory. Any subdirectories are created as needed. The file's modification times are the same as they were at the time the archive was created.

```
ls -A ¦ cpio -pdl /usr/newdir
```

This command takes the list generated by `ls` and copies it to the directory `/usr/newdir`, creating any directories needed and linking instead of copying when possible.

Note

`cpio` with the `-i` and `-o` options is a filter program, meaning that it accepts its input from the standard input and directs its output to the standard output. This means that `cpio` can be anywhere in the pipeline, as long as the input to the `-o` option is a list of file names, and the input to the `-i` option is the result of a previous `-o`. The `-p` option is not a true filter, because the output is the specified directory.

See also

copy, tar, find

cron

A background program started by the system to manage scheduled execution of programs. The system comes installed with `cron`; it runs continuously. You should never have to type this command. `cron` allows you to schedule when jobs will take place by reading a file in `/usr/spool/cron/crontabs/username`, where *username* becomes the name of a user who is allowed to run a job.

Syntax

```
cron
```

Rule

To use `cron` you must have your user name in the file `/usr/lib/cron/cron.allow`. Some sites may have the file `/usr/lib/cron/cron.deny`. At these sites, users on this list cannot use `cron`.

See also

crontab, at, batch

crontab

Informs cron of the programs and the schedule on which they should be run.

Syntax

```
crontab sched-file

crontab -l

crontab -r
```

Argument or Option	Description
sched-file	The name of a file containing the schedule and programs to run. If no file is given, crontab reads from the standard input. The file must be in the following format: M H D m d cmd.
	M The minute of the hour (0-59).
	H The hour of the day (0-23).
	D The day of the month (1-31).
	m The month of the year (1-12).
	d The day of the week. (0-6, 0=Sunday)
	cmd The program to run; the string passed to sh. The first five fields may be a single digit, a list of digits separated by commas, a range of digits using a dash, or an asterisk (meaning all legal values).
-l	Lists what you have told cron to do.
-r	Removes your jobs from cron's tables; cron no longer executes those jobs.

Rule

All jobs are executed with sh from your home directory ($HOME). The environment is setup with HOME, LOGNAME, SHELL=/BIN/SH, and PATH=/bin:usr/bin. If you need your .profile run to set additional environment variables you have to do this specifically in the crontab sched-file.

Messages

```
crontab: you are not authorized to use cron. Sorry.
```

You are not allowed to use cron. Check the cron.deny and cron.allow files.

```
crontab: can't open your crontab file
```

You don't currently have a `crontab` file defined and either tried to list it using the -l flag, or you simply gave a bad flag and `crontab` thought this was a file name.

```
* * * * echo hello
crontab: error on previous line: unexpected character found in line.
```

You receive this message when your *sched-file* is not properly defined. In the example, the file has a line in it without sufficient fields. When this happens, `cron` ignores the entire file. You must change and resubmit the file.

Examples

```
0 8 * * * echo "Good Morning"
0 8 25 12 * echo "Merry Christmas"
0 8 * * 1 echo "Not Monday again"
```

Here are some examples of what the *sched-file* might contain. The first line gives the message of "Good Morning" every day at 8:00 a.m. The second line sends "Merry Christmas" once a year on the 25th of December at 8:00 a.m. (Hopefully, you won't be at work to get it.) And the last line complains about it being Monday once a week on Monday morning at 8:00 a.m.

```
crontab exmpl-crontab
```

Reads in a file called `exmpl-crontab` in the current directory and informs `cron` that the jobs found in it are to be executed.

```
crontab -l
```

Lists the jobs you asked `cron` to execute.

```
crontab -r
```

Informs `cron` to remove your jobs from its scheduling list. You must resubmit a *sched-file* for `cron` to execute your jobs again.

See also

cron, sh, at

crypt

Encrypts a file. `crypt` uses a password to store a file in an encrypted form and requires the same password to decode the file. `crypt` reads from standard input and writes to standard output.

Syntax

```
crypt password
```

Argument or Option	Description
password	The password used to gain access to the file. It is also referred to as the encryption key. If you do not supply *password*, crypt prompts you for it.

Rules

crypt generates files compatible with the editors: ed, edit, ex, and vi when in encryption mode.

crypt, although documented, is not distributed with UNIX. This is because the U.S. Government regulates the distribution of the crypt libraries and crypt is not available outside the United States and its territories. Contact your dealer to obtain these tools.

Examples

```
crypt pickles <letter-to-mom >let.crypt
```

Encrypts the letter using the password of pickles and stores the result in the file let.crypt

```
crypt pickles <let.crypt ¦ lp
```

Decodes the previously encrypted file and prints it.

See also

ed, edit, vi, ex

csh

csh is a command interpreter similar to sh. It is named the C-shell because its syntax resembles that of the C programming language. Like sh, csh is almost a complete programming language itself. To take complete advantage of csh consult the reference manual and user's guide supplied with your system, or consult a book that covers csh exclusively.

Syntax

```
csh
```

IX

Command Reference

Example

```
csh
```

Launches a new shell to work in temporarily. When you exit this shell, your environment is returned to what it was before you launched the new shell.

See also

ksh, sh

cu

Dials into other systems, either through a modem or a direct connect. cu also provides a set of tilde (~) commands to enhance its usefulness.

Syntax

```
cu [flags] system-name

cu [flags] -lline -sspeed telno

cu [flags] -lline -sspeed dir
```

Argument or Option	Description
system-name	The name of the system to call. This requires system-name to be setup in the file /usr/lib/uucp/Systems. The speed, line, and phone number are pulled from this file.
-lline	The device used for the communication link.
-sspeed	The baud rate at which to make the connection. If this option is not used the speed is pulled from the file /usr/lib/uucp/Devices.
telno	The telephone number to dial for automatic dialer. A = indicates second dial tone; a - indicates four second delay.
dir	A keyword used to inform cu that you want to talk directly with the modem. This is useful when you have to program the modem.

Flags

Argument or Option	Description
`-xdebug-level`	Sets cu into a debugging level to give diagnostics on its progress. Normally, cu operates silently, and you don't know what it is doing. *debug-level* may be any digit between 0 and 9; 9 gives the most information.
`-n`	Prompts for a telephone number.
`-o`	The connection is made with odd parity.
`-e`	The connection is made with even parity.
`-oe`	The connection is made with 7 data bits and no parity.

Notes

The system administrator must have properly installed the modems and configured the uucp subsystem to use the modems. At a minimum, the devices connected to the modems have to be setup in the file `/usr/lib/uucp/Devices`.

cu offers several tilde commands. These commands can be used while running cu. Each command is preceded by a tilde (~).

Each time you connect to succesive machines, you need to chain enough tildes to make that command active on the machine you are on. For example, you call the machine "french" and then from french, you call "german." For the tilde commands to apply to the machine "german," you need to have two tildes (~~). The following table lists the tilde commands available.

Item	Description
`~.`	Disconnects from the machine, or quits cu. This is extremely useful if you have to abort a program running on the remote system, or if for some reason you can't log on.
`~!`	Runs a subshell on the local system.
`~!command`	Runs *command* on the local system.
`~%command`	Runs *command* on the local system and sends the results to the remote system.

(continues)

IX

Command Reference

Item	Description
~%break	Sends a break signal to the remote system. This is useful when the speed at which you dialed in is not the speed at which the port is currently set. A break on UNIX systems causes a new baud rate to be selected.
~%b	Same as ~%break.

Messages

```
Connect failed: SYSTEM NOT IN Systems FILE
```

You gave cu a system name it doesn't recognize. uuname may be used to obtain a list of valid system names on your system.

```
Connect failed: NO DEVICES AVAILABLE
```

All the modems are in use.

Examples

```
cu sosco
```

Calls the system sosco.

```
cu -x9 sosco
```

Calls the system sosco with a debugging level of 9.

```
cu -l/dev/tty1A -s38400 555-1212
```

Calls the phone number 555-1212 using the modem attached to the port /dev/tty1A at 38400 baud.

```
cu -l/dev/tty1A -s38400 dir
```

Makes a connection with the modem to program it or test it.

See also

uucp, uuname

cut

Extracts fields from a list of files. Fields may be defined as either character positions, or relatively, with a field separator.

Syntax

```
cut -cchar-pos filelist

cut -ffields -dfield-sep -s filelist
```

Argument or Option	Description
`filelist`	The list of files from which to cut. If no files are specified, cut reads from the standard input.
`-cchar-pos`	The character position to cut out. May be a list separated by commas (,), a range separated by dashes (-), or a combination. (For example, 1, 4, 5 or 1-4 or 1-4, 5-10, 25 are all valid.)
`-ffields`	The fields to cut out. Fields are denoted by a one character separator. If the separator repeats, as in several in a row, they are not treated as one separator. `fields` uses the same syntax as `char-pos`.
`-dfield-sep`	Specifies the field separator. A tab character is the default. `field-sep` may be any character.
`-s`	Suppress the line if it doesn't contain `field-sep` characters.

Note

The `-c` and `-f` options are mutually exclusive.

Messages

```
line too long
```

One of the input lines from one of the files was longer than 511 characters.

```
bad list for c/f options
```

You didn't supply cut with either a `-c` or `-f` flag, or the `char-pos`/`fields` were incorrectly specified.

```
no fields
```

You didn't supply `char-pos` or `fields`.

Example

```
cut -f1,5 -d: /etc/passwd
```

Extracts the user id and names from the password file.

See also

paste

date

Displays the system date and time, or if you are the super user, sets the date and time. You can control how the date is displayed.

Syntax

```
date MMDDhhmmYY

date +format
```

Argument or Option	Description
MMDDhhmmYY	This is the format used to set the date and time. The following table explains each variable. Each part must be two digits.
	MM The month (01–12)
	DD The day (01–31)
	hh The hour (00–23)
	mm The minute (00–59)
	YY The year (00–99) (optional)
+format	Controls how the date is displayed. *format* is made up of a percent sign (%) followed by any of the following:
	MM The month (01–12)
	t Inserts a tab
	m Month (digits)
	d Day of month (digits)
	y Last two digits of year
	D Date as mm/dd/yy
	H Hour (00 - 23)
	M Minute
	S Second
	I Hour in 12-hour clock (01 - 12)
	j Julian date (001-366)
	w Day of week (0-6, 0=Sunday)
	a Sun, Mon, Tue, etc.
	A Full weekday name
	h Jan, Feb, Mar, etc.
	B Full month name
	r AM/PM notation for time

Messages

        no permission

or

        UX:date: error: not privileged

You aren't the super user, and you tried to set the system date. The second message is from UnixWare.

        bad conversion

You didn't give the date setting syntax correctly.

        bad format character

You didn't use a format character from the preceding table.

Examples

        date 0101130091

Sets the date and time to 01/01/91 at 1:00 p.m.

If you type in this command:

        date "+Date = %D Time = %H:%M"

this is the result:

        Date = 01/01/91 Time = 13:00

dc

The desk calculator uses postfix notation (also referred to as reverse polish notation). If you aren't familiar with this format, use the bc command.

Syntax

        dc *progfile*

Argument or Option	Description
progfile	An optional file name containing a set of dc commands.

Messages

        0 is unimplemented

0 is replaced with the octal number of the character you type. This means the character you type has no meaning in dc.

```
stack empty
```

The stack is empty; you didn't push enough arguments to perform the task.

Example

```
4 5 + p
```

This adds 4 and 5 and prints the result.

See also

bc

dd

dd stands for data dump, or device dump. It is useful for copying blocks of data to and from devices. It behaves differently than cp in that it can access the raw devices, for example, floppy drives. You can also use it to convert files so that they are suitable for a different platform of hardware.

For example, the swap argument allows you to swap each byte as it comes through dd. This is useful when migrating from a big-endian machine to a little-endian machine. Archiving programs such as tar write header information in native binary form to the devices they write to. A tar archive created on a Motorola-based machine is not normally readable on an Intel-based machine. By using dd in a pipeline and swapping the bytes, you can exchange tar files across platforms.

Syntax

```
dd [flag=value ] ...
```

Flags

Argument or Option	Description
if=file	Sets the input file, where file is the file name dd is to read. If this option is left blank, dd reads from the standard input.
of=file	Sets the output file, where file is the file name to which dd is to write. If this option is left blank, dd writes to the standard output.
ibs=input_buffer	Sets the read buffer to the size of input_buffer. The default buffer size is BSIZE.
obs=output_buffer	Sets the write buffer to the size of output_buffer. The default buffer size is BSIZE.

Argument or Option	Description
bs=*i/o_buffer*	Sets both the read and the write buffers to the size of *i/o_buffer*. The default buffer size is BSIZE.
cbs=*conv_buffer*	Sets the conversion buffer to *conv_buffer*. This option is only valid with the conversion types of ascii, ebcdic, or ibm.
skip=*records*	Specifies the number of records to skip, before any output takes place. The record length is set by the ibs or bs arguments.
seek=*records*	Similar to skip but applies to the output file. dd seeks past existing records before it starts to copy.
iseek=*records*	Similar to skip except the input records are seeked past and not read (the iseek(S) routine is used).
files=*file_cnt*	Sets the number of input files to be considered as one file. When *file_count* EOFs are encountered the EOFs are ignored. (This option is useful only when reading from tape or floppy devices, as multiple EOFs may be on a tape.)
count=*records*	Copies only the number of records specified.
conv=*conv_type*	Specifies the type of conversion. Valid types of conversions are:

	block	ASCII to unblocked ASCII
	unblock	unblocked ASCII to blocked ascii EBCDIC to ASCII
	ebcdic	ASCII to EBCDIC
	ibm	Slightly different map then ebcdic
	lcase	To lowercase (if alphabetic)
	ucase	To uppercase (if alphabetic)
	swab	Swaps each pair of bytes (reads two bytes and swaps them, then the next two, and so on)
	noerror	Continues to process even if an error is encountered
	sync	Pads each input record to the length of ibs or bs

Conversion types may be strung together separated by commas.

Rules

The numeric arguments *input_buffer*, *output_buffer*, *i/o_buffer*, *file_cnt*, *records*, and *conv_buffer* may be followed by a modifier to specify the unit measures as follows:

k	kilobytes
b	512 byte blocks
wa	word (2 bytes)

These arguments may also be separated by an x to indicate multiplication and the product of the numbers is used as the argument.

Messages

```
dd: bad arg qf=ben
```

You gave dd a flag it didn't understand. In this case it was the flag qf=ben; qf isn't one of the valid flags.

```
dd: cannot open frank
```

You gave dd an input file that it can't find, or you don't have permission to open. In this example, the file it can't find is frank.

```
36+1 records in
36+1 records out
```

Every successful dd command reports the number of records read (records in) and the number of records written (records out). In this case, 36 records plus 1 partial record are read and written.

Examples

Suppose you download a tar file from a bulletin board and you want that file on a floppy disk. You can try to extract the tar file and then use the tar command to get the files you extracted to the floppy disk, or you can use the tar command to get the original tar command file to the floppy. But neither of these ideas really works very well in practice. dd helps. Suppose the file you download is a SCSI device driver and the name you give it is scsi_drive.tar. To get this onto a floppy disk, enter the following:

```
dd if=scsi_driver.tar of=/dev/rfd096ds15 bs=10k
```

This begins dumping the file scsi_driver.tar to the floppy drive in 10k increments.

Also suppose that file is compressed and is called `scsi_driver.Z`. Use the following command:

```
zcat scsi_driver.Z ¦ dd of=/dev/rfd096ds15 bs=10k
```

The `zcat` utility uncompresses the file to standard output. The file is then piped to `dd`, which places the contents on the floppy disk.

If you want to copy a disk but have only one floppy drive, you can use the following command:

```
dd if=/dev/rfd096ds15 of=tmp.file bs=10k
```

This reads the floppy drive and creates a file called `tmp.file`. Now place the formatted blank destination disk in the drive and enter:

```
dd if=tmp.file of=/dev/rfd096ds15 bs=10k
```

This reads the file `tmp.file` and places it on the floppy drive.

See also

tar, cpio, cp, copy, hd

deassign

See assign.

devnm

Reports the name of the directory's file system.

Syntax

```
/etc/devnm dirname
```

Argument or Option	Description
dirname	The name of the directory you want reported and what file system name it resides in.

Example

```
/etc/devnm /
```

This reports the following: `root /`.

df

Reports the amount of free disk space.

Syntax

    df [flags] filesystems

Argument or Option	Description
filesystems	This is an optional list of file systems from which to report the amount of free disk space. If this is left blank, all currently mounted file systems are reported.

Flags

Argument or Option	Description
-t	Normally df only reports the free space. With this option set, the total allocated size of the file system is reported, as well.
-f	With this flag set, df actually counts the number of free blocks instead of reading the number from the mount table (may not be available on all implementations of UNIX).
-v	This causes df to report the percentage free and the number of blocks.

Notes

df reports in blocks rather than bytes. Blocks are typically 512 bytes each; consult your system documentation for more information.

The -v option cannot be used with the other options.

Message

    df: illegal arg badarg

You specified an option listed previously; badarg is replaced by the bad option you supplied.

See also

    du, mount

diff

Compares two text files and reports what must be done to the one to make it look like the other. diff also can be used to create a script usable by the editor ed to re-create the second file from the first. To compare binary files use cmp.

Syntax

```
diff [flags] oldfile newfile
```

Argument or Option	Description
oldfile	This is the file that you want diff to compare and then report what has to be done to it to make it look like newfile.
newfile	This is the name of the file you want to use to compare to oldfile. In a sense this is the control file, as diff reports what it takes to make oldfile look like newfile.

Flags

Argument or Option	Description
-b	Causes leading and trailing blanks and tabs to compare as equal. (For example, "the big tree " is the same as "the big tree".)
-e	Generates a script suitable for the editor ed.
-f	Similar to the -e flag, this produces a script in the opposite order. However, this is not usable by ed.

Notes

The output of diff takes any one of the following forms where each form shows a line number range and the text being referenced after:

```
lineno a from-lineno to-lineno
```

The text in the first file lineno has to have the text in the second file from-lineno to the to-lineno added to it. The text found in the second file is shown preceded by a greater-than sign (>). This shows that these lines were found only in the second file.

```
from-lineno to-lineno d lineno
```

The text in the first file found at line number from-lineno to the line number to-lineno must be deleted. If these lines were to exist, they would fall after the line number in the second file lineno. The text to be deleted follows and is preceded by a less than sign (<). This shows that these lines are only found in the first file.

```
from-lineno to-lineno c from-lineno to-lineno
```

In this line diff shows how two sets of lines are different and have to be changed from the first set of line number ranges to match the second set of line number ranges. The text that has to be changed follows and is preceded by <. The text, as found in the second file, follows this and is preceded by >.

Example

```
diff old-letter letter-to-dad
```

Changes the file old-letter so it looks like the file letter-to -dad.

See also

> ed

diff3

Compares three files at once.

Syntax

```
diff3 [flags] file1 file2 file3
```

Argument or Option	Description
file1	The first file used in the comparison, probably the oldest of the three.
file2	The second file used in the comparison.
file3	The third file used in the comparison.

Flags

Argument or Option	Description
-e	Produces a script for ed to change file1 to reflect the differences between file2 and file3.

Argument or Option	Description
-x	Produces a script for ed to change *file1* to reflect the differences in all files.
-3	Produces a script for ed to change *file1* to reflect the differences in *file3*.

Example

```
diff3 old-letter letter-to-mom new-letter
```

Compares the three letters and displays the results of the comparison.

See also

diff, comm, cmp, ed, sdiff

dircmp

Compares the contents of two directories listing which files only are found in one or the other, and runs diff on each of the files sharing the same name.

Syntax

```
dircmp [flags] dir1 dir2
```

Argument or Option	Description
dir1	The name of the directory to use in the comparison. A period (.) means the current directory.
dir2	The name of the second directory, also can be a period (.).

Flags

Argument or Option	Description
-d	Runs a "full" diff on the files named the same. Normally, dircmp just reports if the contents are the same or not.
-s	Suppresses the displaying of identical file names in both directories.
-w*width*	Sets the width of the output to *width* characters; the default is 72.

IX

Command Reference

Example

```
dircmp /usr/bin /bin
```

Compares the two executable paths /usr/bin and /bin.

See also

diff

dirname

Enables you to extract the directory portion of a path name. This is useful in shell scripts.

Syntax

```
dirname pathname
```

Argument or Option	Description
pathname	The path name for which you want to know the directory portion. If no slashes (/) are used in the string provided, then a period (.) is returned.

Examples

```
dirname /usr/bin/test
```

The result displayed on-screen is /usr/bin.

```
dirname /usr/bin
```

Results in /usr. Even though bin is a directory, dirname doesn't look at the file system to determine what the directory portion of the string is; it just looks for the last slash, and assumes everything before that.

```
dirname usr
```

The result written to standard output is a period (.).

See also

basename, sh

disable

You use disable to disallow terminals to be logged on to the printer or print jobs to be applied to the printer. When you disable a printer, jobs may still be queued for that printer, however; the jobs are not completed on the printer. This is useful when clearing up paper jams or temporarily replacing the printer for servicing.

Syntax

```
disable terminals

disable -c -rreason printers
```

Argument or Option	Description
terminals	The list of terminals you wish to disable. These terminals will no longer accept logins.
-c	Use this flag when you wish to cancel the job that is currently printing.
-rreason	If the printer will be disabled for an extended period of time, you may want to tell the users. reason must immediately follow -r, and if it is more than one word, enclose it in quotation marks (").
printers	The list of printers to disable.

Note

When you disable a printer, the print job currently printing is stopped. When you enable the printer again, this job starts from the beginning, unless you used the -c flag.

Examples

```
disable tty12
```

Disables the twelfth console terminal.

```
disable frontdsk
```

Disables the printer called frontdsk.

```
disable -c -r"servicing, back up in 1 hr." frontdsk
```

Disables the frontdsk printer, cancels the currently printing job, and notifies users checking on the status of this printer why it is disabled and when it will be back in service.

See also

enable, cancel, lp, lpstat

IX

Command Reference

diskcmp

See diskcp.

diskcp

diskcp copies floppy disks and diskcmp compares the contents of floppy disks using cmp. You can make multiple copies of a single floppy disk or multiple copies of multiple source floppy disks. Both diskcp and diskcmp contain self-explanatory prompts for their use.

Syntax

```
diskcp [flags]

diskcmp [flags]
```

Flags

Argument or Option	Description
-f	Format the target floppy before copying; only valid with diskcp.
-d	If you have a dual-drive machine, the floppy disks are copied or compared directly; normally a copy of the source floppy is copied to the hard disk.
-s	This flag uses sum to run a check sum on the copy to verify the accuracy of the copy.
-48ds9	Specifies the 360K floppy.
-96ds9	Specifies the 720K 5 1/4-inch floppy.
-96ds15	Specifies the 1.2M floppy.
-135ds9	Specifies the 720K 3 1/2-inch floppy.
-135ds18	Specifies the 1.44M floppy.

Rules

These utilities work with two floppy disks when both floppy disks are the same density. When you have a 3 1/2-inch and a 5 1/4-inch drive, these utilities work only with the primary drive. Because both utilities are shell scripts, it is possible to modify them to accommodate the secondary drive.

Example

```
diskcp -s -135ds18
```

Copies a 3 1/2-inch floppy disk and runs a checksum to verify the copy.

See also

dd, cmp, sum, format

doscat

Enables you to mimic the UNIX cat utility on a DOS disk or partition.

Syntax

```
doscat -r -m filelist
```

Argument or Option	Description
-r	Specifies a raw copy; no newline translation occurs. (See the "Rules" section for a definition of newline translation.) When copying binary files, such as word processing, spreadsheets, and database files, use this option.
-m	Forces newline translation. Normally, the DOS utilities test to see if newline translations should be done. If the utilities can't determine this, -m forces newline translation.
filelist	The list of files you want to copy to standard output. File names consist of a drive specification followed by the directory specification. Although you access DOS files, use UNIX conventions; don't use backslashes. You may also use drive letters, as defined in the /etc /default/msdos file. This file is a map of drive letters to UNIX devices, and enables you to use familiar DOS convention drive specifications. (For example, a:letter.mom.)

Rules

Newline translation involves the conversion of the way DOS stores text files and UNIX stores text files. DOS uses a carriage return and a line-feed character to signify the end of a line. It also uses Ctrl-Z to signify the end of a file. UNIX uses one line-feed character, referred to as the *newline character,* and no end-of-file marker.

The -r and -m options cannot be used together.

Examples

```
doscat /dev/rfd096:letter.mom
```

Copies the file letter.mom found on the DOS disk in the primary high-density drive.

```
doscat a:letter.mom
```

This is similar to the previous example except that it uses the /etc/default /msdos file to map a to a UNIX device.

See also

cat, doscp, dosdir, dosformat, dosls, dosmkdir, dosrm, dosrmdir, xtod, dtox

doscp

Enables you to mimic the UNIX cp utility on a DOS disk or partition.

Syntax

```
doscp -r -m filelist dir
```

```
doscp -r -m source dest
```

Argument or Option	Description
-r	Specifies a raw copy, that is, no newline translation is to occur. (See the discussion in the "Rules" section for a definition of newline translation.) When copying binary files, such as word processing, spreadsheets, and database files, this option should be used.
-m	Forces newline translation. Normally, the DOS utilities test to see if newline translation should be done. This option forces it to be true if the utilities can't determine if it should be done.
filelist	This is the list of files you want to copy. File names consist of a drive specification followed by the directory specification. Although you are accessing DOS files, UNIX conventions are used; don't use backslashes. You may also use drive letters as defined in the /etc/default/msdos file. This file is a map of drive letters to UNIX devices, thus allowing you to use familiar DOS convention drive specifications (for example, a:letter.mom).
dir	The directory for the list of files to be copied to.
source	The source file name to be copied.
dest	The destination file name of the copy.

Rules

Newline translation involves the conversion of the way DOS stores text files and UNIX stores text files. DOS uses a carriage return and a line-feed character to signify the end of a line. It also uses a Ctrl-Z to signify the end of a file. UNIX uses one line-feed character, referred to as the newline character, and no end-of-file marker.

The `-r` and `-m` options may not be used together.

Examples

```
doscp /dev/rfd096:letter.mom letter-to-mom
```

Copies the file `letter.mom` found on the DOS disk in the primary high-density drive.

```
doscp a:letter.mom letter-to-mom
```

This is similar to the previous example except that it uses the `/etc/default /msdos` file to map a to a UNIX device.

See also

cat, doscat, dosdir, dosformat, dosls, dosmkdir, dosrm, dosrmdir, xtod, dtox

dosdir

`dosdir` produces a directory listing similar to that of the DOS command DIR.

Syntax

```
dosdir drive
```

Argument or Option	Description
drive	The drive for which you want a directory listing. You can use the DOS convention or the UNIX device name.

Examples

```
dosdir a:
```

Gives a DOS-style listing of the floppy disk found in the a: drive as defined by the `/etc/default/msdos` file.

IX

Command Reference

```
dosdir /dev/rfd096
```

This is similar to the previous command, but uses the UNIX device name.

See also

ls, doscat, doscp, dosformat, dosmkdir, dosls, dosrm, dosrmdir

dosformat

Creates DOS 2.0 formatted disks.

Syntax

```
dosformat [flags] drive
```

Argument or Option	Description
drive	The drive to be formatted. You can use the DOS convention or the UNIX device name.

Flags

Argument or Option	Description
-f	Suppresses the interactive nature of dosformat.
-q	Specifies quiet operation and suppresses the messages normally displayed while using dosformat.
-v	Specifies a volume label of as many as 11 characters.

Rule

You cannot use dosformat to format a hard disk.

Examples

```
dosformat /dev/rfd096
```

Formats the high-density drive.

```
dosformat a:
```

Formats the drive mapped to a: in the /etc/default/msdos file.

See also

format, doscat, doscp, dosdir, dosmkdir, dosls, dosrm, dosrmdir

dosls

Produces a directory list of the contents of the DOS floppy or hard disk partition; has the format of ls.

Syntax

    dosls *drive*

Argument or Option	Description
drive	The drive for which you want a directory listing. You can use the DOS convention or the UNIX device name.

Examples

    dosls a:

Gives an ls style listing of the floppy found in the a: drive as defined by the /etc/default/msdos file.

    dosls /dev/rfd096

This is similar to the previous command, but uses the UNIX device name.

See also

ls, doscat, doscp, dosdir, dosformat, dosmkdir, dosrm, dosrmdir

dosmkdir

This allows you to make a directory on the DOS floppy or partition.

Syntax

    dosmkdir *directory*

Argument or Option	Description
directory	The directory you want to create. Directory names consist of a drive specification followed by the directory specification. Although you access DOS files, use UNIX conventions; don't use backslashes(\). You can use drive letters as defined in the /etc/default /msdos file. This file is a map of drive letters to UNIX devices, and enables you to use familiar DOS convention drive specifications (for example, a:letter.mom).

Examples

```
dosmkdir /dev/rfd096:/letters
```

Creates the directory /letters found on the DOS disk in the primary high-density drive.

```
dosmkdir a:/letters
```

This is similar to the previous example except that it uses the /etc/default /msdos file to map a: to a UNIX device.

See also

mkdir, doscat, doscp, dosdir, dosformat, dosls, dosrm, dosrmdir

dosrm

Enables you to remove files found on the DOS floppy or partition. dosrm mimics the rm command.

Syntax

```
dosrm filelist
```

Argument or Option	Description
filelist	The list of files you want to delete. File names consist of a drive specification followed by the directory specification. Although you access DOS files, use UNIX conventions; don't use backslashes(\). You can use drive letters as defined in the /etc/default/msdos file. This file is a map of drive letters to UNIX devices, and enables you to use familiar DOS convention drive specifications (for example, a:letter.mom).

Examples

```
dosrm /dev/rfd096:letter.mom
```

Deletes the file letter.mom found on the DOS disk in the primary high-density drive.

```
dosrm a:letter.mom
```

This is similar to the previous example except that it uses the /etc/default /msdos file to map a: to a UNIX device.

See also

doscat, doscp, dosdir, dosformat, dosls, dosmkdir, dosrmdir

dosrmdir

Enables you to remove a directory on the DOS floppy or partition.

Syntax

```
dosrmdir directory
```

Argument or Option	Description
directory	The directory you want to remove. Directory names consist of a drive specification followed by the directory specification. Although you access DOS files, use UNIX conventions; don't use backslashes (\). You can use drive letters as defined in the /etc/default /msdos file. This file is a map of drive letters to UNIX devices, and enables you to use familiar DOS convention drive specifications (for example, a:letter.mom).

Examples

```
dosrmdir /dev/rfd096:/letters
```

Removes the directory /letters found on the DOS disk in the primary high-density drive.

```
dosrmdir a:/letters
```

This is similar to the previous example except that it uses the /etc/default /msdos file to map a: to a UNIX device.

See also

rmdir, doscat, doscp, dosdir, dosformat, dosls, dosrm, dosmkdir

dtox

Converts DOS text files to UNIX text files. UNIX uses one character to mean the end of a line—the newline or linefeed character,whereas DOS uses two—a linefeed and a carriage return. Furthermore, DOS has an end-of-file marker (Ctrl-Z). Without running a conversion on the files, UNIX does not understand the format of the files you create. Do not use dtox on binary/data files.

Syntax

```
dtox dos-filename
```

IX

Command Reference

Argument or Option	Description
dos-filename	The name of the DOS file you want to convert to UNIX format. If left blank, dtox reads from standard input. dtox always writes to standard output.

Example

```
dtox dosletter >letter-to-mom
```

Converts the file dosletter; places the results into a file called letter-to-mom.

See also

xtod, doscp

dtype

Provides information about the format of your specified disk and presents an exit code from the following table.

Exit Code	Message
60	Error
61	Empty or unrecognized data
70	Backup format, volume *n*
71	tar format (extent *e* of *n*)
72	cpio format
73	cpio character format
80	DOS 1.x, 8 sec/track, single-sided
81	DOS 1.x, 8 sec/track, double-sided
90	DOS 2.x, 8 sec/track, single-sided
91	DOS 2.x, 8 sec/track, double-sided
92	DOS 2.x, 9 sec/track, single-sided
93	DOS 2.x, 9 sec/track, double-sided
94	DOS 2.x, fixed disk
110	DOS 3.x, 9 sec/track, double-sided

Exit Code	Message
120	XENIX 2.x file system (needs cleaning)
130	XENIX 3.x file system (needs cleaning)
140	UNIX 1K file system (needs cleaning)

Syntax

```
dtype -s devices
```

Argument or Option	Description
-s	The messages are not displayed; only the exit status is used. The exit status is valid for the last device.
devices	List of devices to check the format in which the media is stored.

Rule

This command is reliable only on floppy disks. The tar, cpio, and backup formats may not be recognizable if created on a foreign system.

Message

```
/usr/bin   : unrecognized data
```

This command asks for the disk type of the directory /usr/bin. Because /usr /bin isn't a device, dtype gives this message.

Example

```
dtype /dev/rfd096
```

Reports what kind of format is used on the floppy disk in the primary high-density drive.

du

du displays the amount of space being used by the specified directories or files. The information is reported in 512-byte blocks.

Syntax

```
du [flags] names
```

Argument or Option	Description
names	The list of directories or files for which you want to have the space requirements calculated. If left blank, the current directory is used.

Flags

Argument or Option	Description
-s	Causes only a total for each of the specified *names*. Normally, a number for every subdirectory is displayed.
-a	Causes each file encountered to be displayed with its size.
-f	Only the directories in the currently mounted file system are traversed; other file systems are ignored. May not be supported on some implementations of UNIX.
-u	Causes files with more than one link to be ignored. May not be supported on some implementations of UNIX.
-r	Produces a message if the directory cannot be read.

Note

Files with more than one link are counted only once. However, du has a maximum number of links it can table, so when this maximum is exceeded, the sizes used by these files are included in the total.

Examples

```
du -s /usr/bin /bin
```

Reports the total space in 512-byte blocks used by the two directories /usr /bin and /bin.

```
du
```

Reports the space usage of the current directory and gives a number for each subdirectory encountered.

See also

df

echo

This command takes the arguments passed to it and writes them to standard output. echo is useful in shell scripts to prompt for input or to report the status of a process.

Syntax

```
echo -n string
```

Argument or Option	Description
-n	Normally, echo follows all the output with a newline; this option suppresses that.
string	The string of characters you wish to output. The following special characters produce special output sequences:

Sequence	Meaning
\b	backspace
\c	don't print a newline at the end
\f	formfeed
\n	Newline
\r	Carriage return
\t	Tab
\v	Vertical tab
\\	Backslash
\0n	n is a 1-, 2-, or 3-digit octal number, representing a character

Examples

```
echo Hello
```

Prints Hello on the standard output.

```
echo "enter Y or N \c"
```

Prompts the user for a Y or N response without echoing a newline.

```
echo
```

Produces a newline.

```
echo 'Can you hear this \07\07\07?'
```

Demonstrates the use of octal digits. Here it is used to sound the terminal bell three times.

See also

sh, cat

ed

A line editor useful on systems or terminals that don't support full screen editors, such as vi. ed; also can be used to edit files in batch by created ed scripts.

Syntax

```
ed - -p prompt filename
```

Argument or Option	Description
-	Suppresses the messages produced by the e, r, w, q, and ! commands.
-p prompt	Enables you to specify your own prompt string.
filename	The name of the file you want to edit. You edit only one file at a time.

Note

ed is rather complex and powerful. For more information, see the user's guide and reference provided with your system, or use a book dedicated to the usage of ed.

Example

```
ed letter-to-dad
```

Starts ed to edit letter-to-dad.

See also

vi, ex, sed

egrep

See grep.

enable

Allows terminals to be logged on to the printer and print jobs to be applied to the printer.

Syntax

```
enable terminals

enable printers
```

Argument or Option	Description
terminals	A list of terminals to enable. These terminals accept logins.
printers	A list of printers to enable.

Examples

```
enable tty12
```

Enables the twelfth console terminal.

```
enable frontdsk
```

Enables the printer called frontdsk.

See also

disable, cancel, lp, lpstat

env

Modifies the environment for the execution of a command without affecting the current environment. It also can be used to display the current environment.

Syntax

```
env - name=value command
```

Argument or Option	Description
-	Restricts the environment to only those values to follow in the *name=value* list. Normally, env adds the list to environment.
name=value	Allows you to pass environment variables to the command specifying the value of the variable for this execution of the command. You may pass multiple variables simply by repeating the *name=value* format.
command	The name of the command and its arguments to be run with the specified environment.

Examples

```
env
```

Prints the current environment in a *name=value* format, one per line.

```
env HOME=/usr/sue sh
```

Runs a new shell with the home directory set up as /usr/sue.

expr

Enables you to evaluate expressions in shell scripts. These expressions can be mathematical or string-oriented. String functions include returning substrings, the length of a string, and more.

Syntax

```
expr arguments
```

Arguments

Argument or Option	Description
arg1 ¦ *arg2*	*arg1* is evaluated, and if it is neither null or 0, it is returned; otherwise, *arg2* is evaluated and returned.
arg1 & *arg2*	Both *arg1* and *arg2* are evaluated and if neither one is null or 0, *arg1* is returned; otherwise, 0 is returned.

Argument or Option	Description
arg1 { =, ==, >, >=, <, <=, != } *arg2*	*arg1* is compared to *arg2* using any of the logical operators; = and == are functionally equivalent. If both *arg1* and *arg2* are integers, then the comparison is numeric. If either is a string, then the comparison is done lexicographically as defined by the locale; typically, this means an ASCII comparison (for example, "cat" is greater than "car", and "bat" is less than "cat"). If the comparison is true, then the result is a 1; otherwise, the result is a 0.
arg1 { *, /, % } *arg2*	Multiplication, division, or modulo of *arg1* and *arg2*.
arg1 { +, - } *arg2*	Addition or subtraction of *arg1* and *arg2*.
string : *match_expr*	The colon (:) is a matching operator. *string* is compared to the expression *match_expr*. The result of the command is the match, based on *match_expr*. *match_expr* is any regular expression (one exemption is that all expressions are considered to be "anchored" as if a caret (^) had been used). Normally the result of the matching operator is the number of characters that match. You can use the notation \(*reg_expr* \) to return a substring.
match *string* *match_expr*	Same as *string* : *match_expr* but different syntax.
substr *string* *beg_pos* *len*	Returns a substring of *string* beginning at position *beg_pos* for length of *len* characters. expr counts *beg_pos* characters from the beginning of the string *string* and returns each character after that for *len* characters. *beg_pos* must be an integer greater than zero. *len* must be a positive integer.
length *string*	Returns the length of the string *string*. That is, expr counts the number of characters in the string.

(continues)

Argument or Option	Description
`index string char_set`	Returns the location of `char_set` in the string `string`. Typically `char_set` is one character and `expr` returns the offset location of that character in the string. If `char_set` is several characters, `expr` returns the offset location of the first character in the set it finds in the string. If `char_set` is not in the string, a 0 is returned.

Rules

Each argument presented to `expr` must be separated by spaces. All characters that are also special to the shell must be escaped. The output of `expr` is the standard output. Integers are treated internally as 32 bit 2's compliment numbers. Parentheses `()` may be used for grouping.

The exit status may be any of the following:

Argument or Option	Description
0	The expression is neither null nor 0.
1	The expression is null or 0.
2	An invalid expression is encountered.

`expr` recognizes operators only by their values not their position, so it is possible for `expr` to have a problem after the shell expands the arguments given to it. For example, in the following `expr` statement:

```
a="="; b="="# assign the variables a & b the equal sign
"="xpr $a = $b
```

what `expr` sees is

```
expr = = =
```

`expr` thinks it has a bad expression because its first argument is an equal sign (=). The following code segment allows for the comparison of equal signs.

```
expr X$a = X$b
```

which after substitution looks like the following:

```
expr X= = X=
```

Messages

```
syntax error
```

You used an invalid operator, or referenced a variable and did not set it.

```
nonnumeric argument
```

You attempted an arithmetic function and used an argument that is not

numeric.

Examples

When writing a shell script, you need to be able to iterate until you reach a certain limit. Suppose you want to allow the user to pick how many times the date appears on-screen. To do this, you can code the following shell script:

```
echo "Enter number of dates to display \c"
read DATE_CNT
i=0
while ($i < $DATE_CNT)
do
date
i='expr $i + 1'
done
```

With expr you can mimic the function of the basename command with the following:

```
:
# argument passed is the file name to get the basename of.

expr $1 : '.*/\(.*\)'
```

This example is more complicated and not as intuitive as the date displayed in the on-screen example. If you look at this example more closely, you see that the matching operator (:) is used and that it compares what is passed ($1) with the expression (.*/\(.*\)).

Item	Description
.*	A regular expression that matches zero or more occurrences of any character.
/	A single character regular expression matching itself, a slash /.
\(.*\)	The .* is a regular expression matching zero or more occurrences of any character. The \(\) notation causes these "zero or more occurrences of any character" to result in expr.

You read this regular expression as "return the set of characters that follow a slash preceded by any number of other characters or no characters."

See also

awk, basename, bc, dc, sh

fgrep

See grep.

file

Determines the type of a file. file is able to recognize whether the file is 386 executable, 286 executable, command text, ASCII text, C source, and so on. Many of the UNIX commands are only shell scripts. file can be used to report to you which ones are scripts and which ones are not. It also is useful to determine whether the file is "text" based and whether it can be viewed or edited.

Syntax

```
file [ -f ffile ] filelist
```

Argument or Option	Description
-f ffile	Tells file that the list of files to identify is found in ffile. This is useful when many files must be identified.
filelist	A space-separated list of files of which you want to know the type.

Messages

```
filename: cannot open
```

You asked file to type a file that doesn't exist; filename is replaced by the file you requested.

```
filename: cannot open for reading
```

The file you requested exists, but you don't have read permissions; *filename* is replaced by the file you requested.

Example

```
file /unix
```

Examines the file /unix and reports what type of file it is.

See also

The internal type command of sh.

find

find is an extremely powerful tool. It traverses the specified directories generating a list of files that match the criteria specified. Files may be matched by name, size, creation time, modification time, and many more critieria. You even can execute a command on the matched files each time a file is found.

Syntax

```
find dirlist match-spec
```

Argument or Option	Description
dirlist	A space-separated list of the directories in which you want to look for a file or set of files.
match-spec	The matching specification or description of files you want to find. See the "Flags" section for a list of possible *match-spec* values.

Flags

Argument or Option	Description
-name *file*	Tells find what file to search for. If enclosed in quotation marks (") *file* can contain wild cards (* and ?).
-perm *mode*	Matches all files whose modes match the numeric value of *mode*. All modes must be matched—not just read, write, and execute. If preceded by a negative (-), *mode* takes on the meaning of everything without this mode.

(continues)

Argument or Option	Description
`-type c`	Matches all files having a type listed in the following table:
	c Character device
	b Block special
	d Directory
	p Named pipe
	f Regular file (not c, b, d, or p)
`-links n`	Matches all files with n number of links.
`-size n`	Matches all files of size n blocks (512-byte blocks). If n is preceded by a +, matches all files larger than n blocks. If n is preceded by a -, matches those less than n blocks.
`-user user-id`	Matches all files having a user id of `user-id`. May either be the numeric value or the logname of the user.
`-atime n`	Matches all files last accessed within the previous n days.
`-mtime n`	Matches all files modified within the previous n days.
`-exec cmd`	For each file matched, the command `cmd` is executed. The notation { } is used to signify where the file name should appear in the command executed. The command must be terminated by an escaped semicolon (\ ;), for example , `-exec ls -d {} \ ;` Here the command `ls` is executed with the `-d` argument, and each file is passed to `ls` at the place where the { } is found.
`-ok cmd`	Same as `-exec` except the user is prompted for confirmation before the command is executed.
`-newer file`	Matches all files that have been modified more recently than `file`.

Notes

The expressions (flags) may be grouped together and combined to limit the search criteria. Multiple flags are assumed to be ANDs. Both criteria must be met. To offer more control over selection, the following table describes other options:

( )   Parentheses can be used to group selections. Because the parentheses are special to the shell they must be escaped (\ ().

-o   This is the OR operator that overrides the default AND assumption.

!   This is a NOT operator that negates the expression that follows it.

+ -   The *n* arguments may be preceded by a plus (+) or a negative (-) to denote either more than or less than, respectively.

Messages

```
find: bad option -badoption
```

A *match-spec* that is not valid was used. *badoption* is replaced with what was specified.

```
find: incomplete statement
```

find did not have enough arguments for it to understand what you wanted.

Examples

```
find . -name letter-to-dad -print
```

Searches the current directory and its subdirectories for a file called letter-to-dad. When and if it finds it, the full pathname is shown on-screen.

```
find . -name "letter*" -print
```

Looks for all files starting with letter. Note the use of the wild card (*). This allows for a pattern match of all files starting with the characters letter. This finds: letters, letter_to_dad, letter_to_mom, and so on.

```
find . -name "letter*" -exec ls -l {} \;
```

Searches for the files starting with letter and executes a long listing on them. Notice the placement of the {} and the escaped semicolon \;.

```
find . ! \( -name "letter*" -o -name "*dad" \) -print
```

Looks for a list of files that do not start with letter or end with dad.

finger

Displays information about users on the system.

Syntax

```
finger [flags] users
```

IX

Command Reference

Argument or Option	Description
users	This is an optional list of user names. If specified, then extended information about the user is displayed.

Flags

Argument or Option	Description
-b	Displays a more brief output
-f	Suppresses header lines
-i	Displays a quick list with idle times
-l	Forces the long (extended) output
-p	Doesn't print the .plan file
-q	Displays a quick list of users

Rules

Finger reads the information in the comment field of the /etc/passwd file. The comment field is divided into three subfields, each separated by a comma. The second field requires two commas. For example, if the comment field contains Frank Burns, Swamp, Mash, 555-2939, then Frank Burns is displayed under "In real life," Swamp, Mash under "office," and 555-2939 under "home phone."

The extended information about users includes the comment field described previously and two files found in their home directories (.plan and .project). The contents of these files are displayed on-screen.

Idle time is the time elapsed since something displayed on-screen or the user typed something. This is not true idle time, as it is possible for a program to do useful work without requiring the user's intervention.

An asterisk (*) before the terminal name indicates that the user does not give others write permission.

Examples

    finger

Lists all users on the system.

```
finger frank susie
```

Lists extended information about `frank` and `susie`.

See also

who, w

format

Formats floppy disks for use with UNIX. UNIX requires perfect media on floppy disks; it can't deal with bad spots on a floppy disk. `format` verifies the disk to make sure it is writeable and readable.

Syntax

```
format device
```

Argument or Option	Description
device	The name of the raw device you want to format (for example, /dev/rdsk/5h is the primary 5 1/4-inch high-density drive)
-v	Verbose
-V	Verify with one random write/read/compare
-E	Exhaustive verify where every track is write/read/compare

Note

`format` prompts you to enter the floppy disk when ready; however, `format` does not prompt you to format another. You have to reinvoke the `format` command.

Examples

```
format /dev/rdsk/5h
```

Formats a 5 1/4-inch high-density disk.

```
format /dev/rdsk/3h
```

Formats a 3 1/2-inch high-density disk.

grep

grep looks for patterns found in files and reports to you when these patterns are found. The name of the command comes from the use of "regular expressions" in the ed family of editors. grep stands for "Global Regular Express Printer."

Syntax

```
grep [flags] reg-expres filelist

egrep [flags] reg-expres filelist

fgrep [flags] string filelist
```

Argument or Option	Description
filelist	An optional space separated list of files to search for the given string or reg-expres. If left blank, the standard input is searched.
reg-expres	The regular expression to search for. Regular expressions are in the form used by ed. See the man page for the definition of regular expressions.
string	The string you want to find in the files.

Flags

Argument or Option	Description
-v	Lists the lines that don't match string or reg-expres.
-c	Counts the matching lines.
-l	Only the file names containing a match are displayed.
-h	Suppresses the name of the file in which the match was found from being displayed (grep and egrep only).
-n	Each matching line is displayed along with its relative line number.
-i	Causes matching to not be case-sensitive. The default behavior is case-sensitive.
-e reg-expres	Useful when the regular expression or string starts with a dash (-).
-f file	file contains the strings or expressions to search for.

Notes

fgrep stands for fast grep and can only search for fixed strings. Multiple strings may be searched for by separating each string by a newline or by entering them in the -f *file* file.

egrep stands for extended grep and accepts the following enhancements to regular expressions defined by ed.

+	If this trails a regular expression, it matches one or more of that occurrence.
?	If this trails a regular expression, it matches 0 or 1 occurrences.
|	Used to denote multiple regular expressions (for example, this or that expression).
( )	May be used to group expressions.

Messages

```
grep: illegal option -- badoption
```

You gave grep an option/flag that it doesn't understand; *badoption* is replaced by the option specified.

```
grep: can't open file
```

You tried to search a file that doesn't exist or for which you don't have read permission; *file* is replaced by the file you specified.

Examples

```
grep hello letter-to-dad
```

Searches for the word hello in the file letter-to-dad.

```
fgrep hello letter-to-dad
```

This does the same thing.

```
grep "[hH]ello" letter-to-dad
```

Searches for the word hello or Hello.

```
fgrep "hello
Hello" letter-to-dad
```

This does the same thing.

```
egrep "([Ss]ome¦[Aa]ny)one" letter-to-dad
```

Looks for all the words `someone`, `Someone`, `anyone`, or `Anyone` in the file.

```
vi 'fgrep -l hello *'
```

Generates a list of file names in the current directory that have the word `hello` in them and passes this list of names to the editor `vi`.

See also

sh, ed

hd

hd stands for hex dump. Use `hd` to see the hexadecimal representations of the contents of a file. Viewers such as `pg` and `more` are designed for *text-based files*. These files consist of printable characters. *Binary files* are typically files generated by a database. Today, most spreadsheets and word-processing documents are also binary. There are times when you need to look at an area of a binary file and `more` doesn't work.

Syntax

```
hd [ -format ] [ -s offset ] [ -n count ] [ file-list ]
```

Flags

Argument or Option		Description
-format		Format specifies the behavior for generating the output. The default format is -abxA (show addresses, use the bytes output format, the numeric base is hexadecimal, and show the ASCII output on the right side). Formats can be combined to produce multiple output lines per 16-byte record.
	a	Generates the address offset for each 16-byte record read, on the far left side of the output generated.
	c	Shows all printable characters as themselves and nonprintable characters are shown in the chosen output base.
	b	Shows input as bytes in the chosen output base—each 8 bits.
	w	Shows input as a word in the chosen output base—each 16 bits.

Argument or Option	Description
l	Shows input as a long in the chosen output base—each 32 bits.
A	Shows printable characters as themselves and all others as a period (.). This is displayed on the right side of the output generated.
	What the number base of the output should be
x	The output uses hexadecimal as the base.
d	The output uses decimal as the base.
o	The output uses octal as the base.
-s offset	Specifies how many bytes (offset) to read (skip) from the input file before output starts. offset can be specified in decimal, octal, or hexadecimal. For example:
11	(decimal) skip 11 bytes
013	(octal) skip 11 (decimal) bytes
0x0b	(hexadecimal) skip 11 (decimal) bytes
	You can use the following modifiers to change the number's unit of measure:
w	words (2 bytes)
l	long word (4 bytes)
b	"blocks" (512 bytes)
k	kilobytes (1024 bytes)
	Because it is valid for a hexadecimal number to end in a b, you cannot use the preceding modifiers when specifying hexadecimal offsets. You may, however, use the asterisk (*) separated by a space to specify a multiplier (for example, 0x0b * 512).
-n count	Specifies the total number of bytes to process. count follows the same rules as offset for formatting.
file-list	The list of files to process, each separated by a space. If no file is specified, then the input is the standard input.

Messages

```
hd: cannot access ben.1
```

You attempted to dump a file that doesn't exist; in this example that file is ben.1.

```
0000    74 6f 74 61 6c 20 31 35  32 0a 2d 72 77 2d 72 77
   total 152.-rw-rw
0010    2d 72 77 2d 20 20 20 31  20 62 65 6e 61 68 20 20
   -rw-   1 benah
0020    20 20 70 72 6f 67 20 20  20 20 20 20 20 33 37 30
     prog         370
0030    32 31 20 46 65 62 20 31  32 20 31 37 3a 32 33 20
   21 Feb 12 17:23
0040    62 65 6e 0a 2d 72 77 2d  72 77 2d 72 77 2d 20 20
   ben.-rw-rw-rw-
0050    20 31 20 62 65 6e 61 68  20 20 20 20 70 72 6f 67
    1 benah      prog
0060    20 20 20 20 20 20 20 33  37 30 32 31 20 46 65 62
         37021 Feb
0070    20 31 32 20 31 37 3a 32  36 20 62 65 6e 32 0a 2d
   12 17:26 ben2.-
0080    72 77 2d 72 77 2d 72 77  2d 20 20 20 31 20 62 65
   rw-rw-rw-   1 be
0090    6e 61 68 20 20 20 20 70  72 6f 67 20 20 20 20 20
   nah      prog
00a0    20 20 20 20 20 20 30 20  46 65 62 20 31 32 20 31
         0 Feb 12 1
00b0    37 3a 32 38 20 62 65 6e  33 0a
   7:28 ben3.
00ba
```

This sample output uses the default *format*. Notice the address offsets on the left, the hexadecimal output of 16 bytes in the middle, and the ASCII output of those records on the right.

Examples

Suppose someone used a word processor or spreadsheet to create a very unusual file name on the system. This name is corrupt because, when you do an ls ‑C on the directory, everything is scrambled on-screen. You know that some sort of unprintable character was used but you don't know what it was. To figure this out, you can pass a directory listing through hd as in the following:

```
ls ¦ hd
```

Produces a listing in hexadecimal form and enables you to see the nonprintable character's hexadecimal representation. You can then identify the faulty file name and remove it or rename it.

See also

od, ls, more, pg

head

head prints out the first number of specified lines of a file.

Syntax

    head -lines filelist

Argument or Option	Description
-lines	The number of lines to print from the beginning of the file. The default is 10.
filelist	A space-separated list of file names you want displayed. If left blank, the standard input is read.

Example

    head letter-to-dad

Prints the first 10 lines from the file letter-to-dad.

See also

tail, pr, cat, more, pg

hello

hello sends messages to another terminal, if that terminal is set up to receive messages. This command functions in the same way as write, except that as each character is typed, it is sent to the user's terminal. This character-by-character transmission is unlike write, which waits until a newline is encountered to transmit.

Syntax

    hello user tty

Argument or Option	Description
user	The name of the user to whom you want to send a message.
tty	An optional terminal device specification used when the user is logged on more than once.

Example

```
hello frank
```

Initiates a conversation with the user frank.

See also

write

hwconfig

Determines what devices are currently installed. hwconfig is primarily used by the system administrator. This information is then used to determine if any conflicts exist, and where new devices can be installed. hwconfig effectively reproduces the output generated at boot time.

Syntax

```
hwconfig
```

Messages

hwconfig produces a columnar report with the following column headings:

Heading	Description
device	What kind of device it is; not the UNIX special device name.
address	The base address for I/O; the range of the driver working space.
vector	The interrupt vector assigned to the device.
dma	The dma channel assigned to the device.
comment	More useful information about the device.

Example

```
hwconfig
```

Produces a list of devices found on the system.

Caution

Third-party device drivers don't always conform to the requirements of this command. In some cases, you might not see the device in the list, or the information displayed is meaningless.

See also

swconfig

id

id displays your identification to the system. It reports your user name, user id number, group name, and group id number.

Syntax

id

Example

id

Shows the id information.

join

Extracts the common lines from two sorted files. One line of output is produced for each line in the two files that match, based on the specified keys.

Syntax

join [*flags*] *file1* *file2*

Argument or Option	Description
file1	The first file used in the join; may be a dash (-) to tell join to read from the standard input; thus, join may be a filter in a pipeline.
file2	The second file used in the join.

Flags

Argument or Option	Description
-a*n*	The unmatching lines from either *file1* or *file2* also are produced. *n* may be either a 1 or 2.
-j *n* *m*	Joins the two files on the *m*th field of file *n*. If *n* is not specified, then the *m*th field of each file is used.

(continues)

IX

Command Reference

Argument or Option	Description
-t *char*	By default, the field separators are tabs, newlines, and spaces. This option causes *char* to be used as the field separator. All instances of *char* are significant. Multiple instances of *char* and the default are treated as one.

Example

```
join to-do-list old-do-list
```

Reports the lines that the two lists have in common.

See also

sort, comm, uniq

kill

Allows you to send a signal to a process that is currently executing. Usually, this command is issued to cause the process to stop executing.

Syntax

```
kill -signal pid
```

Argument or Option	Description
-*signal*	An optional signal that can be sent. The default is 15. 15 stands for SIGTERM. Two other popular signals are 1, which is the equivalent of hanging up the phone as if on a modem, and 9, which is referred to as a sure kill.
pid	The process id of the process you want to send the specified signal. A *pid* is a number used by the system to keep track of the process. The ps command can be used to report the *pid* of a process.

Message

```
kill: permission denied
```

You tried to kill a process that you don't own and/or you are not the super user.

Examples

```
kill 125
```

Sends signal 15 to the process 125. The default signal is 15.

```
kill -1 125
```

Sends signal 1 to the process 125.

```
kill -9 125
```

Sends signal 9. This works if no others do.

Note

Although -9 is the sure kill, it is often best to try -15 and -1 first. These signals can be caught by the applications and, after they receive them, properly clean up after themselves. Because -9 can't be caught, you may have to do some housecleaning after the process terminates.

Caution

There are instances when even -9 won't kill the process. This is when the process is using a kernel service and can't receive signals. Periodically processes get locked up in this mode. The only way to resolve this is a system shutdown.

See also

sh, ps

l

A link to the command ls. l is just like ls except the default is the long format.

Syntax

```
l [flags] filelist
```

Example

```
l
```

Gives a long listing of the current directory.

See also

ls

last

Reads from the /etc/wtmp file and reports the history of logins and logouts from the system. It can be used to report who has logged in or what terminals have been used.

Syntax

```
last -n limit -t tty user
```

Argument or Option	Description
-n limit	Limits the output to limit lines.
-t tty	Reports the login activity on the terminal device tty.
user	Reports the login activity of the user user.

Rule

last reads the /etc/wtmp file, which grows until cleared. On many systems this file is cleared daily. On these systems, last can only report the information within the last 24-hour period.

Examples

```
last frank
```

This reports the login activity of the user frank.

```
last
```

Reports all information, not restricted to a user or terminal.

See also

who, finger, w, ps

lc

Lists directory and file contents in columns sorted alphabetically.

Syntax

```
lc [flags] filelist
```

Example

```
lc
```

Gives a columnar listing of the current directory.

Note

lf is a link that assumes an invocation of lc -F.

lr assumes lc -R.

lx assumes lc -x.

See also

is

line

Reads a line (a string of text up to a newline character) from the standard
input and writes it to the standard output. This is useful within a shell script
program to read a file and examine its contents or to read a user's input.

Syntax

line

Example

```
while INPUT='line'
do
echo "you entered: $INPUT"
done
```

Reads what you type and displays it on-screen.

See also

sh

ln

Creates a link between two files, enabling you to have more than one name
to access a file. A directory entry is simply a name to call the file and an
i-node number. The i-node number is an index into the file system's table.
Therefore, it is easy to have more than one name to i-node reference in the
same directory or multiple directories.

A benefit of a link over a copy is that only one copy exists on the disk; therefore, no additional storage is required. Any file may have multiple links.

ln is a link to the cp and mv commands and behaves in a very similar manner.
All the rules for these two commands apply here as well, except that ln just
makes a link.

ln allows you to link one file to another or to a list of files to use the same name in another directory.

Syntax

```
ln source-file dest-file
```

```
ln source-list dest-directory
```

Argument or Option	Description
source-file	The original file.
dest-file	The destination name. This is the name you want the file to go by. It is sort of an alias of the original file.
source-list	A space-separated list of files to link.
dest-directory	The destination directory. This is the directory where you want to have the linked files stored. That is, you want to duplicate the names of the files here just as they were given in the source-list.

Example

```
ln letter-to-dad my-letter
```

Enables you to edit either the file letter-to-dad or the file my-letter and modify both of them at the same time.

See also

cp, mv

logname

logname reads the /etc/utmp file to report what name you used to log in to the system.

Syntax

```
logname
```

Example

```
logname
```

Reports the name you used to log in to the system.

lp

Submits a print request to the UNIX system print spooler, or changes the options of a previously entered request. Print requests are spooled, thereby enabling you to move on to other work.

Syntax

```
lp [flags] filelist

lp -i id [flags]
```

Flags

Argument or Option	Description
-c	Makes a copy of the original file. Without this option set, a link is established between the original file and the working area of the lp spooler.
-ddest	Specifies the destination of the print request. *dest* may be either an individual printer or a class of printers. A class of printers is a group of printers accessed under one name.
-f *formname* -d any	Causes the spooler to print the request only when the specified *formname* is mounted on the printer. With the -d any flag set, the request goes to any printer with *formname* mounted. For example, a *formname* may be the company letterhead.
-H *spec-Handling*	Denotes special handling of the request. Valid values for *spec-Handling* are hold, resume, and immediate.
-m	Sends a mail message to the user, making the request when the request is printed.
-n *number*	Prints *number* copies of the request.
-o *option*	*option* is completely dependent on the interface script chosen by your system administrator when the printer was defined.
-q *priority*	Assigns the request priority of *priority*. The range of *priority* is 0 to 39, with 0 being the highest priority.
-s	Tells lp to be silent. Normally lp responds with the print request-id.
-t *title*	Prints *title* on the banner page.
-w	Writes a message to the user's terminal after the request is printed.

Note

If the environment variable LPDEST is set, and no -d*dest* is set, the request goes to the *dest* defined by LPDEST; otherwise, the request goes to the system default printer. The lack of a space between -d and *dest* is necessary.

Messages

```
request id is frontdsk-100 (2 files)
```

A successful completion of requesting two files to be sent to the frontdsk printer.

```
lp: destination "frontdk" non-existent
```

A request to print to a printer called frontdk was not granted because the system doesn't know about any printers named frontdk.

```
lp: can't access file "monday_repots"
lp: request not accepted
```

An attempt was made to print a file named monday_repots. However, no file existed by that name. In this case it looks like reports was misspelled.

Examples

```
lp myfile
```

Prints the file myfile to the default printer.

```
lp -dfrontdsk myfile
```

Prints the file myfile to the printer named frontdsk.

```
lp myfile my_other_file
```

Prints the two files myfile and my_other_file

```
date ¦ lp
```

Sends the date to the default printer. This demonstrates how lp may be used at the end of a pipeline to get a printout of the pipeline's output.

Note

Use the -s option when defining printers for applications. This way a request-id does not show up on-screen and confuse the user.

See also

lpstat, mail, enable, disable, cancel

lprint

Prints to a local printer attached to your terminal.

Syntax

    lprint - *file*

Argument or Option	Description
-	Tells lprint to use standard input for the print request, that is, lprint is at the end of a pipeline.
file	Tells lprint to print the file *file*.

Rules

The - and *file* options are mutually exclusive. The user must have the proper settings on the terminal to communicate with the printer. lprint uses /etc/termcap entries PN and PS to start and stop the print request, respectively. lprint is a direct printer; it is not a spooled operation. The use of your terminal is forfeited until the request is done or the printer's buffer has absorbed the request.

Message

    lprint: terminal does not support local printing

The terminal type as defined by the TERM environment variable does not have the PN and PS entries defined in the /etc/termcap file.

Example

    lprint myfile

Prints myfile to the printer attached to the user's terminal.

See also

    lp, termcap

lpstat

Shows the status of the lp spooler system and print requests.

Syntax

    lpstat [*flags*]

Flags

Argument or Option	Description
-a *list*	Shows the acceptance status of the printers in *list*.
-c *list*	Shows the class names of the printers in *list*, and their members.
-d	Shows the lp spooler's system default destination.
-f *list* -l	Verifies that the forms listed in *list* are defined to the lp spooler.
-o *list* -l	Shows the status of the print request queued for the printers in *list*. The -l flag gives more detail on the request.
-p *list*	Shows the status of the printers in *list*. Usually used to see if the printer is enabled or if not, why.
-r	Shows if the scheduler is running or not. If the scheduler isn't running, then no print jobs can be scheduled to print. No printing takes place.
-s	Shows a status summary of the spooler. Lists if the scheduler is running, the default printer and the printer names and the devices associated with them.
-t	Shows all status information. Equivalent to -acdusr.
-u *list*	Shows the status of the printer request similar to that of -o, but for a list of users instead of printers.
-v *list*	Shows a list of printers and the devices associated with them.

Note

Whenever *list* is used it may be left blank. This causes the flag used to respond with all entries that apply to that flag.

Message

```
frontdsk-100      sue      245      Sep 15 20:13 on frontdsk
```

This is a sample of the output generated by lpstat with no options, when issued by the user sue after making a print request. The first field, frontdsk-100, is the request-id. The second field, sue, is sue's user name. The third field, 245, is the size of the request in bytes. The fourth field, Sep 15 20:13, is the date and time that the request was made. And the last field, on frontdsk, is a status message reporting that the request is currently being printed.

Examples

```
lpstat
```

Shows the outstanding print requests for the user entering the command.

```
lpstat -u
```

Shows the outstanding print requests for all users. Notice how the *list* parameter that caused all users to show was not supplied.

```
lpstat -t
```

Shows all status information.

```
lpstat -s
```

Shows the system default printer, the devices for each printer on the system, and whether the scheduler is running.

Note

When using the -t option and you have more than four printers, this is a lot of information to see on-screen. You can pipe it to lp or a pager, such as more, so that the information does not scroll off your screen.

See also

lp

ls

Lists the files found in the file system.

Syntax

```
ls [flags] filelist
```

Flags

Argument or Option	Description
-A	Shows all files including hidden files. Hidden files start with a period. Does not show the current directory (.) or the parent directory (..).
-a	Shows all files including the current directory and the parent directory.
-C	Columnar output, sorted down the columns

(continues)

Argument or Option	Description
-x	Columnar output, sorted across the columns
-d	Treats each entry as a directory.
-l	Gives a long listing. A long listing shows details about the files, such as the type of file, the permissions, the link/directory count, the owner, the group, the size in bytes, when the file was last modified, and the file name. The file types are as follows:

-	Normal file
d	Directory
b	Block special device (disks)
c	Character special device (terminals)
p	Named pipe
s	Semaphore
m	Shared memory

The permissions are three clusters of three bytes each. Each cluster represents the permissions for the owner, group, and other. The permissions are as follows:

r	Read access
w	Write access
x	Execute access

Argument or Option	Description
-t	Sorts by the time last modified. Used with the -l flag.
-u	Sorts by the time last accessed. Used with the -t flag.
-c	Sorts by the time the i-node information last changed. Used with the -t flag.
-r	Reverses the sort order.
-i	Shows the i-node number of the file in the first column.
-F	Places a / after directory entries, and an * after executable programs.

Message

```
/bin/ls: arg list too long
```

You have asked ls to process an argument list that has more characters in it than can be handled. The maximum number of characters in an argument list is 5,120.

Examples

    ls

Lists the files in the current directory in one long column.

    ls -C

Lists the files in the current directory broken into columns.

    ls -l

Gives a long listing of the files in the current directory.

    ls -ltr /usr/spool/uucppublic

Gives a long listing, sorted by modification time, in descending order of the files found in the directory /usr/spool/uucppublic.

Note

Use -d when you want to find the characteristics of a directory. Otherwise the contents of the directory are shown and not the directory itself.

lc is a link to ls that assumes the option of -C.

l is a link to ls that assumes the -l option.

lx is a link to ls that assumes the -x option.

See also

    chmod

mail

Enables you to communicate with other users not only on your local machine—but with the right kinds of connections—to the larger computing community as well. This is the electronic mail facility of UNIX, an extremely handy and powerful tool. mail provides a means of passing messages throughout the office without having to wait for a scheduled mail run. Furthermore, users can catalog incoming mail and use the mail system as a to-do list and filing system to track correspondence.

Syntax

    mail [flags] usernames

IX

Command Reference

Flags

Argument or Option	Description
-e	Tests to see if there is any mail in your incoming mailbox. There is no visible output when this option is used. Useful for the shells if statement or with the shell's && and ¦¦ operators.
-f *file*	Opens *file* to read mail from instead of your incoming mailbox. If *file* is omitted, then the file name mbox is used.
-F	Stores outgoing mail in a file name the same as that of the first recipient of the message. Useful to keep a log of all the mail messages you've sent.
-H	Shows a header summary of the mailbox contents only.
-i	Causes mail to ignore interrupts while constructing mail messages; can be useful when working over noisy dial-up lines.
-n	Causes mail to not initialize from the system mailrc file. The mailrc file sets various options to customize the mail environment for each site; a user may have a mailrc file also. This is typically called .mailrc in the user's home directory.
-N	Causes mail not to print a summary header of the mailboxes' contents.
-s *subject*	Sets the subject line in the mail header to *subject*.
-u *user*	Reads *user*'s incoming mailbox.

Note

The -u *user* flag is only possible if the system administrator has set the permissions on the incoming mailboxes to allow this.

Message

```
No messages.
```

This means that you have invoked the mail utility with no flags set and your incoming mailbox is empty; you have no mail.

Examples

```
mail
```

Invokes the mail utility and enables you to read your mail.

```
mail -u sue
```

Invokes the mail utility to read sue's mailbox.

```
mail sue -s "soccer games(kids)"
```

Invokes the mail utility to send a message to sue on the subject of a soccer games for the kids.

```
mail sue -s "soccer scores" < scores
```

Sends a message to sue with a subject heading of "soccer scores" from a prepared file called scores.

```
date ¦ mail sue -s "date"
```

Demonstrates how mail is used at the end of a pipeline to mail the results of the pipeline to a user. In this case the date to sue.

```
mail kim john sally
```

Invokes the mail utility to start construction of a message to three people: kim, john, and sally.

Caution

You have to be particularly deliberate when setting up a good structure to catalog your mail files. Otherwise, you might find yourself with mail files throughout the file system. If you want to catalog or save messages, talk to your system administrator about a good approach for this. The administrator may already have the structure in place for you.

Note

For more information, read the user's guide and tutorial provided with your system.

See also

write

mesg

Enables other users to write to your terminal. This controls whether you allow a user to use the write command to your terminal.

Syntax

```
mesg n y
```

Argument or Option	Description
n	Does not allow users to send messages to your terminal.
y	Allows users to send messages to your terminal.
	No option specified shows the status of your terminal availability to messages.

Note

The default state of your terminal. This command enables users to write to your terminal.

Messages

```
is y
```

Your terminal allows others to write to it.

```
is n
```

Your terminal does not allow others to write to it.

Examples

```
mesg
```

Shows whether users can write to your terminal.

```
mesg n
```

Disallows the writing of messages to your terminal.

```
mesg y
```

Allows users to write to your terminal.

Caution

It is a good idea to set root's .profile file to include the command mesg n. Many terminals have an escape sequence that puts them into echo command mode. That is, what is supplied by the user writing to root's terminal is, in effect, executed by root.

See also

```
write
```

mkdir

Creates new directories in the file system.

Syntax

```
mkdir -m mode -p dirnames
```

Argument or Option	Description
-m mode	Sets the directory permissions to mode at the time of creation.
-p	Creates all nonexistent parent directories. See the example that follows.

Message

```
cannot access letters/
```

You attempted to create a directory and a parent in the list didn't exist. In this case, that parent was letters. Use the -p option.

Examples

```
mkdir letters
```

Creates the directory letters.

```
mkdir -p letters/personal letters/work
```

Makes the directories letters/personal and letters/work. If the directory letters had not existed, the -p flag would have caused the directory letters to be created also; otherwise, an error message would have resulted.

See also

rm, rmdir, chmod

mknod

Makes special files. *Special files* are considered one of the following kinds of files: devices, named pipes, semaphores, or shared memory.

Syntax

```
mknod file_name [flags]
```

Flags

Argument or Option	Description
b *major minor*	Makes a block special file with major number *major* and minor number *minor*.
c *major minor*	Creates a character special file rather than a block special file.
p	Makes a named pipe.
s	Makes a semaphore.
m	Makes a shared date (memory) file.

Rule

Only the super user can make block and character special files.

Message

```
mknod: must be super user
```

You attempted to make a block or character special file and you don't have super user privileges.

Example

```
mknod my_pipe p
```

Creates a named pipe called my_pipe.

mnt

Enables regular users to mount and unmount file systems similar to those offered to the system administrator through mount and umount. The system administrator can limit access to some or all file systems.

Syntax

```
mnt -tu dirname
umnt dirname
```

Argument or Option	Description
-u	Causes mnt to behave as umnt, and unmounts the file system.
-t	Prints a table of information about the file system.

Rule

The directory you want to mount must be defined by the system administrator in the file /etc/default/filesys with an entry of mount=yes. Otherwise this command fails.

Message

```
Device busy
```

An attempt was made to either mount a device that is in use, or unmount a device that is in use (an open file, the current directory, for example).

Examples

```
mnt /mnt
```

Mounts a device to the default mount directory /mnt.

```
umnt /mnt
```

Unmounts a device that is mounted to the default mount directory /mnt.

See also

mount

more

more is a general-purpose pager. Use more to view text that scrolls off the screen. more also provides some handy text search capabilities using regular expressions.

Syntax

```
more [flags] filenames
```

Flags

Argument or Option	Description
-n	n is an integer used to set the window size to n lines long. The window size controls how many lines appear on-screen.
-c	As more pages through the text, it draws each line from top to bottom by clearing the line and then drawing the next line. Normally, more clears the screen and then draws each line.

(continues)

IX

Command Reference

Argument or Option	Description
-d	Displays the prompt Hit space to continue, Rubout to abort in place of the default more prompt.
-f	Counts logical lines rather than screen lines. Long lines wrap around the screen and are normally counted as a new line by more; the -f flag turns off the counting of the wrapped portion of long lines.
-l	Does not treat the ^L (formfeed) character specially. Normally, more treats the ^L the same as the window filling up by pausing.
-r	Shows carriage returns as ^M.
-v	Shows all control characters as ^C, where C is the character used to generate the control character. Those above DEL are shown as M-C, where C is the character without the high bit set.
-s	Multiple blank lines are suppressed and treated as one.
-w	Waits at the end of the file for user-supplied control of quit. Normally, more quits at the end of the file.

Note

For the -c option to work, the terminal must support the clear to end of line capability.

Messages

> *filename*: No such file or directory

You tried to view a file that doesn't exist.

> *filename*: not a text file

You tried to view a file that is not a text file. more tries to determine whether a file is a text file before allowing you to view it. *filename* is substituted with the name you asked for.

> *dirname*: directory

You tried to use more to view a directory file. *dirname* is substituted with the name you asked for.

Examples

```
more letter-to-dad
```

Displays a text file called letter-to-dad.

```
ls -l /dev ¦ more
```

Demonstrates how more is used at the end of a pipeline to control the output of the pipeline.

Notes

While using the more utility, press h for a list of other possible actions to use.

Set the environment variable MORE to options you want to have set every time you invoke the more utility. For example, if you always want the -v and -w options set, enter the following in your .profile:

```
MORE="-v -w"; export MORE
```

If, while viewing a file, you realize you want to change something, just enter the v command. This boots the vi text editor and allows you to make the changes you want. Exit the editor, and you are returned to the more utility.

If you know that you want to look at a section of the text that contains a certain set of characters, enter the / command followed by a regular expression. This searches for the regular expression you entered. See the ed command in the reference manual supplied with your system for definitions of regular expressions; these are powerful tools.

See also

vi, ed, pg, pr, cat

mv

Renames a file or moves it to a new directory, or both. mv also lets you rename a directory.

Syntax

```
mv -f file1 file2
mv -f dir1 dir2
mv -f filelist dir
```

IX

Command Reference

Argument or Option	Description
-f	Normally mv prompts you if the destination file exists and write permission is turned off. This causes mv to do the move without prompting.
file1	The source file name.
file2	The destination file name (new name).
dir1	The source directory name.
dir2	The destination directory name (new name).
filelist	A space separated list of file names. When this option is used the files retain their names, but are moved to the new directory *dir*.
dir	The destination directory.

Note

mv cannot physically move a directory, it can only rename it.

Messages

        mv: *filename*: *mode* mode

filename already exists and the mode of the file does not permit it to be overwritten. A response to this prompt with anything starting with a y causes the move to take place; otherwise, the move is ignored. If the -f option is used the prompt is not shown and the move takes place. *mode* is the mode the file has. Modes are numbers representing permissions.

        mv: *filename* and *filename* are identical

You tried to move a file to itself.

        mv: cannot access *filename*

You tried to move a file that does not exist.

Examples

        mv letters letter

Changed the file name letters to letter.

        mv letter $HOME/trashcan

Here trashcan is a directory in the user's home directory. This is a useful way to remove files because they are easier to recover if you did not really want to delete them.

Caution

mv doesn't prompt for confirmation of the move unless the destination file already exists and the mode of the file prohibits writing. Because mv first removes the destination file, you may lose a file you do not mean to lose.

Consider the following directory listing from the lc command:

```
customer.dat   inventory.dat
customer.idx   inventory.idx
```

An accidental entry of mv customer* where you forgot to supply a destination directory causes the customer.idx file to be wiped out. When a wild card expands to only two files and you forget to give the destination directory, you wipe out the second file in the expansion.

Because mv first removes the destination file before performing the move, any links established with the destination file are lost. If you need to maintain those links, copy the file to the destination name and then remove the original file.

Note

ln, cp, and mv are linked to each other; they determine their actions based on how they are invoked.

See also

rm, cp, ln, copy, chmod

newgrp

Changes your current group id, allowing you to work with that group's files.

Syntax

```
newgrp - group
```

With no options, newgrp returns you to the group you are in when you log in.

Argument or Option	Description
-	If this option is given, the user is logged in under this group id.
group	This is the group id under which you want to become active. group must be set up in /etc/group and the user must be in the list; otherwise, access is denied.

IX

Command Reference

Note

With no options `newgrp` returns you to the group you are in when you log in.

Messages

`unknown group`

This message means you asked to change to a group id that does not exist.

`Passwd:`

You asked to change to a group id for which a password exists. You must enter the correct group password or access to the group is denied.

`Sorry`

Access to the group is denied. Either your user name is not in the list of valid users for the group, or you entered an incorrect group password.

Example

`newgrp admin`

Changes your group id to `admin`.

See also

id

news

Reads posted news. Articles are posted to the /usr/news directory. /usr/news is a publicly accessible directory for posting information to share with other users. Articles are simple text files created with any editor. Do not confuse this news facility with USENET news.

Syntax

`news [flags]`

Flags

Argument or Option	Description
-a	Shows all news items, regardless of how current they are.
-n	Shows just the names of the articles rather than their contents.

Argument or Option	Description
-s	Reports the status of the file; shows if there are any articles to read.
*item*s	Enables you to specify which articles you want to read. Separate each item with a space.

Rule

news places a file named .news_time in your home directory. It uses the time and date of this file to compare to the articles in the /usr/news directory to determine if an article has been read.

Message

```
cannot open item
```

You asked to read a specific article and that article does not exist.

Example

```
news
```

Asks that only current articles be printed.

See also

mail, write

nice

Lowers the scheduling priority level of a process. This utility is appropriately named—you are being nice if you use it.

Syntax

```
nice -increment command
```

Argument or Option	Description
increment	The amount by which to change the scheduling priority. Processes are normally given a scheduling priority of 20. *increment* may be any integer in the range 0-39.
command	The command (with its arguments) you want to run with the specified nice factor.

Rule

When using the C shell, this command doesn't apply because the C shell has its own `nice` command.

Example

Suppose you want to run a large batch job called `mass-update`. Running the following command lowers the priority from the default value of 20 to 30.

```
nice -10 mass-update
```

Note

The super user may enter an *increment* as a negative number. –10, for example, increases the scheduling priority of the command.

nl

Adds line numbers to a file. If text files are used by many people, line numbers are a useful reference.

Syntax

```
nl [flags] file
```

Flags

Argument or Option	Description
-b*type*	Specifies how the body of the text is numbered. *type* may be any of the following: a All lines. t Printable text only (default). n No lines (no numbering). p*str* Only those lines containing the string *str*.
-h*type*	Same as -b for the header. n is the default type.
-f*type*	Same as -b for the footer. n is the default type.
-p	Does not restart numbering at logical page breaks.
-v*init*	*init* is the number at which to start the logical page numbering (default is 1).

Argument or Option	Description
-i*incr*	*incr* is the amount to increment the numbering (default is 1).
-s*char*	*char* is the character used to separate the numbering from the text of the file (default is a tab).
-w*width*	*width* is the amount of space the numbering can have (default is 6).

Rules

file can be left blank. If *file* is left blank, then the standard input is assumed; this allows nl to be the filter program in a pipeline.

nl's output is always to the standard output.

nl can distinguish header, body, and footer sections only if lines containing nothing but the following are used to denote the beginning of that section:

Section	Indicated by
Header	\:\:\:
Body	\:\:
Footer	\:

Message

```
INVALID OPTION (-C) - PROCESSING TERMINATED
```

You gave nl an option *C*; *C* is not a valid option. *C* becomes the option you tried to use.

Example

```
nl first-draft ¦ lp
```

Numbers all lines in the file called first-draft and sends the output to the default printer.

See also

pr

od

od stands for octal dump. od shows the octal representations of a file's contents. Viewers such as pg and more are designed for text-based files. Text-based files consist of printable characters. Binary files are typically files generated by a database, but today, most spreadsheets and word-processing documents are also binary. At times, you need to look at an area of a binary file, and more doesn't work.

Syntax

```
od [ -bcdox ] [ file ] [ offset_spec ]
```

Argument or Option	Description
file	The name of the file to process. If left blank, the standard input is used.
offset_spec	An offset specifier that determines when the output starts. offset_spec by default is the number of bytes to skip (expressed as an octal number). You can provide either one or both of the following modifiers:
	. The number given is interpreted as a decimal number, not octal.
	b The number, whether octal or decimal, is not bytes, but blocks (512 bytes).
	If no file is given, then offset_spec must be preceded by a plus sign (+) as in this example: +10.b - -. This example specifies that 10 (decimal) blocks are skipped from the standard input.

Flags

Argument or Option	Description
b	Shows the octal number of each byte (8 bits).
c	Shows printable characters as themselves, non-printable as octal numbers, and the following special characters:
	\b Backspace
	\0 Null
	\f Formfeed
	\n Newline
	\r Carriage return
	\t Tab

Argument or Option	Description
d	Shows decimal words (16 bits)
o	Shows octal words (16 bits)
x	Shows hexadecimal words (16 bits)

Message

```
od: cannot open ben.1
```

You tried to open a file (ben.1) that od cannot find.

Examples

Suppose you are working with an application, and when you press F1 to bring up a help screen, nothing happens. You can double-check the software configuration to ensure that F1 is the correct key. Each key on a keyboard returns a set of characters. You can validate the output of the F1 key against the documentation for this terminal type to see if someone reprogrammed the key.

```
od -c
```

Reads from standard input anything you type until you press a newline (the Enter key) followed by Ctrl-d. It then displays those keystrokes on-screen using printable characters when it can and octal for all others. You press the F1 key, the Enter key, and, finally, Ctrl-d to see what sequence returns.

See also

hd, more, pg

pack

Compresses or packs files so that their storage requirements are less. This is most useful when sending files across a modem because a smaller file takes less time to transfer. pcat works like cat but on packed files.

Syntax

```
pack - filenames
```

IX

Command Reference

Argument or Option	Description
-	If the - is specified, more statistical information is shown about the packing of the files.
filenames	A space-delimited list of the files to be packed.

Notes

pack obtains about a 40 percent reduction on text files, and only about 15 percent on binary files. (This is just a rough estimate; actual compression rates vary for each file.)

Files that are packed are renamed with a .z extension added.

Messages

        pack: *filename*: *xx.xx*% Compression

filename was able to obtain a compression percent of *xx.xx*.

        pack: *filename*: cannot open

filename does not exist, or you don't have permission to access it.

        pack: *filename*: already packed

filename looks as though it is already in a packed format.

        pack: *filename*: cannot pack a directory

filename is a directory; you can't pack directories.

        pack: *filename*: file name too long

If working on a UNIX system that still limits file names to 14 characters, you can get this message. *filename* must have more than 12 characters; therefore, there isn't enough room to append the .z.

        pack: *filename*: has links

The file you wanted to pack has links; you cannot pack a file with links.

        pack: *filename*.z: already exists

There is a file name with the .z extension already; pack won't overwrite it.

        pack: *filename*: no savings - file not changed

Running pack on the file does not result in any savings; nothing is done to the file.

```
pcat: filename: cannot open
```

filename doesn't exist, or you don't have permission to access it.

```
pcat: filename.z: not in packed format
```

A file with the .z extension exists; the file isn't in a packed format.

Examples

```
pack old-letters/*
```

Packs all the files in the directory old-letters.

```
pcat old-letters/letter-to-dad ¦ more
```

Looks at the file letter-to-dad.z, unpacks it, and pipes the output through the utility more.

See also

compress, uncompress, zcat, cat, unpack

passwd

Maintains user passwords. Also, system administrators can use this command to administer the user directory. It is strongly recommended that you use the system administrator's shell provided with your system to administer user directories as they are typically menu-driven and allow you to back out of actually implementing the change.

Syntax

```
passwd
```

The passwd command actually has many options not shown here. These other options are relevant only if you are a system administrator, so they are not discussed here. All features on password management are clearly defined in the system administrator's guide provided with your system.

The following are two of the password management features:

- *Locks.* An account may have a lock on it. This prevents the account from being used. Locks can be applied automatically if there are more than a system-defined number of tries to log in under that user name.

■ *Expiration.* A password can expire after a certain amount of time has passed. This is sometimes referred to as *password aging.* You also may require a user to change his or her password the next time he or she logs in. You can limit how soon a user may change his or her password again, thus discouraging changing the password back to the old password.

Notes

You have to be an administrator to change someone else's password.

Passwords should be chosen so that they are easy to remember but hard to guess. This almost seems like a contradiction in terms. However, good password selection is crucial to a secure system.

Messages

```
Permission denied
```

You attempted to change the password for a user that doesn't exist, or you are not a system administrator or super user and attempted to change a password other than your own.

```
Sorry
```

passwd prompts you for your old password when trying to enter a new one. You entered your old password incorrectly. You have to invoke passwd again to change your password.

Example

```
passwd
```

Places you into the password change program. You are first prompted for your old password. Depending on your system's configuration, you may be allowed to choose a password for yourself, it may generate one for you, or you may be able to choose which to do.

paste

Produces columnar output from one or more files, where each file contributes a column of the output. paste often is used with cut to reorder columns in a file.

Syntax

```
paste -ddelim filelist
paste -s -ddelim filelist
```

Argument or Option	Description
-ddelim	Specifies what character is used to delimit each column (tab is the default).
filelist	A list of files to paste together. Can be - to signify standard input.
-s	Causes paste to traverse each file separately. This uses lines in the file for each column. The first line is the first column, the second line the second column, and so on.

Note

The output of paste is always standard output.

Messages

```
line too long
```

The output of paste using the files supplied exceeds 511 characters on a line.

```
too many files
```

You tried to paste together more than 12 files. You have to do it in two or more passes to complete the job.

Example

```
ls -l ¦ tee /tmp/tmp.$$ ¦ cut -f5 -d' ' >/tmp/sz.$$
cut -f9 -d' ' /tmp/tmp.$$ ¦ paste - /tmp/sz.$$
rm /tmp/*.$$
```

At first this might look like a lot to swallow, but look at it piece by piece. This command takes the output of l and produces a listing with the name of the file followed by its size in bytes. The result of l is piped through tee to allow you to store a copy of l's output for later use (/tmp/tmp.$$). The pipe flows through tee to the first cut command that extracts the field holding the size and stores the field in a file for later use (/tmp/sz.$$). The second cut extracts the name field, piping this to paste. paste accepts standard input as its first column and the file /tmp/sz.$$ as the second column. Lastly, clean up by removing the temporary files.

See also

cut, rm, tee, pr, grep

IX

Command Reference

pcat

See pack.

pcpio

pcpio stands for *portable copy in out* (cpio). It reads and writes the format of
the cpio Archive/Interchange File Format specified in IEEE Std. 1003.1-1988.
pcpio behaves very much like cpio, but it is an archiver. pcpio is useful not
only for making backups, but also for moving files in the file system.

Syntax

    pcpio -o [flags]

    pcpio -i [flags] filelist

    pcpio -p [flags] dirname

Argument or Option	Description
-o	Creates the archive, that is, generates the output.
-i	Copies from a previously created archive.
-p	Accepts a list of files from the standard input and passes them to the specified directory. Useful for copying whole directory structures on the file system.
filelist	A space separated list of files to extract from the archive. May contain wild cards. The wild cards supported are the same as the simple regular expression expansion provided by the shell (sh).
	! Means not
	? Matches a single character
	* Matches any number of characters
	[] Matches the set of characters specified between the brackets
	If you use a wild card, enclose filelist in quotation marks ("). Otherwise, the shell expands them. A weakness of another archiver, tar, is that it doesn't support wild cards; it relies on the shell to expand its list of files.
dirname	The destination directory for the files given pcpio with the -p option.

Flags

Argument or Option	Description
-B	Signifies a blocking factor of 5,120 bytes per record. Used with the -o and -i options and only when sending the output to, or reading the input from, a character special device.
-a	Resets the access times of files after the copy is completed. If used with -l, files with links are not affected. Used with -o or -i.
-c	Creates or reads the header information in an archive in an ASCII character format. This creates headers readable on other platforms. For example, you can move an archive created on an X86 Intel-based machine to a 68X Motorola-based machine. Used with -o or -i.
-d	Creates the directories as needed. If the directories don't exist, pcpio creates them. Used with -p or -i.
-f	Changes the interpretation of *filelist*. Normally *filelist* is a list of files to extract. When you use the -f option, *filelist* is the list of files not to extract. Used with -i.
-l	Links files rather than copying them, if possible. Used with -p.
-m	Retains the modification times of files as found in the archive. Normally the modification times change to the current time. This does not affect directories. Used with -i and -p.
-r	To rename the files in *filelist*. You are prompted for each file in *filelist* for the new name, if none is given, the file is skipped. Used with -o or -i.
-t	Prints a list of files in the archive. Used with -i.
-u	Extracts files from an archive unconditionally. Normally pcpio extracts a file from the archive only if the file is newer than the file on the file system. Used with -p or -i.
-v	Signifies verbose mode. Tells pcpio to give a status report. Used with -i.

Messages

```
pcpio -o[BacLv]
pcpio -i[Bcdmrtuvf] {pattern...}
pcpio -p[adlLmruv] directory
```

The message you most likely see is a usage clause showing you the necessary syntax to use pcpio. If such a message appears, you probably forgot to provide an option; check your command line again.

Examples

    ls ¦ pcpio -oBc >/dev/rfd096ds15

Lists the current directory passing the list through the pipeline to pcpio. pcpio uses the input from the pipeline as its list of files to copy. It copies this list of files to the standard output with a blocking factor of 5120; the header information is written in a portable ASCII format. This output is redirected to the character special device /dev/rfd096ds15 (a high-density 5 1/4-inch floppy disk).

    pcpio -iBcdm "*.ltr" </dev/rfd096ds15

Extracts the files ending in .ltr from the floppy disk, and places them in the current directory. Any subdirectories are created as needed. The file's modification times are the same as at the time the archive was created.

    ls ¦ pcpio -pdl /usr/newdir

Copies the list generated by ls to the directory /usr/newdir, creates any directories needed, and links rather than copies when possible.

Note

pcpio with the -i and -o options is a *filter program*; it accepts input from the standard input and directs its output to the standard output. pcpio can be anywhere in pipeline, as long as the input to the -o option is a list of file names, and the input to the -i option is the result of a previous -o. The -p option is not a true filter, because the output is a specified directory.

See also

    copy, tar, cpio, ptar, find

Prompt Commands

Some of pg's commands may be preceded by an optional *address*. An *address* is interpreted as either pages or lines based on whether the command is a line-oriented command or a page-oriented command. An *address* preceded by either a plus (+) or a minus (-) causes pg to go forward or backward relative to the current line/page. In other words, + means forward *address* lines/pages, and - means backward *address* lines/pages. An unsigned *address* is absolute with respect to the beginning of the file (for example, 100 for a line-oriented command is the 100th line, and 100 for a page-oriented command is the 100th page).

Command	Description
address <return key>	if you press the return key, pg moves *address* pages. The default *address* is +1.
address l	Causes pg to move to *address* line. A signed *address* scrolls forward or backward the number of lines specified. An unsigned *address* displays a full screen starting at the specified *address*. The default *address* is +1
address d or <CTRL> d	Moves in half screens. The default *address* is +1.
. or <CTRL>l	Redraws the screen.
$	Moves to the end of the current input file. When used in a pipe line this command may not behave as expected.
i/*search_expr*/	Search forward to match the regular expression *search_expr*, and look for the *i*th occurrence of this expression. *i*'s default is 1. Searches to the end of the file.
i^*search_expr*^ *i*?*search_expr*?	Same as i/search but searches backward to the beginning of the file. Either form is valid.

Note

Each of the preceding search commands can have a trailing modifier to affect where the found text is displayed. Normally pg displays the found text at the top of the screen. The modifier specified resets the default behavior for all searches. The modifiers in the following table are valid.

Modifier	Description
b	Displays the found text on the bottom.
m	Displays the found text in the middle.
t	Resets the displays to the top.

If no modifier is used, *search_expr* doesn't require a trailing, /, ^, or ?. When using the modifiers, the trailing characters must be included so that the modifiers are not confused with the *search_expr*.

Command	Description
i n	Skip the current file; start displaying the *i*th file in *file_list*. The default for *i* is 1.
i p	Same as n but for the previous file.
i w	Displays another window (screen full). Or if *i* is given, it resets the window size.
s *file_name*	Save the current file to the file name specified by *file_name*.
h	Gives a help message on available commands.
q or Q	Quits pg.
!*command*	Runs your current shell as defined by the environment variable SHELL and passes *command* to it for processing.

Messages

```
ben: No such file or directory
```

You tried to give pg a file that doesn't exist; in this case that file name is ben.

```
Pattern not found:
```

While at the command line (the prompt) of pg, you entered a search string and that string is not found in the file.

Examples

```
pg letter-to-dad
```

Looks at a text file called letter-to-dad.

```
ls -l /dev ¦ pg
```

Demonstrates how you can use more at the end of a pipeline to control the pipeline's output.

See also

vi, ed, more, pr, cat

pg

pg is a general-purpose pager. Similar to more, pg enables you to view text files. pg enables you to go backward through a file, and more does not. However, more enables you to edit the contents you are viewing by invoking the vi editor; pg doesn't.

Syntax

```
pg [flags] filelist
```

Argument or Option	Description
filelist	A list of space-delimited file names; if left blank, pg reads from the standard input.

Flags

Argument or Option	Description
-	Specifies that standard input is used to read the text.
-number	Sets the window size to *number*. The amount of lines shown at a time is *number* (default is 1 less than the li parameter in /etc/termcap).
-p *message*	Uses *message* as the prompt at the end of each window's display. An optional %d may be used in *message* to show the current page number. Enclose *message* in quotation marks (") to ensure that the shell does no wild-card expansion. The default prompt is :.
-e	pg won't pause at the end of each file.
-n	Causes pg to behave like more and recognize the end of the command as soon as a letter is pressed. Normally, each command must be followed by a carriage return.
-s	All messages and prompts use "standout mode." Standout mode is usually reverse video.
+*number*	Starts showing text only after *number* of lines is encountered.
+/*pattern*/	Starts showing text when *pattern* is found. *pattern* uses the rules of regular expressions. See the ed command in your user's reference for a definition of regular expressions.

IX

Command Reference

Note

If the terminal type defined by the environment variable TERM can't be found in /etc/termcap, then the terminal type of dumb is used.

Messages

    pg: *dirname* is a directory

You tried to invoke pg to read a file that was a directory. *dirname* is substituted by the name you gave it.

    pg: No such file or directory

You tried to view a file that doesn't exist, or you don't have permission to read the file.

Examples

    pg letter-to-dad

Displays a text file called letter-to-dad.

    ls -l /dev ¦ pg

Demonstrates how pg may be used at the end of a pipeline to control the output of the pipeline.

Notes

While using the pg utility, press the h command for a list of other possible actions to use.

Pressing / while in pg places you in search mode. ^(caret) or ? places you in reverse search mode. Search mode uses regular expressions as described previously for *pattern*.

Commands preceded by a negative number cause pg to do the action of the command backward the number entered. For example, if the command is preceded by –10, the command performs the action after it goes back 10 pages; it does not perform the action on each page as it goes back.

Some UNIX applications use a pager. Many of these applications look for an environment variable called PAGER. Setting PAGER to the pager you want causes these applications to give you a more consistent feel when viewing the output.

See also

    more, ed, cat, grep

pr

Allows you to do some formatting to a file while printing it to the standard output. pr also has some of the functionality of paste and nl built into it.

Syntax

```
pr [flags] filelist
```

Argument or Option	Description
filelist	A space-delimited list of files. If left blank, the standard input is read. - can be used as a file name to tell pr to read from the standard input. You can combine file names and the -. This causes pr to read both from the standard input and from the listed files.

Flags

Argument or Option	Description
+page	Begins printing with page *page*. The default is page 1.
-col	Specifies *col* columns of output. This flag assumes the flags -e and -i. The default is 1 column.
-m	Merges the files, printing each file in a column, overriding the -*col* flag.
-d	Double-spaces the output.
-eccol	When reading the input, tabs are replaced with character *c* and expanded to positions (*col* + 1), ((2 * *col*) + 1), ((3 * *col*) + 1), and so on. *c* can be any nondigit character. *col* defaults to every eight positions.
-iccol	Works like -e except on the output of pr, replacing whitespace with the character *c*. Whitespace is spaces, tabs, and so on.
-ncwidth	Selects line numbering. *c* is the character to place between the line number and the normal output (the default is a tab). *width* is how many character positions the number occupies +1 (the default is 5).
-wlength	Sets the length of the line to *length* lines. For columnar output the default is 72; no limit is assumed otherwise.

(continues)

Argument or Option	Description
-o*offset*	Offsets each line of output by *offset* character positions (default is 0).
-l*lines*	Sets the length of the page to *lines* lines (default is 66).
-h *string*	Uses *string* as the header rather than the file name.
-p	Causes pr to page the output, pausing at the end of each page (only if the output is associated with a terminal).
-f	Uses a formfeed character between pages. Normally, pr fills the remaining lines with newline characters to cause a page break.
-t	Doesn't print the header or the footer. Normally, pr prints a five-line header and footer.
-s*char*	Separates multicolumn output with *char*. Tab is the default.

Messages

```
pr: can't open filename
```

pr can't access *filename*. Either it doesn't exist, or you don't have permission to read it.

```
pr: bad option
```

You specified an option pr doesn't understand.

Examples

```
pr -n program.c ¦ lp
```

Formats the file program.c with line numbers and sends the output to the printer.

```
ls ¦ pr -8 -i\ 6 -w132 -l51 ¦ lp
```

Takes the output of the ls command and produces an eight-column report separated by a space every six character positions and prints it to a printer that has 8 1/2 x 11-inch paper in it (132 columns by 51 lines).

```
ls /dev | grep "^tty" | fgrep -vx "tty" | \
pr -m - /etc/ttytype | lp
```

Takes the listing of the /dev directory and pipes it through two grep commands, then pipes that result to pr. The first grep extracts all the lines starting with the characters tty. The second grep extracts all the lines that don't exactly match tty (do this to strip out the /dev/tty entry), then merges this with the /etc/ttytype file, sending the results to the printer. This is useful to compare the actual tty devices with entries in the /etc/ttytype file.

See also

cat, grep, fgrep, lp, paste, more, pg

ps

Reports the status of processes. Because processes rapidly progress in their execution path, this report is only a snapshot view of what was happening when you asked. A subsequent invocation of ps can give quite different results.

Syntax

ps [*flags*]

Flags

No options shows you a picture of the currently executing processes on your terminal. The following columns are reported:

Column	Description
PID	The process id number used by the kernel to keep track of the process.
TTY	The terminal with which the process is associated.
TIME	The accumulated time spent running the process (CPU time, not wall-clock time).
CMD	The name of the process running.
-e	Shows status of every process.
-d	Shows the status of all processes, except group leaders.

(continues)

Column	Description
-f	Gives a full listing. A full listing gives you the user name that invoked the process, and also shows you the original command line used to invoke the process. If ps can't get the command line information, it places the name of the process in square brackets [ ]. The following also are shown:

<table>
<tr><td></td><td>PPID</td><td>The process id of the process that invoked this process (the parent process).</td></tr>
<tr><td></td><td>C</td><td>Used for scheduling purposes.</td></tr>
<tr><td></td><td>STIME</td><td>The time when the process started.</td></tr>
</table>

Column	Description
-l	Gives you a long listing. This gives you a snapshot of the following:

<table>
<tr><td></td><td>F</td><td>The status flag of the process (01=in core, 10=being swapped).</td></tr>
<tr><td></td><td>S</td><td>The state of the process (S=sleeping, R=running, Z=terminated, B=waiting).</td></tr>
<tr><td></td><td>PRI</td><td>The current priority of a process. The lower the number, the higher the priority. If a process's priority is less than around 24, it usually means the process is in the kernel, and signals can't be caught. Thus, a kill has no effect until its priority is lowered (unkillable process).</td></tr>
<tr><td></td><td>NI</td><td>The nice factor used in scheduling.</td></tr>
<tr><td></td><td>ADDR1
ADDR2</td><td>The address in memory or disk of the process.</td></tr>
<tr><td></td><td>SZ</td><td>The size of the process's user area. This does not include the size of the text portion.</td></tr>
<tr><td></td><td>WCHAN</td><td>The kernel event for which the process is waiting.</td></tr>
</table>

Column	Description
-t*ttys*	Reports the status of the process associated with the terminals listed in *ttys*. *ttys* can be comma-delimited or space-delimited and enclosed in quotation marks. (You do not need the tty portion of the tty name.)
-p*pids*	Reports the status of the processes with pid numbers of *pids*. *pids* uses the same format as *ttys*.
-u*users*	Reports the status of the processes invoked by the users in the list *users*. *users* uses the same format as *ttys*.
-g*glist*	Reports the status of the processes whose group leaders are in the list *glist*. *glist* uses the same format as *ttys*.

Message

```
ps: illegal option
```

You gave ps a flag that it doesn't understand.

Examples

```
ps
```

Shows you the processes running on your terminal.

```
ps -t01,02
```

Shows the processes running on the terminals tty01 and tty02.

```
ps -usue
```

Shows you what process sue is running.

```
ps -elf ¦ more
```

Shows you everything ps can show you. Pipe the output through more, so that it doesn't race across your screen.

Note

The -t and -u options are particularly useful for system administrators who have to kill processes that have gone astray.

See also

kill, nice, more, w, who, whodo

ptar

Purpose

Creates portable tar output to conform with the Archive/Interchange File Format specifications in IEEE Std. 1003.1-1988. ptar, the *p*ortable *t*ape *ar*chiver, creates archives of the file system.

Syntax

```
ptar -action[flags] flag-args filelist
```

IX

Command Reference

Argument or Option	Description
`-action`	Specifies what action to take on the archive. `action` can be one of the following: c Creates a new archive, or overwrites an existing one. r Writes the files named in `filelist` to the end of the archive. t Gives a table of contents of the archive. u Updates the archive. Adds the files named in `filelist` to the end of the archive if they aren't found in the archive or if they have been modified since the last write (can take quite a bit of time). x Extracts the files named in `filelist`.
`filelist`	The list of files to manipulate, can contain wild cards (see warning below). If `filelist` is a directory, that directory is recursively traversed and matches all files within that directory's substructure.
`flag-args`	When a flag requires an argument, the arguments are delayed until after all flags are specified. The arguments are listed on the command line in the same order as the flags.

Flags

Argument or Option	Description
`-b`	Specifies the blocking factor. Can be any integer between 1 and 20. The default is 1. You should use this only with raw tape/floppy devices. Requires an argument.
`-f`	Specifies the file name to use as the archive. Can be a regular file or a special character device (`/dev/rfd096ds15` for a high-density floppy). If `-` is used, standard input is read from or written to, depending on the action specified. (You cannot pipe a `filelist` to `ptar` as with `cpio`, or `pcpio`.) Requires an argument.
`-l`	Tells `ptar` to display a warning if it can't resolve all links to a file. Normally, `ptar` is silent about archiving a set of files when not all links are specified. Used only with `-c`, `-r`, and `-u` actions.
`-m`	Tells `ptar` to set the modification time to that of the time of extraction. Normally, `ptar` sets the modification time to that stored on the archive. Not valid with the `-t` action.

Argument or Option	Description
-o	Sets the user and group ids to that of the user extracting from the archive, as opposed to that stored on the archive. Used only with the -x action.
-v	Places ptar into verbose mode. That is, the file names appear on the terminal as ptar processes them. When used with the -t option, ptar gives you a listing similar to the long listing of the ls command.
-w	Causes ptar to wait for you to respond with a y or an n before taking action on the file. Any response starting with the letter y means yes, and any other response means no. Not valid with the -t action.

Rules

When listing the file names, you must be careful to use absolute or relative path names. Files are extracted from the archive in the same way they were created. Furthermore, if you request only a single file to be extracted, you must specify that file name on the command line the same way it was created. For example, suppose you created an archive using the following:

```
ptar -cvf /dev/rfd096ds15 /usr/frank
```

This created an archive of all files in the directory hierarchy /usr/frank. If you want to get back a file called letters-to-mom, you must enter the following:

```
ptar -xf /dev/rfd096ds15 /usr/frank/letters-to-mom
```

If you had specified letters-to-mom in the *filelist*, ptar could not have found the file.

Messages

```
ptar: tape write error
```

Means one of two things: you don't have a floppy disk or tape in the drive, or you have filled up the floppy disk or tape.

```
ptar: tape read error
```

Means you don't have a floppy/tape in the drive.

```
ptar: directory checksum error
```

Means one of two things: you specified the wrong media type for the floppy disk or tape drive, or the tape needs to be rewound. Specifying the wrong media type is a common error. Users have been known to place a 360K floppy disk in the drive and attempt to access it with the /dev/rfd096ds15 device.

Examples

```
ptar -cvf /dev/rfd096ds15 .
```

Creates an archive on the high-density floppy drive of the current directory showing all file names it encounters.

```
ptar -xvf /dev/rfd096ds15
```

Extracts all files found on the floppy and shows the file names it encounters.

```
ptar -cvbf 20 /dev/rfd096ds15 /usr/frank
```

Demonstrates the syntax involved when combining flags that require arguments. It creates an archive of frank's home directory using a blocking factor of 20 and places the archive on the high-density floppy.

```
ptar -cf - /usr/frank ¦ wc -c
```

The value of this particular command is questionable. However, it shows how to use the - to send the output to standard output. It creates an archive of frank's home directory and pipes the output through wc to get a count of the characters. You can use this command to find out how big the archive is.

Caution

Special devices are not placed on the archive.

You can use wild cards in *filelist*. However, the ptar command doesn't do any wild-card expansion. The shell does the expansion and passes the result to ptar. This can be a problem for novice users who have deleted files and then want to extract them from the archive. Because the file doesn't exist on the file system, the shell can't expand the wild cards to match the nonexistent files. To illustrate, suppose you have a series of files that all end with the letters .ltr. You can create an archive of the whole directory using the following command:

```
ptar -cf /dev/rfd096ds15 .
```

After realizing that you messed up all files ending with .ltr, you can extract them from the archive:

```
ptar -xf /dev/rfd096ds15 *.lst
```

This restores the fouled .ltr files. However, if the files are deleted, then ptar doesn't find any files to extract. It cannot find any more than the following ls command does.

```
ls *.ltr
```

If the files are deleted, you have to specify each one in full without the use of wild cards. Alternatively, you can use a prepass with the -t option redirected to a file.

```
ptar -tf /dev/rfd096ds15 >list.tmp
```

Use the following to retrieve all files ending in .lst:

```
ptar -xf /dev/rfd096ds15 'grep ".lst$" list.tmp'
```

See also

tar, cpio, pcpio, backup, restore, xbackup, xrestore, ls, wc, grep

purge

Purges files by overwriting them. Because removing files with the rm command doesn't actually change the magnetic image on the disks and tapes, it is still possible to get to the data. This command can be useful when dealing with sensitive data, especially on portable media such as floppy disks and tapes.

Syntax

```
purge [flags] filelist
```

Argument or Option	Description
filelist	A space-delimited list of files to purge. These can be regular files, directories, or special character files.

Flags

Argument or Option	Description
-f	Causes purge to not complain about files that do not exist or on which you do not have sufficient permissions. (A floppy disk or tape not in its drive still generates an error message.)
-r	Recursively traverses any directories specified, and purges all files encountered.
-v	Verbose mode.
-mint	Causes multiple passes. int specifies the number of passes (any integer). The first pass always writes binary zeros. Subsequent passes alternate between binary ones and zeros.

Example

```
purge /dev/rfd096ds15
```

Writes binary zeros to the high-density floppy drive.

pwd

Reports your present working or current directory.

Syntax

```
pwd
```

Messages

```
Cannot open ..

Read error in ..
```

The two previous messages indicate a problem with the file system. Contact a system administrator.

Example

```
pwd
```

Shows the current directory in which you are working.

See also

```
cd
```

rm

Removes files and entire directory structures from the file system.

Syntax

```
rm [flags] filelist
```

Argument or Option	Description
filelist	A space-delimited list of files you want to delete. It can contain directory names as well.

Flags

Argument or Option	Description
-r	Deletes the directories specified in *filelist*. Directories are not deleted unless this flag is used. -r can only delete as many as 17 levels of subdirectories.
-i	Specifies interactive mode. You are prompted for confirmation before the removal takes place. Any response beginning with a Y indicates yes; all others indicate no.
-f	Specifies forced mode. Normally, rm prompts you if you don't have permissions to delete the file. This flag forces the remove without your involvement.
--	Indicates the end of all options. Useful if you have to delete a file name that is the same as one of the options. For example, suppose a file named -f was created by accident and you want to delete it. The command, rm -f does not accomplish anything because the -f is interpreted as a flag and not the file name. The command rm -- -f, however, successfully removes the file.

Messages

```
rm: filename nonexistent
```

You tried to remove a file that doesn't exist. *filename* is substituted with the file name you supplied.

```
rm: illegal option -- ?
```

You supplied rm with an option it didn't understand. It can be that you are trying to delete a file that starts with a -. See the -- flag.

Examples

```
rm letter-to-dad
```

Deletes the file named letter-to-dad.

```
rm -r oldletters
```

In this example, oldletters is a directory. This deletes all the files in this directory substructure.

```
rm -i sue*
```

Prompts you each time it encounters a file starting with the letters sue to see if the file should be deleted.

See also

rmdir, mv, cp, ln, copy, purge

rmdir

Removes directories.

Syntax

```
rmdir -p -s dirlist
```

Argument or Option	Description
-p	Causes rmdir to delete any parent directories that also become empty after deleting the directories specified in *dirlist*. A status message as to what is and is not deleted is displayed.
-s	Suppresses the messages when the -p option is active.
dirlist	A space-delimited list of directory names. Directories must be empty to be deleted.

Notes

If the sticky bit is set on a directory, the directory is deleted only if at least one of the following is true:

■ The parent directory is owned by the user.

■ The user owns the directory in *dirlist*.

■ The user has write permissions to the directory in *dirlist*.

■ The user is the super user (root).

Messages

```
rmdir: dirname non-existent
```

The directory you tried to remove doesn't exist.

```
    rmdir: dirname not a directory
```

You used rmdir on a file name that isn't a directory.

```
    rmdir: dirname not empty
```

You tried to delete a directory that still contains some files.

Example

```
    rmdir letters.1970
```

Deletes a directory that used to hold some old letters.

See also

rm

sdiff

Runs diff with the files compared side by side. This command can be extremely useful when comparing two versions of a file because the output is easier to read than that of regular diff.

Syntax

```
    sdiff [flags] file1 file2
```

Argument or Option	Description
file1	The file in the left column of the output.
file2	The file in the right column of the output.

Flags

Argument or Option	Description
-wwidth	Specifies the output line is to be width characters. The default is 130.
-l	When lines are identical, they appear only on the left side.
-s	Suppresses the lines that are identical.

(continues)

IX

Command Reference

Argument or Option	Description
`-ofilename`	Enables you to merge the two files into a third file specified by `filename`. `sdiff` prompts with a % after displaying the set of differences. Identical lines are automatically copied to `filename`. Valid responses to the % prompt include:

l	Use the left column to append to `filename`.
r	Use the right column to append to `filename`.
s	Silent mode, doesn't print identical lines.
v	Turn off silent mode.
e l	Invokes ed with the left column.
e r	Invokes ed with the right column.
e b	Invokes ed with both columns.
e	Invokes ed with neither column.
q	Exits `sdiff`.

Changes made in the editor are transferred to `filename`.

Rules

The output has three columns. The left column is `file1`, the right column is `file2`, and the middle column is one of the following:

Symbol	Meaning
	No symbol, a space, means the lines are identical.
<	These lines are found only in `file1`.
>	These lines are found only in `file2`.
¦	These lines are different.

Messages

```
sdiff: cannot open: filename
```

You supplied `sdiff` with a file name, `filename`, that doesn't exist.

```
sdiff: Illegal argument: arg
```

You supplied `sdiff` with an argument, `arg`, that it doesn't understand.

Example

```
sdiff letter-to-mom letter.bak
```

Compares the two files: letter-to-mom and letter.bak.

See also

diff, diff3, ed

setcolor

Sets various color attributes on the system console. This allows applications written without any color support to appear as if they have color support. It also enables you to set the characteristics of the bell and the cursor.

Syntax

```
setcolor [flags] color1 color2

setcolor -p pitch duration

setcolor -c first last
```

Argument or Option	Description
color1	The first color argument.
color2	A second color argument for the flags that accept it.
-p	Defines how the bell character (^G) acts.
pitch	Sets the pitch (microseconds).
duration	Sets the duration of the bell (fifths of a second).
first	The first scan line of the cursor.
last	The last scan line of the cursor.

Flags

The absence of a flag accepts color1 as the foreground color, and an optional color2 as the background color.

Argument or Option	Description
-n	Sets the screen to "normal." This takes no color arguments, and sets the screen back to a white foreground and a black background.
-b	Sets the screen's background color to *color1*.
-r	Sets the screen's reverse video foreground color to *color1* and the background reverse video color as *color2*.
-g	Same as -r, except for the graphics characters.
-o	Sets the border to *color1*.

Rules

color1 and *color2* can be any of the following:

blue	magenta	brown	black
lt_blue	lt_magenta	yellow	gray
cyan	white	green	red
lt_cyan	hi_white	lt_green	lt_red

setcolor works only on consoles that support color. The effect of invoking this utility on any other terminal is undefined. Serious damage isn't a real threat, but some really messed-up terminal settings can result.

Messages

```
setcolor: Invalid color name
```

You supplied setcolor with a color that is not listed in the table, or you didn't supply a color when one was required.

```
setcolor: Unrecognized option
```

You supplied setcolor with a flag that is not in the list.

Examples

```
setcolor brown black
```

Sets the console's foreground color to brown and its background color to black; makes the console look very much like an amber terminal.

```
setcolor -r red white
```

Sets the reverse foreground to red and the characters to white.

Notes

Invoking setcolor with no options at all gives a usage clause and displays the color table.

The output of setcolor can be redirected to a tty device. In this way, colors are set inside shell scripts for different applications.

If you type the following at the console, all possible combinations of foreground and background color appear.

```
for i in blue lt_blue cyan lt_cyan magenta lt_magenta \
        white hi_white brown yellow green lt_green \
        black gray red lt_red
do
    for j in blue lt_blue cyan lt_cyan magenta \
             lt_magenta white hi_white brown yellow \
             green lt_green black gray red lt_red
    do
    if [ $i = $j ]
        then
        continue
    fi
    setcolor $i $j
    echo "This is $i foreground and $j background"
    echo "Press enter \c"
    read yn
    done
done
```

Caution

It may be wise not to use the second and fourth command lines. I have experienced instances where, when these colors are used and the application sends the sequence to bold, the characters and the screen misbehave. The screen may start flashing or some other strange behavior can occur. The second line is the bold of the first, the fourth line is the bold of the third, and so on. It seems that the bold of something bolded isn't defined.

sh

sh starts the Bourne shell. The Bourne shell is one of many command interpreters available under UNIX. A shell's job is to take the command line you enter, check its syntax, parse it, and pass it to the kernel in a manner the kernel can understand. sh also is a programming language of sorts; it provides all the control structures found in most high-level languages. It lacks, however, floating-point math, and robust file-reading tools.

Because sh is such a powerful utility, only the basics are discussed here.

Syntax

```
sh [flags] args
```

Argument or Option	Description
args	What you supply for args varies based on what flags you supplied. The common usage is the name of a shell script, or the name of a shell script and arguments to that script.

Messages

```
-c: bad option(s)
```

You invoked a shell with an option it didn't understand. c is replaced with the bad option.

```
script: script: cannot open
```

You asked sh to run a script that doesn't exist, or you don't have permission to read the file.

Examples

```
sh
```

Invokes a new shell. You can now work in this shell, changing directories, setting environment variables, and so on. When you return to the original shell by pressing Ctrl-d or typing exit, you are returned to the directory from which you started the new shell, and any environment variables you changed are returned to their former values. Applications sometimes let you run a UNIX command from the application. Entering sh as the command gives you a subshell to work in, letting you enter an entire series of commands.

```
sh install.prog
```

Runs an installation script.

```
EDITOR=/usr/bin/emacs; export EDITOR
```

Sets the environment variable EDITOR to a popular public domain editor called Micro-Emacs. Applications can access variables, such as EDITOR and alter their behavior based on the variables' values.

```
while :
do
format /dev/rdsk/5h
done
```

This is a bit more tricky. A common task is to format floppies, but no one wants to type in the `format` command repeatedly. You can use the programming capabilities of `sh` by using a `while` loop. The commands listed on the lines between `do` and `done` are executed as long as the last line in between `while` and `do` returns a zero value. `:` always returns zero value, so this loop executes forever. When you're done formatting all the disks, press the interrupt key (usually the Delete key on the console).

```
while :
do
echo "Next floppy? \c"
read yn
tar xvf /dev/rdsk/5h
done
```

A more complex example introduces the `echo` and `read` commands of `sh`. This example is useful when the software product you just bought has a bunch of floppy disks that have to be extracted, and you have to complete the repetitive task of typing `tar` as many as 20 times. `echo` prompts the on-screen message of Next Floppy without moving the cursor to the next line (`\c`). The `read` command pauses for you to enter something and stores the result in the made-up variable yn. Simply pressing enter at the prompt causes `tar` to begin extracting the files. When you're done, you can press the interrupt key.

See also

csh, cd, env, tar

shutdown

UNIX is an operating system which has to be told that you want to turn it off. You can't just turn off the power on a UNIX system; well you can, but you're going to wish you hadn't. `shutdown` lets you control when the shutdown will take place, and it notifies the users on a regular basis. `shutdown` safely brings the system to a point where the power can be turned off.

Syntax

```
shutdown [flags] su
```

Argument or Option	Description
su	After the system goes through the shutdown process, it enters single-user mode without completely shutting down the system.

Flags

Argument or Option	Description
-y	Without this flag set, shutdown prompts you if you want to shut the system down. This forces a yes response to that question, and you are not asked if you want to shut down.
-g*time*	Specifies the grace period before the shutdown occurs. *time* is expressed as *hh:mm* where *hh* is the number of hours, and *mm* is the number of minutes to wait before shutting down.
-f*mesg*	Specifies the message to write to the users' terminals that the system will be shutting down. *mesg* must be enclosed in double quotation marks (-f"shutdown soon").
-F*mesgfile*	Specifies that the message to send to the users' terminals is found in the file *mesgfile*.

Note

shutdown can be run only by the super user. Messages are sent to the users' terminals at intervals based on the amount of time left until the shutdown. The following table shows this:

Time Remaining	Message Sent Every...
More than 1 hour	hour
More than 15 minutes	15 minutes
More than 1 minute	minute

Messages

    shutdown: not found

If you get this message, it is probably because /etc isn't in your search path (PATH), which means you probably aren't the super user. You can't run shutdown unless you are the super user.

    device busy

Part of the shutdown process is to unmount all the file systems. If a file system is still in use at the time of the shutdown, then umount complains. This situation arises if a user ignored the messages about the shutdown and was using one of the mounted file systems.

Examples

```
shutdown
```

Using this command is the simplest way to invoke shutdown. With this approach, shutdown prompts you to see if you really wanted to shut down. It then asks for the grace period and whether you want to send a message other than the default.

```
shutdown -y -g1: -F/etc/shutdown.msg su
```

This line tells shutdown not to prompt for confirmation on the shutdown that will take place in one hour. shutdown sends the contents of the file /etc /shutdown.msg to all the users logged on the system. When the hour is up, the system will go through the shutdown process and go to single-user mode.

See also

wall, haltsys, reboot

sleep

Suspends execution for an interval of time.

Syntax

```
sleep seconds
```

Argument or Option	Description
seconds	Specifies the number of seconds to sleep. This must be an integer.

Note

sleep is not guaranteed to wake up exactly the number of seconds specified.

Example

```
while :
do
    date
    sleep 60
done
```

Shows the date every 60 seconds.

sort

Enables you to sort and merge text files. Sorts can be based on character fields or numeric fields, and multiple sort keys can be specified.

Syntax

```
sort [flags] files
```

Argument or Option	Description
files	An optional list of files to be sorted or merged. If no files are specified or - is used as the file name, then the standard input is read.

Flags

Argument or Option	Description
-c	Checks to see if the files are sorted. If they are, then no output is generated.
-m	Merges the specified files. It is assumed that the files are already sorted.
-u	Makes sure only unique lines go to the output. The uniqueness of a line is based on the sort keys.
-o*file*	Specifies the output file name. This can be the same as one of the input file names. Normally, the output of sort is the standard output.
-yk*mem*	The amount of memory, expressed in kilobytes, to use for the sort area. Normally, sort grows in memory size to satisfy its needs. This flag can specify an amount known to be optimal for this sort.
-z*reclen*	The length of the longest line of the output. Normally, sort determines the longest line while sorting the input files. However, the -m and -c options may need the *reclen* to avoid abnormal termination.
-d	Sorts in dictionary order. Only letters, digits, and blanks are used for ordering.
-f	"Folds," or changes, lowercase letters to uppercase for sort purposes.
-i	Ignores nonprintable characters in the sort keys.
-M	Treats sort key as if it was a month. JAN less than FEB that is less than MAR, and so on.

Argument or Option	Description
-n	Specifies a key is a numeric key; implies the -b flag.
-r	Reverses the sort (descending).
-t*fld-sep*	Specifies that the field separator is the character *fld-sep*, not tabs or blanks.
-b	Ignores leading blanks when determining the value of the sort keys.
+*keybeg*	Specifies that the sort key starts at field number *keybeg*. Fields start counting at zero; the fifth field is a 4. *keybeg* accepts the format M.NF, where M is the field number and N is the character offset within that field. The absence of .N assumes zero. F can be any of the following flags: b, d, f, i, n, or r, which have the same meanings as described previously except that they apply only to this key.
-*keyend*	Specifies on what field number the key ends, and follows the same format rules of +*keybeg*. If no ending field number is specified, the end of the line is assumed.

Notes

When multiple keys are used, the keys specified later in the command line are compared when the earlier ones are equal. For example:

```
sort +2 -3  +5 -6
```

the key defined by character positions 5, -6 are compared only when the key defined by positions 2, -3 does not define a uniq record. All comparisons are governed by the locale of the system; this allows support for international usage.

Because sort distinguishes records by looking for the newline character, the command is not suitable for binary files.

Messages

```
sort: invalid use of command line options
```

You specified a flag that sort doesn't understand.

```
sort: can't open filename
```

You specified a file name that doesn't exist.

IX

Command Reference

```
sort: can't create filename
```

You specified the -o option with a file name in a directory for which you don't have permission to write, or the file name exists and you don't have write permission.

Examples

```
ps -e ¦ sort
```

Because the first column of ps is the PID number, this gives you the processes running on the system in PID order.

```
ps -e ¦ sort +3
```

Because the last column of ps is the name of the command, this gives a list of the processes running by command name.

```
ps -e ¦ sort -u +3
```

Strips out any duplicate process names.

```
ps -e ¦ sort -r +2 -3
```

The third column is the CPU time the process has had. This reverses the sort, pushing the CPU hogs at the top.

See also

uniq, join, ps

spell

Checks spelling of a text file. An option to add and remove words from the dictionary also exists.

Syntax

```
spell [flags] +userdict filelist
```

Argument or Option	Description
+userdict	A file containing a list of words that, although not found in the system dictionary, should be considered correctly spelled. userdict should have one word per line.
filelist	The files to read and spell check. If no files are specified, spell reads from the standard input.

Message

```
cat: cannot open myfile: No such file or directory
```

This message means you tried to spell check the file myfile and that the file did not exist.

Flags

Argument or Option	Description
-v	All words not literally in the dictionary appear along with a list of possible spellings.
-b	Use the British dictionary.
-l	spell supports the troff macros .so and .nx. These are used to chain files together to create a complete document. Normally, spell does not follow the path if the path name begins with /usr/lib. The -l causes spell to look at these files as well.
-i	Causes spell to ignore all chaining requests.

Example

```
spell letter-to-mom
```

Examines the file letter-to-mom and displays the misspelled words.

split

Breaks up a text file into smaller pieces. Periodically, files become too large to load into an editor or some other utility. split lets you handle the file in more manageable pieces.

Syntax

```
split -numlines file tagname
```

Argument or Option	Description
-numlines	Specifies the number of lines to include in each piece.
file	The file to split into smaller pieces. If left blank or - is used, then standard input is read.
tagname	By default, split builds the output pieces by creating the following files: xaa, then xab, then xac, and so on. tagname, if specified, replaces the x in the previous list, thus building the list: tagnameaa, tagnameab, tagnameac, and so on.

Note

There must be enough room for two copies of the file in the current file system.

Message

```
cannot open input
```

You supplied `split` with a file name that doesn't exist.

Examples

```
split -1000 letter-to-dad dadletter
```

Apparently the previous `letter-to-dad` was a large one. This line breaks up that letter into 1,000 line pieces. The output files are `dadletteraa`, `dadletterab`, and so on.

```
cat dadletter* >letter-to-dad
```

Takes all pieces and puts them back together again into the file `letter-to-dad`.

See also

```
cat
```

strings

Extracts the printable strings from an object module.

Syntax

```
strings [flags] filelist
```

Argument or Option	Description
filelist	A space-separated list of file names to be examined for strings.

Flags

Argument or Option	Description
-	Normally, `strings` examines only the initialized data space of an object file. - tells `strings` to examine the entire file.

Argument or Option	Description
-o	Shows the byte offset in the file where the string is found.
-number	Normally, the length of a valid string is four printable characters in a row. This option allows you to control the minimum length of a string.

Example

```
strings /bin/ls
```

Shows all strings in the program ls.

See also

od, hd

stty

Sets the terminal device driver line controls. stty provides many options to control the tty driver. You can set the character size, parity, baud rate, input preprocessing of special characters, and output processing of special characters.

Syntax

```
stty -a -g settings
```

Argument or Option	Description
-a	Shows all current settings of the currently logged on terminal. Normally, stty gives a reduced version of all the settings. stty actually reads from the terminal driver. So, if you want to see what the terminal settings are for another tty, just redirect the input to stty (see the example that follows).
-g	Like -a, but produces 12 hexadecimal numbers separated by colons. This output is suitable for input to stty.
settings	The settings can either be the output of a previous -g flag, or a series of stty commands.

IX

Command Reference

Note

It is important to understand that stty changes how the system's tty driver behaves in reference to what your terminal is physically set to. There are two ends to having a terminal communicate: the physical settings on the device, and how the system thinks it should talk to the device. If these aren't equal, then the communication breaks down. stty only affects how the system thinks the device is talking. You use stty to enable the system to talk to tty devices with varying communication needs.

•

Message

```
/dev/console: cannot open
```

You tried to manipulate a port for which you don't have permission.

Examples

```
stty -a
```

Shows all the settings on this tty.

```
stty -a </dev/tty02
```

Shows all the settings on the second console.

```
(^-J)stty sane(^-J)
```

Occasionally a program crashes, leaving your terminal in a state in which it doesn't seem to be accepting your input. In this case, entering the preceding command returns your terminal to a usable state. Note that the notation (Ctrl-j) indicates that you hold down the Control key while pressing the J key. Do not type in the parentheses or the Enter key.

su

Substitutes another user id for yours. Enables you to become someone else on the system so that you can access his or her files; you need to know his or her password to do this. su is commonly used to become the super user (root).

Syntax

```
su - user arguments
```

Argument or Option	Description
-	Logs you on as this user, running through /etc /profile and her .profile file.

Argument or Option	Description
`user`	The user you want to become. If left blank, `root` is assumed.
`arguments`	Any arguments specified are passed to the program invoked by the shell. A common use is to specify `-c` followed by a command to execute. Runs that command as if you were that user and then returns. You become that user only for the time it takes to execute the command.

Rule

The super user can change to any other user without having that person's password, but if you wanted to change to another user you would need his or her password.

Messages

```
Unknown id: baduserid
```

You asked to become a user that doesn't exist on your system. *baduserid* is replaced by the user you tried to become.

```
Sorry
```

You did not enter the correct password when prompted.

Example

```
su - frank
```

You become the user `frank` and go through the login process as if you had logged on as `frank`.

```
su - accounting -c "close-month"
```

Here you become the accounting user to run a program called "close-month."

swconfig

Lists the software packages installed with the custom utility.

Syntax

```
swconfig -a -p
```

IX

Command Reference

Argument or Option	Description
-a	Shows all information available; a more extensive listing.
-p	Shows the software packages.

Examples

```
swconfig
```

Gives you a concise report of the applications installed, the release number, and indicates whether the application is installed.

```
swconfig -a
```

Gives a much more thorough report.

See also

custom, hwconfig

sync

Writes the current disk image held in the system's disk I/O buffers to the hard disk. You have to make sure that the buffers are written before you shut the machine down; otherwise, the disk does not have a correct image of the information written to it. However, because both shutdown and haltsys do a sync, the need to use sync is limited.

Syntax

```
sync
```

Example

```
sync
```

Causes the system disk buffers to be written.

See also

haltsys, shutdown

tabs

Sets the tab stops on the terminal.

Syntax

```
tabs tabstops -Tterm +mlmrgn
```

Flags

Argument or Option	Description
-Tterm	Specifies what terminal type obtains the codes used to program the terminal's tab stops. If term isn't specified, the environment variable TERM is used.
+mlmrgn	Specifies the left margin. tabstops is expressed relative to lmrgn.
tabstops	Specifies the tab stops; can have any of the following four constructs:

	-code	A predefined set of common programming languages' conventional tab settings. If you don't use these languages or don't like the settings, this option isn't very helpful. See your reference guide for specifics.
	-every-n	Makes the tab stop every-n + 1 characters.
	-list	A comma-separated list of tab stops. If a number other than the first one is preceded by a plus sign (+), the number is considered an increment of the first.
	—file	Specifies that the tab stops are in file file and conforms to the rules outlined in fspec(F).

Rule

The terminal must support host-set tab stops.

Messages

```
illegal tabs
```

You used the *list* form to specify the tab stops, and this list is not in the correct order.

```
illegal increment
```

Message appears if, using the *list* form, you did not specify the increment value correctly.

```
unknown tab code
```

You attempted to specify a predefined tab stop that doesn't exist.

Examples

```
tabs -4
```

Sets the tab stops at 5, 9, 13, 17, and so on.

```
tabs 1,5,9,13,17
```

Performs the same action as the previous command for the first five tab stops.

```
tabs 1,+4
```

Accomplishes the same thing as the previous command.

tail

Enables you to view the end of a text file or track the growth of a text file.

Syntax

```
tail beg-offset -f file
```

Argument or Option	Description
beg-offset	The offset within the file to begin viewing. If beg-offset is preceded with a -, then the offset is relative to the end of the file. If a + is used, then the offset is relative to the beginning of the file. The following qualifiers can be used to specify beg-offset's unit of measure: b The offset is expressed in blocks. l The offset is expressed in lines; this is the default. c The offset is expressed in characters. If beg-offset is left blank, then 10 lines are assumed.
-f	When this option is used, and the input is not standard input, tail monitors the growth of the file. This is an endless loop of output and has to be terminated with the interrupt key.
file	The name of the file of which you want to view the end, or track its growth. If file is left blank, the standard input is used.

Message

```
tail: illegal option -- option
```

You tried to invoke tail with an option other than -f.

Examples

```
tail letter-to-dad
```

Looks at the final 10 lines of letter-to-dad.

```
tail -10c letter-to-dad
```

Looks at the last 10 characters of letter-to-dad.

```
tail +10 letter-to-dad
```

Begins showing letter-to-dad after the first 10 lines are read.

```
tail -f growing-file ¦ more
```

Assuming a file called growing-file was built by some other process, this shows you what is built so far and what is generated on an ongoing basis. Pipe the output through the pager more in case it generates too fast to view on-screen.

See also

more, pg

tar

Used to create tape archives (backups of your file system) or saves and restores files to and from an archive medium.

Syntax

```
tar action[flags] flag-args filelist
```

Argument or Option	Description
action	Specifies what action to take on the archive. action can be one of the following:
	c Creates a new archive, or overwrites an existing one.
	r Writes the files named in filelist to the end of the archive, appending the existing archive.
	t Gives a table of contents of the archive.
	u Updates the archive. Adds the files named in filelist to the end of the archive if they aren't found in the archive or they have been modified since the last write. (Can take quite a bit of time.)
	x Extracts the files or directories named in filelist.

(continues)

IX

Command Reference

Argument or Option	Description
filelist	The list of files to manipulate can contain wild cards (see Caution later in this entry). If *filelist* is a directory, then that directory is recursively traversed matching all files within that directory's substructure.
flag-args	When a flag requires an argument, the arguments are delayed until after all the flags have been specified. Then the arguments are listed on the command line in the same order as the flags.

Flags

Argument or Option	Description
key	A number between 0 and 9999. This number is a key to the file /etc/default/tar that specifies default options for the device name, blocking factor, device size, and whether the device is a tape.
b	Specifies the blocking factor. Can be any integer between 1 and 20. The default is 1. Use this only with raw tape/floppy devices. Requires an argument.
f	Specifies the file name to be used as the archive. Can be a regular file or a special character device (for example, /dev/rdsk/5h for a high-density floppy). If - is used, then standard input is read from or written to depending on the action specified. (You cannot pipe a *filelist* to tar as with cpio or pcpio.) Requires an argument.
l	Tells tar to display an error message if it can't resolve all the links to a file. Normally, tar is silent about archiving a set of files when not all the links are specified. Used only with the c, r, and u actions
m	Tells tar not to restore the modification times. The modification time is the time of extraction.
v	Places tar into verbose mode. The file names are displayed on the terminal as tar processes them. When used with the t option, tar gives you a listing similar to the long listing of the ls command.
w	Causes tar to wait for you to respond with a Y or an N before taking action on the file. Actually, any response starting with the letter Y means yes, and any other response means no. Not valid with the t action.
F	The next argument is a file that holds a list of files to be manipulated.

Argument or Option	Description
k	The next argument is the size in kilobytes of the device. This enables tar to know when it has filled up the device and when it has to prompt for the next media.
n	This tells tar that the device is not a tape drive. For floppy devices, this allows tar to seek the files it wants.
A	Changes all absolute file names to relative file names.

Notes

When listing the file names, you have to be sure you use absolute or relative path names. Files are extracted from the archive in the same way they were created. Furthermore, if you request only a single file to be extracted, you must specify that file name on the command line the same way it was created. For example, suppose you created an archive using the following:

```
tar cvf /dev/rdsk/5h /usr/sue
```

This creates an archive of all the files in the directory hierarchy /usr/sue. If you want to get back a file called letters-to-dad, you have to enter the following:

```
tar xf /dev/rdsk/5h /usr/sue/letters-to-dad
```

If you specify only letters-to-dad in the *filelist*, tar does not find the file.

Messages

```
tar: tape write error
```

This usually means one of several things: you don't have a floppy or tape in the drive; you have filled up the floppy or tape; the tape is write-protected; or you need to clean the drive.

```
tar: tape read error
```

This usually means you don't have a floppy/tape in the drive, the door isn't properly shut to the drive, or you have bad media.

```
tar: directory checksum error
```

This usually means one of two things: you have specified the wrong media type for the floppy or tape drive, or the tape has to be rewound. Specifying the wrong media type is a common error. Users have been known to place a 360K floppy disk in the drive and then access it with the /dev/rdsk/5h device.

IX

Command Reference

Example

```
tar cvf /dev/rdsk/5h .
```

Notes

If no device is specified for `tar`, it uses a default device—usually the floppy drive.

Creates an archive on the high-density floppy drive of the current directory showing all the file names it came across.

```
tar xvf /dev/rdsk/5h
```

Extracts all the files found on the floppy disk, showing you the names of the files it came across.

```
tar cvbf 20 /dev/rdsk/5h /usr/sue
```

Demonstrates the syntax involved when combining flags that require arguments. This line is an example of creating an archive of sue's home directory, using a blocking factor of 20 and placing the archive on the high-density floppy disk.

```
tar cf - /usr/sue ¦ wc -c
```

The value of this particular command is questionable. However, it shows how to use the - to send the output to standard output. An archive of sue's home directory was created, piping the output through wc to get a count of the characters. This tells you how big the archive is.

Caution

Special devices are not placed on the archive.

Wild cards can be used in *filelist*. However, the `tar` command doesn't do any wild-card expansion. The shell does the expansion and passes the result to `tar`. This can be a problem for novice users who have deleted files and then want to extract them from the archive. Because the file doesn't exist on the file system, the shell can't expand the wild cards to match the nonexistent files. To illustrate, suppose you had a series of files that all ended with the letters .ltr. You can create the archive of the entire directory, not just the .ltr files, using the following:

```
tar cf /dev/rdsk/5h
```

After realizing that you messed up all the files ending with .ltr, you can extract them from the archive with the following:

```
tar xf /dev/rdsk/5h *.ltr
```

This then restores the fouled `.ltr` files. However, if the files were deleted, `tar` does not find any files to extract. It does not find anymore than the following `ls` command does.

```
ls *.ltr
```

In a case where the files have been deleted, you have to specify each one in full without the use of wild cards. Alternatively, a pass with the `t` option redirected to a file can be used.

```
tar tf /dev/rdsk/5h >list.tmp
```

Then use the following to get back all the files ending in `.lst`:

```
tar xf /dev/rdsk/5h 'grep ".lst$" list.tmp'
```

See also

tar, cpio, pcpio, backup, restore, xbackup, xrestore ls, wc, grep

tee

Splits the output in a pipeline to one or more files. This enables you to capture what is going to standard output and place that output into a file and still allow the output to flow through standard output.

Syntax

```
tee [flags] filelist
```

Argument or Option	Description
filelist	The space-separated list of files into which you want to capture the output.

Flags

Argument or Option	Description
-i	Causes tee to ignore interrupts.
-a	The files in filelist are appended with the output, rather than overwritten.
-u	The output through tee is unbuffered.

Example

```
l ¦ tee listing ¦ more
```

Places a copy of the file listing generated by l in the file listing, while you view the listing through the pager more.

See also

l, more

test

Most commonly used in if and while statements. if and while are sh control constructs used when programming in the Bourne shell. test returns a zero exit status if what it tested is true.

Syntax

```
test expression

[ expression ]
```

Argument or Option	Description	
expression	This is the expression that test tests. The following can be used to build a valid expression:	
	-r *file*	True if *file* has read permissions.
	-w *file*	True if *file* has write permissions.
	-x *file*	True if *file* has execute permissions.
	-f *file*	True if *file* is a regular file.
	-d *file*	True if *file* is a directory.
	-b *file*	True if *file* exists and is a block special file.
	-c *file*	True if *file* is a block special file.
	-u *file*	True if *file* has the set-user-ID flag set.
	-g *file*	True if *file* has the set-group-ID set.
	-k *file*	True if *file* has the sticky-bit set.
	-s *file*	True if *file* has a files size greater than zero.

Argument or Option	Description
-t *fd*	True if the file with file descriptor *fd* is opened and associated with terminal device. The default *fd* is 1.
-z *str*	True if the length of the string *str* is zero.
-n *str*	True if the length of the string *str* is nonzero.
str1 = *str2*	True if string *str1* equals the string *str2*.
str1 != *str2*	True if string *str1* doesn't equal the string *str2*.
str	True if the string *str* is not a null string.
int1 -eq *int2*	True if the integer *int1* equals the integer *int2*. The following also can be used instead of -eq.
	-ne not equal
	-gt greater than
	-ge greater than or equal
	-lt less than
	-le less than or equal
	! Negates the expression.
	-a A logical AND.
	-o A logical OR.
	( ) Used for grouping.

Note

All the file-oriented tests are false if the file doesn't exist.

Message

```
test: argument expected
```

test was expecting something, and you didn't give it. This can be caused by several factors: you gave it an invalid argument; or quite typically, you were testing an environment variable, and it wasn't set to anything. It didn't expand in the command line and test expected an argument there.

Examples

```
if [ -f letter-to-dad ]
    then
        echo "letter-to-dad exists"
fi
```

Tests to see if the file letter-to-dad exists and is a regular file.

```
if [ -f letter-to-dad -a -f letter-to-mom ]
    then
        echo "both letters written"
fi
```

Tests to see that letter-to-dad and letter-to-mom have been written.

Note

The second form [*expression*] is useful for readability. [is actually a program name found on the file system that is linked to test.

time

Determines how long a program takes to execute.

Syntax

```
time command
```

Argument or Option	Description
command	The command you want to time.

Notes

time reports three different times:

real	The total elapsed time since you invoked the command. This is sometimes referred to as "wall clock" time, because it is the time that has elapsed on the clock on your wall.
user	This is the amount of time actually spent on the CPU outside sys time.
sys	This is the amount of time spent in the kernel; the amount of time spent fulfilling system requests.

The total CPU time is user + sys time. The difference between this and real time is the amount of time the CPU spends on other tasks.

Example

```
time compress letter-to-dad
```

Reports the amount of time it takes to compress the file `letter-to-dad`.

touch

Changes the access and modification times of a file, or creates a new file with specified times.

Syntax

```
touch [flags] MMDDhhmmYY filelist
```

Argument or Option	Description
MMDDhhmmYY	This is the time to which to set the file. The format is as follows:
	MM The month
	DD The day
	hh The hour
	mm The minute
	YY The year
filelist	A space-separated list of the files that you want to have the specified time.

Flags

Argument or Option	Description
-a	The specified time changes the access time of the specified files.
-m	Same as -a, but for modified time.
-c	If a file in *filelist* doesn't exist, then this flag tells touch not to create it.

IX

Command Reference

Note

The flags -am are the default. You cannot modify the creation time of a file. (The term *creation time* is a bit misleading. The creation time is not really the time the file was created, it is better thought of as when the i-node information changed. When the file size changed, the mode changed, the owner changed, and so on.)

Message

```
touch: illegal option -- badoption
```

You tried to specify a flag *badoption* which touch doesn't understand. (*badoption* is substituted with the flag you supplied.)

Examples

```
touch letter-to-dad
```

Sets the modification and access times of letter-to-dad to the current date.

```
touch 0101120191 letter-to-dad
```

Sets the modification and access times of letter-to-dad to 01/01/91 at 12:01 p.m.

See also

date

tr

tr translates or maps characters in a file from one form to another. For example, you can use tr to change all tabs to spaces. This command enables you to do some rather robust character handling with a somewhat simple structure.

Syntax

```
tr [flags] from-string to-string
```

Argument or Option	Description
from-string	This is the string of characters from which to map; the characters you want translated. The following special notations can be used and repeated:
	$[c_1-cn]$ This specifies a range of characters from c_1 to c_n.

Argument or Option	Description
[c*n]	This specifies that character c repeats *n* times. *n* can be zero or left blank, which assumes a huge number of the character c. This is useful for padding the *to-string* (see Note later in this entry).
octal	Specifies the octal value of a character. This is useful for manipulating the nonprintable characters (control characters).
to-string	This is the string of characters to map into; the character to which the *from-string* translates. The special notations noted previously can be used here as well.

Flags

Argument or Option	Description
-c	Normally tr substitutes the characters found in *from-string* with the characters found in *to-string*, with the output showing the original contents of the file with the substitution applied. This option restricts the output to the characters specified in *from-string* and effectively appends the characters in *to-string*.
-d	Deletes the characters specified in *from-string*.
-s	Strips repeated characters generated in the output by those specified in *to-string*, leaving only one of the repeated characters in the output.

Note

The *to-string* must be the same number of characters as the *from-string*.

Message

```
bad string
```

This is usually a case where the number of characters in *from-string* and *to-string* aren't equal.

Examples

```
tr -d "\015\032" <dosfile >unixfile
```

IX

Command Reference

This is one way of translating DOS text files into a format more suitable in UNIX. It deletes the carriage returns and the DOS end-of-file marker (^Z).

```
tr -s "\015\032" "[\012*]" <dosfile >unixfile
```

This is a significantly more complicated way of accomplishing the same task as the previous example. However, it demonstrates two features of tr. In this example, you replace all the carriage returns and end-of-file markers with the UNIX newline character. The -s strips the duplicate newlines, producing only one. *to-string* uses the "padding" option described previously to ensure that the lengths of the two strings are equal.

Note

Enclose *from-string* and *to-string* in quotation marks as shown in the examples to ensure that the special meaning of any characters recognized by the shell is escaped and passed to tr rather than expanded by the shell.

Caution

The range notation can be used with the characters representing the digits as well, such as 0-9. However, such notation refers strictly to the digits themselves and not the value they can represent. You cannot use this to replace all tens with nines, as ten is two digits and nine is only one digit.

See also

ed

true

Returns a zero exit status which in the shell is what means true. This command is useful when programing in the shell to create continuous loops.

Syntax

true

Example

```
while true
do
      format /dev/rdsk/5h
done
```

Formatting floppy disks is one of the rituals of computer use. Rather than typing the format command repeatedly, have the computer do the repetitive work for you. When you're done with the stack of floppy disks, you can just hit the interrupt key at the prompt to kill the loop.

Note

The character : in the Bourne shell gives the same results as `true` and doesn't require the execution of a program.

See also

sh

tty

Reports the currently logged on terminal device name, or tests whether the standard input is a terminal.

Syntax

```
tty -s
```

Argument or Option	Description
-s	This option causes `tty` to test if the standard input is a terminal device or not. No output is generated. The result code is set to zero if standard input is a terminal, one if it is not.

Message

```
not a tty
```

This message displays when you try to invoke `tty`, you haven't used the -s flag, and the standard input is not a terminal.

Examples

```
tty
```

Reports the terminal's device name.

```
if tty -s
    then
        echo "This is a terminal"
fi
```

Tests whether the standard input is a terminal.

umask

Specifies the default permissions of files or reports the current defaults.

Syntax

    umask *mask*

Argument or Option	Description
mask	The mask that is applied when generating the permissions for the files you create. If left blank, umask reports the current setting. *mask* is composed of three digits. The digits represent the permissions for the owner of the file (that's you), the group, and the rest of the world. The mask is called a mask because the value specified is actually masked at the bit level to generate the permissions. However, if you don't think in this way (most people don't), then simply think of mask as the permissions you don't want to give.

0	You don't want to restrict any permissions.
1	You want to restrict execute permissions.
2	You want to restrict write permission.
4	You want to restrict read permissions.

Adding any of these numbers together restricts the combination of the permissions. A 7 restricts all permissions.

Examples

    umask

Reports the current mask setting.

    umask 000

Gives complete access to everyone on the system to every file you create.

    umask 022

Gives you complete permissions on the files you create. However, everyone else is able only to read and execute those files.

    umask 007

Gives you and the people in your group complete permissions and doesn't allow anyone else to do anything.

See also

    chmod

umnt

See mnt.

uname

Reports the system name and other catalogue information.

Syntax

```
uname [flags]
```

Flags

Argument or Option	Description
-s	Reports the system name. This is the default.
-n	Reports the node name of the system. This is used in communications.
-r	Reports the release number of the operating system.
-v	Shows the version number of the operating system.
-m	Reports the machine hardware name.
-a	Reports all the above information, equivalent to -mvrns.

Message

```
uname: illegal option -- badoption
```

You invoked uname with an option it doesn't recognize.

Example

```
uname
```

Reports the system name of the currently logged on machine.

uncompress

See compress.

uniq

Strips out lines that are identical, producing only one unique line.

Syntax

```
uniq [flags] input output
```

Argument or Option	Description
input	The name of the file from which to read; if left blank, the standard input is read.
output	The name of the file to create with the results of the uniq command. If left blank, then standard output is used. If specified, *output* must not be the same as *input*.

Flags

Argument or Option	Description
-u	Causes uniq to output only those lines that aren't repeated.
-d	Causes uniq to output only those lines that were repeated—but only one copy of them.
-c	Produces a report with the left column as the number of times the line repeated and then the line itself.
-fields	When doing the comparison for uniqueness, the first *fields* count of fields is skipped. Fields are separated by tabs or spaces.
+chars	After skipping any specified fields, also skips *chars* number of characters.

Notes

The default operation is to output all the lines in the input file, but with only one copy of any repeated lines.

uniq assumes the input file is already sorted.

Examples

```
who ¦ cut -d" " -f1 ¦ uniq
```

Shows a list of users currently logged on the system; if anyone is logged on more than once, you see them once.

```
who ¦ cut -d" " -f1 ¦ uniq -d
```

This is a slight twist on the previous command. This is an example showing those who logged on more than once.

```
who ¦ cut -d" " -f1 ¦ uniq -u
```

Shows only those who have not logged on more than once.

```
who ¦ cut -d" " -f1 ¦ uniq -c
```

With this command you get a list of each user on the system and a count of the number of times he or she is logged on.

See also

sort

unpack

A companion command to pack. unpack reverses the process of pack, restoring the file to its original form.

Syntax

unpack *filelist*

Argument or Option	Description
filelist	The space-delimited list of files to unpack. You don't have to specify the .z as this is assumed.

Messages

unpack: *filename*.z: cannot open

You've asked unpack to unpack a file that doesn't exist with a .z appended.

unpack: *filename*.z: not it packed format

A filename with .z appended existed, but it is not in packed format. The .z on the end of the file is a coincidence; it didn't mean the file was packed.

Example

unpack letter-to-dad

Apparently you wrote a rather large letter to Dad and had packed it to reduce its storage requirements. This command unpacks it, presumably to modify or print it.

See also

pack

IX

Command Reference

uucp

uucp stands for UNIX-to-UNIX copy. uucp enables you to copy files across a network to another UNIX machine. Typically, this network consists of asynchronous telephone lines.

Syntax

    uucp [*flags*] *source_list destination*

Argument or Option	Description
source_list	A space-separated list of files you want to copy.
destination	The destination name to which you copy. If multiple source files are given, this must be a directory name.

source_list and *destination* can be preceded by an optional machine name followed by a "bang" or exclamation mark (!). The following syntax is valid:

    machine_name!*file_name*

Wild cards (*, ?, and []) are expanded on the appropriate machine. When wild cards are used for the *file_name* on a remote machine, the request is sent and is processed by that machine, and the files are sent later. The actual transfer is not guaranteed to take place at the initial connection.

The special notation of *~user* can be used as part of *file_name*. This tells uucp to look for the file in *user*'s home directory. (For example, uucp mfg!~frank/daily_sales gets the file daily_sales from frank's home directory on the machine mfg and copies it to the current directory of the local machine.) When using this notation for the *destination*, and when *~user* on the remote machine is not accessible by uucp, the file is placed in /usr/spool/uucppublic and the user is notified by way of mail.

The notation of ~/ also can be used as shorthand for /usr/spool/uucppublic.

If a file being transferred is an executable program, then those executable permissions are preserved across the transmission. The owner of the file on the remote machine becomes uucp and the permissions of read and write for owner, group, and other are set.

Flags

Argument or Option	Description
-c	Does not copy the file to be transferred to the spool directory before transferring to the remote machine. This is the default.
-C	Copies the file to the spool directory before transferring. (This option enables you to delete the file from the local system after the uucp request is made.)
-d	Makes all necessary directories for the copy (default).
-f	Does not make the directories.
-ggrade	A single character to prioritize the order of transfer for this request. The lower the ASCII value of grade, the earlier in the connection the request is carried out. (For example, if you had 10 files to transfer, you can give each a different grade to change the order in which they transfer.)
-j	Shows the job number this request is assigned by uucp. This number is suitable for use with uustat to check the status of the job.
-m	Sends mail to you when the copy is completed.
-nuser	Sends mail to the user user on the remote machine when the copy is completed.
-r	Queues up the request, but does not actually start the transfer.
-sfile_name	Logs the status of the transfer to the file file_name.
-xdebug_level	Debugging levels 0-9 are available. Each number gives more detailed debugging information on the status of the connection; 9 gives you the most information.

Rules

uucp can't connect to a remote machine until the following files are properly set up (see your system's administrator's guide for help):

File	Description
/usr/lib/uucp/Devices	The list of valid modem ports on which to dial out.

(continues)

File	Description
/usr/lib/uucp/Systems	The list of machines your machine knows how to call, what modems to use to call, when to call, the phone number to call, and a chat script to send the remote machine's login process.
/usr/lib/uucp/Permissions	The list of machines you now want to call you or send you information if you call them. This contains the list of commands these machines can request your machine to run, the list of directories from which it can read or write, and several other layers of security issues.
/etc/systemid	The name of the local machine for uucp purposes.

If no machine name is given for either the source or destination, then uucp simply uses cp to copy the file locally. You can use uucp and not cp to copy local files.

uucp is a spooled process. That is, uucp takes your requests and executes them for you. You do not have to interact with or watch the file transfer take place. The machine that you want the file from can be called at night to save on phone rates.

Messages

```
can't get status for file /usr/acct/benah/ben
uucp failed partially: 0 file(s) sent; 1 error(s)
```

You tried to copy a file on the local machine that doesn't exist. In this case, that file name is /usr/acct/benah/ben.

```
bad system: frank
uucp failed completely (11)
```

You tried to send a file to, or receive a file from, a machine that doesn't exist in your /usr/lib/uucp/Systems file; in this case, that machine is frank.

```
uucp: illegal option -- Q
unknown flag -Q
```

You tried to give uucp an option flag that uucp doesn't understand; in this example, it is an uppercase Q.

```
usage uucp from ... to
uucp failed completely (2)
```

You didn't give enough arguments; uucp needs both a source and a destination.

Examples

```
uucp -m  -j mfg!~/daily_sales mfg!~/invt_lvl .
```

Calls up the machine mfg and gets two files from /usr/spool/uucppublic: daily_sales and invt_lvl. You are mailed when the transfer is complete and the uucp job number is shown on-screen after you execute the command.

```
uucp -nfrank -m my_file mfg!~frank
```

Gets a file in the current directory called my_file and sends it to frank's home directory if it can be written to by uucp, otherwise it goes to /usr/spool /uucppublic. frank is notified when the file shows up, and you are mailed when the copy is complete.

vi

vi stands for visual ex. vi is the same editor as ex except it is full screen, and you are able to see the changes you make. vi is such a powerful tool that this discussion only provides rudimentary information on vi. If you want to work with vi, consult both the user's guide and user's reference provided with your system.

Syntax

```
vi filename

view filename

vedit filename
```

The three forms all invoke the same editor. The first form is the normal form. view invokes the editor in a read-only mode, thus enabling vi to act somewhat like the pagers more and pg; however, view can't be piped to. vedit places the editor in novice mode, which can be useful for beginners.

Argument or Option	Description
filename	This is the name of the file to edit.

The following are a few of the commands available in vi:

Command	What It Does
Esc	Pressing the Escape key puts you back into command mode, allowing you to enter a new command.

(continues)

Command	What it does
r	Replaces one character
R	Unlimited replacement in the line
i	Insert mode
dd	Delete the line
x	Delete a character
$	End of the line
^	Beginning of the line
:x	Writes the file and exits vi
:q!	Quits vi without saving the file
/	Allows the entry of a search pattern

Example

```
vi letter-to-dad
```

Starts vi to work on a letter to your dad.

See also

ed

W

Reports who is logged on the system and what they are doing. It also reports how many users are on the system, how long the system has been up, and the *load averages*. The load averages are the average number of processes in the last 1, 5, and 15 minutes.

Syntax

```
w [flags] users
```

Argument or Option	Description
users	A space-separated list of users to which to limit the output of w. Normally, w reports all users.

Flags

Argument or Option	Description
-h	Does not show the header information. Normally, w prints a heading line showing the current date, how long the system has been up, the number of users currently logged on, and the load averages.
-l	The default; specifies the long format and produces the following columns:

	User	The user logged on.
	Tty	The terminal the user is on.
	Login@	Indicates when the user logged on this terminal.
	Idle	The number of minutes the user hasn't typed anything at the terminal. This doesn't mean the processes on the terminal aren't doing something useful. It may be that the user launched a process that takes a long time to execute, but requires no interaction (for example, a large sort).
	JCPU	The cumulative CPU minutes used by all jobs run during this login session.
	PCPU	The number of CPU minutes the present process is taking.
	What	The name of the currently running process with its arguments.

-q	The quick output. Lists only the following from the table: User, Tty, Idle, and What.
-t	Prints only the heading line; equivalent to uptime.

Messages

    w: illegal option -- *badoption*

You invoked w with an option/flag it doesn't support.

Examples

    w

Reports all possible information.

    w -t

Reports the uptime, number of users, and load average information.

```
w frank sue
```

Reports information on only the users frank and sue.

See also

who, whodo, uptime, ps, finger

wall

Writes to all users currently logged on the system. This is a broadcast message.

Syntax

```
wall
```

wall reads from standard input until an end-of-file (Ctrl-d) is reached. It then broadcasts this message to all users on the system.

Note

You must be the super user to run wall and to override any write protection the users have on their terminals. The wall executable is found in the /etc directory, and the system default does not enable regular users execute permissions.

Examples

```
wall
Please get off the system in 10 minutes^D
```

Invokes an interactive version of wall and types in a one-line message ending with the end-of-file keystroke (Ctrl-d). The message doesn't go out until the end-of-file is encountered.

```
wall <shutdown-note
```

Redirects the file shutdown-note to wall and sends the contents of that file to all users.

See also

write

WC

Counts the number of characters, words, or lines in a file.

Syntax

```
wc [flags] filelist
```

Argument or Option	Description
filelist	A space-separated list of file names of which to count the contents. If left blank, the standard output is read.

Flags

Argument or Option	Description
-c	Counts only the number of characters.
-w	Counts only the number of words. Words are any string of characters separated by a space, tab, or newline.
-l	Counts only the number of lines. Or, more precisely, it counts the number of newline characters encountered.

Note

Any combination of the flags in the list can be used. The default is all of them. When more than one option is specified, the output is in this order: lines, words, characters.

Messages

```
wc: can't open filename
```

You invoked wc, asking it to count in a file that it can't open. Either the file doesn't exist, or you don't have permission to read it.

Examples

```
wc letter-to-dad
```

Tells you how many lines, words, and characters letter-to-dad is.

```
dd if=/dev/rct0 ¦ wc -c
```

Counts the number of characters found on the tape. In other words, it tells you how much data went on the tape. (It also is a useful way of validating that the tape is readable.)

what

Searches files for the occurrence of the character sequence @(#) and prints the characters following until a ~, >, <, \, null, or newline is found. The file name is shown followed by a colon, and on the subsequent lines the string between @(#) and the terminator is also shown. what is intended to be used by get in the SCCS system (source code control system).

Syntax

```
what filelist
```

Argument or Option	Description
filelist	A space-separated list of files to search.

Example

```
what my-file
```

Looks at the file my-file and, if it finds the sequence @(#), reports those lines.

who

Reports who is currently on the system and other user and login information.

Syntax

```
who [flags] utmp-like-file
who am i
```

Argument or Option	Description
utmp-like-file	This is an alternative file to read to obtain login information. This is usually /etc/wtmp. /etc/wtmp is a history of what is found in the /etc/utmp file, and as it grows larger it must be cleaned up periodically.

Flags

Argument or Option	Description
-u	Reports those users who are currently logged onto the system. The following columns are reported:
	NAME — The name of the user.
	LINE — The terminal they are logged on to.
	TIME — When they logged on.
	IDLE — The number of minutes since they've typed something in at their terminal. A period (.) indicates there has been some activity in the last minute.
	PID — The process-id of the login shell.
	COMMENTS — The comment field as defined in /tcb/files/inittab.
-T	Indicates whether the terminal allows users to send messages to it. A plus sign (+) just before the LINE column indicates the terminal can be written to. A minus sign (–) indicates it cannot be written to, and a question mark (?) can indicate a problem with the terminal.
-l	Shows only those lines waiting for someone to log in.
-H	Prints the header line.
-q	Shows a space-separated list of user names and a count. A quick version of the output. All other options are ignored.
-d	Shows the processes that have expired and have not been respawned by init.
-t	Shows when the system date/time last changed. It shows the old and new values.
-a	Shows all the information available.
-s	This is the default and limits the output to a form like -u but only the following columns are provided: NAME, LINE, and TIME.

Examples

    who

Gives the columns: NAME, LINE, and TIME.

```
who -t
```

Shows when the system time was changed.

See also

ps, whodo

whodo

Identifies who is on the system and what they are currently doing.

Syntax

```
whodo
```

whodo produces a merged output from the ps and who commands.

Example

```
whodo
```

Produces a listing of who is on the system and what that user is doing.

See also

ps, who

write

Communicates with a user interactively, who is otherwise inaccessible.

Syntax

```
write user tty
```

Argument or Option	Description
user	The user name of the person to whom you wish to send a message.
tty	When the user is logged on to more than one terminal at a time, you can specify the terminal to which you want the message to go.

Note

`write` reads from standard input, and each time you press Enter it sends that line to the user. When you press the end-of-file key (Ctrl-d) `write` exits.

Messages

```
Message from sending-user sending-tty
```

This means someone is writing to you. `write` lets you know who is sending the message and from what terminal they are running `write`.

```
(end of message)
```

The user sending you a message is finished.

```
user is not logged on.
```

You tried to write to a user who is not currently on the system.

```
permission denied
```

The user you want to write to doesn't want to be written to right now. The user most likely issued the `mesg n` command.

Notes

When you have finished a line of thought and want the person with whom you are communicating to respond, it is common practice to use the notation (o) to signal "over" and when you are finished with the conversation (oo) to signal "over and out." Multiple newlines are also used. Press the Enter key at least twice to signal the other user it is his or her turn.

If the user has a phone, it is probably just as easy to pick up your phone and call. `write` is very useful when the phone isn't available, but it can be quite cumbersome because you can't begin your response until the other user completes his or her line of thought.

Novice users tend to get frustrated if they are written to because they are not comfortable enough with the system to respond. This is usually because they believe that the writing is messing up the application they are currently running, and some applications available on UNIX don't provide a redraw or shell escape function. This, in essence, cripples that user, even though no real damage has taken place.

IX

Command Reference

Caution

If a user is logged on to more than one terminal, `write` assumes the terminal with the most recent login. This may not actually be the terminal he or she is currently on. Now you have to track down what the current terminal is or it may appear as though the user isn't able to respond. This problem is due to the multiple consoles and screen capabilities of UNIX.

See also

> mesg, mail

xtod

Converts UNIX text files to DOS text files. UNIX uses one character to mean the end of a line: the newline or linefeed character. DOS uses two: a linefeed and a carriage return. Furthermore, DOS has an end-of-file marker (Ctrl-Z). If you do not convert the files, DOS will not like the files you create. Don't use `xtod` on binary/data files.

Syntax

> `xtod unix-filename`

Argument or Option	Description
`unix-filename`	The name of the UNIX file you want to convert to DOS format. If left blank, `xtod` reads from standard input. `xtod` always writes to standard output.

Example

> `xtod letter-to-mom >dosletter`

Converts the file `letter-to-mom`, and places the results into a file called `dosletter`.

See also

> dtox, doscp

yes

Continuously outputs the given string or the letter *y*. You can use this command when you run programs that require a yes response to prompts, but you can't be there to answer them.

Syntax

```
yes string
```

Argument or Option	Description
string	The string to continually output. If left blank, *string* generates the letter *y*.

Rule

yes continues to output the given string until it is aborted/killed. If it is in a pipe, it terminates when the program it pipes to terminates.

Example

```
yes ¦ rm my-file
```

If my-file does not allow for write permissions the rm command prompts for a yes or no response. This command shows the yes response. This duplicates the -f option to rm.

zcat

See compress.

Appendix

Resources for UNIX Users and Administrators

The resources listed in this appendix are selections, not exhaustive lists. Any omissions or errors are not intentional. For a list of hundreds of ftp sites and gopher servers, see *Using the Internet* (published by Que Corporation).

The following chart lists network tools by anonymous ftp, a way of logging into a system for which you don't have a login ID or a password. For information on using anonymous ftp, see Chapter 25, "UNIX Networking Concepts."

The first column in the chart, *Tool*, is the filename you download from the remote computer listed under *Site* (the third column). The file is located in the directory listed under *Directory* (the second column) .

For example, to retrieve gopher, a tool used for searching through the Internet, enter **ftp boombox.micro.umn.edu** to connect to the remote system. At the Name prompt, enter **anonymous**. Then enter **cd /pub/gopher** to change to the directory containing the program. To retrieve (download) the program, enter **get gopher /tmp**. This command puts the program gopher in the /tmp directory on your local system.

Tool	Directory	Site
archie	/pub/archie	ftp.sura.net
gopher	/pub/gopher	boombox.micro.umn.edu
hytelnet	/pub/hytelnet	access.usask.ca
wais	/wais	quake.think.com
www	/pub/www	info.cern.ch
mosaic	/Mosaic	ftp.ncsa.uiuc.edu

The following chart lists, by company, the sites that carry software for UNIX systems. This information is available by anonymous ftp as shown in the example above. The *Site* column lists the remote systems you ftp to.

Company	Site
Apollo	archive.umich.edu
BSD	bsdi.com
Convex	convex.convex.com
GNU	prep.ai.mit.edu
Hewlett-Packard	ftp.csc.liv.ac.uk
	ftp.cae.uiuc.edu
Novell	ftp.novell.com
	ftp.novell.de
Sun	sunsite.unc.edu

The following list presents specific resources available on the Internet:

- **Frequently Asked Questions:**

    bloom-picayune.mit.edu

- **Internet Services List:**

    /pub/inet.services.txt csd4.csd.uwm.edu

- **Inter-Network Mail Guide:**

    /pub/internetwork-mail-guide csd4.csd.uwm.edu

- **Internet Access:**

    /pub/info-deli/public-access/pdial ftp.netcom.com

    /netinfo/internet-access-providers-us.txt ftp.nisc.sri.com

    /netinfo/internet-access-providers-non-us.txt ftp.nisc.sri.com

- **Internet Tools List:**

    /pub/communications/internet-tools ftp.rpi.edu

- **Joe's Editor:**

    /stusrc/joe.tar.Z wpi.wpi.edu

■ **List-of-Lists:**

/netinfo/interest-groups crvax.sri.com

/siglists/internet.lists dartcms1.dartmouth.edu

■ **Pico Editor:**

/pine/unix-binaries ftp.cac.washington.edu

The following chart lists general sources of UNIX information and software available by anonymous ftp (explained earlier in this appendix):

Site
cwis.usc.edu
ftp.uu.net
ftp.cso.uiuc.edu
ftp.sura.net
gatekeeper.dec.com
oak.oakland.edu
prep.ai.mit.edu
sumex-aim.stanford.edu
unix.hensa.ac.uk
wiretap.spies.com
wuarchive.wustl.edu

The following chart lists sources for network information, users guides, and software:

Site
ftp.sura.net
ds.internic.net
is.internic.net
nic.ddn.mil
nic.merit.edu
nis.nsf.net
rs.internic.net
src.doc.ic.ac.uk
uvaarpa.uva.edu

The following chart lists some gopher servers (sites you can access if you have gopher software loaded on your system) you may want to explore:

Site
calypso.oit.unc.edu
csrc.ncsl.nist.gov
dewey.lib.ncsu.edu
feenix.metronet.com
gopher.acm.org
gopher.acs.oakland.edu
gopher.cic.net
gopher.cpsr.org
gopher.eff.org
gopher.gdb.org
gopher.ieee.org
gopher.nosc.mil
gopher.tamu.edu
gopher.tcm.umn.edu
gopher.utdallas.edu
isaac.engr.washington.edu
marvel.loc.gov
rain.psg.com
riceinfo.rice.edu
wiretap.spies.com

The following chart lists a source for various UNIX shells available by anonymous ftp:

Directory	Site
/shells	ftp.uu.net

Index

Symbols

X–Y–Z

GO AHEAD. PLUG YOURSELF INTO
PRENTICE HALL COMPUTER PUBLISHING.

Introducing the PHCP Forum on CompuServe®

Yes, it's true. Now, you can have CompuServe access to the same professional, friendly folks who have made computers easier for years. On the PHCP Forum, you'll find additional information on the topics covered by every PHCP imprint—including Que, Sams Publishing, New Riders Publishing, Alpha Books, Brady Books, Hayden Books, and Adobe Press. In addition, you'll be able to receive technical support and disk updates for the software produced by Que Software and Paramount Interactive, a division of the Paramount Technology Group. It's a great way to supplement the best information in the business.

WHAT CAN YOU DO ON THE PHCP FORUM?

Play an important role in the publishing process—and make our books better while you make your work easier:

- Leave messages and ask questions about PHCP books and software—you're guaranteed a response within 24 hours

- Download helpful tips and software to help you get the most out of your computer

- Contact authors of your favorite PHCP books through electronic mail

- Present your own book ideas

- Keep up to date on all the latest books available from each of PHCP's exciting imprints

JOIN NOW AND GET A FREE COMPUSERVE STARTER KIT!

To receive your free CompuServe Introductory Membership, call toll-free, **1-800-848-8199** and ask for representative **#597**. The Starter Kit Includes:

- Personal ID number and password

- $15 credit on the system

- Subscription to CompuServe Magazine

HERE'S HOW TO PLUG INTO PHCP:

Once on the CompuServe System, type any of these phrases to access the PHCP Forum:

GO PHCP   **GO BRADY**
GO QUEBOOKS   **GO HAYDEN**
GO SAMS   **GO QUESOFT**
GO NEWRIDERS **GO PARAMOUNTINTER**
GO ALPHA

Once you're on the CompuServe Information Service, be sure to take advantage of all of CompuServe's resources. CompuServe is home to more than 1,700 products and services—plus it has over 1.5 million members worldwide. You'll find valuable online reference materials, travel and investor services, electronic mail, weather updates, leisure-time games and hassle-free shopping (no jam-packed parking lots or crowded stores).

Seek out the hundreds of other forums that populate CompuServe. Covering diverse topics such as pet care, rock music, cooking, and political issues, you're sure to find others with the sames concerns as you—and expand your knowledge at the same time.

Enhance Your Personal Computer System with Hardware and Networking Titles from Que!